SURVIVING THE PEACE

Peter Lippman

Surviving the Peace

THE STRUGGLE FOR POSTWAR RECOVERY IN BOSNIA-HERZEGOVINA

VANDERBILT UNIVERSITY PRESS

Nashville

© 2019 by Vanderbilt University Press
Nashville, Tennessee 37235
All rights reserved
First printing 2019

This book is printed on acid-free paper.
Manufactured in the United States of America

Library of Congress Cataloging-in-Publication Data

Names: Lippman, Peter, 1952– author.
Title: Surviving the peace : the struggle for postwar recovery in
Bosnia-Herzegovina / Peter Lippman.
Description: Nashville, Tennessee : Vanderbilt University Press, [2019] |
Includes bibliographical references and index. |
Identifiers: LCCN 2019009076 (print) | LCCN 2019014183 (ebook) | ISBN
9780826522634 (ebook) | ISBN 9780826522610 (hardcover : alk. paper)
Subjects: LCSH: Bosnia and Herzegovina—History—1992– | Bosnia and
Herzegovina—Social conditions. | Bosnia and Herzegovina—Politics and
government—1992– | Peace-building—Bosnia and Herzegovina. | Human
rights—Bosnia and Herzegovina.
Classification: LCC DR1750 (ebook) | LCC DR1750 .L57 2019 (print) | DDC
949.74203—dc23
LC record available at https://lccn.loc.gov/2019009076

To my parents,
Leopold and Eleanor Lippman

Contents

Pronunciation Guide for Bosnian-Croatian-Serbian Words

Consonants. Most consonants are similar to those in English, except for the following modifications:

c   *ts*

č   hard *ch*

ć   soft *ch* like the t in the British "tune"

đ   *dj* in "edge" or the d in schedule (American pronunciation)

dž   hard *j* as in "joke"

j   *y* as in "yes"

r   rolled *r*; syllabic r is like the *ur* in "hurt," but very short

š   *sh*

ž   *zh*

Vowels. There are five simple vowels and no diphthongs:

a   *ah* as in "father," and sometimes *u* as in "cup"

e   *e* as in "egg," and sometimes *ey* as in "neigh"

i   long *ee* as in "seek"

o   pure, rounded *o* as in "oh"

u   rounded *oo* as in "fool"

Glossary

JNA. Yugoslav People's Army

KM. Konvertabilna marka (convertible mark); Bosnian currency, worth about US$0.60–US$0.70

MICT. Mechanism for International Criminal Tribunals, successor to the ICTY ; now International Residual Mechanism for Criminal Tribunals (IRMCT)

NIOD. Dutch Institute for War Documentation (Nederlands Instituut voor Oorlogs-documentatie)

OHR. Office of the High Representative

OSCE. Organization for Security and Cooperation in Europe

PLIP. Property Law Implementation Plan

RRTF. Return and Reconstruction Task Force

RS. Republika Srpska; Serb-controlled entity in postwar Bosnia

SDA. Party of Democratic Action; leading Muslim nationalist party

SDC. Supreme Defense Council of Serbia

SDP. Social Democratic Party; nonnationalist but dominated by secular Muslims

SDS. Serb Democratic Party; Serb nationalist party that led the Serb separatist movement during the war

SFOR. (UN) Stabilization Force

SIPA. State Investigation and Protection Agency; state-level police body

SNSD. Party of Independent Social Democrats; Bosnian Serb nationalist party led by Milorad Dodik

SRRP. Srebrenica Regional Recovery Programme

SRS. Serbian Radical Party

UNDP. United Nations Development Programme

UNHCR. UN High Command for Refugees

UNPROFOR. (Wartime) UN Protection Force

VRS. (Wartime) Army of the Republika Srpska

VOCABULARY AND PROMINENT NAMES

Bosniak. Bosnian Muslim.

Chetnik. World War II Serb royalists and ultranationalists who ultimately collaborated with Nazis to fight Tito's Partisans; their movement was revived in the 1990s.

Dayton agreement. Peace agreement resulting from negotiations overseen by the United States at Dayton, Ohio, signed in Paris in December 1995. Contains annexes covering refugee return; including the Bosnian constitution; and establishing the OHR and other postwar institutions.

Dragan Čović. Leader of the HDZ, Croat nationalist party.

Mirsad Duratović. Concentration camp survivor, politician, and human rights activist in Prijedor.

Federation. With the Republika Srpska, one of the two entities making up Bosnia-Herzegovina. Formed in 1993 and controlled by Bosnian Croats and Muslims.

Herzegovina. Southern region of Bosnia-Herzegovina, geographically and ethnographically distinct from Bosnia.

Alija Izetbegović (1925–2003). Founder and first president of SDA, Bosnian Muslim nationalist party. Leader of Bosnian government and commander of the ARBiH during the war.

Bakir Izetbegović. Leader of the SDA in the 2010s, son of Alija Izetbegović.

kafana. Coffeehouse, restaurant, drinking place, social venue.

Radovan Karadžić. Serb nationalist founder and wartime leader of the SDS, convicted of genocide and other war crimes.

Željko Komšić. Bosnian Croat, leader of the nonnationalist Democratic Front.

Krajina. Northwest region of Bosnia-Herzegovina (part of both entities), overlapping into Croatia.

Ratko Mladić. Commander in chief of the Bosnian Serb army (VRS); convicted of genocide and other war crimes (pending appeal in 2019).

Hasan Nuhanović. Wartime translator for UNPROFOR in the Srebrenica enclave, author, and activist.

Podrinje. Eastern Bosnia along the Drina River.

pozitivci. People who think and act positively.

Republika Srpska. With the Federation, one of two entities making up Bosnia-Herzegovina.

Ustasha. World War II ultranationalist Croats who collaborated with Nazis in ruling Croatia and part of Bosnia-Herzegovina. Their movement was revived in the 1990s.

Bosnia and Herzegovina, 1997. Map by US Central Intelligence Agency, courtesy of Perry-Castañeda Library Map Collection, University of Texas Libraries

Introduction

THE WAR AND THE CAMPAIGNS
FOR RECOVERY

YUGOSLAVIA SEEMED LIKE A FINE PLACE TO LIVE WHEN I moved there in 1981. People had work without being overworked. There was time to spend with family and neighbors. With a Yugoslav passport it was possible to travel east and west with minimal visa requirements, and people generally had the income and vacation time to do so. They went abroad, and they were happy to return home.

But dark forces lurked behind this apparently pleasant scene, and just a few years later the Yugoslav federation was in a state of violent disintegration. The thousand-year history of Bosnia was thus punctuated in a most dreadful way by the 1992–1995 war, which changed the face of the country forever. By far, the most extensive bloodshed took place in Bosnia-Herzegovina.

Many books have been written about that war, but the history of Bosnia did not end in 1995. A struggle is ongoing in Bosnia-Herzegovina, waged by ordinary people against great odds—a struggle for freedom of movement, for equal opportunity in the pursuit of a decent life under peaceful conditions, for a government free of corruption, for the restoration of good relations among the diverse ethnicities, and for justice.

This book is a portrayal of postwar life in Bosnia. It is meant to be more in-depth than the occasional newspaper article and more accessible than the scholarly writing currently available. It is the result of more than two decades of close observation of grassroots human rights campaigns and the struggle for recovery in Bosnia-Herzegovina.

MY CURIOSITY ABOUT OTHER CULTURES LED ME TO settle in Yugoslavia in the early 1980s, a decision that laid the foundation for a lifelong attachment to the language, the country, and the people.

Though my interest began with ethnographic exploration, my activist background led me to get involved in a different way when the country was broken up by war ten years after my first visit. In 1993 I helped put together an organization in Seattle to sponsor a family of refugees who had fled the war. I quickly became close to that family, listening to their stories and trying to imagine the troubles they had lived through.

After the war ended, I went to live in Bosnia for two years. At the beginning of my stay, I volunteered with a small relief agency in Tuzla. There I had the eye-opening experience of meeting survivors from Srebrenica. Looking into the eyes of a widow who has lost all the men in her family is a searing experience.

I also visited Prijedor just as refugee return to that municipality was beginning. I witnessed the transformation of the mostly Muslim town of Kozarac from rubble back into a lovely community facing new, post-return problems.

As I sat with return leaders Emsuda and Osman Mujagić in the garden of one of the few homes left intact in Kozarac, the couple expressed their determination to me. "We will rebuild Kozarac," Emsuda said. "We built this town together before the war, too. We didn't wait for the government to build our roads and our water supply system. We will do it again."

Osman added, "To us, Kozarac is beautiful, even if it is ruined."[1]

I wound up my two-year stay working for the Advocacy Project (a Washington, DC–based human rights organization[2]) as a field researcher on grassroots human rights campaigns. The movement for refugee return, described in the opening chapters of this book, was the first widespread campaign for recovery in postwar Bosnia-Herzegovina. It lasted for six or seven years and was followed in many return communities around Bosnia by an ongoing campaign against ethnic discrimination. In some places this discrimination still amounts to apartheid.

WITNESSING THE STRUGGLE FOR RECOVERY IN BOSNIA

The main part of this book is a description of the cards that were dealt ordinary Bosnians at the end of the war and a depiction of how those people have responded. The whole story is full of detail, and I can recount only a small part of it.

After four chapters that illustrate the larger postwar situation and discuss the refugee return movement, I concentrate on two places where I have spent significant time over the years: Srebrenica and Prijedor municipality.

In general, if people have heard of Bosnia-Herzegovina, they have heard of Srebrenica—and too often the story stops there. Srebrenica deserves attention, of course. But along with the history of the genocide that was committed there, Srebrenica has also become a place where people are fighting for change. Prijedor is another such place, one where there was above-average refugee return after the war, and it has been the location of some of the most concerted struggles for justice under apartheid-like conditions.

I regret that I am not able to give more space to Stolac, Mostar, Goražde, Bijeljina, Višegrad, and many other places in Bosnia where I have spent time and where people have generously shared their experiences with me. In those places I have met people who are likewise fighting for recovery under particular, local conditions of division and separatism; they all deserve to have their stories told.

During the war, over two million people were displaced or made refugees.[3] Somewhat over a million of those people returned home from abroad or from internal displacement, but the return movement was not successful in recreating a multiethnic population in any part of the country. In the places where there was significant return, such as the municipalities of Prijedor, Zvornik, and Mostar, the different ethnicities have lived alongside each other rather than with each other. Nearly one hundred thousand people remained internally displaced as of 2017,[4] with some seven thousand of those still living in collective centers.[5]

The fate of Bosnia-Herzegovina as a recovering nation and a functional state, one that protects and nurtures its people, is as uncertain as ever. But while corruption and division have been pervasive over the years, it has been possible to view the response of Bosnians with hope, simply because, as I will detail, there has been a recurring, courageous response.

At the same time, corruption and the accompanying economic stalemate prompt both an economic and emotional depression, conditions that drive people to leave Bosnia in ever greater numbers. Ongoing instances of corruption are reported in every newspaper—with each outlet focusing on the transgressions of its ideological adversaries. Hypothetically, if one were to read a broad sample of Bosnian news outlets, one could uncover a well-rounded description of the regime of corruption. Ordinary people are well aware of the problem, but hard put to discover effective ways to resolve it; often, leaving for a more stable country where work is available seems the best option.

In recent years one of the salient points of corruption in the Republika Srpska, for example, has been the complex set of scandals surrounding Bobar Banka and Pavlović Banka and shady deals conducted by then RS president Milorad Dodik. After losses of hundreds of millions of KM, leading to the 2014 closure of Bobar Banka in Bijeljina, some fifteen of the bank's employees had been arrested by 2017. They were accused of participating in a joint criminal enterprise to make illegal, unsupported loans that cost the entity's banking sector nearly 125 million KM. Clients of the bank—individuals, corporations, and local governments—lost millions of KM. Between 2014 and 2015 the balance of the banking sector was down more than 100 million KM—posting an 80 million KM loss. Court proceedings against a total of fifteen people accused of organized crime continued throughout 2018.[6]

The shady operations of the Bobar Banka group were possible only with the approval of the highest level of power in Dodik's regime. By 2016 not only was that bank out of business, but several other top banks in the entity were also going into bankruptcy or, at the least, operating deeply in the red. But no legal process has come close to endangering Dodik's liberty, as his partners in plunder continue to enrich themselves.

Also in 2016, Bosnian state police arrested the American-based tycoon Slobodan Pavlović, owner of Pavlović Banka of Bijeljina, together with two other bank officials, for financial crimes related to that bank. The three officials were under suspicion of arranging a fictitious loan to then prime minister Dodik for the purchase of a mansion in Belgrade.[7] Dodik received a loan for 1.5 million KM a year *after* he bought the mansion, thus prompting suspicion that the loan was a cover-up for a money-laundering maneuver.[8] Pavlović, a crony of Dodik, managed to remain at liberty.

The ongoing plunder of social wealth is perpetrated by the highest-echelon leaders of the Croats and Muslims as well, though with somewhat less drama and media exposure—and the criminal records of those leaders seem as Teflon-coated as that of Milorad Dodik. On the Croat side, the apparently lifelong supreme leader among Croat nationalists, Dragan Čović, has emerged from one criminal court proceeding after another without a conviction. And on the Bosniak side, scandals and rumors of corruption have dogged nationalists and nonnationalists alike.

There are midlevel and one or two high-profile prosecutors and ministers who have made it clear they know right from wrong and are in favor of prosecuting crooked politicians regardless of their party. But politics prevails, and the sense of the overriding political dynamic in Bosnia-Herzegovina is that multiethnicity still lives mainly at the level of the three ethnonationalist profiteering leaderships. There is tacit cooperation, even amid apparently rancorous election campaigns, to ensure that the elite confound the public and retain their positions.

My portrayal of Bosnia-Herzegovina and the campaigns for postwar recovery takes a turn at the end of the book, where I discuss the problem of war crimes denial and revisionism. The demand for justice requires that the truth be told and that the memory of crimes committed during the war be preserved. For there to be recovery, that memory must not be besmirched by denial and revisionism or consigned to oblivion. And there is a corps of people who are working overtime to generate lies about the war and to distort the truth.

Although the nature of the war is not the heart of this book, what happened in the early 1990s naturally influenced everything that has taken place since then. While I do not consider myself biased, I expect to offend some readers because of my considered positions on the history of the war. Some will be convinced that I take a position against one ethnicity or another, but this is not the case.

I have already used the word *genocide*, and I assert that the crime was committed not only in Srebrenica but also in other parts of Bosnia during the war. In addition, I agree that war was imposed on Bosnia-Herzegovina through aggression by Serbia and Croatia.

That said, my position on the matter of aggression during the war is more nuanced than that of some analysts. It is very clear that separatists among the Bosnian Serbs could not have prosecuted the war in Bosnia without the material, logistical, and strategic support of the Serbian regime led by Slobodan Milošević, and there is also convincing evidence to show, beyond reasonable doubt, that Croatian president Tuđman's government gave crucial military and financial support to the Bosnian Croat separatist effort. At the same time, I find compelling reasons to accept that at least in some parts of the country, Bosnians of different ethnicities truly experienced the conflict as a civil war. This will be discussed in subsequent chapters.

The remainder of this introduction gives a very short description of Yugoslavia before the war, followed by a similarly brief outline of wartime events. But first, a few words about terminology.

The three main ethnicities of Bosnia-Herzegovina are known as "Croats," "Serbs," and "Muslims." Generally, Croats are of the Catholic faith or descended from Catholics, and Serbs are of the Orthodox Christian faith or descended from Orthodox believers. As nationalism developed in Bosnia in the nineteenth century, the Catholics and Orthodox Christians gradually took on political identities tied to neighboring Catholic Croatia and Orthodox Serbia, respectively. Gradually, they adopted the ethnopolitical designations of their neighboring co-religionists.

For clarity, common usage generally designates people living in Serbia as "Serbians," and their co-religionists living in Bosnia as "Bosnian Serbs." Likewise people living in Croatia are generally called "Croatians" while their co-religionists in Bosnia are called "Bosnian Croats."

Unlike the Croats and the Serbs, Bosnian Muslims retained the status of a religious community, as opposed to a political body, well into the twentieth century before their political status as an ethnicity with rights equal to those of other ethnicities was enshrined in law. Terminology that gave the Bosnian Muslims a political name lagged behind this historical development, but this finally changed during the war of the 1990s.

In 1993, the semantic confusion about the ethnicity of Bosnian Muslims was resolved at the official level when Muslim political activists of Bosnia formally adopted the name "Bosniak" as their own. This name provides a secular ethnic designation that parallels "Croat" and "Serb," tying its bearer to a nation without explicit religious implications.

It satisfies those secular Muslims who consider the term "Muslim" to refer only to religiously observant people.

The word has received mixed acceptance from all sides. There are secular Muslims who oppose the politicization of ethnic or religious identification and insist that members of all three ethnicities are simply "Bosnians." There are those who recall that Bosniak, originally a Turkish word, once referred to all Bosnians. And there is a component of antinationalist Muslims who energetically oppose the use of the term Bosniak because they see it as a way of unconscionably forcing Bosnian Muslims into an artificial ethnic corral.

The reader will notice that at times I refer to Bosnian Muslims as Bosniaks and at other times simply as Muslims, as if the names were interchangeable. In common English usage, for the most part they are, but among many in Bosnia-Herzegovina, they are not. I have opted not to take a position on this issue.

In a similar vein, the reader will notice that I sometimes refer to the country in question as Bosnia-Herzegovina, and often just as Bosnia. The two names are primarily geographical and ethnographic designations; in these realms there are significant differences between Bosnia and Herzegovina, even though they have been part of one country since early Ottoman times. Most foreigners simply say Bosnia—but Herzegovinans are proud of their region and their culture, and they insist on the recognition of the special attributes of their identity.

METHODOLOGY

Regarding my research methods, my writing has been based, first of all, on personal relationships with activists and on the interviews and informal conversations that I have conducted with them over many years. I conducted hundreds of formal interviews and also learned about the lives of the survivors and ordinary Bosnians through countless informal conversations.

I regularly visited the staff of local and international nongovernmental organizations, and I visited numerous refugee return settlements from the time that they were rudimentary tent encampments until when they were reconstructed villages and towns. I also periodically consulted with local officials dealing with refugee resettlement and other problems of recovery, and I kept in touch as well with some domestic and international analysts as well.

Added to that has been my ongoing study of available information from such sources as grassroots organizational journals, dozens of books on the war (and the few available on postwar life), and ongoing correspondence with Bosnians when I was not able to be in the country. I have made use of available case history information not only from court trials in the International Criminal Tribune for the former Yugoslavia, but also from relevant trials taking place in Bosnia, Croatia, and Serbia.

BEFORE THE WAR

It took Yugoslavia a couple of decades to recover physically and economically from the devastation caused by World War II. By the late 1960s, with urbanization, massive infrastructure development, international aid, and crucial remittances from abroad, the country was in relatively good shape, with a living standard that was the envy of other East European nations.

However, by the mid-1980s the Yugoslav economy was in great distress, as inflation began to go out of control. Massive debts incurred during Tito's time started to come due, and politicians and bureaucrats failed to salvage the economic order. The country's constituent republics competed, more and more on an ethnic basis, for scarce resources. Regional representatives to the federal government fought to ensure perks for their constituencies, generating hostility among republics and the ethnicities they represented.

Marshal Tito, lifelong president of Yugoslavia, died in 1980, leaving a power vacuum that responsible leaders were unable to fill. Growing instability provided fertile ground for the surfacing of old animosities and new demagogues. One of the most prominent markers of the breakout of national chauvinism was the 1986 Memorandum of the Serbian Academy of Arts and Sciences (SANU). The memorandum, in an expression of ethnic nationalism, shrilly articulated a sense of Serbian victimhood and advocated the "complete national and cultural integrity of the Serbian people." This was recognizable code language calling for a rearrangement of the constitutional order of Yugoslavia. It was a short step from this rhetoric to the advocacy of a "Greater Serbia."[9]

In 1986, the banker Slobodan Milošević engineered a takeover of the Serbian Communist Party, and in the same year he made a belligerent speech in Kosovo exploiting friction between Serbs and Albanians in that province.

The year 1990 saw the first multiparty elections throughout Yugoslavia, resulting in the endorsement of nationalist parties in all republics. By then, the Yugoslav Communist Party had disbanded, and the only institution holding the country together was the Yugoslav People's Army (JNA), which was dominated, for historical reasons, by Serbian officers.* The officer corps of the JNA was already recorded as 60 percent Serb in 1983, with a greater percentage of Serbs taking the high command positions.[10]

---

* The predominance of Serbs was the case because, first of all, during World War II there was a higher percentage of Serb soldiers among the ultimately victorious Partisans than of other ethnicities, and throughout the postwar period there was likewise a predominance—or at least a plurality—of Serbs in the Communist Party.

  One factor contributing to the high proportion of Serbs in federal politics and in the military was that positions in these institutions were delegated by republic rather than by ethnicity. Each ethnicity, other than the Serbs, was primarily located in one republic (Croats in Croatia, Macedonians in Macedonia, and so on). However, there were significant Serb populations in Bosnia-Herzegovina and in Croatia. So in these two republics and in Montenegro, high officials in politics and in the army were often Serbs. This skewed the ethnic representation not only in the army, but also in the federal political structures.

The ethnic Serb domination of the army was made all but complete when, in the early 1990s, nationalists under the leadership of Slobodan Milošević were making preparations to take control of a large part of Yugoslavia. By the end of the war in Croatia in late 1991, Milošević was reshaping the JNA to ensure that it was controlled by officers known to be loyal to the idea of a Greater Serbia.[11]

In Bosnia-Herzegovina, three new political parties had formed: the Serbian Democratic Party (SDS), the Croatian Democratic Alliance (HDZ), and the Bosniak-dominated Party of Democratic Action (SDA). Each of these ascendant parties retained elements of the authoritarian, centralist political culture of the earlier period.

Ethnic politics filled the vacuum left by a vanished Yugoslav patriotism, as citizens who had previously identified and voted as "Bosnians" or "Yugoslavs" gravitated to the party representing their ethnicity. Leaders of each ethnic group rushed for the political openings created by the introduction of multiparty politics, and each leader told a story of his own constituency's victimization. One extremism answered another; Croat, Serb, and Bosniak representatives each inspired their followers with talk of past injuries and future greatness.

Serbian expansionists called for the annexation of Serb-populated areas of Bosnia and Croatia; likewise, Croatian expansionists strove for annexation of Croat-populated areas of Bosnia. During the 1990 Croatian electoral campaign, presidential candidate Franjo Tuđman, as described by the writer Lenard Cohen, "emphasized the special ties between Croatia and Bosnia-Herzegovina and suggested that it might become necessary to raise the question of the republic's territorial reorganization in future negotiations about the restructuring of Yugoslavia along confederal lines."[12] As soon as such map-based resolutions arose, a free-for-all competition for control of territory became the imperative.

In Bosnia, leading up to the November 1990 elections, Serbs agitated in the predominantly Serb-populated areas, and Croat nationalists organized in Croat-majority parts of the country. Each ethnicity created local nationalist party organizations in all areas where they had any significant representation. Political polarization was accompanied by heightened rhetoric, threats, and sporadic violence.

The wars of Yugoslav dissolution began in earnest in June 1991, when Slovenia and Croatia declared secession from Yugoslavia. The Yugoslav National Army (JNA) responded with a halfhearted attempt to take control of Slovenia, a venture that lasted only ten days before the army withdrew. A genuine war, however, ensued in Croatia. By late summer, Serb militias, with the backing of the JNA, had taken control of a third of Croatia.

The militias and JNA played cooperative roles, each reinforcing the other body's work. From the point of view of the Serb extremists in Croatia, the creation of independent paramilitary groupings was essential to the initiation of separatist actions because, at the beginning of the hostilities, the public still viewed the JNA as the army of all Yugoslavs—an institution that existed to safeguard the entire population and to preserve the integrity of the Yugoslav federation. Thus the war in Croatia commenced with sporadic paramilitary actions, and a pattern developed wherein the JNA would intervene after such incidents.

The goal of the intervention was presented as simply to restore order, but the pattern showed that the JNA consistently reinforced the separatist goals of the Serb militias.

The international community wavered in its policies with regard to the breakup of Yugoslavia, sometimes encouraging one side, sometimes the other. Although signs of turbulence in Yugoslavia had been evident at least since 1987, Europe and the United States were caught unprepared when the violence began. International officials gave lip service to the protection of minorities within each republic without exerting significant leverage to reinforce their message. Finally, toward the end of 1991 Germany recognized the independence of Slovenia and Croatia; the European Community (EC) followed suit in January 1992. The United States held back.*

By early 1992 there was little prospect for reconciliation among separatist forces in Bosnia. In December 1991, President Alija Izetbegović applied to the European Community for recognition of Bosnia as an independent state. The EC responded by requesting that Bosnia hold a referendum on independence; the government of Bosnia scheduled this for the end of February 1992.

Nationalist Serb leaders called on Bosnian Serbs to refrain from participating in the referendum. The Serbs had already held their own referendum in November 1991, resulting in a strong vote in favor of Bosnia remaining part of Yugoslavia. They announced the formation of their own republic in December and formalized this entity with the January 9 establishment of the Serbian Republic of Bosnia and Herzegovina, later renamed the Republika Srpska (RS), the "Serb Republic."

When the referendum was held on February 29 and March 1, 1992, the Serbs, constituting over 30 percent of Bosnia's population, in large part obeyed the call to boycott. However, there was very strong Croat and Bosniak turnout, with about 65 percent of the total electorate voting. Approximately 99 percent voted in favor of Bosnian independence.[13] On April 6, the European Community, followed by the United States, recognized the independence of Bosnia-Herzegovina. But if Western officials expected that this move would prevent war, it was too late.

WAR

In the spring of 1992 an assault by Serb separatist units, backed up by the Yugoslav People's Army (JNA), began in several parts of Bosnia-Herzegovina almost

---

* I note here that the meaning of the phrase "international community" is vague; it most often refers to whichever powers are involved in the situation under discussion. On the whole, it can be taken to refer to those powerful states that are in a position to respond to a given political problem. In the case of the Bosnian war that means, foremost, the United States and the European Union, often via their intergovernmental alliances and organizations such as NATO and the UN. The phrase can also, at times, refer to nongovernmental organizations as implementers of state policy. And in situations where Russia, China, or other powers are involved in a significant way, they too can be considered part of the international community.

simultaneously. Military groupings instituted a reign of terror, killing or expelling the non-Serb population.

For the first couple of months of the war in Bosnia, the cooperation between local Serb militias and the JNA replicated that of the war in Croatia; Serb paramilitaries attacked non-Serb communities, and the JNA "intervened" to restore order but reinforced the ethnic cleansing carried out by the Serb militias. By May 1992, the JNA had officially withdrawn from Bosnia, but to a large extent this involved leaving the Bosnian Serb portion of its staff and ranks in place with new insignia, under the control of the Army of the Republika Srpska (VRS). Logistical, financial, and material support continued to flow from Serbia.

Serb separatists took over the entire eastern part of Bosnia, save a few enclaves. Srebrenica, Žepa, and Goražde held out, and thousands of refugees from the rest of the region fled to those places. In this same period, Serb forces conquered the northern part of Bosnia as well, and much of central Bosnia. By midsummer 1992, 70 percent of Bosnia was under Serb control,[14] and by the fall, over two million people had been displaced.[15] Tuzla, Sarajevo, part of central Bosnia, and western Herzegovina remained under Bosniak and Croat control.

The result of Serb military operations was to create ethnically homogenous zones under Serb control. The process of enforced displacement quickly came to be known as ethnic cleansing, a euphemism for forced population transfer (at times accompanied by genocide) based on ethnicity. The separation of people of different ethnicities, who had been living side by side for centuries, was one of the main goals of the war.

Sarajevo came under siege, surrounded by Serb forces that shelled the city and subjected its residents to sniper fire. There were days when a particularly harsh atrocity punctuated the passage of time. One of these was the first Markale massacre. On February 5, 1994, a bomb fell on that crowded market as people were buying and selling, killing more than sixty-five people and wounding hundreds.

In mid-1992, news broke of Serb-run concentration camps. Journalists released chilling stories of brutality at several camps near Prijedor. British and American journalists managed to enter Omarska, a mine complex near Prijedor, and the nearby Trnopolje camp. With the news of the concentration camps, Western public opinion was shocked into awareness of the atrocities taking place in Bosnia. There followed a series of conferences, peace plans, and negotiations that would, for the next three years, nevertheless do next to nothing to save Bosnia.

SREBRENICA AND THE ENCLAVES

By mid-1992, Serb forces created dozens of concentration camps and expelled hundreds of thousands of non-Serbs from areas under their control. The military situation remained static in most parts of the country, except for the eastern territory around Srebrenica, Žepa, and Goražde. These enclaves were stumbling blocks in the Serbian plan to annex a geographically compact area to Serbia or, at the very least, have it function with de facto independence from the rest of Bosnia.

Bosniak forces in the eastern enclaves mounted resistance to the Serb siege. The military structure of Bosniak defense in the enclaves was formed in an ad hoc way, with commanders taking authority based on their personal following. Prominent among these leaders was Naser Orić, a young ex-policeman. Early in the war, he became one of the leading commanders in the Srebrenica area.

In the Srebrenica enclave, Orić fought to expand territory under government control. In the fall and winter of 1992 he came close to breaking through to the Bosniak/Croat-controlled area around Tuzla, to the northwest of Srebrenica. By January 1993, nine hundred square kilometers of territory had come under Bosniak control.[16] The enclave reached from the Drina to within five miles of the Tuzla front line.

During this period, the people of Srebrenica and its surrounding villages were usually hungry. Emir Suljagić, a young local translator for international officials, described the town as being so crowded with refugees that thousands were sleeping in the streets. Conditions were worse in the town than in the surrounding villages, where people could at least find some wild food and occasionally cultivate a garden.

At the beginning of the war, Serbs living in Srebrenica left or were driven out of the Bosniak-controlled enclave, just as Bosniaks were expelled from the surrounding areas. Periodically Naser Orić would lead forays against the Serb villages on the periphery of the enclave. On these occasions, civilians would follow the army and take whatever food they could find. Bosniak troops and civilians alike participated in assaults against Serb civilians. One particularly notorious attack on Serb civilians was perpetrated in January 1993 in the village of Kravica.

Some hundreds of Serb soldiers and civilians were killed as Orić fought to unite the enclave with government-controlled territory. The Serb forces that controlled most of eastern Bosnia were determined to prevent this from taking place. In February 1993, Bosnian Serb commander General Ratko Mladić launched a counteroffensive against Srebrenica.

Within a short time, Serb forces recovered most of the territory that Orić had taken over. The Serb offensive threatened over forty-five thousand people who were trapped in the Srebrenica enclave. At this point, aware of the desperate siege conditions in the east, the UN Security Council declared Srebrenica a "safe area." Bosniak troops within the enclave were required to surrender their weapons, and in return an UNPROFOR (UN Protective Force) contingent would establish bases in the enclave, intended to deter attacks from the surrounding Serbs. The concept of a "safe area" or "UN protected zone," though, was never thoroughly defined.

A small, rotating contingent of international troops established the UNPROFOR base in Srebrenica town and several observation posts around the enclave, eventually staffed by a Dutch battalion (Dutchbat). A UN Security Council resolution attempted to define UNPROFOR's role in the enclave, promising that the UN was going to defend the population against attack by the surrounding Serb forces. The resolution further authorized UNPROFOR, "acting in self-defense, to take the necessary measures, including the use of force, in reply to bombardments against the safe areas by any of the parties or to armed incursion into them or in the event of any deliberate obstruction in or around those areas to the freedom of movement of the Force or of protected humanitarian convoys." This language seemed clearly to promise the defense of Srebrenica by UN forces.[17]

Hasan Nuhanović, another translator for UN forces in Srebrenica, said, "At every meeting where I was translator, the question was posed, 'How do you think you will defend this place in case of attack?' The answer was, NATO airplanes are covering the skies of Bosnia, and they can arrive at the 'protected zone' within two to three minutes after our call, and eliminate any attacking formation."[18]

THE CROAT-BOSNIAK WAR

In the summer of 1992, Bosnian president Izetbegović and Croatian president Tuđman formalized an alliance between government and Croat forces, but it was not to hold for long, as tensions between Bosniaks and Croats grew. A year into the war, fighting broke out between the two forces on several fronts.

Asked to sort out the origins of the Croat-Bosniak conflict, writer Željko Ivanković said, "The Croats and the Bosniaks fought for their self-interest. One part of the Croats, led by Mate Boban, fought for Tuđman's expansionist goals and for a Greater Croatia. But some fought in self-defense, to protect their own homes. Then there were Croats in some places such as Usora, and Tuzla, where they fought together with the Bosniaks against the Serbs."[19]

In April 1993, fighting between Bosnian Croat armed units called the Croatian Defense Council (HVO) and the government army (the ARBiH—Army of the Republic of Bosnia-Herzegovina) broke out in full force, starting in several towns in central Bosnia. Within a couple of months after the onset of the fighting, the towns and villages of central Bosnia had been divided up in a patchwork between Croat and Bosniak forces.

In mid-April the HVO committed a massacre in the village of Ahmići as part of an ethnic cleansing campaign in the Lašva valley. There were war crimes committed by Bosniak forces as well, including expulsions, arson, rape, and killing of civilians. Bosniaks ethnically cleansed several dozen Croat villages in the summer of 1993.[20] They committed massacres in the Croat villages of Križ and Uzdol, and Bosniak soldiers murdered two Catholic priests at a monastery in Fojnica.

The Croats of central Bosnia fared the worst in this part of the conflict, as they came to be the victims simultaneously of the HDZ's aggressive policy and of the Bosniaks' war goals. When the conflict was played out, tens of thousands of Croats had been expelled from central Bosnia, to end up as displaced persons in Croat-controlled Herzegovina or as refugees in Croatia and beyond. Much of this movement was the result of Bosniak attacks on the Croat population. It was also the result of the Croat policy of "humane resettlement," a euphemism concocted by aides of Croatian president Franjo Tuđman.[21]

The movement of Croats into western Herzegovina and the expulsion of Muslims from that region was part of a plan to establish a Croat-controlled statelet called Herceg-Bosna. It is probable that the long-term intention was to annex Herceg-Bosna to Croatia.

During the summer of 1993 the HVO drove Bosniaks out of towns and villages throughout western Herzegovina; many of these people ended up in east Mostar. Bombarded by the HVO, east Mostar became a Bosniak enclave under siege. The prewar population of that part of the city was estimated at ten thousand; by mid-1993 at least fifty-five thousand people were crammed into the besieged area, suffering from increasing hunger.[22] People were being killed or wounded by bombs and snipers every day. The situation was described as being worse than that of Sarajevo.[23]

After the war, suspected Muslim war criminals and Croat separatists and military leaders of the HVO were put on trial at The Hague for a variety of war crimes. Of these trials, the most prominent, widespread, and drawn out one was that of *Prlić et al.*, the prosecution of six prominent Croat separatists for forced deportation of Bosniaks, along with detention, torture, murder, and the use of civilians as human shields and for slave labor, among other things. After a first-instance conviction of the six in 2013, an appeal resulted in confirmation of the initial judgment in late 2017.[24]

By the spring of 1994, military developments made a significant change in the trajectory of the war possible. Bosniak forces had begun to win victories against the Croats on the battlefield, especially in central Bosnia. Meanwhile Western officials put pressure on Croatia to halt support of Bosnian Croat separatists. Croat and Bosniak representatives went to Washington to work out a cease-fire agreement.

The Washington Agreement of spring 1994 ended the fighting between the Croats and Bosniaks and, at least on a formal level, re-created the alliance between the two parties that had existed at the beginning of the war. However, the relationship had been changed permanently. Two-way ethnic cleansing in Herzegovina and central Bosnia was all but complete, with at least eighty thousand Croats and Bosniaks displaced in that region.[25]

With Croat and Muslim forces cooperating, the route was opened for an eventual tipping of the military balance against the Serbs. The Washington Agreement also created a Croat- and Bosniak-controlled Federation of the territories controlled by the respective forces. A new military/political reality was born.

CORRUPTION IN WAR

It is critical to introduce the fact of wartime corruption here, because it is the root of the dynamics that have flourished in Bosnian-Herzegovinan politics to this day. As the war continued, a regime of corruption flourished. There was potential for profiteering at many levels, from that of the petty smuggler up to the high political echelon. The new elite, engaged vigorously in implementing ethnic cleansing, was at the same time involved in enriching itself.

Whether the plunder and corruption were end goals or secondary but inevitable to wartime dynamics is open to discussion. There has been a spectrum of motivations; for some people involved in the war, the establishment of a Greater Serbia or a Greater

Croatia was paramount. It would not be accurate to accuse Slobodan Milošević, nor many of his high-level collaborators in the Serbian political and military infrastructure, of working simply to enrich themselves. After all Milošević and his family, for example, were already quite well situated, with their millions pocketed away in secret bank accounts in Cyprus and Switzerland.[26]

It would be more appropriate to describe Milošević's motive as the desire for increased power. As has been the case with leaders before and after Milošević, reinforcing one's power often turns out to be the only way to stay out of prison. Other military and political leaders involved in the Yugoslav wars were similarly motivated by lust for power, but also, at times, by a seriously misplaced sense of patriotism colored by national chauvinism. It tended to be the lower commanders who took advantage of opportunities to smuggle goods or engage in plunder; the higher-level leaders had more refined ways of enriching themselves.

In any case, the massive transfer of wealth from ordinary citizens to all manner of profiteers, war criminals, and political leaders commenced during the war and continued in the postwar period. From the beginning of the war the dynamic of corruption was in force throughout Bosnia-Herzegovina; for military leaders on all sides, killing and getting rich often went together.

Describing the development of an alliance between criminals and the new state, the Sarajevo journalist Gojko Berić wrote, "[The war's] character was determined by mass gangsterism against civilians and general plunder. The war . . . brought onto the public stage thousands of killers and violent robbers. It was their war, the occasion they'd been waiting for. Yesterday's riff-raff, headed by local nationalist leaders, were given the chance to vent their brutal energy. At the head of the gangster lines were the people who had thought up, organized and led the whole thing. Cloaked in the mantle of State and Nation, they all reeked of blood."[27]

Munir Alibabić, wartime head of Sarajevo's Central Intelligence Service, wrote about dishonest practices among police and officials in the Sarajevo government. He noted an "oligarchic group" that "acted as a team, divided up property and powers without regard to rights, mainly keeping goods for themselves: real estate, merchandise, position, and travels."[28] These practices took place while thousands of honest Sarajevans fought and died to protect their city. Alibabić termed the dishonest regime a "mafiocracy."

WHILE THIS PASSAGE HAS FOCUSED ON PERSONAL enrichment and other motives for the killing spree that was the Bosnian war, it is important to note the role of genocide in the overall wartime picture. Whether Tuđman or Milošević set out to exterminate the members of another ethnicity, in whole or in part, is up for debate; it is demonstrable that either of these leaders would have been satisfied to annex significant territories of Bosnia-Herzegovina and to subjugate or expel vast numbers of members of the target ethnonational groups. It is equally clear that military commanders and some political leaders, such as Radovan Karadžić, Ratko Mladić, and Mate Boban, among others, were avidly and intentionally involved in the mass targeting of Muslims for murder. In any case, while there was a spectrum of motivations for the aggression against Bosnia-Herzegovina, genocide was one of the outcomes.

MOVING TOWARD THE END

Throughout the war, the inhabitants of Bosnia-Herzegovina lived through cycles of desperation, false hope, and disappointment. The front line changed little after the early months of the war. The eastern enclaves remained under siege, and Serb forces continued to expel Bosniaks and Croats from areas that they controlled. However, there were certain developments that would bring the war to an end in the course of 1995.

After the creation of the Croat-Bosniak Federation in the summer of 1994, a new peace plan was drafted by a "Contact Group" composed of the United States, France, Germany, Great Britain, and Russia. The plan proposed to allot 49 percent of Bosnia-Herzegovina to the Serbs, and the rest would go to the Federation.

Although the Contact Group's proposed map gave Srebrenica, Žepa, and Goražde to the Federation, geography and military logic worked against such an arrangement, and many international officials recognized this. By early 1995, members of the US administration had more or less given up on preserving the eastern enclaves, and they were considering a land trade.[29] Bosniak leaders saw the problem as well, although none of them was willing to openly propose giving up the enclaves. Early in 1995 President Izetbegović had told US negotiator Richard Holbrooke that he "knew that all three eastern enclaves were not viable and would have to be given up."[30]

For three years after the establishment of the "safe area," there was an uneasy standoff between the huddled residents of Srebrenica and surrounding Serb forces. Although a condition for UNPROFOR protection of the enclave was the handover of firearms owned by the Muslims, residents turned in their less useful weapons and kept what they could. And as the reach of the safe area was ill defined—both geographically and in the sense of UNPROFOR's responsibility—units of the Army of Bosnia-Herzegovina were able to operate defensively on the periphery of the enclave. However, after the spring of 1993 their struggle was for survival, not for expansion or breakout of the enclave.

In March 1995, for reasons that have never been explained, Naser Orić's superiors in Sarajevo ordered him to leave the enclave. This was a serious blow to the Bosniaks' defense of the enclave, because Orić's leadership was a critical factor in promoting cohesion among the local troops.

Determined to hasten the outcome of the war in 1995, Serb leaders increased pressure on Srebrenica early in the year. In April and May, Serb forces intensified bombardment of some of the settled areas on the edges of the enclave. Their encroachment on the enclave escalated in June 1995, when Serb forces took over all of Dutchbat's southern observation posts one by one. The Muslim population and its lightly armed soldiers fully expected that the UN was going to defend the enclave and drive back the advancing army; without antitank weapons or an air force, there was no other possible salvation. But during critical days in early July, NATO did not appear. The enclave fell on the eleventh of July.

Many writers have concluded that responsibility for the capture of Srebrenica does not fall squarely on the Dutch. In *Yugoslavia: Death of a Nation*, one of the most authoritative books on the breakup of Yugoslavia, the authors declare, "The Dutch had done what they could. . . . They were poorly placed to do anything to halt the offensive that was taking place."[31]

This statement seems logical, given the small number of Dutch troops present in the enclave, and it is true that the Dutch are not alone in their responsibility for the fall of Srebrenica. However, the book was written at the end of the war, when much information had not yet become available, at least not to most foreigners. In 2005, Hasan Nuhanović published his book *Under the UN Flag*. This book focuses on the actions of Dutchbat in Srebrenica, and it demolishes the assertion that the Dutch "did what they could." *Under the UN Flag* describes in painful detail the steps Dutch authorities took throughout their stay in the enclave that undermined the Bosniak defense. In many instances, Dutchbat went overboard to thwart the Bosniak defense, thus making the Serb takeover easier.

Nuhanović relates that on various occasions, Dutch troops prevented the Bosniaks from constructing defensive positions in the southern part of enclave. They stopped the army from digging trenches near the boundaries of the enclave and at times even filled them in.[32] Between 1993 and 1995, when the Serb army took over parts of the enclave that were important for its defense, the Dutch did not react. Periodically, they confiscated weapons from Bosniak soldiers who were trying to patrol the periphery. And during the Serb offensive, the Dutch also refrained from defending their own positions that the Serbs fired on.[33] When the enclave fell, as Dutch soldiers evacuated their observation posts they consistently handed over their weapons to the Serbs.[34] The behavior of Dutchbat helped Srebrenica fall.

As the fall of the enclave came closer, its population divided into two groups. Most men of fighting age embarked on an overland trek toward government-controlled territory around Tuzla. Women, children, and the elderly moved toward Potočari, a suburb several kilometers to the north of Srebrenica town, hoping to find safety at the Dutchbat headquarters. By the time Serb forces arrived in Srebrenica on the afternoon of July 11, some twenty-five thousand people were streaming into Potočari. The Dutch opened a section of fencing on the side of their base in order to allow people to enter. Around five thousand people were let in; then, the Dutch welded shut the opening, saying that the base was becoming overcrowded.

Twenty thousand terrified people were left stranded on the road and in the fields surrounding the base. Hasan Nuhanović reported that the Dutch concern about overcrowding was fraudulent, because there was much space that could have housed more refugees.[35]

The evacuation of the crowds around the Dutchbat base proceeded quickly. By two days after the fall of the enclave, the Serbs had removed most of the refugees who had not been admitted to the base, separating out the men of fighting age and sending them off to be killed. Serb officers then directed the Dutch to allow the evacuation of the roughly five thousand people located on their base. Some Dutch soldiers cooperated with the evacuation, even though they were aware of the killings that had been taking place around the base. Some individual Dutch soldiers objected to the separation and expulsion, but they were powerless.[36]

Hasan Nuhanović mentions several reasonable actions that the Dutch could have taken to save lives. Immediately upon taking over Srebrenica, General Mladić requested that the Dutch supply vehicles to remove the Bosniak population. When there was no response forthcoming from the Dutch, Serb troops took over this task, making the separations and abuse more likely.[37] Nuhanović points out that a UN-coordinated convoy from other parts of Bosnia could have transported the refugees in a secure manner.

The men captured at Potočari were driven to the nearby town of Bratunac and confined in a warehouse. Meanwhile, a column of ten thousand to fifteen thousand men had set out from the enclave through the woods toward Tuzla. Around a third of them were armed. These men, accompanying Srebrenica's military and political leaders, headed the column. The march was to be a hideous experience that the majority of the men would not survive.

The column proceeded through the woods slowly, short on food, water, and sleep. Men became disoriented and wandered in circles. The Serb army ambushed the unarmed middle and rear portions of the column several times and captured large numbers of men. The captured men were taken in groups and gunned down in summary executions and then buried in mass graves. Larger groups of captives were taken to collection points and killed. Over a thousand men were mowed down by automatic weapons and grenades in a warehouse in Kravica. The final phase of the atrocity was under way.

The vanguard of the column managed to fight its way through Serb troops near the front lines, and it reached free territory in less than ten days. Other people straggled in after a few weeks or even months, having lost their way, or simply having waited for a safe time to cross through dangerous territory. At most, only around five or six thousand men arrived safely.

THE CROATIAN OFFENSIVE IN THE KRAJINA

Launching Operation Storm in August 1995, the Croatian army attacked Serb forces occupying the Croatian Krajina, part of a region that stretched from northwestern Bosnia westward across the border into Croatia. The entire Croatian Krajina fell within three days. The largest single expulsion of the war ensued, with at least two hundred thousand

Croatian Serbs fleeing eastward along routes that the Croatian army had left open. Some Croatian soldiers committed war crimes against the civilian population. Around twenty thousand Serb homes were looted and burned.[38] Elderly Serbs who had chosen to remain in their centuries-old homeland were murdered by the dozens, and, in some instances, Croatian forces bombarded the roads on which Serb refugees were fleeing.[39]

The combined Croatian, Bosnian Croat, and Muslim forces then began to take back control of part of the Bosnian territories conquered by Serb forces three years earlier. By a week into August, the military balance of the war in Bosnia had turned. Serbian ambitions to create a "Greater Serbia," all the way across northern and western Bosnia and into Croatia, were curtailed.

On August 28, Serb forces launched a bomb into Sarajevo that landed on the Markale open-air market where, eighteen months before, a similar attack had caused a gruesome massacre. The second Markale massacre was a shock to a newly sensitized world and served as the pretext for the ensuing NATO intervention. NATO's bombing soon forced the end of the siege of Sarajevo, and a final cease-fire came into force October 12, 1995. The next step was to prepare for the Dayton peace conference, to be held in Ohio in November.

THE DAYTON PEACE AGREEMENT

To a large extent, the negotiations at Dayton enshrined wartime territorial acquisitions as they stood in late 1995; these facts on the ground, together with the Contact Group's 51/49 percent agreement, dictated the Dayton map. The Dayton peace agreement (officially titled "The General Framework Agreement for Peace in Bosnia and Herzegovina") recognized the territorial and political division of Bosnia into two "entities" in that territorial ratio: the Serb-controlled Republika Srpska, and the Croat- and Bosniak-controlled Federation of Bosnia-Herzegovina. The RS was granted 49 percent of Bosnia's territory, and the Federation received the rest—excluding Brčko, which was later decreed a "District."

A new constitution was promulgated as Annex 4 of the peace agreement. The constitution set up a state where its subjects were defined as "Serbs," "Croats," "Bosniaks," and "Others." In this way Bosnia-Herzegovina became a state where people's political rights were tied to their ethnicity.[40] The enshrining of ethnic differences as a constitutional factor contributed to cementing the wartime ethnic divisions. The Republika Srpska was understood to be the "Serb entity," and the Federation was a place for Bosniaks and Croats.*

---

* The International Crisis Group's Balkans Report "Is Dayton Failing?" notes, "The Preamble to Annex 4 mentions three constituent nations of Serbs, Croats and Bosniaks. 'Others' are recognised as an afterthought, with mere 'citizens' barely worth mentioning. Note that the Serbs, Croats, Bosniaks and Others are not categorised jointly as citizens—the 'citizens' are an additional, fifth group of people in the state. It is already evident in the Preamble, therefore, that the DPA BiH state was to be hijacked from the citizens and transferred to the three ethnic groups."

Annex 7 of the Dayton agreement provided for freedom of movement and for return of displaced persons to their prewar homes. But there was no guarantee that the return called for under Annex 7 could take place. Dayton also established the Office of the High Representative (OHR), an international envoy with governing powers over Bosnia. The OHR was designed to be a guiding administrator, rather than a commanding one, in the hope that in peacetime there would be a strong desire among Bosnian leaders to re-create a unified nation and a functional state. It was an illusory hope.

The Dayton constitution bequeathed most political power to the ethnically domi-nated entities. At the state level, voters were to be represented by a three-member presidency, composed of a Croat, a Serb, and a Bosniak. The Serb was to be selected in the Republika Srpska, and the Croat and Bosniak members of the presidency were elected in the Federation. This disenfranchisement of Serbs in the Federation and of Croats and Bosniaks in the RS was a reflection of the fact that, under Dayton, Serbs had constitutional protection, or "constituent status," only in the RS, and Croats and Bosniaks only in the Federation. The fact that this built-in discrimination flouted inter-national rights conventions that were also enshrined in the Dayton constitution was but one of many internal, self-defeating contradictions of the document.[41]

The competencies of the central state were limited by Dayton to such spheres as foreign policy, foreign trade, customs enforcement, monetary policy, and immigration. The resulting power arrangement was one in which the entities took on the character of autonomous statelets, while the central authority remained essentially powerless, especially regarding domestic policy. The Federation's unity was symbolic as well, since the territory that had come to be controlled by Croat separatists during the war contin-ued to be dominated by those wartime leaders and their political heirs. The resulting postwar Bosnian state, deformed by partition, has been pithily described as a legal fiction, or a "customs union with a foreign ministry."[42]

The Banja Luka artist Alojz Čurić characterized the Dayton setup in a more col-orful manner, saying, "This is a traffic accident in the United Nations, an unnatural division. The system of two entities reminds me of a monster, a Hollywood creation. There should be decentralization along regional, not political lines: Herzegovina, the Krajina, Semberija, and other parts Bosnia; this unnatural, pathological Bosnia-Herzegovina can't go to Europe."[43]

But Čurić provided a metaphor for Bosnia that echoed many people's expectations: "Bosnia is a phoenix." More than one Bosnian has said to me, "We have outlived all previous occupations; we will recover from this as well."

The postwar period was to be characterized by a struggle to survive what was pos-sibly the greatest threat in Bosnia's thousand-year history: the division of the country as ratified by Dayton.

PART I

AFTERMATH OF WAR

1

Postwar Bosnia

A NEW NATIONAL DISORDER

THE DESTRUCTION WROUGHT IN BOSNIA-HERZEGOVINA WAS staggering to contemplate. Nearly half a million houses and apartments were destroyed,[1] and hundreds of mosques and churches were demolished. Serb forces destroyed more than eleven hundred mosques and over five hundred Catholic churches, according to the International Court of Justice.[2] Croat nationalist forces also destroyed mosques, and Serbian Orthodox Church sources counted nearly two hundred Orthodox churches and related buildings that were destroyed in the war.[3]

Fully half the population of Bosnia-Herzegovina was displaced. Of that number, well over a million fled to a hundred countries around the world. The rest were internally displaced persons who ended up in makeshift temporary residences called collective centers or with relatives in the zones controlled by their ethnicity: Serbs to the Republika Srpska, and Croats and Bosniaks to the Federation.

Although the Croats and Bosniaks were formally allied at the end of the war, the Federation was ethnically divided. The nationalist elite of each ethnic population remained in control of an army. Territory under the control of Bosnian Croat forces (HVO) amounted to about 20 percent of Bosnia, with another 30 percent under Bosniak control. Bosnian Serbs controlled half the country.[4]

The ethnic homogenization of these territories was nearly complete. "Ethnic cleansing" had succeeded in driving all but a few thousand Croats, Bosniaks, and other non-Serbs out of the Republika Srpska. Likewise, at the end of the war Croat-controlled territories in western Herzegovina and several other parts of the Federation were predominantly Croat-populated, and the rest of the Federation was mainly populated by Bosniaks.[5] For the first time, Croats, Bosniaks, and Serbs were designated as "minorities" in areas where the other ethnicities held control. Only Sarajevo and Tuzla, under Bosniak control, were not completely ethnically cleansed, but Bosniaks still constituted around 90 percent of the population in those two cities.

Bosnia was scattered with hundreds of mass graves. Shortly after the war's end, thirty thousand people were reported missing.[6] At least seventy-five hundred people were missing from Srebrenica alone. The impact of not knowing the fate of a lost loved one became clear to me when I volunteered at a relief agency in Tuzla. Many displaced people from Srebrenica, most of them widows, had ended up in Tuzla in 1995. Some of them frequented the place I worked. It was not rare that a middle-aged woman would look at me through eyes burning with grief and exclaim something like, "I had six sons!"

Compounding the personal upheaval and sorrow caused by the war was the physical discomfort caused by damaged infrastructure, systems that didn't work, and poverty. In homes where I lived in Tuzla and Sarajevo, it was necessary to fill jugs full of water and save them on the kitchen and bathroom shelves, as running water was only an occasional thing. Electricity was often shut off, and one was lucky if both utilities were working at the same time for a short period. Telephoning was difficult and expensive, with most pay phones out of order. Good fruit and vegetables were rare in the cold season. Mail delivery was spotty. As my landlady remarked, "Well, you have come to a country where they have been making war."

Thousands of windows in Sarajevo were covered only by a sheet of plastic with the logo of the UNHCR printed on it in blue ink. The chill of the continental winter made living uncomfortable in an unheated building in this mountain city, where a meter of snow could fall in a couple of days and a temperature below freezing was not unusual.

Gas for heating was piped from Russia and was not turned on until well after the cold season had started. The lack of fuel and a shortage of electricity meant people bundled up and lived by candlelight at night. In the first few years after the war, people in Sarajevo were saying that "the only difference between now and the war days is that there are no bombs falling."

POVERTY

My Sarajevo landlord, Riza, said to me:

> Before the war, everything was good. All schooling and health coverage was free. When you went to the dentist, you didn't have to pay ten marks before you could say "aah." You could sleep in any park anywhere, and no one would steal from you. The police didn't bother you, either. No one told you that you couldn't go into a mosque or a church. You had enough to eat and go on vacation. You could go to the coast, or to Slovenia, or Macedonia, and prices were the same there as here. In the evening, you sat in a kafana [coffeehouse] and sang the old songs from all over Yugoslavia with your friends; that was our simple satisfaction.
>
> Now, I would croak from hunger if it weren't for the 150 marks the government gives me for a retirement pension. But I had to spend 700 marks on wood to heat this room, and another 100 for electricity.
>
> The Serbs will never live as they did before the war. Neither will we. It used to be, you'd sit in the Ćiro [the old Austro-Hungarian narrow-gauge train] at the station and ride up to a Serb village and buy *kajmak* [a salted, creamy specialty farm cheese]. No one cared what people you belonged to; you just cared about the taste of the kajmak.
>
> Now we won't ever live as well as we did, nor will the next generation. You live in order not to die, that's all. You work, but you aren't paid.

The factories of Bosnia had been looted during the war, and most of those that remained intact were shut down. Production remained around 20 percent of the prewar rate for several years. Unemployment was widespread, and many of those who were lucky enough to find work were employed by international relief organizations or by international governmental organizations. A family was lucky if there was one employed member to support it. Others lived on miserly retirement pensions or equally small benefits that were afforded to some demobilized veterans or widows. The unluckiest were the thousands of displaced people who had no support and were forced to pay rent to stay in other people's homes.

In Sarajevo and Tuzla, where I spent my first months in postwar Bosnia, the sidewalks were lined with people selling things. These informal vendors were all over town, at the parks and on the side streets, piling their wares on card tables or crates. They sold cartons of cigarettes, stacked up Lincoln-log style, three or four feet high. They hawked cigarette lighters, chocolate, chewing gum, plastic shoes, plastic bowls, and music cassettes. Here and there they sold a bit of produce. Others prepared popcorn or French fries right on the street. Used books were in abundant supply. I saw a woman with nothing for sale but three bags of potato chips and a plastic bowl.

The wretchedness of life after the war struck me when I saw how some people struggled to make ends meet. One old man stood with a satchel by his feet, holding a few boxes of cigarettes and a couple of paper twists of pumpkin seeds in his hands. He didn't have a card table or crate. He stood in the cold, not looking at anyone. Many people out on the street selling things stayed until well after dark, with most of those who were better off passing them by, or occasionally stopping for a pack of cigarettes.

In such impoverished circumstances, smuggling and tax evasion are survival tactics for the poor, and a means for enrichment for the more well-off (at the expense of the country's budget). One prominent showcase of these practices was the "Arizona market" north of Tuzla. Reporters were fond of going there and writing articles to the effect that "this is the last little bit of Yugoslavia," where people came from every surrounding country to sell cheap goods, and no one asked where they or their goods were from. What the reporters often neglected to mention was that this tax-free market was one of the great wounds in the Bosnian economy, which was bleeding from a thousand cuts.

I began to take trips to Prijedor and the surrounding area soon after the war. There, retired economist Mirjana told me:

> Many people are living below the poverty line. Here in front of my building there are dumpsters. I have lived here for thirty-eight years. People used to pass this way coming back from the paper factory; over three thousand people worked there. Now that factory is closed. I see an engineer looking in the dumpster for bread. I'm embarrassed to look at him, because I know him. I would help him, but I don't want to take away that last bit of dignity. These people have a pension of 120 marks. They buy discarded vegetables and eat at home. There is no money for medicine or the clinic; many people just die from their sicknesses, with no help. There has been a rise in suicide, for economic reasons. This is taking place among older people, and among younger people who don't see any future, who won't even get a pension. Those who work can't live from their pay.

When I was volunteering at the relief center in Tuzla in 1997, one of my co-workers was Mina, a displaced person from a nearby area that had been absorbed into the Serb-controlled entity. Mina told me that she owed eight hundred marks (about US$500) for her electricity bill. There were five refugee families living in the house with her, and none of them wanted to pay their share. I asked her what she was going to do. She said, "Get out the candles, I guess." When Mina's mother was sick and needed an injection, if she had not had twelve marks to pay for this care, she would have simply died. Twelve or fifteen marks for medicine was a significant sum for people who, if they were working, earned three hundred marks per month.

Esma, director of the relief center, told me, "All our lives, we paid into the health and pension systems, and now that money is gone. If you go to the clinic now and don't have money, they just tell you to go home. I look at the death notices that are posted on the walls and telephone poles, and people are dying younger. There is a certain population that is hungrier than during the war. Then, at least you knew you were going to get an aid package, no matter who you were. You might not have had any vegetables, but you could count on those beans. Now, everything is available in the stores; there's just no money to buy anything."

In late 1997, I visited a family in an outer neighborhood of Sarajevo Canton. No one in the family, headed by a demobilized veteran named Refik, was working. They had small pensions; there was not much help for veterans. Refik said that the people who had nice cars in Sarajevo were people who left during the war and earned money elsewhere. The ostentatious display of privilege in Sarajevo offended him, a displaced person who had fought bravely during the war and had lost his home. Refik said that there was no opportunity or future for the refugees and veterans. "There is a future for the children," he said. "If we take back the rest of Bosnia, that future will come earlier." As a Bosniak who fought the Serb forces and was displaced from eastern Herzegovina, Refik considered the entire Republika Srpska to be territory stolen and separated from Bosnia.

Raba, the matriarch of the family, was receiving a pension of twelve marks a month. At seventy years old—no small age for someone who had lived through two wars—she was alert and lively, wearing *dimija* (baggy Turkish pants) and a scarf. She rose at 6:00 every morning to bake bread for the family. She took her worry beads and went to a back room to pray before dinner. When the topic of conversation turned gloomy, she muttered, "Poor people, poor people. All split up, all spread out everywhere."

While under the prewar socialist system the elite possessed material privileges, there was nevertheless a significant amount of leveling, accompanied by substantial economic security for the average Yugoslav. Citizens who worked for their whole lives after World War II took it for granted that they would not have to worry in their old age. So it was with great affront and disappointment that masses of people realized that the security they expected was no longer there.

After the war, Bosnians found themselves living in a "kafana republic." That phrase could encapsulate the economic arrangement of the country, just as "banana republic" does for some Central American lands. That is, the new managers of the economy enriched themselves through high-end profiteering; smugglers and looters who had come out ahead during the war opened kafanas, and the ordinary people were lucky if they had a half mark to buy a coffee in those venues.

The Zagreb journalist Ivica Bašić summed up the losses that affected all ex-Yugoslavs: "We lost the peace, and we got war, over twenty thousand graves [in Croatia] and still more disabled. . . . We lost our unity, and we got madness. We lost the socialist society and got capitalism, the state of criminality and thievery. We lost brotherhood and unity and love among people, and we got nationalism and hatred. We lost worker self-management and social ownership, and we got tycoons who took away that ownership and turned workers into ordinary slaves who could easily lose their jobs. We lost secure employment and regular payment, and we got unemployment, insecurity, and irregular payment even for those who are employed."[7]

TRAUMA

To walk in Sarajevo after the war was to see the signs of destruction everywhere. Entire buildings had been reduced to piles of rubble. There was not a single block that was free of shrapnel holes in the walls or small bomb craters in the sidewalk. Some of these craters had been filled in with red plastic, creating the "Sarajevo rose" that was an enduring memento of the destruction.

One could not help but think of the damage a small piece of metal could do to human flesh, if it could cut through an iron fence or a brick wall.

There was a bullet hole in the refrigerator of my apartment in downtown Sarajevo. Someone had fired this shot from Mount Trebević—visible about five miles away in a direct line of sight—through a narrow passage between two buildings.

Living through nearly four years of hell was bound to take a toll on people's long-term emotional state. The broken glass from every window in Sarajevo had been cleared away and replaced with plastic by the time I arrived in 1997, and eventually with new glass. But the psychic wounds were not so easy to repair.

Different people experienced the war in different ways. Mirza, a young acquaintance in Tuzla, was about twelve when the war broke out. Looking back, he said casually, "It was fun during the war; you didn't have to go to school all the time. My mother worried about me when I was playing outside, though."[8]

Slavenka, an artist from Sarajevo, endured a much more fraught contact with risk and death in her besieged city. On one occasion she was attending a funeral when snipers began firing on the cemetery. She had to jump into an empty grave for shelter. She was stuck there while the snipers kept shooting, as if they were playing with her. Slavenka told me she would like to lock a door on some memories; there were some things from the war that she just wanted to forget. But she could joke about other events, such as the time a sniper's bullet grazed her hair and left a burning smell in the air.

In Tuzla, Emina missed a date with death when she was delayed from going to the Kapija, a central pedestrian zone, on the night that a bomb killed over seventy young people there. She said, "I knew one of those girls who was killed. She loved to dance; she was sixteen. Many of my friends were wounded. Thank God I wasn't wounded. What I carry in myself, I can't describe with words. It is not easy to fall asleep at night, because I don't know what I will dream."

Indira Čečo, director of the Sarajevo counseling center Corridor, founded by counseling professionals during the war, spoke about the problems soldiers faced. Čečo said, "Before the war, the issue of mental health simply meant 'to be crazy or not.' Or someone was just called 'nervous.' It was bad to say you needed help."[9] Čečo recalled that a small group of soldiers snuck into the counseling center for a time.

> They needed the most help, because they saw the worst things, murder, arson. If a man was head of the family, he lost his role during the war by being absent much of the time. He had been a hero, but then after the war, he started drinking, and he lost the role of husband and father.
>
> With younger men, reintegration into society is easier; it is easier for them to get work. Older men, no one needs them. There is no work. They were on the front, and they didn't learn computers, and other new skills—they don't fit in whatsoever.

The disruption of the traditional role of men in Bosnian society is one of several things that people often referred to when they told me that "values have been disturbed." Čečo continued, "Before the war, neighbors helped take care of children. You would leave your key with the neighbor to help take care of your apartment. Now, you don't even know who lives next door. You can no longer call for outside help; you have to fix things yourself. You have to take all the responsibility. It is a big problem."

It was clear that survivors were reeling in the aftermath of the war, many of them at a loss to heal their emotional wounds. These wounds were bound to be much deeper for the thousands of victims of torture in concentration camps during the war. Women had often been singled out as targets of sexual violence; the number of victims of rape is undocumented, but estimates range in the tens of thousands. The physical and emotional effects of this treatment were devastating; one survivor told an interviewer, "I will never be okay."[10]

The saddest history is that of the children, of whom an estimated twenty thousand were killed in the war and another eighty-five thousand injured or subjected to serious trauma.[11] Postwar studies reported that between 20 percent and 50 percent of Bosnian citizens have suffered from post-traumatic stress disorder.[12] Widespread unemployment continues to compound this problem. Domestic violence, chronic disease, and suicide have been startlingly common in Bosnia-Herzegovina.

Indira Čečo said:

> War trauma can't be fixed; it can only be ameliorated. It is a question of the moment. For example, say an eighteen-year-old was in a concentration camp, or in five camps. If he has help, and he was able to work immediately, he feels very good. He is working and has money for food and clothes. But then if his company fails, he gets no pay. He sweats, doesn't sleep, has nightmares, and is nervous, has bad concentration.
>
> For some people it is easier, and for some harder. The loss of a child is the worst thing. You can't cure it like pulling a tooth.

VALUES

Hearing that I was preparing to live in her country after the war, a Bosnian immigrant to the United States said to me, "Be careful over there. People have changed." I did not know what she meant, but I was uncomfortable with the implication that a whole people was not to be trusted. However, I found that much more than buildings had been destroyed in Bosnia. A way of life had disappeared.

The transition from a society that provided security to one in which people had to fend for themselves came unannounced, without guidebooks to help people navigate the changes. Indira Čečo noted that the changes in values happened covertly, that "people are not aware of the transitions, neither the internal nor the external ones." Mostar activist Huso Oručević commented, "There is no reflection about it here. It is as if fifty years of socialism just disappeared. It as if there were no causes, just a conspiracy." Learning how to cope with the chaotic postwar order was a long-term process.

Social commentator Vojislav Vujanović said that "socialism hated an elite, and that brought about mediocrity."[13] That mediocrity continued to thrive in the new system formed under the banner of ethnic nationalism. Party operatives rose to prominence based on conformity with the ethnochauvinist ideology of their organization rather than because of any excellence in leadership. This dynamic was similar to what had functioned under socialism, but in the "old system" (as the Tito-era socialist government has come to be called) there was an expressed ethic of egalitarianism.

People were not treated equally during the Tito era, when there was a not-so-covert system of privilege. But the average worker had much more of a chance to live securely during the Tito period than in the postwar system, in thrall to a new national elitism that works to divide friends, suppress talent, and enrich a new aristocracy. The writer Ivan Cvitković described this as a situation where "nationalism enables a nobody to become a somebody."[14] The new leaders were willing to ignore truth, forget right and wrong, and commit crimes in the name of their ethnicity. They were also people who were skilled at jumping ship ideologically when they saw a change in the wind.

The new leaders have excelled at destroying, not healing. Their leadership encourages a culture of mediocrity. Indeed, in the words of Slavenka, what reigns in the postwar period is "the revenge of the bad students." Those who were previously not able to thrive and succeed because of their lack of talent or energy found opportunity during the war and afterward to even the score.

The postwar regime of mediocrity began in the concentration camps. In some instances, notoriously at Omarska, the civic leaders and notable talents of an entire community were wiped out based on lists that had been drawn up in advance. (This practice came to be called "elitocide.") Camp survivors have recalled people who acted out resentments against their former teachers. The mediocre student made a good concentration camp guard and a good midlevel police official.

A century ago Bosnia-Herzegovina, like the rest of Yugoslavia, was an agrarian society beginning to join the modern industrialized world. Urbanization took place in fits and starts, and every war saw a new wave of peasants arrive in the cities. The war of the 1990s was no exception, but there was a new twist: "ethnic urbanization" was the name of the latest country-to-city migration. Bosniak refugees from Srebrenica and Foča went to Sarajevo. Croats went to west Mostar, and Serbs to Banja Luka. Meanwhile, intellectuals left Bosnia altogether. The result was a wrenching change—not only demographically, but also culturally.

To walk down the street in Sarajevo after the war was to notice contrasts between the newcomers, who were mostly villagers, and the city folk. The differences in style were obvious, with women from villages tending to wear scarves, while city women looked like those of any other European city. Those who were of the city felt not only outnumbered but also endangered. Their multiethnic cultural life had been destroyed. They mistrusted the *papci*, a disparaging word for villagers.

Slavenka said, "After World War II, the people in government in Bosnia were mainly villagers. They brought their entire families to cities. Sarajevans waited thirty years for the children of those villagers to become city people, and create careers, and then those were the people who fled. Now after this war the same thing is happening. People are coming to the city, where 90 percent of the intellectuals left during or after the war. We are in same position that intellectuals were in after World War II."

It was a commonplace to say that the recent war was in fact a war of the countryside against the city. One intellectual told me, "People from the village wanted to destroy the city, to have the schools moved out to where they are, so that they could go to school in their slippers." The truth was more complicated. In fairness, the villagers were least of all the masters of their own destiny. They did not choose to be driven from their ancient homes, and they had little or no choice where to land.

One must imagine how painful the adjustment has been for displaced villagers, faced with such compounded insults and thrust into an entirely new way of life, without a way of making a living in the devastated postwar economy. Both sides of the cultural divide had sustained great losses. For at least a time, both the village and the city were murdered, to use a phrase of the writer Ivan Lovrenović, who vividly summarized the "end of urbanism" thus: "There is no imaginable manner in which the Bosnian cities have not been murdered. Visible and invisible . . . the result: one knows not where there is less civility. In Sarajevo, around which until yesterday there was an iron Serbian ring that spewed sulfur and steel every day for almost four years, with all its countless negative consequences, or in Banja Luka, in which there was no war, but all the same it became a monstrous place, a live example of the action of 'pure ethnic ideology' in a Serb rendition."[15]

With so much ruin and dislocation, postwar Bosnia-Herzegovina was a place of disappointment. While Bosnians were living through the war, they did not know what to expect afterward. It was easier for them to hope that things could go back to an old "normal" than to imagine the seemingly permanent wreckage the war made of society.

People even remembered good times during the war. Miki, a Sarajevan who lived through the war in his home city, recalled the way people stayed together and helped each other. "There was nothing else we could do; there was no television, and rarely any work. So we sat and talked and played cards. Happiness came when there was water, or oranges. Once I got five oranges, and there were four of us. How to divide up the five oranges for four people, that was happiness."

When ordinary people saw what the politicians and the privileged made of the peacetime for which they had paid so much, then came the disappointment. It came, as journalist Senka Kurtović wrote, "when those who defended Bosnia from abroad received the 'Golden Lily' award [the highest award in the Bosniak-controlled zone]; when prewar greengrocers . . . became wealthy; when villas, hotels, and motels began to spring up throughout Bosnia, and managers and businessmen overnight became their owners; when the cheats, the liars, and the troublemakers came to power."[16]

When someone can say that life was "better during the war," when bombs were falling, that is disappointment.

IDENTITY

> I am a European, a Bosnian, a citizen of Stolac,
> and my religion is my own business.
>
> —*Amer Medar, Stolac*

> I hate Bosnia
>
> —*graffiti in Banja Luka, Republika Srpska*

Where "Yugoslavism" had previously been the uniting patriotism of a country of twenty million, now there were three newly enforced patriotisms in a country of under four million.

The dissolution of Yugoslavia, the demise of socialism, and the rise of three mutually hostile nationalisms in Bosnia-Herzegovina demolished the foundation of people's identity before the war even began. In the decades before the war it was nearly universal to think of oneself as a Yugoslav. One's definition of identity was never simple; other layers of identity were present as well. Some people identified more consciously with their locality—be it a mountain village or a neighborhood of Sarajevo—than with any political designation.

Religion was not forbidden during the Tito era, but neither was it encouraged. In general, there was an underlying awareness of one's ethnicity, at least to the extent of knowing where one's ancestors came from and what their religion was. The ethnic designations in Bosnia-Herzegovina, while extensively politicized, derive from those religious backgrounds. For a time the differences that defined the ethnicities became minor matters and faded into the background; then they returned with a vengeance.

Ivan Lovrenović described the cultural pluralism that existed in Bosnia as "a matter of ongoing interaction"—being Bosnian is not simply a matter of "algebraic adding-up of nations or national cultures . . . more than that it is a civilizational process . . . of a constant culturally creative relationship of give and take."[17] For Lovrenović, Bosnian Croat and Bosniak cultures were not mutually antagonistic, but they actually reinforced and enriched each other. Only crude political manipulation in the interest of territorial division managed artificially to introduce discord between the ethnicities.[18]

Before nationalist extremism broke loose throughout Yugoslavia, there was something special about being Bosnian and being recognized as such. One could be a Bosnian Serb or a Bosnian Croat, but one was still a Bosnian. Vanja said, "We are different from them in Serbia. I'm glad that I'm a Bosnian Serb." Bosnian Croats have told me that they are culturally the richest and most interesting Croats, less adulterated in their "Croat-ness" than those of Croatia. Centuries of Bosniaks, Serbs, and Croats living together and mixing had necessarily created a varied and specific culture. Bosnia was Bosnia; it was not Serbia, Croatia, nor any other land. Lovrenović even asserts that there was one Bosnian culture, where "cultural differences . . . operated as nuances, and far more dominant was the cultural homogeneity of the entire Bosnian-Herzegovinian space."[19]

The demagogues and the profiteers took control of the media and the army and worked to eradicate that multiculturalism and that intangible, unifying Bosnian-ness. The crude nationalisms, each exalting a mythical version of its own "pure" culture, forced apart the peoples of Bosnia-Herzegovina by promoting a xenophobia that was quickly underpinned by wartime atrocities. The mediocre minds that administered the dissolution were not capable of grasping the concept of richness in diversity, or else they simply rejected it. They specialized in shattering nuances. After the murder of Bosnia there were still thousands of people who believed in tolerance. But the tolerant community, the collectivity capable of healing a society, was gone.

Identity theft thus took place on a grand scale, and people were forced to find substitutes for the Yugoslav or Bosnian component of their identity. Most, prompted by fear, gravitated toward the new prefabricated collectivities whose leaders promised them security. These leaders tacitly worked together as if they were a three-way protection racket, effectively collaborating with their "enemies" to keep their flocks separate.

In his book *Places of Pain*, anthropologist Hariz Halilovich describes this process as an "orchestrated collective 'remembering'" that prepared the ground for ordinary people "to kill . . . in the name of their people, to avenge lost mythological battles and (re)create mythical homelands for their nations."[20] Halilovich connects the transformation of people's identities with what he calls the "war over memory," where different historical narratives compete for the establishment of new identities—and, for that matter, for the erasure of old ones.[21]

One of the dynamics underway as the newly isolated, "de-Bosnianized" flocks were regrouped was the process of "re-traditionalization." The religions of the Bosnians' pre-Tito era ancestors were taken off the shelf and dusted off. It is questionable to what extent the revived religiosity answered spiritual needs. The traditional Bosnian way of being religious was not an exaggerated thing. Thus, when it became "politically appropriate" to be seen as religiously observant, many ordinary, religious people refrained from jumping on this bandwagon. However, others did, zealously turning to religion.

Miki told me, "It's very 'in' now to be an observant Muslim. It helps you get a job to be seen in a good section of one of the elite mosques. I know a woman who was already observant before the war, and now she can't even get into her old mosque, for lack of room."

For many, on the other hand, the restoration of their ethnic identity is a rectification, the patching of a perceived hole in their identity. Vanja's return to a Serb identity is as much a cultural expression as a religious one. She said, "Maybe it's sad that I hardly knew I was a Serb during the Communist period. In those days it was not important what religion or ethnicity you were. Now, I tell my kids that they are Serbs, but also that there are other nationalities that need to be respected. One should know one's identity."

With the demise of a politically united Bosnia-Herzegovina, the citizens of the new chaotically arranged state were forced to adopt new political allegiances alongside their redefined ethnic and religious identities. Vanja, speaking for Serb citizens of the Republika Srpska, said, "Before the war it was very big to say that you were from Bosnia. Now we say we are from Bosnia, but the majority of people do not have a strong sense of belonging. It is not from the heart. Sometimes I feel lost, I don't know where I belong."

Slavenka, a Sarajevo-born Bosnian Croat, feels discriminated against in her home city, dominated by Bosniak nationalists in the postwar period. She described the trajectory of changes in her identity: "Tito abolished personal identity after World War II; there were not Muslims, and Croats, and so on, just Yugoslavs. We all called ourselves Yugoslavs. Maybe 60 percent of us were satisfied with that situation. I called myself a Buddhist, that's how little I cared about my Croat identity. Now that I'm endangered, I care. I don't have a 'reserve country'; I have nothing to do with Croatia, but they are pushing me there."

"Before, we didn't pay attention to religion," said Vesna, a Serb living in the eastern part of the Republika Srpska and married to a Bosniak. "Now it is different. When they ask what religion you are, I say, 'What's it to you?' That's a personal thing."

Pero, a Tuzla Serb married to a local Bosniak, came from a family that observes its religion modestly. He said, "I like to maintain the tradition. I don't go to church every week. I go when I want people to live in peace, when I want the dead to rest in peace."

Nationalist division created a polemic between those who require every individual to adhere to one ethnoreligious bloc, and antinationalists, who would divorce ethnicity from political affiliation. "I am Bosnian Orthodox Christian, not a Serb," Pero said. "This is a small country, fewer than four million people live here. It is too small to divide up into separate nationalities and languages."

The danger to Bosnia as a multicultural place has not come from those who want to defend their own culture, but from those who exaggerate a perception of endangerment, an overemphasized state of victimhood, as a way to separate people. They are sometimes called "professional Croats," or "professional Bosniaks," or "professional Serbs," because they profit from their enhanced, exaggerated ethnicity. This new "profession" was not a by-product of the war; rather, it was a conscious endeavor in the service of separatism.

Meanwhile, there are those who still identify themselves simply as "Bosnians," regardless of their ancestors' religion. Some of these people continue to struggle for the restoration of a secular Bosnia-Herzegovina that protects all its citizens equally. Of these people, writer Gojko Berić lamented, "What worries me is the gradual drift away of those Bosnians who are committed to Bosnia as a single state, as the homeland of all its peoples, and who have been with us all these years. I would say that their energy, too, is dwindling, and that there are fewer of them than when the war came to an end. Many of them have stopped tilting at windmills, realizing that the villains have already brought their work to a close in Bosnia."[22]

SEPARATION

Postwar Bosnia-Herzegovina was divided into three de facto ethnic territories, with three armies and police forces and three nationalist political infrastructures. The Dayton constitution called for reintegration, but Bosnia's postwar rulers worked actively against this. Separation had been a main goal of the wartime commanders and their political leaders, and they accomplished their goal. The memories of the violence and of neighbors killing neighbors, and the relentless fear-mongering of the nationalist media, cemented this division.

There were many who insisted that there was no possibility of restoring the prewar cultural mixture. Political leaders continued to promote the idea that Bosnia's ethnicities could never live together again. Only by preserving ethnic homogenization could the nationalist leaders retain a constituency that would follow them. People had been frightened into believing that ethnicity took priority over more concrete common interests, such as their needs as workers, residents of a given environment, taxpayers, or citizens of a European state. People who felt compelled to vote as "Serbs," "Croats," or "Bosniaks," were ready-made "voting bodies," as the Bosnian saying goes, for their nationalist leaders.

Mayor Umičević of Banja Luka announced, "There can be no return for Bosniaks. But if they really want to come back, they must realize that they will have to learn Cyrillic and listen to the national anthem of Republika Srpska."[23] Many displaced Bosniaks yearned to come back to their prewar homes as soon as possible after the war, but such overt hostility sent a clear message to would-be returnees. I asked one Bosniak, displaced from Zvornik (an eastern Bosnian city now located in the Serb-controlled entity), if he wished to return home. He told me, "I will go home, but not if my children are required to study the Cyrillic alphabet."

A Bosniak woman, displaced from Kozarac, who was wounded during the war, told me that she knew that her neighbor had killed her husband. In spite of this she said she didn't hate him, but only pitied him. "As far as I'm concerned, life goes on. In Bosnia ethnicity should not be important. It is important that someone be a Serb who loves Bosnia, or a Croat who loves Bosnia, or a Bosniak who loves Bosnia."

After the war there were regular surveys that showed Croats and Serbs coming out strongly against a unified Bosnia-Herzegovina. The surveys tended to show that Bosniaks, on the other hand, believed that Bosnia should be reunited.[24] It was the Bosniaks who pressed most actively to return to their prewar homes in areas now controlled by other ethnicities, and their leaders gave at least rhetorical support to reunification of Bosnia. Serb and Croat leaders, on the other hand, worked most persistently to consolidate their constituents in separate, compact territories. They had not given up on their wartime dreams of connecting those territories to neighboring Serbia or Croatia.

The separatists managed to divide localities; Mostar, the most well-known of these, became divided between Croats and Bosniaks, as did Gornji Vakuf in central Bosnia. The core of Sarajevo came to be controlled by Bosniaks and some of its suburbs by Serbs, and the reverse was true in Doboj.

Before the war the population of Trebinje, in southern Herzegovina, had been 20 percent Bosniak. Most of the rest was Bosnian Serb, and Trebinje remained under Serb control after the war. When I visited the town in 1997, no Bosniaks remained. Dobrivoje, a local Serb, worked as a driver for an international organization. He told me, "We can never live with the Muslims again. It just doesn't work. We should live separately and learn to be good neighbors, like France and Germany."

But as I was leaving Trebinje, Dobrivoje said to me, "Please keep in touch. It's boring to live only with one people."

YOUTH

Bosnians, physically displaced after the war, struggled with emotional trauma, impoverishment, and the dislocation of their identity. The young people, who should have been the most hopeful, were quite tragically affected. Many were caught up in the nationalist fervor, and some participated enthusiastically in religious revivalism. Others cultivated a sense of victimhood, focusing on the most convenient enemy, placing the responsibility for their problems outside of themselves and their community. But many were aware that their elders had failed them.

Regardless of their ethnic background or wartime experiences, the youth felt the loss of a protective state and the vanishing of a promising future most keenly. They could go to college, but there was little promise of employment afterward. They didn't have money to travel or even to shop. Bosnia-Herzegovina was a devastated and partitioned country on bad terms with its neighbors.

There was not much for young people to do after the war. It was very common for them to spend much of the day frequenting kafanas, socializing with friends, and sharing coffee.

In a Serb-controlled eastern suburb of Sarajevo, I was introduced to Ljubo, who told me that he wanted to move to Canada. His parents were in the process of trading their house in Sarajevo for one on the other side of the border between entities. Ljubo said to me, "Here, there is no hope. Not here, not on the other side. Maybe in twenty or thirty years it will be better, but that is a long time from now. We have all been swindled by a few people who made a profit out of this."

For a time in 1998 I worked at a media agency in Sarajevo. One Friday when things were slow, young Maja started asking me questions. She said, "Do you still have discos in America?" and "How much do drugs cost?" Maja told me that entertainment was in short supply in Sarajevo, where one could go to the discos only one or two nights a week. And they didn't have what she needed at the library. She would go to the library, and it would take her a half hour to find something to read.

Drugs had been a minor problem in Yugoslavia before the war, but their importation increased via well-used smuggling channels during and after the war. Mira, director of a youth center in Tuzla, told me, "Alcoholism has risen, as well as drug use. There are twelve- and fourteen-year-olds who are using drugs."

Mira explained, "A large part of the young population is burdened with events; it is a period of social catastrophe. Parents are struggling to survive, and they are taking care of their children less and less. Before, close attention to children was very characteristic of families here. There was extra attention for young people. Now governmental involvement in youth activities is disappearing; there are fewer resources. The socialist system preserved it, but that is lost. It is as if this country existed only since 1995, and everything starts from today."

Tens of thousands of Bosnians, especially younger people, were following wartime refugees out of their homeland in the first postwar years. A study by the non-governmental youth organization KULT (Institute for Youth Development) reported that between the end of the war and late 2013 some 150,000 young people had left the country, never to return.[25]

Summing up many people's resignation, one young Sarajevan, frustrated after struggling through his university studies and then failing to find employment, wrote me, "The same old thieves are running Bosnia. I'm sick of this country. As far as I'm concerned, this whole region, with the exception of Slovenia, should go to hell. It should be buried under the mud. Then you can come back here as an archaeologist in fifty years and sort it all out."

HOPE

The end of the war brought shock and rude disappointment to the mass of Bosnians. Once they saw that they had survived the war, they understood that life would never again be the way it had been before. Postwar Bosnia brought a scene of disabled men or widows hawking smuggled cigarettes in the public market; retired professors searching for food in garbage dumpsters; and frustrated young people fantasizing about leaving their ruined homeland behind.

And yet there was something positive among the people, something that compelled more than a few of them to work against the division, to speak out against crime and corruption wherever they saw it. That natural impulse for justice was not entirely killed or co-opted. After the war, some Bosnians and Herzegovinans showed that they knew their rights. They knew they had the right to define their own identity and that they had the right to dignity, justice, and a livelihood. And they knew that they had to fight for these rights.

Principal among the forms this struggle would take in the coming years was the campaign waged by tens of thousands of displaced people to return to their prewar homes. Naturally, people were more aware of their own struggles than of those of other people, but they were often able to comprehend that the principles of justice they held dear must also be applied universally—even to their erstwhile enemies. There were those who held fast to the ideal of coexistence. In this comprehension and in this universal struggle there was hope. That hope was not among the international officials, the politicians, or the new elite of the fractured Bosnian society, but among the ordinary people who had the energy to agitate for their own needs. Whatever recovery was to commence in the next few years was above all their responsibility, and there were people who were ready to join the campaign for recovery that has continued up to today.

PART II

OVERVIEW OF THE RETURN MOVEMENT

Most of us displaced persons from Višegrad wish to return there. But with conditions as they are at present, it is very difficult. We will have to live together again; we were together for a thousand years. There will be no survival if we try to continue on as separate ethnicities.

—*Amir, 1998*

2

Introduction to Refugee Return

AMIR WAS A DISPLACED PERSON FROM VIŠEGRAD WHOM I met in Sarajevo soon after the war. He had found refuge in Srebrenica during the war, and when that enclave fell, he escaped across the Drina to Serbia. He was beaten and held prisoner there for eight months, and then the Red Cross facilitated his release. He ended up in Sarajevo, where he became an activist for the return of displaced persons. His story is one variation on the theme of a million internally displaced persons who were trying to make their way back home after the war.

If the war was fought to divide Bosnia-Herzegovina into separate, ethnically homogenized territories, one of the main goals of the separatists in the postwar years was to keep the displaced Bosniaks, Croats, and Serbs from returning to their prewar homes. The separatist forces on all three sides, working with the advantage of fait accompli, employed an ongoing, low-level terror to cement the division. However, hundreds of thousands of displaced persons were determined to return.

The central question in the reconstruction of Bosnia-Herzegovina in the half dozen years after the war was that of return. The international community had helped put an end to the fighting, and it provided significant assistance in the reconstruction of the country when the war ended. But without the persistent struggle of ordinary displaced people, Bosnia's final division would have been a simple matter.

Zehra spoke to me of her despair as a displaced person and her hopes for return when I met her in Tuzla after the war. She was from Bratunac, an eastern Bosnian town not far from Srebrenica. "I was expelled from Bratunac in 1992. There were no war activities there at that time. The Yugoslav People's Army and the paramilitary formations came into the town with no resistance on April 17. On May 10, they took us all from our houses to the stadium and then took us to the outskirts of Tuzla in cargo trucks."

Zehra was one of forty thousand displaced persons in the city of Tuzla; there were another one hundred thousand displaced people living in the rest of Tuzla Canton. Most of them were Muslims from Podrinje, the eastern region along the Drina River. Some lived in crowded collective centers or imposed themselves on relatives. Some adopted homes abandoned by Serbs who had left Tuzla. Some paid rent to live in private apartments or houses. And as in the rest of the country, there was little employment to be found there after the war.

Zehra commented:

There is a very small percentage of all these people who can make their way under these circumstances, with employment so scarce. Most would like to return home. Every morning when I wake up, I ask myself, "What am I doing here?" The people of Tuzla have gotten tired of us. We are second-class citizens here. Our last name is "refugee."

Bratunac is where I finished college and worked, and I was not involved in politics. Neither was my father or any of my other relatives. My father was one of the most reputable people in Bratunac. He died here in Tuzla during the war, of sadness. Now my mother is sick. The tragedy makes one go crazy. I can't start from zero here, but I can, there in Bratunac. I don't need anything to go home, just the minimal conditions. I would go home without anything, as I came here. I have my hands, my brain. That energy to return has potential. With all my energy, to the end of my life, I will fight to go home.

Help is needed, just a little, to harness that energy, that dissatisfaction. There are women here who have lost several men in their family. I ask them, as a devil's advocate, "How can you think of going home?" They say, "I want to die in my own village." And they tell me, "After *that* war [World War II], there were also no men left in the village." We are very connected to our homes. We survive without help from the government. The younger people help the older ones.[1]

An "Agreement on Refugees and Displaced Persons" was incorporated into the Dayton peace agreement as Annex 7. This crucial "return annex" articulated principles supporting the protection of refugees and displaced persons and promoting their return. But while the annex called on all sides to make way for return, it failed to arrange for enforcement mechanisms to be applied in the event of obstruction.

As Zehra said, "The desire to return is one thing, but the reality is something else. It is obstruction if we can't physically visit our homes because of the danger. There is still not freedom of movement. We cannot visit our homes alone. We need to go in a vehicle belonging to the international community. OK, we are prepared to take risks. Maybe there would be a first attack, but later it would be easier."

The nationalist leadership on all sides made sure that there were no intact empty homes waiting for their rightful prewar inhabitants. Houses and apartments that had not been destroyed during or soon after the war were taken over by displaced members of the newly dominant ethnicity, or by profiteers. Serbs from Drvar living in Banja Luka could not return home until Croats living in their homes moved out. Those Croats could not return home to Travnik until Bosniaks moved out of homes that belonged to them. And those Bosniaks who were expelled from Banja Luka, Jajce, or Doboj could not leave Travnik without their own homes being rebuilt or evacuated.

This Chinese puzzle of occupied homes was the most prominent obstacle to return, but there were two more factors: the will of displaced persons to return, and the will of the local authorities to allow return to take place. If a displaced person or refugee found herself in a better living situation than the one she was to return to, or if she had any reason to fear for her security on return, then she was likely to decide to remain in her new, "temporary" home. And the local official who welcomed returning refugees of the "minority" ethnicity was extremely rare, especially in the first few years after the war.

Local officials had an extensive repertoire of obstructionist techniques that they could employ to prevent return. In the early postwar years, violence was a common means of prevention, but it was a short-term tactic. In the long run, other forms of obstruction—a myriad of ways of destroying hope—were more effective. "Everything is being drawn out, and this dulls our desire to return," Zehra said of the effect of the long-term stalling strategy.

However, very soon after the war's end, organizations that advocated refugee return were springing up all around the country, from the local level to the national. These grassroots organizations, leaders in the struggle for return, constituted the infrastructure of a mass movement. They helped to counter the personal frustration of many displaced people.

Immediately after the war, even before many return advocacy organizations had the chance to form, ordinary people and a few leaders began to attempt to visit their homes.

Vahid Kanlić, from Goražde in eastern Bosnia, told me of his first experience: "In April 1996 we sent two busloads of people to visit our cemeteries in Kopači [across the interentity border from Goražde, in the Republika Srpska], and thousands of Serb civilians blocked our way. There were a hundred Serb policemen, and there were snipers on the roofs. I took a chance and got out of the bus. A sniper was holding me in his sights. The IFOR [UN Implementation Force] representative asked me what to do. I told him that it was his job to solve this problem. We left."

Such blatant incidents of violent obstruction to return continued. During 1996 and 1997, bands of Croat extremists expelled Bosniaks and Serbs from apartments in Croat-controlled west Mostar, where some had managed to remain throughout the war. In February 1997, a couple hundred Bosniaks tried to cross into west Mostar hoping to visit a cemetery on Liska Street during the concluding days of the holy month of Ramadan. Some Croats, including several dozen uniformed and plainclothes policemen, blocked their way. Television footage captured out-of-uniform policemen firing on the Bosniak visitors. They killed one man and wounded twenty others.[2] On the same day, armed bands evicted about one hundred Bosniaks.

Local officials tried to thwart return by throwing up financial obstacles as well. In Tuzla Canton, against the instructions of the entity government, officials were requiring returnees to pay "a certain sum for each month that they were out of the country during the war."[3] Returnees were also, on occasion, being required to pay overly high fees to take out identity documents or for restoration of utilities hookups. These practices were common in the Republika Srpska as well.

Displaced Serbs started returning from the Republika Srpska to Drvar, just across the interentity border in northwestern Bosnia, in late 1997. Previously nearly 100 percent Serb-inhabited, this area had been taken over by Croats at the end of the war and repopulated by displaced Croats. For a couple of years, men had torched dozens of uninhabited Serb-owned houses. In April 1998, an elderly Serb couple was murdered and their house set on fire. A week later, a mob of displaced Croats attacked the municipal building; assaulted Mayor Mile Marčeta (a Serb, and himself a returnee) and left him in critical condition; attacked and torched the offices and vehicles of the UN Mission in Bosnia; and attacked apartments inhabited by returning Serbs as well. An International Crisis Group report described a "criminal network that has a grip on key aspects of governance, policing and the economy in Drvar."[4]

During the same week as these incidents, a group of about 650 Croats who had been expelled from the northern town of Derventa returned, with Cardinal Vinko Puljić, to celebrate a St. George's Day Mass in the ruins of their cathedral. A crowd of around one thousand local Serbs gathered and besieged the church for six hours. They threw stones at the Croats as SFOR (the UN postwar Stabilization Force, formerly IFOR) troops finally escorted them to buses.[5] Members of the mob turned cars over and attempted to set the church on fire. Republika Srpska media and government officials ignored the incident.

Clearly, there were serious hurdles in the struggle for refugee return; Zehra was not dramatizing when she spoke of risks. But the displaced people and their leaders were not easily deterred.

One of the first organized group returns of displaced persons was that of Bosniaks to the "pioneer village" of Jušići, not far from Zvornik in the eastern part of the Republika Srpska. In October 1996, with the encouragement of the activist and return leader Fadil Banjanović, dozens of returnees set up tents and got to work clearing rubble from their demolished farmhouses. They had to repair an access road to the village and watch out for mines, which hampered planting of their first crops. During that month there were "more policemen than returnees, to show that we were not wanted, even among the ruins," as one villager reported.[6] Despite threats and occasional gunshots, the returnees persisted.

By the spring of 1998, more than half of the prewar population of this village had returned. Bosniak return to numerous villages in that part of the Republika Srpska, on the road between Tuzla and Zvornik, was underway. In Jušići returnees began to install utility poles in order to receive electrical power from the Federation, but RS authorities ordered the poles removed. Returning children were bused to the Federation to attend school. With time, the security situation around Jušići improved, but transportation and water supply continued to be problems for several years.

RETURN IN THE KRAJINA

I attended a conference held in the spring of 1998 by a local association of displaced persons from Kozarac, a town in Prijedor municipality in the Bosnian Krajina, the northwestern part of the country. The local association Srcem do Mira (Through Heart to Peace) was based across the interentity borderline in the nearby city of Sanski Most, in the Federation.

During the war, thousands of people from Kozarac and other parts of the Krajina had been displaced to Croatia and central Bosnia. Soon after the war's end, many of them gravitated to Sanski Most, around a half hour's drive from Kozarac. From there, they mounted their campaign for return. The first attempted visit to Kozarac took place early on, in 1996. A convoy of displaced people, traveling from Zagreb, headed for the town. However, in Prijedor, the convoy was blocked by a group of people who threw stones at the visitors. The convoy continued south without reaching their goal.

The next year the activists planned a visit from Sanski Most. "When we went to Kozarac, the SFOR found out about our plans and followed us," return activist Emsuda Mujagić said of this visit, recalling that the international organizations in the area were not enthusiastic about the idea. "I must say that in 1997 we had great resistance from SFOR, the Organization for Security and Cooperation in Europe [OSCE], and the International Police Task Force [IPTF]. They wanted to prevent our trip to Kozarac, because they thought the time was not ripe. They were angry that we were so persistent."

The return activists did persist, and visits to Kozarac picked up in early 1998. Srcem do Mira held a conference about return in Sanski Most in May, on the sixth anniversary of their expulsion. One rainy day, I traveled with displaced people and international visitors to Kozarac. We passed through Prijedor, the municipal center of the area. Demolished farmhouses along the roadside set an ominous mood in the otherwise pleasant terrain of gently rolling hills and farms. The ceramics factory Keraterm, during the war a place of torture and death for captive Bosniaks, was on our left. The turnoffs for Trnopolje and Omarska, locations of other wartime concentration camps, were further down the road.

The road to Kozarac was lined with dozens of wrecked houses and a ruined mosque, with its downed minaret lying in chunks beside it. We passed a Muslim cemetery overgrown with weeds. The weather was gray and drizzling.

Five thousand houses were destroyed in Kozarac; we saw ruined homes in varying states of wreckage. Some only lacked a roof, while others were missing whole walls. Piles of rubble stood next to many houses, here and there stood a stripped, rusty car. Weeds grew where gardens had once been cultivated. Fruit trees stood unpruned. All along the main street of the town stood houses with walls, but no roofs, doors, or windows.

Only half of Emsuda's house remained, missing its roof and a couple of walls. In the driveway was what remained of her car, overturned, rusting, and missing the doors and wheels. Shards of dishware were strewn about the yard; inside, tiles were falling off the bathroom wall. Weeds poked through the concrete slab in the basement, now exposed to the sunlight. The handrail had fallen off the steps.

I walked down the street with Rozalija, another local person displaced from Kozarac, to look at her house. There was rubble in the front yard, and more dishes on the floors inside. Someone had chipped out the mortar from the front wall to remove the electrical wiring. We stood on the back balcony. The backyard was lush, overgrown with untended flower bushes. Nearby someone had cultivated a vegetable garden. Rozalija pointed out where the shade arbor had been, and where they used to grill food, and hoped to do so again one day. It was the first time Rozalija had been home in six years.

Thinking back to the time she left Kozarac, Rozalija said, "I was stupid. I didn't take anything. I believed we would be back soon. I just locked the door. Now I have a key, and no house."

Some of us congregated on the main street across from the partially repaired local government building. Some SFOR troops on security duty served us warm drinks in the rain. The atmosphere was gloomier for the presence of some straggling, displaced Serbs, some of the 150 or 200 who inhabited the local elementary school. They hailed from central Bosnia and from the Croatian Krajina, across the border to the west. While the visiting Bosniaks were acting in hope of return, these displaced Serbs, intimidated by their own leaders, had very little hope at all.

I said to Emsuda and her husband, Osman, that it was depressing to see such a ruined town. They felt the same way. They told me that their son said he would never go back to Kozarac. The first time they visited there after the war, he was speechless and did not say anything for hours.

However, depression did not amount to despair; Emsuda and Osman were determined to restore their prewar community. In the next few years, their persistence paid off.

Some factors made return to Kozarac smoother than return to other places. A large number of people who had been displaced from the town were massed in nearby Sanski Most, which made it easier for them to organize. The returnees were determined, and they had competent organizations and strong leaders. Furthermore, their town had been nearly entirely Bosniak-populated, and all but a handful of the houses were destroyed. This meant that usurpation of homes by displaced Serbs was not an obstacle.

An important factor that facilitated return to Kozarac was the wartime creation of the Seventeenth Krajina Brigade, largely composed of people displaced from Kozarac. In *Re-Making Kozarac*, author Sebina Sivac-Bryant (herself a native of a village not far from Kozarac) describes how this military formation within the Bosnian government army functioned as a "liberation movement within the Bosnian army," a disciplined group of fighters who held fast to the goal of return to their local homeland. Although circumstances at the end of the war prevented the Seventeenth Krajina Brigade from accomplishing this goal, survivors regrouped around Sanski Most after the war and participated in the return movement.[7]

With a tentative easing of tensions several years after the war, people were able to start rebuilding their homes. Assistance from international governmental and non-governmental relief organizations was crucial in this phase. In mid-1998, several organizations set up field headquarters in Kozarac and began to repair houses.

The returnees persevered, and the atmosphere in Kozarac gradually changed. By early 1999 between fifty and one hundred families had returned to the town, and at least two hundred houses were either repaired or in the process of being repaired. The change in mood in Kozarac, from the tense and dreary times of early 1998, was palpable, with Bosniak returnees strolling the main street as if wrecked houses were the most normal thing in the world.

Bosniaks cooperated with Serb contractors and workers—some of whom were displaced persons from central Bosnia—without serious tension. In a place where six or seven years earlier several thousand people had been killed or had gone missing, this was a remarkable sight.

GORAŽDE: AGITATION FOR RETURN TO SOUTHEAST BOSNIA

While return was starting up in other parts of Bosnia-Herzegovina, it was still blocked in the area around Goražde, the only eastern enclave that was not taken over by Serb forces with the fall of Srebrenica. The Dayton agreement preserved Goražde as part of the Federation, a canton jutting like a thumb into the Republika Srpska, about fifty kilometers southeast of Sarajevo. But the creation of the canton did not solve the problem of the seventy thousand Bosniaks who were displaced from Foča, Višegrad, the suburbs of Goražde, and other towns in southeastern Bosnia. These Bosniaks took refuge in Goražde and Sarajevo; likewise, there were thousands of Serbs in Višegrad, in Foča, and throughout the region who were displaced from Goražde and from much further afield.

In early 1999 return activists formed the Regional Committee of Refugees of Southeast Bosnia. Its president, Vahid Kanlić, was a displaced person living in Goražde. He had been a social worker before the war and owned a house and fifteen hectares of land in the Goražde suburb of Kopači. With the upheaval of war and displacement, Kanlić became a vigorous leader of the regional struggle for return.

Kanlić complained bitterly that the international community seemed to be ignoring obstruction to refugee return in eastern Bosnia. "When incidents of obstruction and violence take place in Bugojno or Stolac, it is all over the news. What is the OHR doing about this situation? If this were Stolac or Drvar, there would have been big changes by now. Who has been fired?

"We're going to put pressure on the international community to implement Dayton's Annex 7, and to remove from their positions those who are responsible for the obstruction. If this doesn't happen, then we will have to make it known that the international community is obstructing return, which helps solidify the ethnic cleansing that took place."[8]

Kanlić was just impatient enough to step up the campaign for return in southeast Bosnia, together with fellow activists, without waiting for the international community.

He organized a conference on multidirectional return in southeast Bosnia in Goražde. Serb and Bosniak activists represented displaced persons from the region, including eight municipalities between Sarajevo to the west, Foča to the south, Višegrad to the north, and Goražde in the center. A couple of dozen displaced Serbs were there, an early sign of improvement in collaboration between the two ethnicities in this part of the country.

Activists, members of international NGOs, and domestic and international governmental officials held hundreds of conferences about refugee return after the war. They were often billed as news. Some were useful, but too often they were just talk sessions. The Goražde conference, however, was an opportunity for me to meet activists and to learn about the state of return in southeastern Bosnia.

I met Himzo Bajrović, president of the local Association for Return to Srpsko Goražde. "Srpsko Goražde" was the name given by the Republika Srpska authorities to a new municipality including Kopači, the suburb of Goražde that had been taken by Serb forces in the spring of 1994, and several surrounding villages. Kopači was important to Goražde before the war, as it was the location of an industrial zone. Kopači's former residents, overwhelmingly Muslim, were well educated and prosperous. Now it was filled with displaced Serbs from many other parts of Bosnia.

Bajrović described the obstacles to return to his prewar home:

Kopači is four kilometers from here; we can see our houses, but we can't return. There were over three thousand Bosniaks living there in 1991, in what is now Srpsko Goražde, and several hundred Serbs. Ninety percent of those Bosniaks are now in Goražde. We can't return to our houses because the Serb government won't allow us to. They say that their people do not have places to go.

There are now three hundred houses in Kopači—twelve hundred were destroyed. Most of the institutions—the post office, the Red Cross—are in private houses, because that's almost all that there is. The government settled displaced Serbs in Kopači, but they are residing in private property, which should be untouchable. To date, 650 families have now submitted applications to return, but we are continually blocked by demands for new paperwork.

Bajrović mentioned that to that point, some thirty families of displaced Serbs had returned to Goražde, and that almost three hundred more Serb families had applied to return. When I asked him what would happen to the displaced Bosniaks living in their houses, he replied, "We are prepared to live in tents, if we have to."

Ahmo Žigojević was displaced from Kopači when it fell in 1994. His wife had been killed when tank fire hit his house. He told me, "Before the war, I was a shoemaker, and I had two shops in Kopači. One was destroyed, and the other is now a bakery. I don't know what happened to my equipment. I have gone to visit the bakery a few times without any problem. I want to fix my house; I am waiting for permission from the government of the Republika Srpska to do that."

Vahid Kanlić explained the work of his organization: "The prerequisites for return are the establishment of multiethnic police forces and local governments, and an in-creased SFOR presence to provide security. Before the creation of this committee, there were no contacts between Serbs and Bosniaks. But now we have established commu-nication with people in Višegrad, Rudo, Rogatica, and several other places. We have a mutual language of displacement; we think the same way."

Kanlić estimated that, counting displaced Serbs in the region, his organization represented around one hundred thousand people. It was significant that participants in this conference included displaced Serbs living in Višegrad and several other mu-nicipalities—people who for the first time were starting to organize themselves and press for their right to return to Goražde.

Return organizers viewed Kopači as the "key to southeast Bosnia." One Bosniak refugee from Čajniče told me, "There are officials in the Serb-controlled part of this region who want to cooperate, but they lack resources. For example, the Čajniče mayor is a good person, and he is supporting everything we're trying to do. The town of Rudo is more difficult. The mayor has invited people to return, but Rudo is at the end of the road, near where Bosnia, Serbia, and Montenegro all meet. Also, the Army of the Republika Srpska has a base there, and people are afraid to return to the areas of southeast Bosnia that are controlled by the RS. This is why Kopači is the key to return to all of the towns around the region."

Hilmo Bajramović commented, "When people know that we have returned to Kopači, they'll be encouraged to go to their homes farther away. Kopači can serve as a point of departure for return to Višegrad, Rogatica, Rudo, and other locations further afield."

I met with three displaced Serbs living in Višegrad who were return activists. One, a woman from Goražde, was returning to her hometown for the first time in six years; the others were displaced from Sarajevo. They mentioned that many displaced Serbs were anxious to return to their prewar homes and explained that although the political atmosphere had relaxed somewhat in recent months, local authorities still failed to provide displaced Serbs in Višegrad with information regarding return.

During an open session of the conference, the energetic refugee return advocate Fadil Banjanović, based in Tuzla, strode on stage. Himself a displaced person from Kozluk near Zvornik, Banjanović gave a hoarse and rousing speech, yelling, shaking his fist, pounding the podium, and proclaiming, "The Drina area is part of Bosnia. We want to return to Foča! We are in a deep sleep. It is time to wake up. *We* will make return happen, not the international community. Everyone is for return, but for three years, nothing has happened. Something is wrong, either with the international community, or with us, or both."

Goražde itself was a depressed place. Many young people were leaving. The most common term I heard for Goražde was "dead end." It was isolated from the rest of the Federation, surrounded by the RS, and there was very little employment.

That evening when I was walking around Goražde, I met a young couple, Elvir and Sanela. Both of their fathers were dead, and neither Elvir nor Sanela was employed. Elvir told me, "It's very hard to have a good time with no money. If there were only a factory where I could work, it would be a lot better. The way it is, I'd like to leave Goražde and go work somewhere for a couple years. I think things will be better here in about ten years." Sanela parodied an old woman with a cane and said, "Yes, when we're like this, things will be better."

As the conference ended I made a foray into Kopači with some journalists from Sarajevo. We made an unannounced visit there to the mayor of Srpsko Goražde, Slavko Topalović, who had been a high school literature teacher in Goražde before the war. He received us in his office, but he was visibly uncomfortable at our presence.

Topalović's small office was decorated with a picture of St. George and the Dragon, a framed *kokarda* (Serbian nationalist symbol), and a portrait of Nikola Poplašen, then president of the Republika Srpska. Topalović sat behind a desk looking defensive and unhappy. On the bookcase was a plaque bearing the emblem of the SDS, the dominant Serb nationalist party, and the book *Who Is Who in Serbia*. On another wall hung an old map of Yugoslavia.

Topalović told us that he felt sorry for all the citizens of Goražde. Dayton should be observed, he said, but in Kopači there were 350 families of displaced Serbs living in Muslims' houses on the right bank of the Drina alone. Where could they go?

The journalist asked about the possibility for return to the region, and Topalović asked, "Do you mean two-way return?" The journalist responded, "Of course." The mayor told us that there were five thousand displaced Serbs in the municipality, and the lack of housing, as well as of infrastructure, was an obstacle to Bosniak return. Furthermore, the displaced Serbs from Goražde were not planning to return home. He said, "There have been unpleasant incidents. We have gotten used to living here." In response to the journalist's question "Can the Bosniaks return here?" Topalović said, "When the conditions permit."

The Coalition for Return was a prominent and effective umbrella organization of the grassroots return movement. The organization's main function was twofold: to inform prospective returnees of their rights in the face of massive obstruction and periodic changes of property laws, and to inform governmental and humanitarian relief organizations of these people's needs.

The Coalition for Return sponsored visits by legal experts to local associations for return throughout the country and published a magazine for refugees and displaced people. The magazine contained legal information, updates on progress (or obstruction) in return, and news about the international community's activities.

Financed by international governmental organizations, the Coalition for Return worked closely with domestic agencies at various levels to coordinate return efforts. Prominent among them was the Commission for Real Property Claims (CRPC), established by Dayton's Annex 7. The CRPC reviewed and made decisions on claims filed by displaced people for the return of their property. The Coalition directed property claims and information about claimants to the CRPC, and the CRPC directed displaced people in need of legal advice and advocacy back to the Coalition. The Coalition also provided similar critical services to other agencies at the local and regional level.

For its staff, the work of the Coalition for Return was more than a job. Employee Željka Slišković told me, "Almost all of us who work here are former displaced persons and refugees. I myself was out of the country for four and a half years. So we know what the people we're trying to help are going through. What other organization has been able to accomplish what we have, with so little money? We've worked 'from the heart,' without asking what we were going to be paid."

Nearly all return activists throughout Bosnia-Herzegovina cooperated with the Coalition for Return. One who stood out was Fadil Banjanović, who struck me as a force of nature. His moral and political sense and his impatience made him responsible for some of the most extensive multidirectional return in the country, including a large proportion of those tens of thousands of displaced persons who, like him, had landed in Tuzla during the war.

Banjanović was a large and imposing man, director of the Tuzla Canton's Office for Return of Displaced Persons and prominent in the NGO movement. As president of the Regional Association of Refugees and Displaced Persons of the Tuzla region, he spearheaded countless preliminary visits at a time when displaced people who were trying to return to their ruined villages were greeted with hostility by their former neighbors. He fought not only for Bosniak return to Doboj and Zvornik, but also for the return of displaced Serbs to Tuzla and the surrounding area.

Banjanović described the early period of return: "In many places we have a significant number of people who are highly motivated to return, who push that entire process forward. Sometimes I call them fanatics, but in fact they are just brave and hardworking. In Gajevi the international community, local police, and paramilitary groups attacked us. All of that against a little group of people from Koraj; one day they would be attacked, and the next day they would return. When they attacked, they would torch our houses, but then we would return again, and in the end that persistence bore fruit. Now return is a normal thing in the largest and richest places in the area of Koraj. There, we have countless examples of neighborly assistance between Serbs and Bosniaks. . . . None of that would have happened if it had not been for the persistence of those people."[9]

I visited Banjanović's office in a decrepit building on the outskirts of Tuzla in 1999. Interruptions were constant as he carried on with his work. The phone rang every few minutes. Banjanović opened letters, signed papers, and filled envelopes as we talked. He referred to himself in third person. At one point, with his booming voice, he yelled to an unseen secretary in an adjoining room, "Send Mustafa in Jušići fifty kilos of flour!"

Between interruptions Banjanović told me, "There is no alternative to return. We are for return in all directions. We won't call it two-way return, or minority return—just return. The return in this area started with Jušići in 1996. Then Dugi Do, and Mahala Kalesija. We are the only organization in the region that has accomplished this number of returns." Making a comment that explained his impatience at the Goražde conference, Banjanović said, "We are an organization that doesn't hold panel discussions, or publish lofty declarations. That is political manipulation and a way of getting money."

Asked about the rate of return to and from Tuzla, which was better than elsewhere in the country, Banjanović replied,

> There are too many people here in Tuzla. The rent is very high, and there are very difficult social conditions. There are nearly 150,000 displaced persons, so there is more pressure to leave. One of the main reasons is that the displaced persons here are very well organized via NGOs and governmental organizations. The Tuzla Canton government helps. It has provided a positive example. So let the Federation government help, let the Republika Srpska help.
>
> This association has contact with local organizations in the Republika Srpska, and with the international community. We do concrete work in the field, and that's why we get results. Croats have returned to Pelagić, Serbs to Lukavac and Kalesija, and Bosniaks to Zvornik and Doboj.

I asked whether people had returned to the urban core of those cities. Banjanović said, "There will be return. But the first focus is on empty houses, to places where people can work in the fields and gardens, and herd sheep. Because for us, our fields, our gardens, and our forests are our factories. That's where people can fix their lives. You can see for yourself there that people are working in the countryside."

The Coalition for Return had a branch organization in the central Bosnian town of Zenica, one of the largest cities in Bosnia. There was no fighting in Zenica during the war, but displaced Bosniaks inundated the city from many directions. Meanwhile, since central Bosnia was the scene of much fighting between Croats and Bosniaks, there were many Bosniaks displaced to Zenica from nearby places taken over by Croats, such as Busovača and Vitez. Likewise, many Croats had left Zenica for places under the Croat control.

On a trip to Zenica in 1999 to visit the local office of the Coalition for Return, I left the bus station and walked through the busy public market, not far from the Bosna River. I heard traditional Bosnian folk music being played on a cassette tape recorder in the market and noticed two sellers holding hands, dancing a lively *kolo*, the traditional line dance of the region, in the rain.

When I arrived at the Coalition's office, I saw that two rooms and one telephone served the Coalition and eight or ten local return associations working under their auspices. Indicative of the meager resources of grassroots return organizations at that time, the office boasted one typewriter, but no computer.

The activists of the Coalition for Return were more ready to criticize the obstruction to return they personally experienced than obstruction in the reverse direction. But one person commented that all obstruction in the Federation takes place at the local level. Another activist responded, "There is really no local power. It looks like obstruction and 'incidents' are fomented on the local level, because it is intended to look that way. But none of this would happen without the approval and management of the top powers." Employing a saying common throughout Eastern Europe, a third person said, "The fish stinks from the head. Obstruction is a centralized operation."

I caught a ride back to the bus station with Dževad, a Bosniak displaced from the nearby town of Busovača. This municipality had suffered through the Croat-Bosniak conflict and was divided along the former front line. Busovača came under the control of Croat forces, and Bosniaks controlled the nearby village of Kačuni. Most of the Croats left Kačuni, and Bosniaks from Busovača were displaced to that village.

Dževad told me he was living in a Serb's house in Zenica. The Serb was visiting him occasionally, and waiting patiently until Dževad could move home to Busovača. There was a displaced Croat living in Dževad's house. That man, according to Dževad, had a house in a nearby village, but he was unwilling to move home. Dževad told me that he hoped to be able to return home that year, but that if he could not, he was going to buy some explosives and blow up his own house.

DOBOJ

I traveled to Doboj from Tuzla in the winter of early 1999. The bus followed a ridge for many miles through the gentle hills of northern Bosnia, the southern edge of the vast Pannonian flatlands. From that ridge one could see rolling hills and farms covered with snow, an idyllic scene stretching to the distant horizon in all directions.

Doboj is a pleasant town flanked by two rivers, in a broad valley surrounded by hills. Just off the center of town is a steep narrow promontory with a medieval fortress on top. Its stark lines can be viewed from every part of town.

In Doboj I met with Aleksandar Šakota, an activist with Klub 92 Doboj. He shared an office with Milutin Mikerić, an attorney who provided legal advice and assistance to displaced persons of all three ethnicities who wished to return to their prewar homes. Klub 92 was also organizing visits of displaced persons to their prewar homes.

Some twenty-five thousand people, primarily Croats and Muslims, had been displaced from Doboj during the war, and approximately two thousand had returned as of early 1999. While a relatively small number, this was more progress than in most parts of Bosnia-Herzegovina at that time. Meanwhile, about twenty thousand displaced Serbs were living in Doboj.

Mikerić and Šakota described their organization's goals and the obstacles that confronted them:

> We founded the organization because we realized that we can't work for democracy in this city without the citizens who were displaced from here. We need to solve problems for everyone. People ask us, "Why are we, local people, working to help return?" It's the fair thing to do. We're not representing the displaced persons; we're representing the citizens.
>
> We placed an advertisement for return to Doboj on Sarajevo radio in June 1997, and there was significant response. But we were attacked on the local radio station here in Doboj for seven days in a row after we placed that ad. They said, "Why have you invited twenty-five thousand Muslims back to Doboj?" People called us on the telephone to harass us. They accused us of working illegally. We did not respond. There is no point in talking to those "primitive" people, nationalists. As a result of our announcement, we were able to start working with associations of displaced Doboj citizens throughout central Bosnia.

Listing some forms of obstruction faced by Klub 92, Mikerić noted:

> The day after Dayton was signed, there was no change here. The government does not respect the law. There are currently over one thousand requests for settlement of property claims on file via this office alone. Many of these claims have been rejected, and few settled. The procedure for these decisions is supposed to take no longer than thirty days. But there is only one man who does this work. This is a form of obstruction, drawing out the process. The local government would prefer to do nothing.

There is a big problem with passports. For example, there are people from here, Muslims and Croats, who worked in Europe for twenty years. They come here to renew their passports, and they are faced with bureaucratic obstruction. They have troubles renewing their identification cards, with submitting proof of residency. And their children who were born in Germany are treated as complete foreigners. There are children who turned eighteen while absent from here. They have a right to an identification card, but this is obstructed as well.

It's very difficult for us in the NGOs to get our point of view into the media. They want money for announcements, but we don't have it. Here in Doboj there was an alternative newspaper, the *Nova Alternativa*, that carried articles in favor of return. This newspaper's offices were bombed twice, and now it no longer exists. This month, there was supposed to be a public discussion of a new property law, but no one here provided information to the public about it. The NGOs didn't receive the information, so how can citizens have it? We are best represented on Sarajevo television, not in the Republika Srpska.

Speaking of obstacles to return throughout the country, Šakota added, "There is similar obstruction to return in the Federation. Among all three ethnicities, there is a political structure organized along nationalist lines. These structures, in fact, cooperate with each other. Any return that is happening has had to take place under pressure. For more return, the police and the municipal administration in both entities need to become multiethnic. The biggest problem for return is that the entity governments are against it.

"The obstruction comes from the top, but it is manifested on a local level, at the office counter where people have to go to fill out request forms. There are special obstructions that come down through the political parties."

For Mikerić and Šakota, obstruction was an attempt to cement the corrupt practices perpetrated by nationalist leaders during and after the war. "Many apartments changed hands during the war," they told me. "At least 30 percent of the relevant arrangements are invalid. Local politicians are living in larger apartments than they did before the war. If people return to these apartments, those politicians would have to move out. Furthermore, people's rights were violated here during the war. Many people were fired from their jobs. Among those who have returned to the area, there are forty legal cases pending related to return of employment.

"What's good for the politicians is not good for the citizens. How much right do citizens have to take part in creating the laws? Only personal will reigns here in Doboj. Ordinary people have no information. There is none available about the privatization process. The politicians are buying firms; other people do not know what to do, what is for sale, and so on. Everything on the main street of Doboj has been sold. Ordinary citizens cannot participate in privatization. Or else they can buy firms that have already been ransacked, or those whose equipment is outdated."

Returning to overt forms of obstruction, Mikerić described the manipulation of displaced Serbs in Doboj, a practice that was widespread among all displaced populations throughout the country: "There are many displaced persons here who have no property. These people are being held here, with no assistance to return. They constitute a voting machine for the ruling parties. People are not thinking for themselves. The political parties are providing people with humanitarian assistance in exchange for their votes. They are giving out bags of flour, for instance. Perhaps I am giving a banal example, but that's the situation all over the country. It is similar in the Federation; there is much crime and corruption, and government is totalitarian.

"During the war, there was propaganda that people who came here would be able to keep the abandoned properties they were taking over. People were naive. Now, as return is slowly starting, the Republika Srpska government is deceiving people, saying that it will build them their own new houses. With what resources? There is no money. There is also an organization, 'Ostanak' [Remaining]. They are fighting against refugee return. They have the right to stay, but nothing gives them the right to usurp someone else's property."

Šakota took me to visit the ancient fortress high on the hill near the center of town after our meeting. On the way we passed a few houses that had been destroyed. Šakota told me that these houses had belonged to Bosniaks. He pointed out the yard where there had once been a mosque. There was anti-Muslim graffiti on the nearby buildings.

As we walked up to the top of the hill, we could see the rivers and all the surrounding hills. Šakota pointed out which parts belonged to the Federation, which to the Republika Srpska, and which villages Bosniaks were moving back to. He showed me where the front line had been during the war.

Pointing to one hill area, Šakota said, "I was there for two years." I imagined him, around fifty-five years old, braving the cold, the mud, and the winter's fierce snow. I struggled with the realization that he had been on the front line. I felt a discomfort, trying to reconcile my sense of this honorable human rights activist with the fact that he had fought against those I considered the defenders of Bosnia.

I asked Šakota if it was not a strange thing, having fought against those people and now working to bring them back. He said, "Of course. But we understand each other. I have no problem at all with my old friends who fought on the other side. We were all cold, hungry, and uncomfortable. We visit each other now. I want them to come back, and they want to come back. The problem is with those people who stayed in the city here during the war, abusing citizens. They don't want them to come back."

I recalled a line from Hemingway, as mentioned by the Sarajevo journalist Gojko Berić: "The closer to the front, the better the people."[10]

SARAJEVO

For many years after the war, one's first sight of Sarajevo was the view of tall buildings that had been wrecked. There were five-story buildings without their roofs. Then, ten- and fifteen-story buildings with most of their windows gone, their glass or concrete facades missing as well. Here and there a pristine new building appeared, or a bright new house next to a demolished one. There were signs of direct mortar hits high up on apartment buildings, with splatter patterns from bombs that had struck the sides. Some bombs had scored direct hits, striking windows. No one who was inside at such a time could have survived.

Arriving in Sarajevo in 1997, I found the train station bombed and blackened. I took the half-hour walk to the center of town. Sarajevo has an ancient Turkish core called the Baš Čaršija, surrounded by an Austro-Hungarian section, and from there, tall apartments and office buildings stretch out to the village suburbs. The Baš Čaršija is famous for its Ottoman flavor. Wooden storefronts line narrow, winding pedestrian alleys. It is traditionally an artisan's neighborhood, and now predominantly a kafana and tourist district, graced by several mosques.

Throughout Sarajevo, I found that every building facade had been damaged. Walkways and courtyards were pockmarked. Many windows without glass were covered by plastic UNHCR sheeting, although there was also much new glass. In 1997 repair was still underway throughout the city.

In front of the garish blue Sarajka department store, a couple dozen retired men watched a game of chess played with two-foot-high chess pieces on an outsized chessboard. All kinds of people walked the streets: teenagers smoking cigarettes and lounging, enjoying the last days of warm weather; Bosnian soldiers strolling alongside SFOR soldiers from France, Turkey, Italy, and Pakistan. Canadian and Arab businessmen walked to their appointments past buildings covered with scaffolding.

Displaced men and women from villages sold cigarettes, hand-knitted socks, or other household items in the outdoor markets. Some sat on the pedestrian walkways and begged.

Several stories of displacement were unfolding at once in Sarajevo. Tens of thousands had been displaced to the capital city from surrounding towns and villages. Some wanted to go back to their prewar homes, and some wanted to stay. Others wanted to leave for another country. And there were just as many Sarajevan refugees in neighboring countries—or countries on the other side of the globe—and others who were displaced throughout Bosnia-Herzegovina to localities controlled by Serb or Croat nationalist forces.

Although there was not the kind of systematic ethnic cleansing in Sarajevo that had been practiced in much of the rest of the country, some local gangsters and local commanders had committed acts of intimidation and brutality against Sarajevo's non-Muslims. It was understandable that anyone might wish to leave a city that was under siege. Those who remained were primarily Bosniaks, either local residents or refugees. However, Sarajevo was one of the only cities in the country with even a symbolic multiethnic presence remaining immediately after the war.

Not all ethnic cleansing in Bosnia-Herzegovina took place during the war. The practice continued for a short time afterward, some of it perpetrated by an ethnicity's leadership on its own people. The most notorious instance of postwar self-ethnic cleansing took place during the reunification of Sarajevo. The displacement of tens of thousands of Sarajevo Serbs by their own leadership was to have long-term, damaging consequences for two-way return to Sarajevo.

During the war, Sarajevo was divided between neighborhoods controlled by Serb separatists and by government forces. Five municipalities that surrounded the city came under the control of Serb forces; and Bosniaks and Croats were terrorized and expelled from those areas. Serbs who had been displaced from other parts of the country moved in, increasing the Serb population in those outlying municipalities. With the end of the war, the Dayton agreement mandated that these five municipalities were to be reunited with the city as part of Sarajevo Canton, under the administration of the Federation.

In the lead-up to the mid-March 1996 transfer of this territory, Serb police and soldiers persuaded or intimidated the Serbs of these municipalities to leave for the Republika Srpska. Ultimately more than sixty thousand of the approximately seventy thousand Serbs left. Rada, one of those who was forced to leave, told me how it happened:

The war ended in late 1995. After Dayton was signed, my family left our neighborhood. We had no choice. The authorities told us to stay, but we could see the trucks loading up and leaving. They were removing whole factories. I asked, "Why are they leaving? And what happens then?" People were removing their dead from the cemeteries.

Officially, we were told to stay, but unofficially, we knew that we were expected to leave. The authorities told the people in my neighborhood to go to a town in the eastern part of Bosnia, on the border with Serbia. And there were bandits that were coming into the neighborhood, both Serbs and Croats, who were stealing things, beating people up, and torching apartment buildings. The only way to leave was via Lukavica and over Mount Trebević.

Now I think this was our mistake. We should have stayed. We should have blocked the road.

On the first of January, there was a huge exodus of Serbs from all the outer neighborhoods of Sarajevo, which were being reunited with the core of the city. I watched the exodus from the office where I had a job; there was an endless line of cars. The weather was bad; it was very cold, with deep snow. There were many car accidents. There were cars, trucks, tractors, horses and wagons, and people on foot. Some were carrying dead bodies. I couldn't do anything to help. Some people had tried to go through Sarajevo, but they were stoned.

I watched these people and knew that my family could be among them. In each vehicle there were at least four people. That's four lives, four life stories. Tens of thousands of people left.

My family arrived with thousands of others at the town assigned to us, and there was not much room. Years later there were still some people living in collective centers. My relatives slept in an outbuilding. For that they paid 150 DM a month (US$80). My parents and another whole family stayed there. It was better than nothing. I was lucky, because I was working and could pay for their lodgings. Later we were able to move into one floor of a family house. But it's still crowded, after the big house we had before the war.

I was hoping to move back to my old neighborhood. But when I went back there, I found out that our family house had been destroyed. I was shocked at the situation; I didn't imagine it would be so bad. I had been dreaming about going back, but I saw that this would be impossible. This is what they wanted.

I hope somehow to be able to live normally again, to be in an honest place. I would like to go away from the Balkans, away from Europe as far as possible, where no one will ever again ask me what my last name is.[11]

When Rada said, "This is what they wanted," she could have been referring to officials on either side of the interentity borderline. Serb authorities took advantage of the influx of displaced Serbs to create demographic facts on the ground, directing the flood of refugees to Brčko, Zvornik, Bratunac, and Srebrenica. Later their propagandists described the exodus purely as the result of Bosniak pressure. Meanwhile, statements by Bosniak leaders in Sarajevo discouraged Serbs from remaining, and some Bosniaks committed attacks and vandalism against those who did attempt to stay.[12]

The human rights disaster of the Serb exodus was compounded by the shameful conduct of the NATO troops. IFOR troops stood by as buildings in the outlying municipalities were torched and burned.[13] This behavior conveyed an emphatic message that the protection of multiculturalism and citizens' rights in Bosnia-Herzegovina was not a priority of the international community, and that separatist leaders on all sides could continue to hold sway over their beleaguered constituencies.

RETURN OF SERBS TO SARAJEVO

We knew that no one has the right to seek justice only for himself and not to struggle for justice for all people at the same time.

—*Dušan Šehovac, leader, Democratic Initiative of Sarajevo Serbs*

One of the most active and determined NGO members of the Coalition for Return in Sarajevo was DISS, the Democratic Initiative of Sarajevo Serbs. DISS was led by Serbs who had lived in Sarajevo's outlying municipalities throughout the war and either stayed in their homes during the postwar reunification, or had come back soon thereafter. DISS fought for the return to Sarajevo of displaced Serbs, and for the rights of those who had stayed.

DISS activists traveled throughout the Republika Srpska, wherever there were displaced people from Sarajevo to be found. They organized seminars on return, advising would-be returnees of their rights and the procedures through which they could realize those rights. DISS had to help clients cope with obstruction, both from Serb nationalist leaders who wished to prevent displaced Serbs from returning home, and from Bosniaks in Sarajevo who wished to prevent that return.

At one such seminar in Brčko, DISS activist Goran Kapor told his audience, "You are being deceived, first of all by the Serb leaders and authorities in the RS who led you into your exodus. Then they lied to you that you would come into permanent ownership of someone else's property; they promised you building lots, houses, work, and everything else. Now you are being evicted, and they are still lying to you that there aren't secure conditions for return, because the division is useful to them. . . . I know that in the Federation you'll come up against bureaucratic tricks when you want to go back to your property, but just as you may not stay on other people's property, they must also return yours to you. Think hard and don't be taken in by tricks."[14]

Kapor noted, "In many meetings people told us that we were the first to visit them and explain their property rights, and to tell them the news from their old home." Kapor told me that in one meeting a listener asked, "Can you really walk around Sarajevo?" "I said that we can walk and take the streetcar," Kapor recalled, "and the person asked, completely seriously, 'Do the streetcars really work in Sarajevo?'"[15]

Kapor said, "There is a lack of information, and there is misinformation. For instance, in the RS, there was no printed copy of the Dayton agreement until 1998. The only good information comes either from us or from the international community."

Jovo Janjić, another activist with DISS, told me, "We are the stepchildren of both entities. No one loves us. The leaders of RS call us 'traitors,' 'weak Serbs,' or 'Alija's Serbs.' This is a problem between us and the Serb politicians, not the Serb people. Then people in the Federation call us 'Chetniks,' 'aggressors,' and other ugly things. Neither side is correct. We are ordinary people who want to stay in our own city. We have been here for centuries, and we have a right to be here."

Janjić and his colleague Božidar Stanojević, head of DISS's human rights program, listed ways that Bosniak authorities worked against Serb return to Sarajevo:

> There is fear among people who have returned. Right after the war, there were threats by Alija [Izetbegović]. There is also a fear of secret arrest lists held by the Federation government. And there is fear of the actions of local citizens, especially in the case of the return of small groups of people. Some of the Bosniaks have organized harassment, even physical attacks.
>
> There is no organized method of dealing with abandoned property. If someone's property has been declared abandoned, then it is under the jurisdiction of the government agencies. If it has not been declared abandoned, then it is illegally inhabited, in which case it is a matter for the courts. In any case, people are waiting for two, three years for their cases to be settled.
>
> On return, the government requires proof of ownership from the returnee, which is expensive and takes months to establish. Some people never transferred ownership from their father or grandfather who died, so they have to do that. And there were many unlicensed buildings, which therefore do not legally exist.[16]

There seemed to be no limit to the repertoire of bureaucratic entanglements that were cooked up by those obstructing return. For example, at a DISS seminar in Višegrad, one displaced Serb noted that when he went to the Sarajevo neighborhood of Dobrinja to submit a property returns claim, he saw that the record books listed him as being dead. He thus had to prove that he was alive, and he was asking DISS for help in determining the correct procedure to do this.

Especially in the first several years after the war, when property laws were chaotic and often contradictory, the legally prescribed time period for delivery of the decision on a property claim was rarely observed. Jovo Janjić stated, "Say a decision is supposed to be made in thirty, sixty, or ninety days. In no case is the decision ever made within that time period. And suppose someone receives a resolution on their case. Even if it is positive, there may not be any eviction because the illegal occupant refuses to leave, or the government will give him extra time to find a new place. Then that obstruction requires a whole appeals process, which takes a lot of time. In other words, a positive decision can be as bad as a negative one! If there is a negative decision, then there is also a very slow appeals process. Finally, a case may go to the international human rights ombudsman, and they have their own slow processes."

Where there was a tenant residing unlawfully in a would-be returnee's home, a positive decision on a property claim was supposed to result in an eviction. But it was not uncommon for the "temporary" inhabitant to organize to resist it. In such cases, Janjić said, "the government will not help. The police attend the evictions, but they haven't used compulsion to evict, except in rare instances when they're making a political point."

Echoing another complaint heard all around Bosnia, Janjić and Stanojević brought up the problem of resistance to Serb return by displaced Bosniaks in Sarajevo:

> Displaced Bosniaks who live in Sarajevo are working against the return of Serbs. They prevent evictions of illegal occupants of houses. When there is an eviction, a hundred or so women will go out and block it.
>
> Some of the displaced persons voted in the municipalities where they lived before the war, and say that they want to return there. But many of them don't want to, because the quality of life is much better for them here, richer, more comfortable. They lived in villages, in old houses, sometimes without running water. Here, they live in houses that belonged to Serbs, and they have water, gas, electricity, buses, and schools. Many people are now living in someone else's home.

In those first years after the war, DISS made it clear that it was campaigning for Serb return to Sarajevo and for the reestablishment of a multicultural atmosphere in the city. There was a prominently posted sign on the wall of its office announcing that DISS was there to assist people who were interested in return, not those who wished to sell their prewar homes.

Stanojević told me, "Now, there is massive selling of property. Serbs are cooperating with Muslims who act as brokers to help them sell their property to a third party, usually from another country, since people here don't have any money. Many of these buyers are Muslims from the Sandžak [a predominantly Bosniak-populated region of Yugoslavia] and, lately, people arriving from Kosovo. These people have no papers legitimizing their presence in Bosnia, yet they are allowed to freely purchase property or build here."

Returning to the subject of obstruction to return by Serb authorities, Janjić said:

> The Republika Srpska government considers it a defeat for them whenever a Serb leaves the RS to go home to the Federation. It doesn't want a reunified Bosnia. It works against return at the expense of ordinary Serb citizens. An oft-quoted poll of Serbs in the RS supposedly showed that 97 percent of them had no desire for return. Under present conditions, polls are no way to determine the real wishes of the people. People will say one thing in public, because they're afraid of consequences. But in private, half of them will ask for advice about how to return.
>
> In the RS there is pressure, trickery, and unfavorable speech against people who want to return, so that people lose their desire to return. Or else they conceal their true wishes and plans. If we were in the RS right now, we wouldn't be talking openly like this.

At the seminar in Brčko, Goran Kapor examined the root of the obstruction: "The heads of both entities are getting rich. You should understand that some 2 percent of the Serbs, Bosniaks, and Croats will grab most of the wealth of Bosnia-Herzegovina. You are making their job easier, because you are not returning, and you're offering them your property for a song. The majority of you will end up poor. The politicians are getting rich and giving you advice, especially before the elections. They are tricking you, and you are voting for them."[17]

Stanojević concluded gloomily, "If the things that were promised last year don't happen in 1999, then there will be no return. People will go to New Zealand, South Africa, Canada. It is a sad thing to have to leave. It's logical when younger people go, but what about older people? If I go to the United States, what am I going to do there? How much longer would I live?"

3

Obstacles to Return and Breakthroughs in the Late 1990s

THE INTERNATIONAL COMMUNITY PLAYED A CRITICAL ROLE in the process of refugee return from the beginning. Its handling of the problem paralleled its behavior throughout the breakup of Yugoslavia and the Bosnian war. Top international officials made deals with the nationalist leaders, looked after their own careers, and often ignored the representatives of the grassroots return movement. It would be unfair to completely condemn of the international community in this capacity, as far less return would have taken place without international pressure and economic assistance. However, from the start the international role was chaotic and experimental.

For the first several years after the end of the war, the only significant "return" was that of refugees coming home from abroad, usually from countries where they had not been granted permanent residency status. "Minority returns," that is, return to homes people had been expelled from during the war, amounted to fewer than 10 percent of the approximately four hundred thousand returns that had taken place by early 1998.[1] And this was before tens of thousands more refugees, mainly Bosniaks, were pressured to leave Germany, where nearly 350,000 had sought refuge during the war. The arrival of hundreds of thousands of returnees, overwhelmingly to places that were not their prewar homes, compounded the problem of return and recovery.

The international community experimented with a variety of approaches before arriving at a comprehensive plan to promote return. At the outset, it focused on "easy cases," hoping that minority return via the path of least resistance would set a chain reaction in motion. This was a logical assumption, but it did not take into account the long-term commitment of nationalist authorities to ethnic separation.

The easy cases were those where displaced persons could return to their prewar homes without fear of violence. This excluded such hard-line areas as most of the eastern half of the Republika Srpska and most of the Croat-controlled part of western Herzegovina. The places most conducive to return were monoethnic villages and small towns that had been destroyed. Since they were destroyed, those homes were thus not usurped by squatters who were themselves displaced members of the now-dominant ethnicity, as had happened on a wide scale in the cities. Such localities were also more conducive to return if they were not far from the interentity borderline, and near where a critical community of displaced persons from the target area for return had gathered.

As mentioned earlier, the predominantly Muslim town of Kozarac was just such a target; the fact that large numbers of its displaced people were able to resettle temporarily in nearby Sanski Most, and that Kozarac itself was mostly empty of squatters, contributed greatly to the relative success of its repopulation. Similar circumstances existed in the demolished Muslim villages between Zvornik and Tuzla.

On the other hand, the cities were full of displaced people who had become squatters. Villagers who gravitated to the cities controlled by their own ethnicity tended to land in apartments belonging to expelled members of another ethnicity. Usurpation of tenancy rights by displaced persons was a major obstacle to the return of displaced persons to the cities, and international officials avoided confronting it for a long time after the war.

The international community identified "axes of return," as it termed twinned municipalities for two-way return. These included the Zenica-Doboj axis, Tuzla-Bijeljina, and Sanski Most-Prijedor (including Kozarac). Return focused primarily on the villages surrounding the municipal centers, rather than the urban centers themselves.

In the spring of 1999 I met with Helena Holme-Pedersen, a Sarajevo-based staff member of the Return and Reconstruction Task Force (RRTF). In her office behind

Sarajevo's main Catholic cathedral, she explained this international agency's strategy. The RRTF's approach was a pragmatic one of "geographical prioritization," meaning focusing on areas where there was a "less threatening situation." For example, over three thousand displaced Serbs had by then returned from the Republika Srpska to villages around the Federation city of Drvar. Holme-Pedersen explained that it was strategically effective to begin with returns to villages where ownership of private houses was not contested, and then to gradually work on return to the towns.

In response to the criticism that eastern Bosnia was being ignored, Holme-Pedersen pointed out that the eastern half of the Republika Srpska was still under the control of hard-line nationalists. "It is hard to encourage return to a place like Rogatica, where the mayor bragged to us about how during the war he put Muslims through the wood chipper—alive," she told me.

Economics played a large part in the international community's strategy for return. From a simple cost-analysis point of view, concentrating on areas of lesser resistance resulted in the most returns accomplished for effort and money spent. Holme-Pedersen emphasized the importance of "bribing, rather than penalizing" political leaders in order to open the way for return.[2]

This approach was key in the Republika Srpska. Throughout the first two years after the war, that entity received a mere 2 percent of international aid coming into Bosnia.

In 1999 the RRTF announced an evolving strategy of three "pillars": space, security, and sustainability. Creating space for return involved evacuating usurped homes and reconstructing houses. Establishing security required ending the low-level terrorism practiced against returnees during the first several years after the war. And sustainability, an oft-repeated watchword, referred to the most difficult aspect of return: reestablishing life and livelihood for returnees in their prewar home.[3]

International officials were barely beginning to confront these problems in a coherent way in the late 1990s. However, here and there, they implemented elegantly simple solutions that made a great difference in overcoming obstruction. One such solution was the UNHCR-coordinated program of busing displaced persons to their prewar homes for preliminary visits. In most cases these bus trips were the only way people could make the visits safely. The buses were occasionally met with violent resistance as people in the target location stoned the vehicles or even robbed the passengers, so the buses initially had to be accompanied by IFOR troops. But several hundred thousand visits were undertaken within the first few years of the program.

Another simple but crucial measure was to standardize vehicle license plates and remove indications of residence. After the war, as before, all license plates displayed the car owner's municipality of residence, and Cyrillic lettering was used in the Republika Srpska. Such identification caused serious problems for potential returnees visiting a prewar home. In Teslić, for example, drivers with license plates from outside of the RS were stopped and required to go to the police station for questioning.[4] When the international community's High Representative Carlos Westendorp abolished this identification by decree in mid-1998, the drive across the entity border to visit one's prewar home, neighbors, or relatives suddenly became much easier.

In spite of these measures, minority return remained at an insignificant level. A menacing atmosphere was pervasive, particularly in areas under nationalist Croat and Serb control. Radovan Karadžić's SDS party wielded ongoing control throughout the Republika Srpska. Karadžić himself, indicted for war crimes in 1995, seemed to move freely throughout the RS in the first years after the war. International community officials regularly vowed that Karadžić would be arrested. In one of what came to be hundreds of such statements, Louise Arbour, then chief prosecutor of the International Criminal Tribunal for the former Yugoslavia (ICTY),[5] announced that the handover of Karadžić would take place "in a matter of days."[6] But at the same time, NATO troops in Bosnia stated that only local officials had the authority to arrest war criminals, and that foreign troops could detain them only if they happened upon them. Thus there were several reports of Karadžić wandering freely, even passing through checkpoints undisturbed.

At the end of 1997, only nineteen of seventy-three people known to be indicted for war crimes had been arrested. One of those indicted was Simo Drljača, former police chief in Prijedor and organizer of nearby concentration camps. In one of the very first moves by international forces to apprehend war criminals, British troops went after Drljača in July 1997. He was killed when he fired on the soldiers. Drljača had been the subject of a secret indictment, together with the director of the Prijedor hospital, Milan Kovačević.* Kovačević, charged with genocide and crimes against humanity in connection with the operation of concentration camps, was captured successfully during the same operation.[7]

In spite of these rare operations, persons indicted for war crimes often had more security than displaced persons. This certainly put a chill on the freedom of movement

---

* For fascinating background information on the nexus between the war criminals and the postwar nationalist mafiocracy, see "Aiding and Abetting," an article by Diane Paul in the May 1997 issue of *War Report: Bulletin of the Institute for War and Peace Reporting* (no. 51, 30). which describes the nature of Drljača's and his confederates' operations in Prijedor. For example: "Last year, Stakić and Drljača demanded that the NATO implementation Force (IFOR), which was managing grants from Britain's Overseas Development Administration (ODA), give all construction contracts to public construction companies—companies reported to be under their direct control. 'When the MIC [Civilian-Military Centre] gave money only to private companies,' a well-placed source told Human Rights Watch, 'Simo's guys came' and threatened the private construction workers. The owners of private businesses feared that if no contracts were awarded to public companies, Drljača's men would burn their businesses down. They asked IFOR to give some contracts to publicly owned companies. 'Everything is controlled by Simo,' the source said, adding that Drljača and other town officials were behind everything that is going on. There's no way [to implement] projects just with the private companies, 'because everything's controlled by the [local] mob.'"

of would-be returnees. Movement and early attempts at return continued to be rebuffed by the stoning of buses, mining of repaired houses, and assassination of returnees.

One international official even factored violence into his appraisal of the return process. In late 1999 when I talked to Nigel Moore, Mostar director of the RRTF, I asked whether violence was decreasing in the region. "Anyone who believes that return will take place without violence is not living in the real world," he answered. "This is not a very humanitarian thing to say, but it may be a small price to pay. Anyone who thinks this can take place without incidents is fooling himself."[8]

In 1997 a political development promised to mitigate the hard-line political atmosphere in the Republika Srpska. Biljana Plavšić, a close collaborator with Radovan Karadžić during the war, became president of the RS after Dayton, when Karadžić was forced to leave politics. In mid-1997 Plavšić precipitated a crisis in the SDS after she began an anti-corruption campaign in which she targeted officials of the party, all the way up to the Serb member of the three-part Bosnian presidency, Momčilo Krajišnik. After she fired the RS minister of the interior and dissolved the RS Parliament, she was expelled from the SDS. However, with strong support from the international community, she drew part of the RS population over to her side.

Plavšić then formed her own coalition, named Sloga (Accord). Her party, the SNS (Serb Popular Alliance), supported Milorad Dodik of the small Alliance of Independent Serbian Social Democrats (SNSD), in his bid for prime minister of the RS. In parliamentary elections late that year, Plavšić won just enough support to shepherd Dodik into power the next January, by a slim parliamentary majority vote.*

Milorad Dodik had credentials as a "moderate," someone who would deal with the West more willingly than previous leaders. When Dodik was elected there was great

---

* I worked on those November 1997 elections with the OSCE, supervising what they termed the "most complicated elections in the world." In the part of eastern Bosnia where I worked, not far from Pale, the hard-line parties were still by far the most popular. As ballots were being counted, whenever a vote for Plavšić's party came up, the counter would call out not "SNS," or "Biljana," but "*kurva*" (whore). The final ballot count gave a plurality to the SDS, but even together with the Radicals, they barely lacked a majority. Plavšić tried throughout December to put together a "government of national unity," but the SDS stonewalled by missing and disrupting meetings. Finally in mid-January Plavšić nominated Milorad Dodik for prime minister.

The way Dodik won his post on the night of January 17 was rather entertaining: At a thirteen-hour parliamentary session in Banja Luka, procedures started out as usual with a long agenda and little progress. Hard-line delegates spent most of the evening protesting against the "betrayals by Biljana Plavšić." Around midnight the Speaker of Parliament, an SDS member, adjourned the session against the wishes of some of the delegates, and the hard-liners left. Realizing that there was still a possibility for a majority of forty-two out of eighty-three votes, the remaining SNS, Coalition, and independent delegates decided to hold a vote for Dodik.

One Croat representative, however, had left for Zagreb. Deputy High Representative Jacques Klein, present to observe the meeting, put out a call for his retrieval. Cooperative NATO troops found this representative on the road home to Zagreb. He was brought back, a count was taken, and at 2:30 a.m. Dodik was elected prime minister in a 42–0 vote.

enthusiasm among international officials. A member of the International Crisis Group called this "the best thing that had happened since Dayton." Dodik declared strong support for Dayton and called for the separation of church and state, an apolitical police force, and freedom of the press. He declared the war crimes tribunal at The Hague to be fair, and promised the eventual surrender of all war crimes indictees. He vowed to solve the refugee problem, ensure equal rights for all citizens, and privatize the economy. These promises pointed to a historical change in the political climate of the Republika Srpska.

Dodik had tenuous support from the population of the Republika Srpska, so how much he was going to fulfill his promises remained to be seen. He appeared to make a serious start. He replaced all the SDS government ministers and moved the Republika Srpska capital from Pale to Banja Luka, the entity's biggest city. He also replaced tax and customs officials, theoretically cutting off an important source of income for the separatists. But Dodik also appointed new ministers with a wartime record of support-ing separatism. His new interior minister, for example, was Milovan Stanković, during the war a colonel under General Ratko Mladić in the Republika Srpska army. Manojlo Milovanović, the new defense minister, was Mladic's chief of staff.

Another of Dodik's early promises was that he would encourage the return of seventy thousand displaced people to the Republika Srpska in 1998. At the beginning of that year, this seemed like an impressive number, and the international community enthusiastically shifted significant economic aid to those parts of the RS that cooperated with Dodik. International NGOs increased their reconstruction support in the entity as well. At the same time, international officials increased their emphasis on minority return, as opposed to refugee repatriation, as the true measure of the reconstruction of a multicultural Bosnia.

Still, return trundled along without picking up great speed. The eastern part of the RS, except for the villages around Zvornik, remained closed to return. Estimated return to the RS in 1998 topped out at roughly ten thousand.[9] In the Croat-controlled areas the region around Stolac was similarly blocked, and, only Drvar and some villages around Mostar saw return.

The international community poured some five billion dollars in reconstruction aid (separate from its military expenses) into the recovery of Bosnia-Herzegovina in the first five years after the war. International NGOs and governmental agencies financed the repair of roads, public buildings, private houses, and large-scale infrastructure projects. That physical recovery took place, gradually, but where return was con-cerned, a coherent strategy was a long time coming. Often international NGOs spent money in a hurry toward the end of their budgeting period in the fear that other-wise they could not justify new grants in the subsequent period. This led to wasteful spending and the creation of useless projects. International NGOs and governmental officials alike quite often cooperated with war criminals who had remained in power on the local level, because, as during the war, they were the people who wielded power. It was common to hear that people who had destroyed houses were working as building contractors, in some cases rebuilding the very houses they had earlier bombed or torched.

The international community's unwitting collaboration with war criminals and extreme nationalists reinforced separatist politics. At the same time, its reckless and wasteful expenditure in the years immediately after the war encouraged local NGOs to sprout like mushrooms. It was crucial for international relief agencies and human rights workers to learn how to assess the sincerity of local NGO workers, because domestic activists of all stripes quickly learned to espouse exactly the correct terms, such as "two-way return," "multi-ethnic organization," "no party affiliation," "tolerance and coexistence," and "reconciliation." Many times these phrases were uttered with complete insincerity.

Phantom NGOs with a bank account, and perhaps a brochure, sometimes came into existence solely for the purpose of raking off the dollars and deutschmarks that were flowing. In addition to these obviously criminal NGOs, there was a spectrum of NGO operations of varied usefulness, from feel-good "trauma counseling" with short-lived or nonexistent results, to the truly sincere, even heroic, multiethnic organizations (such as the Coalition for Return) where former enemies worked together for recovery.

The international community, as represented by agencies from the OHR and UN departments on down to smaller international relief organizations, struggled as it came up against obstructionist tactics that local separatists skillfully updated as needed. The International Crisis Group noted that bribes (formally known as "aid conditionality") to local authorities failed to be effective, as those authorities were adept at making promises they never planned to keep.[10]

The atmosphere in the northern and western part of the Republika Srpska did relax somewhat after Dodik's election. The roughly ten thousand minority returns to that area in 1998 were a leap from the previous two postwar years—but that figure still represented only approximately 1 percent of those expelled from the RS territory during the war. Return remained at a symbolic level. And as people were starting to return, they were confronted with the next dilemma, a more long-term problem than bare return: sustainability. It was rare that returnees had a way to make a living. In the long run, lack of economic viability proved to be the ultimate obstruction to return.

Fadil Banjanović made some pithy remarks on the subject of sustainability: "Neither our authorities nor the international community want those people [the returnees] to be self-sufficient. . . . If that were not the case, then in the area of Zvornik, where return is ongoing in forty villages, there would be forty plantations with vineyards, strawber-ries, blackberries, because that area, in former Yugoslavia, was the first in production of berries. Many people lived well from that, and that is work that grandmothers, and grandfathers, and children can do."[11]

By late 1999, UNHCR public affairs liaison officer at Mostar Olivier Mouquet was able to report that "in the Federation, there is no municipality where minority return has not taken place. There is widespread village return. This must be put in context. It doesn't mean that young people are returning. Reconstruction is not taking place at the same rate as return, and only partial families are returning. In general, the average returnee's age is over 50. Youngsters are not going back. Those who were 14 when the war broke out are now 21. So if only the parents return, this still could be the last generation of a multi-ethnic Bosnia."[12]

In mid-1999, Helena Holme-Pedersen of the RRTF responded to criticism from Bosnian return activists by characterizing the Kozarac return organization Srcem do Mira as "very demanding." She said, "There seems to be an idea of 'milk the international community.' Where's the gratitude? People have to be realistic."

When I suggested that the assertive nature of this group was part of the reason that Kozarac had, at that time, the highest reconstruction activity in all Bosnia, Holme-Pedersen admitted that she would rather see organizations push hard for their rights than remain passive. However, she commented that domestic NGOs needed to better understand the limitations of reconstruction.

"There are cases where returnees refuse to accept the key to a repaired house, because there is a toilet seat missing. People need to understand that they had a pile of rubble, and that this reconstruction is free for them. We did not destroy the houses, and we know that they didn't either. But we can't make everything perfect. The international community has spent $5.1 billion to date on fixing Bosnia, and there will be more. But people need to be patient."

In late 1997 the Peace Implementation Council (PIC), the institution of fifty-five states and agencies established to oversee the implementation of the Dayton agreement, held its semiannual meeting in Bonn. At that meeting, the PIC authorized the Office of the High Representative to decree laws that would impose provisions of the Dayton agreement in cases where domestic officials obstructed fulfillment of the treaty's goals. These "Bonn powers" significantly increased the status of the High Representative—at the time Carlos Westendorp—as the governor or proconsul of Bosnia-Herzegovina. Westendorp soon used these powers to standardize license plates, currency, and passports for the country, as well as to choose a flag and a national anthem. With advice from the OSCE Democratization section, Westendorp began removing political officials from office, and some obstructionist candidates from electoral lists.

DISRUPTIONS IN SPRING 1999

Activists and international officials alike were hopeful that 1999 was going to be more truly a year of return, but domestic and regional turbulence temporarily put a brake on the process.

Several very disruptive events made the spring of 1999 one of the most chaotic post-war periods for Bosnia-Herzegovina. These were Carlos Westendorp's dismissal of the president of the Republika Srpska, Nikola Poplašen; the Brčko arbitration commission's decision to create a Brčko District rather than awarding the municipality to one entity or the other; and NATO's intervention in neighboring Yugoslavia in response to the Serbian regime's mistreatment of the Albanian majority in Kosovo. With these three events taking place practically at the same time, cooperation between the two entities at the state level was interrupted, numerous violent incidents took place in the RS, and refugee return was brought to a standstill.

As backdrop to the events of spring 1999, political developments in the Republika Srpska in 1998 had been disappointing for the international community. The "Dodik promise" had not come to fruition; and while postwar tension had eased in the western half of the entity, refugee return to the RS for the most part remained blocked. To make matters worse, in the general elections in September 1998 Nikola Poplašen of the Serbian Radical Party (SRS) ousted Biljana Plavšić in the contest for presidency of the entity.

Poplašen, formerly a professor of Marxism in Sarajevo, fought with the army of the Republika Srpska and became head of the SRS. In his office in Banja Luka, Poplašen kept a large photograph of himself in full Chetnik regalia, with a skull-and-crossbones insignia and a large knife in his belt. He once stated that Dayton was a "pause between two wars," and that he never would have signed it himself.

Soon after he was elected, Poplašen tried to thwart cooperation between the Republika Srpska government and international officials. He worked persistently to remove Dodik from his position, but he was unable to find a candidate that the RS Parliament would approve. The stalling process became an increasing source of tension in the entity over the next six months, as Dodik remained at his post as caretaker prime minister. On March 4, 1999, High Representative Westendorp used his Bonn powers to remove Poplašen from office.

Meanwhile, an arbitration decision on the status of Brčko was also looming. The signing of Dayton left this strategically placed city temporarily under the control of the Republika Srpska, with the stipulation that it would be supervised by an international representative, and that an internationally appointed arbiter would decide to which entity it should belong. The international arbiter's decision was delayed for three years under pressure from Serb politicians, who considered it essential that the RS retain exclusive control of Brčko city. Their claim was that anything less would split the entity in two, and that the RS must remain a territorially contiguous unit.

Finally, on March 5, the same day Westendorp dismissed Poplašen, international arbitrator Roberts Owen decreed the formation of the Brčko District. The new district included the city of Brčko, theretofore controlled by the RS, and its surrounding suburbs, previously controlled by the Federation. Brčko District, according to the arbitrator's decision, was to belong to both entities, and it was to be completely demilitarized. The territorial integrity of the Republika Srpska, as guaranteed by

Dayton, was not to be interrupted, but the district was to have its own autonomous, multiethnic government.

The government of the Federation accepted the decision, but the reaction in the Republika Srpska was almost unanimous rejection. Angry protest demonstrations broke out in many cities. Scattered but ongoing incidents of violence also took place as people attacked offices and vehicles belonging to UN and other international organizations. As a result, the staff of most international organizations soon withdrew to cities in the Federation.

Looming over all this domestic turbulence was the specter of war in neighboring rump Yugoslavia (Serbia and Montenegro). Throughout the 1990s Milošević's regime had increased pressure on the Albanian population of Kosovo to the point where the presence of Serbian special forces and paramilitaries constituted a military occupation of the province, whose autonomy Milošević had abolished in 1989. The Serbian authorities had systematically disenfranchised Albanians, firing agency and company directors, expelling Albanians from their schools, and dismantling the health system. In the mid- to late 1990s Serbian forces began arresting Albanians, torturing and assassinating activists, and conducting military raids on villages where there was resistance to the regime.

The fighting in Kosovo, the ratcheting up of tension, and the looming threat of a NATO intervention were felt strongly in Bosnia at the same time that the political upheavals of March 1999 were underway. Albanian refugees fleeing the violence in Kosovo had been arriving in Bosnia since the middle of the previous year. When negotiations between the West and Milošević's representatives broke down, an intervention was just a matter of time.

The NATO air campaign against Yugoslavia finally began on March 24, 1999. It sent a flood of refugees into Bosnia-Herzegovina, significantly destabilized the country's economy, and accelerated agitation by Serb nationalists. By the time the NATO intervention was well underway, a reported thousand refugees had come into Bosnia.[13]

Unrest in the Republika Srpska continued throughout the spring of 1999, and the war's economic repercussions in the RS were severe. At least half of RS companies did business with those in Serbia, and over three-fourths of the RS's exports went to that country. As factories in Yugoslavia were bombed and firms shut down, companies in the RS were forced to close as well. Several tens of thousands of workers in the RS lost their jobs.[14]

The infuriated Serbs continued to criticize the internationals, but in the Federation, many people who felt themselves to be victims of Milošević's expansionist policies celebrated.

Serb officials in the RS—excluding extreme nationalists grouped around Poplašen—took note of the fact that the Serbian militarist impulse from neighboring Yugoslavia was no match for international military force when the international community resolved to block Milošević's aggression. With this understanding, that spring Dodik and other RS politicians gradually renewed cooperation with the Federation and returned to the Bosnian state institutions. With economic cooperation with Serbia severely damaged for the time being, Dodik worked to improve trade between the RS and Croatia, and eventually with the Federation as well.

Dodik also called on Serb member of the three-member state-level presidency Živko Radišić to "do his work or leave the job."[15] President Poplašen objected that resumed cooperation would "contribute to the disappearance of the Republika Srpska,"[16] but Dodik expected the opposite, and he was correct: cooperation with the international community meant the preservation of the Serb-controlled entity. Radišić gradually came back to participation in state government affairs.

During the spring turbulence, displaced persons throughout Bosnia-Herzegovina never gave up trying to return home. After all, while 1998, the "Year of Return," had proved disappointing, international officials and domestic activists alike were determined that 1999 would be better. But return was blocked in the spring. Dozens of attacks were perpetrated against returnees, especially after the NATO intervention began. Anonymous attackers bombed or torched the houses of Bosniak returnees in several cities, and returnees were subjected to threatening telephone calls.[17]

The war in Kosovo ended in early summer, and the mood in Bosnia began to simmer down. But violent obstruction to return continued. Separatists were also learning how to obstruct return through bureaucratic procedures. Local governments provided inadequate budgets to staff local housing offices and turned a blind eye toward offensive harassment and attacks aimed at returnees. There was an increase in the distribution of state-owned property—and, often, private property belonging to expelled residents—to displaced persons. Housing was then built on this land, increasing the number of permanent residents of the dominant ethnicity.

Activists around the country were identifying the elected representatives of all three ethnicities as part of the problem of obstruction. A Coalition for Return activist in Banja Luka told me, "There can be no return as long as the nationalist parties are in power; they all oppose return of their own people to where they came from. This is true on all three sides. It would be best to remove those who were involved in conducting the war; things would be 100 percent better."

Deputy High Commissioner Hanns Schumacher, resigning in early July 1999, stated that he could not name a single Bosnian politician who was working toward the reintegration of the country.

At the height of the return season in 1999, refugee return was, certainly, more than a trickle. Over five thousand Serbs had returned from the Republika Srpska to the villages around Drvar and Bosansko Grahovo. Croat returns to central Bosnia were tentatively increasing, and there were signs of the ice breaking in some of the most return-resistant areas of the eastern half of the RS.

But the critical mass required to restore Bosnia-Herzegovina as a multiethnic state was not moving. Since Dayton, only around seven thousand Bosnian Muslims, out of hundreds of thousands displaced, had returned to their prewar homes in the RS. These returnees were mostly older people going home to semirepaired houses in villages. The return of ethnic minorities to town centers was still negligible. With an estimated eight hundred thousand people still displaced within Bosnia-Herzegovina, it was clear that the obstructionists still had the upper hand.

PROPERTY AND THE RULE OF LAW

In the course of 1998 and 1999, representatives of the international community realized that they must revamp their approach to refugee return in Bosnia for there to be any hope of long-term implementation of Annex 7. The Peace Implementation Council declared at its Madrid meeting in December 1998 that reorienting the focus of return projects from an area's ethnic makeup to a focus on rule of law would accomplish return more effectively and equitably. "Constructing the rule of law in BiH" became the international community's main priority for 1999.[18]

The task of legal restructuring was complicated by the fact that in prewar Bosnia, as throughout socialist Yugoslavia, there were two forms of property ownership. Besides traditional private property, there were thousands of apartments whose inhabitants held tenancy rights under the system of "socially owned property." Socially owned property was generally built and administered by state-controlled institutions such as banks, schools, mining companies, and the armed forces. These institutions, called "allocation rights holders" controlled the distribution of this socially owned property to their employees.

During and after the war, thousands of internally displaced persons took over the socially owned apartments for which other people, now displaced elsewhere, had held tenancy rights. For example, during the war in Sarajevo, approximately 130,000 Serbs, Croats, and Bosniaks left the city, and tens of thousands of displaced persons, predominantly Bosniaks, arrived from areas of Bosnia that had been ethnically cleansed.

It was inevitable for displaced persons to occupy empty houses and apartments. Sometimes people would simply find an empty home and take it over illegally. Often a home was declared legally abandoned, because the tenancy rights holder had been absent for longer than the six-month limit. Such apartments were then legally allocated to a new resident.

In both entities new laws annulled former tenancy rights holders' claims to their apartments, legalizing the handover of abandoned apartments. Thus at the end of the war, refugees hoping to make a smooth transition back to their former homes were usually disappointed to find that they could not return, because their houses and apartments were occupied.

The governments of both entities ostensibly established procedures for the recovery of occupied property. In reality, these arrangements were forms of obstruction. In the Federation, people who had left their apartments were required to return to them immediately, within fifteen days of the end of the war for refugees, and within seven days for internally displaced persons.[19] Those who missed these deadlines forfeited their tenancy rights. However, even if returnees were able to arrive on time, they would not have been able to take over their apartments within the deadline, since they were occupied. In any case, few displaced persons who could have been helped by this ruling even heard about it, since it was not announced until the time limit had expired.

In the Republika Srpska no time limit was imposed, but return was based on "reciprocity." This meant that the prewar occupants of an apartment were allowed to return only if the new occupants were also able to return to *their* old homes, and only if they so desired. In practice this law prevented minority return to the RS.

The international community's attempts to untangle the legalistic web of obstruction to return began with the creation of the awkwardly named "Law on the Cessation of the Law on Abandoned Apartments," which went into effect in the Federation in the spring of 1998. Prewar occupants were now able to file claims for their apartments, and government bodies were set up to process property claims. Authorities were required to process claims within thirty days. After this took place, the present occupant was given ninety days to evacuate the property. If this occupant did not have a place to move to, the government was responsible for supplying alternative accommodation.

The newly-confirmed right to file claims to reinstate prewar tenancy rights did not produce significant effects in the near term. In mid-1999 Carlos Westendorp was replaced as High Representative by the Austrian diplomat Wolfgang Petritsch. Seeing that obstruction was still significantly slowing down return, in October of that year Petritsch decreed a new set of laws that reconciled the property laws of the two entities. Stiff penalties were introduced for noncompliance to these laws, including fines and jailing of uncooperative officials.

The new property laws stipulated that double occupants, people who were illegally occupying more than one property, would receive notice that they had to evacuate and return to their prewar property. A deadline of fifteen days after notification from the municipal housing office was introduced for eviction of illegal occupants.

In late 1999 I visited David Howitt, coordinator of property returns at the OHR in Sarajevo. Howitt's shelves displayed a bust of Josip Tito, and a Tito screensaver floated across his computer screen. Chain-smoking as he spoke of recent developments in property law, Howitt said, "There are problems of territorialism. The achievement of the ethnic objectives of the war is being carried out through other means. Until recently, this process [of encouraging refugee return] was dealt with in the context of deals. But these are deals that shouldn't be negotiated. Recently, the international community has started another approach to establishing return. Now, we are working on the coordination of the implementation of property law. This is all very interventionist, but we need to take away the steel lid that is preventing civil society from doing anything."[20]

Under the new standardized laws, filing of property claims accelerated; by late 1999 over 220,000 claims had been filed.[21] However, local housing commissions failed to process these claims on a host of pretexts. For example, late in the winter of 1999–2000 in Banja Luka processing of claims for the return of apartments was a mere 0.2 percent.[22] Most other parts of the country were not far ahead of Banja Luka.

In this period, as the international community pressed its "rule of law" agenda, separatists were gradually moving from violent resistance to bureaucratic obstruction to return. Local officials found ways to circumvent every new law that required them to allow property restitution and return. One of the first lines of obstruction was the assertion that temporary occupants of claimed property had nowhere else to go. It was the responsibility of local officials to provide such people with temporary housing in order to free up occupied apartments for their original tenants. Since the local nationalist officials wished to discourage such return, they usually dragged their feet where providing alternative accommodations was needed.

Stalling on evictions took place in various ways. At times a simple lack of office materials slowed down the process. OHR spokesperson Alexandra Stieglmayer accused the Republika Srpska Ministry for Refugees and Displaced Persons of failing to ensure "the most basic conditions for work; they [municipal branch ministries] don't have a phone, vehicles, often not even paper on which they could write decisions and resolutions."[23] And in Brčko, local officials held up evictions for several weeks in 2000, on the grounds that their "typewriters were not working."

As laws were promulgated that streamlined the path toward eviction from temporary housing, residents often simply refused to leave. Their situation was fraught with conflict, because most people who were about to be evicted had been expelled from another part of the country—or even from the same municipality—during the war. They had arrived to places where they were assured that they could stay in their new homes without ever having to fear a second displacement. Although the international community increased pressure to evict, local officials resisted identifying candidates and implementing the evictions. When evictions were scheduled, local police often simply failed to show up.[24]

Resistance to eviction, like resistance to refugee return, was implemented at the local level, but it reflected the intentions of the highest domestic authorities. President Alija Izetbegović himself had spoken out against evictions on one occasion, declaring that no soldier was going to be "thrown out on the street" to make way for the return of "some grandmother."[25]

Resistance to eviction took more direct forms, from civil disobedience to extreme violence. When local authorities cooperated and tried to perform evictions, people protesting against evictions were arrested. In Novo Sarajevo, one illegal occupant went after a police officer with an axe, but he was disarmed.[26] In Banja Luka several policemen who were carrying out an eviction were injured when a man about to be evicted poured gasoline on them and on himself. His wife then lit a match. The evictee was burned to death.[27] In addition to policemen implementing evictions, those deciding them were also targets: In Zvornik the head of the local housing office was stabbed by a person slated for eviction.[28]

Finally, when eviction did take place, often those who were being evicted stripped their temporary lodgings bare upon leaving, removing not only furniture and appliances, but parquet flooring, doors, windows, and even personal belongings and mementos of the prewar owners.

ANKA, DISPLACED IN HER OWN CITY

The story of Anka, a displaced Croat, illustrates many of the problems of minority refugees trying to return to Sarajevo. Anka fled the country a few months after the beginning of the war. At the end of the war, she said, "a friend from Sarajevo told me that the Dayton agreement had been signed, and peace had started in Bosnia, so that we could go home. But when I arrived, I saw that returning wasn't as simple as I had imagined, and that I could not just go to my apartment and get resettled. There was a very ugly atmosphere. Wherever I went to some office to seek the return of my apartment, they all but said, 'Oh, you left, why didn't you defend Sarajevo?'"

Anka's struggle to regain her prewar apartment lasted several years, during which she persisted in the face of obstruction that would have made less determined returnees give up and leave permanently.

When I returned, I found out that there was someone in my apartment who had just moved in. The man who took my apartment sent me a message that I would never get it back. I went to the police and told them about the person who had taken my apartment, without any papers. And they said, "And what should we do, throw him out? We can't help you."

Then I went to the municipality offices, and to the ministries; I knocked on every door, everywhere. To the Ministry for Refugees and Displaced Persons, then the canton ministry for housing, and nothing happened. Everyone supposedly filled out forms and wrote letters, but nothing happened. They just lied to me.

Then the canton Ministry for Housing decided to get rid of me, since I had been bothering them for months. They sent me to the municipality office and said, "Go see if they'll give you a written statement that they will return your apartment to you." And I went there, and they told me that the apartment had been declared permanently abandoned. And I had been going around for almost a year trying to get my apartment back. I asked them how they could declare it abandoned, when I was there, alive and well.

They said it didn't matter, and that they would give back apartments to returning people if the displaced people in them went back to where they had come from. [This was at a time when approximately a quarter of the population of Sarajevo were displaced persons.][29] So then I realized exactly what was happening there: that they were kicking me around like a ball.

Later the man in my apartment sent me another message, saying that he had received permanent rights to my apartment. I went to the OHR office to ask what I could do. They sent me to the UNHCR, and the UNHCR sent me to a collective center, where I lived in one room. Until then I was going from one friend's apartment to another. If I had known that I was going to live like that for so long, I would have gone crazy. But the days go by, and you think you're doing something, something smart.

I forced myself to go to that room, but I was all alone. Nothing happened with my apartment, but something was happening in the collective center. They decided that because I was alone, they had to put someone else in there with me that I didn't know, between those four walls, those sixteen square meters. I asked, "How is someone I don't know going to live there right beside me?" They replied, "What's it to us? You can kill each other, if you want." These were people from the Ministry for Refugees and Displaced Persons.

At the ministry they said, "You've been here too long. We can't kick you out, but we can make you want to leave." I asked, "How can you do that?" They said, "We can do it." I asked, "Where am I supposed to go, onto the street?" They said, "On the street. What's it to us? Go wherever you want." Then I went to the UNHCR and asked, "Can you send me to some other country? So many people have left, so help me to leave, too. You can see that they're not returning my apartment to me." They said, "Don't pay attention to what they say, you'll get your apartment back."

But they won't return our apartments, because the people who are passing those laws are people who are living in others' apartments. They don't want to get out of those apartments that aren't theirs.

When I returned to Sarajevo I saw that the city was crawling with people carrying furniture around, couches, armoires. I asked myself, "What is this? Are things being distributed?" I asked a friend, and because we were on the streetcar, she told me to be quiet. When we left the streetcar, she whispered, "Be quiet. Don't be stupid, they're carrying furniture from one apartment to another, before the owners return."

Anka concluded her story by saying, "This is like another war. The war was more honest than this. But I'm not going to give up. I have nothing else. I'm prepared for them to kill me, I don't care. If I could have left, I would have gone somewhere else, to a completely different place, a long time ago."

After a couple of years of frustrating campaigning, by the end of the 1990s Anka got her apartment back. She succeeded because of her determination; many other would-be returnees were not so doggedly persistent in the face of obstruction.

RULE OF LAW MAKES HEADWAY; GRASSROOTS RESOLVE INCREASES

High Representative Wolfgang Petritsch had all this obstruction in mind when, as part of his October 1999 package of property reform laws, he set up PLIP, the Property Law Implementation Plan. At the heart of the PLIP program was a shift to across-the-board enforcement of property laws in the city and the countryside, in both entities, without regard to ethnicity. It replaced return campaigns that emphasized rural return, quotas, or exchanges. PLIP set up a network of regional RRTF offices that met regularly for monitoring and enforcement.

Laws accompanying the establishment of PLIP required local governments to provide alternative accommodation to displaced persons evacuating contested housing; it also provided for temporary residents to be evicted—even forcibly—if they were standing in the way of implementation. PLIP officials kept tabs on double occupants as well.

With these moves to prevent stonewalling by local housing agencies came increasing resolve. Local officials were expected to become more cooperative, or face sanctions. In this vein, the OHR's David Howitt commented, "Our policy is ruthless implementation so that all property is returned to its owner. We are using the law to subvert ethnic territorialism."[30]

By late 1999, tens of thousands of property claims were streaming into local housing offices and the Commission for Real Property Claims. PLIP implementation began moving upward throughout the country. Now there was a measurable mechanism for supervising property restitution.

Toward the end of the year Petritsch used the Bonn powers to remove twenty-two obstructionist officials. In one move, nine Serbs, seven Muslims, and six Croats—mayors, canton governors, housing commission authorities, and others—were banned from participation in politics for obstruction to return. Among the most notorious were Džordže Umičević, mayor of Banja Luka; Slavko Topalović, mayor of Srpsko Goražde; Pero Pazin, mayor of Stolac; and Dževad Mlaćo, delegate to the Bosnian Parliament. Mlaćo was a hard-line Muslim nationalist who had previously been removed from his position as mayor of Bugojno. Under Pazin's tenure Stolac had experienced high levels of violence and other obstruction against Bosniak return. Topalović, who displayed photos of war criminals on his office wall, had stonewalled Muslim return to the outskirts of Goražde. Umičević had blocked the reconstruction of the Ferhadija Mosque in Banja Luka.

RETURN TO KOPAČI: A TENT ENCAMPMENT IN THE SNOW

Meanwhile, return activists were stepping up the drive for return in their own way. As Petritsch was decreeing his new set of property laws in October 1999, displaced people in Goražde set up a tent encampment on a hill at the interentity border, overlooking their homes in the nearby suburb of Kopači.

Displaced people from Kopači had worked hard in the years after the war to overcome obstruction to their return. They pressed their case with the Office of the High Representative (OHR), with Bosnian government officials, and with intermediaries from the Serb-controlled entity, without concrete results. International humanitarian relief organizations had promised to rebuild seventy Bosniak-owned houses that had been destroyed during the war. They initiated a pilot project to repair some of the houses, but the local government put a stop to it. Local authorities, employing displaced Serbs, also blocked efforts by displaced people to plant winter wheat in their fields.

By late October 1999, their efforts having been repeatedly thwarted, the displaced people resolved to take stronger measures. With the cold weather approaching, around two hundred people set up tents on the main highway north out of Goražde and vowed to stay there until they were allowed to go home to Kopači.

That fall I should have been in my hometown of Seattle, where grassroots action was bubbling over. But it was happening in Goražde as well. When I visited the camp at the beginning of December, the weather was brisk, not much above freezing. As I stood talking to campers, a man walked up to me with that day's edition of the Sarajevo daily newspaper, *Oslobodjenje*. On the cover was a photograph of police violence that had erupted in downtown Seattle during protests over the World Trade Organization conference taking place there.

The man said to me, "I see you have problems in your country as well," and showed me the newspaper. We talked about globalization and nonviolent direct action for change. Behind us a man chopped wood, and others hung around outside the tents, walking from one to another, talking and visiting. From time to time a truck drove up with a delivery of food or fuel. An occasional delegation of visitors from another town came to offer moral support to the campers.

The tent encampment stood immediately by the road out of Goražde, not far from the Drina River. Just a few meters down the road was the border between the Federation and the Republika Srpska. Hand-painted signs on the tents read, "Kopači is the key to Annex 7 of the Dayton agreement," and "Kopači is the key to return to southeastern Bosnia." Lined up in front of several houses that had been destroyed during the war, there were five tents of varying sizes, most of them large enough to hold twenty to thirty people.

A huge pile of donated firewood was stacked in a clearing between the houses. Nearby was a pile of coal. A canopy sheltered an outdoor campfire, where several men and women sat on benches around the fire. One woman was knitting; a man read a newspaper. Up the road at the end of a field, a stream ran down to the Drina. An improvised outhouse was built nearby.

With colder weather the encampment shrank to around a hundred people, aged from seven months up to eighty years. Most of the camp residents were out of work, but others left during the day to work or attend school. Before the encampment was formed, these people were living with relatives or in a collective center. Some told me they had been living in ruined houses. Some of them were about to be evicted to free up their houses for returning Serbs.

One man said, "I have to be out of the house by December 22." I asked him where he would go. He said, "To the tents, and then to my home. My house in Kopači is fine, but others need to be fixed. Do you see that house in the field over there? That's my house. It's right on the interentity borderline. If I were allowed to reenter my house, I'd be cooking dinner in the Republika Srpska and sleeping in the Federation."

I entered a tent. It was fairly well lit, with beds around the perimeter, and a table for coffee in the middle. A couple of women made coffee at a wood stove in the corner. This was the women's tent, but it was the center of the socializing, and people came and went constantly. Some older women sat quietly around the edges of the tent. Men came in and talked boisterously. Some flirting and joking took place; one man pointed to a middle-aged woman and told me that I should find a husband for her—"her teeth are good." I replied that I was not there in the capacity of a matchmaker.

Activist Akifa Dučić told me: "There are seven families in this tent. Some of the people here were living in the collective center. In Goražde, I was in a house belonging to a Serb. I'll never say that it is my house; he earned that house. He should be in his house, and I in mine.

"I have four children and a husband. We lived in the collective center for a year. Before that we were in Germany for three years. The Red Cross has brought us some food here, but the children won't eat their vegetables. It doesn't bother me to be here, but I'm sorry for the children."

A member of the refugee association who was making a video of the encampment took me to the clinic, a bare room in one of the ruined houses nearby. A young nurse there was taking an older woman's blood pressure. In another room in the same house, three older men were sitting.

One of them, Ismet Ćosović, told me:

In Kopači, I had sixty-four beehives before the war. That produced three tons of honey a year. Now I live on a pension, and it comes five months late. I want to return to my land. I would have cows, bees, and fifty chickens. If I could go home, the pension I get now would be like pocket money. I had a tractor. My only wish is to return to what is mine.

If only ten families could return, within six months return would really be moving. But the Serb government is telling displaced Serbs that they would have great difficulty living in Goražde. However, over there the pension is around sixty or seventy DM, and on this side it is two hundred.

I'd like to go home—today rather than tomorrow—because I'd like to work on my own property. I'd be the most happy when you could visit me at my home.

In a tent that held about eight men, two were playing chess, and two more were watching the game. Others, all in their sixties and older, were lounging on cots and smoking. While I talked with them, a younger man came in and loaded a wood stove.

The men took turns telling me their stories. One told me that he lost a daughter and three grandchildren in the war. His son was wounded. "I owned 120 dunums of land, with two houses and three barns. That was all torched. The houses in lower Kopači survived, but all those in the hills were burned."

Another man told me, "I have been left all alone. My property was destroyed too. My son-in-law, brother, and grandson were all killed."

Someone nearby muttered, "God preserve him."

Ćosović's companion Ragib Mašić told me:

I am seventy years old. In 1941 there was a catastrophe too. I was finishing elementary school then. When the war broke out, I escaped to Kosovo. The Chetniks were killing us then too, not the Germans. I walked all the way to Mitrovica, carrying a pack on my back that weighed sixty kilos. Now I'm struggling to return, again.

My grandfather died in World War I. My father died in World War II. In this war it was my turn, but I lived. My son was wounded. They had his stomach out on the table, but he lived.

I had three houses in Kopači. There are twenty-one people in my family. Some of them are now in Sarajevo, but most of them are here. Instead of being in a tent, I should be resting, enjoying my last years. I left behind two cows and a horse and escaped with only my head.

When we went to plant in the fall, we had around twenty people and a couple of tractors. The Serbs made a barricade and cursed at us, and the police said that it was not safe. Then we decided to stay here. We didn't ask anyone for permission.

The campers held on throughout the winter, showing great persistence and creating a headache for both local and international officials. But the response of these officials was sluggish. Then in mid-December, the biggest snowstorm in Bosnia in over fifty years shut down most of the country, blocking roads and causing extended power outages in many towns. At the Goražde encampment two of the five tents were knocked down, and some of the children and older people were sent to shelters in town.

International officials expressed impatience and suggested that it was time to fold up the tents. This produced a spirited response from Džemila Hubjer, who said: "If they are not helping us now, while we're freezing out here, what would they do if we returned to Goražde? Those who are telling us to go back are telling us to reoccupy Serb houses."

Akifa Dučić said, "It's no worse for us here than in the wrecked houses where we live in town. We will not even speak about leaving." The campers were adamant that the idea to set up the tents was theirs alone. Dučić told me, "I want the world to know that this is not a political action. I am not interested in politics. The politicians lied to us for seven years. All I want is to be in my home. No one can come in here and tell me where to go. No one can tell me to go back to Goražde. No money, gold, or the riches of the world can keep me from my house."

BREAKTHROUGH

Finally in the spring of the next year, international officials convinced the Serb authorities in Kopači that they must allow the displaced Bosniaks to return home. An agreement specified that returnees would first occupy two Bosniak-owned houses that were in good repair. More than forty returnees moved into these houses. Serb separatists immediately began a harassment campaign, throwing a rock through the window of one of the returnees' houses, setting off a bomb in front of another, shooting at the houses, and plastering Kopači with posters of Nikola Poplašen. Local authorities also continued to build homes for displaced Serbs on Bosniak-owned land.

The returnees persisted. Return to Kopači gradually accelerated during the year 2000. What is more, a regional thaw slowly took hold that year, and returnees began to trickle into eastern parts of the Republika Srpska where their presence had been inconceivable in the years just after the war. The hard-liners' grip on the area was loosening.

For the first time since the war hundreds of people were visiting their prewar homes in villages around Foča, Žepa, Višegrad, and other municipalities notorious for obstruction. Most returns to these places were to tent encampments, as the homes destroyed in the war had yet to be rebuilt. In some places returnees were living in the basements of demolished houses while they cleared away rubble from other homes. Bosniaks were not the only returnees; a large-scale return of displaced Serbs took place in Dubište, a village under Federation control just outside of Goražde.

By mid-2000 dozens of returnee tent encampments were reported in the eastern part of the RS alone, with estimates as high as eighteen thousand people inhabiting those tents.[31] In Kopači evictions were picking up, and houses were finally beginning to be rebuilt, although occasional violent incidents still occurred. Houses were being rebuilt in Kozarac. The OHR reported that the process of return and evictions had begun in all municipalities in the Federation, except for a few hard-line Croat-dominated centers.[32]

Over sixty-seven thousand minority returns took place by the end of 2000. Nearly 250,000 property claims were filed by this time as well; around 111,000 of them had been resolved, and somewhat over fifty thousand of those resolutions had been implemented. At the end of 2000 PLIP implementation stood at 21 percent.[33]

On the local level, return in the RS was highest in Prijedor municipality, where well over ten thousand non-Serbs returned. This figure included at least five thousand returns to Kozarac, where several mosques were rebuilt. Return to the Zvornik area, where return was taking place in forty villages, was just as impressive. Fadil Banjanović estimated that between 80,000 and 120,000 people were involved in return in northern and eastern Bosnia; at least ten thousand families had already returned in this area. In an interview, Banjanović said, "at one time it was unthinkable that someone would return to Zvornik, because for a long time that was impossible . . . and return to some village near the entity line or a couple of kilometers further, at one time, was a bogeyman."[34]

Approximately two hundred thousand minority returns took place in the first five years after the war. At some 10 percent of the displaced, this number was too small to be able to say that Bosnia-Herzegovina was on the way to a multiethnic recovery. Meanwhile, there were still around ten thousand displaced persons in collective centers (down from forty-six thousand immediately after the war). And while some displaced persons were returning home, the Bosnian Helsinki Human Rights Committee reported that other people—as many as one hundred thousand—had left Bosnia since the end of the war.[35]

In Sarajevo, progress in returns was mixed. After five years of obstruction, threats, and torment, Anka won her tenancy claim and was allowed to move back into her apartment. However, that was not the end of the story. The man who had lived in her apartment for all those years claimed that he had invested 8,000 KM in its repair, even though the apartment had not sustained any war damage.* He sued Anka for those expenses, and she was faced with another long court battle.

Other Croats were leaving Sarajevo. Down from a prewar census of thirty-four thousand, in 2000 Sarajevo's Croat population was estimated at twenty-one thousand. Some had left during the war, but many more were still leaving.[36] Serbs were reported to be returning: fifteen thousand came back in 1999 and the first half of 2000,[37] while DISS reported that over twenty-three hundred Serb families returned in the year 2000.[38] Edin Beća of the Coalition for Return noted that around seven hundred people were coming to the Coalition for legal advice each month in 2001, and that fifty families a month were retaking possession of their apartments.

Commenting on the speed-up of return, Beća said, "Just now, people are slowly starting to come to their senses. During that time when people had not yet crossed the interethnic barrier of fear, we represented people. People were confused, but we knew the time would come when they would start to think for themselves. It is just now starting. Times are changing, and people are seeing that no one can live from promises alone. The old leaders are going to The Hague. So each day we have more clients." Around 80 percent of the Coalition's clients in 2000–2001 were Serbs hoping to return.

Beća mentioned that the local government, taken over by the Social Democrat Party in 2000, had even been willing to evict high functionaries and noted, "With the new government, there is a real change in Sarajevo Canton in implementation of the laws. It is all much more efficient. They don't oppose return, because their composition is multi-ethnic. Unfortunately, this is only in Sarajevo Canton. In other places, there has not been a change of government. In the Republika Srpska, the SDS [Serb separatist party of Radovan Karadžić] has even gotten stronger."

Father Franjo Radman, a Sarajevo-based Franciscan priest and advocate for Croat return, had a less optimistic comment on the nature of the Social Democrat–led coalition government: "There has not been much change with the SDP. Before, there was open manipulation of people. These people don't talk the same way. But they are only doing superficial things. They paint a door while the house is burning."[39]

With heightened return the nationwide count of internally displaced persons (IDPs) decreased significantly by early 2001, from around 800,000 to somewhat more than 518,000. A reregistration of IDPs had been held at the end of 2000. The lower figure is explained in part by real return, that is, minority return of internally displaced people to their prewar homes. Besides this internal return, a few thousand Croatian

---

* One KM (Bosnian konvertabilna marka, or convertible mark) and one DM (deutschmark) hold roughly the same value, which fluctuates between US$0.60 and US$0.70. So 8,000 KM would equal approximately US$6,000

Serbs returned to Croatia, and some displaced Albanians from Kosovo returned home. Meanwhile, a significant number of displaced persons decided not to reregister as displaced, opting to set down roots in their postwar residences.

Return continued to accelerate in all directions in 2001. In northeastern Bosnia between Zvornik and Bijeljina, tens of thousands of Muslims returned, primarily to villages. Returns to Kozarac, where displaced Serbs finally evacuated the high school, doubled to ten thousand. In addition to receiving significant assistance from international relief agencies, hundreds of returnees in Kozarac rebuilt their houses at their own expense.

By the end of 2001, property claims throughout Bosnia-Herzegovina passed one hundred thousand, bringing the implementation rate to more than 40 percent. Minority returns in that year surpassed ninety-two thousand—an increase of twenty-five thousand from the previous year. Return was peaking, but whether this movement would restore a multicultural Bosnia was still very questionable.

It was becoming apparent that property claims resolution did not translate directly to refugee return. Immediate sale of repossessed apartments was forbidden, but tenants who had privatized their flats found ways around this or simply rented the apartments out. In mid-2001, the High Representative abolished the law forbidding sale of a flat before two years of residence.

One could look at want ads in the newspapers of most cities, or even at signs pasted on lampposts, and see that brisk trading and selling of apartments was underway. Displaced Serbs living in Banja Luka were offering their Sarajevo apartments for sale or trade for an apartment in Banja Luka, as were Muslims trading apartments in Banja Luka in order to remain in Sarajevo.

CROATS AND RETURN

Croats were displaced by the tens of thousands during the war, and they had particular problems in their attempts to return. As with the Serbs, their leaders, on the whole, wanted them to stay displaced and corralled in ethnic enclaves. The HDZ, by far the strongest party representing the Bosnian Croats, strove to consolidate a Croat population in western Herzegovina, with its center in west Mostar. These nationalist leaders effectively disowned much of the ancient Croat-populated region in central Bosnia and in Posavina to the north.

Father Radman discussed the role of the HDZ with some anger: "HDZ destroyed the Croats. In Zenica the Croats fought the Bosniaks, and in Doboj the Serbs. Croats from these places went to the new settlements around Mostar; there are Bobanovo Selo, Šuškovo, Domanovići, and others. There, they signed papers that they would not sell their new houses for twenty years, and therefore would not try to return to their prewar homes. These settlements, with about 150 houses in each settlement, are considered the 'first wall of defense.' They were built without an infrastructure."

Radman opposed the transfer of Croats to an ethnically consolidated territory: "What they call 'humane resettlement' we call robbery because, for example, Drvar [taken over by Croat forces] was over 90 percent populated by Serbs before the war."

Thousands of displaced Croats from central Bosnia ended up in the new "buffer settlements" in western Herzegovina and, according to Radman, eighty thousand landed in Croatia, on the coast and in Knin. Real estate agents there were buying evacuated Serb-owned property in those locations and selling it to the newcomers at low rates.[40] There was fierce pressure from nationalist leaders both in Croatia and in western Herzegovina to prevent displaced Croats from returning to their prewar homes.

The obstruction was not all from the inside; nationalist Bosniak and Serb leaders in the territories they controlled also mobilized to prevent Croat return. And there were few Mile Marčetas or Fadil Banjanovićes among the Croats; this lack of leadership hurt their chances for return. However, many Croats were not ready to give up their ancient homelands, where they had lived for at least as many centuries as the Bosniaks and Serbs in theirs. Some Croat return activists arose, notably from among the progressive clergy—especially in central Bosnia, where support for separatism was much weaker than in Herzegovina.

Before the war Croats in Bosnia-Herzegovina numbered around eight hundred thousand, some 17 percent of the population. Without a census it was difficult to estimate the postwar Croat population, but its decrease has been drastic. Father Radman estimated that it had been cut in half, to four hundred thousand. Thus, although the Bosniaks suffered the highest number of casualties, in the long run, with continuing attrition, the Croat population in Bosnia is arguably the most in danger of disappearing.

BUGOJNO

> For five and a half years I did not drink coffee in Bugojno.
> —Ivica Marina, Bosnian Croat displaced from Bugojno, 1999

Situated at the western approach to central Bosnia, Bugojno came out of the war dominated by Bosniaks. Its prewar Croat population of some sixteen thousand people had fled, thousands of their houses demolished. During the first couple of postwar years, the former high school teacher turned strongman Dževad Mlaćo, favorite of the SDA, sponsored fierce obstruction against return of the Croats, who had previously constituted one-third of the city's population. The eight thousand–odd displaced Serbs were discouraged from returning as well. Regular harassment and beatings of potential returnees, and even looting, arson, and bombing of their homes, terrorized the Croats. Buoyed by pressure from the international community, however, an intrepid group of some one thousand Croats did return over the first few years.

Croats increasingly presented claims for the return of their property in Bugojno; by the end of 1998 over twenty-three hundred had been filed. Under the Mlaćo administration, these claims were ignored or processed very slowly. Those Croats who did return faced widespread discrimination. Croats were barred from inclusion in a local economy that was operating at one-fifth of its formerly robust power. In a standard move to "redraw the demographic map," the city government was also distributing state-owned land to displaced Bosniaks for home construction. Some of this was land formerly owned by Croats and nationalized under the socialist government, now subject to ongoing restitution litigation. Mlaćo ignored those proceedings.

Under pressure, Mlaćo consented to allow some degree of integration of the Bugojno police force. The presence of Croat police on the force would reassure Croat returnees of their security. But Mlaćo was slow to assist those Croat police in regaining their own homes. Commenting on the problem of housing for returned police officers, Mlaćo commented, "where police officers live isn't important."[41]

The OHR struggled for three years to pressure Mayor Mlaćo to cooperate with the return effort, with little success. The last straw for the international community came when Branka Raguž, one of Bosnia's three human rights ombudsmen, filed a complaint about Mlaćo's obstruction of property claims resolutions. The mayor's response was to call Raguž a "war criminal." The OHR then suspended Mlaćo in mid-February 1999. Soon afterward, the SDA elected Mlaćo member of the Bosnian Parliament's House of Peoples. This move effectively removed Mlaćo from the scene of controversy in Bugojno, but it simultaneously served as a vote of confidence from his party. A more conciliatory politician became mayor of Bugojno.

I visited Croat return activists in Bugojno the day after Mlaćo's suspension. The Coalition for Return had recommended that I go see Father Mirko Majdandžić, a Franciscan priest. Throughout the war Father Mirko had stayed in Sarajevo, helping people of all faiths in the besieged city. He was subsequently transferred to Bugojno.

I took the four-hour bus trip to Bugojno via Zenica and Travnik, going over Mount Komar, one of the most ravishing scenes in Bosnia. From that pass, one of the highest in the country, you can see forever in three directions: east, west, and down.

I met Father Mirko in his rectory behind the church of St. Ante. In his early middle age and solidly built with dark but thinning hair, he wore black jeans and a black leather jacket. Father Mirko could have been a truck driver.

There was a crucifix in the room, a painting of the Last Supper, and a two-foot-diameter loaf of bread with "Merry Christmas" written on it in Bosnian. We sat at a long table as nuns came out from the kitchen to serve us soup, stuffed cabbage, salami, ham, bread, and fruit. There were three bottles on the table: slivovitz, lozovača (brandy from grapes), and red wine. We ate and watched the news about tensions in Kosovo, the upcoming Brčko decision, and a new war between Ethiopia and Eritrea.

Father Mirko told me that he was originally from Busovača, and he had been in Bugojno for a year and a half. Adding to the list of obstacles facing Croats desiring to return, he noted that not only were Croat-owned homes occupied by hundreds of displaced persons from Jajce and Prozor, but there was also a high incidence of double occupancy: "For example, before the war, a family of five lived in one house or flat. Now, people from that family would have moved into one or two abandoned Croat houses. As many as 30 percent of the Croat houses are occupied by Bugojno citizens, and not by displaced people. The problem is that no one will evict them. If they did, that would solve a large part of the problem."

After describing the bureaucratic obstruction of property claims and misuse of public land, Mirko said, "When you put all these things together, it adds up to an ugly picture for the Croats. People look at this and conclude that it's a bad idea to return. The mayor is the main person responsible for this, but he didn't do anything alone. He had support from the highest levels of his party. Nevertheless, his suspension is a big plus."

I asked how long the obstruction could last without displaced Croats becoming discouraged. Father Mirko replied, "It's already very late. Around fifteen thousand Croats from here should return, but they won't. If half of that number returns, I'll be happy. Many already went over to America. There are around a thousand Croats from here in Livno, another thousand in Dalmatia between Makarska and Šibenik. There are more in Glamoč and Drvar, some in a camp in Grude, and others in Čapljina, Knin, Austria, and Germany."

Mirko was traveling regularly to these locations to encourage return. He found that if displaced Croats found work or were given permanent lodging in their place of refuge, they tended to give up on return. And those who were returning lacked their own school, a problem that was a major obstruction to Croat return throughout Bosniak-dominated areas: "In the local schools they have to learn the Bosniak language [sic], their geography, and history. So this is a deterrent to their return. In the Federation there are two equally valid school programs: Croat and Bosniak. I went to talk to Mlaćo several times about this problem and suggested to him that we make a combined curriculum, but he did not accept this. So now the Croat school is in the parish center."

Eventually this split curriculum was applied in a "separate-but-equal" system called "two schools under one roof," guaranteed to raise children who are foreign to each other, in both Croat- and Bosniak-dominated areas.

That night I slept in a modest room upstairs in the rectory. On the wall over my bed was a picture of the Virgin Mary, with a flaming heart portrayed on her chest. The next morning Father Mirko took me to meet an ethnically mixed group of activists who were determined to work against the perpetuation of ethnic tensions in Bugojno. They had recently founded Feniks (Phoenix), an organization with Croat, Bosniak, Serb, and Jewish members. Some of their leaders were tradesmen who wished to rebuild Bugojno. They spoke of leading a mass return to the city after the end of the school year, when returnees could be housed temporarily in the school buildings.

One Feniks activist complained to me about corruption: "I am not so familiar with how things work in your country under capitalism, but I know Germany. It usually takes two or three generations for someone in a family to get rich. Here, there are people who got rich in a few years; they are millionaires. The international community allowed that.

"Four months ago, Mlaćo took away seventeen thousand square meters of property that belonged to my family. He also confiscated land from thirty other families. Then he sells this land to profiteers. That was land that had been nationalized. By law, it must be returned to us, but he takes it and sells it. So what reason is left for us to stay?"

Father Mirko and I visited Vesna Tustonja, a Croat returnee and local activist with the Coalition for Return. Tustonja was a mother of five young children ranging from about three to fourteen years of age. Tustonja wore a cross around her neck, and one of the little girls wore cross earrings.

Father Mirko played with the kids while Tustonja told me how the family spent part of the war in Dalmatia. "I had to leave home with my kids one night, going through the woods. We really suffered during the war. We slept in a room in a collective center in Podgora with three beds for seven people. I am the only one left in my family now. My two brothers were killed, and my parents died of sickness. I returned to Bugojno last spring. I was the last to leave and the first to come back. If I can return, others can too."

In the next couple of years, other Croats did return, thanks in part to the efforts of return activists. With the mayor's replacement, the atmosphere for returnees in Bugojno eased somewhat. Evictions picked up, and security for returnees improved. By the end of 1999 more than 150 double occupants were evicted and over four thousand Croats had returned.[42] The trend in return in 2000 and 2001 followed the acceleration taking place in the rest of the country. In this period, return to Bugojno was among the greatest in the country. By late 2002 more than half of Bugojno's displaced Croats, about eighty-five hundred, had returned.[43] What Father Mirko had hoped and worked for came true.

MUJAHEDIN IN CENTRAL BOSNIA

Some three thousand to four thousand Arab soldiers, known as mujahedin, came to fight in the Bosnian war as early as mid-1992. They fought on the side of the government army against Serb forces, and when the Bosniak-Croat conflict broke out in early 1993, they fought against the Croats as well. There were two fighting groups based in central Bosnia: the Seventh Muslim Brigade, composed exclusively of local Bosniaks, and El Mujahedin, which included both Bosniak and foreign soldiers. The latter force, while officially under the command of the Army of Bosnia-Herzegovina, often operated quite independently. It was responsible for a number of war crimes committed against Croats and Serbs, and its foreign members were also known to harass local Muslims who did not adhere to their strict form of religious observance.

By the end of the war, Serbs were dispersed far from their homes in the cities and villages of central Bosnia, but the Croats, in many cases, did not end up far away. Rather than experiencing expulsion to another entity, as did the local Serbs, part of the local Croat population was removed to nearby places that remained under Croat control. Most municipalities in Central Bosnia Canton, which includes Bugojno and Travnik, ended up divided in this way. This proximity to their prewar homes left displaced Croats with greater possibility for return than the Serbs.

At the end of the war, the removal of the foreign mujahedin was a primary concern to most of the drafters of the Dayton agreement. The final draft of the agreement required foreign military forces to withdraw from Bosnia. All signatories including Alija Izetbegović agreed to this condition. Some mujahedin left, but at the same time, Bosniak officials were issuing hundreds of Bosnian passports to others who remained.[44]

Information as to who illegally gave out citizenship to foreign fighters, and why they did so, remains murky. Gratitude for wartime support has been cited, but at least as strong a motive for helping mujahedin stay in Bosnia was their potential for furthering the separatist goals of some of the Bosniak leaders. Naturally, these goals were not publicly espoused by Izetbegović or other top leaders, but they were nevertheless promoted.

Some of the remaining mujahedin had honest motives for staying, and others not. There were those who had married Bosnian women and simply wished to settle down, although some of those women had married under pressure. There were also former fighters who were wanted for criminal or political offences in their home countries, and who faced persecution if they returned. Finally, some mujahedin wished to continue what they perceived as the struggle for Islam in Bosnia.

It is estimated that around fifteen hundred mujahedin remained in the country, settling primarily in central Bosnia.[45] Some lived quietly, but others formed secret organizations and practiced terror against would-be returnees. The mujahedin forces had opposed the formation of the Croat-Bosniak Federation under the Washington Agreement of 1994 because they favored a Muslim-dominated state (or statelet). Thus, after the war they worked to prevent Croat-Bosniak cooperation and reconciliation. Their actions were significant in preventing return of Croats to their central Bosnian heartland in the first few years after the war. In a de facto manner, then, they collaborated with the Herzegovinan separatist Croats, led by a hard-line faction of the HDZ, who also wished to prevent the Bosnian Croats from returning to central Bosnia.

During the war, mujahedin forces had helped to expel thousands of Croats from their villages around Travnik, including from the village of Guča Gora. Travnik and this village, with its Franciscan monastery, represented the heartland of the central Bosnian Croat cultural identity. Hundreds of mujahedin occupied the village during the war. After the war, the mujahedin launched terror attacks on Croat targets in this area. The Travnik area was a target not only because it was a base of mujahedin residence, but also because its municipal government was more receptive to Croat return than was the case in Bugojno.

Terror attacks were launched in the region between Zenica, Travnik, and Bugojno when the ink on the Dayton agreement was barely dry. For the next several years, the mujahedin and their accomplices desecrated cemeteries, bombed churches, and assassinated Croat policemen. The formation of a joint Croat-Bosniak police force in

Travnik, a move to promote security for returning Croats, was apparently particularly objectionable to the mujahedin. At least eight policemen were murdered in a campaign waged against this police force in 1998.

The terror campaign moved further afield and reached new heights when a car bomb was set off in Mostar in front of the central police station, injuring around fifty people. Numerous threats were issued against Pope John Paul II on the occasion of his April 1997 visit to Sarajevo. During the visit, police discovered a powerful bomb mounted under a bridge, but it was disarmed before it could harm the Pope or his entourage. Meanwhile, during this period Catholic churches were attacked and desecrated in other parts of central Bosnia such as Kakanj and Donji Vakuf, and all the way to Sarajevo. The monastery at Kraljeva Sutjeska, the ancient home of the Catholic royalty of pre-Ottoman Bosnia, was bombed as well.

Local Bosniak authorities in central Bosnia seemed to be tolerant toward those who were practicing terrorism against Croats. Efforts to apprehend the culprits were lackadaisical; those who were prosecuted and convicted received short sentences, and some who were sentenced received pardons well before their time was served. For example, six Bosniaks and one veteran from Yemen were jailed for conspiracy to acquire arms and explosives in 1997, and all were subsequently pardoned.[46]

This lenience paralleled the authorities' tolerance toward double occupancy and other obstacles to return. Nevertheless, the determination of Croats to return in the face of such intimidation was great; by the end of 1998, nearly thirty-five hundred Croats had returned to Travnik,[47] and return accelerated in subsequent years. By the end of the year 2000, Travnik was noted as having one of the most efficient implementations of refugee return, with 54 percent repossession of prewar property, double the average for that year in the Federation.[48] Translated into actual return, in 2001 this meant that after Sarajevo Canton, return to Central Bosnia Canton was the highest in the Federation.[49]

4

Return to Mostar and Other Parts of Herzegovina

A COUPLE OF YEARS AFTER THE WAR'S END I WAS INTER-viewing Azra Hasanbegović, director of the women's organization Žena BiH (Woman of Bosnia-Herzegovina), based on the east side of Mostar. Hasanbegović had been displaced from her apartment on the west side of Mostar and was as yet unable to return. I asked her how her application for return to her apartment was progressing. She looked at me with a quizzical expression, as if there were only one possible answer, and said, "I am in the phase of waiting."

Hasanbegović spoke of going to look at her apartment: "I saw my home but didn't go in. I can walk by my house, but I can't go in. Another family is in my house now, a family that lived in a village before. A woman in that family has been wearing my hat all summer."

Azra Hasanbegović's hometown, with its Mediterranean sun and its rushing, crystal-blue river, was one of those rare places in the world made astonishingly beautiful by nature. When humans settled there, they managed to add to the beauty, rather than effacing it. Before the war around one-third of Mostar's 125,000 population were Croats, and one-third were Muslims. The remainder were Serbs, "Yugoslavs," and "others."

After an initial offensive by Serb nationalist forces in 1992, and then the yearlong Croat-Muslim conflict, most local Serbs had left or were expelled from the city. By the end of the war Mostar was divided into a Muslim-controlled east side and a Croat-controlled west side, each part almost completely emptied of the other ethnicity. Roughly thirty-five thousand Muslims were driven out of the west side, and around seven thousand Croats from the east side.[1]

Croats from central Bosnia and Muslims from the rest of Herzegovina swelled the numbers of the displaced in their respective zones. Mostar's overall population had been reduced by some twenty thousand, and of those remaining, nearly half were displaced.[2]

The postwar atmosphere in divided Mostar—the administrative seat of the region—influenced political dynamics in the rest of Herzegovina. It was in Mostar that the Croat political infrastructure staked out its center of operations. A minority in the Federation, Croat nationalists held onto their separatist aspirations and worked to maintain the ethnic homogenization they had created. Not only did they fiercely oppose Bosniak return to areas they had conquered, but they also violently evicted hundreds of additional Bosniaks from west Mostar in the first couple of years after the war. And in addition to this, they continued to work in manifold ways to prevent Croats from returning to their own prewar homes in other parts of the country.

Bosniak leaders advocated for Bosniak return to west Mostar and other parts of Herzegovina that the Croats had taken over, such as Stolac. But while they were not as fiercely obstructionist as the Croat leaders in preventing return, for a time Bosniaks prevented Croat return to east Mostar. Ultimately it was the impoverished and traumatized displaced people of both sides who suffered, unable for years to return to a stable life.

Toward the end of 1997 I visited east Mostar. Ramiz, head of a displaced family from Gacko, met me at the bus station. As we walked away from the station we passed the aptly named "Beirut Café." East Mostar had borne the brunt of bombing from both directions throughout the war, and there was not much left unscathed. Piles of rubble still lay where houses and buildings had stood, and the antique Ottoman core of the east side was just beginning to be restored. As we arrived at the decrepit Serb-owned house that Ramiz and his family were occupying, he said to me, "Here we are, in someone else's house."

During the war Gacko was taken over by Serb forces. Ramiz hid in the nearby woods for a couple of months with his family, who were eventually allowed to leave by bus. Ramiz made his way on foot, at night, to Mostar. The walk took him eight days. He spent the next three years on the front lines.

Ramiz told me that he would have three, seven, or fifteen days at the front line, and an equal number of days off to rest. At home, there was no electricity, and sometimes no candles. Mortars and grenades fell on east Mostar often, day and night. Once one fell outside the window of the living room in which four people were sleeping and showered the room with glass. Another time shrapnel came through the upstairs window, passing within inches of Ramiz, and made a hole in the television screen.

Ramiz said that, bombing or no, people would go out to get firewood, and stand in line for food. He said, "There were a hundred times that I could have been killed." Ramiz was never wounded. I asked him if he had been frightened during the fighting. He said that of course, he was afraid at first, but then he got used to it.

After years of fighting, Ramiz had nothing, and he said that he could lose his home any time the owner came back. Now, when he could find employment, Ramiz worked as a construction laborer for twelve dollars a day. He showed me the calluses on his hands and said that all he had to feed his kids was what he could earn from that occasional work.

Ramiz's wife, Nermina, worked as a housekeeper for an international agency, and this made it possible for the family to make ends meet in their poor lodgings. The house had only a kitchen, a living room, and two bedrooms. Only the ground floor was heated, by a wood stove. Nermina said to me, "What can we do? We're refugees." Ramiz said that if it were his house, he would fix it up. But he feared that he would be displaced again if the former owners came back.

ACTIVISTS FOR RETURN

In the Mostar area, like nearly everywhere else in Bosnia-Herzegovina, return activists got busy soon after the end of the war. Capable people, regardless of their prewar profession, found their way into local and regional associations that agitated for return. Most of these organizations received financial assistance and training from international relief agencies.

The organization Žena BiH (Woman of Bosnia) was one of the more stable and effective NGOs formed in Mostar during and after the war. In that period this organization devoted most of its resources to helping displaced women who were coping with the demands of chaotic postwar life. Many were widows or single mothers who were attempting to regain control of their prewar homes. Some were dealing with domestic abuse. Most had lost whatever security they possessed before the war.

Director Azra Hasanbegović commented that women were natural leaders in the postwar NGO sector, because they had remained active during the war—practically creating this sector on their own—while "the men were away fighting." Afterward, activist women were able to cross bridges—literally—that were off limits to men as demobilized veterans. In this way, activists from Žena BiH reached out to Croat women in west Mostar, and to displaced Serb women from Mostar who were now living in eastern Herzegovina.

Milan Jovičić was a Mostar Serb who lived on the west side before the war. He was not an "ordinary citizen" then but was active in business and politics. He had served as director of the energy plant in Gacko and was also a delegate in the Bosnian, and then Yugoslav, parliaments for a time. When Serb forces attacked Mostar in 1992, Jovičić opposed the nationalist assault and remained in his hometown. He stayed in Croat-controlled west Mostar throughout the war.

Soon after the war Jovičić became involved again in local politics, serving on the Mostar municipal council as a member of a multiethnic coalition. His luck turned bad at this point when, as he recounts, demobilized veterans from a brigade of Croat extremists came to "liquidate" him in mid-1996. He took refuge at the office of the EU, whose special envoy to Mostar gave him new identification and helped him to hide for a time. However, Jovičić complained that the international community took no steps to apprehend and punish his persecutors.

In early 1999 Jovičić told me, "I can't return now. If I did, I would have to be armed, because it's still too dangerous. It is known exactly who is where, their first and last names. It is ridiculous and sad that I am a displaced person in my own city. I live one hundred meters from my own home, and I can't return there. I see it every morning when I leave my apartment."

However, Jovičić did not remain inactive and in hiding. Instead, he helped form a multiethnic advocacy organization, the Association of Refugees and Displaced Persons of Mostar, representing the displaced of all ethnicities. In the early period following the war, there were some twelve thousand displaced people living on both sides of the city. The association also tried to stay in touch with thousands of other Mostar citizens scattered throughout the world, keeping them informed of property law changes, deadlines, and other local developments.

Jovičić was harshly critical of separatist leaders, particularly on the Croat-controlled west side of the city, whom he considered much more resistant to return than were the Bosniaks. He said, "On the east side of the city, there are many displaced persons from east Herzegovina—Gacko, Trebinje, and Nevesinje—as well as from Stolac and Čapljina. The east side is crowded, but goodwill exists for the problems to be solved. But it simply does not exist on the west side. The war profiteers who operate there, some of them control five apartments and rent them out.

"The HDZ [the leading Croat nationalist party] says, 'The Serbs got their entity; why can't we get ours?' They want to revise Dayton. They want a third entity, and so they are obstructing all the executive organs of the government." Asked whether there was obstruction to return on the east side, Jovičić responded, "Yes, certainly, but less than there was before. There has been some movement on the east side; some evictions, but only a minimum. There has been no movement on the west side."

When High Representative Wolfgang Petritsch removed twenty-two local officials throughout Bosnia-Herzegovina, Jovičić was optimistic. He said, "Petritsch has given us hope. He hit the target. It was good that they removed Stipe Marić [mayor of Mostar Southwest municipality], but they need to do more. We know exactly who is obstructing return. We need to eliminate them, and to eliminate whole parties, if necessary. We can't do these things without the West, and SFOR. If they were to leave, tomorrow there would be war again."

It remained to be seen whether Petritsch's removals would make a significant difference in return in Mostar. Jovičić focused on the HDZ, together with groups of demobilized veterans, as the principal obstruction to return. He pointed at Croatian president Tudjman as their sponsor: "Croatia is the mentor of everything that has happened here. Nothing is decided here; they just wait for the green light from Zagreb. The international community knows all of this."

I spoke with Zinka Cerić, the director of Swiss House, a local return organization supported by the relief organization Swiss Labour Assistance. Cerić described the nature of return in the Mostar region:

> Only older people, in the rural areas, are coming home. They want to die at home. The younger people will not come home. It's common that part of the family will return, and the other part will stay where they are.
>
> Meanwhile, people are building new houses on someone else's land, or taking state land. And someone is financing that. Each nationalist party is taking over state land in the areas that they control, and building houses. This is true here on both sides of the city, as well as in Brčko, Nevesinje, and so on. Until the political climate changes, there will be no change. You don't need to write that; the international community already knows.[3]

In this period, return to villages in the Mostar area was accelerating gradually. The Croat nationalists could even boast that areas under their control witnessed the most return—but this was because they controlled most of the region. Serb return to villages near Mostar was picking up as well. However, Croat return to the east side was weak, and Bosniak return to west Mostar remained fiercely obstructed. Arsons and physical attacks against Bosniaks continued.[4]

CONTINUING DIVISION

Over the years, it became less physically dangerous for Croats and Bosniaks to cross the invisible border between west and east Mostar. However, the city has remained a divided one. Croats and Bosniaks keep to their respective bus stations, markets, schools, and hospitals.

At the governmental level, police departments have remained separate, as have municipal courts and budgets, relying on parallel taxation systems. The international community participated in cementing the division of the city by contributing funds for construction of separate institutions—even while international officials were pressing for reunification. International financing was available for separate transportation companies, water systems, post offices, and other divided companies.[5]

Bosniak authorities were striving both to integrate Mostar and to cultivate a connection between their city and the Bosniak power center, Sarajevo. Croat leaders were holding fast to de facto autonomy and consolidation of their wartime parastate of Herceg-Bosna, which had been made illegal by the Washington Agreement.

For many years after that treaty was signed, Herceg-Bosna remained a fact. A spring 2000 report by the International Crisis Group (ICG) noted that the international community had crafted over thirty major agreements about reunification of the city—and that the Croat leaders had broken every one of them. Deadlines were set, to no avail, for removing separate pension and health insurance systems, as well as for abolishing parallel financial institutions. Clearly, the HDZ separatists were determined to perpetuate their soft secession, and they were ever more skilled at manipulating the internationals. The ICG criticized international officials for "rely[ing] on the good will of the HDZ—the party responsible for the ethnic cleansing of west Mostar," and it stated that the HDZ "worked against the national interests of Croats in Bosnia and Herzegovina."[6]

At the end of 1999 president of Croatia Franjo Tuđjman died, his departure creating a tentative opening for change in Croat separatist policies. Since the war, the government of Croatia had supplied copious funding to the Herceg-Bosna parastate in support of its parallel institutions. Now, with the impending election of a more liberal, less virulently nationalist government in Croatia, there would be less financial and political support for Bosnian Croat separatism. At the very least, there could be greater transparency in Croatia's material support for Bosnian Croats.

International officials concerned with Mostar attempted to open the way to multidirectional refugee return. By late 1999 several thousand families had returned to their prewar homes within Herzegovina-Neretva Canton, of which Mostar was the capital. Even this meager beginning was a struggle to achieve, as return plans were often formulated with no enforcement mechanisms.

Bosniaks began to return from Mostar to eastern Herzegovina in the Republika Srpska—especially to nearby Nevesinje—as well as to places in western Herzegovina that had been completely ethnically cleansed by Croat forces. Displaced Serbs returning from eastern Herzegovina were spending the winter in improvised shelters, without water or electricity, in their villages near Mostar.

At the end of the year Olivier Mouquet, UNHCR public affairs liaison officer at Mostar, told me, "The year 1999 was not a totally lost year."[7] He outlined a familiar return plan wherein the first target was empty houses and those easily fixed, followed by returns to occupied houses and those needing more extensive repair. He noted that most returns to date were of elderly people, and he expressed frustration about continuing obstruction of return to the city centers.

Describing Croat obstruction of Croat return, Mouquet said, "Their main method is use of propaganda to manipulate the population; they offer work in their territory, and they say that there is no work in the Muslim-controlled areas. They play up every incident of violence against Croats in central Bosnia. They put pressure on the friends and family of people who are thinking about going home. Croat return has actually increased, especially intracanton return, but the Croat authorities are also building whole new settlements for displaced people."

I asked Mouquet, "Where does the money come from for this construction?" He said, "Officially we don't know." I asked, "In other words, the government of Croatia is financing it?" Mouquet did not respond, except to smile.

Displaced Croats were reluctant to return to their former homes one at a time, Mouquet noted:

> The Bosniaks and Serbs will fix one house and use it to shelter many men who will then work on the other houses until they are livable. The Croats want all their houses to be finished at the same time.
>
> We have made the mistake in the past of fixing an entire village of houses, and then the people did not return. Now, since there are fewer financial resources available for reconstruction, we focus on places where people have already displayed a clear intent to return. For instance, where people are working to recreate ties in their old homes, are clearing the rubble, and starting to garden.

With the international community mounting its campaign for rule of law throughout Bosnia-Herzegovina, Mouquet was concerned that too much time had been lost, but he expressed hope that recently standardized property laws could be implemented. Petritsch's recent removal of obstructionist officials also bolstered his optimism.

CONTINUED OBSTRUCTION, SEPARATIST MANEUVERS, SFOR RAIDS

Throughout 1999 and 2000 two-way return in Mostar accelerated slowly. Grassroots return activists and their advocacy organizations, from the local to regional level, pressed on. Obstruction continued as well; it was more pronounced in the case of return to the city core on both sides of the ethnic division than to the villages. Resistance on the Croat-controlled side continued to be more organized than on the east side of the city.

Meanwhile, the movement for the political separation of Croat-controlled territory remained active. Posters appeared around the west side of Mostar that read, "No Identity without an Entity." This slogan was supported by the HDZ and other Croat nationalist parties, together with the Croat war veterans' associations.

The separatist movement appealed to some ordinary Croats, many of whom, aware that their numbers were steadily decreasing in Bosnia, felt beleaguered and outnumbered. To them it seemed perfectly logical that "if the Serbs have their entity, why should we be stuck together with the Bosniaks, with whom we fought a war?"

On the other hand, there was a solid constituency of Croats, especially from Posavina and central Bosnia, who rejected secession and wished to cooperate with the Bosniaks. Many of them, with reason, had strong reservations toward the Bosniak political infrastructure. There had, after all, been vicious fighting between the two populations in central Bosnia—and for that matter, most of the prominent Bosniak leaders had clear nationalist leanings of their own. However, the "pro-Bosnia" Croats wished to return to their own prewar homes and remain in their own country. Given this sentiment, they were aware that cooperation with the Bosniak population, rather than an eventual split-up of the Federation, was indispensable for their survival.

It was the covert parastate of Herceg-Bosna that was behind the resistance to multidirectional refugee return, and for the time being, the separatists had the upper hand.

One of the principal leaders of the Herceg-Bosna separatist movement was Ante Jelavić. Before the war, Jelavić had been a lieutenant in the Yugoslav People's Army, stationed for a time in Pale. Early in 1992 he left his post. He then began working for Bosnian Croat separatist leader Mate Boban as a logistics officer for the HVO (the Bosnian Croat army) in Grude, a center of Croat separatist operations in western Herzegovina.[8]

Soon after the war Jelavić was appointed as director of the Grude-based company Monitor M, which performed lucrative military and civilian construction work worth tens of millions of dollars, primarily in Croatia, but in Bosnia as well.[9] Jelavić's colleagues on the steering board of the company were military and political figures from the top levels of the wartime Herceg-Bosna leadership. He became minister of defense for the Federation of Bosnia-Herzegovina in 1996. After he became president of the HDZ in 1998, Jelavić was elected Croat member of Bosnia's three-part presidency.

Financial support was critical to the maintenance of the illegal postwar parastate of Herceg-Bosna, and significant funds came from Croatia. The Dayton agreement had arranged that funding for the Federation Ministry of the Defense would come not only from the Federation budget, but also from the Croatian government. These donations were directed toward the HVO (Croat) component of the Federation army and were to be used for salaries of Croat officers, for pensions for demobilized veterans, and for support of their families.

For more than five years after the war, tens of millions of dollars in assistance to the HVO flowed into Bosnia from Croatia, and its dispensation was quite nontransparent.[10] Millions of dollars of this assistance never reached its intended recipients. Starting in 1997, the Croatian donations were funneled through the newly created Hercegovačka Banka. This bank was set up for the purpose by Jelavić and other Bosnian Croat nationalists.[11]

The Hercegovačka Banka was one leg of the foundation of what has been called the "clandestine political economy" of postwar Herceg-Bosna. The numerous companies that founded this bank were headed by other HDZ leaders, many of whom, like Ante Jelavić, had entered the war as midlevel officers and who rose through the ranks. By the end of the war, some of them were already wealthy thanks to wartime business dealings, and the rest were poised to profit from their participation in the group of businesses known as "Herzegovina Holding," which included powerful media, financial, and communications businesses.

The HVO had founded Hercegovačka Banka; upon privatization, the network of funders became the owners and then raked off millions of dollars in Croatian assistance that was deposited in the bank. The Croatian government donated US$175 million in 1999 alone; the OHR later reported that the intended beneficiaries received very little of this money.[12] Rather, the nationalists who formed Herzegovina Holding channeled millions to the HDZ in support of its separatist operations.

In just one of many illustrations of this corruption, later court proceedings showed that US$4.4 million in Croatian funding was used for luxury homes for high officials in the HDZ.[13] More significant to the separatist project was the fact that funds were used to build "buffer settlements" between Mostar and Stolac for displaced Croats from other parts of Bosnia. Funds were also diverted to support Croats accused of war crimes, as well as to finance the associations of demobilized veterans. All these illicit uses of embezzled funds contributed to strengthening the hard-line faction among the Croat nationalists.

In addition to money diverted from legal Croatian donations meant for the HVO, the separatists had several other sources of funding: they also diverted money from the Federal budget, and they received donations from various Bosnian Croat nationalist parties, as well as from smuggling operations.

Reviewing the corruption practiced by the Herzegovinan separatists in the late 1990s, a report by the Institute for War and Peace Reporting noted in 2002 that "Jelavić and his supporters appointed themselves or their acolytes to key positions in ministries, related agencies, private companies and banks, which enabled them to exercise control over the bank's funds. Without such a network of highly-placed and interconnected people, fraud on such a scale would have been impossible." Officials associated with Hercegovačka Banka took out successive loans without repaying previous ones, without prompting any corrective action from the bank. The report further noted that this group created over one hundred fictitious companies, which they then used as foils to avoid paying taxes while importing valuable commodities such as oil and other goods—"at least 13 million euro were embezzled in this way."[14]

A report on Mostar issued by the ICG in April 2000 summed up the nature of the separatist operations by quoting a confidential report from a major international organization in Bosnia-Herzegovina: "Herceg-Bosna is a functioning parallel state and its politics are about capital accumulation. . . . Once this financial base of Herceg-Bosna is addressed, the rest of its parallel institutions, its symbols, and its resistance to minority return can be overcome."[15]

Thus the essence of the resistance to reunification of Bosnia-Herzegovina: enrichment of the separatists, who depend on a misled, ethnically homogenized constituency for support.

Much later, a commentator described Jelavić's role in more down-to-earth terms, writing that "Jelavić had not come to power as a representative of the Bosnian-Herzegovinan Croats, but as representative of a Zagreb-based criminal gang that, to the detriment of the least numerous Bosnian-Herzegovinan ethnicity, emptied the Croatian state budget for years. . . . Ante Jelavić served that gang."[16]

Here it is pertinent to recall the words of wartime intelligence operative Munir Alibabić, who soon after the end of the war wrote that "fascism is the highest form of organized crime" and described its practitioners as "implementers of high-intensity plunder."[17] In this vein, the operations of the Herceg-Bosna group displayed a continuity between wartime murder and ethnic cleansing by the separatists, and the postwar plunder of socially created wealth perpetrated by the same people.

The practices mentioned here were just the tip of the iceberg of widespread corruption, and such operations were found not only among Croat extremists. To one extent or another, very similar practices carried on among Serb separatists and Bosniak profiteers as well. In varying degrees, in all the monoethnically controlled areas, nationalists have enriched themselves while preventing refugee return. And in the Federation, there is ongoing collaboration between the Croat and Bosniak nationalist infrastructures in the division of the spoils. The HDZ and the SDA, as the two most powerful parties, have regularly made deals to split up control of the large state-owned companies.

In the spring of 2001 Croat nationalists attempted to improve their ability to commit high-intensity plunder by seceding from the Federation. In early March the HDZ organized a Croat National Congress of seven nationalist parties. The Congress voted to separate from the Federation and began drafting a constitution that would create a complete set of parallel governing bodies. The attempted secession backfired when international officials intervened in response to what had become a constitutional crisis. A few days after the meeting of the Congress, the OHR removed Ante Jelavić from his post in the presidency of Bosnia.

The HDZ had moved to establish its own entity without the political strength necessary to pull off the move. Several prior events had begun to threaten the HDZ's monopoly on power among the Bosnian Croats. Most obvious of these was the death of Croatian president Tudjman and subsequent election of a far less nationalist government in that country. Croatia's new president, Stipe Mesić, expressed the intention to discontinue support of the parallel institutions; shortly before the Croat National Congress took place in Bosnia, Croatia discontinued its aid transfers to the HVO.

Secondly, political developments in Bosnia-Herzegovina weakened the separatist movement. In late 2000 the nonnationalist coalition led by the SDP had won the nationwide elections, driving the HDZ and its coalition partner the SDA out of power. This encouraged and strengthened pro–Bosnia Croat forces throughout the country.

Finally, in addition to the cutoff of Croatian financing, there were other constraints on the ability of the separatists to fund their operations. The international community was working to reduce smuggling into Herzegovina, and the OHR had recently appointed an international auditor to investigate illegal funding of parallel bodies.[18] Furthermore, word of an impending investigation of Dragan Čović (rising leader of the HDZ after Jelavić's removal) was circulating. These developments made HDZ leaders nervous about their continued ability to function.

The international community did not stop at removing Jelavić from power but resolved to strike at the financial heart of Herceg-Bosna, the Hercegovačka Banka. Early in April 2001, SFOR troops raided the Mostar branch of the bank. The ill-planned raid resulted in a fiasco when hundreds of local Croat nationalists surged on the bank in protest and violently attacked the international troops. In the course of daylong rioting, more than twenty soldiers and several civilians were injured. Rioters turned over SFOR vehicles and flooded into the building, where they destroyed files. Some soldiers were temporarily taken hostage.

SFOR came back, better prepared, a couple of weeks later. This time, with hundreds of soldiers supported by dozens of tanks and helicopters, and even two air-support jets, they entered the bank in the middle of the night.[19] For several hours until dawn they searched every room and carted away boxes of documentation.

The OHR froze the bank's accounts and appointed a temporary administrator of the Mostar branch, an international official tasked with sorting out the evidence. Later examination of the material collected during this raid showed that directors of the Hercegovačka Banka were involved in embezzlement of funds that were directed to the HDZ. Investigators found that these funds were being used to support the creation of a parallel political infrastructure that would become a Croat-controlled entity. Another move by the international community following the raid was to break up Herzegovina Holding and to sell off its component firms.

Several top figures in the scandal were eventually arrested, including Ante Jelavić. Jelavić was charged with twenty-one counts of tax evasion, abuse of office, undermining of the constitutional order of Bosnia-Herzegovina (by supporting an illegal parastate), and embezzlement.[20]

The intervention in the Hercegovačka Banka's operations was a qualified success. The separatist plan was put on hold, as the leaders of Herceg-Bosna were no longer able to adequately finance parallel state structures. Evidence of corruption was exposed to the light of day, helping some Croats understand the character of their leaders. The HDZ, with some success, had been urging thousands of Croat members of the Federation army to desert their posts. Those soldiers returned to the army after the raid. The weakening of the Croat separatist leaders shored up the Federation, at least for the time being. However, sentiment among many Croats still reflected separatist tendencies. One slogan painted on a wall in west Mostar after the April raids read, "ICTY/SFOR/USA = Murder."

RETURN ACTIVISM CONTINUES

Obstruction by nationalists on both sides of Mostar did not deter the campaign for return. There was a special case of multiethnic cooperation within the city: the campaign of the tenants of the apartment buildings on the former front line, on Bulevar and Šantićeva Streets. The scene on these broad roads in the aftermath of the war was reminiscent of Beirut or Grozny, with every building, one after another, reduced to a ragged hulk.

In September 2001 I met with Silva Memić, an activist in the Association of Residents of Šantićeva Street. Memić described how her street and her campaign represented the best hope for the reunification of Mostar: "I'm from Šantićeva Ulica. Since 1996 I have been advocating the renewal of that street. I lived there all my life. The ethnic composition in my building was one-third, one-third, and one-third [Serb, Croat, and Bosniak]. This was a multiethnic area, but it is now divided. When the main roads are renewed, then there will be a united city. I will do that road."

Silva Memić and her activist colleagues accelerated their struggle for reconstruction of the apartment buildings of Šantićeva and Bulevar in the fall of 2000, when they wrote to the leaders of Mostar.

> In the last five years, we residents of Šantićeva Street, refugees in our own city, have addressed all institutions including yours, with the question, "when will renewal start in our torched and destroyed homes?"
>
> We hear how you talk about return, multiethnicity and togetherness, but you don't do anything for the reconstruction of our homes, and we are reminding you that Šantićeva Street was a street of all nationalities and as long as it remains destroyed, the city will be divided, because it is a reminder of the evil that happened.
>
> You have installed lighting and greenery on our street and told the media how you returned life to it, but we wish to inform you that it is a sad life without residents.
>
> We are wondering if you were waiting for us to die or to leave for some other town, and then in the most attractive location in town, you would build business spaces and houses for some new "citizens?"[21]

At the time of our meeting, Memić was director of the tax office for Herzegovina-Neretva Canton. She told me that she had remained in her building until August 1993, well past the outbreak of the Croat-Bosniak conflict: "I was in the building with the fighters until it burned." Afterward she cooked for soldiers and was once lightly wounded. Memić escaped the war and lived in Italy for a time, but she returned home, explaining, "I was in Italy. They have golden, talented hands, but I have a talented mind. I never thought to stay there."

Upon coming back to Mostar, Memić began to fight for return to Šantićeva. Describing the animosity and obstruction she encountered, she said, "When I started this campaign, I was treated like a prostitute." She showed me a petition with ten pages of signatures, calling for assistance in reconstruction of the buildings on the former front line. The petition read, "We know that money has arrived for the reconstruction of Mostar and that it has been spent for various purposes, but there was nothing left for the people of Bulevar, except a feeling of bitterness that they have become marginal people."

I met with the architect Krešimir Krtalić, another prominent member of the organization for Šantićeva and Bulevar. His small office was lined with art and travel photos. A fishing pole leaned against the wall in one corner. He provided me with some background about his home street: "Before World War II, Šantićeva was an elite neighborhood of ministers and rich people. Then it became a workers' neighborhood. There were builders, locksmiths, doctors, and people who worked in the railroad. We are the children of that generation. We were poor, but we love this city. I was born here and stayed here. I won't go anywhere, dead or alive."

Krtalić told me that throughout the war, he had fished every day, even as grenades were falling nearby. I asked him if he had been bothered by the grenades. He said, "For the first twenty days or so there was fear, but then it came to seem normal. If you hear the bomb go by, things are OK. It's when you don't hear them, then you're already dead. But things are all right now. You don't dwell on the evil that happened." During the war Krtalić continued his professional work, and he ran a restaurant on the side. "Then the restaurant was bombed, and I wrote everything off."

During several years of campaigning, reconstruction went slowly. When I spoke with Krtalić and Memić in late 2001, only two buildings had been restored, out of dozens of wrecks.

Memić encountered ongoing difficulties as a displaced person and an activist. Since her return, she had been evicted eight times. But her work was showing results. She described a meeting of the return organization, with displaced people from Šantićeva and Bulevar coming from all directions: "There was a city meeting with people of all ethnicities there. There were old neighbors who were seeing each other for the first time since the war, and they were kissing each other."

Memić showed me a magazine article about her, which named her the "Iron Lady of Šantićeva Street." In the article, Memić described her home street as the "street of the lindens," after the spreading trees with their fragrant flowers. In the face of continuing obstruction and superficial declarations of support, she said, "We are not giving up, we are going ahead, until the smell of the linden pervades life behind all the windows of our street."[22]

In late 2001, six years after the signing of the Dayton agreement and over seven years after the Washington Agreement, activists and international officials in Mostar were ambivalent as to the prospects for successful return. On one hand, obstruction was not dead, and the ghost of Herceg-Bosna still lurked along the Neretva. Meanwhile, international interest and economic assistance had peaked, and, while the UNHCR and dozens of international nongovernmental relief agencies were still sinking millions into recovery, aid was decreasing significantly. As return was peaking throughout Bosnia-Herzegovina, what lay around the corner for the Mostar region troubled everyone I met.

On the other hand the internationals had shown resolution in their robust confrontation of the corruption that supported Croat separatism. Furthermore, the international community's comprehensive rule-of-law strategy, with its consistently applied set of procedures, was making a difference in property restitution.

Ignacio Matteini of the UNHCR was optimistic about increased return in Mostar: "Our rates of return today are comparable to Sarajevo, and this would have been considered utopia two years ago," he said. "There has been a big change since last year. The biggest event has been the implementation of property law. There is a much greater ability to repossess property, implement evictions, and return to a more-or-less livable home."[23]

Matteini noted that the evictions, which had previously taken place in a chaotic manner, now also reflected the imposition of order. Stripping of apartments upon removal of illegal tenants had been halted. During evictions, the owner was now invited to be present, along with the tenant and a representative of the municipality. The representative was to take notes on the proceedings, and the owner was able to file a complaint if necessary. The IPTF (UN International Police Task Force) was present at evictions as well.

Matteini said, "This is the first time that local authorities are putting money into reconstruction of minority accommodations. Before, it was like Beckett, *Waiting for Godot*. Now, they are speaking our language. This is a big change, both in the Federation and in the Republika Srpska. In the Federation, materials are going to areas where minorities are returning. The army is supporting reconstruction by cleaning and building bridges."

Matteini summed up the situation by saying, "Mostar is becoming more normal. There is a positive trend. But I don't know if it will ever really become normal. The division is in people's minds."

RETURN TO GACKO

Before the war, Mostar was the cultural and economic center of all Herzegovina. People from the entire region visited there on the way to the sea, or simply for an afternoon's getaway. Now, many of the surviving Bosniaks who had been expelled from the part of Herzegovina taken over by Serb separatists were living as displaced persons in Mostar. For several years, return to eastern Herzegovina stalled.

I had heard many stories about eastern Herzegovina from refugees from Gacko who ended up in my city in the United States. They had described their lives before the war, when they had work and security, summer cottages in the villages, long vacations on the Adriatic, and friendly relations among the ethnicities. The thought of leaving all that for America or another country was nothing but an idle fantasy. I was often told about the legendary waters of a spring called Sopot: "Once you drink from Sopot, you will always return."

Speaking of those times Fahira, a displaced person in Mostar, told me, "My father was born in Gacko, but his father was born in Fazlagića Kula, which was a collection of villages near the town. My father raised cattle on land that he had outside Gacko. He had modern farm machinery, and he sold milk and cheese. People from Gacko were special. Although it is a small place, we were well educated, and we all tried to accomplish something with our lives."

Hasan, another refugee from Gacko, told me, "Before the war, no one thought that they would have to leave their homeland. No one talked about who was a Muslim and who was a Serb. We all lived together, went to the kafanas together, to school, on summer vacations, fishing, to the mountains."

When the war in neighboring Croatia began in 1991, columns of Yugoslav troops rumbled through Gacko on their way to Dalmatia. Hasan recalled:

> Immediately after the attack on Sarajevo on April 6, 1992, a column of tanks and trucks full of Serbian soldiers came through the main street of Gacko. The column was so long that you couldn't cross the street for three hours. You couldn't look out from the windows above the column, because they would shoot at you. They were shooting at the mosque with rocket launchers.
>
> When the war started, people that I had worked with and lived with started to destroy Muslim-owned buildings, kafanas, and stores. These were people who were from Gacko, with the help of those from Serbia, who were doing this.

Hasan and many other men from Gacko were rounded up and put in concentration camps in eastern Herzegovina. Hundreds were tortured, and dozens were killed. Others, together with the women and children, fled to the hills surrounding Fazlagića Kula. Serb forces destroyed several dozen villages, bombing or torching every house and mosque. Eventually the men fled on foot through the mountains to safe territory, and the women and children were sent into exile by bus.

When the war started, Fahira took her children and went to Dubrovnik and then went by boat to Slovenia. Her husband, Šerif, hid with others in the mountains for two months. They had prepared a store of food and hidden it in barrels in caves. During this time soldiers were firing grenades into the woods, and people hiding in the hills watched as their villages below were torched and bombed.

After two months, Šerif walked through the woods at night to Mostar. This escape took ten nights, during which time he and his companions ate only the plants they could find in the forest. Many of the men from Gacko who wound up in Mostar went on to fight in the Bosnian army on the east side of the city, and dozens of them were killed there.

Of her exile in Slovenia, Fahira said, "I lived in an empty warehouse with my children for ten months. Everything was difficult. The life of a refugee is a slow death. I had nostalgia for everything I had lost. My children were unhappy because they missed their father. Finally, my husband found out where we were and called us. We then returned to east Mostar."

In August 1999 I learned that return to Fazlagića Kula (or simply "Kula") had begun. In December I visited Dževad Memić, director of an association of displaced Bosniaks that served as Gacko's government-in-exile, based in Mostar. Memić was optimistic about the possibilities for return to eastern Herzegovina and to his prewar municipality. Return had started late there, but it had been underway since the spring in the nearby town of Nevesinje and was beginning in other parts of the region as well.

Dževad Memić showed me a large display on his wall, more than one hundred photos of Gacko citizens who were killed during the war and brought me up to date on the efforts for return to Gacko. Donors financed the repair of a house in Kula for several families to live in while they were fixing other houses, and they donated six cows as well. Returnees had built a barn and sheds.

Ten days after the first return, someone began sniping and firing mortars on Kula from the hills above. SFOR and the IPTF came out to Kula with the local (Serb) police and found six mortar launchers in the hills, but no one was apprehended. Not long afterward a car carrying four people drove over an antitank mine and was blown up. Three of the people were hurt, but fortunately their injuries were minor. It was Memić's optimistic opinion that the mine could have been a leftover from the war, although there had been no battlefront there.

The atmosphere in Gacko town was also unfriendly. Only one shopkeeper would sell food to the returnees, and then someone bombed his store. Memić told me, "At the beginning, returnees went into Gacko town several times. Some people spit and yelled at them. But then gradually there has been less of this harassment. There are around ten local people who should be in The Hague. If they were arrested, Gacko would become a completely normal place."

Dževad Memić arranged for me to meet with several people who were planning to return to Gacko. They knew only that I was an acquaintance of Memić. When I took photographs of my friends from Gacko in Seattle out of my wallet, one of the returnees said of me, "Ovaj stranac nije bez veze." ("This foreigner is not irrelevant.") Not surprisingly, some of the returnees were related to my friends. At that point they opened up and began to tell me their stories.

One returnee, Dževad Jugo, spoke of the war damage: "All the farms were destroyed, in Bašići, Ćatovići, Branilovci." He leaned his head on his neighbor, remembering all the people who were killed. "There wasn't a soul left there. If they're not here in Mostar, they're in the United States, or Australia. Since the war ended, life is a little better, but there is no work, none whatsoever. We just barely survive. Some of us are getting help from our relatives abroad."

The next summer, in 2000, there were around thirty returnees to the returnee settlement in Kula, and restoration of houses was taking place in a half dozen villages. Dževad Memić told me that around fifteen houses had been repaired, and that electricity and water were going to be hooked up for twenty houses in the near future. He did not seem as optimistic as he had been when I saw him the previous winter, however.

Memić arranged for a driver, Enes, to take me to Gacko and to the returnee settlement in Kula. We drove from Mostar through the woods and over a ridge to where we could see the high Herzegovinan plains between sparsely forested mountains. The first sight on the approach to Gacko is the towers of the energy plant where most of my acquaintances had worked before the war. Passing through Gacko, we turned toward the hills and continued on to Kula. Enes told me that there were some fifty people working to restore life to the villages, including some women who were staying permanently.

When we arrived at Kula, Enes showed me the central village where there used to be a high school, a mosque, and some stores. All the buildings stood without roofs. One of the shops had been rebuilt as a community center and store. There was no one in sight. We wandered over to the cemetery by the ruined mosque. I recognized the names of some of my friends' relatives. A little further up the road was Sopot, the legendary spring.

At one of the rebuilt houses, a half dozen returnees were lounging. They offered rustic Herzegovinan hospitality; sitting at a plywood table, we shared a bottle of homemade brandy and some smoked meat that we cut with a jackknife and ate with our hands, without bread.

A dog was tied up in the yard, and a cow grazed in a field nearby. People complained about the lack of electricity, but they were otherwise optimistic. One of the old-timers said that the young people would come back when there was a school, work, and health insurance.

As we sat at the table, the sun shone, and the air was the finest in all Bosnia-Herzegovina. I looked out at the hills. Those were the hills where my friends had run to escape from the invading army in 1992, and where they lived for the next months.

I had heard all these stories from my friends. Sitting there in the Herzegovina sun, I realized that my association with those refugees in Seattle was what led to my obsession with Bosnia-Herzegovina. Finally spending time in Kula, I had come full circle.

Back in Mostar, Memić expressed a plea for coexistence: "This area is so small, it's beyond human sense to try to divide it among ethnicities. We are one nation. We all speak the same language; we don't need a translator. There will be Muslims in Gacko, and the war will be forgotten."

Back in Seattle I conveyed Dževad Memić's message of hope and trust to Hasan and Šefika. Too little time had passed for them to forget the torture of 1992, and too much time had passed for them to return. To Memić's exhortation to maintain good relations with the "normal" Serbs and Croats, and to come back and help with the restoration of Kula and Gacko, Hasan responded, "Maybe when the time comes for me to pass to the other world, I'll go back to Gacko. But it is nicer to be in Seattle than to be in Mostar or Sarajevo.

"There, they will call you a refugee—they call those who defended Sarajevo and Mostar that—and they blame you for having left Bosnia. The displaced people have no work or apartments of their own in Mostar. It is 100 percent bad there for people from Gacko. So they go to Austria, to the United States—there's nowhere that they haven't gone, except to Russia and Serbia. People are leaving Gacko. In Gacko, they are only leaving bones, the bones of those who defended Mostar."

Sopot was calling Hasan, but the call was fading. "Before the war, I spent a lot of time in Mostar, Trebinje, Sarajevo, but I don't dream of those places, only of Gacko. I dream of Gacko, the river, the lake. But mostly, I dream about the concentration camp."

In the first years of the new decade, the elderly returnees in Gacko struggled to rebuild, surviving on help from outside and on subsistence agriculture. Low-level terrorism against them continued, with thirteen mine-related incidents just in the year 2000.[24] The rebuilt mosque was bombed in 2002. Return stagnated, with only around forty families remaining in Kula. The one Bosniak family that returned to Gacko eventually left. By the end of 2003, nearly eight hundred property claims had been resolved.[25] Most of the people whose property was returned sold it and resettled elsewhere.

THE PEAK OF RETURN, CONTINUED PROBLEMS

While every locality throughout Bosnia-Herzegovina has its particular history and its own troubles, in broad terms Mostar at the beginning of the new century resembled the entire country. Some of the militant wartime leaders had died or been removed from office, replaced by more refined politicians who were ostensibly more cooperative with the international community and more open to refugee return. Meanwhile, international officials were making progress in their rationalization of the legal system, and the OHR was showing its teeth in enforcement of housing law. Return was picking up.

Internationals and local activists alike were calling 2001 "the *real* year of return." The property law implementation system was taking effect, but even more important to concrete return, momentum was truly gathering among activists and the mass of displaced people. Return was taking place in areas such as the eastern part of the Republika Srpska, where it had been unthinkable a couple of years earlier.

Reviewed year by year, annual minority return figures can be seen to peak in 2001 and 2002. In the late 1990s these figures averaged around 40,000 per year. The year 2001 showed a minority return total of over 92,000, and in 2002 the figure topped 102,000, bringing total minority return to that date up to approximately 389,000. After 2002 minority return halved, and it continued to decrease from then on.[26]

Property return figures under the PLIP system likewise rose from around 20 percent implementation at the end of 2000 to 40 percent a year later, and nearly 70 percent at the end of 2002. Property restitution in the Republika Srpska lagged behind that in the Federation but began to catch up toward the end of this period. By late 2003, of some 250,000 claims filed, more than 90 percent had been resolved.

With increased return, a new set of problems arose: returnees in all directions had great difficulty obtaining pensions and health care in their prewar residences. Discrimination on the basis of ethnicity was nearly universal. And the greatest problem was unemployment; this was a problem for all Bosnians and Herzegovinans, but especially for returnees. Addressing this issue, Edin Beća of the Coalition for Return told me, "We need the international community to stimulate the economy. Will they do that now, so that people can work? Everything now works on smuggling. Without employment, refugee return is only fictitious. It is the same everywhere. Now, the main return is happening among older people who have a pension. Some families are dividing, with one part staying where they have a job, and the other part returning."

In late 2001 there were still approximately seventy thousand displaced persons in Sarajevo Canton. A couple thousand illegal occupants of apartments faced eviction; such evictions alone would not free up the housing that was needed.[27] The greater part of displaced persons in Sarajevo were from outside of the canton, particularly from eastern Republika Srpska, but there were a significant number who were displaced in their home city. Those whose prewar homes were in the RS were returning at a much faster rate than were Serbs coming back to Sarajevo.[28]

In 2002, hoping to accelerate implementation of property claims resolutions, the OHR initiated a new program that required that property claims be resolved chronologically, in the order they had been filed. The hope was that the program would reduce corruption among obstructionist local authorities, and promote impartiality and transparency. The increased rate of property claims resolutions in 2002 and 2003 noted above could be attributed to this heightened international pressure. Aware of the possibility for removal from office and banishment from politics, local officials complied. However, they meanwhile practiced other, less obvious ways of discouraging return. The awareness that they could still prevent return in these other ways, in fact, probably factored into authorities' decision to ease up on property repossessions.[29]

Property repossession accelerated apace, but it became obvious that repossession was not equivalent to return. The international community's centerpiece strategy for return thus failed to reverse ethnic cleansing on a massive scale. Continued obstruction to return through various forms of discrimination, coupled with the general lack of employment, discouraged those who had regained their prewar property from returning. It was estimated that out of all those people whose property in the Republika Srpska was restored, only some 20 to 30 percent actually returned. Return continued to be stronger in rural areas where people could support themselves through subsistence farming. But in urban areas throughout the country, a disheartening 75 percent of repossessed property was resold.[30]

In the early years of the 2000s the state of return in Bosnia remained in an ambiguous position. Return figures, and especially property repossession figures, were up. The number of internally displaced persons went down from approximately eight hundred thousand in 2000 to half that figure in 2002, after a recount of the displaced population.[31] The new lower figure, however, reflected permanent relocation as much as return. One of the most discouraging figures was that of Croat return to the Republika Srpska. Before the war there were some 220,000 Croats in the territory that came to form that entity, but by 2001 only around eighty-five hundred had returned.[32]

Of those people (of all ethnicities) still displaced, several thousand lived in collective centers throughout the country. Somewhere between twenty thousand and thirty thousand victims of the war were still missing. Meanwhile, over six hundred thousand refugees remained in more than forty countries outside of Bosnia-Herzegovina, with half of them lacking permanent residency status. Half of that six hundred thousand were living near Bosnia, in Croatia and the rump Yugoslavia.[33]

Prijedor and Zvornik municipalities, along with the rural area around Mostar, saw significant numbers of return that broke out of the symbolic realm. However, while the overall situation of security was much better than immediately after the war, harassment and occasional incidents of serious violence still took place. Some of the worst violence in 2000 involved several days of rioting against Muslim returnees in Janja near Bijeljina, and there were vicious attacks in 2001 thwarting the attempted reconstruction of mosques in Trebinje and Banja Luka. Discrimination and attacks also took place against Serbs trying to return to areas in the Federation, and against Croats trying to return to central Bosnia.

At this point the greatest obstacle to return was, nevertheless, economic. It was reported that fully 60 percent of the population lived near or below the poverty level.[34] A 40 percent unemployment level was commonly cited. These figures explain why as many as one hundred thousand people left Bosnia in the first five or six years after the war, as others were trying to return home.[35]

Thus in the early years of the new decade, in a country where everyone except a few profiteers had suffered, ordinary people struggled to create a new life amid the ruins of their country. The leaders of the Bosnians were working against their own people to keep them divided, confused, and impoverished. The international officials themselves were often confused and inept. It remained for those ordinary displaced persons and returnees, and their extraordinary representatives among the grassroots activists, to carry on the fight for survival and dignity.

PART III

RETURN TO SREBRENICA AND THE CAMPAIGN FOR RECOVERY

5

Postwar Srebrenica

TO THIS POINT I HAVE DESCRIBED THE AFTERMATH OF THE war in Bosnia-Herzegovina, and discussed the movement for refugee return throughout the country in detail—except for Srebrenica. The following half dozen chapters are devoted to that municipality, which endured great atrocities during the war, and afterward confronted particular obstacles to recovery.

Just as was the case during the war, in the postwar years events in Srebrenica took their own special, tormented course. The war and the genocide at Srebrenica left that city's scattered, traumatized community at a formidable disadvantage where recovery was concerned, and for a long time the new Serb masters of the municipality strove to hinder that recovery. The obstruction put the return movement to Srebrenica several years behind that of other localities.

The postwar story of Srebrenica municipality is the story of postwar Bosnia-Herzegovina depicted in high contrast. The survivors of Srebrenica needed the same things as other survivors throughout the country. These needs fall into two broad categories: return and recovery, and truth and justice.

Srebrenica in the period immediately after the war was a particularly grim place, stripped of the prewar charm and vibrancy so beloved by its citizens. All Bosniaks had been expelled from the town, and many of the several thousand Serbs living there were displaced people, removed by their own leaders from the urban center around Sarajevo. To these people Srebrenica was a great comedown, an insignificant burg without so much as a theater; one could not even purchase a needle without traveling ten kilometers to Bratunac. Srebrenica was but a shell of its former self, and the displaced city folk felt out of place and manipulated.

Local Serbs who had been displaced from Srebrenica during the war were slow to return. Those Serb returnees who had disagreed with the ethnic cleansing and genocide perpetrated by the Serb nationalists kept their opinions to themselves. Work was scarce. Wartime profiteers and war criminals walked the streets openly, as was the case in many other parts of the country.

The depressing and dislocated nature of people's personal lives in Srebrenica was mirrored in the physical surroundings. The single street traversing the town split at one square, forming two back streets and reuniting at another square half a kilometer uphill. All the town's buildings were pockmarked with shells, their roofs leaking and, for a time, their window glass replaced by plastic sheeting. Some six thousand buildings and residences had been destroyed in the municipality.[1]

The water from the town's supply system was not fit to drink, and people fetched home canisters of potable water, just as during the war. The spas and the mines were closed down, and the factories were empty and pillaged. There was no street lighting. Supply of electricity to the schools and hospital was intermittent at best.

Srebrenica's administration was in the grip of the SDS, the party that had led the war and that oversaw the destruction and genocide. The political leaders of the municipality were either displaced Serbs themselves or locals who had participated in the conquest of the town.

Even the UN forces (IFOR and then SFOR) only reluctantly visited the municipality, one of the most remote in all Bosnia.

The survivors—those for whom the recovery of Srebrenica mattered—were in a wretched state. Between eight thousand and ten thousand of their men and boys, and more than a dozen women,[2] had been murdered, leaving around fifteen thousand children without at least one parent.[3] The more than six thousand widows and bereaved mothers asked about the fate of their loved ones and, for an eternity, received no answer. With the perpetrators of the great crime controlling Srebrenica, many survivors brushed off the idea of returning.

While working in a relief agency in Tuzla shortly after the war, I had occasion to meet and talk with some of the many survivors from Srebrenica. Sadeta told me, "I was a housewife, and my husband, a truck driver, died before the war. I have two daughters. My son disappeared upon the fall of Srebrenica. My husband's brother also disappeared, and so did my sister's husband and son. It hurts to lose a son, and it hurts for all of our people. This is the biggest pain you can have in life, if you lose someone you gave birth to."[4]

Nura, from Pusmulići, told me that her husband, a tile layer, disappeared at the beginning of the war, in 1992:

> We were in Srebrenica until 1995. Before the fall of the town, there was much shooting. We escaped to my father's house for a couple of months, and then we had to go back to my home, with my father-in-law and brother-in-law. They killed my father on July 11, 1995, in Potočari. My brother, father-in-law, and brother-in-law all disappeared on the same day.
>
> We were brought to Tuzla in a military truck, with our children and daughters-in-law, to Dubrave. We lived for two months in a collective center there, then nine months in a school in Tuzla. Now [2003] we are in a collective center with nineteen families. There is a communal kitchen and bathroom. We have one room for the three of us. We don't have to pay rent, but soon we will have to pay for the electricity. I do various kinds of work, cleaning windows, hallways.[5]

Sadeta's and Nura's stories were those of thousands of mothers, wives, sisters, and daughters. It was not unusual for one extended family to have lost ten or twenty male relatives. In the first couple of years after the war, a cruel rumor circulated that some of the missing men were alive—enslaved, for example, in a mine in central Serbia.[6] Widows grasped at any possibility that their loved ones would reappear. One woman whose son was killed during the exodus of the large column of men from Srebrenica asked me, five years after the war, "Do you think they will ever find my son?"

Emina and Muša came from Podosoje village, near Srebrenica. When Serb forces surrounded the "safe area" and it was obvious they were going to take over, the sisters came with their children to Potočari to be evacuated. Emina burned all her personal documents, because she was told that she would be killed on the way out if she carried any of them with her. Emina's son and husband were taken away. Muša told me that when she came to Potočari, she was allowed to leave on foot with other women and children from Srebrenica. One of her sons was in the army. She heard from a witness that her son was captured on the twentieth of July, nine days after the fall of Srebrenica. When I spoke with Muša in 1998, she had received no further news of her family. She said, "We hope, but there is no hope."[7]

Tens of thousands of displaced Srebrenicans found a sorry refuge at the bottom of society in Tuzla and Sarajevo, with little work, few prospects, and no security. It was not unusual for those who were displaced to live three or four families to a house, unemployed, impoverished, in danger of having their electricity cut off at any time. Many families lived on a pension of US$60 a month or less and made ends meet by selling newspapers or cigarettes on the street, unwelcome foreigners in their own country.

Srebrenica lay two hours from Tuzla by car, and three hours from Sarajevo. The hills on the way to Srebrenica were littered with the bones of the Srebrenicans. How were the displaced survivors going to reconstruct their lives?

The prospect of return in the face of hostility and physical danger was a daunting one. But soon after the war there were those who were determined to return to the place where they had spent the best years of their lives. They needed organizational support for their return. They needed transportation to visit their homes and assess the damage in the villages, and they needed financial support from international organizations to rebuild their houses. Once home, they would need more assistance to begin farming operations, and they would need jobs. But first, they had to overcome the hostility and threat of physical violence from those who had taken over the municipality.

Besides the matter of return, there were those who were more preoccupied with issues that fell under the rubric of "truth and justice." These people were, first of all, the widows and mothers of the missing men. Early on, they formed several organizations, including the Sarajevo-based Movement of the Mothers of the Srebrenica and Žepa Enclaves (Pokret "Majke enklava Srebrenica i Žepa") and the Tuzla-based Women of Srebrenica (Žene Srebrenice). These organizations called for the discovery and opening of the many mass graves that dotted the countryside around Srebrenica and for the identification of the remains exhumed from those graves. They advocated for a common memorial burial place for their loved ones. And they demanded that the war criminals responsible for the massacres be brought to trial.

The goals of these two groups of survivors overlap, and their struggles continue to this day.

SURVIVING THE PEACE: THE FIRST YEARS

While working in Tuzla in the fall of 1997, I witnessed a demonstration of several hundred women from Srebrenica. It was on the eleventh of the month. Each month on that date, Women of Srebrenica held a demonstration to call attention to and to pressure the international community to locate their missing loved ones. Some three hundred women carried pieces of fabric embroidered with the names of their missing. Most of the women were dressed in the village style, wearing scarves and long dresses. They started their march from a park on one edge of town and marched to a mosque in the center of town, where they made a circle and stood quietly for a while.

During the same period, I happened on a march in Sarajevo of several hundred women from Srebrenica, ending up at the International Red Cross headquarters. These were solemn middle-aged women, mostly in raincoats and scarves. They carried many banners and signs: "Holland, you betrayed us," "Srebrenica is the guilt of the world," "Son, where are you?," "Europe, why are you silent?," "We want the truth."

I met Fatima, a woman from Srebrenica who was working as an activist for the Social Democrat Party (SDP). Fatima informed me that there were displaced people from Srebrenica in 137 countries around the world, and in ninety-three municipalities in Bosnia. Regarding return, she said, "We are ready to extend the hand of reconciliation, ready to go home." Srebrenican activists from the SDP were making contact with some of their former neighbors, Serbs still residing in Srebrenica. Fatima and her colleagues' approach was to cultivate relationships with Serbs still living in Srebrenica, former neighbors who were interested in promoting return. Her thought was that small steps in building trust among old friends would pave the way to return.

Those first couple of years after the war's end could be called the "dead years" when, on the surface, there was no justice, no return, and only a false peace. The ordinary survivors dared not visit Srebrenica, but they had not given up. One woman, Samila, told me that she had lost two brothers in the genocide. "I'm not interested in my house. I'm just interested in knowing what happened to my family," she told me. But when asked whether she had hopes regarding the fate of the disappeared, she answered, "Why shouldn't we hope? And why wouldn't we return to Srebrenica?"

Just hoping seemed a valiant act in that period. In May 1998 Physicians for Human Rights reported that approximately one thousand remains, out of seventy-five hundred people reported missing, had been exhumed. But in early 1998, only fifteen of the remains had been identified.[8]

Adding to people's emotional burden were the various rumors swirling around among the survivors regarding the fate of Srebrenica and its citizens. Rumors circulated about the whereabouts of missing men; there has also been fierce discussion ever since the war as to the role of the SDA in "selling" or trading Srebrenica for the Serb-controlled suburbs of Sarajevo. Accusations and counteraccusations along these lines have been launched in many directions. This polemic has been augmented with theorizing about why Naser Orić was removed from Srebrenica at a critical moment before the fall of the enclave.

Furthermore, not only did the Serbs who had conquered Srebrenica hold all the strings of power in the municipality, but former soldiers and paramilitary operatives who had directly participated in the abuse of Srebrenica's Bosniak population and in the atrocities were still walking freely in Bratunac, Zvornik, and other towns on the way to Srebrenica. Some of these war criminals had been indicted by the International Criminal Tribunal for the former Yugoslavia (ICTY), but many other lower-ranking individuals who had committed war crimes were also present.

In those dead years no progress was made on the establishment of a memorial cemetery; another polemic involved its location: should it be in Srebrenica, or in the Federation?
The Serb-controlled government of Srebrenica firmly opposed local establishment of a
cemetery, and Srebrenica survivors in the Federation were somewhat divided.

Nor was any progress made in return to Srebrenica. While Fadil Banjanović was
leading displaced persons back to Jušići and Zvornik, and others were returning to
Kozarac, Srebrenica was still a grim place where potential returnees dared not venture.
But behind the scenes there were capable activists preparing to lead Srebrenicans back
to their homes; and there were thousands of ordinary Srebrenicans who did not give up.

BREAKING THE LOGJAM

In the early postwar years a combination of security threats and political obstruction
posed serious obstacles to return. In other parts of the Republika Srpska, preliminary
return visits were taking place, and there was at least a trickle of return. But progress
was much slower in Srebrenica and other parts of the eastern half of the RS. The
international community's response to the obstruction in that region was to impose
economic sanctions on several municipalities including Srebrenica. These sanctions
lasted until well into 1999, preventing any reconstruction in the area.[9]

Obstruction came from all sides, in fact. The July anniversary of the fall of Srebrenica
was an occasion for the widows and mothers' organizations to try to reach Srebrenica
and to remember their missing loved ones. In July 1997 some survivors, with assistance
from organizers in the Society for Threatened Peoples, attempted to visit a cemetery in
Nezuk, a small town in the Federation near the border with the Republika Srpska. It was
one of the entry points where surviving members of the column escaping Srebrenica
crossed into safe territory. But on that occasion, when survivors were attempting to
return simply to honor their dead, soldiers from SFOR stopped them, held them for
several hours, and searched them for weapons.[10]

A memorial was held on July 11, 1997, the second anniversary of the genocide, in
the village of Ravne, near Kladanj in the Federation. Kladanj was another place where
surviving members of the escaping column had crossed into the Federation in 1995. In
1998, a public memorial was conducted at the Mejdan sports center in Tuzla. It would
be some years before a public event was possible in Srebrenica.

With obstruction coming from those who were supposed to protect all Bosnians
and enforce Dayton (including freedom of movement under Annex 7), combined
with hostility from the Serbs controlling Srebrenica, visits to the municipality were
all but out of the question for the time being. However, early on, various activists
from among the displaced began making contact with their Serb former neighbors
in Srebrenica.

In early 1999 Fatima, the activist from the SDP, described to me work her organization had begun more than a year earlier. The women's association of the SDP in

Tuzla conducted a survey among displaced Srebrenicans; Fatima reported to me that 95 percent of the respondents said that they wished to return to Srebrenica. Fatima and her colleagues also visited Srebrenica periodically in 1998. She told me, "We have had no problem when we went to Srebrenica, but they try to prevent local people from having contact with us. There was a meeting last month, attended by UN special envoy Elisabeth Rehn, We were allowed into the meeting hall, but the police blocked the way to the local people."[11]

An independent organization was formed in Tuzla around this time, led by Hakija Meholjić and Vesna Mustafić, both displaced persons from Srebrenica. Displaced people had begun working together informally by 1997, and the organization Srebrenica 99 was formed in 1999. In that year, Srebrenica 99 succeeded in organizing a summer camp for Serb children living in Srebrenica and displaced Bosniak children living in other parts of the country. The summer camp took place in the Federation at a lake near Teočak, not far from the interentity border.

Around 120 people between the ages of ten and thirty spent two weeks together, swimming, playing ball, and singing together. "This shows that people can still live together," Mustafić explained to me. "We speak with people [prewar neighbors] and try to recreate the trust that we had, because we used to live together; we intermarried, became godparents, and friends. That cannot all be erased—it's impossible."[12] Together with the Tuzla Citizens Forum, Srebrenica 99 continued to organize low-profile encounters between displaced Srebrenicans and their Serb former neighbors.

Vesna explained her organization's strategy for return. "Our approach has been to cultivate relationships with Serbs still living in Srebrenica, former neighbors of ours, who are interested in promoting our return," she said. "In 1998 and 1999 we invited some of these people to Tuzla, where there are many displaced Srebrenicans, to build friendly ties with them gradually."[13]

While these very grassroots contacts were underway, Serb officials in Srebrenica made every effort to keep the municipality under their control and to obstruct return. They ruled the municipality unchallenged until municipal elections took place in September 1997.

In that election, voting by absentee ballot, displaced Srebrenicans in Sarajevo, Tuzla, and other places around the Bosnian Federation won twenty-four out of forty-five seats on Srebrenica's municipal council. Srebrenica thus became the only municipality in the Serb-controlled entity in which Bosniaks won a majority. The Bosniak victory in Srebrenica was possible because the population of the municipality had been approximately 75 percent Bosniak before the war, and displaced Srebrenicans were allowed to vote in the municipal elections from wherever they now resided.

This victory seemed to point toward an opening for return. But return remained thwarted as a string of incidents discouraged any progress. At a session of the Srebrenica municipal council in early 1998, Serb members opened the meeting by singing the nationalist hymn of the Republika Srpska, and the Bosniak council members, interpreting this as a provocation, walked out of the meeting in protest. They were not to return for over a year.

In 1998 UNHCR began to organize regular bus visits for displaced persons living in Tuzla and Sarajevo. When people began tentative visits to property in and around the town, their reception was often hostile.

Finally, in June 1999, a multiethnic municipal government was formed in Srebrenica according to an agreement worked out with the assistance of organizations from the international community. A Bosniak mayor and a Serb deputy mayor presided over the municipal council's first meeting that month. The municipal assembly prioritized its tasks: renewal of infrastructure and two-way return of people displaced by the war.[14]

With multiethnic governance, Srebrenica took on an air of tentative normality. But this initial rapprochement suffered a serious setback in late 1999, when an assassination attempt was carried out against Munib Hasanović, a Bosniak who was secretary of the municipal council. On October 6, two men wearing ski masks attacked Hasanović in a restroom of the municipal building. He was beaten, strangled, stabbed, and left for dead. Fortunately he survived, but his attackers were never arrested. Bosniak councilmen boycotted sessions again for several months, calling for increased security measures.

The attack was meant not only to disrupt the functioning of the municipal council, but also to frighten potential returnees into giving up. After the attack, all cooperation between Serbs and Muslims was frozen again. The Muslim members of the municipal council boycotted meetings for over two months.

It wasn't until January 2000 that the UN International Police Task Force (IPTF) stationed a complement of more than fifteen international police observers in the town, and the Muslim representatives resumed their participation in the municipal council. Meanwhile, the international community decided that the nationwide municipal elections, scheduled for the coming spring of 2000, would be postponed for six months in Srebrenica.

Dysfunction in the municipal council—a reflection of the determination of governing Serb authorities to prevent return—and lack of security for potential returnees were two important factors that continued to discourage return as the 1990s wound to an end. Not long after the assassination attempt I spoke with Ibrahim Hadžić, an employee of the municipal court. He described the situation in Srebrenica:

> Srebrenica is now one of the least-developed municipalities in Bosnia, in all senses: physically, economically, and politically. It will take a lot of money to fix this. Ninety percent of the people who live in Srebrenica now need social assistance. For us to be able to return to Srebrenica, first the economy must be activated. There is nothing to live on. If we just return and add to that 90 percent figure of welfare cases, social problems there will increase.
>
> Srebrenica is the farthest place in the Republika Srpska from the Federation. It is 70 kilometers from Kladanj, 150 kilometers from Sarajevo. For return to Srebrenica to take place, first it needs to happen in Zvornik, Vlasenica, Bijeljina, and Bratunac; only then

will people want to return to Srebrenica and beyond. There are unburied skeletons in the woods around Srebrenica, and the people there know this.[15]

In spite of these obstacles, activists were escalating their agitation for return, and making concrete plans. Officials and grassroots return activists differed about the best strategy for return. Hadžić commented:

We [Bosniak municipal officials] are not in favor of individual return. Return must start with at least one hundred families. And the international community says that return must be in two directions.

We have good relations with the Serbs who are from Srebrenica. They are all in favor of our return; they say they can hardly wait for us to come back. But they are a small minority of the people there. Only two out of the eight people in the government are locals.

We also have good relations with our colleagues among the displaced persons of Srebrenica. But there is fear; you will see it. It can't be described. People look pathetic, sad. It can be seen that they are poor and hungry. Everyone knows who the criminals are. Until they are arrested, nothing will change. That is basic. Serb friends of mine in Srebrenica tell me to be careful, and they know. Until they make arrests, there will be no change. We go to Srebrenica, park our car, go into the hotel to meet, and then we leave. We are the government, but it is as if we are in a jail.

Speaking of his personal situation, Hadžić told me, "A former co-worker of mine from the mines lives in my apartment now. We know each other well. He is not a displaced person. He had an apartment that was not as nice as mine, so he took mine. We talk, but not about that. My things are there in the apartment. I have heard that I will receive permission to return, but I can't go home alone."

I visited Srebrenica for the first time in late 1999, a couple of months after the attack on Munib Hasanović. On a cold and dreary day just before deep winter set in, I rode with my colleague Elissa Helms up into the town. It is situated in a very tight valley, practically a ravine. The flat part of the valley could not have been more than two blocks wide, and at the south end of town it quickly rose into the mountains toward the Drina and Serbia. The physical setting was magnificent, but the town was poor.

People from Srebrenica had often told me that to them it was beautiful, and that they would never like to live anywhere else. The clean mountain air, the paths into the woods, and the mineral springs nearby supported this sentiment. But on that first visit, Srebrenica was a shabby place with mortar-pocked buildings whose facades were deteriorating, a place inhabited by displaced, unhappy Serbs. Most of the buildings in the center were war damaged. The large Robna Kuća (department store) on the square stood empty, plastered with old election campaign posters for Vojislav Šešelj and Nikola Poplašen, Serb nationalists who led the extreme right-wing Serbian Radical Party (SRS).

Elissa and I visited Dragan Jevtić, deputy mayor of Srebrenica, a member of the Serbian Radical Party. We sat in his office in the municipal building, at that time the only restored building in Srebrenica. The office was decorated with a few nondescript paintings and a large flag of the Republika Srpska. On the back wall were a couple of framed certificates, including one that read, in English, "Dawgs of War," given to Jevtić by an outfit of British troops.

Himself displaced from Sarajevo, Jevtić began by saying, "My job is to help people return. The main problem is that this area needs a financial injection in order for anything to happen. However, not many people want to return. The Srebrenicans who now live in Sarajevo are happy there; they've gotten used to it. And I don't want to return to Sarajevo. I'm doing all right here; I have a pizzeria, and I can support my family. I want to sell or trade my house in Ilijaš [suburb of Sarajevo]. Many other displaced people who are here don't want to go back, either. We want to help people return. But if they don't want to, there's nothing we can do. After a time, people will forget about the tragedy that happened here, and it will be easier to solve things," he said.[16]

Jevtić's implicit argument was that all the problems of trauma and displacement were going to disappear of their own accord. It was true that there were many Srebrenicans who did not care to return home, but there were a significant number who did wish to return. Likewise, many displaced Serbs who had come to Srebrenica from Sarajevo and beyond, from Donji Vakuf or Glamoč, yearned to return to their ancestral homes. But Jevtić was polite, personable, and almost convincing.

I recognized Jevtić's approach and his discourse as similar to that of Republika Srpska prime minister Dodik, who together with Biljana Plavšić had led the "moderate" Serbs to power in that entity. Their strategy was to appeal to the West for international aid by softening their rhetoric, while working behind the scenes to salvage as much of the Serbs' separatist wartime gains as possible.

However, Jevtić had referred to an important problem of postwar Srebrenica: it was full of displaced Serbs. These people had their own urgent problems to address, and it was necessary to facilitate two-way return.

I spoke with Milorad Marjanović, representative of a group of Serbs displaced from villages around Srebrenica. Many of their villages had been destroyed; some of them remained without electricity. Many of these villagers preferred to remain settled in the town. Marjanović dwelt on the prospect of Bosniak return, saying that he expected that return, but that alternative housing had to be created for the Serbs who were in his situation.

This visit took place just as a new High Representative, Wolfgang Petritsch, was gaining momentum in office and as the recently launched Property Law Implementation Plan was beginning to be enforced. The direct result of this plan, throughout the country, was the widespread eviction of squatters in displaced people's homes. This trend prompted displaced persons living in "abandoned" homes to focus on ways to resolve their newly insecure residential status.

Marjanović hoped he would be able to find alternative housing in the town. He told me:

My village was destroyed on June 13, 1992. After that I lived in Bratunac, and then I moved here in 1995. I fixed up the house that I moved into here in Srebrenica. When I came here, I found it empty. I took care of it for the owner, who is in Tuzla. Some people don't let the owners in, but I did. The woman who owns it came to visit and was very pleased at the shape that it is in. Now, it wouldn't be nice if she were to return, and I ended up on the street. She wants to return. But there is simply not a place for everyone to return to now.

Now, the atmosphere for return to Srebrenica is good, but not for throwing anyone out onto the street. The right to one's property is not in question. If people had work and another place to live, there would be no problem. My goal is to have return take place in a correct way. Because, you see, if ten Muslims return to Srebrenica, and then you have ten Serbs on the street, that is not a solution. What we are most afraid of now is eviction.

GOING HOME: THE FIRST RETURNS

In the face of the obstacles, local organizations of displaced persons pressured the international community for support, drew up agreements with relief agencies for reconstruction of homes, and conducted preliminary visits to prewar homes and to cemeteries. One attempted visit that took place on May 11, 2000, was attacked by local residents. With agreement from the local authorities, four buses carrying approximately two hundred women traveled toward Srebrenica, getting as far as Bratunac. A large crowd of Serbs surrounded the buses and began throwing stones at them. Unchecked by the local authorities, the crowd broke the windows of the bus and injured many of the women. The visit was called off and the women returned to the Federation.[17]

By this time, however, the first full-time returnees had come back to Srebrenica to stay. In March 2000 Šaćir Halilović and his wife, Mevlida, returned to their home on a hill above the center of Srebrenica. Šaćir was eighty years old and Mevlida was five years younger. They had been among the last Bosniaks to leave the town when it fell in 1995.

I visited the Halilovićes in their modest, half-renovated house, where we talked in a tiny kitchen. Mevlida, who moved slowly and with difficulty, wore the traditional hand-embroidered slippers, vest, and scarf. She cried when Šaćir mentioned their son, a doctor, who had been killed during the war in Srebrenica.

Šaćir was a bricklayer before the war. He spoke of his work partner, "He was a Serb, I was a Muslim, and that didn't bother anybody." He continued, "This is my home, my land. I had a house, but they knocked it over. They haven't fixed everything; it is as you see it. I still work with my hands, in the garden; what else can I do?" He pointed across the creek to another hill and said, "There is the cemetery; I have buried everyone with my own hands. I have no one. If it weren't for the war . . ."

The couple received no pension and survived on income from a tenant and on assistance from friends.[18]

For the time being, the Halilovićes' return to Srebrenica was an aberration. But by spring of 2000 more preliminary visits were underway, and several organizations were making plans to establish return settlements in villages outside of Srebrenica. Srebrenica 99 was one of the most active of these organizations.

In much of the rest of the country, returnees were setting up tent encampments as a foothold toward return. Srebrenica 99 was planning the same tactic in Sućeska, a remote complex of villages in the hills above Srebrenica town.

Hakija Meholjić described the organization's difficulties in preparing for return:

> We talked to the international community for three years, telling them we wished to go back to our homes in Srebrenica. For three years, they did not take us seriously. There was no assistance from the international community. So we decided to take our own steps to return. Our first target is Sućeska. That is not one village, but a complex of around twenty villages.
>
> We don't know the reason why the international community has not helped us; maybe it suits their goals for us not to return. Now that we have started the project in Sućeska, representatives from the international community are saying that this is the first time they've heard about our work. Some of the international officials we are dealing with are third-rate politicians who don't know what they are doing.
>
> All of the nationalist-oriented organizations have plenty of money. We have nothing. We can't even afford paper for the office, let alone a connection to the Internet.

Venting his frustration, Hakija concluded, "We would be better off if the international community was not here."

Hakija and Vesna Mustafić made it clear that theirs was an antinationalist organization composed of both Bosniaks and Serbs who wished to return to their prewar homes. These goals and the multiethnic character of the group put Srebrenica 99 at odds with both Serb and Bosniak nationalist political parties.

Vesna argued that in spite of obstruction, many displaced persons from Srebrenica were still determined to return:

> The atmosphere is how it is, but we can still return. The fact is that Srebrenica is under the control of the extremists, that is, the SDS, the SRS, and the SDA. But we're getting more members every day. There has been progress in the last year, much more than we expected. We simply decided to solve the problem, to do something about it.
>
> The biggest obstacle is lack of money. To get return going, more houses need to be fixed. The desire to return exists. Whoever says otherwise is wrong. We've been focusing on two villages: Sućeska and Bektići. People from there are ready to go to work fixing up their houses, but they need money to do so. Many international organizations have come to look at the situation, but no one has started yet.

Srebrenica 99 had requested support for their project from several governments, including Holland, Denmark, and the United States. There was no answer from the

United States. Vesna showed me a letter from the Dutch Embassy, politely declining to support the project on the grounds that the Dutch were concentrating on minority return to other regions. "Some organizations are looking to the past. The Dutch government is supporting SDA-affiliated organizations, and not talking to multiethnic ones like us."

Vesna expressed her determination to resolve her own displacement in Tuzla: "It is very difficult here; there are no jobs and no assistance. We must return. I love Srebrenica very much, and will do all I can to return. All of my memories are there. It was a very beautiful town. Now it is sad and ugly, but we will fix it."[19]

The Sućeska return project began in mid-2000 with residents clearing rubble around their devastated houses and preparing them for reconstruction. Before the war, around three thousand people lived in the Sućeska complex of villages. After the war, these people were scattered around Bosnia and the world. Hakija estimated that approximately fifteen hundred could repatriate.

With the beginning of the return project, house repairs were underway. The UNHCR and the Muslim relief organization Merhamet provided some assistance. The first group of displaced persons moved back in early June, setting up UNHCR-donated tents. They threw up a kitchen and dining shelter and went to work preparing their houses for reconstruction. Within a month of their arrival, contractors and owners were replacing roofs, doors, and windows in at least a half dozen homes. Hakija informed me that if things went well in Sućeska, Srebrenica 99 planned to resettle four more villages in a similar way that summer.

Early in July 2000 I visited Sućeska with Hakija Meholjić and Zulfo Salihović, of Drina, another Tuzla-based organization for displaced persons. We traveled from Tuzla to Srebrenica in Zulfo's jeep, and then up into the hills. As we left Srebrenica, Zulfo pointed out the house he had lived in before the war. He mentioned that the displaced Serb who lived there would not let him enter the house.

The road to Sućeska resembled a remote backwoods Appalachian route, a grueling forty-five minutes of dusty, ill-maintained dirt road with switchbacks, no railings above sheer drop-offs, and plenty of ruts. Beautiful views of green hills and woods compensated for the hard driving.

We climbed further into the mountains, passing forests, spying ridges ever further in the distance. This was an isolated area, with few villages along the way. As we rode, Hakija told me that the people of Sućeska were renowned for their strength and good health because of the pure air and water, and the natural food they eat there. "In Sućeska, they don't need Viagra," he said.

During our rough ride to Sućeska, something was bothering Hakija. In the vein of his criticisms of the international community, he said, "I want to ask you, sincerely, what Americans think about people from Srebrenica. Do they think that we are morons?" Hakija was referring to international officials. His impression was that these representatives think of people from Srebrenica as "backward."

We arrived at Sućeska, dropping down from the last ridge to a high plateau. Passing a ruined community center building, we came to a clearing where ten white tents stood, each large enough to sleep five or ten people. There was a rustic common kitchen built from rough posts and beams, with a long table that could seat twenty-five. It was midday in the middle of the most severe heat wave in fifty years, and a half dozen men were lounging around the table. On the road by the kitchen, a couple of trucks were unloading rafter beams donated by the Tuzla Canton government, to be used for repair of the houses.

On Hakija's arrival, the men perked up and listened to his report of a meeting with High Representative Petritsch. His conversation with the Sućeska returnees resembled a pep talk.

I spoke with Abid Salihović, Zulfo Salihović's relative and coordinator of the camp's activities. He had grown up in Brakovci, a village fifteen minutes from Sućeska by foot, and lived there until the fall of Srebrenica in 1995. He told me, "We feel safe here now. There are Serbs who come here, and we talk to them. There is a Serb construction firm from Banja Luka working on the community center, and they sleep here without any problem."

Hakija commented, "We can live together with the Serbs without problems, when the politicians don't get involved."

After the fall of Srebrenica, Abid lived with his wife and three children in Zenica. He had no work there. He received some oil and flour from a relief organization, but no money. Now he was in the process of clearing rubble from his house and preparing it for reconstruction. Abid told me that nearly eight hundred people from Sućeska, mostly men, had been killed during the fall of Srebrenica. The resulting low proportion of able-bodied men made reconstruction difficult without international help.

Abid asked, "Have you ever seen such a bad road? It was built more than a hundred years ago by the Austrians, who came here to develop the silver and bauxite mines. This is the only complex of villages in the municipality whose main road was never paved. If the roads were better, we would do well with a factory here. We could grow fruit and raise cattle and sell them in town. The road needs to be asphalted."

Zulfo told me:

We tried for a year and a half to return directly to the city of Srebrenica, but our efforts were always blocked. Now we are here, and we must work on establishing return settlements closer to the city. If this doesn't succeed, all our efforts will fall through.

We are very disappointed with the small amount of help we have received from the international community. And the Republika Srpska has said that they have no money for reconstruction. But their budget declaration from the last session shows that they spent 360,000 deutschmarks on flowers! This was from their quarterly budget, not the annual one. When I read that, I wanted to faint.

People were snacking as we talked. Hakija cut up an onion and dipped a chunk of it directly into a box of salt. He then ate it with a piece of bread and liver pate. He resumed his pep talk. "It's up to us to show the world that we are serious about return. There are plenty of people who doubt us." "Fuck those who doubt us," someone interjected. Another added "We have already shown that we are serious."

An older man complained to Hakija, "I lost my whole family; I'm alone here. How can I take care of myself?" Hakija replied, "And I lost two brothers and my father. You're not alone here. We are all in this together."

Returnee Ahmet Mehmedović showed me his house, a couple hundred meters down the road toward a communal water source. On the way, he pulled a few bottles of beer out of the trunk of his car, wiped them off, and placed them in the well to cool. Behind the well stood the ruins of the village's mosque.

Ahmet had worked for ten years in the bauxite mines before the war, and he built his own house. Since the fall of Srebrenica he had lived in Lukavac, near Tuzla, with his wife and children. He said, "Every night when I go to sleep, I'm thinking about how I'm going to get ten deutschmarks the next day to feed my family. There is no life for us there. Here, maybe. But my wife and children don't want to come back here. They want to go to America, where we have relatives. My youngest son was in third grade when all that happened in Potočari. He remembers everything."

I asked Ahmet, "Maybe if your wife and kids came back here and saw how things are being rebuilt, they would become enthusiastic?" He made eating motions with his hands. "There's nothing to eat," he said.

A couple of men were working on Ahmet's house, filling in gaping holes caused by mortar strikes in the cinderblock walls. The windows had been replaced. A large pile of rafter beams and roof tiles lay in the front yard. We sat in the shade drinking the chilled Tuzla beer. Zulfo and the others discussed whether drinking beer was a sin.

From this hill you could see several green ridges stretching out to the horizon. Ruined villages were barely visible here and there, their gray houses standing roofless. Zulfo pointed out a Serb village a few kilometers away, its red-tile roofs standing out against the green landscape. "They fired mortars at us from above that village. That's when they wrecked the mosque. They really fucked us."

Walking back from Ahmet's house, I asked him whether he talks to the Serbs who are there working on the reconstruction. He said, "Why not? They are not responsible for what happened to us. If I were in the United States, I would talk to Serbs. I would talk to Croats, and I would talk to Jews. I have to be civilized."

BEGINNING RETURN TO SREBRENICA TOWN: IZET AND ZEKIRA

While the return project was unfolding in Sućeska, a second couple returned to Srebrenica town in August 2000. Izet Imamović, seventy-five, had been a driver for the company that ran the huge battery factory, one of Srebrenica's biggest employers, in nearby Potočari. He worked for the company for twenty years, until its closure at the start of the war.

Izet had been forced to leave home before. As a teenager during World War II, he had been taken to Germany to work in forced labor. Fortunately for him, the war ended a few months after he arrived. Izet came back to Srebrenica and returned to school.

As a young man Izet loved singing Sevdalinkas, the popular Bosnian folk songs. He told me that he became so well known as a singer that people would start clapping when he walked into a kafana, even before he sang.

In the early 1970s, Izet was hired to work as a driver at the new battery factory, a place that would subsequently gain notoriety during the war as the headquarters of the UN's Dutch battalion and the staging point for taking thousands of Muslim men off to the killing fields. Izet's wife, Zekira, also worked at the factory, and that is where the two met.

Early during the war the couple managed to escape from Srebrenica to Tuzla. Izet told me, "We lived in Tuzla for the whole war. For a time, there was a displaced Serb who let us live in his house for free, for eighteen months. We had to change our living place nine times. In the winter people would raise the rent. In the end, we were paying 200 KM (approximately US$135) a month for rent."[20]

In Tuzla Izet and Zekira's pension left them only a few dollars after rent, and humanitarian aid was decreasing. They decided to return to their own house in Srebrenica in order to be able to live rent-free.

When I asked Zekira whether she had been afraid to return to Srebrenica, she answered, "I forced my husband to return; I insisted. My husband was not in favor of it, but I was not afraid. It was so hard to live in Tuzla that I preferred they kill me here, rather than stay there."

Izet described his first days back home:

When I left Srebrenica in April 1992, this house was fully furnished, with a heater and everything. When I came back this year, I saw that everything had been taken out. Three families lived here. Each one took things. The second person took the most. He is now a driver for the municipal government. There's nothing I can do about it.

The last person was a sanitary inspector for the municipal government. He was from Ilijaš. We tried to get permission via the Ministry for Refugees to return to one floor of our house. He refused to give us permission, because he said there would be an incident. If we lived here together, someone would throw a bomb. I understood that as more of a threat than a warning.

Then we went to the ministry and asked for the whole house. We documented the fact that the man and his wife both had employment, and that his mother received a pension. The ministry gave a decision that he would have to leave, and we could return. I said that I would bring a tent and camp in front of the house until he left. All of my things had been taken away, the sink, six light switches, electrical outlets, light fixtures—everything but the bathtub, which was built in. On the top floor, they took away three doors and the flooring. The UNHCR, when we returned, gave us two beds and a stove.

Describing the atmosphere in Srebrenica upon his return, Izet said:

I went to the market on the first day I was here, and I said hello to people. They turned their heads away from me. It was the same the second time. On the third time, they said hello back.

I said to one man, "How are you?" He said, "I don't know you." But I was his driver for twenty years. There have not really been incidents though, other than some small things, insults.

People's attitudes have softened since then. They decided that they like me. I want to do good things for anyone. Yesterday a pregnant Serb woman came to visit. She needed help getting clothes for her baby.

OBSTRUCTION CONTINUES, BUT RETURN PICKS UP

By mid-2000 incipient return to a couple of villages was underway, and two or three families had returned to Srebrenica town. Significant return had yet to begin, but these first brave returnees had opened the gates.

The UNHCR had been organizing weekly preliminary visits to villages in Srebrenica municipality since May 1999, when people would come to clean up their damaged houses. These visits were now taking place twice a week. By the end of 2000, sixty families had returned to Srebrenica town and several villages.[21] Around one hundred returnees had come back, mainly to Sućeska and Bajramovići, a second village return project near Potočari, led by Srebrenica 99 and Drina.[22]

A couple hundred houses in the villages had been cleared of rubble, and several dozen houses and apartments within Srebrenica town had also been returned to their prewar owners.[23] Approximately three hundred displaced persons had applied for the return of their apartments in the city.[24]

The security situation remained volatile in the first year of return. In early January 2000 the IPTF had stationed fifteen officers with monitoring capabilities in Srebrenica. The SFOR commander for the area of Bratunac and Srebrenica characterized the safety situation in Srebrenica as "completely satisfactory," noting that families were conducting regular visits to their apartments and property in the municipality without obstruction.[25]

However, in that same period unidentified Serbs in Srebrenica were reported to have threatened potential Bosniak returnees.[26] In early May the house where the Bosniak municipal council members were spending their weekdays was burglarized, in spite of an increased security presence. In the next several months, arsons and other attacks were committed against Bosniak property. Fifteen houses were torched by early August 2000.[27]

During my mid-2000 visit to the Sućeska return settlement, Hakija Meholjić complained to me at length about the security situation, saying that it was the main factor
preventing people from returning to Srebrenica. He advocated the formation of a multiethnic police and court system as a way of recreating trust. "The police must have Mujo
and Djuro out there together," he said, using typical Muslim and Serb names. "The
people are not just worried about food or work, but also security—that's number one."

The first Bosniak policeman was assigned to join the Srebrenica department one
month after my visit. Meanwhile, displaced Srebrenicans advocated the establishment of
an SFOR base closer to Srebrenica as a concrete measure that would encourage return.

In the period of the arsons, Srebrenica 99 published a serious accusation against
Dragan Jevtić and local SDS leader Momčilo Cvijetinović, asserting not only that these
two officials were behind the arsons, but that they also owned companies that were
involved in the reconstruction of damaged homes.[28]

No investigation into these accusations was conducted, but it is understandable
that return activists would be extremely mistrustful of Cvijetinović. During the war he
had been a member of the municipal presidency of the part of Srebrenica controlled
by Serb forces. Later, Radovan Karadžić appointed him head of the Srebrenica branch
of the SDS immediately after the fall of Srebrenica, in the middle of the period of the
massacres.[29] And in the immediate postwar years, Cvijetinović repeatedly denied that
the genocide had ever taken place.[30]

THE PRESENCE OF WAR CRIMINALS

In late 2000, the International Crisis Group (ICG) issued a report titled "War Criminals in Bosnia's Republika Srpska: Who Are the People in Your Neighborhood?"[31]
This report provided a quick overview of suspected war criminals residing in eighteen
municipalities throughout the RS, many of them still holding positions of authority. It
noted that there was a "code of silence" that penetrated the RS where these war criminals and their history were concerned.

The report outlined criteria for indictment for various kinds of war crimes. In addition to naming a few suspects from each municipality and describing their actions, the
report recommended more robust response on the part of the local and international
authorities. To that point, there had been few arrests of persons indicted for war crimes,
and none had been carried out by the RS authorities.

One prominent suspect named in the ICG report was Dragomir Vasić, who had
been chief of police in Zvornik during the fall of Srebrenica and its aftermath. Vasić
served in this office from 1993 to 1998, "during which time he allegedly played a significant role in the massacres and ethnic cleansing of Srebrenica," according to the
ICG report.[32] As of the date of the report, he was serving as a member of the Zvornik
municipal assembly. He subsequently became a delegate to the Republika Srpska national assembly and held crucial committee positions in that body.

Another participant in the atrocities testified that he had met with Vasić at the SDS office in Bratunac and had "talked openly about the killing operation."[33] Evidence confirms that Vasić received orders directly from General Mladić, and in one communiqué sent during the fall of the enclave (dépêche 283/95, sent July 13), Vasić describes the efforts of his police units in preventing the escape of Muslim men in a column through the woods.[34]

In 2003 High Representative Paddy Ashdown removed Vasić from office for providing support to suspected war criminals in hiding. However, in October 2014 he was again elected representative to the Republika Srpska Parliament. It was very shortly after that election that he was indicted for genocide. His trial, together with four other suspects, began in April 2015. The suspects were accused of the forced removal of the inhabitants of Srebrenica upon the fall of the enclave; separation of men from the population; and the killing of men and boys in the area of Srebrenica, Bratunac, and Zvornik.

In spite of Vasić's indictment, he was allowed to continue to serve in office as his trial dragged on into 2019. Bosnian law prohibits political office only to those who have received binding secondary convictions. In October 2018 he was elected delegate to the state-level House of Representatives in a victory that was clouded by an extremely suspicious vote count.[35]

This is just one example of the menacing personalities who openly roamed Srebrenica and the surrounding municipalities, wielding great power, just as the displaced Bosniaks were mounting their most serious attempts to return home. In light of the presence of these people, the fears of the displaced persons for their security were understandable. The IPTF unit that had been established in Srebrenica was insufficient to assuage those fears, and the displaced population's calls for the creation of an SFOR base near Srebrenica were unheeded for several years.

BOSNIAK LEADERS DISCOURAGE RETURN

Obstruction by hard-line Serbs was only one of the problems confronting would-be returnees to Srebrenica. Some return activists bitterly criticized the Bosniaks' own governing party, the Party of Democratic Action (SDA), for working against return.

The substance of this accusation was that the SDA played on the fears of displaced people, encouraging their perception of themselves as permanent victims, fearful of persecution. The assumption was that they would respond to favors from the SDA (such as permission to stay in Serb-owned houses in Sarajevo) by keeping the SDA in office.

Some displaced Srebrenicans wanted to return home, but some did not—they had established comfortable lives in the suburbs of Sarajevo, or they were fearful of return. Some were clearly manipulated by leaders who claimed to speak for them. Senija Purković, a displaced person from Srebrenica and member of Srebrenica 99, explained how her government really approached return:

> When I went to Srebrenica for the first time after the war, in spring of 1997 with the accompaniment of SFOR, the minister for refugees in the Tuzla Canton government, Adib Đozić, called me. He is from Srebrenica. First he told me that I didn't need anything in Srebrenica, that there was nothing for me there. Đozić told me, "You had a nice big house, that's all fine, but the best thing would be to trade Srebrenica for Vogošća or, say, for Ilijaš; that would be the best, and Ilijaš is the most similar to Srebrenica . . ." and how that's already been arranged. And we expect them to support return, but that's a sheer illusion.[36]

It appears that Đozić was doing the job for which he was paid. On this topic, for many years the journalist Hasan Hadžić has openly condemned the SDA for its role in obstruction of return. Hadžić had written of Đozić and several other Srebrenicans well positioned in the SDA hierarchy, as people who were "fighting to stay in the Federation."[37] He wrote of Đozić's role as minister for refugees in Tuzla Canton, where thousands of Srebrenican refugees had ended up. Hadžić described Đozić as "ready to profit in every way from the Srebrenica tragedy," and that he was "installed . . . with the instruction to obstruct return with all means possible."[38]

Hadžić wrote that "the 'minister for return' Đozić had received from Sarajevo a special budget to move Srebrenican and other Podrinje refugees from Tuzla Canton, from where return to their houses in Podrinje had been in full force, to Sarajevo Canton, where priority was given to filling abandoned Serb houses and neighborhoods with displaced Bosniaks. Later, High Representative Petritsch removed Đozić from his position because of various shady activities, but by then a critical mass of Srebrenicans had already been torn from the Tuzla source of return."[39]

It was Hadžić's conclusion that Đozić was "simply the implementer of works designed according to the will of the then Bosniak leadership," which must be held responsible for its part in the failure of a more robust refugee return to Srebrenica.[40]

Hakija Meholjić had particularly harsh words for the SDA. He told me, "The international community gives a large part of its assistance directly to the government, and too much of this money ends up in the pockets of influential politicians. Some of these are people who did not even own a bicycle before the war, and now they are driving Mercedes, living in fancy villas, and they own companies that are worth ten million deutschmarks. This includes some Srebrenicans who have bought houses in Sarajevo and Tuzla, and so now they are not interested in promoting return."[41]

International officials were also critical of the SDA in this period. Eleanor Gordon, Zvornik-based staff member of the UNHCR, told me, "The SDA has exaggerated security concerns to discourage return. However, they are now changing their strategy, because ordinary displaced people are clamoring to go home."[42]

The OHR special envoy to Srebrenica, Charlie Powell, also criticized the SDA, calling it a "Muslim nationalist party that ... opposes the return of refugees to this town." The SDA responded with outrage, calling this statement a "pure lie" that "could probably be published in 'Believe It or Not.'"[43]

Evidence of official Bosniak discouragement—if not obstruction—of return to Srebrenica came from the mouth of President Alija Izetbegović himself. Fadila Mujić, a return activist, reported that in May 1999 she had attended a meeting with the president in which she asked about the possibility of return to Srebrenica. Izetbegović encouraged his audience of displaced people to remain as permanent squatters on the outskirts of Sarajevo, responding, "What return?! Take care of those [Serb-owned] houses; you'll be getting cows."[44]

It was very common in this period to hear from return activists that the SDA was reluctant to allow thousands of Srebrenicans living in and around Sarajevo to leave, because they represented a "voting machine" for the Bosniak nationalist party in the Federation. The implication of this accusation was that the SDA was essentially willing to cooperate in the partition of Bosnia into three ethnically dominated zones, in order to have the greatest power in the Bosniak one. This suspicion of the SDA's capitulationist position had its roots in divisions that had already developed during the war.

A couple of years after the beginning of return to Srebrenica municipality, a former SDA member, now a return activist and wishing to remain anonymous, confirmed for me the antireturn position of SDA's leadership. He spoke of an SDA meeting he had attended in Sarajevo where there was discussion of scaring returnees by firing weapons in the vicinity of the return settlements.

However, as Eleanor Gordon noted, the SDA discontinued its practice of direct discouragement of return when it became clear, in 2000, that displaced Srebrenicans were determined to return home with or without the SDA's assistance.

Activists and displaced persons continued the campaign to come back to Srebrenica throughout 2000, that first year of return. Srebrenica was one of the last municipalities that opened to return, and the fact that it did so at all, against the odds, was owing to the persistence of these activists. At the same time, circumstances that favored return to Srebrenica were mounting.

The international community's Property Law Implementation Plan had been put into effect, and, as a direct result, not only were Serbs who lived in usurped housing in Srebrenica faced with eviction, but displaced Bosniaks in Tuzla, Sarajevo, and elsewhere in the Federation were under the same pressure. After the war there had been nearly nineteen thousand refugees from Srebrenica residing in Tuzla Canton alone,[45] and these displaced persons were under pressure to resolve their residency status. By 2000, many had already emigrated abroad. Some found ways to settle permanently in the Federation. But with increased international attention on Srebrenica—and with the example of Sućeska beckoning—displaced Srebrenicans (especially those living in substandard conditions in collective centers) gradually came to consider return to the municipality as an option.

Addressing one of the more daunting obstacles to return, Srebrenican survivors and returnee activists agitated fiercely for increased security measures. In response, during 2001 SFOR took steps that would significantly bolster the confidence of potential returnees. In the spring SFOR established Forward Operating Base Connor at the village of Glogova, in a prominent position on the road between Bratunac and Konjević Polje, an area that had predominantly been populated by Bosniaks before the war. The new base guarded the main approach to Srebrenica, a road that was dotted with the derelict shells of Bosniak-owned houses.

In the same period the High Representative removed the mayor of Bratunac for obstruction of return and for numerous other violations of the Dayton agreement, including tolerating attacks on returnees.[46] Since passage through Bratunac was the only practical route to Srebrenica for the returnees, these two moves by the international community encouraged an acceleration in return to Srebrenica.

In addition, the international community was implementing better-coordinated plans with regard to the municipality, principally by creating the "Srebrenica Action Programme (SAP)." This program was described by its organizers as a "coordination mechanism to encourage humanitarian and development organizations to increase support for reconstruction and revitalization of Srebrenica."[47]

At this time, the UN Mission in Bosnia-Herzegovina (UNMIBH) donated funds for the rehabilitation of critical infrastructure including roads and electrical supply, and for the renovation of schools, the hospital, and the police station. In November 2001 a Bosniak became deputy chief of police in Srebrenica, and five new Bosniak policemen joined the force.[48]

By the end of 2001, twice as many people (118 families) had returned to Srebrenica as in the previous year.[49] Still behind most of the rest of the country, property return implementation tallied between 15 and 20 percent.[50] Just as significant was the fact that hundreds of families returned in that year to Bratunac municipality. The road to Bratunac, passing by Connor Base, was coming to be lined by repaired Bosniak-owned houses with their gleaming new red-tile roofs.

The truth for us, punishment for the criminals; that has been our message since the first day of our search for the truth about our disappeared loved ones and we will persist in that search until we learn the fate of the very last murdered Srebrenican and until every criminal has been punished.

—*Nura Begović, secretary of the Association of Women of Srebrenica*

To remember them is indeed a matter of moral hygiene of sorts. . . .

Remembering this crime is the only apology.

—*Bogdan Bogdanović, Serbian architect, mayor of Belgrade, essayist*

6

Truth and Justice—Another Version of Activism

WHILE THE SURVIVORS OF SREBRENICA STRUGGLED TO return home, their campaign for recovery involved much more than just return. Put simply, they needed to know where the remains of missing loved ones were and for those remains to be identified. They needed a place to put those remains to their final rest where the survivors, relatives, and friends could visit the dead and honor them. Arriving at an appropriate resolution for the reburial and commemoration of those killed was an urgent part of the struggle for justice—and it faced as much obstruction as did the campaign for return of the displaced Srebrenicans.

Another overriding component of justice was the arrest and trial of those guilty for the war crimes that had been committed. The survivors needed to see that the truth about those crimes was exposed to the light of day. They needed that truth to be established in court, in the media, and in public opinion. The perpetrators had to be convicted and punished. The story of who committed which crimes—and who conceived of the expulsion and mass extermination—had to be told. Denial and distortion of that story had to be refuted.

This is a daunting list of needs, but from early on, survivors fought for them to be addressed. The activists for truth and justice have made headway over the years, achieving some significant successes. But this struggle will go on as long as there is memory. And there has been the least satisfaction in hearing an acknowledgment by the perpetrators of the suffering they caused. There has been next to no expression amounting to "I'm sorry"; and next to no confrontation with the official denial that dominates the mainstream discourse in the Republika Srpska and in Serbia. In this last matter there has been precious little progress, and that progress has mostly taken place under great pressure from the courts or the international community.

The heart of the postwar movement for truth and justice regarding Srebrenica has been the organizations of the "mothers," those thousands of bereaved women who were left without their sons, husbands, and other male relatives. These are the survivors who suffered the greatest injury of the war. What they lost can never be returned, but there is a measure of healing in the struggle for redress of their needs. The mothers and widows joined this struggle instinctively and waged it relentlessly over the years.

Several organizations of survivors were formed after the war; of these groups two stand out, the Tuzla-based organization Žene Srebrenice, or Women of Srebrenica; and the Sarajevo-based Pokret "Majke Enklave Srebrenica i Žepa," or Movement of the Mothers of the Srebrenica and Žepa Enclaves (henceforth "Mothers of Srebrenica").

Early on, the Tuzla-based organization initiated regular marches and demonstrations on the eleventh of every month, with a column of women and their supporters carrying embroidered *jastučice*, or pillowcases. The pillowcases showed the names, birth dates, and birth places of their missing loved ones. Similar demonstrations—and on occasion, protests blocking traffic—were held in Sarajevo. Reporters regularly covered these events in the newspapers and on television, helping to create a prominent public image for the women's organizations.

The existence of mass graves of Srebrenica victims was known before the end of the war. Investigators sponsored by the Federation government began exhumations soon after the war's end, and collections of remains accumulated in storage facilities in Tuzla and Visoko. Initially, lacking sophisticated technology, the rate of identification of the remains was so slow as to be practically insignificant. But with or without identifications, the survivors knew that the remains would ultimately have to be reburied. At the same time, they wished to have a location where they could regularly pay respects to the victims.

International officials were compelled to meet with these activists and listen to their demands. Representatives of the organizations called for the exhumation and identification of the missing and the apprehension of the war criminals. On every possible front, they pressed the demand for a memorial cemetery for victims of the massacres.

In mid-2000 I visited the Women of Srebrenica office near the center of Tuzla. When I arrived, there were five members of the organization there, all women who had lost most of their family members in Srebrenica. Only Nura Begović, one of the organization's leaders, was under fifty.

The office was lined with cushioned benches, and the walls were covered with newspaper clippings and posters related to Srebrenica. One showed women demonstrating, holding signs reading "Tell Us What Happened to Our Men," "We're Looking for Our Disappeared," and "Srebrenica: End of the World's Morality."

Begović told me that her organization's primary goals, as she phrased it, were to "learn the truth about our disappeared relatives, and to get justice and punishment of the war criminals."[1]

The disposition of the identified remains of the victims was a critical issue for the Women of Srebrenica, who saw burial in a publicly accessible memorial cemetery as paramount. Begović said, "Some people can go into the tunnel where they are stored, to try to identify their relatives, and others can't bear it. Imagine your son lying in a bag there. Let him be in a grave, where people can visit."

The establishment of a cemetery was a contentious issue for the Serbs who controlled the municipality of Srebrenica. To allow a cemetery and memorial center to be built at Potočari would be to acknowledge that war crimes were committed. Far from letting this happen, Serb authorities had begun to resettle Potočari, formerly populated overwhelmingly by Bosniaks, with their own displaced people. At the time of my meeting with the Women of Srebrenica, they had also permitted the construction of an Orthodox church in this location; work on this church was just beginning.

Begović said, "The Serbs will never allow us to build the cemetery. Someone must put pressure on them, and only the High Representative can do that."

Around the same time, I met with the Sarajevo organization Mothers of Srebrenica, led by Munira Subašić and Kada Hotić. Hotić told me, "My son, husband, and brother-in-law were all killed. But my neighbor, a war criminal, is free. . . . We seek world recognition of the truth; this was not a conflict, but genocide. It was not a civil war or a religious war."

Addressing the relevance of religion in her organization's struggle, Hotić told me, "Among us, religion is a custom. It's not good when there are fanatics. God is for human rights. There are no bad religions, except when they are politicized."[2]

Tied to the demand for establishment of a burial ground and memorial complex was the need for a place to conduct ceremonies of remembrance on the anniversary of the fall of Srebrenica. Well before a resolution of the dispute about the cemetery's location was reached, survivors wished to gather every year on July 11 to hold this ceremony.

Security concerns and the obstruction of Serb authorities in Srebrenica prevented such a large gathering from being held in Potočari in the first few years after the war. Thus in 1997, three thousand people attended a memorial service in a village near Kladanj in the Federation (near one of the exit points for the women who were bused out of Srebrenica after the fall of the town).[3]

The next year, as Munira Subašić recounted, "The first commemorative visit to Srebrenica was in 1998. We visited some wartime graves with police protection. We weren't allowed to visit our houses at that time. Only two buses were able to go, and many people were not able to participate."[4]

The campaign for the memorial complex in Srebrenica continued into the fifth year after the war. In 2000, activists and officials collaborated in planning a commemoration to be held on July 11 at Potočari. Srebrenicans decided to caravan there, hold a religious ceremony, and if possible, lay a foundation stone for a new memorial center.

SFOR (UN Stabilization Force) informed the commemoration organizing committee that only fifteen buses, or 750 people, would be permitted in the convoy. The committee responded that one hundred buses would travel, regardless of SFOR's decision. They questioned how much the problem was truly one of security, and how much it was the Serbs' desire to minimize the atrocity.

Committee leader Abdurahman Malkić asked rhetorically, "If the international community can't guarantee the safety of five thousand people who want to return to Srebrenica for half an hour or forty-five minutes, how can they guarantee security for twenty thousand returnees?" Finally, on the weekend before the eleventh, international officials consented to allow forty-five buses on the caravan.

The effort to organize a commemoration drew accusations of manipulation from all sides. Serb politicians in the Republika Srpska said that the event was "politicized" and organized with "dishonest intentions." Opposition politicians in the Federation accused Žene Srebrenica and similar groups of being front organizations for the SDA and lashed out at the party for cynically manipulating the victims.

At 6:30 on the morning of July 11, I parked my rented car near the field in Tuzla where buses were to leave for Srebrenica. Two buses were parked nearby, bearing signs that read "Srebrenica Ekspres" and "We Do Not Forget." People were already gathering around the bus doors, waiting to board.

There were far more would-be riders than spaces. I arranged to take some women with me. Hajra, around sixty, shook my hand and introduced herself: "I lost my only son, and I can't get on the bus." She started crying and continued, "My son was a policeman, and he disappeared when Srebrenica fell. My husband is here in Tuzla. We've received approval to get our apartment back, and we're waiting for it to be fixed. I'm fighting to go back home."

A busload of French people arrived to join the caravan. Srebrenica survivors crowded around the door of a bus, hoping to get on. Soon a Dutch bus arrived, but it was full. A man asked me for a ride and told me that from his village, only he and one other person had survived. He had lost his father and two brothers. He said, "I can't go to clean my mother's grave in Srebrenica. I can only go like this, with an organized group. Otherwise, it's too risky."

We headed south for Kladanj, where buses coming north from Sarajevo were going to join the caravan. As I drove, Hajra's daughter Munevera told me that her former neighbor had moved into her apartment after the fall of Srebrenica. "This was not a displaced person, just someone who wanted a better apartment," she told me. "That person was evicted two weeks ago and took everything out of the apartment. Not only did he take the furniture, but the water heater, the electrical switches and outlets, the locks on the doors, and the plumbing fixtures."

Around sixty buses arrived at Kladanj, the last stop in the Federation before the Republika Srpska. Well-known figures also arrived with their entourage and bodyguards: prime minister of the Bosnian Federation Edhem Bičakčić, Social Democrat leaders Sejfudin Tokić and Gradimir Gojer, and others.

Ten kilometers out of Kladanj, a sign read "Welcome to the Republika Srpska." A Muslim and a Serb policeman stood together at the border, while a couple of helicopters circled high overhead.

A dozen other cars were in front of me, and many more behind me. As we arrived at the border, all but one of the other cars were turned away. I doubted my cardboard press sign would help me; anyone could have printed it up. But a policeman casually waved me through.

I drove through fifty kilometers of Republika Srpska territory. It was wooded and hilly, undeveloped except for an occasional village or farmhouse. Every one or two hundred meters, a lone Serb policeman stood by the side of the road. I followed the convoy and drove with several buses, SFOR armored vehicles, and an ambulance. An RS police car followed behind me, blue lights flashing.

After we passed the town of Vlasenica there were many bombed houses beside the road. Fields of corn, already two meters high, grew between ruined homes. Here and there people stood at the side of the road watching. There were no welcoming waves, nor did I notice particular hostility.

I wondered what kind of country all these people, and all these policemen lining the road, hoped for, and whether they thought that they could thrive in an "ethnically pure" territory. I remembered what a Serb driver had told me when I supervised an election in the Republika Srpska: "We can never live together again. One day, we will learn to be good neighbors, like France and Germany." But the scenario of separation was looking less and less likely.

We passed through Bratunac, a few miles north of Potočari, without incident. There, it seemed that there were more police on the streets than civilians. SFOR and IPTF police crowded the streets. Later I heard that there was a stoning incident, and one woman was arrested. All I saw, however, were several children giving the three-finger gesture, a provocative Serb nationalist symbol. I took down my press sign.

We made the turn toward Potočari. This is a former "industrial suburb" of Sre-brenica, stretching along the road through the hills, with factories on both sides. These factories, to the extent that they were working at all, functioned at 10 percent of their prewar capacity. Here and there stood a kafana, with displaced Serbs fanning them-selves in the ninety-degree heat. Between the coffeehouses and defunct factories, there were cornfields and run-down houses. The temperature in my car rose to 95° F. At Potočari, I parked between an IPTF jeep and an armored SFOR vehicle and headed for the ceremony.

The grounds adjacent to the former battery factory, surrounded by empty buses, had been converted into a large prayer field. Altogether over fifty buses had made it through to Potočari.

An elderly woman cried out, grieving at the first sight of the place she had left in terror five years earlier. Helicopters circled over nearby ridges. A woman fainted near me and was fanned by her friends. The mood was solemn and quiet. Here on this field, mothers and wives had been separated from their sons and husbands; most of them still did not know where their men were.

I climbed onto a small hummock and saw around three thousand people lined up to pray—men in the front rows, and at least twice as many women behind them. The head of the Bosnian Islamic community, Reisu-1 -ulema Mustafa Cerić, was giving a sermon and leading prayers, in Bosnian and Arabic. A sea of women in white scarves listened; all repeated "Amin" at the end of a phrase.

I walked down toward the front of the line of praying men. They were raising their hands to their faces in the traditional manner of prayer. Cerić spoke, "We are not here to condemn, but we won't give up on justice. Give us strength, and save us from hate. Give bravery and kindness to those who survived. And for the criminals, give them the strength to change their bad intentions." Behind him I could see Edhem Bičakčić praying. President Izetbegović was not far away. This was his first time in the Republika Srpska.

Croat member of the Bosnian state presidency Ante Jelavić stood near Bičakčić, as did UN special representative Jacques Klein. High Representative from the international community Wolfgang Petritsch and Ambassador Thomas Miller (US ambassador to Bosnia), were there, as were many other diplomats.

Jelavić and the diplomats participated as a political act. The Serb member of the presidency, Živko Radišić, did not attend, although Ambassador Miller had personally called on him to do so. All top Republika Srpska politicians had been invited—from mayors to members of Parliament—but none had come, nor had any representative of the Orthodox Church.

Cerić announced, "We have finished. Please go home peacefully now." Bodyguards in black surrounded the public figures, and everyone walked off the field. People ap-proached Alija Izetbegović and kissed his hand.

ESTABLISHMENT OF THE MEMORIAL GROUNDS

At the time of the commemoration, the status of the prospective cemetery grounds had not been formalized. The issue was under deliberation by a special committee in the Srebrenica municipal assembly. The committee was composed of two Serbs, two Muslims, and an international official.

The Serb and Muslim sides each made proposals for a location, but there was no progress toward an agreement. The Serbs proposed several remote village sites. Abida, a member of Women of Srebrenica, argued, "They are suggesting places far from the public eye. But my son was slaughtered there in Potočari. His blood was spilled on that ground, so let him be buried there."

In response to the obstruction and confusion about the location of the memorial complex, the Sarajevo-based survivors' organization conducted a survey in 1999. They asked more than ten thousand respondents whether they wished the center to be created in Sarajevo Canton, Tuzla Canton, or Potočari. The respondents answered overwhelmingly, by 83 percent, in favor of Potočari.[5]

In November 2000, High Representative Wolfgang Petritsch, overriding Serb obstruction, decreed that the memorial complex should be built within Srebrenica municipality. Upon this decision, Dragan Jevtić resigned his position as deputy mayor, calling on other Serb officials to do so as well.[6] But Petritsch's decision was final.

For the time being, the memorial complex at Potočari was to be administered by the OHR through the Srebrenica-Potočari Foundation, an administrative body formed for that purpose. Funding for its construction was donated by the Netherlands and several other countries, and from numerous other sources including the government of the Bosnian Federation.

In a ceremony held during the July 2001 anniversary of the massacres, a symbolic cornerstone was placed on the designated grounds of the cemetery. The block of white stone, guarded against vandalism by a local policeman, sat alone for some time waiting for the memorial complex to be constructed around it. Early the following year, the Srebrenica municipal council issued a "Resolution on Special Treatment of the Area of Srebrenica Municipality" that, among other things, supported the construction of the memorial center. This represented a significant evolution in the official attitude in Srebrenica.[7]

A first reburial of hundreds of identified remains was scheduled for March 2003, to take place before the construction of the memorial complex was quite finished. This was to be a moment of high emotional impact for the victims' families, thousands of people who had waited for a place to mourn their dead and for some kind of closure. Shortly before the event, Munira Beba Hadžić, director of the Tuzla-based women's organization Bosfam, herself from Srebrenica, wrote me about the mood of her organization's members in the period leading up to that first reburial.

"They are preparing to bury 582 victims from Srebrenica; those are identified people who will be buried in Potočari on the 31st of March. For all of us this is a very difficult time. Sometimes we really ask ourselves where the limit of human endurance is, how much pain a person can stand. The women are very sad and depressed. We'll see what comes; after this funeral there will be a funeral of 400 victims, on July 11, and then some new date and new funeral . . . you have to stay sane, if you can."[8]

The reburial and commemorative ceremony took place on March 31. Attendance at the event was more than twice that of the previous year, with 115 buses, and many private vehicles, traveling from various parts of the Federation. An estimated ten thousand to fifteen thousand mourners came to Potočari. Reis Cerić, the High Representative, and Sulejman Tihić, Bosniak member of the Bosnian state presidency, all attended. From the Republika Srpska, Foreign Minister Mladen Ivanić came in a private capacity.[9] Six hundred new graves had been dug in advance for the remains that were to be reburied that day.

Vesna Mustafić, Srebrenica return activist, attended the reburial in her capacity as a member of the NGO Snaga Žene (Women's Power), along with members of other Bosnian NGOs. Their mission was to provide moral support for the mourners.

Vesna wrote describing the event. Following are excerpts from her letter:

Yesterday was one of the most difficult days in my life. All that I feel is a great sadness and helplessness. A thousand questions without answers.

All evening on television there has been footage from Srebrenica. Mixed, old and new film. Everything is the same as 1995. The entire road from Kladanj to Srebrenica, every 50 meters—a policeman. And it was like this in 1995, only then they wore military uniforms and had automatic weapons. Today they only have pistols.

Now they are watching to make sure that no one will cause an incident of harassment, but in 1995 they were concerned that no one would accidentally remain alive.

What do these women think, who were there? And they came along the same route, only in the opposite direction?

Then, they were concerned about all those who had no chance to board a bus in Potočari, which was the only chance for survival. And now many were left without bus transportation, only in Tuzla, because there weren't enough buses. Then, they were not able to help their sons and husbands to survive, and today perhaps some of these women were not able to get to Potočari to see them off. Perhaps to a better world. Maybe there, they will find peace?

There was a huge crowd. Everyone was looking for someone else. . . . The rows were horribly long, the grave markers arranged in alphabetical order. Six hundred of them. 599 men, and one woman. By each one, a bouquet of flowers.

I have never seen such a thing. All were crying; with each car, bus, person, more and more sadness. So much sadness in one place.

If only this were the end. But there are still 13 times this many graves unfilled.

They finish the religious ceremony and now everyone is going back toward the graves. Each will lower her relative into the grave and bury him. Everyone is the same. Here you can only listen and feel.

We return home. It's silent in the car. A horrible silence that hurts the ears. We drive slowly, in an endless line of cars. We stop often. Policemen are everywhere, the whole route. Like in 1995.[10]

Shortly before the March 31 reburial, the Bosnian Human Rights Chamber delivered a judgment that supported the ongoing construction of the Potočari memorial complex. The previous year, forty-nine relatives of Srebrenica victims had filed a lawsuit against Bosnian Serb authorities for the massacre, demanding compensation and that they provide details on the crime, along with official admission of responsibility.

In early March the Human Rights Chamber found that the Republika Srpska government's ongoing refusal to provide details about the massacres was violating the human rights of the victims' families. The chamber ordered the RS to form a commission to investigate and draft a comprehensive report about the events of July 1995. The decision also required the RS to pay 2 million KM into a fund for the Potočari Foundation. This sum was to be paid by early September of the same year. A further 2 million KM was to be paid later.[11]

The next reburial, of 282 identified remains, took place on July 11, 2003. Approximately twenty thousand visitors were present. Among them were high officials from the Bosnian Federation, along with Dragan Mikerević, prime minister of the Republika Srpska. Mikerević was the most senior politician from the RS to attend the ceremonies to date.

People of conscience from Serbia were able to cross the border and attend the commemoration. Members of the antiwar organization Women in Black (Žene u crnom) came from several Serbian cities and traveled in one busload across the border. This display of solidarity was welcomed by the mourners. Women in Black had tried to attend the year before but were turned back by the Bosnian Serb police when they crossed into Bosnia.

Once the memorial complex at Potočari was built, the July 11 commemoration would become a tradition, more massively attended each year. But there was one more founding event of consequence that took place after the first two reburials in 2003. The official opening of the cemetery was held, with great fanfare, on September 20.

It was announced that the ceremonial opening would be attended by former US president Bill Clinton. This decision by the Potočari Foundation Advisory Board was met with mixed emotions from survivors. Given that the Srebrenica massacres took place during Clinton's term in office, some people faulted Clinton for having allowed the genocide to take place. Some were adamant, calling the decision a "scandal."

Others were more ambivalent. Munira Subašić later told me, "It was important that Clinton came. His participation in the opening gave importance to the event. But there was some confusion. He was aware that there had been mistakes and a missed opportunity to protect the citizens of Srebrenica. He talked with us and promised to help us. Most of us wanted Clinton to participate."[12]

The symbolic foundation stone had been laid, and the cemetery was built. Some US$6 million was to be spent on the memorial complex.[13] In 2002 I spoke with a return activist who had already come back to live in Srebrenica, but was unemployed and desperately trying to support a family. She said, "The people must be buried, but this is overdone. It doesn't help us at all. They should use some of those funds for a factory, and put us to work. What do we get out of this? The dead don't eat bread. But we do, by God. Put me to work so I can feed my family."

However, by 2003 any simmering division between return activists and those working for the establishment of the cemetery was disappearing. The returnees had all lost relatives, after all, and most of them were hoping to see the remains of those victims reburied in the memorial cemetery.

THE SEARCH FOR THE MISSING

The search for the missing remains of the Srebrenica victims, and the complicated task of their identification, were goals of a campaign that went hand in hand with the establishment of the cemetery. Unlike the project of the memorial complex, the hunt for the missing will never be completed.

The existence of some mass graves was already known during the war from the results of US satellite surveillance of the terrain behind Serb lines. Excavation of a few known sites commenced soon after the end of the war, and this activity picked up as information about the location of other sites trickled in.

In order to identify the remains that were being discovered, a first requirement was to create a list of the names of the missing. The International Red Cross (ICRC) initiated a list to be used to trace missing persons; this list came to be used for identification as well.[14] Problems arose with this part of the process immediately as the information was being collected by the ICRC, which did not allow informants to provide data about anyone other than members of their own immediate family.

When Srebrenica fell and the Serb army expelled masses of refugees from that enclave, thousands of them took shelter at Dubrava airport near Tuzla. Speaking of those first days, Nura Begović told me:

> There were many of us who were staying in tents at Dubrava. We had to come to the Red Cross office in Tuzla. They didn't even invite us; the families would tell each other about the possibility of registering their missing. We came and waited in front of the office. The war was still going on, and bombs were falling, but we waited.
>
> The Red Cross asked for information only about the immediate family. I was not allowed to give information about the sons of my two brothers who were missing, or about my neighbor's family. I know that there were complete families killed who had no one to give information about them.[15]

In the course of 1996, the collection of data about the missing took a step toward better organization when President Clinton created the International Commission on

Missing Persons (ICMP) to work on the problem of thousands of missing in various parts of former Yugoslavia including those from Srebrenica. This institution, along with commissions representing each of the three main Bosnian ethnicities, carried out exhumations, which were originally led by the ICTY.

Another step toward better coordination of a very chaotic process was taken in 1997, when the OHR's creation of the Joint Exhumation Process facilitated the implementation of exhumations in one entity by representatives from the other.[16] Nationalist officials in the local governments continued to conceal dozens of mass graves, but the step provided a measure of freedom of movement. But the process of identification of exhumed remains was excruciatingly slow in the first half dozen years.

The ICRC created a "book of the missing" with photographs of clothing and personal belongings found with the remains of the Srebrenica victims upon exhumation. Staff members took the book around to show to survivors, who could also view it at the Tuzla office of the Women of Srebrenica. This resulted in disappointingly few identifications. In 2001, only seventy-three victims had been identified.[17]

Then, in late 2001, an unexpected breakthrough occurred that sped up the identification process. The technology for DNA identification of remains had been introduced in Bosnia that year. In November an ICMP DNA analysis center in Sarajevo made the first successful matching of DNA from relatives' blood samples with DNA from the exhumed bones of a victim—in this case, a fifteen-year-old boy from Srebrenica. Identifications picked up rapidly with the new technology. In 2002 there were 518 official identifications.[18]

The acceleration of identifications made it possible for that first reburial to take place at Potočari in March 2003, giving some sort of relief to the relatives of the victims. I avoid the use of the word "closure" here. The identification and reburial were owed to the survivors, but they were no cure for their suffering. One woman, when asked if the reburial would bring an "end to the healing process," responded, "The end? There is no end. Only when we die."[19]

The process of exhuming and identifying missing victims pertained not only to the Srebrenica massacre, but also to victims throughout Bosnia-Herzegovina and beyond. Roughly thirty thousand people were missing at the war's end. Regionally, the project of identification was unparalleled in previous war history; after World War II the missing in former Yugoslavia were, for the most part, simply commemorated with monuments dedicated to a mass of victims. The identification project after the more recent war was a vast and costly one; by 2007 the ICMP had a staff of 170.[20] The monthly bill for chemicals alone (used in the identification process) was calculated to be US$100,000.[21]

In the early 2000s the ICMP became one of the world's leading organizations in this kind of search and identification, owing to its expertise in DNA identification. Over the ensuing years it provided assistance in this field in Kosovo, Iraq, New York after the 9/11 terrorist attacks, and Asia after the tsunami of late 2004.

Compounding the difficulty of identifying remains was the fact of "secondary graves." Originally, victims of the Srebrenica massacres were buried in a relatively small number of graves in a wide circle spreading from Srebrenica to Zvornik and beyond. But in the months after the killings, as Serb officials involved in the conquest of Srebrenica became aware that authorities in the West had learned of the mass graves, those officials took measures to conceal them. This involved digging up the graves with bulldozers and trucking the remains to secondary sites in more remote places. Of some ninety-five mass graves found to be holding victims of the Srebrenica genocide, only seven were primary graves, and the rest secondary.[22]

One dreadful result of this crime upon crime was that parts of individual remains were separated and scattered among two or more secondary graves. This made identification, upon recovery of the remains, extremely difficult because the presence of a complete set of bones was unusual. With ongoing exhumations, by late 2002 there were already seventy-five hundred bags of remains. But of these, around two thousand were complete sets, another two thousand contained partial sets of the bones of one body, and the rest contained mixed remains from more than one victim.[23]

The locations of the mass graves, both primary and secondary, were known to the perpetrators and to some local residents who lived near them. There was precious little cooperation in finding the sites. People would call in information, but this information was evaluated as being between 10 and 20 percent accurate.[24] The lack of information about the location of mass graves was yet another factor that made the relatives of the victims desperate.

In mid-2004, under pressure from the international community and after much delay, the Srebrenica Commission, a body formed by the government of the Republika Srpska, published a report that owned up to some amount of responsibility for the Srebrenica massacre. The report named the locations of thirty-two theretofore undiscovered mass graves.[25] There was dispute as to whether all these sites were truly previously unknown.

By this date several dozen mass graves had been opened, and sites containing high numbers of remains continued to be discovered. There was Crni Vrh near Zvornik, opened in mid-2003 and containing remains buried up to four meters deep. This secondary grave was found to contain 629 remains.[26] For a time Crni Vrh held a record as the largest mass grave, but a complex of a dozen graves opened in mid-2002 at Kamenica surpassed that record as work at the site carried on for years. One after another, associated sites were discovered, finally amounting to thirteen sites related to the 1995 genocide. By 2008, some five thousand collections of bones had been exhumed at those sites. This amounted to at least thirty complete bodies and 851 partial remains.[27]

While time passed and more graves were opened, still there were thousands of widows and mothers who had no news of their missing relatives. In April 2005 Amor Mašović, chairman of the Federal Commission for Missing Persons, noted that there were still twenty-two unexcavated mass graves related to the Srebrenica killings.[28] The prolonged delay in locating the missing victims was an agony for the survivors; Amnesty International characterized it as "one of the largest continuing human rights violations in Bosnia-Herzegovina."[29] The international human rights organization considered that, since most of the missing were victims of "enforced disappearances," and local officials were participating in the obstruction of their discovery, this amounted to an ongoing abuse of the survivors' rights.

In the mid-2000s new mass graves were discovered practically on a monthly basis. By spring of 2005 some sixty-five hundred remains of victims of the Srebrenica massacre had been exhumed, and around four thousand of those were identified.[30] In that same period the Potočari Foundation published a preliminary list of 8,106 names of disappeared victims. The search continued, but Gordon Bacon, chief of staff of the ICMP, said, "I don't really know if there will ever come a time when finding bodies will stop."[31]

The number of identified remains continued to rise, but since most of the remains were found in secondary graves, complete remains were few. It was not unusual to discover a set of bones without a skull, or to identify just one bone from a missing person. Some bags of remains that were delivered to the DNA analysis laboratory contained the bones of up to ten people.[32] Just as gruesome was the fact that parts of one skeleton could be found in more than one secondary grave; there has been more than one instance of a victim's remains being found in as many as five different sites.[33]

The fact that many remains have only been partially identified leads to a dilemma for the ICMP. When do officials notify the families, and when should the remains be reburied? If partial remains are buried and then new bones are identified, then a grave must be opened up and there must be a new reburial; this customarily takes place after the July 11 commemorative funeral. The ICMP and other missing persons agencies have decided to let the family know after a given percentage, often 50 percent, of a victim's remains are identified, and then to let the family decide when to hold a funeral.[34] Some families have opted to delay a funeral pending discovery of additional remains. Thus in the later 2000s there was a significant number of victims whose partial remains had been identified, but which were not destined for an early reburial.

An integral part of the identification process is the donation of blood samples by relatives of the missing victims, without which there can be no identification through DNA matching. The ICMP campaigned widely to encourage the survivors to provide blood samples and has sent officials to far-flung parts of Europe and the United States to collect them. By the spring of 2007, over twenty-one thousand blood samples had been collected, related to nearly eight thousand missing persons.[35]

The number of blood samples collected continued to rise, but one obstacle to efficient identification, besides further location of burial sites, was a lack of blood samples pertaining to specific victims. In some cases an entire family was killed, or relatives subsequently died without giving blood, so that there was no DNA sample to identify a set of remains. In cases where a DNA match takes place, the accuracy rate is 99.95 percent. But there are limits to DNA matching. Analysts may possess multiple samples from parents and other relatives. However, if parents lost two or more sons, the DNA cannot differentiate between siblings.

Yet another difficulty in DNA identification has to do with the quality of the bone samples taken from the remains of the exhumed victims. In some cases the weather, or the passage of time, can deteriorate the DNA beyond recognition. Furthermore, there have been cases where people wishing to conceal the evidence poured damaging materials such as liquid whitewash over the graves.[36] On the other hand, identification technology has improved over the years since the end of the war, and more identifications are possible than before. While DNA is the strongest aid to identification, there are additional lines of evidence that augment the process, including forensic anthropology, dental records, and material evidence such as clothing.[37]

For these and many other reasons including the sheer number of victims, an identification that can be undertaken in the course of one day can nevertheless take many years to come to fruition. One woman who provided a blood sample waited ten years for news of an identification.[38] Because of delays in identification, some remains found as early as 1996 were not reburied until 2009.[39]

One factor contributing to the delays was structural; there were numerous lists of the missing that were not reconciled for over a decade. There were also several organizations throughout Bosnia-Herzegovina that cooperated only minimally in the search for the missing. It took many years to resolve these problems. The two entities of Bosnia-Herzegovina initially ran separate missing persons commissions that carried out separate searches. It was not until 2008 that entity-based missing persons agencies were abolished and the Missing Persons Institute, working at the state level, coordinated searches regardless of the ethnicity of the missing persons. But that coordination continued to be hampered by political obstruction and ethnic division.

Early 2011 finally saw the creation of a central database of missing persons, coordinated by the Missing Persons Institute in cooperation with the ICMP and the ICRC. The unified list was compiled from thirteen different sources, and its existence made political manipulation of figures of the missing more difficult. At that time it was estimated that some two-thirds, or around twenty-three thousand, of those who were missing at the end of the war had been found and identified.[40] And as late as mid-2018, that number had not risen greatly, standing at 25,500—with two thousand of these remains yet to be identified.[41]

As the search continued, mothers were dying before the remains of their missing sons were located. The Women of Srebrenica held protests in late 2011 calling for accelerated search activities, saying that the ICMP was ignoring eight known mass graves in the Podrinje region. Hajra Čatić warned that Srebrenica survivors might undertake their own searches if necessary. Čatić noted that she herself had entered into a minefield in search of the remains of her own son.[42]

It has not been unusual that people with knowledge of the whereabouts of a clandestine grave offered to share that information in return for payment. Some of these people were probably involved in the war crimes or removal of remains to secondary graves; others were local residents who live near the sites. In either case they have taken advantage of the survivors, sometimes contacting them directly, other times contacting the ICMP or the Missing Persons Institute.[43]

In late 2008 the list of victims of the Srebrenica massacres was updated to include 8,372 names. A long, curved stone slab sits in the Potočari memorial complex, inscribed with the name of each of these victims. As the search went on Kathryne Bomberger, director-general of the ICMP, noted that it was doubtful that the remains of all the Srebrenica victims would be found, because "the criminals hid them very well, or destroyed them to a point that makes identification impossible."[44]

Nevertheless, searchers and laboratory technicians continued to make progress over the years. The ICMP has estimated that between eight thousand and eighty-one hundred people had been missing as a result of the Srebrenica massacres, and Amor Mašović of the Missing Persons Institute gave an estimate of 8,262.[45] By early 2018, 22,268 family members of 7,743 victims had given blood samples. Of the roughly eight thousand people missing, at least partial remains of nearly seven thousand victims had been identified by that year, with the work still in progress.[46]

Between 2016 and 2018 an additional 233 remains were reburied; that brought the total of remains reburied at Potočari to 6,610, with more than two hundred reburied in other cemeteries. These remains had been discovered at 150 different locations, including ninety-five mass graves.[47] There were more than one hundred partial sets of remains that had been identified but that were deemed incomplete for burial, and over one hundred sets that were unidentified. The Podrinje Identification Project further reported that there were still some eleven hundred victims missing in the case of the Srebrenica genocide.[48] In the mid-2010s a handful of sites were still being searched for remains, and searchers still hoped to find additional sites.[49]

A FUNERAL IN 2006

I attended the commemoration of the massacres and the reburial of identified victims on the eleventh anniversary of the genocide, in July 2006. To that date the identified remains of 1,937 victims had been reburied. Among another 505 victims reburied on this anniversary was Azem Pašalić, the uncle of my friend Suljo Pašalić. Only six years older than Suljo, Azem was more like a brother. His remains were discovered in the mass grave at Crni Vrh.

I asked Suljo how the discovery and identification of his uncle's remains affected him. He said, "Until this year I never had the time to go to see all the remains as they lay in the warehouse; this year I had to go because it was my uncle. I looked at those five hundred coffins, and I wondered, 'What kind of soul could do such a thing?'" Suljo's wife, Magbula, told me, "I went to the funeral in 2001; I won't go again. I don't think I'm capable of that."

As I took the bus to Srebrenica, some people were on a several-day hike through the woods, retracing the path of approximately fifteen thousand men who had tried to escape the massacre in 1995. From 2005, local human rights activists organized this annual event as a powerful demonstration of remembrance. The hike began at Nezuk, one of the points where fleeing Srebrenicans had arrived at safe territory. It ended at Potočari the night before the funeral.

In Potočari, next to the battery factory that served as the wartime headquarters of the Dutch battalion, was a warehouse holding the 505 coffins waiting to be buried. They were not coffins, in fact, but the traditional *tabut*—a board carrying the remains, with a stick frame covered by a green cloth.

Tens of thousands of people attended the reburial on July 11. People started carrying the tabuts out of the warehouse, in one long green-tinged procession. Among the open graves were temporary boards naming the victims, sometimes two brothers beside each other, or a father and son. I followed Suljo Pašalić and his family to gravesite number 99.

I watched with great sadness as Suljo, his son, and cousins shoveled dirt over Azem's coffin. Suljo's daughter began crying, and it was all I could do to hold back my own tears. But no one else cried.

I reached out to touch Suljo in consolation. But he was somewhere else, unreachable, lost, absently shifting pebbles in the dirt as others shoveled.

When the burial was finished the family sat in silent contemplation around the grave, just as hundreds of other families were doing throughout the complex.

On the bus back to Sarajevo, after the commemoration, I spoke with a fellow passenger who told me he had lost his father, three brothers, and his disabled mother in the massacre. "I wish to God I had been killed too," he told me. We passed the cemetery at Potočari. Referring to the Serb politicians who must pass the vast cemetery in order to reach Srebrenica, he asked, "How could they not be ashamed?"

Back in Sarajevo it was pouring rain in the middle of July. My landlady Fata said, "All this rain is falling because of so many unburied victims. As the people behave, that's how God will react."

INCIDENTS OF OBSTRUCTION

Bosniaks were returning to Srebrenica, making their presence felt more strongly, and conducting memorial ceremonies. Some members of the local Serb population resented this return to what they apparently believed should remain an exclusively Serb-inhabited territory. While the arsons of the early 2000s were a thing of the past, periodic actions continued to make the Bosniaks feel unwelcome. In general it is difficult to say definitively who was behind these "incidents," as they were termed, but it was clear that Serb authorities in the municipality turned a blind eye.

For example, in 2005, just days before the tenth anniversary commemoration of the massacres, two bombs were placed near the memorial complex—one at a power transformer station not far from the main road, and one near a fence.[50] Investigations never led to an arrest.[51]

Provocations, insults, and assertions of Serb domination over Srebrenica municipality have taken many forms. In 1999 the Serbian Orthodox Church began to build a church in the heart of Potočari, a settlement that was more than 90 percent Bosniak before the war, not far from the site of the first massacres in 1995. The OHR halted construction of this church in late 2000. A similar marking of territory through use of religious symbols took place on a hill above Srebrenica in 2003 when unidentified individuals raised a cross on the day of the commemoration. In 2010, individuals erected a large cross in the immediate vicinity of the mass grave at Budak, shortly before the anniversary commemoration. Later in the same year, builders began to construct a church in this village that was still overwhelmingly inhabited by Bosniaks.

Self-styled "Chetnik" activists have visited Srebrenica in a very public manner nearly every year on July 12, the day after the anniversary of the genocide and the vastly attended commemoration. After the commemoration in 2006, I witnessed the occupation of the city by militarized units of the Serb police forces. July 12 is the anniversary of the 1992 killing of Serb civilians on the outskirts of Srebrenica by Bosniak troops led by Naser Orić. The date coincides with Petrovdan (St. Peter's Day), and so the provocative demonstrations by Serb nationalists conflate the anniversary of the attack on Serb villagers with a religious observation.

Serb politicians in the Republika Srpska have chosen to use this anniversary as a counter to the anniversary of the genocide. On that day Serb visitors from out of town have strolled through Srebrenica wearing T-shirts inscribed with the slogan, "Republika Srpska—we are all Mladić."

In 2009 the media reported a similar, intensified invasion of black-shirted roughnecks from Pančevo, a Serbian city. These were reportedly members of the organization Obraz (Honor), an extreme Serbian nationalist organization that glorifies the World War II Chetnik leader Draža Mihailović and nurtures the idea of a Greater Serbia. Wearing T-shirts with the likenesses of Ratko Mladić and Draža Mihailović, around seventy of these people roamed the town, played Serbian nationalist songs through a loudspeaker, carrying a "Chetnik" flag. Toward the end of the day, they tore down the Bosnian flag from the municipal building and spat and urinated on it. The police arrested no one.[52]

The July 12 anniversary continued to gain prominence as an annual commemoration of Serb casualties in the war. For many Serbs the Parastos, or requiem for the fallen, came to be held in the spirit of a counterweight to the July 11 anniversary of the massacres. The massive July 11 commemoration was an implicit accusation against the Serb extremists who had committed the genocide, and their political heirs found it appropriate to remember the fallen Serb fighters and civilians of the broader Birač region. Authorities reckon the number of Serb casualties at 3,267. In the later 2000s, in addition to Petrovdan ceremonies in Srebrenica on July 12 commemorative ceremonies were held in nearby Bratunac at a military cemetery, attended by high officials from the Republika Srpska.

The combination of mourning with political manipulation and provocation was unfortunate but widespread. Finally, in 2010 Serb authorities in the eastern part of the RS took measures to curb the provocations. On July 12 of that year members of Obraz and two similar organizations, "1389" and the Ravna Gora Chetnik Movement, were turned back when they tried to cross the border from Serbia. But the next year the organization Serbian National Movement Naši (Ours) posted an announcement on the Internet reading, "Happy July 11, day of liberation of Srebrenica," noting further, "On that day in 1995, the Army of the Republika Srpska liberated this Muslim military stronghold, thus halting the genocide against Serbs that had lasted since 1992."[53] And shortly before the annual commemoration, provocateurs from Serbia were back in Srebrenica, driving through town playing loud nationalist songs from their cars, and waving the SRS (Serbian Radical Party of Vojislav Šešelj) flag.[54]

Expressions of hate with the intent to provoke have by no means been limited to Srebrenica and vicinity. Further afield, impudent or insensitive young sports fans and others have adopted a slogan launched in November 2002 at a Banja Luka soccer match between the local team and one from Sarajevo, when a local fan unfurled a banner that read, "Nož, Žica, Srebrenica." This translates as "Knife, Wire, Srebrenica."[55]

This chilling slogan stood throughout the match, and Serb fans sang songs about Radovan Karadžić and displayed his portrait. After the match, some Serbs threw stones and flares at the buses returning to Sarajevo and fought with police, who prevented them from further attacking the opposing team's fans.

Afterward, no one was prepared to take responsibility for this skirmish. The local police arrested some of the hooligans, but none of the Serb political parties expressed an opinion about the incident. The Serb team was suspended for a few games. There were Serb fans who didn't like the offensive banner, but when interviewed they said they were afraid to do anything about it.

Later the slogan showed up again and again.

7

Justice in the Courts

AS SURVIVORS OF THE SREBRENICA GENOCIDE WERE MAKING progress in the creation of the Potočari memorial complex and in the discovery of their missing relatives, the search for truth and justice was also underway on a parallel track at The Hague. There, war crimes prosecution under the auspices of the ICTY picked up in the early part of the 2000s. Along the way, details about the atrocities of July 1995 became clarified through eyewitness and expert testimony.

One by one, the convictions of greater and lesser actors in the crimes cemented the record of the genocide in history. In some cases crucial information was provided by high-placed participants, thus putting to rest the case of those who denied the facts of the massacres—at least, for those who were willing to consider the evidence. A large body of information about the fall of Srebrenica came to be enshrined in legal history.

Numerous valuable books have been written on single war crimes cases; what follows will necessarily be a brief and partial overview of the search for justice in the courts, covering cases related only to the Srebrenica crimes.

The first soldier involved in the Srebrenica massacres who was tried at The Hague was Dražen Erdemović, a sergeant in the RS army's Tenth Sabotage Battalion. Erdemović pleaded guilty to participating in the shooting of dozens of men at Branjevo farm near the village of Pilica, saying, "I had to do this. If I had refused, I would have been killed together with the victims. When I refused, they told me: 'If you are sorry for them, stand up, line up with them and we will kill you too.'"[1]

Somewhere between fifteen and twenty busloads of prisoners—estimated at twelve hundred altogether—were delivered to Branjevo farm for execution. Erdemović recounted how the prisoners were lined up in groups of ten; the firing squad of which he was a part shot prisoners from 10:00 a.m. to 3:00 on the afternoon of July 16, 1995. Erdemović recalled, "I could not shoot anymore; my index finger had gone numb from so much killing."[2] When Erdemović was called on to participate in a subsequent killing shift, he refused.

Erdemović's initial sentence of ten years in late 1996 was subsequently reduced to five years because of his expressions of remorse and his assertion that he committed the murders under duress. It is not surprising that his short sentence for the killing of around seventy civilians was very distressful to the survivors, but Erdemović's cooperation in subsequent trials of higher officers has been critical.

The trial of Republika Srpska Army general Radislav Krstić, commander of the fifteen-thousand-member Drina Corps, delivered a verdict of high impact. General Krstić, arrested in 1998, was convicted in August 2001 on eight counts including genocide. This was the first conviction for genocide related to the Srebrenica massacres, and it remained the only one for many years. Krstić was sentenced to forty-six years in prison.

Krstić was involved at the beginning of a chain of events leading to genocide, and testimony from his trial described Krstić's role in organizing the transportation of the victims.[3] Records revealed planning meetings that Krstić had attended, called by General Ratko Mladić during the massacres.

In summarizing the decision, an ICTY judge said, "By deciding to kill all the men of fighting age, a decision was taken to make it impossible for the Muslim people of Srebrenica to survive. Stated otherwise, what was ethnic cleansing became genocide."[4]

Upon appeal, Krstić's conviction was reduced to "aiding and abetting genocide," rather than genocide, and the sentence was reduced to thirty-six years. Again, the sentence reduction greatly pained the survivors. Munira Subašić, leader of the organization Mothers of Srebrenica, said in protest, "I feel humiliated as a victim and, in some way, dead."[5]

Nevertheless, the reduced conviction still retained the fact of genocide as a matter of court record. In an essay published in 2005, Srebrenica survivor and journalist Emir Suljagić explained the significance of the genocide conviction: "In the judgment upon

Radislav Krstić, commander of the Drina Corps, whose main force took part in the genocide of July 1995, the judicial council of the Hague Tribunal confirmed certain basic facts. First, the Bosniaks of eastern Bosnia were a protected group, under the terms of the [genocide] convention; secondly, a mass killing of males took place in Srebrenica; thirdly, through the killing of males, the reproductive part of the community was killed, so that the latter was brought to the brink of extinction; fourthly, the leadership of the Bosnian Serbs, which planned this crime, had the intention of destroying the Bosniaks of eastern Bosnia, in part or in whole."[6]

It is significant that the Krstić conviction pertains to military command responsibility for the genocide, rather than to the political decision making that made the genocide possible in the first place. This would prove to be more difficult to demonstrate in court.

After the Krstić conviction, a plea-bargaining process led to the conviction of Momir Nikolić in a trial that was extremely important for case history in another way. Nikolić was not convicted of genocide, but of the lesser count of crimes against humanity. The significance of Nikolić's agreement was that he was the first VRS (Army of the Republika Srpska) officer to plead guilty for the crimes in Srebrenica, and he was intimately involved in carrying out the massacres. As such, he was in a position to reveal details of the war crimes to such an extent as to provide an effective bulwark against denial of those crimes.

Nikolić had been indicted in 2002 as part of a case including three other officers, Vidoje Blagojević, Dragan Obrenović, and Dragan Jokić. He pleaded guilty on May 6, 2003, for the "widespread and systematic attack on the civilian population of Srebrenica," and to the murder of over seven thousand boys and men between the ages of sixteen and sixty.[7] The plea arrangement, Nikolić's expressions of remorse, and his promise to testify in upcoming war crimes cases resulted in the dropping of a genocide charge. He was sentenced to twenty-seven years in prison.

Activists for justice for Srebrenica were again very distressed by Nikolić's plea bargain, especially by the fact that the ICTY traded away a genocide conviction for the confession. One survivor commented that "the Hague Tribunal is not a market where you can bargain about such things as genocide."[8]

Discussing the significance of the plea arrangement, Emir Suljagić wrote, "until the moment Nikolić confessed, I had never heard a Bosnian Serb admit that the massacre even happened. . . . The confessions have brought me a sense of relief I have not known since the fall of Srebrenica in 1995. They have given me the acknowledgment I have been looking for these past eight years. While far from an apology, these admissions are a start.* We Bosnian Muslims no longer have to prove we were victims. Our friends

---

* Nikolić's guilty plea was by far not the only one; about twenty others accused of war crimes pleaded guilty as well. The motivations varied; while Nikolić seems to have been truly contrite about his crimes, it has become clear in several other cases, such as those of Biljana Plavšić and Darko Mrđa, that their guilty pleas were matters of expedience. They received reduced sentences because of their feigned remorse and later made it clear to their supporters that they had no such sentiment.

and cousins, fathers and brothers were killed—and we no longer have to prove they were innocent."[9]

In a confession as part of his plea bargain, Nikolić admitted that he had had direct knowledge in advance of the plan to separate the men of Srebrenica from the women and children, and to kill them. He recounted, "On the morning of 12 July I met up with . . . lieutenant-colonel Vujadin Popović, head of security, and lieutenant-colonel Kosorić, head of the intelligence unit, of the Drina Corps. On that occasion Popović told me that all Muslim women and children in Potočari would be taken from there toward the territory in the vicinity of Kladanj under Muslim control, but that the men of military age found in the Muslim civilian mass would be separated off, imprisoned temporarily in Bratunac and soon afterwards killed."[10]

Nikolić subsequently coordinated the transport of Bosniak women and children to the front line at Kladanj, and the men to their places of captivity and execution. He reported having met and planned these operations with his co-indictees, as well as other officers all the way up to General Ratko Mladić.

Not only was Nikolić involved in logistics for the extermination of thousands of Bosniaks from the Srebrenica enclave; he also subsequently took part in the exhumation and reburial of the remains of these victims in secondary graves as a maneuver to conceal the original crime. Noting another cover-up, Nikolić testified that documents that would have provided evidence of the killing were also destroyed.[11]

Momir Nikolić appealed the length of his sentence, which was longer than what the prosecutors had recommended. In 2006 he won a reduction to twenty years. Nikolić has testified at important trials after the conclusion of his plea arrangement. During testimony in the trial of General Zdravko Tolimir he further described his motivations, apologizing in particular to "my students who were killed in the crimes in Srebrenica."[12]

SLOBODAN MILOŠEVIĆ'S ABORTED TRIAL

The trial of Slobodan Milošević began in early 2002 and promised to bring up critical questions related to the Srebrenica survivors' search for truth and justice. Milošević was president of Serbia and then of Yugoslavia between 1989 and 2000. In the capacity of his high position he bore personal responsibility for manipulating extreme nationalist sentiments among his Serb constituency, not only in Serbia, but also throughout those parts of Yugoslavia where there were Serb populations.

Milošević was charged with sixty-six counts of genocide and complicity in genocide, deportation, murder, persecution, crimes against humanity, plunder, attacks on civilians, and other grave breaches of the Geneva Conventions and violations of the laws or customs of war.[13] In short, he was charged with being the intellectual author of an entire range of abuses and atrocities that took place during the war. The hope and expectation among seekers of justice was that Milošević's trial would, above all, expose two facts: the involvement of the government of Serbia in the Bosnian war, and the commission of genocide not only in Srebrenica but in many other parts of Bosnia-Herzegovina. Unfortunately, Milošević's death from heart failure in a prison cell before the end of his trial thwarted these hopes.

The trial was handicapped from the beginning; nevertheless a modicum of truth was revealed, and some case history was created that could be called on in later trials. One handicap to the trial was Milošević's insistence on defending himself, coupled with the tribunal's ongoing patience with his courtroom behavior. Milošević turned his trial into a political forum primarily for the benefit of his followers back home; the court's forbearance with his strategy surpassed reasonable boundaries. Beyond compromising the dignity of the court, this dynamic prolonged the trial for so long that it was ultimately unable to conclude, because of the defendant's death.

The functioning of the prosecutor's case was also handicapped by virtue of the fact that throughout his leadership of the Yugoslav war effort, Milošević had been clever enough to avoid leaving a paper trail that would provide proof of his directing Yugoslav involvement in the war and the accompanying war crimes. Whether the trial could result in a genocide conviction was always in question. However, it was not possible to erase the public secret of the rump Yugoslavia's participation in the war, and of the Yugoslav regime's direct support of the Bosnian Serb separatists. In the course of the aborted trial, certain solid evidence and incriminating facts were revealed.

Evidence from a Human Rights Watch report illustrating Yugoslavia's support of the Bosnian Serb separatists in the war—and thereby incriminating Milošević—revealed "how leaders in Belgrade and the Federal Republic of Yugoslavia financed the wars; how they provided material to Croatian and Bosnian Serbs; and how they created administrative and personnel structures to support the Croatian Serb and Bosnian Serb armies. The report traces the mechanisms, some of which were previously secret, by which Belgrade fueled the conflicts."[14]

Another Human Rights Watch document, titled "Weighing the Evidence: Lessons from the Slobodan Milošević Trial," notes that the Serbian government was compelled to release evidence of its collusion with and support of Bosnian Serb separatists that had not previously been exposed. One witness testified, "The [Bosnian Serbs] relied almost entirely on the support they got from Serbia, from the officer corps, from the intelligence, from the pay, from the heavy weapons, from the antiaircraft arrangements."[15]

On rare occasions the direct participation of operatives from Serbia was not even concealed. In one instance that came to light during the trial in April 2005, an order by the Bosnian Serb interior minister directed special police from Serbia, stationed within Bosnia, to relocate to an area near Srebrenica to participate in the conquest of that enclave. The order was dated July 10, 1995, just a day before the fall of Srebrenica. It commanded units of the Serbian interior ministry police, based in Trnovo near Sarajevo, to move to Srebrenica.

While evidence that the Serbian units moved to Srebrenica was not subsequently produced, the fact that they were operating within Bosnia, a sovereign state, placed responsibility for Serbia's involvement in the Bosnian war on Milošević, the ultimate holder of authority over Serbia's police force. Even without evidence of his knowledge of the Serbian police operations in Bosnia, their presence was grounds for an accusation of crimes against humanity.[16]

A similar, but far more dramatic piece of evidence of Yugoslav collusion in the war—this time, directly related to the Srebrenica massacres—was presented at Milošević's trial. An amateur film showed the execution of six young captives from Srebrenica at the hands of members of the military organization from Serbia known as the Scorpions. Filmed by participants in the murders, the film was shared among soldiers, one of whom turned a copy over to Nataša Kandić, a human rights activist and head of the Belgrade-based Humanitarian Law Center. Kandić released the film to the ICTY, and it was shown as part of the proceedings during Milošević's trial early in June 2005.

The involvement of the Scorpions was another proof of direct Yugoslav military and police involvement in the Bosnian war. Detractors tried to assert that the Scorpions were a "paramilitary" unit operating on its own, but in fact they were part of the Red Berets, a formation of special police under the command of the Serbian Ministry of the Interior.

While the film had questionable impact on a doomed trial, its footage was made public and spread quickly beyond the sober courtrooms of The Hague. The film was shocking in its raw portrayal of the brutality committed in a casual manner by the killers, who were quite aware of being filmed. When the film was aired on Bosnian television, the mother of one of the young men whose murder was filmed recognized her son. When the film was aired in Serbia soon after, it shocked the part of the Serbian public that was willing to be confronted with factual evidence of the country's role in the atrocities. This was the first significant crack in the wall of denial and impunity that surrounded Serbia.[17]

Milošević himself never acknowledged the truth of the film, saying, "Those units had no connection to Serbia," and that there was "something suspicious" about the film, that it was "some kind of compilation."[18] But members of the Scorpions shown in the video to have participated in the murders were quickly arrested and put on trial in Serbia. Four members ultimately received sentences between four and twenty years in prison.[19]

On the whole, Milošević's aborted trial had a mixed effect on the development of justice with regards to Srebrenica and its tormented survivors. While it failed to result in a verdict, the proceedings did constitute an important step in revealing a body of evidence about the background to Srebrenica (as well as to the rest of the war in Bosnia-Herzegovina). It arguably succeeded in showing that Serbia and the rump Yugoslavia played a direct role in the destruction of Bosnia and in the atrocities at Srebrenica. But the trial's premature ending left open the question of Serbia's complicity in genocide, one of the thorniest issues in the whole thicket of "postconflict" justice.

In customary midtrial deliberations, the court rejected a motion to acquit Milošević of genocide. Two out of three of the court's three-judge panel felt that they had heard enough evidence to support the eventuality that they would convict Milošević of genocide. They agreed that all but one of the genocide charges should be retained, finding that "the prosecution could show a joint criminal enterprise existed, the aim of which was to commit genocide against Bosnian Muslims, and that its participants did indeed commit genocide in Brčko, Prijedor, Sanski Most, Srebrenica, Bijeljina, Ključ, and Bosanski Novi."[20]

Because of his early death, Milošević was convicted of neither genocide nor anything else. As of early 2006, more than ten years after the Srebrenica massacres, the results of legal proceedings pertaining to Srebrenica were mixed. Convictions were paltry, with only one related to genocide, for the time being. But the body of evidence enshrined in case history was growing. Krstić, a high officer in the VRS, was convicted of complicity in genocide; Nikolić and Obrenović pleaded guilty and provided crucial evidence, as did Erdemović; the Scorpion tape made a dent in Serbian indifference; Milošević's aborted trial provided evidence of participation in the war from abroad; and there was more to come.

LAWSUIT IN THE WORLD COURT

Another sort of deliberation, equally relevant to the campaign for justice in Srebrenica, was taking place at the International Court of Justice (ICJ). In 1993, while the war was still raging, the government of Bosnia filed a lawsuit against the rump state of Yugoslavia for genocide. The case gathered dust for thirteen years, until it was finally heard in early 2006.

The lawsuit argued that Yugoslavia had "planned, prepared, conspired, promoted, encouraged, aided and abetted and committed" genocide against the population of Bosnia-Herzegovina.[21] The government of Bosnia, as plaintiff in the case, called for reparations from Yugoslavia for war damages to its infrastructure and economy and to the property of private individuals.

The suit introduced evidence of numerous war crimes, including various massacres and the maintenance of concentration camps such as Omarska. It described war crimes that took place thus: "Serbia and Montenegro, through its agents and surrogates, has killed, murdered, wounded, raped, robbed, tortured, kidnapped, illegally detained, and exterminated the citizens of Bosnia and Herzegovina."[22] Events that took place after the suit was filed, such as the Srebrenica genocide, also became relevant to the case.

The Bosnian lawsuit was to be the first one pertaining to the UN Genocide Convention heard in the ICJ. As with other trials for genocide, proving genocidal intent at the highest level was going to be key. For Serbia and Montenegro (as the rump Yugoslavia was then called) to be found responsible for genocide, that state had to be shown to have been in control of the Army of the Republika Srpska as it was committing that crime in Bosnia.

Judges at the ICJ were able to review some of the publicly accessible material that was presented during the Milošević trial, such as the film of the Scorpions murder, and the letter revealing the presence of Serbian police within Bosnia upon the fall of Srebrenica. Other evidence amply illustrated Yugoslavia's financial and logistical support for the VRS. However, crucial evidence, in the form of minutes from the meetings of Serbia's Supreme Defense Council (SDC), was unavailable to the ICJ.

The Supreme Defense Council was the rump Yugoslavia's highest decision-making body at the time of the war. Formed in 1992, it was composed of the country's top military and political leaders, along with Bosnian Serb leaders of the war. The government of Yugoslavia had supplied the SDC minutes to the ICTY for use during the Milošević trial, on the condition that they not be shared with any other court.

It is probable that Yugoslavia wished to restrict access to the SDC minutes to avoid contributing to a decision in the ICJ lawsuit that would financially burden that country, potentially in the amount of billions of dollars. For that matter, a court decision finding Serbia-Montenegro responsible for the genocide, and thus implicitly defining the Republika Srpska as having been created through genocide, could reinforce calls for the abolition of that entity. But the decision on the part of the ICTY—supported by the US administration—to comply with this constraint was arguably irresponsible and became the subject of much speculation and criticism.

When the lawsuit came to court in February 2006, representatives of Yugoslavia argued that that country had had no intention of destroying the Muslim population of Bosnia, and that thus there was no genocide. Meanwhile, the legal team representing Bosnia stated that the ethnic cleansing and killing of tens of thousands of non-Serbs in that country was the result of a carefully laid plan. The team introduced footage from the Srebrenica massacres and the siege of Sarajevo and discussed verdicts from some of the ICTY trials in which defendants were convicted of such crimes as "mass forcible transfer."

To the argument that Yugoslavia had withdrawn its army in 1992, the plaintiffs responded, referring to the siege of Sarajevo, that "Belgrade was never absent during this longest siege in history."[23] General Richard Dannatt, commander of British troops in Bosnia toward the end of the war, argued that Belgrade was in control of Bosnian Serb forces, asserting not only that Serbia provided financial and logistical support for the war, but that operations that the VRS conducted were planned in Serbia. Dannatt also noted that Serbian and Bosnian Serb troops had carried out some of these operations together.[24]

The ICJ's hearings lasted nine weeks, and the court took another ten months for deliberation. During this period Montenegro seceded from its union with Serbia and argued that the lawsuit no longer pertained to it. The ICJ accepted this argument.

In the end, the ICJ delivered a mixed verdict that predominantly exonerated Serbia. While one part of the decision laid a modicum of blame on Serbia, the fifteen-member panel of judges rejected the charge of genocide, stating that it failed to find evidence of intent to commit genocide on the part of the state. Another element of the decision found that Serbia nevertheless "*violated the obligation to prevent genocide*, in respect of the genocide that occurred in Srebrenica in July 1995." The decision likewise found Serbia guilty of the same violation for not having turned over General Ratko Mladić, who was indicted for genocide.[25]

Thus, the ICJ affirmed ICTY rulings that genocide had been committed in Srebrenica, and that Serbia had supported the VRS logistically and financially. But while it was demonstrable that Serbia supported the war, this was not deemed equivalent to planning genocide.

The decision left Bosnian Serbs and Serbian officials relieved, even exultant that they would not be labeled a "pariah nation," nor be required to pay onerous reparations. Even though the decision was to find Serbia guilty of violating the Genocide Convention, Serbian nationalist commentators were able to overlook that serious finding and celebrate the decision. It made it easier for them to continue to assert, ignoring evidence to the contrary, that the Bosnian war had simply been the result of a long-standing conflict between ethnicities.

Meanwhile, the plaintiffs were gravely disappointed. One of the early proponents of the case had said, "If the Court establishes that a genocide has been committed, it would undermine the [1995] Dayton Accords built on that genocide. In that case, it would become clear that the RS must cease to exist."[26] But the campaign for the fulfillment of that vision of justice was thwarted.

The relatively mild ICJ decision did not move either of the resentful sides from their positions. Although the decision was primarily experienced as a defeat by the Bosniaks—especially by the Srebrenica survivors—their spokespersons held up the court's judgment that Serbia was in violation of the Genocide Convention, and its affirmation of the genocide in Srebrenica, as proof that the Republika Srpska was founded on the basis of the gravest crime and should thus be abolished.

One lingering conflict stemming from the ICJ lawsuit is the matter of the notes from the Supreme Defense Council meetings, which has remained controversial many years after the ICJ decision was rendered in 2007. During a subsequent ICTY trial, some of the SDC minutes were made public. Former chief of staff of the Yugoslav Army Momčilo Perišić was put on trial in 2008 for war crimes related to the siege of Sarajevo, the shelling of Zagreb, and other acts including murder and persecution.[27] Leading up to the closing arguments of that trial in the spring of 2011, the ICTY announced that it was lifting the seal on relevant documents including the SDC minutes, without objection from the Serbian government.

The minutes of the SDC meetings provided an extensive, theretofore "strictly confidential" record of top-level discussions of Serbia's intimate involvement in the wars in Bosnia and Croatia. Not only had the Serbian government retained on its payroll thousands of army officers stationed in Bosnia, but it also continued to transfer

Yugoslav Army personnel to Bosnia, and to provide "training, health insurance, and accommodation."[28]

The documents provided details about the establishment of "Personnel Centers" to provide support for officers all the way up to VRS commander General Ratko Mladić. In segments of the SDC notes leaked the previous year, it was revealed that Mladić was on the payroll of the Yugoslav Army all the way to 2002.

The leaks even revealed the outright admission by RS president Radovan Karadžić in 1994 that "without Serbia nothing would happen; we do not have the resources and we would not be in any condition to make war."[29]

On balance, surveying the significance of the case and its mixed resolution, the lawsuit satisfied no one and failed to achieve any of its intended results. Rather than aid the process of reconciliation as hoped for by some, the process just reinforced the feeling of victimhood on both sides.

The expectation that reconciliation could result from a finding of genocide was far-fetched. But the defeat of the lawsuit was still a defeat in the campaign for justice. The disappointment at this result was as great as that caused by the premature death of Slobodan Milošević before the conclusion of his trial.

NASER ORIĆ

Not only Serbs were sent to The Hague. As these trials were taking place, a handful of Croats were also convicted of war crimes, primarily for actions that took place during the Croat-Bosniak conflict. Likewise, a few Bosniaks were put on trial as well. The only Bosniak sent to the ICTY for actions related to Srebrenica was the most well-known commander in that enclave, Naser Orić.

Orić was the most prominent of a number of commanders operating independently of each other, and on occasion cooperating with each other, in the Srebrenica enclave. Orić had been responsible for leading missions to expand the enclave in late 1992, and he was in general a respected—and sometimes feared—figure in Srebrenica. His military role became less significant after the spring of 1993, when Srebrenica was declared a "safe area" and UN troops were stationed there. Orić was mysteriously removed from the enclave in March 1995, thus unable to participate in the failed defense of Srebrenica during the final attack in July of that year.

Orić's arrest and his lengthy trial brought up disturbing questions for those who survived the long siege and fall of Srebrenica. Orić was accused of command responsibility for a host of attacks on Serb villages in the vicinity of Srebrenica municipality, attacks that resulted in much destruction and numerous deaths.

Apologists for the Serb extremists referred to these attacks as the cause of the Srebrenica massacres, which they called a "retaliation." They ignored the context of the long-term siege of Srebrenica and the desperate conditions under which the enclave's trapped inhabitants lived. This pained the survivors, and the arrest of Orić looked to them like a way for the ICTY to present to the world an artificial "evenhandedness."

The leader of the Sarajevo-based Srebrenica survivors' organization, Munira Suba-šić, told me, "I can't say what happened with Orić, but I think that the truth is already known. Orić is a man who protected his people. If there is no right to do that, then there are no rights."[30]

In the spring of 2003, Orić was charged with five counts of war crimes for failure to prevent troops under his control from looting and burning villages, and similarly for failure to prevent the cruel treatment, including torture and murder, of Serbs who had been held captive in Srebrenica during the war.

Addressing the charges against Orić, Zulfo Salihović, who had participated in the defense of the Srebrenica enclave during the war, told me, "There is no material proof for the accusations that he committed crimes in Kravica. But he had to go to The Hague because of politics, for balance. I don't believe that he ordered killing. In Srebrenica in 1992, there was no legal continuity, no law. Actions were carried out in the interest of getting food, even though they ended with murder. Civilians were shooting. There was no food for forty thousand to fifty thousand people. There were actions where there were five hundred to one thousand people, with some soldiers. The civilians would follow, to get food. Those who have not been hungry can't understand what happened there."[31]

During Orić's trial, the prosecution depicted him as a ruthless "warlord" who was "drunk with power," and determined to practice ethnic cleansing against all the Serb villages within his reach. The defense insisted on illustrating the context of the siege and accompanying starvation and chaos, wherein as many as seventy thousand people were packed into the enclave, subjected to daily bombardment, and left with precious little to eat. They pointed out that between March 1992 and April 1993, only one convoy of around twenty trucks was allowed through to the Srebrenica enclave to provide food and medicine.[32]

Among the main points that the defense presented were, first, that Orić was not the de facto commander of all fighters in the Srebrenica enclave, and that chaos reigned when it came to military resistance to the siege. Second, conditions of starvation caused people to be so desperate that, as Bosniak troops were trying to extend the amount of territory under their control, civilians followed them and there was nothing to prevent them from looting food in Serb villages.

One point of contention during the trial was whether the targets of the Bosniak offensives were military or not. The most well-known target was Kravica, on the main road between Bratunac and Zvornik. There, on Orthodox Christmas day in January 1993, Orić's men attacked an unprepared Serb population and dispersed them, burning many homes and killing dozens of people, both soldiers and civilians. Orić's defense argued that Kravica was inhabited by a significant military detachment, but this did not negate the fact that civilians—and soldiers—were involved in looting, and that the attackers harmed civilian inhabitants.

One defense witness after another affirmed that Naser Orić had not functionally been the commander of all other commanders, even though he had officially been designated as such during one staff meeting.

Overall, the prosecution presented a weak case. Its assertion that Orić was supreme commander of troops in the Srebrenica enclave was not convincing. In addition, witnesses from among the Serbs held captive in Srebrenica did not prove that Orić was involved in their mistreatment. They did recount brutal treatment by guards in Srebrenica—but they did not associate this treatment with Orić.

Furthermore, the weak preparation of the prosecution's case was underlined by the fact that some of its witnesses gave conflicting testimony. When the prosecutors finished presenting their case Emir Suljagić, then working as a journalist at The Hague, commented, "This is one of the sloppiest trials I have seen so far at the tribunal."[33] In June 2005, judges dropped two of the six charges against Orić related to the plundering of public and private property.

The trial continued until the spring of 2006, with the prosecution requesting an eighteen-year sentence and the defense calling for acquittal. In the end, Orić was convicted solely of the charge of failure to prevent the mistreatment and murder of Serb prisoners. He was sentenced to two years' in prison and, since he had already been held in custody for three years, was released immediately.

Orić's partial conviction was then overturned in mid-2008 when the Appeals Court at The Hague found that the prosecution had not supplied sufficient evidence that Orić knew that his subordinates had committed war crimes. While Orić returned from The Hague to a second hero's welcome, the highest officials of Serbia and of the Republika Srpska slammed the decision.

The Orić episode left most Serbs entrenched in their defensive position that the ICTY was an "anti-Serb" court, and most Bosniaks convinced that the court made a weak attempt to show fairness by prosecuting a hero.

Orić landed on his feet in Tuzla toward the end of the war and embarked on a new career. Following the pattern of some other war heroes, he became involved in suspicious business activities and garnered a reputation as the leader of Tuzla's gangster clan.[34] Later arrests and trials of Orić for racketeering and illegal possession of weapons seemed to support this reputation. He was sentenced in 2009 to two years in prison on an illegal weapons charge. But the trajectory of his life after the war was as much a reflection of the pervasive criminality in the failed state of Bosnia as it was a result of all that happened during the war.

In early 2016 Orić found himself before the Bosnian state court for war crimes, charged with the 1992 killing of three Serb captives in the Srebrenica enclave. He had appealed to the ICTY to release him from these charges in light of his previous acquittal, but that court deemed the new case to refer to "fundamentally different" events.[35]

The first instance trial, that is, delivering a verdict that was nonbinding pending appeal, was concluded in late 2017, with yet another acquittal of Orić, with the presiding judge finding insufficient evidence for a conviction. This outcome, predictably, outraged public figures among the Serbs and pleased survivors from Srebrenica. However, the acquittal was overturned on appeal, and a retrial was commenced in the fall of 2018. The retrial also ended in an acquittal, when the presiding judge in the state Appeals Court found that the main witness testifying against Orić was inconsistent and not credible. The decision was not subject to appeal.

SLOW JUSTICE: FURTHER TRIALS CONNECTED TO SREBRENICA

As the 2000s wore on, trials regarding Srebrenica continued to be processed at the ICTY, resulting in several significant convictions.

The year 2010 saw the very significant conviction for genocide of seven higher-level officers in the *Popović et al.* case. Former chief of staff of the Yugoslav Army Momčilo Perišić was convicted in 2011 of aiding and abetting war crimes in Croatia and Bosnia-Herzegovina. And former senior commander of the Bosnian Serb army Zdravko Tolimir was convicted of genocide in late 2012.

These convictions in the ICTY, while providing a measure of hope and a sense of justice to the victims, were only "first instance" convictions. They would ultimately be subject to drawn-out appeals, with unpredictable outcomes.

Prosecutions for the Kravica massacre were slow to develop, but the crime was included in the trials of higher-ranking officers that gradually came before the court in the 2000s. Kravica, a Serb-populated village in Bratunac municipality, where several dozen Serb soldiers and civilians were killed when it was attacked by troops led by Naser Orić, was also the location of one of the largest massacres perpetrated during the fall of Srebrenica in July 1995.

On the night of July 12, approximately one thousand prisoners held captive in a warehouse were executed without warning by their guards. For four hours, guards shot with automatic rifles into the warehouse at the mass of prisoners and also threw hand grenades into the building.[36]

Lower officers and soldiers who were directly involved in the massacre faced prosecution. Between 2008 and 2012 more than a dozen men were convicted of participation.

Meanwhile, a far-reaching trial of higher officers at The Hague, covering Kravica and the broader catalogue of atrocities associated with Srebrenica, concluded in June 2010. In the case of *Popović et al.*, the International Criminal Tribunal for the former Yugoslavia convicted seven men for charges ranging up to genocide.

The seven men had been in the top levels of command that oversaw the massacres. Two received life sentences for genocide, and all seven were convicted of crimes against humanity (or aiding and abetting such crimes) and violation of the laws and conventions of war.

The ICTY's decision was significant because it reinforced other somewhat less definitive court findings about genocide. General Radislav Krstić had earlier been convicted of genocide, but on appeal, his conviction was reduced to that of "aiding and abetting" genocide. The *Popović et al.* convictions attached specific names to the authorship of the crime.

The four-year-long trial laid bare the full extent of the defendants' plans and actions in what the prosecutor termed a joint criminal enterprise to remove the Muslim population from Srebrenica and Žepa, and to murder the able-bodied Muslim men.[37] Witnesses described how Bosnian Serb forces lined up tanks to shell the forest where men were trying to escape, and how thousands of men were captured and detained in holding centers. Several chance survivors of mass executions described those events in painful detail. Survivors testified as to the presence of top officers, including Krstić, Vinko Pandurević, and Ratko Mladić, at the executions.

Attorneys for the defense claimed there was no evidence that the Bosnian Serb army command "ever took any decision to murder all men and young males from Srebrenica."[38] They said their clients bore no responsibility for the crimes. Calling for acquittal, they also denied that genocide had taken place in Srebrenica.

After a long deliberation, in 2010 the court found Vujadin Popović and Ljubiša Beara guilty of genocide and sentenced them to life imprisonment. Drago Nikolić received thirty-five years for aiding and abetting genocide. The other four officers were sentenced to prison terms ranging from five to nineteen years for committing (or aiding) crimes against humanity. On appeal, the convictions were upheld and made binding in 2015.

PERIŠIĆ

While the *Popović et al.* trial was taking place, another equally important trial began, that of Momčilo Perišić, who was chief of staff of the Yugoslav Army from 1993 to 1998, including a critical period during the Bosnian war. Given that Perišić was the highest Yugoslav military figure to be tried at the ICTY, his trial was expected to clarify the relationship between the Belgrade leadership and wartime events, not only in Bosnia-Herzegovina, but in Croatia as well.

Perišić was described as a "key figure in the murky relationship between Yugoslavia proper and its armed forces and the Bosnian Serbs, whom Yugoslavia furnished with arms, funds, men and materiel."[39] He was charged with war crimes and crimes against humanity for acts committed by officers under his command. Those acts included murder, extermination, and persecution of civilians, notably including the siege of Sarajevo and the Srebrenica massacres. Perišić pleaded not guilty to the charges.

During the trial, the prosecutor worked to demonstrate not only that Perišić had command responsibility for subordinates who were involved in these crimes, but that he directly participated in the "planning and execution of a military campaign of artillery, mortar shelling and sniping on civilian areas of Sarajevo," including "aiding and abetting the Bosnian Serb siege of Sarajevo, and the Bosnian Serb forces which massacred up to 8,000 Muslim men and boys after the fall of Srebrenica in July 1995."[40]

Evidence that was submitted in the trial showed that Perišić had created the "Thirtieth Personnel Center" as a mechanism to deploy his subordinates from the Yugoslav Army covertly in Bosnia. Members of the Thirtieth Personnel Center were involved in the Srebrenica massacres. These included the seven officers convicted in *Popović et al.* All these figures were on the payroll of the Yugoslav Army. Given this, prosecutors argued that Perišić must have known of the crimes that his subordinates were committing.

At the time of the fall of Srebrenica, Western intelligence operatives intercepted radio conversations with Perišić instructing Ratko Mladić on how to attack the enclave.[41]

Dražen Erdemović testified in the Perišić trial that members of his unit, the Tenth Sabotage Detachment, went to Serbia for military training. A second training session was provided by officers of the Yugoslav Army in the Republika Srpska. Erdemović described how, upon entry into the RS from Serbia, officers from the Yugoslav Army switched the license plates on their vehicles, attaching Republika Srpska plates so as to avoid detection as military interlopers from a foreign country.

In the course of the nearly three-year trial, prosecutors made the case that units of the Yugoslav Army were very well integrated into the Bosnian Serb army; that Yugoslavia provided crucial logistical support and supplies to the Serbs; and that Perišić participated intimately in the war crimes that the Bosnian Serbs committed.

The verdict issued in September 2011 found Perišić guilty on twelve out of thirteen counts, including crimes against humanity and war crimes, such as "aiding and abetting murders, inhumane acts, persecutions on political, racial or religious grounds, and attacks on civilians in Sarajevo and Srebrenica." He was also found guilty of failure to punish his subordinates for their commission of war crimes. Perišić was sentenced to twenty-seven years in prison.[42]

Perišić filed an appeal in late 2011. He admitted that he had participated in the support of the Bosnian Serb army; however, he denied that he had any knowledge of the war crimes that had been committed. Perišić criticized the judges of the ICTY for "criminalizing" war, saying, "If the ruling remains, every commander and national leader who gives military assistance to a foreign country or a third party in an international armed conflict will be considered responsible for aiding and abetting crimes by the very act of helping in waging war."[43]

TOLIMIR

A year after Perišić was convicted, another important verdict was handed down in the case of Zdravko Tolimir. A former assistant commander for intelligence and security of the Bosnian Serb army, Tolimir had been the third most wanted fugitive sought by the ICTY after Radovan Karadžić and Ratko Mladić. He had been one of General Mladić's closest wartime colleagues. Prosecutors considered Tolimir, Karadžić, and

Mladić to be the figures most responsible for the atrocities committed upon the fall of Srebrenica.[44]

Tolimir's intelligence and security authorities were vested in him as a member of the Main Staff of the Bosnian Serb army. According to testimony by Radislav Krstić, Tolimir had been a member of a group of officers "hand-picked" by Mladić to oversee the military operation in Srebrenica. Krstić asserted that these officers were the "main order-makers and executioners of everything that took place between 12 and 20 July 1995."[45]

Tolimir's indictment accused him of overseeing the notorious massacre of more than fifteen hundred Muslims from the Srebrenica enclave at Pilica. He was also suspected of having directed the support network for the fugitive Mladić for several years after Mladić went into hiding.

Apprehended in May 2007, Tolimir was charged with war crimes and crimes against humanity, including genocide, conspiracy to commit genocide, murder, and extermination. The genocide charge against Tolimir referred not only to the crimes committed at Srebrenica, but also to the subsequent expulsion of the Muslim population of nearby Žepa.

Tolimir's trial started in 2010 and lasted for two years. His prosecutor characterized him as "making sure that the murder operation did its evil work until the last bullet was fired and the last body was buried."[46] In the course of the trial one witness after another testified about the executions around Srebrenica and illustrated a pattern of the capture, detention, and murder of thousands of men fleeing from the fallen enclave.

In his defense, Tolimir asserted that the formation of the column of men fleeing the Srebrenica enclave was actually a military offensive and, as such, was a legitimate military target.[47] He also denied that the execution of captured prisoners from Srebrenica was a preplanned operation, saying that he was not aware of the killings as they were taking place, and insisted that the Bosnian Serb army treated prisoners in a correct manner.[48]

In December 2012, the ICTY found Zdravko Tolimir guilty; he was sentenced to life imprisonment for genocide, crimes against humanity, and murder as a violation of the laws or customs of war, as well as extermination, persecutions, and inhumane acts through forcible transfer. It is significant that the court found Tolimir guilty of genocide in connection with Žepa as well as with Srebrenica, because the crime there involved mass expulsion, rather than mass murder. This conviction helped to reinforce the fact that the legal definition of genocide does not involve numbers, but the "intent to destroy, in whole or in part, a national, ethnical, racial or religious group."[49]

Tolimir appealed the court decision, but in April 2015 the second-instance court confirmed his conviction and authorized his life sentence as well.

In years to come, the legal case history partially described above will be helpful to historians and students of crime and justice in the former Yugoslavia. But those who have stated that "justice is the first step toward reconciliation" have been disappointed.

An expression of contrition or empathy on the part of the supporters of the convicted war criminals—not only among the Serbs but also among the Croats and Bosniaks—has been exceedingly rare. The denialism practiced in the courtroom has its echo in the home media.

JUSTICE DELAYED, CONFUSED, DENIED: SOME LEGAL DETOURS

After the disposition of the cases described above, subsequent developments served up a series of confusing events in the courts. Upon the reversal of some first-instance ICTY verdicts on appeal, and with the surprise acquittal of other accused war criminals in the first-instance judgment, the response among advocates for justice ranged from perplexity to outrage. The reliability, the impartiality, and even the rationality of the judicial process were called into question.

In February 2013, the Appeals Chamber of the ICTY reversed the guilty conviction of Momčilo Perišić, setting him free. From 1993, that is, during much of the Bosnian war, Perišić had been chief of staff of the Yugoslav Army. Evidence presented during his trial showed that he had wielded command responsibility for subordinates who were involved in war crimes in Bosnia and that he directly participated in the planning and execution of the siege of Sarajevo, and had provided military support to the forces that conquered Srebrenica and committed the genocide there. This support was characteristic of the relationship between the Serbian regime in Belgrade and the Republika Srpska from the beginning of the war until quite some years afterward.

In the face of the compelling evidence that had led to Perišić's conviction, the startling decision of the Appeals Chamber hinged on one legal issue: that of "specific direction." The principle of specific direction holds that aiding and abetting war crimes by, for example, providing weapons, can be proven only if there is evidence of explicit instructions to use the weapons to commit certain crimes. In this thinking, it is not sufficient for it to be implicitly obvious that the weapons were going to be used to commit those crimes; the explicitly expressed intent that they were to be thus used must be demonstrable.

The majority in the five-member Appeals Chamber, headed by ICTY president Judge Theodor Meron, decided that the evidence in Perišić's original trial had not proven conclusively that Perišić had explicitly directed Serbia's assistance to be used in the commission of the war crimes. The fact that the aid to Bosnian Serb forces was indeed used in ethnic cleansing, mass murder, and long-term perpetration of terror against civilians was in the end deemed irrelevant to Perišić's command responsibility or personal involvement in the crimes.

In the Perišić case, the ICTY Appeals Chamber found that since it did not see proof of specific direction from Perišić in the case of provision of military support to the VRS, that support therefore constituted "general assistance that could be used for both lawful and unlawful activities." As such, the court could not fault Perišić for crimes committed by the VRS. As sociologist and commentator Eric Gordy wrote, "By this standard, the only way that Perišić's conviction [could have] been upheld would have been with evidence that showed him telling the VRS, 'here is some money, weapons and personnel, please use them to commit crimes.'"[50]

The acquittal of Perišić was greeted with celebration in Serbia, where the prime minister said that it "proved there was no aggression by the Yugoslav army against Bosnia and Croatia." On the other hand, Sandra Orlović, director of the Humanitarian Law Center in Belgrade, said, "Perišić was the personification of Serbia's institution-alised support for these two armies. I should note that . . . individual responsibility was not established, nor did the judges' explanation of their ruling deny the fact that the Yugoslav army supported the VRS . . . for years."[51]

A similarly confounding decision was reached in the trial of Jovica Stanišić and Franko Simatović, which lasted from mid-2009 to May 2013. Stanišić was head of the State Security Service of the Serbian Ministry of the Interior throughout most of the 1990s, and Simatović, as commander of that agency's Special Operations Unit, was Stanišić's close colleague. The two were accused of establishing, organizing, and financing training centers for Serb forces, in order to carry out military activities in Croatia and Bosnia-Herzegovina.

Stanišić and Simatović were charged with having participated in a joint criminal enterprise that, as their indictment read, "directed, organised, equipped, trained, armed and financed units of the Serbian State Security Service which murdered, persecuted, deported and forcibly transferred non-Serb civilians from Bosnia and Herzegovina (BiH) and Croatia between 1991 and 1995."[52]

The trial was one of the last opportunities for the ICTY, after the midtrial death of Milošević and the acquittal of Perišić, to prove and convict Serbian officials for their involvement in Serbia's fomenting of the aggression in Bosnia and in Croatia.

The trial proved this involvement. For example, Slobodan Lazarević, a former Serbian counterintelligence operative, testified about the role of Stanišić and Simatović. Repeating what he had said at the aborted trial of Milošević, Lazarević stated that "all military, police and political structures of the Republika Srpska Krajina [Serb rebel–held territory in Croatia] . . . were controlled from Belgrade."[53]

Nevertheless, on May 30, 2013, at the end of the trial, the three-member Trial Chamber headed by Judge Alphons Orie acquitted Stanišić and Simatović by a two-to-one majority. The judges agreed that the two men had supported military units in Croatia and Bosnia financially and logistically, and that they provided assistance to those committing murder, deportation, and other forms of persecution. But the court, again calling on the principle of specific direction, failed to find evidence of Stanišić's and Simatović's intent to participate in a joint criminal enterprise to commit those crimes.

Even the fact that the two men "must have known that the members of that unit killed and expelled civilians in 1992 in Bosanski Šamac and then carried out the deportations and forcible transfers in Doboj," as the judges acknowledged, was not deemed to be evidence that they had ordered the crimes. And where the Trial Chamber accepted the fact that Stanišić and Simatović had helped plan an attack on a village, the judges stated that it had not been established that the attack had actually taken place.[54]

Judge Orie found Stanišić's and Simatović's support of military units in Croatia to be of a "general nature," rather than given with the purpose of facilitating war crimes, and said that it was "not possible to conclude that the defendants shared the aim of the alleged joint criminal enterprise of forcibly removing the non-Serb civilian population."[55]

As with the Perišić decision, the acquittal of Stanišić and Simatović pleased Serb nationalists and stunned advocates for justice in Bosnia-Herzegovina, especially the victims of war crimes. In Serbia, head of the Helsinki Human Rights Committee Sonja Biserko said, "It now looks like the Serbs in Bosnia organised this war all by themselves, and that Serbia wasn't involved at all." She noted ironically, "Yet here in Serbia we have 400,000 veterans of the war. These are facts that cannot be overlooked."[56]

British Columbia law professor James G. Stewart weighed in on the specific direction criterion, saying that it had "no basis in customary international law or scholarly thought." Relating the results of a study of 362 international cases involving aiding and abetting, Stewart concluded that specific direction was not mentioned at all in the vast majority of cases—98 percent of them—or mentioned only in passing. He noted that prior to the Perišić case, no war crimes suspect had been acquitted for lack of specific direction of assistance in an international crime. He also found that in academic literature concerning international crime, there was no conspicuous mention of specific direction as an important element of complicity in a crime.[57]

In late 2015 the ICTY Appeals Chamber overturned the acquittal of Stanišić and Simatović and ordered a retrial. The five-judge panel accepted several appeals claims by the prosecution, including the assertion that the "specific direction" criterion was used inappropriately in the first trial.[58] The new trial began in June 2017 under the auspices of the Mechanism for International Criminal Tribunals (MICT), the successor to the now-closed ICTY. The retrial was still underway in 2019.

There is a point where law becomes so abstract, and prosecution becomes so circuitous, that the connection between law and justice seems to be lost. The judgments sowed confusion and reduced confidence in the tribunal as a legal institution. Survivor Sabaheta Fejzić said, "That is no longer a court, that is an institution that does good deeds for those who committed crimes. I no longer believe in the Hague Tribunal, because this [the acquittal of Momčilo Perišić] is a political decision."[59]

Politics certainly appear to have been involved in the functioning of the ICTY, from the time of its creation to the end. But another important factor in the court's apparent weakness and capricious nature of its findings is simply the fact that different judges presided over different cases, and they clearly did not unify their strategies with regard to the matter of genocide and related issues. This led to results that seem confusing or contradictory when reviewed from a distance; one obvious contradiction is the fact that there were convictions of genocide for officers who were lower in rank than other officers who were convicted of lesser charges.[60]

THE TRIALS OF RADOVAN KARADŽIĆ AND RATKO MLADIĆ

It is important to mention the outcome of the first-instance trials of Radovan Karadžić and General Ratko Mladić. Both figures lived as fugitives for quite some years after the war's end; Karadžić was apprehended in 2008 and Mladić in 2011. Karadžić's trial was finished in 2016, and Mladić's in November 2017.

Both men were charged with crimes against humanity; persecution; participation in several joint criminal enterprises; violation of the laws and customs of war; and genocide. Each was charged with two counts of genocide: one pertaining to Srebrenica, and the other pertaining to ten other municipalities: Bratunac, Brčko, Foča, Ključ, Kotor-Varoš, Prijedor, Sanski Most, Višegrad, Vlasenica, and Zvornik. (In both cases the number of municipalities was later reduced.) The defendants' charges also included the siege of Sarajevo and the establishment of many concentration camps.

The two trials had similar conclusions: both Mladić and Karadžić were convicted of genocide in Srebrenica, but not in the other municipalities. Few on any side of the issue were satisfied with the partial convictions for genocide. Even the Srebrenica survivors felt only partial satisfaction; upon the conviction of Ratko Mladić former mayor of Srebrenica Ćamil Duraković stated, "I think we can be partially pleased with the life sentence for the person most responsible of commanding the army that committed all those crimes, on the order of politicians, but not with the fact that genocide hasn't been confirmed in other places."[61]

Mladić's and Karadžić's convictions were appealed by both the prosecution and the defendants, with Karadžić's convictions upheld in the spring of 2019 (with an increased sentence), and with the Mladić decision still pending in mid-2019.

DOMESTIC TRIALS; FRUSTRATION OF JUSTICE

While the ICTY was operating, a war crimes court was established in Bosnia-Herzegovina to try numerous lesser cases. The record showed that in the eight-year history of the Bosnian war crimes court between 2005 and 2013, it had tried more than two hundred war crimes cases, but that there were still thirteen hundred cases pending.[62]

All the above-mentioned U-turns in justice took place at a time when many survivors were still waiting for news of their missing relatives; new mass graves were still being discovered; and an untold number of war criminals were still walking free in Bosnia and abroad. Trust in both the Bosnian court and the Hague Tribunal were at a new low. In early 2014, out of seventy-four people convicted at the ICTY, forty-nine were already free.[63] One commentator wrote to me, "Of the people convicted by ICTY, 66.2 percent have now been freed. Of the people they killed, 100 percent are still dead."

Meanwhile, justice has also been thwarted to a significant extent in the domestic courts. Among other causes, numerous persons suspected of war crimes have fled to Serbia and have found a haven there, safe from extradition or local prosecution. These include Milorad Pelemiš, former commander of the Tenth Sabotage Detachment of the Bosnian Serb army, which was responsible for the massacre at Branjevo, and Tomislav Kovač, wartime minister of the interior. Both men, along with a half dozen others, have been charged with genocide.[64]

The victims are focused on absolute justice. One essay that was published shortly after the Perišić acquittal commented that "the ICTY fostered unrealistic hopes of local communities that their individual and collective suffering would be fully acknowledged and addressed through convicting those directly responsible and those who designed policies that led to war crimes being committed. Furthermore, the ICTY was projected as the institution that could and would dispense absolute justice to all those who were wronged."[65]

In the Srebrenica area alone, thousands of people had committed war crimes. When the appeal of Vujadin Popović and Ljubiša Beara was rejected in 2015, the March First Coalition, a grassroots human rights organization, recalled that the 2004 report by the Srebrenica Commission had listed the names of 810 participants in the war crimes. In an announcement marking the genocide conviction for Popović and Beara, the organization noted that some four hundred of those people were still employed in various public service jobs.[66]

At the same time, hundreds of individuals had participated not only in logistical support, but in the intellectual authorship of those crimes. With the ICTY strained for resources, there is no court in the world with the capacity to handle such a load.

The failure of judicial bodies at any level to grapple with the source of the war crimes is not simply a matter of lack of resources but, also, a lack of political will. And the lack of interest in pursuing justice to greater ends cannot entirely be ascribed to inattention nor even lack of institutional capacity. The international laws and conventions that apply to political responsibility for crimes exist and could be implemented, if the desire existed. No, the failure of the most powerful nations in the world to enforce the ideals that they have enshrined through international law must be explained as a manifestation of conflict of interest.

That is, on one hand, the powerful states of the world express an interest in upholding the principles that are delineated, for example, in the Universal Declaration of Human Rights and the UN Conventions on Genocide and on Apartheid. But the same states are more concerned with maintaining the orderly conduct of business among countries that do not respect those principles. As a result of this conflict of interests, it is the victims of gross violations of human rights who seem to lose out every time, as one dictator after another, and one authoritarian regime after another, is deemed an entity "we can do business with."

Eric Gordy weighed in on this subject, commenting that "the interests of the powerful states in the Balkans and powerful states in the world converge" in the failure to cross certain lines in the prosecution of crimes committed during the wars of the 1990s. Those lines dictate that the lower level of perpetrators receive punishment but, as Gordy put it, "the barriers to justice get higher the higher one reaches up the chain of command."[67]

The result of such discrimination in prosecution is that the broader picture of the crimes of war is seen as a succession of unconnected incidents, rather than as a process orchestrated (and supported) from central positions of authority. The failure to work toward a closer examination and a coherent understanding of the nature of the nationalist regimes that fomented the war enables the powerful states of the world, ultimately, to ignore the criminal nature of those regimes.

All this, of course, describes realpolitik and a mindset that prevents the greater powers from recognizing genocide and taking the responsibility to prevent it. It is the same mindset that, during the Dayton negotiations, ended the war, partitioned the state, and confoundingly allowed one entity to be named after one ethnicity, while simultaneously enshrining equal rights for all ethnicities throughout Bosnia-Herzegovina. In other words, it is the blinkered mindset that equates the lack of war with peace but, in reality, leaves the conditions in place for ongoing conflict.

A NOTE ABOUT "RECONCILIATION"

This chapter has discussed some of the more important court cases dealing with major war crimes. Prosecution of war criminals is an integral component of justice. In this vein, people who are not closely involved with the survivors of those war crimes, and who are not particularly acquainted with the nature of postwar life in Bosnia-Herzegovina, often think of the process of recovery (of which the struggle for justice is an important part) in abstract terms. One of those abstractions is the idea that justice leads to reconciliation.

As an outside observer to activism in promotion of justice in Bosnia-Herzegovina, I have avoided using the word "reconciliation." Outsiders who use this word are, it seems, more often than not either careerists, politicians, or simply people who are not informed as to the entire sequence of steps that are necessary to take before reconciliation can even be approached. For such people, "reconciliation" is not much more than the vague, feel-good representation of a goal.

It is for those who may eventually be reconciled to think about ways to promote that goal, if and when it seems possible. But it is clear that the revelation of the truth about war crimes and the achievement of justice, to the maximum extent possible, are significant prerequisites to the accomplishment of any reconciliation.

8

Reporting History

RECKONING VERSUS DENIAL

SURVIVORS FROM SREBRENICA HAVE TOLD ME, "THERE IS enough blame to go around the whole world."

After the fall of Srebrenica and after the end of the war, the various actors involved in the debacle at Srebrenica worked in various ways, always slowly, to come to terms with their responsibility for what Bosnians sometimes call a crime of "planetary" proportions. The French, the Dutch, the UN, and the Republika Srpska each reported on their own involvement, providing their own interpretation of events. Each report—with the partial exception of that of the UN—avoided blame and shifted it elsewhere.

On November 15, 1999, UN Secretary General Kofi Annan issued the first significant report on the crimes at Srebrenica. From 1993 to 1996, Annan had worked as undersecretary general for UN peacekeeping operations in Bosnia, and he was made head of the UN in 1997. The UN General Assembly ordered the report in late 1998.

The 113-page report, detailing the events leading to the fall of the Srebrenica enclave, found that the UN demonstrated institutional failings and errors of judgment in allowing the enclave to fall. While assigning the preponderance of guilt for the atrocities to the Bosnian Serb forces, Annan's report admitted that the UN leadership, UN forces in the enclave, and the Contact Group (a monitoring group of diplomats from five nations)[1] lacked a realistic understanding of what the Serb forces were prepared to do.

The UN Protection Force was extremely reluctant to exercise military force in order to protect the "safe areas" that it had established. The UN member states that were involved in Srebrenica were not able to agree on a coherent and robust strategy for defense of the Srebrenica enclave. The UN was prepared to base a few hundred armed soldiers at Potočari, but it was not prepared to provide the necessary logistical support that would have enabled them to save Srebrenica.

In his report, Kofi Annan stated, "The cardinal lesson of Srebrenica is that a deliberate and systematic attempt to terrorize, expel or murder an entire people must be met, decisively, with all necessary means, and with the political will to carry the policy through to its logical conclusion."[2]

The report noted that it was a critical error to place peacekeeping forces in a situation where there was no peace and, at that, to try to do so when there was no strategic agreement with the besiegers of Srebrenica about the UN's presence there. Annan admitted, "We tried to keep the peace and apply the rules of peacekeeping when there was no peace to keep."[3]

A serious shortcoming in the UN's approach during the war was its official stance of neutrality; in order to defend the enclave in an effective manner, it would have needed to acknowledge the fact that there was an aggressor and a victim in this situation. Annan's report admitted that international officials viewed Serb forces and the inhabitants of Srebrenica through a prism of "moral equivalency through which the conflict in Bosnia was viewed by too many for too long."[4]

Annan also acknowledged that the international arms embargo, decreed by the UN in 1991, left the pro-Bosnian forces without weapons with which to defend themselves. Nor did the "safe areas" that the UN established keep people safe; of the approximately one hundred thousand people killed during the war, some twenty thousand of them were killed in or near the safe areas—as were most of the 117 UN troops who were killed in Bosnia.[5]

The report noted that UN officials working in Bosnia during the war failed to provide their superiors in New York with a realistic picture of the gravity of the situation in the Srebrenica enclave. Annan concluded that "negotiations with Bosnian Serb General Ratko Mladić at various times during the war amounted to appeasement,"[6] and, finally, "even in the most restrictive interpretation of the mandate, the use of close air support against attacking Serb targets was clearly warranted. The Serbs were firing directly at Dutch observation posts with tank rounds as early as five days before the enclave fell."[7]

Overall, the UN report broke precedent with its level of self-criticism. It provided clarification, for the historical record, regarding the fall of Srebrenica. Coming before the delayed series of court cases, this was an early step forward in uncovering the truth about the crimes. However, while criticizing the decision-making mechanisms and other failures of the institution, it did not assess the conscious decisions leading to the abandonment of the enclave to the Serb forces, and it was not sufficient to satisfy the organizations of Srebrenica survivors. An early attempt at litigation on their part involved a request to chief prosecutor of the ICTY Carla Del Ponte, calling on that court to prosecute top UN officials and Dutch military officials.[8] Del Ponte rejected this request, but there would be subsequent attempts to call the Dutch government and the UN to task.

"THE NETHERLANDS IS NOT GUILTY, BUT IT IS TO BLAME": DUTCH REPORTS ON SREBRENICA

The government of Holland also commissioned a report on the fall of Srebrenica, but it was not released until long after the UN report. In late 1996 the government engaged the Dutch Institute for War Documentation (Nederlands Instituut voor Oorlogsdocumentatie or NIOD) to undertake a full inquiry. No deadline was set for the project, and many years were to pass before publication of the report.

The NIOD report finally came out in April 2002, a cumbersome multivolume set running to some seventy-six hundred pages. While somewhat chaotic in organization and dauntingly long, the report's overall thrust was easy on the Dutch government. An official summary of the report that was released for the press began by assigning the bulk of the guilt for the genocide to the Serb political leaders, acknowledging that the international intervention suffered from "muddling on," and noting that the "safe area" concept was an ill-defined notion that ruled out an effective military defense of the enclave. The report described the Netherlands' motivation for participation in the defense of the enclave as founded both on humanitarian principles and on political ambition, adding that the Dutch went into the enclave without fully understanding the local situation.[9]

The report criticized the Dutchbat mandate as very unclear, with a role of keeping peace where there was no peace, with a lack of in-depth information or training, with "misplaced confidence in readiness to deploy air strikes," without any exit strategy, and "virtually without military and political intelligence work to gauge the political and military intentions of the warring parties."[10]

The report also acknowledged that Dutchbat was uninformed when it arrived at its Potočari base and made little attempt to add to its knowledge. Troops lacked motivation, and they assimilated prejudices against the people they were supposed to protect. The Dutch force is portrayed as navigating a tenuous balance between local forces and the surrounding Serbs, and the summary denies that there were clear indications of a planned Serb takeover of the Srebrenica enclave.

Dutchbat forces were in no way sufficient to rebuff a serious Serb assault and thus relied on international intervention from the air. Srebrenica fell when Dutchbat offered no resistance to escalating attacks, and when Serb forces saw that such resistance from the air was not forthcoming. The NIOD report further excuses UN commander-in-chief General Janvier for having blocked air strikes, with the explanation that Janvier was unwilling to endanger international troops on the ground—and he had also already advocated, to the UN, relinquishing the eastern enclaves in order to support stronger international action.

The summary of the report goes on to describe the flight of refugees from the Srebrenica enclave and to discuss the ensuing massacres. It explains the collaboration of Dutch troops in the evacuation of the refugees, including participation in the separation of the men from the rest of the population, as a way to "avoid a humanitarian disaster." Deputy Commander Franken was quoted as saying that he had not recognized the "danger of excesses" and excused Dutchbat's refusal to protect nonstaff inhabitants of the enclave, citing fear of their discovery and reprisal by conquering Serb forces.[11]

On the whole, the NIOD report was partially apologetic, recognizing systemic failings of the UNPROFOR effort in Srebrenica from the level of the Dutchbat all the way up to the heights of the Dutch government. At the same time, it tended to deflect criticism in the direction of the UN. And the report itself was confounding in its monumental length and lack of organization. One analysis noted that its index was "poorly organized and full of errors" and went on to say that the report was "full of inaccuracies and amounts to a whitewash designed to clear the Dutch of any wrongdoing."

The same analysis called into question the overall usefulness of the report, saying that "the sheer abundance of information makes it possible for anyone to pluck from it whatever they need to make their point." In fact, it happened that in subsequent war crimes cases before the ICTY, attorneys both for the prosecution and for the defense referred to the NIOD report to support their arguments.[12]

The NIOD report, with its lack of structure and its conflicting conclusions, was published hastily, without an overall preliminary reading by a critical editor. Independent Dutch journalist Alain van der Horst wrote that the report was unreadable "due to its size; therefore, it is practically impossible to check it, and in fact it is unreviewable." He concluded that the NIOD report and the subsequent parliamentary inquiry served to obscure the subject for most of the Dutch public—and that it perpetuated injustice for the Srebrenica survivors.[13]

Upon the release of the NIOD report, Dutch prime minister Wim Kok announced, "I will face responsibility for what my predecessors and I have done."[14] In mid-April 2002, less than a week after the release of the NIOD report, Wim Kok and his entire cabinet resigned from office. Explaining the resignations, he said simply, "The international community has failed to protect the people in the UN safe areas."[15] With new elections due to take place one month later, Kok's government continued on in an interim capacity.

Survivors of the fall of Srebrenica were dissatisfied with the content of the NIOD report, and they were not placated by the Dutch government's resignation, which took place, after all, only very shortly before the end of its mandate. In Srebrenica at the time, I heard from activists that the resignations were a "moral act," but that activists wanted the Dutch government to admit its responsibility more completely. In Sarajevo, widows demonstrated angrily in front of the Dutch Embassy, blocking the limousines of diplomats and shouting furiously.

Activists wanted officials in the chain of command, from Commander Karremans on up to the high military and political officials mentioned in the report, to be named and prosecuted. Survivor Hasan Nuhanović viewed the resignations as an empty gesture, saying, "I want justice—and it's not done by the resignation of ministers."[16] He explained, "It's very simple. Dutchbat was complicit in genocide. They should investigate properly any accusations of criminal activity by Dutchbat, indict them, arrest them, and try them in court."[17]

Recriminations over the NIOD report, and their deflection by the Dutch and others, were traded back and forth over the next few months. In June, Prime Minister Kok stated, "We are no murderers, we were there as part of the international community in order to safeguard security and safety, which proved to be impossible. The blame is to [be] put on those who were really responsible for what happened seven years ago in Srebrenica. It was not the Dutch." He further stated that an apology was "absolutely out of the question." In response, survivor and activist Kada Hotić said, "I don't want an apology or mercy. I want someone to be held responsible for this."[18]

The Dutch Parliament released its report the following year, in January 2003, without taking the survivors' objections to the NIOD report seriously. Continuing in the same vein as that report, the new inquiry acknowledged Dutch responsibility but again directed the bulk of the blame toward the UN. It concluded that the Serb assault on the "protected" enclave fulfilled all the requirements for a UN air attack, and that massive air strikes against Serb forces should have been implemented.[19]

The report also stated that there was no evidence of criminal action on the part of Dutch troops, and it particularly faulted UNPROFOR commander general Bernard Janvier for having blocked the air strikes.[20] The new report did little to satisfy the need on the part of the Srebrenica survivors and others for a more complete exposure of the truth about Srebrenica.

As described in the introduction to this book, an important part of the story of the fall of Srebrenica that is familiar to those who lived in the enclave through the "safe area" period is told in Hasan Nuhanović's book *Under the UN Flag*. There is much that has not been presented to the public through any court process or official report. The reports discussed here contributed in a piecemeal way to a public and official gathering of the truth. But fulfillment of the need for truth, essential to the struggle for justice, was proving to be a long and painful process that has yet to be concluded.

The lower house of the Dutch Parliament revisited the inquiry into the events at Srebrenica in early June 2003, once more debating the responsibility of the Netherlands for the genocide. Parliamentary deputies agreed unanimously that the Netherlands bore special responsibility. Some deputies proposed that traumatized survivors from Srebrenica receive refuge in the Netherlands, but the proposal was not passed. Deputies also urged the government to admit its guilt and issue a formal apology, but this was rejected as well. Bert Bakker, head of the investigation, objected that the use of the word "guilt" could have "dire legal consequences," and that it would be a "cheap and hollow gesture." He summed up his position with the curious statement, "The Netherlands is not guilty, but it is to blame."[21]

REPORTS FROM THE REPUBLIKA SRPSKA

Later in 2002, the Republika Srpska government issued the first of two reports on the Srebrenica genocide—denying that a massacre had taken place. Published in September of that year, the report was written by Dr. Darko Trifunović on behalf of the RS Bureau for Cooperation with the ICTY. The report immediately prompted expressions of outrage for its far-fetched attempts at refutation of the historical details of the Srebrenica genocide, which had already been revealed in the Erdemović and Krstić trials.[22]

The remarkably amateurish report, leaning heavily on unsubstantiated figures, weak logic, and quotes out of context, estimated that some two thousand to twenty-five hundred Muslims had been killed, the majority of them in combat with Serb troops. It attributed additional deaths to exhaustion or Muslims fighting with each other, and allowed that Serbs killed approximately two hundred Muslims for "revenge" or "unfamiliarity with international law after the fall of Srebrenica."[23]

Among other assertions, the report called the allegations of the Srebrenica genocide a "masterpiece of the public relations campaign" pulled off by the Muslim-led government of Alija Izetbegović, whose main goal, together with his "Islamic fanatics," was the establishment of an "Islamic Bosnia and Herzegovina."[24]

The report also stated that thousands of the missing Muslims from Srebrenica were located in the Tuzla enclave, having made their way through enemy lines without reporting themselves, and that the high number of missing was partially attributable to "duplicate tracing requests."[25] It attempted to undermine court evidence of the massacres by calling Dražen Erdemović "mentally ill."[26] Another feeble attempt at evading responsibility was to assert that mass graves that were found had been created for "hygienic reasons," and that "mass graves does [sic] not always mean mass execution."[27]

The report was met with outrage by survivors, domestic officials outside of the Republika Srpska, and international officials alike. Spokesman for the ICTY Refik

Hodžić called the document "simply outrageous and an attempt at revisionism."[28] And High Representative Paddy Ashdown blasted the report, saying, "Pretending it [the Srebrenica massacres] didn't happen is an insult to people of all ethnic groups in BiH. If the accounts given in the media are correct, the report published today is so far from the truth as to be almost not worth dignifying with a response. It is tendentious, preposterous and inflammatory."[29]

In a halfhearted retreat from the flagrant denial encompassed in the report, then-president of the RS Mirko Šarović stated that "the report should not be dismissed entirely, but does warrant further investigation."[30] Likewise, RS prime minister Mladen Ivanić stated that the report "did not represent his government's position,"[31] even though the agency that produced the report was part of the RS government.

It would be nearly two more years before officials from the Republika Srpska were prepared to release a report that was more forthcoming, but a process was already underway that led to a more honest review of the fall of Srebrenica. In March 2003 the Dayton-established Human Rights Chamber had directed the RS government to create a commission that would provide an in-depth report on the events between July 10 and 19, 1995.[32] The chamber's decision initiated a process that would culminate, after significant foot-dragging, in the publication of the first relatively sincere examination of the massacres on the part of the RS.

In early 2004 the Republika Srpska established the independent Srebrenica Commission (formally known as the Commission for the Research of Events in and around Srebrenica between July 10 and 19, 1995) to produce an in-depth report about the atrocities. The commission was primarily composed of RS military officials and civilian government employees, but it also included Smail Čekić, director of the Sarajevo-based Institute for Research of Crimes against Humanity and International Law, as deputy chairman. The commission promised to deliver a report within six months.

In mid-April, when that time limit expired and no report was forthcoming, Paddy Ashdown removed three Republika Srpska officials from the commission and demanded that the report be delivered by early June. He also threatened to remove top RS officials including President Dragan Čavić and Prime Minister Dragan Mikerević. In response to the implied threat against the RS, Čavić complained that "only Ashdown has power in BiH. . . . I can value Ashdown or not, but the fact is that he can do a lot. . . . The only thing he can't change here are natural phenomena—rain, snow, hills, and valleys."[33]

In June 2004 the Srebrenica Commission issued its report, which for the first time included a detailed account of events and preparation leading to the massacres. The report identified over thirty mass graves—although, as it turned out, many of the graves were already known to researchers. It detailed the involvement of certain military and police units belonging to the RS, also mentioning participation of forces from Serbia.[34] The forty-two-page report also acknowledged that over seven thousand people had been killed, and that "the executioner undertook all measures to hide the crime by removing bodies."[35]

The report was released with the implicit understanding, in an atmosphere created by Ashdown's threats and removals, that the Republika Srpska's international legitimacy was endangered and that fulfillment of the Srebrenica Commission's promises was a way to save the RS's reputation. Leaders of the RS, at this time mainly members of the same political party that led the war and committed the crimes, were on the defensive. Dragan Čavić implicitly admitted as much when he stated, "After years of prevarication, we will have to finally face up to ourselves and to the dark side of our past. We must have courage to do that."[36]

Shortly after the release of the report, Dragan Čavić addressed the public and acknowledged publicly, for the first time, that a massive war crime had been committed in the region surrounding Srebrenica. This was the first public admission by a Bosnian Serb leader that his own people had committed the crimes. Čavić stated that those who committed the crime committed it "against their own people" and that the event represented a "dark page in the history of Serb people." Čavić did not apologize but was said to have "made his regret clear."[37] Survivors responded with qualified approval of Čavić's gesture, while acknowledging that it was made under strong pressure from the international community.

October 2004 saw the publication of a follow-up report by the Srebrenica Commission, bearing the names of over seventy-eight hundred persons who had been killed during the massacres. An annex to the report provided information about two newly discovered mass graves. The report, whose contents were not open to public review, also provided a list naming 810 possible participants in the massacres.[38]

Leader of Srebrenica survivors Munira Subašić criticized the reports for restricting their coverage to the ten-day period, when the killing had extended considerably beyond July 19. Subašić also stated that the names of many of the perpetrators of the war crimes were known, and she called for them to be published.[39]

Disputes over identification of perpetrators and the Republika Srpska's full cooperation with the ICTY dominated the following months as pressure mounted for release of the names of the guilty. Smail Čekić, former deputy chairman of the Srebrenica Commission, stated that the report was just one step in a series that the Republika Srpska needed to take in processing the crimes that were committed in Srebrenica in 1995.

LAWSUITS IN THE HAGUE

Domestic institutions in Bosnia and international intergovernmental organizations thus made their imperfect contributions to the establishment of truth and justice regarding the history of Srebrenica. Meanwhile, grassroots actors from Bosnia filed two important lawsuits in the Netherlands that brought up the responsibility of that country and of the international community.

One of the lawsuits was announced in 2003 by the Sarajevo-based Movement of the Mothers of the Srebrenica and Žepa Enclaves, in collaboration with the Tuzla-based organization Women of Srebrenica. The idea to sue the government of the Netherlands and the United Nations for criminal negligence—and even collaboration—in the genocide at Srebrenica was born after the publication of the 2002 NIOD report and the resignation of the Dutch government. The 1999 United Nations report had also contributed to the decision.

The two above-mentioned reports provided background for the plaintiffs' argument that both the Dutch government and the UN bore responsibility for the massacres of their loved ones. The lawsuit was intended to take the Dutch government and the UN to court to compel both institutions to pay damages related to the genocide at Srebrenica, principally for their failure to protect civilians. Lawyers for the case pointed out that, on one hand, the UN was negligent in its responsibility to protect the "safe area" enclave that it had established; at the same time, the Dutch battalion present in the enclave violated procedures by circumventing UN command channels, at times taking orders directly from the Dutch government.

Discussing the case, Munira Subašić told me:

> The goal of this lawsuit is to receive monetary compensation. But the most important thing is that Holland and the UN admit their responsibility for the fall of the two municipalities. We want, first, an admission of responsibility, and second, funds for each surviving family, according to the number of people in each family.
>
> Holland is directly responsible for what happened because they were there. They were supposed to provide protection. We have a moral right to compensation. They can't pay for my son who was killed, but my pain, my sleepless nights, they can pay for that. And our survivors are in the streets, begging; our wives are left without their husbands. The humanity of the world will pass or fail on this test. They must admit their responsibility for what happened. They can't pay for our lost children; even if they gave us all of Holland, that wouldn't compensate.[40]

The formal lawsuit was finally filed at the Dutch District Court at The Hague in June 2007. Reports included in the filing recounted how Dutch soldiers had stood by helplessly as Serb forces rounded up fleeing civilians from the Srebrenica enclave and separated the men from the women. Some Dutch soldiers even helped the Serbs by maintaining order and assisting with the selection process. Quotes for the amount of compensation sought varied from one billion to several billion dollars.

Attorney Axel Hagedorn said, "We can prove that the fall of the enclave was only possible because the Dutch battalion and the UN didn't do what they said they would do and also what they had to do, and therefore the genocide could take place."[41]

Providing background on the lawsuit, attorney Liesbeth Zegveld told Radio Netherlands:

> The UN safe area was divided into several territories, one could say. One of those territories was the United Nations compound. Legally speaking, this was a protected area and

not only protected in the sense that it was proclaimed by the United Nations as a safe area, but also by treaty. United Nations areas are inviolable and no one should enter them. And no one did enter the United Nations compound, where the Dutch battalion were deployed in 1995. No Serb ever went in. It was the decision of Dutchbat to send away the people who had sought refuge in the compound and turn them into the hands of the Serbs. That's legally a very important point and should be distinguished from, for example, the refugees that were sent away from areas around the compound.[42]

Referring to the dual target of the lawsuit, Zegveld continued, "In our view, they are both responsible, the principal rule being that it's the United Nations who was responsible, with a number of exceptions, for example when the Dutch government interfered in the UN command and control structure, which it did in our view."[43] Attorneys for the lawsuit contended that Dutch soldiers conferred directly with the Dutch Ministry of Defense in crisis moments, indicating that there was a de facto double system of command.

Compounding the matter of the "double command" was the failure to protect Dutch troops, and by extension civilians in the enclave, with air support. The Dutch government itself, according to lawyers filing the lawsuit, obstructed this. "The Dutch state has always said its troops were abandoned by the U.N. which gave them no air support, but public documents show a network of Dutch military officials within the U.N. Protection Force blocked air support because they feared their soldiers could be hit by friendly fire," the lawyers said.[44]

The lawsuit effort was met by early and sustained unwillingness to see the plaintiffs' point of view. The UN immediately invoked immunity under the 1948 Convention on the Privileges and Immunities of the United Nations, which states that the UN "shall enjoy in the territory of each of its Members such legal capacity as may be necessary for the exercise of its functions and the fulfillment of its purposes" and "shall enjoy immunity from every form of legal process except insofar as in any particular case it has expressly waived its immunity."[45]

The legal team pressing the lawsuit responded that "genocide . . . is not the fulfillment of the purposes of the UN, and an appeal to immunity is irreconcilable with the UN's own objectives and its international obligations."[46]

In turn, a Dutch veterans' organization, attempting to shift blame from the Dutch government to the UN, stated, "There were no real Dutch troops. They were international UN troops, so the Dutch government was not in the lead, the UN was."[47] At the same time, legal representatives of the Netherlands continued to assert that the case was not in the jurisdiction of Dutch courts.

The Dutch District Court initially ruled that the plaintiffs could sue the UN. However, in July 2008, the same court reversed its stance and ruled that "in international law practice the absolute immunity of the UN is the norm and is respected."

In April 2010, the Dutch Court of Appeals upheld the District Court's ruling. The judges, sidestepping the plaintiffs' charge of Dutch responsibility, stated that "it was not the UN that committed genocide." They further argued that "although allegations of failing to prevent genocide are serious, it is not that pressing that immunity should be waived or that the UN's invocation of immunity is straightaway unacceptable." In response, Hagedorn asked, "It's strange because, what else could happen [other] than a genocide? What could be worse to make an exception?"[48]

After another failed appeal, it remained for the plaintiffs to take their case before the European Court of Human Rights in Strasbourg, which they did in 2012. On that occasion, Munira Subašić stated, "It is important that the world comprehends that we Muslims in Bosnia have the right to justice, and we thus expect that a fair judgment will be rendered, not a political one. After that, we will believe in justice in the world and in Europe."[49]

However, on June 27, 2013, the court at Strasbourg unanimously rejected the Mothers of the Srebrenica and Žepa Enclaves' appeal of last resort, confirming the United Nation's immunity from prosecution and saying that "the granting of immunity to the UN served a legitimate purpose."[50] The plaintiffs expressed strong disappointment at this negative decision in their long struggle for satisfaction in the courts.

The decision pertained to the lawsuit's complaint against the UN, but consideration of the complaint against the Dutch government had been put on hold until the conclusion of this part of the proceedings. In April 2014 attorneys for the plaintiffs launched their lawsuit all over again in the Dutch District Court, again calling on the Dutch government to admit its part of the responsibility for the war crimes at Srebrenica, and to pay compensation to the bereaved families of the victims.

A turnaround in this extended series of appeals and rejections took place in July 2014, when the District Court in The Hague decided that the Netherlands was in fact responsible for the deaths of some of the Srebrenican men who were killed upon the fall of the enclave.

One judge involved in the decision stated that the Dutch soldiers should have known that the men were facing mortal danger: "At the moment that the men were sent away, Dutchbat knew or should have known that the genocide was taking place and therefore there was a serious risk that those men would be killed."[51] Presiding judge Larissa Alwin commented, "By cooperating in the deportation of these men, Dutchbat acted unlawfully."[52]

It was a small victory; the court's decision pertained only to some three hundred men who had been inside the Dutchbat base at Potočari, whom Dutch soldiers had compelled to leave the base. On the other hand, the decision also held that the Netherlands was not responsible for the deaths of those thousands of men who had fled through the woods, nor for those who had sought safety in Potočari but had not been on the base.

The relatives who had filed the lawsuit were, understandably, dissatisfied. Munira Subašić stated, "Obviously the court has no sense of justice. How is it possible to divide victims and tell one mother that the Dutch state is responsible for the death of her son on one side of the wire and not for the son on the other side?"[53]

The District Court decision did not specify the amount of compensation to be paid out to the surviving families. And predictably, in October 2014 the Dutch state announced that it would appeal the ruling, creating expectations of an ongoing legal battle. In June 2017 the Hague Court of Appeals upheld the 2014 judgment, affirming the Dutch state's liability for the actions of its soldiers at Potočari.[54] In September of that year, the Dutch government filed a further appeal with the country's Supreme Court. The appeal was due to be released in the spring of 2019, and shortly before that time, the court's advocate general stated that the Appeals Court's decision was "incomprehensible" and advised the Supreme Court to reverse it.[55]

THE NUHANOVIĆ-MUSTAFIĆ LAWSUIT

In the spring of 2005, relatives of several Bosnians killed during the Srebrenica genocide initiated proceedings in the Dutch District Court at The Hague, in preparation for a civil lawsuit against the Dutch state. Relatives of Rizo Mustafić initiated the lawsuit on his behalf, and Hasan Nuhanović filed on behalf of his father, Ibro; his mother, Nasiha; and his brother Muhamed. Ibro Nuhanović and Rizo Mustafić had worked for Dutchbat in the enclave, and Nasiha and Muhamed Nuhanović were present on the Dutchbat base when Srebrenica fell.

Nuhanović and the Mustafić family believed that Dutchbat and, by extension, the Dutch state, failed in their responsibility to protect the lives of these four people. All of them perished at the hands of Serb troops after the Dutch forced them off the base.

Dutchbat troops removed Hasan Nuhanović's family from the base upon the fall of the enclave. Hasan's father, Ibro, was employed by the Dutch and thus had the right to remain under their protection, but he chose to leave with his wife and younger son, rather than abandoning them as they were being expelled. In a tense and traumatic situation, under pressure, Dutch officers rejected Hasan's plea to include his brother Muhamed on the list of employees of the base. In response, as he was being forced to leave with his parents, Muhamed demanded that Hasan stay on the base, so that he would stay alive.

Rizo Mustafić was an electrician employed on the base by Dutchbat. His name, along with those of Ibro and Hasan Nuhanović, was on a Dutchbat list of local employees to be evacuated. However, he too was required to leave the base when Srebrenica fell.

Upon initiation of the investigatory stage of the case, attorney Liesbeth Zegveld said, "The big legal question is to establish liability, and the Dutch government and the United Nations have both turned that down. There is a legal gap here. There have been grave human rights crimes and the victims should have remedy and receive damages." In response, a spokesperson for the Dutch government stated that the plaintiffs should rather be seeking redress from Serbia, from "the people who committed the murders."[56]

The lawsuit was filed in June 2008, but in September of that year the District Court at The Hague decided against it, saying that the Dutch government was not responsible for the failings of the UN operation in the Srebrenica enclave, because Dutchbat was not under command of the Dutch state.

The plaintiffs appealed the District Court's decision before the Dutch High Court, where proceedings languished for several years. During this time, the remains of some members of Nuhanović's family were discovered.

It is rather overwhelming to contemplate being in Hasan Nuhanović's shoes, having lost his entire family under traumatic circumstances, and carrying on his fight for the truth about their fate for many years.

At the time that Nuhanović's family was expelled, as attorney Zegveld stated, chaos reigned: "It was a complete mess there, but there was also a [Dutch] policy, spoken or unspoken, to get rid of everyone," she said.[57] Nuhanović had to live with the fact that the Dutch officer who ordered his family off the base had previously been a guest of the family and had enjoyed his mother's cooking. And when it came time to deliver the expulsion order to all the Bosnian men on the base, Nuhanović himself was ordered to translate it.

In the years following the war, Nuhanović studied, he wrote *Under the UN Flag*, he prepared his lawsuit, and he worked with Srebrenica survivors. Throughout all this time, he had no idea of the whereabouts of his father, mother, and brother. Finally, in 2006, the remains of his father were identified, having been discovered in one of the thirteen secondary mass graves at Čančari near Kamenica. Ibro had been executed at Branjevo farm near Pilica.

Nuhanović kept searching for information about the fate of his mother and brother. Here and there, he paid some ghoulish profiteers a hundred or several hundred marks for information that started to fill out the story of what happened to his mother, but that did not lead to the discovery of her remains. They were finally located in a creek bed near Vlasenica, Nuhanović's hometown, together with the remains of six other victims. The remains had been burned and then covered with garbage.

Shortly before Nasiha Nuhanović's remains were to be reburied next to those of Ibro Nuhanović in the memorial cemetery at Potočari, the remains of Hasan's brother Muhamed were also located. He too had been killed at Branjevo. On July 11, 2010, Nasiha and Muhamed Nuhanović were reburied next to Ibro at Potočari.

When Hasan filed the lawsuit in 2008, he said, "If I had not done this, I would not be able to go on with my life. I am seeking justice."[58]

The Dutch Appeals Court reversed the District Court's rejection of Nuhanović's lawsuit in early July 2011. The court ruled that although Dutch troops in the Srebrenica enclave were technically under the command of the UN, the Dutch government and military had wielded significant control over Dutchbat's actions. The court further noted that it should have been clear to the Dutch troops that they were putting Bosnians they were expelling in mortal danger, since Dutch soldiers had even witnessed that Serb forces around the base were killing Muslim refugees from the enclave.

Thus, the court ruled, Dutch soldiers acted wrongly in removing the men from their protection on the base, and the State of the Netherlands was responsible for their deaths.[59] However, the Appeals Court did not find the Dutch government guilty in the case of Nasiha Nuhanović's death, but only regarding the deaths of the men in question. The death of Nasiha was excluded from the case at this point because Hasan Nuhanović had not been able to make a case that there was demonstrable knowledge that women would be killed, while "it was clear that the men would be killed. The Dutch did everything they could to narrow the case," Nuhanović stated, "but there was indisputable evidence of the danger to the men."[60]

The Appeals Court decision did not signal the end of the lawsuit, however. A year later, the Dutch Defense Ministry announced that it would appeal the decision before the Dutch Supreme Court. The hearing took place in January 2013. Once again, Hasan Nuhanović explained to the court that "the Dutch . . . expelled my family and handed them to the Serbs, who killed them," and the Dutch state again responded, "The behaviour of Dutchbat troops can exclusively be laid at the UN's door."[61]

Finally, on September 6, 2013, the Dutch Supreme Court, upholding the Appeals Court decision from 2011, ruled that the Netherlands was indeed responsible for the deaths of Ibro and Muhamed Nuhanović and Rizo Mustafić. This ended the tortuous, ten-year struggle for one small bit of justice for Hasan Nuhanović, the Mustafić family, and for their murdered relatives.

Responding to the decision, Amnesty International commented, "Nearly two decades on from Srebrenica, this Dutch case marks the first time an individual government has been held to account for the conduct of its peacekeeping troops under a UN mandate." While Hasan Nuhanović was elated at the ruling, he stated that it was "but one of the battles being fought . . . hundreds of war criminals still roam the streets. The man who ordered my mother's killing works in the same building as me. I have to live with this every day."[62]

RESOLUTIONS COMMEMORATING SREBRENICA

Between the tenth and fifteenth anniversaries of the fall of the Srebrenica enclave, international actors successively passed a series of resolutions addressing the massacres. All these resolutions were political measures; to varying degrees each acknowledged the atrocities and commemorated the date of their occurrence. Equally significant was the failure of some states to adopt relevant statements.

In June 2005, the US Senate passed Senate Resolution 134, a bipartisan measure commemorating the tenth anniversary of the genocide. SR 134 termed the actions of Serb forces as "aggression and ethnic cleansing" and noted that they "meet the terms defining the crime of genocide in Article 2 of the Convention on the Prevention and Punishment of the Crime of Genocide."[63] A similar resolution, HR 199, was passed in the House of Representatives.

At the beginning of 2009, the European Parliament passed a resolution calling on all member states of the European Union to observe July 11 as a day of commemoration of the Srebrenica massacres. Encouraging all countries including those of the western Balkans to follow suit, the measure "commemorate[d] and honor[ed] all victims of the atrocities during the wars in the former Yugoslavia" and expressed condolences and solidarity with the victims.

The European Parliament resolution went further, not just calling the Srebrenica atrocities a "tragedy," but referring directly to the ICTY findings that the event constituted genocide. It acknowledged that both Bosnian Serb units and police forces from Serbia were involved in the war crimes. The resolution urged the relevant parties to apprehend the remaining fugitives, acknowledging that there "cannot be real peace without justice."[64]

The resolution also recognized the "importance of reconciliation as part of the European integration process." It passed by a vote of 556 to 22. However, Milorad Dodik, then prime minister of the RS, immediately rejected the measure, criticizing it for underlining "only one event." Dodik said that the date was "unacceptable to the RS," and that Bosnian leaders should agree on a date to honor the victims from all sides.[65]

A year after the adoption of the EU resolution, the Serbian Parliament underwent a drawn-out and difficult process that resulted in a declaration condemning the crimes at Srebrenica and apologizing for them on behalf of Serbia, but falling short of calling the crimes "genocide." This politically useful pronouncement satisfied only those who could view it as "better than nothing," or as the best possible statement under the circumstances.

In January 2010, then-president of Serbia Boris Tadić proposed to Parliament that it adopt a condemnation of the massacres. Discussion on the proposal carried on in Parliament for a couple of months before a vote was taken. Nationalists worried that a condemnation of Serb war crimes in Srebrenica would amount to a determination of "collective guilt" for the Serbian nation, and that any resolution about war crimes should equally condemn those committed against Serbs. Meanwhile critics from the other direction deemed that a failure to mention genocide would leave the resolution falling seriously short of its mark. A survey among ordinary citizens of Serbia found that only some 20 percent of respondents supported the proposed declaration.[66]

In late March 2010 Tadić's coalition submitted to Parliament a draft resolution that acknowledged the 2007 ICJ finding and acknowledged the UN Convention on Genocide. It strongly condemned the crimes at Srebrenica, supported the processing of war criminals, and called for reconciliation. It also expressed "condolences and apology to the victims' families" because not enough was done to prevent what it termed a tragedy.[67]

A spokesperson for the coalition stated, "Today we are taking responsibility for lifting the heavy burden off the shoulders of future generations." Another politician voiced the sentiments of the opposition, saying that the resolution would amount to a self-imposed declaration of collective guilt.[68]

After a thirteen-hour debate, the resolution was adopted by a narrow majority of two—127 votes out of a possible 250. Bosnian Muslims and survivors from Srebrenica immediately condemned the declaration, faulting it for omitting the word "genocide." Fadila Memišević of the Society for Threatened Peoples called the resolution a "slap in the face to surviving victims of genocide."[69]

The response on the street among Serbs in Banja Luka, the capital of the Republika Srpska, was also angry, for opposite reasons. People interviewed there by Agence France Presse (AFP) stated, "I am outraged. I feel like Serbia stabbed us in the back," and "Shame on them [Belgrade]. We have been branded forever."[70]

It was clear that President Tadić had pressed the parliamentary resolution as part of his long-term drive to bring Serbia closer to the European Union, with a view to eventual membership. In this vein, response from the EU to the resolution was cautiously positive. Officials welcomed it as an "important step" but reminded Serbian leaders of their obligation to continue to cooperate with the ICTY, especially in the search for the fugitive Ratko Mladić who, at that time, had still not been apprehended.[71]

Among those who wished for a sincere apology and reckoning with the past on the part of Serbia, the remark that the resolution was clearly motivated by political expedience was widespread. But Hasan Nuhanović commented, "We do not have to reject things that Serbia does because it is doing them in its own interest." As to his own feelings about the resolution, he stated, "Serbia needs this declaration; I do not need it. Serbia needs to face its own past; it is their problem, not mine. What I need from Serbia is to get actively involved in war crimes prosecutions, particularly by prosecuting its citizens who committed crimes in Bosnia."[72]

In other parts of Europe, the European Parliament's resolution on an official remembrance of the Srebrenica atrocity was widely adopted. Bosnia-Herzegovina itself stood out for being unable to pass a resolution commemorating the atrocity that took place on its own territory. A draft of such a resolution, inspired by the bill in the US Senate and identical to it in language, was proposed in the Bosnian House of Representatives on the eve of the tenth anniversary of the fall of Srebrenica. Representatives from the Republika Srpska objected to the use of the word "genocide," and the proposal was shelved.

9

Return and Recovery, Continued

A "NEW NORMAL" IN SREBRENICA

IN THE COUPLE OF DECADES SINCE THE END OF THE WAR, the campaign for truth and justice in Srebrenica has continued without pause. There have been victories and defeats, but the survivors of Srebrenica and their supporters have never lost sight of their goals.

The struggle for return to Srebrenica and recovery in the municipality also continued. From the outset there were questions to be answered: Will people return? Will there be security? How will returnees make a living?

There are activists and local officials who have the answers. People devoted to the idea of healing Srebrenica—while not always agreeing on the means—stepped up and worked to perform the work that reviving a devastated municipality demanded. As one question came to be resolved, another arose. The work goes on.

Return to Srebrenica increased in the early part of the 2000s and then leveled off after a few years. The majority of people who returned were those who had not found sustainable alternative residency either in the Federation or abroad. There were exceptions; there were people who were fiercely loyal to their home region, who could not imagine leaving it forever, and who were prepared to fight and organize to help their past and future neighbors. They were the "pozitivci," people with a positive attitude—a small minority, but one that made a difference.

As with return, resolution of property claims in Srebrenica started later than in many other parts of the country because of obstruction. By 2002 the fulfillment of the Property Law Implementation Plan was around 50 percent, and by the end of the year nearly all claims for property return were resolved.[1] Nevertheless, clearing away of that significant obstacle was not equivalent to return.

By 2005 authorities recorded the return of somewhat over three thousand Bosniaks, with the return rates having peaked in 2003.[2] Return figures covering both Serbs and Bosniaks for 2014 assert that a total of 4,057 families, or 9,648 people, had returned by that year.[3]

These figures are not to be taken as gospel, for several reasons. They are based on reports to the UNHCR of registered returns. Not everyone who registered their return actually came back to Srebrenica to stay. Some of them registered in order to acquire funding for the repair of their devastated houses, which they then sold or used as vacation homes.

Conversely, a significant number of people made real return without registering. These returns take place beneath the radar of the authorities. Some who return in this way simply prefer not to engage with the local or entity government. Many retained their residency status in the Federation for reasons of security—they wished to retain their higher pensions in that entity, or they felt their options for receiving health care were better there.

The number of returnees in Srebrenica municipality has thus been a fluid one, with some returnees coming and going, some becoming discouraged and leaving to live abroad, and some using their restored homes only as vacation houses. For some years the return figure that I heard from people who work for the municipality, or in local NGOs, hovered around five thousand with the breakdown between Serbs and Bosniaks being roughly equal.

A VISIT TO OSMAČE

After the initial return to Srebrenica and the village of Sućeska began in 2000, displaced Srebrenicans straggled back to the municipality. A couple reclaimed their apartment in town; a few dozen returnees begin clearing rubble in a village. The security situation improved, but the economy did not, and jobs were scarce. However, as evictions of displaced persons increased throughout Bosnia and Herzegovina, return to one's prewar home became an alternative to consider—and sometimes an imperative—even for Srebrenicans.

By spring of 2002, several hundred people had made tentative returns to villages around Srebrenica. At that time, members of thirty-five families arrived at Osmače, a complex of seven villages, to begin reconstruction of their homes. These people started at the same point that the returnees to Sućeska found themselves two years earlier—not at zero, but less than zero. The returnees could not rebuild their houses until the rubble was cleared out. Most houses were a total loss, but they still had to be cleared.

In April of that year I traveled to Osmače to see the start of return efforts there. It was a cold spring, and there was still snow on the ground. However, although Osmače is almost as isolated as Sućeska, more support for return existed at that time than when the pioneer returnees had arrived at Sućeska, as I had witnessed two years earlier.

The local NGOs Drina and Srebrenica 99 were assisting the returnees to Osmače. I rode to Osmače with Zulfo Salihović, the leader of Drina, to visit the new settlement. The route led steeply up out of Srebrenica, winding along a narrow ridge through the green hills and passing a few devastated houses. A little further along it passed Zeleni Jadar, a rural industrial zone tucked into a mountain ravine. There was a furniture factory, a stone processing plant, and a lumber mill. Before the war, twenty-five hundred people worked here. Now, only the lumber mill was operating.

Eighteen kilometers out of Srebrenica, a muddy dirt road split off toward Osmače. The village lay another three kilometers up the road. Zulfo's white pickup truck got stuck in the mud, and he stepped out and switched to four-wheel drive. Soon ruins of houses appeared. These were not houses anymore, just foundations—completely shattered. Trees grew where living rooms and kitchens used to be.

Osmače, like Sućeska, is situated on a mountain plateau from which one can see for miles around. Other ruined villages were dotted here and there in the woods. When it was intact, it must have been idyllic.

There used to be around a hundred houses in the central village of Osmače, and another several hundred in the other villages of the complex. Around two thousand people lived in the area. Everyone in Osmače was employed—many at the factories in Zeleni Jadar, or in the nearby bauxite mine. The houses of Osmače were not poor; they were solid houses, some of them quite big.

The village was destroyed in 1993, and its inhabitants fled to Srebrenica town. Grenades and arson were not enough to put those big houses in the state I saw them; they were also mined with explosives. Someone truly did not want these people to return.

Zulfo parked in the muddy field at the end of the road to Osmače; four bright-white tents were pitched in a nearby clearing. Equipment was stored in some of the tents, and people slept in others. Other people slept in the basement room of a nearby house, one of the few that wasn't damaged beyond repair. Four cots and a wood stove were crammed into the one ground-floor room that was roughly intact.

Zulfo explained that returnees were living in difficult conditions. "On the fall of Srebrenica," he said, "390 people from Osmače alone were killed. There are many women without men, and men without work. Some people have come back to Srebrenica, seen how bad it is, and then left to live abroad."

Osmače's problems were typical of those at all the villages that were being resettled around Srebrenica. Availability of cement and other materials for reconstruction depended on donations from international agencies and the various levels of the domestic government. There was nowhere among the ruined houses to shelter and feed animals. There were springs, but no electricity to pump water. Security was not a problem, but some areas were still mined. On one downed tree in the ruined village, fenced off by yellow police tape, there was an impromptu display of various types of mines and bombs that had been discovered in the area.

The elementary school in Osmače had been destroyed during the war, and there was no clinic operating at the time of my visit. For the time being, returnees were leaving their children behind, in the Federation. They hoped that if all went well, conditions would allow the children to arrive in the summer. Furthermore, returnees did not have medical coverage at the clinic in Srebrenica, so until a clinic was established in Osmače, they were risking their health.

Dževad Delić was the coordinator of the return project to Osmače. During the war he had taken refuge in Banovići near Tuzla, and at the time of my visit he still had three children in school there. Dževad commented that people could earn a living in Osmače if they had a chance to sell agricultural products. They hoped at least to plant potatoes right away, but they had no tilling machines. From the forest, medicinal teas, wild blueberries and strawberries, and mushrooms could be harvested and sold.

Basic conditions for anything more than rough camping did not exist in Osmače. As they waited for assistance, the returnees to Osmače cleaned the rubble around their bombed houses, when the weather permitted. Zulfo told me that perhaps 30 percent of the population of Osmače would return home if there were donations to rebuild. If not, he expected that they would emigrate to America, or wherever else they could find employment.

Returnees to Osmače persevered, and conditions did improve over the next couple of years. By late 2003 the muddy road where Zulfo's jeep had gotten stuck was paved, and the next year, USAID connected Osmače and about thirty other villages to the electrical grid.

One woman who hoped to return around this time said, "I have decided to come back. In the Federation, I have no security. When they restore my house, my children and grandchildren will return as well. I don't wish to have anything that belongs to someone else. There, I'm cold even when the sun is shining. Here, I'm warm even when the snow falls."[4]

Around the time people were first returning to Osmače in the spring of 2002, the United Nations Development Programme (UNDP) had held a widely publicized donor conference in New York announcing a plan to raise US$12.5 million for recovery and reconstruction in Srebrenica and its two neighboring municipalities, Milići and Bratunac, under the auspices of the Srebrenica Regional Recovery Programme. Promised funds did not reach the US$12.5 million figure—and delivered funds did not reach the amount promised. But at least five or six million dollars were channeled to Srebrenica recovery in the several years after the conference.[5]

The funds were delivered in such a chaotic way that it was impossible to monitor their total, their origin, and their destiny. A large number of reconstruction projects, such as the electrification program mentioned above, were accomplished. Roads and houses were repaired, and schools and clinics were rebuilt. Some of the work implemented was excellent, some of it shoddy.

One outstanding problem was that of communication between the implementors and donors and the beneficiaries, the population of the three municipalities involved in the program. To the returnees, who saw that some people were receiving more aid than others, aid distribution seemed to be random or, even worse, influenced by favoritism. There was clearly a disconnect between (usually) well-meaning international relief officials and their beneficiaries. Chaos and poor communication led to a proliferation of rumors about the disposition of aid funds.

An accompanying part of the chaos was that the local authorities themselves were not kept sufficiently involved in the decision-making process about allocation, nor were they even sufficiently informed. Mujo Siručić, in late 2002 serving as head of the Department of Urbanism and Area Organization, was quoted as saying, "Donors choose which buildings to repair. Houses are fixed for those who will never return, while others who have already returned are living in tents, shacks, or other people's houses."[6]

In the aftermath of the donor conference, misuse of newly available donations could have served as a textbook illustration of the ills of postwar "humanitarian profiteering." Reports summarized by *Oslobodjenje* in late 2002 noted that there was "big competition among businessmen who are opening offices in Srebrenica because they think there is money there, after the May donor conference. But the quality of the work done is zero. Few returnees are satisfied with the work done, especially on a repair project of 75 houses by the Malaysian government. That work was done quickly, in the winter, and then returnees must find other workers to fix leaks, bad plumbing, falling tiles, and bad paint. The worst possible quality of building material has been used. Nothing that has been built is worth half of what is being paid for it."[7]

ACTIVISM IN SREBRENICA TOWN

> Srebrenica is not just something I do. Srebrenica is my obsession.
>
> —*Vesna Mustafić*

Activism has evolved and passed through several phases since the early days after the war. My collaboration with activists in the early postwar period afforded me the privilege of being acquainted with some brave and persistent people.

One of these people is native Srebrenican Vesna Mustafić, who was a chemist in the laboratory for the mines before the war. She is a Serb by descent, in a mixed marriage, and Bosnian by conviction. She said to me, "Before the war, I was a Yugoslav. I always felt that way, that I belonged to everyone, and everyone belonged to me. And I feel that way today, that I'm a Bosnian."

Vesna and her husband left Srebrenica on April 17, 1992, at the last moment before the "Arkanovci," a paramilitary group led by Željko Ražnatović Arkan, attacked the town. They had wanted to remain in their home, as they believed that the soldiers would leave soon. When they left, they thought they would be able to return after two or three days. As they had no gas in their car, they left in an unscheduled bus, packed with fleeing people. Vesna recounted, "There were colleagues in the bus—we all knew each other. We were stopped at the yellow bridge [between Srebrenica and Bratunac municipalities]. We hadn't heard about what happened in Bijeljina; we just thought there was some disturbance. That's why most people didn't leave. They thought, 'We're not guilty of anything, so there won't be a problem.'"

I asked Vesna about her development as an activist for return and recovery in Srebrenica. She answered:

Here in Srebrenica, it is a really specific situation. What happened here didn't take place suddenly. We who lived in Yugoslavia had illusions that we were all okay, that we were blessed, that we were better off than the other communist countries. The people who stirred things up during the breakdown of Yugoslavia found old wounds. Before, we didn't pay attention to religion. Then they played the fear card, pitting Serbs against Croats, and so on, and then the media got involved. People had learned to listen to someone else rather than thinking for themselves. It was not the ordinary people who generated the fear and tension. Doctors and other educated people popularized these ideas.

World War II was not long ago; there were memories of the Chetniks murdering, the Ustashe murdering, and so on. These things returned, the idea that one whole people should be killed. That is the easiest way to do it, the bloodier the better. I never imagined that it could happen the way it did, that someone would do this. I was an ordinary person; I worked with people, and had good friends. Then mistrust arose. In those days before the war, the ideologues were manipulating all kinds of facts, recalling the story of Jasenovac [a World War II concentration camp in Croatia], for example.

At first I was not afraid, because I didn't believe that it would last. But I saw the growth of nationalist parties, including the SDA, who were consciously frightening people. I saw in my friends, suddenly, a fear of their neighbors. Then people were putting signs on their houses, so that it would be known that "my house is a Serb house." I saw this sign on one person's house. I doubt he did that, but someone did it as a way to frighten people.

Then there was constant talk about weapons. There were many stories about things that happened in Croatia, and about things that were starting up in other parts of Bosnia, but there wasn't real information. Something was happening, but we didn't know exactly who was doing it. People always said, it was "someone else," but they didn't know what was going on, or didn't want to know. Either people were naive, or they didn't want to accept what was going on. For example, what happened in Vukovar, we thought it would end there, that it wouldn't happen to us.

Discussing the aftermath of the war and her feelings about Srebrenica, Vesna said:

I was in Bosnia throughout the war. I love Srebrenica very much, and I was very unhappy when I heard the news about the massacres. I wanted to return, but it was too slow; it could not happen just like that. Then, to help return happen, I had to get to work.

I simply can't believe that we're all that way. Maybe I'm trying to show myself that there is a connection among people. That's my obsession, to show that we are not like that. There are many good people—more, I hope, whose consciences have awoken, and they will do something. We must be done with that hate and tension, so that we can live normally. I have faith in people, that we can tip the scales. Sometimes I think negatively, then I say to myself, "Stop, go back, and do what is needed." I simply don't want to accept that everyone in Srebrenica hates. I wanted to show that there are people who are ready to show a different face of Srebrenica. But there are still big obstacles, such as the abuse of religion.

Asked about personal responsibility as a component of activism and recovery, Vesna responded:

There was the war, and then most people were displaced persons. Then the international community came and distributed relief assistance. People got situated and received assistance, a bag of flour, some cooking oil. With time people got used to getting assistance. When someone gives something, you don't try to do something for yourself. Now we have a problem, because people are always saying, "I'm not getting something, and I lost everything." Looking at myself, I don't want flour; I want help from the government so that I can earn something, and then I will buy flour for myself.

I look at the international community: they start something, and then they withdraw. In Srebrenica the recovery started late compared to other parts of the country. Here it is a completely unresolved situation, and some people who have returned are already leaving [in 2004]. They fix their house, and then they leave. The coordinators of international organizations are mainly working with the municipal government, and those in the government want to help their friends, people who are in the same party as they are. Most of the politicians don't live in Srebrenica; of twenty-seven politicians, only six live in Srebrenica. Others live in Doboj, Bijeljina, or even in Serbia. They come to work, get good pay, and they decide how people in Srebrenica will live. It is really ridiculous. They earn, but they are not concerned.

ZULFO SALIHOVIĆ

On the afternoon of September 11, 2001, I was sitting in Piccolo Mondo, a crowded and noisy kafana in the Brčanska Malta neighborhood of Tuzla. A television mounted high on one of the walls showed the burning World Trade Center towers of lower Manhattan; someone was waving a white scarf from one of the upper floors, hoping for rescue. But it seemed that the people in the kafana were not paying too much attention to the drama on TV; rather, they were simply socializing and drinking their coffee as if it were another ordinary day.

I was speaking with Zulfo Salihović; I had had the honor of meeting him when he was involved in the movement for return to Srebrenica, as that movement was just beginning. In the late 1990s Zulfo and his organization, Drina, were very active in promoting return to Sućeska. I accompanied Zulfo on a visit to the return encampment at Sućeska in 2000, the first village that people were returning to outside of Srebrenica town.

In that conversation in Piccolo Mondo on September 11, just over a year after the first return to Sućeska, Zulfo described the state of return in Srebrenica. "The security situation is adequate, although you can never be sure," Zulfo said. Pointing at the television on the wall, he said, "You see, even in the United States you can't. Lately there have been fewer attacks, although on July 17 a returnee girl was killed in Vlasenica. Maybe this was a reaction to our first attempts to establish the new memorial cemetery."

Activists and returnees persevered, and Srebrenicans established a foothold in the villages around Srebrenica town. Sućeska grew to become one of the most advanced locations of return in the municipality, with a rebuilt school and clinic, and restored electrical and water services. Within a few years there were a couple dozen young pupils studying in the school.

During a conversation in 2004 I asked Zulfo an open question about what he worked for, and he said, "Right now in the NGO sector, we are trying to advance democracy, which, unfortunately, is beneath all standards. I work to change things for the better, for the improvement of the general situation, and of the political and economic situation in Bosnia and Herzegovina. In these ten postwar years we have not seen a satisfactory amount of improvement."

Zulfo grew up in Brakovci, a small settlement that is part of the Sućeska complex of villages. He went to elementary school in the village, but classes only went through fourth grade, and then he had to walk down the hill to Derventa—eight kilometers away—to get to school. In order to go to technical high school in Bratunac, Zulfo rented an apartment and lived there on his own. He went to Serbia each summer to do odd jobs so that he could continue to study.

In 1985 Zulfo got a job as a mechanical design technician with one of the mining companies based in Milići. He eventually bought a lot in Srebrenica and built a house in town. On becoming politically active before the war, Zulfo told me, "I was not in politics under Tito. I was a kid from the village. I joined the SDA and ran in the first multiparty elections in 1990, and I remained in that party until 1998." At the time of its founding, the SDA was the only political party in Bosnia that represented Muslims.

When the war started extremist Serb forces attacked Srebrenica, ultimately surrounding it and leading to its establishment as an enclave. Of that period, Zulfo said:

> In Srebrenica it was the ordinary people who fought to defend the enclave; the others, the intellectuals and the elite portion of society, were already outside Srebrenica. It happened that the Serbs got their worst people for leaders; a personality cult was established. Karadžić made promises and paid people in the drive to establish a Greater Serbia. The leaders of the Serb nationalists had taken on the task of forcing other Serbs to work for these goals.
>
> Intellectuals were involved in the local Serb nationalist organization for the attempted takeover of Srebrenica. Goran Zekić, a lawyer, was local president of the SDS. Paramilitary formations, the Red Berets and other groups, were also involved. They attacked us and burned houses and killed families. We had a moral right to defend ourselves. There was no organization on our side in the beginning, and those people who had been our leaders escaped to Tuzla. The ordinary people who were left in Srebrenica organized after they saw the killing that had taken place in Bratunac. That was the strongest impulse, simply to defend ourselves.

In 2003 I hitched a ride with Zulfo from Srebrenica to Sarajevo via Milići, the rugged back route through the hills. We headed off toward Sućeska. As we left Srebrenica, Zulfo pointed out the house he had lived in before the war. He said that the man who was living there, a displaced Serb from central Bosnia, would not let him enter the house.

We climbed up the dirt and gravel—and sometimes mud—road out of Srebrenica. Around a half hour out, we stopped at Vijogor, at a viewpoint where you could see just about to Srebrenica to the south, and almost to Sućeska to the west. We were in the mountains, above everything, with a view of many shades of green all the way to the distant horizon.

We passed Zulfo's home village of Brakovci, across the valley. Zulfo pointed up a ravine and said, "I spent much of my youth in these woods." I said, "Then you're not a city kid like me." He answered, "And I'm not ashamed of it."

Coming down through the mountains toward Milići we stopped for water at a fountain in the woods. An inscription on the fountain read, "Good works are the measure of a good person."

There was a hefty slug climbing on the fountain. After we drank, Zulfo looked at it and told me, "I had to eat a lot of those during the hike through the woods. At first, I couldn't eat them, but after a few days, I learned to."

While some people managed to escape to safe territory in little over a week, Zulfo's walk, with some other men from the army, lasted over a month. The people in his group were stuck on one mountain for eighteen days, waiting for a signal to break through to safe territory.

North of Konjević Polje, Zulfo pointed out Udrč, the mountain where he and his fellow refugees had been stranded. "We ate snails, leaves, and mushrooms, and waited," he said.

> After a while there was nothing more to eat. Then we came down to one of these villages at night, and stole a cow. We cooked in the mountains, in the dark. The Serbs hunted us, fired bombs at us. Some people tried to escape from here into Serbia, but most of them were captured.
>
> I walked thirty-two days through the woods before I arrived in Tuzla. Around one-third of those who left, fewer than five thousand people, arrived. No one knows the real figures, because it hasn't been in the interest of even one government to find out.

Along the way through the mountains, we stopped occasionally as Zulfo met someone fixing a house or doing an errand. Zulfo would stop and say, "Hello friend, how's your father?" These were Serbs from the area between Srebrenica and Milići, people he had worked with and was friends with before the war. Zulfo told me that one person he had just greeted had fought on the side of Serb forces during the war. I asked if it was strange for him to be interacting with that person. Zulfo said, "The war is over now, and people have to accept that."

After the war Zulfo found himself living in Tuzla as a displaced person. The trauma of the siege of Srebrenica and the terror of escape led to a health crisis, and Zulfo was in the hospital for nine months. Zulfo commented that the SDA "used this opportunity to get me out. I was driven out by the hard-liners. This is because I faulted those who were in government during the war. I am convinced that Alija Izetbegovic was responsible for the fall of Srebrenica. The Bosnian Army did not hold the line, and thus thousands of people died. So, while I was in the hospital, the party removed me."

Zulfo had a number of political and strategic disagreements with the SDA. Having heard about the SDA's obstruction, I asked him if he believed the party had worked to prevent return to Srebrenica. He responded:

> After the war, the government ordered refugees from Srebrenica to go to areas around Sarajevo, to live in places that had been abandoned by the Serbs. I couldn't find a place to live in Tuzla, Vozuća, or Zavidovići, but in Ilijaš [a suburb of Sarajevo], there were Serb houses that were being offered to people from Srebrenica.
>
> SDA officials were talking as if they wanted to help us return, but they didn't really help. When we started to return in June 2000, some SDA activists from Vozuća who went to the hills; there were people who admitted to me later that there had been a plan to use

firearms to scare us. But we had brave people in the return encampment, and they didn't have the nerve to try to frighten us.

However, they did mount a campaign against return, saying, "You will lose your house . . . you can't live in Srebrenica and earn anything . . ." There were a thousand arguments against return. People criticized us, saying, "What right do you have to try to return? What security do you think there will be? We don't have security there." I responded by saying, "I'm not trying to persuade you to return, but you can't live in houses that belong to other people." I warned people that they would be evicted from the houses that belonged to displaced Serbs, and this started to come true in 2001. At that time, the High Representative put pressure on the SDA by starting the evictions. Then the SDA began to change its policy, but it really only changed in 2003.

Returning to the topic of Zulfo's postwar activism, Zulfo said:

After the war, I tried to go to Srebrenica as soon as conditions allowed. I went to Srebrenica for the first time in 1999. There was a chance to meet people there who were for change, who wanted to establish contact with the outside.

Conditions for working with those people between 1995 and 2000 were blocked because the Serbs in Srebrenica were isolated, and all democratic processes were stopped. The SDS and their friends ran things. There were physical attacks on activists. Conversations were carried out in whispers, not publicly. But Muslims in Tuzla and Serbs in Srebrenica were starting to communicate. Those Muslims and Serbs in political positions didn't like that we were talking to each other, but we succeeded. By 2003 there came to be sixteen or seventeen organizations that worked together, with mutual goals.

I asked Zulfo if it was true that some NGOs were corrupt. "We were aware of this," he said, "and people broke laws—first, from not knowing them. Then, there was illegal importing for the displaced persons, to avoid paying taxes. There was a 20 to 30 percent tax imposed on such goods. Building materials would come in for houses damaged in the war, and people would avoid paying taxes on them. Some of these materials went to people who had not been displaced, who got rich on account of the displaced persons. People helped their friends first."

Over the years Zulfo worked with people who favored return and reconstruction of Srebrenica, regardless of their ethnicity. Asked how he felt about cooperation with Serbs after what happened during the war, he responded, "It is unavoidable for them *and* for us. Even during the war, I was already convinced that we were not going to be able to live separately. I was shown to be right. We have to work together."

During that rough ride between Srebrenica and Milići, we came upon a tall cherry tree growing in the woods. We stopped and picked a few cherries, and then Zulfo, who is at least six feet tall, climbed up into the tree and started picking sprigs of branches with handfuls of cherries on them, and throwing them down to me. We filled two plastic bags that way.

Assessing the toll that the traumas of the 1990s had taken on his psyche, Zulfo said, "I can't say that I'm a completely healthy person. I think I am reasonably intact, but I often have dreams, after all that happened."

I admired Zulfo's ability to recover, to reach out to his former enemies, to focus on rebuilding his homeland—and to stop and pick the cherries.

Once, I commented to him, "I suppose you are an optimist." He answered, "If I weren't, I would not have started the work that I started after the war. Bosnia is still at a low level of functioning. Young people are our strength. I hope Bosnia can revive; I don't know whether it can happen in ten years, but maybe in ten to fifteen, there will be success. It will be freer; there will be democracy. The majority of ordinary people are dissatisfied. There always needs to be a strong movement for change."

Over the years of contact with activists in Srebrenica, I have noticed signs of wear and tear. It is hard to imagine constantly living under the conditions that confront them, and still persevering. Most of the activists are or have been displaced persons. Many have at some time been victims of discrimination; some have been threatened with eviction. In other words, they are faced with the same problems of their constituency.

Activists in Srebrenica have been interrupted regularly in their work by one problem or another: snow piled up in the winter, broiling weather in the summer, bad cars, poor health, bad telephones, computer breakdowns, electrical blackouts, water cutoffs; the list of problems goes on and on, and it truly affects people's moods. It is good to keep in mind that there was a war in the region, and as many people have commented, "It is much easier to start a war and destroy things than to fix them afterward." In that vein, the aftereffects of the war are long-term in nature, and they affect not only infrastructure, but people's mental health.

The ordinary people of Srebrenica, including the activists, are not well-off. One activist had to pay 1,000 KM just to have a power pole erected in front of her house in Srebrenica, and then she had to come up with more money to pay for the hookup. This, because she was not one of the "politically favored." Once, in desperation, she asked me how one may get to America. I did not have a useful answer. But I said to her that if people like her left the country, there would be no Bosnia.

NGO ACTIVISM AND THE SREBRENICA YOUTH COUNCIL

While people returned to the villages of Srebrenica municipality and struggled to rebuild a very rudimentary life there, a different kind of struggle was ongoing in the town itself. Once the most serious problems of obstruction and physical insecurity were overcome, there were still many difficulties that continued to confront returnees. Chief among these were unemployment and the poor economy. There were continued discrimination and favoritism in hiring, and uneven services in the health sector.

Srebrenica was cut off from most media in the rest of the country; people often spoke of an "information blockade." Returnees needed legal advice, employment training and assistance, and reconstruction materials. The elderly, the disabled, widows, and youth all had special needs.

The municipal government tried to take care of as much of these needs as it could, but it was strapped for resources. International assistance was also scarce, and both its origin and its destiny were often a mystery to those who could have benefited the most from aid. Lack of information and suspicion led, again, to rumors of corruption, profiteering, and money laundering.

Into this mix, soon after return began, came a proliferation of nongovernmental organizations that sprouted in Srebrenica like mushrooms in the woods. These NGOs inhabited a spectrum from useless or parasitical to helpful and indispensable. Over time, the less positive organizations folded and disappeared. Some of the more honest and constructive groups failed as well, simply because of lack of resources. But eventually, Srebrenica was left with a number of well-meaning and capable NGOs that cooperated with each other and tried to make up for the shortcomings of the municipal budget.

Throughout Bosnia-Herzegovina there has been a discussion of the role of nongovernmental organizations in the struggle for justice in the postwar period. One position holds that NGO work does not constitute grassroots activism, because members of registered local organizations receive funding from national or international organizations, including both governmental agencies and NGOs. This funding often compromises the position of NGO activists; in addition, it is often the case that work in an NGO in Bosnia-Herzegovina simply constitutes a stepping stone in an "activist's" career.

In this vein, the famed Indian author Arundhati Roy once provided an evaluation that eloquently expresses a popular negative attitude toward NGOs. She stated in an interview that "the NGO-ization of politics threatens to turn resistance into a well-mannered, reasonable, salaried, 9-to-5 job. With a few perks thrown in. Real resistance has real consequences. And no salary."[8]

Certainly, what Roy described is a widespread phenomenon: the co-optation of potential grassroots activism via the corrupting influence of corporate or state financing. This is a problem in Bosnia-Herzegovina. However, many activists who work in NGOs receive little or no compensation and work because of their convictions alone. And there is an entire spectrum of work done by registered NGOs that includes everything from thinly veiled political campaigning to very principled work for justice in a range of issues. At the latter end of the spectrum, there is overlap between NGO work and grassroots activism.

There is a current of distrust on the part of grassroots activists—and ordinary people—for those who are employed by NGOs and receive funding. This is partly but not entirely justified. It is true that there is a background of dishonesty on the part of some NGOs, which, in the heady period of proliferation of such organizations after the war, exploited the opportunity to receive free money from the international community. When I mentioned the case of one corrupt NGO to a local leader whom I trusted very much, he responded, "We were all involved in something like that."

These anecdotes contribute to the mistrust that many ordinary people have toward NGOs. The Institute for War and Peace Reporting (IWPR) has discussed investigation of several NGOs for misuse of donations. IWPR pointed out in a 2011 article that those who should be receiving assistance from NGOs—which receive up to sixty million euros per year—are not getting the benefit of the funding. The article noted that transparency in spending and governmental controls over distribution are lacking. Poor accounting practices were mentioned as a serious problem for NGOs. The article quoted the chief of financial police, who listed some problems with NGOs thus: "When we investigated the financial transactions of some of these associations, we found out that they made per diem payments to their staff for field trips that never took place," he said. "Money was also paid for services that were never rendered. There were cases where conferences or other big events were organised and individuals were paid large sums of money without any description of the services they were supposed to have provided."[9]

The story of dishonest NGOs is wide ranging. However, without putting aside healthy skepticism, one can observe that many NGOs help their constituencies. Their employees, rarely compensated at a comfortable level, suffer along with their communities and go to great lengths to be of assistance. Identifying these organizations requires the development of an internal gauge. And a caveat here: it is not unusual that an organization will be useful and helpful for a period, and will then run out of steam, or adjust its practices, to the extent that it outlives its usefulness and begins to exploit its good reputation and its position as a recipient of funding.

One organization that has campaigned for the needs of an important portion of society in Srebrenica is the Savjet mladih Srebrenice (Srebrenica Youth Council), which for more than a decade has worked to provide services to young people in Srebrenica. The organization is based at the Youth Center, a former movie theater by Srebrenica's main square. For some years this building stood empty, devastated and derelict, as the city had no money to repair it.

Former director of the Youth Council Milena "Mikica" Nikolić, a bright and energetic young woman, talked about how her organization got started.

> The Youth Council was founded in 2002, and the next year young people got together and cleaned out the building that we presently occupy, without asking permission from anyone. That was our first action, during Dani Srebrenice [the annual festival, "Srebrenica Days")] in 2003. This building was in ruins then; that day we pulled off a guerilla action, cleaning the building.
>
> From then, step by step, we have built the organization. We had the good luck to get

support from then-mayor Abdurrahman Malkić, and the municipality consented to allow our group to use the building for twenty years.

Describing the motivation of the Youth Council, Mikica said, "The first thing that connected us all was prejudice from the outside against Srebrenica, the attitude that there was no youth here, and no creativity. We took this as a challenge and worked to build a space in Srebrenica for creativity, organizing young people in the local community. Our activities were mainly cultural, including performances that we held here."

Members of the Youth Council started from scratch in learning how to become activists, coming to collaborate nationally, in both entities, with the most prominent and effective youth organizations. Mikica noted, "We are working on all levels advocating for the creation of laws that advocate for better conditions for young people and for the development of a strategy for youth services."

One young member of the Youth Center told me, "Srebrenica is a great place; it has spirit. But there's no economy, few people, and jobs are hard to get here. Voting doesn't seem to help anything," he continued. "The politicians are just campaigning in order to have four more years of good salary. People are leaving because there is no work here. A huge number of those who finish college elsewhere stay there."

Young Serbs and Muslims alike frequent the Youth Center. One of teenagers there said to me, "There's no hate here among us young people. I think that's normal; why would I hate someone?"

The Youth Council played an active part in the organization of Srebrenica Days, an annual summer festival at Srebrenica. The festival was the most ambitious public event to take place in Srebrenica since the war, a way for the recovering community of Srebrenica, especially its youth, to celebrate life and being with each other. It was an acknowledgment that, while it is difficult to live in postwar hardship in a place where a dreadful war crime has taken place, nevertheless life goes on.

While people know that Srebrenica will never be what it was before the war, they feel they have the right to recreation and enjoyment, and that Srebrenica should be defined not only by a museum and a cemetery. There are other people, especially survivors, for whom this causes discomfort, and this is understandable. But it is also quite understandable that younger people, especially those who did not live through the war, wish for entertainment.

In 2003 Mayor Malkić encouraged the organization of the Srebrenica Days cultural festival set to take place in the second week of June. With the support of the municipal government, many local NGOs got involved. They organized a rock concert, a foot race and other sports competitions, a "graffiti party," a theater performance, and many more events.

When news got out that a rock concert was to be held in the high school in Srebrenica, people in other places criticized the plan, saying that it was "too soon after the tragedy" for such a concert to be held, and that the idea of holding a concert was "worse than scandalous." Another criticism was that the concert was to be held near the spot where many young people were killed in 1993, struck by a bomb that landed while they were playing football.

Malkić responded by saying, "Many people died by the school, but tell me where people did not die. Among my circle of friends and relatives 113 people were killed, including my father, and I was wounded twice. Gentlemen, life goes on. We can't forget the past, but we have to look to the future."

Another pointed comment came from Sakib Smailović, reporter for the Sarajevo daily *Oslobodjenje*, who wrote, "[Critics] should know that people have returned to Srebrenica, and they are struggling so that their children can have a decent future. . . . Even if they wanted to, the returnees couldn't forget the evil that was done to them. That's why those 'concerned from a distance' should not try to give them lessons, and not try to kill what slight heartbeat still lives in this town."[10]

The festival went ahead; the rock concert was well attended. Bands and DJs came from Serbia, Croatia, and both entities of Bosnia, and people stayed until after 3:00 a.m. "Električni Orgazam" came from Banja Luka. A rap group came from Bugojno. There were no "incidents"—no scuffles of the kind that happen all over the West at such concerts.

I joined the celebration that wound up the week's festivities. A couple hundred people were there: Serbs and Muslims, activists from the nongovernmental associations, and local government officials. Food and drink were served. Bosfam, a women's crafts collective based in Tuzla and Srebrenica, staged a fashion show featuring the handiworks created by members of the group, and modeled by young women. The women pranced up an improvised catwalk, stepping onto a stage covered with Bosfam's hand-woven carpets, fully capturing the attention of all the diners.

A folklore group from Tuzla performed some traditional Muslim and Serb dances. The party evolved into a dance with live music. People of all ages stood up and danced all kinds of dances, improvising, and laughing. At one point the duo performed a traditional kolo (line dance), and all the people in the room were on their feet. Mayor Malkić danced the kolo along with everyone else.

The party lasted almost until sunrise. As I was leaving, Senad Subašić, who worked for the municipal government, said to me, "Do you see? Srebrenica isn't a dying town. It's a place for living."

FURTHER NGO ACTIVISM IN SREBRENICA

Subašić's comment was implicitly in response to the view of the municipality from afar as nothing more than a monument to genocide. This essentially fatalistic attitude toward Srebrenica dominates writing by outside journalists who know what happened there in 1995, but are not aware of the vital struggle that has been underway for many years to restore the city to a livable condition. To counter the dour media presentation, one organization has worked from inside Srebrenica to present a different view.

Supported by the Dutch government, Prijatelji (Friends) has distinguished itself by contributing greatly to overcoming the "media blockade" that kept Srebrenica isolated for so many years after the war. The organization secured financial support for the local installation of a radio transmitter and acquired equipment capable of transmitting a radio and television signal throughout Bosnia, in both entities.[11]

When I spoke with Prijatelji's director, Dragana Jovanović, in 2012, Prijatelji employed twelve journalists who worked in various media, especially in the creation of radio programs. Jovanović stressed that the organization's radio studio operates all year:

> We are trying to get out information that lets people know that Srebrenica has to do with things other than July 11. People in the United States have the wrong idea about this place; they don't know very much about Srebrenica—and the reverse is true, too.
>
> We produce between forty and sixty reports a month. In improving the image of Srebrenica we hope that, among other things, this can improve the possibility of return to Srebrenica. There is a better exchange of information now than there was before.

I asked Jovanović if she felt that there was progress in the quality of people's lives in Srebrenica as compared to previous years. She answered, "The good side is that the security situation has been good. But on the other hand, belonging to an ethnic group is still felt to be the most important thing for many people. In such circles, as soon as someone goes out of their own group, there's labeling and criticism. We may have to wait for a new generation to get beyond that problem."

As my conversation with Jovanović drew to a close, she made a comment that summed up the attitude of activists, whether grassroots or NGO–based: "People need to believe in the power of their own influence."

BOSFAM: A CRAFTS COOPERATIVE OF DISPLACED WOMEN

While living in Tuzla soon after the war, I had the opportunity to get to know the members of Bosfam, a women's craft cooperative. I was impressed by these displaced women from Srebrenica—mostly widows—gathering to create a place of support and security for themselves. Led by Munira Beba Hadžić, Bosfam is one of the older NGOs in the country, having been formed before the war's end.

Hadžić, who was the principal of Srebrenica's elementary school before the war, told me that she and others began organizing as displaced persons in Tuzla in 1992.

> There were many of us. Many people were lost, had nothing. We sat together and said, "Let's think about what we can do by ourselves." We began to go around to the collective centers. If nothing else, we could at least talk to people. But it turned out that we didn't just talk. We began to try to find out information about who was where. Some people who

had been displaced from Srebrenica were in Croatia, some in Serbia, and so on. We tried to find out who was killed, who was captured.

In 1993 we were ready to work as an organization, but we had no resources. Then I found someone at the international relief organization Oxfam, a young man who came to visit. That meeting was very significant; he asked if he could work with us. We wanted to try to start working with the displaced women, who were only sitting. But when you sit, you can knit. With the help of Oxfam, we started a pilot project in three schools—all the schools in Tuzla were collective centers at that time. Oxfam got us some wool, and we started making sweaters and hats. We worked while the bombs were falling.

We didn't sell the goods we created but gave them away. The point was to give the women something to do to keep their minds off the bombs. The second project we undertook was to open a center for women to keep each other company. We created a center near the refugee camps, so that women could come visit.

In 1994 my director told me that Oxfam was preparing to change the work it was doing. I asked, "What can I do to help these women?" He said, "I don't know. No organization exists to help them." I said, "OK, I will make an NGO; just tell me what an NGO is." I had been working with Oxfam, but I did not really know what an NGO was.

In the late 1990s Bosfam grew into an organization that supported the women's craft cooperative in Tuzla, and it opened a center in Srebrenica as well. There, Serb and Bosniak returnees gathered to talk, knit, and earn a little money from their work. In the early years of return Bosfam provided administrative and logistical help, and a temporary haven for women who were returning or just visiting the city and encountering an unfriendly atmosphere. In 2002, Hadžić described the organization's work in that period thus:

Last year when we opened, we brought a van full of women, and a truck with furniture. When we arrived, everyone who was around on the street disappeared. No one wanted to say hello. One man, a neighbor, instinctively helped us move the stove. He was carrying one end of it. Then his wife called him from the balcony, saying that he had a telephone call. He went home, and didn't come back. Later people told me that they had been afraid of being seen there with Muslims.

Women were coming to Srebrenica to arrange their documents for return, but they had no place to sit and wait, or keep each other company. The first thing that we did was to tell them to come in and wait with us. They would not go into a kafana or a restaurant; it felt unpleasant.

As Bosfam's presence in Srebrenica grew, women congregated at the apartment that constituted the organization's center for the time being. One local Serb, Milena, described her experience with Bosfam:

Because of this organization, forty-five women here are earning a piece of bread. From 1993 Beba [Hadžić] helped many displaced persons in Tuzla, people from many municipalities in Podrinje.

I started working with Bosfam on the first day that they came here in 2001. I have been doing handiwork. My husband and I had no assistance in returning to Srebrenica; we lived like two animals in that concrete building. After a year or so we received something from friends in Sarajevo, basic necessities for living. We had a big circle of friends of all ethnicities, and we still do. Now, here at Bosfam, I have received material and psychological help. I don't have words to thank Beba.

Over the years, the value of Bosfam has arguably been as much its contribution in the psycho-social realm (to employ a bit of NGO-speak) as in any material assistance it provided. While donor funding—along with sales of handicrafts—has risen and fallen over the years, Bosfam continues its work, providing a haven and a small income for some displaced women, as well as legal counseling.

Over the years, I have visited Bosfam regularly, whether in Srebrenica or in Tuzla. During one of my visits, Hajrija worked on a weaving project. Winding a skein of wool as we talked, she discussed her life as a displaced person from Srebrenica and as a member of Bosfam:

I learned how to weave kilims [traditional flat-weave rugs] from my parents when I was young. Before the war, I was a housewife. I have three children: one daughter, and two sons. I stayed in Srebrenica throughout the war, with my daughter and my younger son.

During the war I lost around fifty relatives, including one brother, all of my closest family, all of my cousins. My husband died before the war, when the children were young.

I left Srebrenica in July 1995, on the fall of the town. It was a very dangerous situation. I came to Tuzla with my daughter—my son was expelled from Bratunac, where he was at the time. We had two houses; the one in Srebrenica was destroyed, but the one in Bratunac is still standing. They stole all my belongings, including eleven kilims.

When we came to Tuzla, we stayed in an empty apartment. We were evicted from there and then moved to another flat. I have submitted a request to return to my home in Srebrenica. I received an approval of this request, but have not yet found a donor to repair my home. We had four dunums of land with fruit trees—plums, walnuts—all this has been neglected.

Such are the stories of the women at Bosfam, a haven for many widows and displaced women from Srebrenica. As the years have gone by, some of the women have been able to return to their reconstructed homes in Srebrenica. For the others, time goes very slowly, and hope is an elusive thing. As I was talking to the women about marketing their products in the United States, one of them said, "Good, let's start a kilim factory in America! You can send us the papers, and we'll come over there and work. Are there sheep in your country?"

ONE FAMILY'S RETURN: TRAUMA, HARD WORK, AND RECOVERY

During a visit to Srebrenica I went with Hessie, a German activist, to visit my friends Magbula and Suljo on their farmland in a valley by Potočari. The couple were prewar residents of Srebrenica who had returned in 2001. Before the war Suljo had been a forestry inspector, and Magbula was a secretary in the same company. Upon their return, for a time they shared their house with a Serb who had been displaced from central Bosnia.

Hessie and I had a picnic with Magbula and Suljo on the land where they tilled several acres of vegetable gardens. They cultivated fields of potatoes, tomatoes, onions, and corn and tended a couple of greenhouses as well. Suljo lit a fire, Magbula roasted some chicken, and we ate pita and fresh cherries as well.

Magbula and Suljo had stayed in Srebrenica throughout the war. At different times, Suljo and their two children were all wounded. When Srebrenica fell, Suljo fled the enclave in the escaping column, walking through the woods with thousands of other men. Suljo told me that he walked for fourteen days, and on the fifteenth he arrived in safe territory, near Tuzla. Telling this story, Suljo made a face with hollow cheeks to show me how he arrived starving in Tuzla. The only time he had something to eat was when he found a cherry tree laden with overripe cherries.

As we talked, the moon, just shy of being full, came up over the hills to the east of the valley. Hessie recalled her own story of trauma; she was born in Germany just a few years before World War II. Her father had been a soldier, and he didn't return after the war. She never found out what happened to him. Hessie said that after the war, people didn't take the time to deal with what had happened to them psychologically. Now, she said, many Germans came to help after the war in Bosnia. For some of them, it was a way to work through their own wartime experiences.

Hessie recalled how once, in the mid-1990s, she heard a noise in her house and ran out into the street in fear, not even knowing what she was doing. This happened three times in a row before Hessie realized that a malfunction in the heating system was creating a noise just like the sound of the air-raid siren she had heard fifty years before.

Suljo looked at the moon coming up. He said, "When we were going through the woods, we had the good luck to have the full moon to light our way. I like the full moon, but now when I see it, sometimes it reminds me of that horrible experience. At times I still wake up dreaming of that long walk through the woods. This is what I have to live with."

Magbula and Suljo had stayed in Sarajevo for six years after the war, but they always wanted to come back home. Now they were there, but their children were still in school in the capital. After they came home to Srebrenica, the couple were nervous for the first five or six months. There were "incidents," they said, with people throwing bottles or rocks at their house. "You slept with one eye open," Suljo said. But by the time of my visit, these hostile incidents were a thing of the past.

Suljo and Magbula were better off than some returnees to Srebrenica because they had each other, and they worked hard on their land. That night of the picnic, their hands were torn up with blisters from the work. Suljo hoped that they would earn money and things would be easier. He said, "After what we lived through, we can live through this. People are made of steel."

Hessie nodded, and said, "I know."

As we sat around the fire, Suljo told us that he was happy that we were there as his guests. But he was one of the only surviving male members of his family. His brother and most of his cousins had been killed in the massacres. He wished that there were twenty or thirty other people at the picnic to welcome us, as there would have been in the old days.

In 2005 the UNDP secured milk cows for ten families and, along with this donation, organized a marketing and delivery system for the resulting milk. The system was called the "Milk Route."[12] Over the next year, the program grew to include over one hundred families, and the Pašalićes were beneficiaries of the program.

The UNDP provided ten cows to the Pašalić family. But first, Suljo had taken out a loan to purchase three calves, and he built a barn to shelter the cows. In the eyes of the UNDP donors, Suljo had justified the donation. In this way, Magbula and Suljo had obtained relative security, but they had implicitly signed up for the back-breaking and relentless work schedule of a dairy farmer.

On another day I arrived to the valley to find Magbula working in the barn, and Suljo up in the house, with a three-day beard, dirty work clothes, and his hands still calloused. He cleaned up, and we sat and had coffee and dinner.

Magbula and Suljo were keeping busy with the cows; at this point they were taking care of nine cows and four calves. But Suljo told me that they had not been paid for the milk they produced in over four months. When I asked why not, Suljo said, "No money. The state is failing." I asked if they would pay. He answered, "Yes, they'll pay. When our eyes fall out."

Magbula explained to me that they were usually paid late for their milk. Indeed, payments were resumed soon. But, she said, the Republika Srpska acted as the middleman, and, when RS officials evaluated the milk they purchased, they would downgrade it below what it was worth, and thus pay less for it. Then they would sell it to a milk processing plant in Tuzla as a higher grade of milk.

I first met Magbula in Srebrenica when she was alone there, having just returned home ahead of her husband. Ten years later, she was alone again. Suljo had suffered from heart disease, and he died in 2009. When I visited Magbula after that, at first I had a hard time recognizing her, because her customary bright smile was missing. We drank coffee under the *šadrvan*, a shade pergola near her house. Magbula's dog Ringo sat nearby. Magbula told me sadly, "Suljo was sixty when he died. Sixty, that's not many years." Then she asked me, "Do you know why he died? It was the lack of justice that killed Suljo; he could not get used to the new system, and that ate him up." She started to cry.

Particularly hard times came a couple of years after Suljo died. One winter the snow load crushed her greenhouse, and then in the spring there were floods that carried away all the firewood that Magbula had stored by the riverbank for winter. The flood took away the riverbank as well. Then in the summer of 2012, there was a killing drought, and the crops didn't grow very well; some did not grow at all.

Fantasizing about leisure, Magbula said that if she could rent her house in town, she would be able to live, and not work, "only spend." But, on consideration of that prospect, she realized that she would last only a few days living that way. She was used to working, and, with the help of her son and daughter, she carried on tending the cows. Magbula complained, however, that "other people have gotten used to not working," and during the summer, she was unable to hire anyone to help her with the farm. "No one wants to do such hard work. They have gotten used to humanitarian aid here. People received tractors and sold them; we need a tractor, but we can't get one. So much international humanitarian aid has come into Srebrenica, the place should be paved with gold. But people used that aid to fix up their houses here, and then went back to the city. That was a mistake."

Besides Magbula's personal difficulties, the worldwide economic crisis was ongoing and it hit Bosnia particularly hard. Discussing this, Magbula said, "There are people from here who live in Germany, and they come here two or three times a year. They have started coming less often, because of the economic crisis, they say. If the crisis affects them that way, then how does it affect us?

"But I'm not afraid of the crisis, after what we lived through in the war, with no food, always worrying that someone would get hurt or killed. Now we can work; whoever wants to work doesn't have to worry. I don't feel the crisis; the crisis doesn't interest me."

10

The Economic Life of Postwar Srebrenica

THE DESTRUCTION OF THE WAR MEANT THE ECONOMIC recovery of Srebrenica had to start from just about zero. To the extent that that recovery could eventually take place, it was going to depend on a complex combination of events and assistance including refugee return, political will, domestic and international aid, NGO assistance, hard work, and honesty.

STARTING FROM SCRATCH

In early 1999, while the municipality was still under sanctions and before any Bosniak return had taken place, the Repatriation Information Centre posted a report detailing economic life in Srebrenica. It stated that there was no agricultural production in the municipality, that all industries were working at 5 percent of their capacity, that there were no income-generation projects, no microcredit providers, no specialized schools, no hospital, and only one clinic.[1]

The destruction of private and public infrastructure as well as industrial capacity meant the economic situation in postwar Srebrenica was "bleak," according to a 2002 report from the United Nations Development Programme (UNDP): "Employment in Srebrenica municipality has fallen from a prewar high of 3,500 in 1991 to less than 200 in the year 2000. Similar unemployment levels exist throughout the region. Until the beginning of the year 2000 the region did not benefit economically at all from any international community involvement in Bosnia and Herzegovina."[2]

That was a stark contrast to the economy before the war, when, the UNDP reported, "prewar Srebrenica municipality was one of the top five municipalities in Bosnia and Herzegovina as measured by production output and average wages. Based upon a wealth of mineral resources, mining, ore processing, metal fabrication and related services, the area flourished. Today the picture could not look more different. The population has declined from over 37,000 to less than 7,500."[3]

In the early years of return and recovery, activists and returnees often recounted to me their memories of life in Srebrenica before the war. Ibrahim Hadžić, an employee of the municipal government, told me, "Before the war, the hotels were full. Everything worked toward tourism. There were competitions to see who had the nicest balcony. There were seventy-five hundred people living in Srebrenica town, and now there are probably only that number in the whole municipality."[4]

Svetlana, an NGO activist, recalls with pained nostalgia the prewar years in her hometown. She told me, "Then, Srebrenica was a city of flowers. Of a population of thirty-seven thousand in the municipality, thousands of people were employed. There were eleven working factories. There was a cultural/artistic association and an amateur theater. There were sports: a soccer team and a basketball team. In the Cultural Center there were performances in the evening from all over Bosnia. When the spa worked, there were tourists here from all over Yugoslavia. Each window, every balcony, was full of flowers. Every day the streets were cleaned."[5]

Senad Subašić, economic consultant to the municipal government, described the economic value of the spa in more detail, including the impact on his own life:

> Up to 1992, Srebrenica, as a well-known spa, registered seventeen hundred to two thousand visitors a day! Guests stayed in private homes as well as in hotels. The owner of a house with space for such guests could buy a car from the income from one season.
>
> I had a business, and a 440-square-meter house, with twenty beds available to visitors to the spa. I worked as an engineer for Energoinvest. My wife was the head of research for the bauxite mining company. Our income was around 8,000 DM per month. Now [2004], we earn around 500 KM each. You see how much the war killed me. And after nine years, I had to make an apartment in another town. This cost me dearly.

I'm an ordinary person, but I'm losing capital; I need 200,000 KM to fix my house in Srebrenica, and Srebrenica will still need five or six years to fix the spa. So the war set Srebrenica back at least fifteen years. Meanwhile, the world's arms producers can't keep up with demand.

So how rational is a war? During the war, the profiteers received 140 DM for a box of cigarettes, 80 DM for a liter of oil, and 60 DM for a kilo of flour. A person had to pay, but there was no work. So an ordinary person was completely destroyed.[6]

On the positive side, Subašić showed me a study, about two inches thick, of 250 sources of drinking water in Srebrenica municipality. Showing me a bottle of Jana water from Croatia, he said, "This water can't be better than what we have here." Ever the visionary, Subašić continued, "In order to have recovery here, we need to concentrate on the economy, to work with the potential of our resources. The conditions for real life exist in Srebrenica. There could be a factory of bio-plastics here. If you plant a ton of potatoes, you get sixty tons back. You can make the plastic from potatoes, from corn."[7]

The return activist Hakija Meholjić summed up the memory of the prewar period in one sentence: "Under Tito, the question was, where on the sea are you going to for vacation?"[8]

Life in Srebrenica after return began in the early 2000s could hardly be more different from these pleasant memories of prewar days.

Aleksa Milanović, NGO activist, told me:

The outstanding problems here are in the areas of employment, health care, schooling, and pensions. After the war I was in school to become an electrician, but there are no jobs. Srebrenica was once a developed place; now it is nothing. Nothing of the old economy works, only forestry. This employs around fifty people. The lead and zinc mines were closed three months ago [in late 1999], and four hundred people were laid off. There were fifteen hundred employed there before the war.

The biggest problem is that people don't want to return, because there is no work. They fix houses to which no one returns. Meanwhile, there is very little help for the Serbs, and that is not OK. That increases the resentment.[9]

In 2003, three years into the period of refugee return, Enes Đozić, an attorney for the Srebrenica branch office of the Ministry for Refugees, expressed pessimism about the prospects for recovery:

Time is the biggest enemy. Since it has taken so long for infrastructure and homes to be fixed here, people moved to places where they could find a better situation. It's been a long time since Dayton. Seven years compels people to make the best of where they are. They, especially the younger people, got used to the places where they ended up during or after the war. They got work, resolved their housing situation.

You can see for yourself that this is a dead town; there's no place for kids, only the older people are returning. It's better in the villages. There, they can raise something to live on. But even there, there's no support, fertilizer, electricity, schools, clinics.[10]

Aware of the daunting material conditions in Srebrenica in the early days of the new century, international officials developed a comprehensive plan for assistance not only to Srebrenica, but also to the neighboring municipalities of Bratunac and Milići. In May 2002, the United Nations Development Programme (UNDP) launched its Srebrenica Regional Recovery Programme (SRRP) during a widely publicized donor conference held at the UN's New York headquarters.

About twenty-five countries attended the conference. Over US$5 million was pledged toward a budget of US$12.5 million. Early on, the Republika Srpska was one of the largest donors and was the only donor not to earmark funds for any specific activity. Projects that the UNDP supported included road and bridge reconstruction, provision of seed and fertilizer to over two hundred families, and development of a mobile clinic in cooperation with Srebrenica municipality and the local hospital.

A number of international nongovernmental organizations worked within the framework of the SRRP to contribute to reconstruction in Srebrenica. Together with agencies of the governments of the Federation and the Republika Srpska, these organizations worked to restore hundreds of houses in at least a dozen villages and towns in the municipality.

Besides repair of homes, the SRRP undertook to implement a number of important development projects as well. The UNHCR donated equipment to a dairy in Zvornik, which agreed to buy milk from returnee communities in Srebrenica. Over one hundred families in the municipality signed contracts to sell milk. International NGOs provided credit and grants for agricultural production and small businesses support.

During this start-up period of the SRRP, I traveled the steep, rough road to Sućeska with Zulfo Salihović, high up into the dense mountains surrounding Srebrenica town. The road was just as bad as it had been a couple of years earlier, when I traveled there with the first returnees to the village. We came to a summit where there was one damaged house and one that had been repaired, in which Zulfo's uncle, also named Zulfo, lived with his wife, Sejda. We stopped to visit them.

Uncle Zulfo and Sejda told me that they had returned to Srebrenica the previous year, in the spring of 2002. They were living there on the top of the world, in a place called "Spasin Do," all alone without even a hint of a neighbor. Uncle Zulfo said, "There are no trucks or airplanes coming by here." They had running water, but no electricity. They showed me the electrical poles that were being erected to carry in a new power line.

Uncle Zulfo told me, "It has been a struggle to survive. During the winter, the snow comes up to one's chest." When he and Sejda were snowed in for ten days the previous winter, a mobile phone was their only connection with the outside world.

All the houses and barns in the vicinity had been destroyed during the war. Uncle Zulfo was hoping to get a donation from a relief organization to rebuild his barn. He said, "It is a shame for a farmer to be without a cow, but you need a barn first."

As part of the SRRP recovery project, the UNDP announced the establishment, together with the Canadian government, of funding for "Quick Impact Projects" that would provide between 5,000 and 15,000 KM for activities within the three relevant municipalities.[11] The recovery program began to be implemented just as refugee return to Srebrenica was peaking. Alongside this project, in the mid-2000s a number of international companies, and a few domestic firms as well, established a foothold in Srebrenica. While there may have been an altruistic motive to this development, the presence of an unemployed and inexpensive workforce was also a draw.

In 2008 Cvijetin Maksimović of the municipal Department for Social Activities and Public Services outlined the decade's economic trajectory to me:

> Economic recovery began around the year 2000. All people from Srebrenica, Serbs and Bosniaks, have been displaced. But there is no longer obstruction or fear for one's security, except of some land mines. The problems have to do with the lack of infrastructure. Electrical power, water, and roads will have been connected to all return settlements by the end of this year. We have fixed roads, and there are more repairs every year.
>
> In employment, there has been some development, with several small factories opening up for production. The zinc and bauxite mines are working. Not only people from Srebrenica are working in them. There is a zinc-coating factory in Potočari, and a wheelchair factory is going to be opened. Foreign development agencies are supporting agricultural development and cattle raising. And there is more agricultural work here than there was before the war.

It has also been a problem that workers have been hired to work in local factories, only to be laid off before their employers would be required to pay them benefits. In this way, corporations coming from other parts of Bosnia or abroad are able to exploit start-up subsidies for the establishment of local production but do not share that economic advantage with the workers.

In 2005 the Slovenian company Cimos opened an auto-parts factory in Potočari. Ultimately the factory employed upward of one hundred workers. While such small industries were being established, development in the agricultural sector focused on berries for jam and juice, with possibilities for organic produce. The Srebrenica region was amenable to small farms that could independently supply fruit to local processing plants. A winery was later established, employing another twenty people.

By 2006, the regional economy around Srebrenica was perking up. At least several hundred returnees, both Serb and Bosniak residents of the municipality, were finally employed. In 2008 Albina Beganović of the legal aid organization Vaša Prava told me, "This is the beginning of a turnaround. Not only elderly people have returned to the villages or Srebrenica; there are also plenty of young people. Life is returning to Srebrenica."[12]

FRUSTRATION

The Robna Kuća (department store) dominating the center of Srebrenica had stood empty and devastated since the war. Its imposingly dreary visage, with boarded-up windows and, more often than not, posters touting extreme nationalist Serb figures, presented an ominous message to people arriving at what passed for the main business section of town. In 2008, I found that it had been refurbished. Now there stood a bright and colorful three-story multiple-use building. The ground floor was filled by a supermarket; one no longer had to travel ten kilometers to Bratunac for trifles. The upper floors were occupied by a kafana, along with offices for NGOs and a political party or two.

While economic life in the late 2000s was markedly different from ten years earlier, conditions were perceived differently by various returnees. Not all was rosy, and not all were satisfied. Young Arifana complained to me, "If I didn't have a job here I wouldn't stay here for two seconds longer. I came back in 2002, and it took me four years to get a job—and for low pay. Bosniaks can't get a state job here. They hire Serbs from Serbia, from Belgrade, or from Banja Luka."

Hakija Meholjić evaluated the economic situation for Bosniak returnees to Srebrenica: "Returnees are second-class citizens. For example, people can't get health care, and that prevents more return from happening. The social situation is such that the state is not concerned with the welfare of the people. They [the state officials] are a group of criminals. A person is nothing, whether he is Muslim, Croat, or Serb. If people had work to do, it would be okay. Now Albania is better off than we are."[13]

The worldwide economic recession that started in 2008 was felt throughout Bosnia, and particularly in Srebrenica. During the next few years economic growth in the municipality slowed and fewer opportunities for a livelihood presented themselves to ordinary returnees. The stagnation exacerbated feelings of frustration that had been stewing since the early return period.

One common target of the frustration was the UNDP and its development project, the results of which were obscure to many returnees. Throughout the 2000s one often heard the comment that "the UNDP has done nothing," often accompanied by expressions of suspicion as to the fate of vast donations for recovery. While it is clear and demonstrable that the SRRP program implemented a broad array of development projects, over the years there has been a disconnect between the implementers and ordinary local citizens, who have often felt that time was standing still in Srebrenica. And it is impossible to refute the accusation that large portions of donor funds never reached the municipality.

As early as 2003 and 2004, Senad Subašić criticized the incipient SRRP thus: "Perhaps the UNDP is doing the wrong strategy by giving equally to three municipalities. Between 1990 and 1995, Milići and Bratunac were not destroyed and were stable economically. But the UNDP is dividing the funds equally by thirds. Our mayor sought

50 percent of the funding, but the UNDP in Sarajevo did not allow this. They should set aside 60 percent of the funding for Srebrenica."

Voicing criticism of the funding process, Subašić added, "Our biggest enemy is uncontrolled transfers—for example, 34 million KM was donated by the Dutch government, but very little of it arrived here.[14] Some of the donors should be *here* to control these things."

At the same time, Subašić offered another side to the story, countering the widespread criticism of the UNDP projects:

> We need a lot of money to fix things. People are not seeing this, and their representatives are not telling them. There is more change for the better than can be seen. The progress that has happened has mostly been in the last year [2004], but after fifteen years, people are depressed. No one wants to work for 20 KM (US$15) a day, even though this is not negligible money in the Bosnian situation. Many people have become used to living on a pension.
>
> It took a long time after World War II to create the riches of Germany. Here, everything has been ruined, and there is very little money coming in from the international community. The municipality can only borrow 450,000 KM at a time, so it can't do very much.

In addition to the criticism of the UNDP projects, there has also been suspicion of long-distance rule over Srebrenica from Banja Luka, the capital of the Serb-controlled entity. At the very least, this is understandable because the majority of Srebrenica's returnees never asked to live under the control of the political heirs of those who destroyed their hometown. But comments from a number of activists and local officials alike also point to a kind of economic discrimination against Srebrenica, the only municipality in the RS that has had a Bosniak-dominated local government for most of the postwar period.

Consultant to the municipal government Ibrahim Hadžić told me, "All of the economic decisions are controlled from Banja Luka. We don't know who is buying the companies, but they are not hiring. The local government writes letters that no one answers. Directors are appointed from Banja Luka. Even that portion of income that should return to Srebrenica does not. So the Banja Luka government is doing all it can to impoverish Srebrenica."[15]

In 2006 Hakija Meholjić, always the most acerbic commentator, said, "Banja Luka is robbing the forestry and the mines, and the local administration is robbing the international donations. There's a rule among elected politicians that they must steal as much as they can in two to four years, to support their grandchildren. They cooperate very well. The goal of government is not to secure better living conditions for people. Five percent of the population is abnormally rich, and the rest are poor. Human norms have been devalued here. People only want power for the privilege it brings."

Senad Subašić elaborated, "Regarding Srebrenica, in the RS all decisions are made centrally, without consulting Srebrenica. For example, they sold the concession for the mine to a company in Gradiška, so the money goes to Gradiška, not to the Srebrenica municipality. They didn't ask us. So in that way, they are continuing to kill Srebrenica. We do not have a way to defend ourselves from that."

In attempting to comprehend the economic development of Srebrenica in the more recent postwar period, one must thus take into account the whole range of perceptions, and certainly the actual living conditions of returnees. Those conditions have improved, but recalling the devastated state of the municipality after the war, that is not saying much.

A worker at a local kafana said to me upon my arrival in 2013, "Suffering, Peter, suffering—that is Srebrenica." She explained that her electricity bill was 100 KM (US$60) a month, and that it did not leave her with enough money to visit her children, living in another town: "I don't have time, and I can't send them any money."

During that visit, while walking home one evening, I chanced upon a pair of elderly Serb residents of the town. As we were chatting, one of them said to me, "Did you come here to watch us starve? My pension is meager, and I have no help from the municipality. If things don't get better soon, the only thing left to me will be to take a rope and hang myself."

A REGIME OF CORRUPTION

Annual reports from Transparency International regularly place Bosnia-Herzegovina at or near the bottom of the scale in Europe concerning public perception of corruption. Corruption in Srebrenica is a local manifestation of the problem that afflicts all Bosnia. It has been reported since the early 2000s that sums of around a billion KM have disappeared annually owing to dishonest practices.[16] In September 2013 the Bosnian Agency for Prevention of Corruption announced that 1.4 billion KM was lost to corruption each year. The report calculated this as equivalent to the daily needs for a family of four being lost each second of the day.[17]

In many parts of Bosnia, corruption is routine, and ordinary citizens know quite accurately how much money they need to bribe a doctor, a professor, or a judge. The journalist Hasan Hadžić has reported a similar situation in Srebrenica, where relief donations have been channeled to recipients with an obligatory "commission" paid to local authorities. He wrote, "The exact tariff was known: building materials for one floor of a house costs 2,000 KM." Hadžić added that it even happened that a shipment of building materials was brought from the Federation to Srebrenica or another part of Podrinje; the delivery would be broadcast over television—and then it would be brought right back to the Federation.[18]

Looking at assistance to Srebrenica, unofficial estimates for the first ten years after the war placed donations at 300 million KM.[19] Overlapping with that period, the UNDP coordinated the donation of 70 million KM to Srebrenica by 2010.[20]

Very soon after the end of the war, Saudi Arabia donated US$130 million, but there was scant record of the fate of this money ten years later. The funds arrived in Tuzla, where three companies were formed and received 50,000 KM each, but there was no trace of the rest of the money. In 2005 the Tuzla Canton prosecutor announced an investigation into the donation, and Srebrenica's Mayor Malkić commented, "It is obvious that we have a disproportion between funds that have been raised and the restoration of houses and assistance in return. . . . There have been many [project] implementers and many donors who do not wish to give information."[21]

Regarding a total donation of 120 million euros by the Dutch government by 2013, the Organized Crime and Corruption Reporting Project (OCCRP) announced that "large amounts of that money were lost to corruption," noting further that "little aid that should have gone to rebuilding homes for families affected by the genocide or the Bosnian war has reached those people." A member of the Dutch Parliament called for an investigation of the corruption.[22]

The state of the municipal water supply in Srebrenica provides a good illustration of the dynamic of reconstruction, waste, corruption, and suspicion. The water supply infrastructure suffered from wartime damage, as well as deterioration due to age. Water lost through leakage approached 50 percent and, to make matters worse, the water that did arrive in people's homes was not deemed potable.

With the establishment of the UNDP projects, donations were provided for repair of the water system. And yet, year in and year out, the pipes still leaked, and the water was still not fit to drink. These problems were not resolved until late 2010. In 2008 Cvijetin Maksimović told me that the water reservoir "sometimes freezes, and sometimes there's no water." Referring to the millions of dollars earmarked for water supply repair, Maksimović said, "No one knows where the donations for the water repair went to." This, after I had been hearing every year for the previous eight years that donations had been provided.

As with other donations via the UNDP, part of the problem has been poor transmission of information to returnees. In fact, the organization was working on the water problem. By 2007 it had installed water systems in eight villages and provided water treatment for a couple thousand households.[23] But trust in the authorities was so low, and information so scarce, that even in 2010 Srebrenicans were still hesitant to drink the water coming out of their faucets at home, and they were still asking what happened to the donations.

Cronyism and corruption connected to political favoritism significantly hold back Srebrenica's development. The postwar fates of two industries that were once mainstays of the Srebrenica region exemplify the problem. Significant obstruction, tied to the granting of development concessions, has blocked the development of mining and tourism. The clearing away of these obstacles to development would make all the difference to the regional economy and to the local people, who scarcely feel the effects of the millions invested in Srebrenica.

CORRUPTION IN THE MINES

Srebrenica takes its name from the Bosnian word for silver. The ground under Srebrenica, exploited since Roman times, has been rich with lead, zinc, silver, and bauxite. For most of the 1990s the lead and zinc mines that had employed up to fifteen hundred workers before the war were inactive. In 1999 Ibrahim Hadžić, formerly an engineer in the mines, told me, "The mines in Srebrenica were the biggest lead and zinc mines in Bosnia. They employed around thirteen hundred workers and were the municipality's biggest source of work. There was still some silver. The mines had modern equipment. Nothing has been maintained since 1992; now it's probably no good and will need replacing."

The lead and zinc mines were located near a village called Sase, named after early Saxon immigrant miners. The Sase mines were closed during the war—except when they were used as an internment center for local Muslims captured by Serb forces. It has been reported that during the war the prewar reserves of the mine simply "disappeared," and outstanding debts to workers were never paid.[24]

Work at the mines started and stopped several times in the first postwar years. A few hundred workers were employed, but their pay was sporadic, and the mine administrators failed to pay into their retirement funds. In the spring of 2002 Charlie Powell, director of the Srebrenica branch of the OHR, told me, "The mines are closed for now. The RS government closed them, and they are running the mines into the ground in order to buy them more cheaply. The RS privatization agency is stalling. There are not enough international officials to go around and see everything that is happening. In the higher scheme of things, this area is not a priority."

Between 1999 and 2003 the lead and zinc mines operated at around 30 percent of their capacity. In 2003 it was reported that "weak results in production, aged technology, unprepared excavation sites and a lack of trained personnel have resulted in a loss of six million KM. . . . Most of the credit [received for mining] has been spent on unpaid wages. Two million KM would be required to reactivate production that was interrupted at the beginning of last year. More than 400 workers are unable to retire because pensions were not covered in the postwar period."[25]

In mid-2004 the Republika Srpska government signed an ill-fated five-year contract with the Russian mining company Južuralzoloto. The company promised to pay off the Sase mines' 2 million KM debt to workers as well as a 13 million KM debt to bankers, and to invest nearly 11 million KM in the mines for updating technology over the period of the agreement. In mid-2005 domestic and international officials, examining the agreement, warned that it allowed the Russian company to retain for itself the entire potential monthly income of 700,000 KM.[26]

Critics also noted that the agreement did not in fact ensure payment to the workers, and that there were no stipulations to protect nearby rivers from lead and arsenic pollution. In response, then RS prime minister Dragan Mikerević stated that "the opinion of the international community and journalists on this does not interest me at all. . . . I stand behind everything I signed."[27]

When miners filed a lawsuit against Južuralzoloto because of its failure to pay them for their previous work, the Russian company's bank account was blocked. In response, the company's financial director formed a private company through which to funnel income from the mines. Many of the fifty-two miners who participated in the lawsuit were fired. A lawyer representing the miners threatened to file a criminal complaint against the mine administrators.[28]

In 2005, a Banja Luka court found in favor of five Bosnian and foreign creditor banks and temporarily prohibited Južuralzoloto from running the Sase mines. The company was given three days to arrange to pay its debt not only to the banks but also to unpaid workers.[29]

At the same time, news outlets reported that the mines owed 630,000 KM in unpaid taxes, but that "no one has expressed an interest in paying that debt." The Russian company was not paying wage taxes to the RS government, a lapse made possible by the 2004 agreement, but an arrangement the RS tax administration stated was illegal. The then minister of finance Svetlana Cenić called for a series of changes to the agreement.[30]

The court decision was not enforced, and workers continued to be mistreated. In early 2006 the miners' union stated that there had been fifteen injuries and one fatality on the job since Južuralzoloto took over, but that the Russian company refused to pay the workers' health insurance. A representative of the miners stated, "We are signing blank work contracts, so the workers do not know how much they will be paid. No one can complain about such arrangements, because they will lose their work." Mayor Malkić complained that the mine administrators had failed to pay taxes to the municipality as well.[31]

Evaluating this situation, Toby Robinson, provisional banking administrator for the OHR, declared that the RS government was "not interested in a resolution to the situation in this mine." She added that she had called and sent messages to the relevant authorities in Banja Luka "countless times to find a solution," but that no one had responded to her messages.[32]

In March 2006 the Basic Court in Srebrenica prohibited export and sale of ore from the Sase mine, but in spite of this order, immediately afterward the company exported ore worth nearly US$300,000 to Serbia. Although the Bosnian tax administration and customs officials had been informed of Srebrenica's decision, trucks bearing the ore nevertheless slipped across the border with Serbia.[33]

Discussing the incident, the director of Sase mines stated that the export was undertaken because the court decision "was not final." It seemed that the fact that Južuralzoloto and its front companies in the Republika Srpska were evading local and entity taxes, flouting their debt to numerous banks, failing to pay workers, and violating clear prohibition orders from two local courts did not overly disturb the RS minister of the economy.

It was tempting to conclude that the arrangement that was so clearly damaging to the ordinary people of the RS was of benefit to the powers that agreed to it. Indeed, in such situations, the common response is "Nekom to odgovara"—"someone" is benefitting from this.

This suspicion was shared by the Bosnia-Herzegovina Office of the Prosecutor's Special Department on Organized Crime, which opened an investigation against former prime minister Mikerević and two of his former cabinet ministers, along with ten other persons for "abuse of position and authority" (the common euphemism for corruption) in the case of the Sase mines.[34] The accused all the way from Mikerević down to the director of the mines were charged, among other things, with driving the mining concern to bankruptcy. Prosecutors asserted that the director and the inspector of the mines had received bribes from the Russians.[35]

Prosecutors also noted that in spiriting ore out of Bosnia, the mining company had gleaned over five tons of silver and nearly a ton of gold, at an estimated value of nearly 25 million KM.[36]

It was also revealed that Južuralzoloto had formed second-tier and third-tier corporations, such as the Gradiška-based D.o.o. Gross, to evade financial sanctions by rerouting payment for ore through parallel bank accounts. This process was developed to such an extent that prosecutors were no longer certain that the Russian company was even involved in the violations.[37]

Toby Robinson closed the Sase mines by decree for a year; they reopened in the spring of 2007 after a period of investigation. By 2008—one year before the five-year agreement with Južuralzoloto was to expire—the mines were privatized. They continued to be administered by D.o.o. Gross in its capacity as a subsidiary of Mineco, a company based in Great Britain and Switzerland.

Former prime minister of the Republika Srpska Dragan Mikerević and some of his associates were jailed in the spring of 2009,[38] but the investigation against them was ultimately dropped. In the years since the end of the Russian exploitation of Sase mines, news reports have alternately announced that the mine was going into bankruptcy and that business was thriving.

Bankruptcy proceedings started in 2009 and lasted for at least five years. In 2014, former mine workers sued for more than a half million KM in back pay. This, in spite of the fact that the present owners were reporting successful functioning of the mine and employment of five hundred workers. But the unpaid former miners, some of whom had worked for the mine for over four decades, were experiencing difficulty in even finding an audience for their grievances, and they threatened to blockade the mines.[39] This threat was not carried out, and to date, the former miners have not been compensated. In the years after this, D.o.o. Gross continued to report growth in production at the Sase mines.[40]

The story of Sase mines is but one example of a broader operation that began during the war, of corruption and plunder by a network of regional and international corporations sometimes known locally as an "octopus." The plunder of local resources starts with the blessing of local or regional authorities, who receive kickbacks from companies that exploit those resources with little regard to either the environment or the well-being of workers—in the case of Srebrenica, be they Serb or Muslim.

This crooked operation is sometimes called "ethnic privatization," because it benefits the corrupt ethnonationalist political infrastructure that is in place in any given part of Bosnia-Herzegovina. What has been described above takes place throughout the former Yugoslavia, from holdings under the Mostar-based Aluminij corporation to the Zenica- and Prijedor-based holdings of ArcelorMittal. Although the Muslims were the greatest victims of the aggression on Bosnia-Herzegovina, ultimately the "transitional" free-for-all that amounted to the wrecking of the country's economy for the profit of a few was practiced with equal enthusiasm by the Bosniak, Croat, and Serb leaders and their cronies.

It is true, as is the case with Sase mines, that there have been periodic work stoppages due to local court decisions, along with criminal investigations and occasional arrests. But just as with Sase, local courts have little power to advocate for the ordinary residents of their municipalities. The vast majority of such cases are dropped either because of "lack of evidence," or because of statute of limitations expirations.

Sase is a textbook illustration of postwar plunder. And the bauxite mines, another potential source of economic stability for the Srebrenica region, were subject to similar crooked maneuvers. In 2006 the bauxite mines were temporarily closed because of "improper procedures" having to do with operating without appropriate documentation and licenses.[41] The following year companies operating the bauxite mines sued the Banja Luka–based company Balkal, which had privatized the mines, for failure to pay nearly a million KM for exploitation work undertaken at the mines.[42] And as recently as spring of 2014 workers were protesting about missed wage payments.

In the case of the Sase mines, the "octopus" in question traces back to Mineco. A search for information on that company, combined with the word "corruption," opens up a topic that is worthy of an entire separate book. Mineco has been involved in wrecking companies, with accompanying environmental destruction and impoverishment of workers, in Serbia, Romania, and Bosnia at the very least, and its "tentacles" reach to Russia and Cyprus.

Providing just one quote here is illustrative:

> Mineco AG, a Swiss-based company run by Serbian businessmen, owns a number of Balkan companies involved in mineral exploration, mining, and agriculture. But the firm has been dogged by allegations of corruption and poor business practices.

Mineco board member Dimitrije (Miki) Aksentijević is accused along with a key aide by Romanian authorities of corruption. Yet they appear to live freely in England, where they manage their Balkans business empire.[43]

Mineco and the fate of the Sase mines at Srebrenica are examples of Bosnia-Herzegovina's postwar, Dayton-approved economic destruction. And compared to other practitioners of cronyism and plunder, the operators of Mineco are relative amateurs among the long list of opportunistic parasites who have taken advantage of "transition" to enrich themselves at the expense of the ordinary people of Bosnia-Herzegovina.

In the mining sector overall, industry managers have continued the characteristic practice of fulfilling obligations to all parties involved except the miners. In the spring of 2014 bauxite miners went on a series of on-and-off strikes, punctuated by negotiations with the mining company AD Rudnik Boksit. The forty or so company employees demanded back pay for four months of work, as well as payments into the benefit funds. This followed a work stoppage the previous December, when the miners were promised several months' wages that were due to them, but were only paid for one. As a union representative said, "If the mine is working, but the workers are not receiving their pay, then we do not see the logic of working."

The fact that working without payment for extended periods of time was under discussion is an indication of the scarcity of work in Srebrenica and the general economic desperation in the municipality.

GUBER SPA

The Guber spa was central to the thriving prewar economy of Srebrenica. During the Tito era visitors from throughout Yugoslavia and beyond came to Srebrenica, stayed at the hotels, enjoyed the healthful effects of the mineral waters, and left large sums of money in the region. Ibrahim Hadžić recalled that Guber was so popular that one practically had to have "connections" to reserve a room at one of its hotels.

The restaurant at the spa was bombed and torched during the war. Two hotels closer to Srebrenica town survived, though in neglected condition. For quite some years afterward, the gloomy remnants of the Domavia and Argentarium hotels were used primarily as collective centers for Serbs displaced from Muslim-controlled parts of Bosnia-Herzegovina. The spa has remained a ghostly, nonfunctioning hole in the heart of Srebrenica's economy.

In 2002 Izet Imamović took me for a tour around the outskirts of Srebrenica and up to the Guber mineral springs. A pleasant cobblestone road built by the Austrians a century ago winds through the woods, passing springs beside the road. People used to walk the several kilometers to the top. Spring was just beginning, with fruit trees flowering. One hillside was covered with purple wildflowers.

There were benches to rest on every so often, but on this visit, we noticed that the wood had been removed from most of their concrete pedestals, to be used for kindling. As we rode up into the hills, we passed a couple of people coming down with a wheelbarrow loaded with firewood.

There are more than forty mineral springs around Srebrenica. Izet pointed out the different springs, describing their medicinal properties. One spring is good for rashes and other skin problems. One is good for eye problems; another, for heart disease.

We arrived at the ruins of the restaurant at the top of the road, in a beautiful wooded setting between two springs. Izet pointed out the plaza next to the restaurant, where vacationers and townspeople used to sit and listen to live music while they ate. He said that they used to roast lamb there every day. One can imagine that once upon a time it was an exquisitely pleasant place to relax after walking up through the forest.

A couple of years later, by which time several thousand Srebrenicans had returned to live in the municipality, I visited the town on May Day, traditionally a popular workers' holiday throughout Eastern Europe. Some local leaders were trying to revive the once thriving cultural life of the town.

Local activists sponsored the revival of a traditional walk up to Guber mineral springs. A few hundred people participated, and there was meat roasting, socializing, and folk music and dancing in the parking lot next to the burned-out motel. Younger people came from Sarajevo and Tuzla to visit their birthplace and their older relatives on this day, and there was a cheerful atmosphere. I shot a few hoops with other visitors on the potholed basketball court. I had the impression that, for Srebrenica, there could be life after death.

Historical records show that Guber spa and its mineral waters were highly regarded in the scientific community during the Austro-Hungarian occupation—and that they had been popular for centuries before the Austrians developed them. Centered around two main sources, Crni Guber and Mali Guber, are dozens of springs that contain iron, copper, cobalt, manganese, and other minerals. Certain of the springs, containing different combinations of these minerals, have been identified as relieving rheumatism and sinus problems, counteracting loss of weight and appetite, improving sight, slowing the progress of multiple sclerosis, and healing skin diseases.[44] Indeed, the name "Guber" derives from the Turkish word for leprosy.

The Austrians began industrial bottling of Guber mineral water, exporting hundreds of thousands of bottles a year to places as distant as the United States and Canada.[45] After World War II Yugoslav analysts published reports about the restorative effect of Guber waters on people with anemia, and bottles of the water were sold in pharmacies throughout the country.[46] In that period the Yugoslav government constructed two hotels and a sanitarium with tubs and bathing pools, and health tourism began to thrive.

People taking advantage of the healing waters could also hunt and fish in the vicinity. The Jadar and Drina Rivers were nearby, and, after a dam across the Drina was constructed in 1966, Lake Perućac offered another recreation point. Near the spa, areas for sports such as basketball were also developed. The entire complex of tourism in the Srebrenica region grew to the point where, up to the outbreak of the recent war, as many as ninety thousand overnight stays were recorded annually. The income to local recipients was numbered in the millions of dollars.[47]

A PRIVATIZATION SNAFU AT GUBER

In the decades since the war, the healing waters of the Guber mineral springs flowed into drainage ditches. Although the land around the old restaurant was privatized, development leading to the revival of the spa, and thus of the Srebrenica economy, was obstructed by legal maneuvers from Banja Luka.

First privatized in 2004, the concession to the spa was purchased by Prnjavor businessman Radojica Ratkovac in 2008. Two years later Ratkovac began construction of two buildings, a bottling plant and a hotel and restaurant, on the old spa site. Down the hill, reconstruction began on the old Argentaria sanitarium as well. It was hoped that Guber spa could be receiving guests by mid-2011.

However, politics intervened, and construction was halted. When I visited Srebrenica in 2012, the two buildings were fenced off, nearly finished but empty, without windows or façade. I ducked around the fence to see that the face of the old spa grounds had changed radically; the construction was truly grandiose. The opening of the spa heralded hundreds of new jobs for the region. But it appeared that Banja Luka had other ideas.

In May 2011 Srebrenka Golić, RS minister for planning and construction, declared that the land on which the Guber reconstruction was situated fell under the legal category of the "common good," or protected natural wealth as of a 1961 law, and that only her ministry had the authority to grant concessions for its use. With this, Golić annulled the municipality's decision to grant Ratkovac the concession to build on the Guber lands.[48]

Officials in Srebrenica's municipal government, naturally, disagreed with Golić's decision. Senad Subašić, director of the municipal department of urbanism and housing affairs, declared that Ratkovac's firm AD Guber was entirely within its rights to build on the land, and that all relevant decisions by the municipality had been made according to law. Minister Golić responded that Srebrenica had not delivered appropriate documentation about the building concession. She characterized this as a "classic case of disrespect for RS institutions" and announced the initiation of court proceedings against municipal authorities.[49]

Citizens of Srebrenica circulated a petition in support of the construction, gathering forty-seven hundred signatures—no small number in a municipality with, at most, a couple thousand more inhabitants than that. But the building site remained quiet as the municipality appealed the stop-work order in court.[50] The case slouched from one court to another, with construction sporadically resuming and then being halted again. Time went by without development of the promising spa. In mid-2012, with construction still halted, acting mayor Duraković stated, "If the municipality were in control of its natural resources, in three years Srebrenica would be a developed city."[51]

The example of Guber spa brings into focus the nature of the relationship between Banja Luka and Srebrenica. Here, Guber and Srebrenica serve as an extreme example of all minority return communities in the Serb-dominated entity. Added to neglect and plunder is the obstruction of attempts at significant economic development for return communities.

Cronyism is a significant element of the relationship. Bosnian politics is governed by the dynamic known as "partyocracy" (*strankokratija*). Each of the half dozen most powerful political parties in the country replicates in miniature the old autocratic paradigm from the Tito era, with the party working as an extension of the personality of its strongman leader. One commentator has characterized this system as a "constellation of oligarchs in an accountability-free pseudo-democracy."[52]

In this system, each party in power takes control of the lucrative state-owned corporations under its purview and appoints its functionaries to manage them to the benefit of party favorites. Different parties cooperate in managing this system of corruption—but they also compete fiercely at times, especially in election periods.

This dynamic of Bosnian politics was manifested in the case of the Guber spa when, in June 2012, the government of the RS granted a concession for the exploitation of most of Guber's mineral waters to the Potočari-based company Argentum 09. This company thus came into direct conflict with AD Guber, which was occupying the Guber spa and constructing a bottling plant in that location.

The concession Argentum received granted the company access to 80 percent of the waters from the Veliki Guber spring. Argentum had privatized a defunct factory in Potočari for eventual conversion into a bottling plant. Conditions of the concession grant stipulated that Argentum was to invest 32 million KM in development, and to construct the bottling facility within a half year of the grant (from mid-2012). Argentum was also required to restore the road to Guber spa.

But Argentum was unable to access the Guber waters because of the fence constructed around the area after the RS government placed a stop-work order on construction by AD Guber.

Some months after the concession grant to Argentum was made public, *Glas Srpske* (Voice of Srpska), an RS newspaper loyal to President Dodik, published an article describing Radojica Ratkovac, majority owner of AD Guber, as "building on someone else's land." The article devoted most of its space to a complaint from Milorad Motika, the owner of Argentum 09. In December 2012 Motika stated that the concession granted to his company required Argentum to take possession of Guber lands by that month, but that he was prevented from doing so by the presence of AD Guber on the land.[53]

Moving from complaint to threat, Motika announced that he was going to sue the municipality of Srebrenica for lost income in the case of Guber.[54]

Control of the Guber waters thus became tied up in ongoing court proceedings. A year later, president of the Srebrenica Municipal Assembly Dr. Radomir Pavlović stated, "This is a political problem [in which] the citizens of Srebrenica are the losers. . . . Let the municipality sell one of the two buildings [in construction at Guber] and then the spa can be put to work using that 20 percent to which the local community has access regardless of the concession."[55]

It is relevant to consider the party affiliations of the figures mentioned here. In the course of 2012, municipal elections shaped up as a fierce mayoral contest between Ćamil Duraković, a Bosniak, and Vesna Kočević, a local Serb running as a member of Milorad Dodik's SNSD party. Radomir Pavlović was the head of the Srebrenica branch of that party. And entering into this mix, Radojica Ratkovac, a Serb from Prnjavor, ran for mayor as an independent candidate.

So principals in the Argentum-versus-Guber conflict were also rival candidates in the upcoming mayoral race. Duraković promoted local control of resources, while Kočević, despite a stated desire for the well-being of Srebrenica, was part of the political apparatus directed from Banja Luka. Ratkovac was the wild card, an ambitious independent businessman who had ventured to invest a large sum of money in development in Srebrenica.

In mid-2016, a reporter from EuroBlic questioned Motika about his role in blocking development of the spa at Guber. He asserted that he had no relationship with Argentum 09 and admonished, "That is very complicated, and it would be better if you didn't fool around with that." But EuroBlic investigated further and learned from the District Commercial Court in Bijeljina that Motika was indeed one of the founders of the company and that he was its authorized representative.[56]

THE ROLE OF MILORAD MOTIKA

There are well-documented instances when certain RS businessmen have received concessions from the RS government because of a close personal relationship with President Dodik. Available information on Milorad Motika, owner of Argentum 09 (and president of a large Zvornik-based bauxite processing company), leads one to conclude that such a personal relationship between Motika and Dodik exists. What's more, media sources present fascinating evidence of Motika's close involvement in the implementation of violence and plunder that gave birth to the Republika Srpska and that are at the roots of the thriving ethnonationalist mafiocracy that runs that entity today.

Going back to the war period, Motika, a mechanical engineer, was director of the Sarajevo-based Pretis company, a massive munitions factory. "Pretis" was a contraction of the full name of the company, "Preduzeće Tito Sarajevo" (Tito Enterprise Sarajevo). A complex spanning eleven kilometers based in the Sarajevo municipality of Vogošća, before the war Pretis employed fifteen thousand people. The company possessed the most up-to-date manufacturing equipment in Europe and, among other products, manufactured a million bombs a year.[57]

Early in the war, when Serb separatist forces took over the outer municipalities of Sarajevo, including Vogošća, Pretis factory continued working under Serb control, with Milorad Motika at the helm. Testimony in the International Court of Justice in 1998 mentioned Motika as the person who, in cooperation with Serb separatist leaders, was tasked with distribution of artillery grenades and other munitions to Serb forces around Sarajevo.[58]

Other testimony, given in 2004 during the trial of Slobodan Milošević, describes communication between Motika and RS Ministry of Defense concerning supply from Serbia of explosives and other material needed for manufacturing munitions.[59] In revisiting this testimony during the ICTY trial of Radovan Karadžić in late 2013, the prosecutor shared an intercepted conversation between Karadžić's right-hand man Momčilo Krajišnik and Milorad Motika: "In the conversation Krajišnik and Motika agreed that the artillery should retaliate by firing 'directly on the town.'"[60]

Clearly, Motika performed important tasks in support of the Serb nationalist prosecution of the war.

When the war ended, the Dayton agreement decreed the reintegration into Federation-controlled Sarajevo of the municipalities controlled by the Serbs during the war. Vogošća was handed over to the Federation—without its factories—a "relocation" of immensely valuable manufacturing equipment not only from Pretis, but also from the TAS automobile factory, the Famos auto parts factory, and a power plant equipment factory owned by the giant Energoinvest.[61]

Soon after the Dayton peace was established, Milorad Motika presided over the plunder and transfer of 600 million deutschmarks' worth of equipment from Pretis in Vogošća to the eastern Serb-controlled part of Sarajevo, then called "Srpsko Sarajevo" (Serb Sarajevo). An eyewitness recalled seeing that forklifts were employed to remove large machines from the factory. To remove immense machines that the forklifts could not move, several thousand square meters of roofing were removed so that helicopters could carry the equipment away. And what the departing Serb forces were not able to plunder they destroyed on the spot.[62]

A postwar manager of the reduced Pretis firm expressed disbelief that international troops in IFOR failed to notice helicopters taking away the company's machines. The valuable equipment ended up in the hands of newly constituted, ethnically homogenous companies in Srpsko Sarajevo and nearby Pale, the wartime capital of the Republika Srpska. Some of it ended up rusting outdoors in fields.[63]

A direct effect of this plunder was the long-term unemployment of as many as fifty thousand workers in the metal industries, workers who had earned up to a thousand deutschmarks a month before the war. Since then most of them have either been on permanent layoff with paltry pensions or none at all, or they have left the country.[64]

Milorad Motika's war record illustrates the strong continuity between wartime corruption and postwar practices that continue to this day. Motika is but a small part of that story, but he is relevant because of his role in the obstruction of development of Srebrenica's economy. The concession that Motika's Argentum 09 was awarded in 2012 to exploit 80 percent of the Guber mineral waters placed him in direct conflict with the company that had already been granted construction rights on the land.

The only conclusion that can be drawn in the case of Guber is that the RS government chose its favorite, Motika, over the maverick Ratkovac, who was not in the good graces of President Dodik's apparatus. That Ratkovac has perennially been on the outs with Dodik is further evidenced by the fact that he has been involved in a legal dispute with the RS government over land ownership in his home base of Prnjavor. The RS-controlled agency "Press RS," clearly waging a media campaign against Ratkovac, noted with alarm that he won a first-instance hearing of the five-year-old lawsuit in late 2013.[65]

Previously, the government-owned news agency called Ratkovac a "controversial businessman," a code phrase reserved for alleged practitioners of organized crime.[66] The fact that the bigger corrupt operator, that is, the government of the RS under Dodik, used this implicitly accusatory term against Ratkovac does not mean that he is entirely honest. His role in the story of Guber, however, stands out as that of a businessman who got in the way of Dodik's goals.

On the other side, an accumulation of evidence shows that Milorad Motika, who served the RS government as deputy minister for industry, energy, and mining, has functioned in peacetime as a facilitator of the corruption and cronyism perpetrated by his superiors, just as he had previously facilitated the accomplishment of the wartime goals of separatist leaders.

By 2016 Motika had left his position in the Ministry for Industry, Energy, and Mining to become chairman of the board of directors for the Zvornik-based company Alumina, a prominent processor of bauxite and other minerals. Alumina, favored by President Dodik, registered increasing profits in 2016 and 2017 but was also beset by heavy financial claims from other companies owing to earlier economic problems. In the spring of 2017 Motika filed for bankruptcy on behalf of Alumina in order to forestall further demands of payments. He caused a controversy in the midst of this (at this writing unfinished) process, when his company bought a luxurious Mercedes automobile for some 80,000 euros. In response to questioning from journalists, Motika responded, "What's the problem? What if we did buy it? . . . Do I have to travel to Banja Luka on a donkey?"[67]

The details of the nearly decade-long dogfight over Guber are murky, and they are, at times, difficult even for advisers to the Srebrenica municipal government to outline with precision. But an assertion by consultant to the municipal government Cvijetin Maksimović seems accurate, that "if Guber spa were somewhere around Banja Luka or Laktaši [home of Milorad Dodik], it is certain that by now it would have been functioning for a long time."[68]

Put simply, in Srebrenica the stakes are high, and the political/profiteer apparatus in Banja Luka apparently feels no inducement to cooperate with the survivors and return-ees of Srebrenica. It is not only the Bosniaks who are victimized by this approach; as one commentator expressed it, the Serb residents of Srebrenica are "collateral damage."[69]

The year 2015 heralded a possible turnaround in the development of Guber spa when Argentum 09 lost its court case against Radojica Ratkovac's AD Guber, presumably clearing the way for resumed construction. Ratkovac predicted that the spa would be functioning soon, but the construction site remained quiet for the next several years.[70] Mayor Grujičić repeated enthusiastic predictions in January 2019, announcing that, with support from the RS government, he would be meeting with Ratkovac to discuss moving the project forward.[71]

Moving beyond the destructive effect of the Republika Srpska government's policies on Srebrenica's economy, there is at least one outstanding difficulty stemming from obstruction by the Serbian government. In the 1960s a massive dam was constructed on the Drina River, the border between Serbia and the Srebrenica municipality. Con-struction of the dam created the vast Perućac Lake, leaving a significant portion of Srebrenica municipality's shoreline permanently under water. Having benefited from the inundation of part of the RS's land, Serbia was required to compensate that entity for its loss. But for over twenty years, since the beginning of the Bosnian war, Serbia never paid this debt. Reckoning from a yearly debt of 1.4 million KM, Senad Subašić calculated that, twenty years after the beginning of the war, Serbia owed Srebrenica approximately 30 million KM.[72]

In late 2013, Mayor Duraković discussed the potential benefits of payment of Serbia's debt to Srebrenica, bringing the Guber spa into operation, and a thorough auditing of the mining industry. The combined economic effects of such developments would attract young returnees to Srebrenica municipality. Duraković stated that "within five years we could make Srebrenica into one of the most developed municipalities in Bosnia-Herzegovina, as it once was."[73]

However, the economic pulse of Srebrenica continued to be weak in the ensuing years, owing to the blockages and corruption described above. The economic weakness compounded itself by discouraging return and prompting some returnees to leave. In 2016 this resulted in the closure of the last butcher shop in Srebrenica, as well as an agricultural outlet. A bakery that had been opened a couple of years earlier also closed.[74]

11

Life in Sućeska

SERBS OF SREBRENICA

IN 2000 I VISITED SUĆESKA, THE FIRST RETURN SETTLEMENT in Srebrenica municipality. I saw that all the five hundred–odd houses and buildings in this complex of several small villages had been destroyed during the war. The first brave returnees were living in tents and putting up new cinderblock walls in their ravaged homes. Life was difficult, but the returnees were determined to make a go of it in their ancestral villages.

REVISITING SUĆESKA

Life remained difficult. There were far more widows and elderly pensioners than intact families. Pensions hovered around 300 KM per month. Returnees lived in half-finished houses and worked fields overgrown with weeds and strewn with mines left over from the war. Employment was scarce; those who would stay and survive were compelled to work the land. Over the ensuing years, more than a few gave up and moved abroad.

The hilly terrain lent itself to subsistence farming and cattle raising, but Sućeska was also held back by a lack of motorized farming implements and milking machines. And the cobblestone roads that had not been repaved since Austro-Hungarian occupation posed at least as much of an obstacle to return and recovery. The only way to market surplus milk that was produced was to deliver it to Tuzla, one hundred miles away.[1]

While ultimately some three-fifths of the destroyed houses in Sućeska came to be repaired with the help of donations from international relief agencies, in the first few years people who had been displaced were reluctant to return. They preferred to stay in vacated Serb-owned houses in places such as Vozuća, in the Federation, but by the late 1990s, they regularly faced eviction as Serbs reclaimed their prewar homes.[2]

With the assistance of the UNDP, gradually the roads to Sućeska were rebuilt, and return picked up, along with donor interest. Sućeska came to be the biggest center of return in Srebrenica municipality, outside of the larger towns of Srebrenica and Skelani. Social infrastructure developed; an elementary school, a clinic, and a youth center were restored, and with time, even a folklore ensemble was established.

Not long after the reconstruction of the main road to Sućeska I ventured up to the village to see how it fared, some eight years after my first visit. There, I met Mujo Hasanović, the mayor of the complex.

Sućeska forms one of Srebrenica municipality's nineteen administrative units known as *mjesne zajednice*, or local communes. Hasanović, who had returned to Sućeska in 2001, was living in a house that was being restored as we spoke. Hasanović and I stood in front of his house and chatted as workers applied stucco to it. Bringing me up to date on conditions in the commune, he told me that around two hundred to three hundred families had returned to live in the twenty villages of the commune.

Hasanović spoke of daily life in Sućeska:

We all know each other here. Everyone goes to see each other for coffee, whenever they want. No one invites anyone, they just go, and drink coffee, or have lunch. You might sit and visit all day. It's not like that in the cities. There, if someone invites you, you go, and if not, you don't. You might see someone once or twice a month. Here, I'll see my neighbor twenty times in that period.

Our return here is somewhat of a surprise, that people wanted to return to where they were practically killed off. And we are having children again. There are now around a hundred children from this commune in elementary school and high school.

"And I am the oldest student here," Hasanović, roughly fifty years old, continued. Referring to the new Srebrenica-based extension of Sarajevo University's law school, he said, "Last year 150 students enrolled. Fifty of us finished our first year and are going into the second year of this four-year school."

Hasanović was a member of Srebrenica's municipal assembly; his income from this function afforded him a measure of security that most returnees do not have. He told me, "People are barely living. No one is employed. Mostly people live from farming and cattle, and there are many women who get pensions for a husband or son who was killed. And these people who don't get anything, demobilized soldiers, see here, these people who are working on my house, I pay them whatever I can. But there is no guaranteed support for them. They only have enough to keep alive, that's all."

THE FUNERAL IN 2010

The mass funeral in 2010, on the fifteenth anniversary of the fall of Srebrenica, was the largest funeral to date at Potočari—and with 775 identified remains of victims pre-pared for reburial, probably the largest there ever would be. To this point, out of some sixty-five hundred identified remains, more than thirty-seven hundred had already been interred.

I arrived at Potočari late in the afternoon on Saturday, the day before the funeral, along with thousands of other people, after participating in the Marš mira, the peace march that traced the 1995 escape route. Men in a long double line were relaying the "tabuts," wooden frames draped with green cloth, from a building in the defunct battery factory, where they had been stored, out to a field in the memorial compound. Carrying so many tabuts to the field took a long time. Throngs of mourners and visitors sat on the ground or milled around while this was going on.

Sunday warmed up quickly as I trekked down to Potočari from Srebrenica, where I had stayed the night. Nonstop traffic slowed down, eventually to a standstill, as tens of thousands of people tried to get to the cemetery. By late morning people had given up on their buses and started walking the rest of the way. And by that time it was almost impossible to enter the compound. Thousands of people waited, seeking a little of the scarce shade around the edges of the factory across the street.

The customary speeches held at the opening of the day's ceremony were beginning. The US ambassador, Serbian president Boris Tadić, the Turkish prime minister, and the French foreign minister all spoke. (No official from the Republika Srpska attended.) Haris Silajdžić, then member of the Bosnian presidency, spoke about the need to pro-hibit the formation of fascist or neo-Nazi parties in Bosnia-Herzegovina.

President Tadić, attending the ceremony for the second time, said that he had come "as an act of reconciliation." The Srebrenica survivors present displayed mixed feelings. Some welcomed him, and others asked, "Where is Mladić?" Ratko Mladić, the wartime general indicted for genocide in connection with the Srebrenica mas-sacre, was still at large at that time and was believed to be living in Serbia under the protection of supporters.

Finally Bosnia's head imam, the Reis Mustafa efendija Cerić, spoke before a prayer. The central *dova* (prayer) of the ceremony was delivered in a most powerful and moving way. All the emotions of the fifteen years of waiting and the loss of one's family members seemed to be contained in that Arabic prayer.

Masses of praying men and women stood, bowed, and kneeled in the traditional way. Then the Reis spoke again, longer than before. Everything about the day's event was bigger than previous years: more people attended; more than ever before were interred; the speeches were longer; and the temperature was hotter. In the course of the lengthy ceremony, attendees started fainting and were rushed to the first aid station. Some people became impatient with the Reis as he was speaking angrily in both English and Bosnian about the faults of the international community. Most just waited.

After several hours, the speeches ended and family members began carrying the tabuts to their final destinations throughout the grounds of the cemetery. Rows of the green-clothed tabuts, each one carried by five or six men, wound through the crowd and up the hill. Readers announced the full names of each victim over the loudspeaker, one by one, as the remains were being moved. This reading took a couple of hours. Among the remains to be buried were those of nearly seventy boys who were between sixteen and eighteen years old when they were killed.[3]

Mothers cried for their sons at the burial sites.

Postwar leader of return Hakija Meholjić buried the remains of his father and one of his brothers. Activist Hasan Nuhanović buried the remains of his brother Muhamed and his mother, Nasiha.[4] As the tabuts were delivered to the gravesites the crowd thinned out. Family members lowered the tabuts into the earth and began to shovel soil into the pit. The work went very quickly, and in an hour or so, 775 more victims rested in the Potočari earth.

Numerous Srebrenicans have publicly—and especially privately—voiced resentment at the increasing trend in speechifying and politicking that has taken over the anniversary commemoration. Discussing this phenomenon, Hariz Halilovich noted that "there has been a strong tendency to appropriate these events for broader political, ethno-religious and nationalist agendas. The experience from Bosnia has shown that the larger the funeral, the greater the opportunity to politicise the event." Halilovich added that to the extent that such an event took on the nature of a "genocide festival" or a "religious pilgrimage," many ordinary survivors resent such manipulation.[5]

On the politicians' exploitation of political capital derived from victimhood, Halilovich has written, "for Bosniak nationalist-opportunists, involved exclusively in amoral, materialistic manipulation . . . genocide has become their privatized political cloak."[6]

Widespread resentment of such speeches led to the announcement that the next year's commemoration would take place before the funeral and in a different location.

As the 2010 funeral and commemoration were underway in Potočari, related expressions—both of solidarity and of hate—were taking place elsewhere. SDS, the party founded by Radovan Karadžić, awarded him a special decoration in absentia, in celebration of the twentieth anniversary of the founding of that party.

In Belgrade, the solidarity and human rights organization Women in Black organized a temporary monument displaying thousands of shoes. The shoes were stuffed with such messages from Serbian citizens as "I will never forget," as a memorial to the Srebrenica victims.[7] Meanwhile, a demonstration in the same city celebrating the "liberation of Srebrenica" had been banned.

Mercifully, the extremist adherents to the Chetnik movement who had rampaged in Bratunac and Srebrenica in 2009 were prevented from a repeat performance in 2010. Members of the organizations Obraz, 1389, and the Ravna Gora Chetnik Movement who attempted to enter Bosnia from Serbia were turned away at the border.[8]

In the mid-2000s Serbs in the region surrounding Srebrenica began to develop a tradition of commemorating their co-religionists killed during the war. The attack on the Serb village of Kravica took place in January 1993; estimates of the number killed in that attack range from forty to eighty, and how many of those were civilians is disputed. It is also alleged that on St. Peter's Day (Petrovdan), July 12, 1992, Naser Orić's forces killed nearly seventy Serb civilians in three villages in the Srebrenica region. In remembrance of this attack, and of all the Serbs who were killed, the Republika Srpska government and demobilized veterans now annually organize Petrovdanski dani (Petrovdan days), a series of public events centering on a memorial held in the military cemetery at Bratunac.

While there should be no objection to survivors remembering their fallen, regardless of ethnicity, it is clear that the annual commemoration has been exploited as a counter to the anniversary memorial and reburial of Srebrenica massacre victims at Potočari. The Petrovdan event, falling one day after the Potočari commemoration, has become a regular occasion for revisionist expressions on the part of some Serbs, who attempt to deny the occurrence of genocide against the Muslims at Srebrenica. One Serb activist called the killings a "lie" and characterized the Potočari commemoration thus: "It is propaganda, created to portray the Serbian people in a bad light. The Muslims are lying and are manipulating the numbers and exaggerating what happened. Far more Serbs were killed in Srebrenica than Muslims."[9]

On July 12, 2010, the day after the massive fifteenth-anniversary massacre commemoration at Potočari, I went to Bratunac with a colleague to attend the annual ceremony at the military cemetery. When we arrived, a few dozen people were waiting in the sweltering heat, huddled up against the cemetery administration building in the scant shade.

I walked around the cemetery, which contained a few hundred graves of Serbs killed during the war. One tall headstone bore a poem in Cyrillic reading, "Here I am in the grave, mother. I did not want to desert the army."

An old man walked among the graves, wearing a šajkača, the traditional Serbian military cap. He stopped and lit a candle at a shrine. One mother sat by a tombstone.

Weeping, she told me with obvious heartbreak of her son who had been killed in the war fifteen years earlier.

Priests, politicians in gray suits, and bodyguards started arriving. A dozen young people wore buttons favoring the accused war criminal Vojislav Šešelj of the Serbian Radical Party, then incarcerated at The Hague and on trial for war crimes and crimes against humanity. The politicians and their assistants gathered under a long canopy, the priests under a nearby café-style umbrella advertising Tuborg beer.

After a wait of nearly two hours, a crowd of two or three hundred had collected. Boys and youth sported t-shirts with the *kokarda* (a cross with four Cyrillic "C's"—the initials of a nationalist slogan)[10] and other nationalist messages; one boy had draped the flag of the Republika Srpska around his shoulders. Prime Minister Dodik arrived and spoke at length to the press. Finally, the ceremony began with people lighting sweet-smelling wax candles. Two soldiers laid wreaths by a three-meter-high cross. The priests chanted their harmonious liturgy, and Dodik spoke to the small crowd.

Dodik spoke about "the legitimacy of the Republika Srpska" and "preserving the memory of the liberation war." He was also quoted as saying, "Republika Srpska does not deny that a large-scale crime occurred in Srebrenica, but by definition it was not genocide as described by the international court in The Hague. . . . If a genocide happened, then it was committed against Serb people of this region where women, children and the elderly were killed en masse."[11]

Later in 2010, Milorad Dodik became president of the Republika Srpska and carried on with his escalating rhetoric. At the *parastos* (requiem) for Serb victims held at the military cemetery in Bratunac on July 12, 2011, he said, "Among us there is no hatred nor revenge, but it is high time for the processing of the monstrous crimes committed against Serbs. We cannot accept the selective justice as it has been to date, that one side, the Serb side, is guilty for everything, but that no one is to answer for so many Serb victims."[12]

Addressing this statement, the Banja Luka psychologist and social commentator Srđan Puhalo deconstructed the figure of 3,267 that has been enshrined as the official number of Serb war victims killed in the Birač region (surrounding Srebrenica). Working with figures supplied by the Republika Srpska Department for Investigation of War, War Crimes, and Processing of Documentation, Puhalo found that the total of casualties from Birač numbered 2,385. Of these, 1,974 were soldiers, 387 were civilians, and 24 were of "unknown status."[13]

This figure is supported by information from the Research and Documentation Center (RDC), an NGO based in Sarajevo that has performed extensive research on casualties of the war on all sides. In 2007, the RDC arrived at an overall figure of fatalities close to one hundred thousand—similar to corresponding figures provided independently by the ICTY,[14] and less than half the figure that had been popularized for quite some years. The RDC notes that a significant number of Serbs who were killed during fighting around the Srebrenica region early in the war were people who came from central and other parts of Bosnia—and some had arrived from Serbia as well.[15]

Puhalo concluded by saying, "If the government of the Republika Srpska wishes well for its people it may not abuse the Serb victims and manipulate them with the goal of gathering cheap political points, and thus in any way justifying everything that happened in July 1995. Confronting the past means establishing the truth . . . because if we do not do this, our children and grandchildren will go to war."[16]

It is clear that, in the spirit of Milorad Dodik's rhetoric, all too often the figures and historical interpretation regarding Serb victims are presented simply as a counterweight to the much more concrete figures of Bosniak victims. The practice of inflating the figures of Serb victims serves as an implicit exoneration of the war crimes perpetrated against the Bosniaks of Srebrenica.

While recognizing the genocide that was committed against the Bosniaks, it is also imperative to acknowledge the pain of the Serb mothers whose sons were killed in the war—a pain that was so clearly shown to me in the Bratunac cemetery. The manipulation of Serbs through the exploitation of hazy statistics simply adds to the tragedy.

SERBS—OPINIONS ACROSS THE SPECTRUM

I took a taxi ride in the hills above Srebrenica. The taxi driver, a local Serb, immediately told me, "My wife is a Muslim." He proceeded to share his version of events at Srebrenica, saying that the memorial cemetery at Potočari contained many bodies that had been moved there from other cemeteries. He asserted that the Muslims who were killed were all soldiers. He also reasoned that, since they were soldiers, it was legitimate to kill them, as "they would have killed someone." The driver finished by telling me, "I'm not on one side or the other."

In recent years, estimates have held that the Serb and Bosniak returnee populations in the municipality were roughly equal. The Serbs of Srebrenica and the surrounding area play an integral part in the story of the recovery of the region.

Uninformed people may tend to think that, since it was Serb forces that expelled the Muslim population from Srebrenica and committed the massacres, then Serbs in general should be considered to be the enemy of peace, justice, and recovery in Srebrenica. But we have already seen that a significant number of Srebrenica's population in the first years after the war were Serbs displaced from other parts of Bosnia-Herzegovina, who had had nothing to do with the crimes committed during the war. Neither did many of those Serbs who had always lived peacefully with their Muslim neighbors before the war, and who were displaced from their homes at the beginning of it.

For most of the Serbs of Srebrenica—locals and displaced persons—postwar life was a matter of bare survival. Life was different for Serbs and Muslims in that the former had not been subject to genocide—although in many cases, they too had lived out the war years in great fear. But making ends meet in Srebrenica after the war was not any easier for Serbs than for the Bosniak returnees.

Because of their differing wartime histories, Muslims and Serbs have afterward generally had separate and conflicting narratives, differing interpretations about what happened—even different "facts." Their wartime experiences on opposing sides colored their attitudes in the postwar period, and the fact that their lives were stagnating on the economic level added to the cementing of those attitudes.

Still, we have seen that, while there are many Serbs and Muslims who have a resolute mistrust and animosity toward each other, at the same time there are those who have thrown themselves into working together to recreate some kind of "normal."

The story of Srebrenica's Serbs in the postwar period is thus a complicated one, with individuals occupying positions on the spectrum all the way from sincere coexistence to hatred.

Jovan

Jovan, a native of a village near Donji Vakuf in central Bosnia, was born during World War II. Toward the end of the more recent war he was expelled from his village, where he had raised fruit all his life. Donji Vakuf had come under Serb control during the war but was recaptured by government forces in 1995, and after the Dayton agreement, it ended up as part of the Federation. It was then that Jovan found himself "relocated" to Srebrenica, a place he had previously hardly thought about.

I met Jovan in Srebrenica in 2002, seven years after the war's end. By this time, the Property Law Implementation Plan was well underway, and people who had occupied houses that did not belong to them were being evicted. Jovan was living in a house that the local government had allocated to him, that had been abandoned by its Muslim owner upon the fall of the enclave.

Now, Jovan had to think about either returning to Donji Vakuf, or finding alternative accommodation. At the time that I met him, the woman who owned the house he and his family stayed in had filed a claim for the return of her property, and it had been granted. Jovan faced eviction. He told me that his monthly income was a meager pension of 130 KM (around US$80). But because two of his sons were working, his family was not eligible for alternative accommodation that would be provided by the state. When he was evicted, they would have to find a home to rent.

Jovan hoped to avoid this outcome by returning home to Donji Vakuf. He said, "I would leave tomorrow if I could reclaim my house. The problem is that it is now inhabited by a Muslim from another village, and that person's house was destroyed in the war." Jovan had filed his own claim for the return of his property three years earlier, and he too had received a favorable resolution. The legal procedure that should have brought him home was clear: the resident of his home should have been evicted and, if necessary, provided with alternative accommodation.

But according to Jovan, officials in the government of Donji Vakuf were obstructing his return and that of many other displaced Serbs. Activists for return who were working in the NGOs of Srebrenica corroborated his assertion.

Jovan told me:

> Whenever we go to Donji Vakuf, the mayor is out of his office. When he sees us coming, he goes to a kafana or home. He only works from 1 to 3 p.m., and then he leaves.
>
> Most of the people from Donji Vakuf would like to go home. I have to fix the plumbing and the woodwork of my house, which is 30 percent destroyed. The person occupying my house allows me to enter it, but he won't leave. He has the support of the mayor. They are intentionally dragging out the resolution for the return of property. This is a typical obstruction to return.
>
> If I can't return within two months from now, I will have to rent a home here in Srebrenica. The rent may be as much as 200 KM. So I would have to go and dig in the fields. There is no work here, or there is work, but no pay—and that is regardless of one's ethnicity.

Addressing the effects of the war, Jovan told me, "The higher-up, powerful people did this. My three sons are not married. If the war had not done what it did, I would have grandchildren.

"I own ten dunums of fruit orchards, apples and plums. I could live from that property. My only wish is to return. There needs to be justice for all. The law is the same for everyone," Jovan concluded.

Vanja

Vanja is an activist in one of the more well-organized and effective Srebrenica-based nongovernmental organizations. She moved to Srebrenica after the war, having grown up in a Serb family in a small town in northeastern Bosnia. She had lived as a refugee for a time, and her fiancé's village was torched. Vanja described to me the changes that she went through under the pressure of the wartime trauma:

> Before the war, many of my friends were Muslims. When Yugoslavia started falling apart, I couldn't believe that there would be troubles among the people of Bosnia. I'm generally an optimist, but maybe I was confused. Seeing things get worse, I did not have feelings of hatred; I just wanted the violence to end.
>
> Then, for the first time in my life, I hated—Muslims, but not the people I knew. I saw my friends die. One girlfriend who was pregnant was killed. One of my friends lost his mother and his wife. Civilians were being killed. I had a strong feeling of hate, which was a completely new feeling for me. I did not know, or I did not think about the fact that at the same time, innocent people were being killed on "the other side." The media were separating us, just as were the politicians.
>
> My prejudices were the logical result of what I lived through. There was a dominant

atmosphere in which everyone felt that way. I suppose everyone on both sides felt that way. We were simply in a struggle for survival. That really lasted the whole war. However, I had Muslim friends that I wanted to hear from, and there were Muslim friends in Novi Pazar, Serbia, who invited me to come be with them, to be safe.

Then, during and after the war, I had the feeling that I didn't want to see any Muslims. But with time, much changed. I started working with NGOs, and probably for me that sped up the change. It helped that, luckily, I came out of the war without big losses.

A couple of years after the war ended I started to volunteer. I started taking classes in English and computers. I started providing home care to the elderly and disabled. During a seminar in Doboj I met the people I work with now, and we decided to start an organization. As parents, we wanted something better for the youth.

Soon after that, we had our first meeting with Muslim women in Tuzla, many of whom were displaced from Srebrenica and the surrounding region. It was difficult at first. In Srebrenica, they called us "traitors," and in Tuzla some people spat on us. You weren't OK with either side; people would talk behind our backs.

And in our meetings at first, the women separated at lunch; Serbs and Muslims ate separately. But after a time, that changed; we were really not thinking about who was of what ethnicity. At the end of one series of workshops, we had a party where we danced together until dawn, and by that point I no longer had any reservations about working with Muslims. We talked about our experience without confrontation; we women can do that differently. We are still in touch.

That series of meetings was a turnaround. There were not big attitude changes, but it gave me the opportunity to think, "maybe I was not right about them; they are not all the same." I got rid of the idea that I would never talk to them.[17]

Going back to the subject of identity, Vanja continued, "A person can change her personality, depending on her surroundings. I would like to return to the time where we were unworried, when we didn't even know how precious our freedom was. I would like to return to real values, not disturbed ones like we have now."

I asked Vanja what she meant by the phrase "disturbed values," which I had heard numerous times around the former Yugoslavia.

I was alive during Communism, and I hardly knew I was a Serb. Maybe that's sad. Before the war, it was common, though not universal, to consider oneself a Yugoslav, or a Bosnian. Often the identification as a Serb, Croat, or Muslim came second. Now we still say that we are from Bosnia, but we don't feel a strong sense of belonging. It is not from the heart. Regarding the Republika Srpska, it is a little strange. Sometimes I feel lost; I don't know where I belong. Many people feel there is a border between the RS and the Federation.

Identities are artificially created, but one should know one's identity. Some of my attitudes have changed. During Communism, you couldn't say what you were. Now we celebrate Christmas and *slavas* [religious holidays]. Before, we had Christmas, but May 25, Tito's birthday, was a bigger holiday. Some people in Bosnia identify more with Serbia if they are Serbian and more with Croatia if they are Croats. In some cases people feel that way, but I do not.

My ethnicity is not my primary identification. There are more important things, for example, that I am a mother; it is more essential how my children will grow up in this country, and then everything else comes after that. I have that identity, which is more important to me.[18]

Of course those cultural elements of my identity are important, but there is no flag, state, or ideal worth it to me to send my children into a bloody war, where our children would be killed. It was really senseless, all of this that happened. If it were to happen again it would be that much more senseless in the end. But I really fear war, and if I saw even one indication of another war coming, I would leave forever.

I had been in Srebrenica during the municipal election campaign of 2008, and I commented to Vanja about the fierce mudslinging, with ethnic undertones, that had dominated the campaign. She replied, "It is really silly and absurd. But these days, such speech occurs mainly in the election years. It is all for the purpose of dividing up power, not for anyone's real national interest or for the good of the people. People are still responding out of fear. They are still under the influence of the war events. If people are afraid, then they are susceptible to manipulation. And then they can be, in a way, blackmailed to frighten them about what could happen *if* so-and-so wins. So I think that people are still quite afraid and aren't in a position to see an accurate picture of what's going on."[19]

True to the nature of an activist, in spite of her dark assessment, Vanja expressed hope for improvement—especially on the local level, in Srebrenica and in the neighboring municipalities. "Srebrenica has many positive examples of coexistence; there really are many positive things, which perhaps are not interesting to the media—exactly because they are positive. Some truly good results are being achieved by well-intentioned people, regardless of whether they are in local government, in NGOs, or international organizations."

SERBS IN KRAVICA

The village of Kravica, on the main road that connects Bratunac to the rest of Bosnia, is notorious for one thing, the massacre of more than one thousand captive Muslim men after the fall of Srebrenica. Among local Serbs, however, Kravica is better known for the incident that took place earlier in the war, when, Naser Orić's forces fell on Kravica, destroying buildings and killing Serbs.

I have not related these two incidents in order to imply a cause-effect relationship between them. I bring it up here because the interpretation of the two events—in fact, the "facts" surrounding them—vary like night and day depending on who is remembering them. The differing narratives, right or wrong, reinforce each side's sense of victimhood and influence the relationships they have with one another in the postwar period.

In 2003, ten years after Orić's attack, I spoke with Nada, a resident of Kravica and a Serb. At the time that we spoke she was a member of a local nongovernmental organization. Her words revealed a kind of ambivalence; she occupied the position of victim and conciliator at the same time. She was burdened by the memory of wartime trauma, but, like Vanja, she also remembered the time before the war, when everyone lived peaceably together. One could see that she missed those times, but also that she was influenced by the Serb nationalist interpretation of events.

Nada related a story not only of trauma and devastation, but also of current dissatisfaction. She told me:

> Before the war, there were some two hundred families here. Around forty-eight hundred people lived in twenty Serb villages near Kravica. Of those people, around three thousand have returned.
>
> On January 7, 1993, our Christmas, Kravica was burned to the ground. Seventeen buildings were destroyed, including the post office. They [Orić's forces] organized groups to destroy things quickly. They dug up our graves to look for gold, brandy, and cigarettes. This is the living truth; not everyone did this, but some people did.
>
> It was written on the school and on my house: "Islamic Bosnia," "Serbs move out," "Long live Naser." Few people have ever heard about this. Serbs suffered a thousand attacks, and we never had freedom until the fall of Srebrenica. It had to come to something in Srebrenica, because you never knew when you were going to be attacked. Srebrenica was a protected area, while people here were killed. When General Morillon testified at The Hague during Milošević's trial, he said that revenge was inevitable. They had burned eighty-five villages.
>
> During the war, I worked in Bratunac, and didn't get any pay; I was paid in flour. Kravica was in a very bad material situation at the end of the war. All that we had was ashes. It is bitter to be alive when you don't have anything. Eventually the elementary school was rebuilt. There was a doctor who came to the clinic twice a week, but then funds dried up.
>
> I am dissatisfied here; there are few organizations that have done anything to help. The Serbs are not treated as returnees, even though we also lost everything. They plowed fields at Konjević Polje and Glogova [Muslim villages] for free, and around thirty organizations repaired the Muslim-owned houses. But in Kravica there were over seventy families in collective centers, some staying there while they fixed their own houses. There are many old people, and there are 145 single women or single mothers, widows.
>
> It is a very gloomy place. Most people manage however they can. We feel discarded. There is nothing to do here in Kravica. There is mostly seasonal agricultural work, raising raspberries, cattle, chickens, and pigs. There is some work in the trades.

Nada compared life before and after the war:

> Before, we all worked in the factory in Bratunac, and we traveled in the same buses. We didn't want the war, but the nationalist parties did. It is ugly, what happened. I have always

been sorry about the breakup of Yugoslavia. We will never have what we had before. We used to travel to Slovenia, Croatia, Montenegro, as we wished.

I grew up surrounded by Muslims. Around 1990 to 1992 they offered my parents money to leave Bratunac. But really, some of them are good people. It is best to work together, although not all people work that way. We Serbs, somehow, are more flexible.

Those relationships have been fixed now. There are no problems; we come and go freely. We see each other, and we talk. They have people who are really very fine. There was a mother who lost sons, but she says, "What can we do; we must live together."

But still, there are divisions between the Serbs and the Muslims. They blame the Serbs for everything. Many people from here disappeared and still haven't been found, including some of my relatives. As for Srebrenica, the figures of those killed are inflated. Some of the people on the lists are alive; some are in the United States.

12
Elections, Repression, and Resistance

FROM 2000 UNTIL 2012, SREBRENICA'S MUNICIPAL GOVERN-ment was headed by a Muslim mayor, someone sympathetic to the cause of recovery and reconstruction in Srebrenica. Thanks to the weight of votes both from Muslim returnees and from absentee voters, Srebrenica was the only municipality in the entire Serb-controlled entity that retained a Muslim-dominated government.

Before the 2008 municipal elections, in an acknowledgment of the injustice done to the prewar majority Muslim population of Srebrenica, the Bosnian state Parliament passed an electoral law specifically concerning Srebrenica. The law allowed prewar citizens of Srebrenica to vote based on their place of residence at the time of the 1991 census. Thus in 2008, Osman Suljić was elected, with returnee and activist Ćamil Duraković chosen as his deputy mayor.

Suljić died in the spring of 2012; soon after his death, controversy loomed as it became known that voting in elections scheduled for the coming fall was to be based on residence. Only those registered as living in Srebrenica municipality would be allowed to vote there. Bosniaks feared that the expiration of the special 2008 voting rule would guarantee that a Serb candidate would become mayor.

THE 2012 ELECTION

In the face of the possible loss of Muslim power in Srebrenica, grassroots activists in the municipality and beyond organized a campaign under the name of "Glasaću za Srebrenicu" (I will vote for Srebrenica) to register voters in the municipality. Glasaću za Srebrenicu worked to unite all "pro-Bosnia" parties and voters in a coalition that would elect Ćamil Duraković. Their argument for this unity was not that they were anti-Serb, but that Srebrenica must have a mayor who did not deny that genocide had taken place in the municipality. That ruled out the Serb-run parties including RS president Dodik's SNSD, which was sponsoring Vesna Kočević as its candidate.

There were many Bosniak returnees to Srebrenica who had never registered their residence in the municipality. They had various reasons for this, particularly having to do with favorable pensions and health care coverage that were accessible to them in the Federation. Secondly, there were still many survivors from Srebrenica living in the Federation, and abroad, who had never returned to their prewar homes. The registration campaign encouraged both groups of people to register their residency in Srebrenica so that they could vote there in the fall.

While the ethnic breakdown of Srebrenica's population has consistently been described to me as roughly even between Serb and Bosniak returnees, the pre-2012 registration showed Serbs as the majority within the municipality. This discrepancy was due, at least in part, to the fact that a significant number of Bosniak returnees never registered their residence in Srebrenica.

I was in Bosnia during the run-up to the elections, and I volunteered to work as an observer during the Srebrenica polling. With the elections approaching, I met with Emin Mahmutović and Nedim Jahić, activists with the registration campaign. They spoke to me of extensive harassment of fellow registration campaign workers during the campaign. Nedim and Emin feared that there would be escalated harassment of voters during the election, along with fraudulent voting from the other side. They explained that voters were required to show valid local photo identification, and that many of the newly registered voters, Serbs residing in Serbia, did not have that. There were rumors about voters being supplied with false identification, and even with ballots that were already filled out.[1]

In June, activists from the registration campaign reported that Republika Srpska police were accosting them on the streets of Srebrenica and asking questions about citizens who had recently registered to vote in the municipality. Obstruction continued at the police station, where people who were attempting to register were told that their birth certificate identification numbers were invalid. These were people who had been born in the Federation during the war. Officials who rejected the applications failed to give a written explanation for the rejection, although they were legally required to do so.[2]

At the end of the registration period, in late August, campaign coordinator Emir Suljagić noted that police officials had violated regulations covering secrecy of personal information by publishing activists' names, addresses, and photographs of their houses in media that were inciting readers against the campaign.[3]

While the Serb nationalist political infrastructure was obstructing voter registration and harassing activists, it was also involved in spurious registration of Serb voters. Activists from the campaign noted the voter status of Serbs who had been displaced from the Federation and had once lived in collective centers in Srebrenica. They were still registered as voters in the municipality, even though they had moved on and the collective centers had long since been emptied.[4]

Toward the end of the registration period, activists called on the Central Election Committee to audit the voter rolls. They pointed out that several thousand Serbs who had registered to vote in Srebrenica actually lived in Serbia. Many of these people had never lived in Bosnia but were illegally granted Bosnian citizenship during the war and would not have fulfilled the requirements to receive it at the time of the registration drive.

Shortly after the closing of the registration period, the Republika Srpska minister of the interior acknowledged that citizenship had illegally been granted to 1,721 voters from Serbia. A commission for review of citizenship in Srebrenica municipality then annulled all illegal registrations that had taken place between 2000 and 2004.[5]

Zulfo Salihović, who had recently joined the SDP, commented on complications that he saw arising from the Glasaću za Srebrenicu campaign: "The parties that deny genocide cannot be defeated without the outside votes of people who are from here, but who live elsewhere. Unfortunately, when there starts to be a campaign to register them all, then the other side starts and registers people who may have lived here once, who were not from here, and who now live in Serbia. It becomes complete chaos and manipulation."

There were people who criticized the voter registration drive because it was encouraging people who did not live in Srebrenica to participate. But as one Bosniak politician expressed it, "You cannot kill 8,000 people, drive out their families, and then say that only those who stayed in Srebrenica can vote."[6]

In other words, one must consider the full course of local history and the fate of the historical inhabitants of Srebrenica when discussing who should vote.

The term "electoral engineering" is used quite frequently, but it is usually forgotten that genocide is the greatest electoral engineering of all.

THE VOTE

The elections took place on Sunday, October 7. From early in the day, I was stationed as an observer at the central voting location, set up specifically to receive "tendered ballots," that is, ballots of people whose names were not found on the central voter list.

A relatively small number of legitimate tendered ballots was expected, around seventy, to accommodate people who had registered on time but whose names had not been entered properly into the voter rolls. In addition to this number, the polling station committee had on hand several hundred more ballots to accommodate any other unregistered voters who appeared. Those hundreds of would-be voters did appear, and well over 90 percent of them were from Serbia.

Predictions about voters arriving from other parts of Bosnia-Herzegovina and abroad came true. Many of voters at the central station—none of whom were properly registered—were appearing with a stamped certificate of permission to vote, given to them by the local police department within the previous couple of days. Most of them did not have proper Bosnian identification and could show only their newly acquired certificates.

One older woman showed me her certificate and told me that she had citizenship in both Bosnia and Serbia. I saw that her official place of residence was a village near Skelani, but she spoke in the dialect of people living across the river in Serbia. She told me that she just wanted to come vote for her grandson to be elected to the municipal assembly.

The chairman of the local elections commission decided to allow people with identification to vote with the tendered ballots. These ballots would, according to standard procedure, be placed in envelopes and sent to Sarajevo to be evaluated, and either counted or rejected later. Ultimately about two hundred people were allowed to vote. In the course of the voting, numerous times I witnessed "family voting," that is, more than one person occupying a voting booth.

The crowd of voters subsided around 5 p.m. Meanwhile, I received information from my colleague Suleyman, who was observing the voting at a polling station in Skelani. He told me that it had been a tense situation there, where busloads of people were crossing the nearby bridge from Serbia. Although their voting permits were of suspicious quality, most of these people were allowed to vote.

Suleyman observed that there was much drinking taking place outside the polling station, and that one of the polling station committee members was drunk. He also reported that the cars of several of the polling station committee members bore license plates from Serbia. He overheard a comment to the effect that "We can't do anything with this Turk hanging around," referring to Suleyman's nationality. Suleyman had been keeping a close eye on the identification documents of the voters.

Voting closed on time at 7 p.m. at my polling station, and I watched the drawn-out process of ballot counting in a neighboring station where regular voting had taken place.

There, Vesna Kočević won easily. The counting ended at midnight, and I walked out into the rain. All the kafanas that I could see were closed and dark. But at one bistro there was a crowd of the young activists from Glasaću za Srebrenicu who were celebrating joyously with their friends. Counting on a victory for Ćamil Duraković based on absentee ballots, the activists from the registration campaign were letting loose, even though the official count was not to be released until much later.

Contention over the results of the election played out within the Central Election Commission (CEC), with some members favoring recognition of the existing vote count, and others bringing up a variety of objections.[7] After a series of appeals, in mid-December the CEC confirmed the Srebrenica elections in favor of Duraković's victory.

No more obstructionist tactics remained available to the Serb separatists. But elections were only one of many avenues for those who wanted to control Srebrenica in service of their separatist aims.

HARASSMENT OF RETURNEES AFTER THE 2012 ELECTION

After the elections, authorities lost no time in exerting repression on the activists who had made Duraković's victory possible. In Srebrenica, the district prosecutor began conducting nighttime raids in search of activists and hauling them to the police station for interrogation.

The district prosecutor and other RS officials alleged that the activists had pressured those who voted for Mayor Ćamil Duraković to register their residence in Srebrenica and to vote there. There were insinuations that the campaign paid people to do so.

By January 2013 police in Srebrenica had questioned "many dozens" of Srebrenica citizens who had voted in the elections, according to news reports. Police were asking questions about the citizens' "motives for voting, and about their connections with key leaders of the registration campaign." Activists responded to the harassment by charging local police with suspending freedom of movement in Srebrenica and in the Podrinje region, in violation of Annex 7 of the Dayton agreement.[8]

The RS police devised a set of requirements for verification of residency that recalled the bureaucratic obstruction of return that was carried out in the early postwar period. With no basis in existing law, police started requiring that returnees who were registering their residence in Srebrenica declare their residency within eight days of their return. The police also demanded any number of documents from an arbitrary list, primarily calling for proof of ownership or tenancy at a given address. These requirements were newly invented and randomly applied.

An example of the out-of-hand removal of newly registered residents of Srebrenica from the voter rolls was Kadrija Malkić, who had registered his return to Srebrenica in June 2012. The owner of a construction company, Malkić was born in Srebrenica. He had restored his war-damaged house and property and tended to his fruit orchard. Malkić had lost two brothers during the war and was himself wounded.[9]

With the annulment of Malkić's residency in Srebrenica, his identification card was taken away. Malkić received the notification of the annulment at his prior address in the Federation. He said, "I don't know on what grounds they have annulled my identification card. Because they are annulling my identity."[10]

In early 2013 the RS government, hoping to chip away at Bosnians' freedom of movement, attempted to legalize its restrictive criteria for returnees' registration of residency. President Dodik announced that a proposal to change the existing law on residency in favor of stricter criteria would be submitted in the state Parliament, and if it were not accepted there, the new law would be promulgated in the Serb-controlled entity.[11]

In that period the "March First Coalition," an ambitious organizational successor to the Glasaću za Srebrenicu campaign, lodged a complaint with the RS Ministry of the Interior concerning the annulment of the residency of five Srebrenica citizens. In April the Basic Court in Srebrenica found that the arbitrary cancellation of residency of returnees by the local police was illegal. The court called a halt to the cancellations, which the March First Coalition termed a "criminalization of free movement."[12]

In April 2014, after the state Parliament failed to pass a comprehensive law on residency, the Republika Srpska Parliament enacted new statutes that enshrined its repressive practices in law, requiring returnees to provide more documentary proof of return than was required in the rest of Bosnia-Herzegovina.[13]

In the following months, the state-level Constitutional Court evaluated the legality of the Republika Srpska's exaggerated usage of verification procedures in appraising the residency of returnees. In July 2014, the court annulled the RS government's decisions justifying such practices.[14] For the time being, this particular form of attack on returnee rights was blocked.

CONTINUED ACTIVISM AND REPRESSION

The continuing struggle for human rights clashed with the repressive police apparatus of the Republika Srpska in another venue in mid-2013. This time, police mistreatment of survivors took place as the result of an attempt by the organizations of Srebrenica mothers and widows to commemorate the killing of over a thousand of their loved ones in the village of Kravica.

Over the years as return increased and the survivor organizations consolidated, the drive for memorialization expanded beyond Potočari. While some victims of the Srebrenica genocide had been killed at Potočari, far more were executed at places such as Pilica, Branjevo farm, Petkovci, and Kravica. The mothers had established the custom of visiting these venues annually,[15] but they were always barred from going to Kravica, where about one thousand of their men had been killed in a single night.

In June 2013, as they had done before, activists announced that they planned to visit Kravica. Hatidža Mehmedović of Mothers of Srebrenica stated, "Every time, we are met by chains and padlocks in Kravica. . . . We are going to enter into Kravica and lay flowers at all costs."[16]

The attempt at memorialization at Kravica did turn out to be somewhat costly. A group of some 150 activists from the women's organizations, together with male supporters, visited several of the sites where men had been killed after the fall of Srebrenica. Three buses of mourners were met at Kravica by a cordon of RS special police. The women asked the police to allow them to pass through to the warehouse, but they were refused. Then, while some of the women formed a shield around them, others cut through a wire fence next to the padlocked gate to the building.

Police physically attacked the women, kicking them and hitting them with their elbows, according to some of the activists. Some eight women were injured, including leaders Hatidža Mehmedović and Munira Subašić.[17]

In response to this incident, there followed a period of police retaliation against the activists lasting nearly a year. Prosecutors and police authorities in Srebrenica began by summoning for interrogation participants who had gone to Kravica.

Šuhra Malić, seventy-eight, a member of Mothers of Srebrenica, was called for interrogation in March 2014, accused of "disturbing the public order and peace." Malić had lost two sons during the massacres; one, Fuad, had been killed at the Kravica warehouse. All told, she had lost twenty members of her family. Threatened with a 200 to 800 KM fine, Malić stated that she had come to Kravica only to pray at the place where her son was killed. She also announced that she would "show up in court, but that would not prevent her from showing up at Kravica as long as she lived."[18]

The Basic Court in Srebrenica dropped the charges against Šuhra Malić. This was an apparent turnaround by the government or, at the very least, a wish for the entire affair to disappear from the public eye. In the course of subsequent anniversary commemorations of the massacres, survivors were allowed to include the Kravica warehouse on the itinerary of their visits to the various killing sites. The persistence of the activists was instrumental in the breakthrough.

REVERSAL IN 2016

Municipal elections were held on schedule in Srebrenica in October 2016. Conditions were quite different from previous elections and, for the first time in the postwar period, a Serb was elected mayor, defeating incumbent Ćamil Duraković.

The new mayor, Mladen Grujičić, was a member of President Dodik's SNSD party, and he was on record as denying the Srebrenica genocide. Like other prominent Serb officials, he acknowledged that a "crime" had taken place at Srebrenica, but he refused to recognize that crime as genocide. Furthermore, Grujičić repeated a standard revisionist assertion, saying that some of the people alleged to have been buried at Potočari were still alive.[19] On the other hand, Grujičić uttered placating statements and promised to be the mayor of all Srebrenicans.

Grujičić's father was killed during the war, when Grujičić was a young boy. He grew up to become a high school teacher. He also served as the president of the municipal committee of the association for fallen (Serb) soldiers. As candidate, on one hand, he advocated "looking forward" and trying to solve local problems for all citizens of Srebrenica. On the other hand, he primarily spoke to fellow Serbs, building his base among that community, denying genocide, and promoting a picture of Serbs as victims of Muslims over the centuries.

After a turbulent voting day, ballot recounts, and many protests, Grujičić won the election by roughly one thousand votes. Several factors contributed to his victory. First, no pro-Duraković voter registration campaign along the lines of Glasaću za Srebrenicu was mobilized; the voting drive for the incumbent was largely in the hands of the SDA, which failed to generate the enthusiasm of the 2012 campaign. The unity among Bosniak party activists was simply not present to anywhere near the extent it was in 2012. Second, in 2012 Radojica Ratkovac's candidacy had been a spoiler that divided the Serb voting bloc. Furthermore, the trickery that was in play in 2012 on the part of pro-Serb voters—many of whom crossed the river from Serbia—was again in full operation.

Another factor contributing to Duraković's defeat was the sustained arbitrary and discriminatory enforcement of residency laws against would-be returnees to Srebrenica. In summer of 2015 a residency law was enacted at the Bosnian state level that legalized this discrimination. This law was enforced particularly robustly in Srebrenica municipality. This behavior on the part of local law enforcement worked to reverse the gains that the registration drive of 2012 had accomplished.

The strictness of the residency law was such that a grown child living with his or her parents would need a rental contract from them in order to prove residency in the municipality. Candidate Duraković was quoted as saying that he himself would not be able to prove residency in Srebrenica under the current laws. He noted that by the time of the election campaign, some six hundred to seven hundred Bosniak voters had been erased from the rolls—and about twenty-five hundred Serbs living outside of the municipality had been added.[20]

On the day of the election, it was estimated that some three thousand people crossed into Srebrenica from Serbia;[21] Duraković stated that on that day, there were more vehicles from Serbia in the municipality than local ones.[22] He added that local police officials were at work the entire day giving out residency documents to these voters.

In the wake of the election, appeals for a recount and for investigation of corrupt voting practices were ignored, and Mladen Grujičić became Srebrenica's mayor. He promised to pursue a policy of reconciliation and to promote a better life for all Srebrenicans. For example, he spoke of pushing through the completion of the Guber spa, as well as other development projects.

I asked Zulfo Salihović, early activist for return, and more recently a member of the municipal council, how it was that Grujičić was able to win the elections. He answered, "The numbers between the Bosniaks and Serbs were about equal. But the Serb voting body was better organized." I asked if that was particularly the case in 2016, and Zulfo said that it was true in 2012 as well, but that in those elections the Serb vote was divided. This year all Serb parties decided to unite behind Grujičić's campaign.[23]

Activists who had supported Duraković's candidacy were in shock, and recriminations were plentiful. In response to the accusation that Grujičić had denied the fact of genocide, the new mayor stated, "I cannot deny something that did not happen,"[24] and, "There was no genocide and that will be my position as long as I live."[25] At the same time, Mayor Grujičić called for Bosniaks to stay in Srebrenica and promised to work with all parties in the municipality to improve people's lives.

While the presence of a mayor who denies genocide is intolerable to people who care about justice for the survivors and returnees, the question of how much difference Grujičić's victory really makes persists. The first couple of years of Grujičić's term passed uneventfully on the whole, and the July 11, 2017 and 2018, commemorations of the genocide also took place without incident—and without the presence of any Serb officials from Srebrenica municipality.

However, there were worrisome reports of increased provocations by extreme nationalists from Serbia. In Grujičić's first year in office it appeared that there was greater space for such provocations and for increased activity of atrocity deniers in Srebrenica. Grujičić enhanced his reputation as an extremist when Ratko Mladić was convicted of genocide at Srebrenica in late 2017 by glorifying Mladić and saying that his guilty verdict confirmed that the purpose of the ICTY was simply "to persecute Serbs."[26]

In a similar vein, Mayor Grujičić shocked Bosniak returnees to Srebrenica by announcing that the Srebrenica municipal assembly would award Milorad Dodik an "honorary certificate of thanks" for his assistance to Srebrenica.[27] Meanwhile, there were no significant improvements in economic development that would make a difference in the lives of all Srebrenicans.

Of Grujičić, Zulfo Salihović told me, "He is not organizing any development projects. Nor are any foreign NGOs here to spur projects anymore. The Serbian and RS governments give some money, but it's just money laundering. The stories of development are just tales for the gullible . . . but there are no new workplaces, no jobs. Or, there's a job for 350 to 400 KM. It's barely equivalent to what you would receive on welfare. You work for ten hours, and you only get ten euros. So people are just thinking about how to leave. Between those who have left and those who have died, the population of the municipality has gone down from some twelve thousand to probably about seven thousand to eight thousand."[28]

Senad Subašić, technical adviser to the municipal government, said of the new mayor, "He doesn't have that much power, in fact. This is the way it was when there was a Muslim mayor as well. At the municipal level the mayor only has the power to solve some local issues. It's all the same as before; Grujičić is no different. The state is the problem. Here, we only have influence over local services, but we have no authority over the companies that most strongly affect our municipality, for example, the mining companies such as Mineko and Boksit. We can't make anything happen; it's all with the entity."[29]

On the person-to-person level, for the most part local Serbs and Bosniaks continue to get along and collaborate; this is especially true among younger people. And according to school registration and the recent census, Bosniaks are in fact the majority in the municipality. Some 70 percent of pupils in elementary and high school today are Bosniaks, and about 60 percent of the children in daycare centers are Bosniak as well.[30]

FIGHTING DISCRIMINATION IN THE SCHOOLS

In the same years that Srebrenican activists were fighting to ensure pro-Bosnian representation in the mayoral office and experiencing repression after that campaign, there was also a campaign to make the municipality's schools more responsive to the needs of the Bosniak returnees.

In the early period of return, the number of Muslim children in the local schools could be counted on the fingers of one hand. During the 2000s the Muslim influx grew, while more and more Serbs displaced from the Federation returned home or left for other parts of the Republika Srpska.

In 2002, in all Srebrenica there were twelve Muslim students in elementary school and six in high school, with one Muslim teacher on the staff.[31] By the end of the decade the proportion of students was quite different, although Muslims were still underrepresented on staff. During the 2011–2012 school year a campaign developed at one school, where 201 out of 405 students were Muslims, and the rest Serbs.[32] The nearly fifty-fifty split among the student body motivated the parents of the Muslim students to form an organization called the Association of Parents of Bosniak Children.

In the 2011–2012 school year parents of Bosniak children attending the elementary school called for an adjustment to the composition of a school board and teaching staff that would better reflect the ratio of Bosniak to Serb students, and they sought the appointment of a Bosniak assistant director of schools. Expressing the most substantive of demands in this campaign, the parents called for the right of their children to study what is called the "national (ethnic) group of subjects."

This demand referred to the wish to study a curriculum that was not colored by the Serb nationalist worldview. Throughout much of the postwar period, the atmosphere in schools in the Republika Srpska has been heavily influenced by Serbian Orthodox symbolism—including schools named after Serbian nationalist figures, celebration of Serbian saints' days, and even the display of Serbian Orthodox icons on the walls. Furthermore, the curriculum has predominantly presented the Serb nationalist interpretation not only of recent historical events but of earlier history as well. It has often been the case that the curriculum, including textbooks, comes from neighboring Serbia.

The wartime divisions had, for the most part, demolished a secular approach to education. Reflecting this fact, in the postwar period the establishment of a "national group of subjects" was institutionalized. This new arrangement recognized that the Croats, Serbs, and Bosniaks wanted their children to study history, language, literature, what is called "nature and society," geography, and religion according to the customs and beliefs of their own communities. As soon as students from the three different ethnic groups were separated during the war, three separate sets of textbooks were established.

For the most part students have continued to study in ethnically separate schools ever since the war. In the Federation, in locations where Croats and Bosniaks lived in the same community, more than fifty schools were established in a Jim Crow–style system called "two schools under one roof." In the Republika Srpska, on the other hand, the schools were simply dominated by a Serbian-based curriculum. However, in the early 2000s it was agreed, on a temporary basis, that if (non-Serb) returnee students in a school numbered more than one-third of the student body, they would be allowed to study their own curriculum, while still sharing classes in such subjects as math, physical education, and science.

This "interim agreement on meeting the special needs and rights of the students of returnees" was signed in 2002 by the Ministries of Education of both entities with the understanding that a long-term system of educational administration in venues of mixed ethnicity would be developed in the subsequent years. This never took place, and as return communities in the Republika Srpska grew and reestablished roots, dissatisfaction about the lack of attention to the needs of students in those communities reached the level of conflict.

Parents of Bosniak pupils complained that their children were being served objectionable historical interpretations, for example, that Srebrenica had been "liberated" in July 1995. The war of the 1990s was termed the "Serb War of Independence." The parents' association demanded that their children be allowed to study in a curriculum developed in the Federation.[33] In January 2012 some 150 parents signed a petition presenting these demands to RS minister of education and culture Anton Kasipović, a Bosnian Croat and career political official in Banja Luka.

By March 2012 the parents had decided on a school boycott to press their demands. After meeting with parents in the middle of the boycott, Minister Kasipović directed the Pedagogical Bureau of the Republika Srpska to work with the Tuzla school district (in the Federation) to standardize a study program that would allow Bosniak children to study their preferred "national subjects."[34]

The next fall, a Bosniak educator was appointed as assistant school director, and the new school board was composed of four Serbs and three Bosniaks. The Tuzla curriculum was introduced as well. In the new school year, the ethnic ratio of students had meanwhile shifted to 176 Serbs and 226 Bosniaks.[35]

The concessions granted in Srebrenica were a victory for Bosniak parents who campaigned for their children, as members of a constitutionally recognized ethnicity, to study their own subjects. But this was just an advance skirmish before similar struggles were to take place in other parts of the Serb-controlled entity.

Another form of discrimination that has manifested in RS schools where there is a significant minority of Bosniak returnee students is the refusal of entity authorities to permit the use of the term "Bosnian" for the language that Bosniaks speak. Bosniaks designate their language in this way. However, officials in the RS Ministry of Education, wishing to impose an artificial ethnic separation in terminology referring to the same language as spoken by different people, insist that the language Bosniak students use be called the "Bosniak language."

This rule has been imposed in Srebrenica, in spite of the fact that the Bosnian-Herzegovinan Constitutional Court had recently ruled that students had the right to call their language whatever they wished. From 2016, Bosniak parents and students fought an inconclusive campaign for this right against the Ministry of Education.[36]

"RECONCILIATION" WORK AT THE GRASSROOTS LEVEL

In Chapter 7, I explained my reluctance to use the word "reconciliation," owing to the superficial usage and incessant manipulation of the concept, especially by foreigners. It is best to leave discussion of reconciliation to those who may practice it someday, rather than holding it out as an ephemeral prize to induce everyone to "get along." However, there are those at the grassroots level in and around Srebrenica who have striven to lay the groundwork for a healthy coexistence.

The struggle for true peace—not just the absence of war—requires taking control of "collective memory" away from the manipulators and creating, as psychiatrist Stevan Weine describes it, a "civic dialogue" where the past is not buried and where people listen to each other.[37] If there is to be any hope for the creation of such an atmosphere, the effort must come from the grassroots; international officials have proven themselves worse than useless in such an endeavor.

In the context of Srebrenica, the work to create dialogue and an atmosphere where different groups of people listen to each other can come from a variety of directions. First, there are the ordinary Serbs and Bosniaks, who have shared the same territory for generations and continue to do so after the war. There are religious officials. There are human rights activists from Serbia, and young people—and veterans—from the Netherlands who are examining their own country's involvement in Srebrenica.

In 2004, an activist from the Serbian branch of Youth Initiative for Human Rights (YIHR) sent a letter to the Movement of the Mothers of the Srebrenica and Žepa Enclaves, thanking them for their visit to the central Serbian town of Leskovac. The letter read, in part, "I am getting in touch with you with shame in my heart and mind, because it is nearing nine years since the loathsome crime which was committed in my name and in the name of my fellow citizens. . . . My parents, and the parents of my friends, did not do much to prevent or to raise their voices against the genocide. I do not know whether those voices could have prevented the criminal intentions, but I know that there would be less shame in my heart if I knew that the people around me, nine years later, were prepared to recognize and accept the truth."

The fact that even a few people in Serbia are confronting their past and fighting against historical amnesia matters to Srebrenica. It is an open question how much progress has been made in this work in the course of the postwar decades. The 2005 release of the Scorpion film depicting the murder of six captive young men from Srebrenica made an impact on the consciences of at least some viewers in Serbia. And the Belgrade-based Humanitarian Law Center, directed by Nataša Kandić, has done crucial work in promoting awareness of Serbia's role in the Bosnian war. Likewise, the Belgrade-based Women in Black and the Helsinki Committee for Human Rights in Serbia, directed by Sonja Biserko, have also been relentless in their advocacy for the truth about Srebrenica and other crimes committed in Bosnia.

During a panel discussion around the time that the Scorpion footage was released, journalist Gojko Berić commented that "people in Serbia have not yet felt shame, and there is little hope that this will happen."[38]

Berić's view of the future of Serbian national awareness was a dark one, although he did acknowledge the essential work of Kandić and Biserko. In an essay from the same period, Berić recalled the formulation of the German psychiatrist and philosopher Karl Jaspers, who wrote of three kinds of guilt: criminal, political, and moral, and that "every person carries a part of the responsibility for his government." Berić's conclusion was that criminal guilt is individual, but political and moral responsibility are collective. He added that "a generation of Serbs will have to live with the burden of Srebrenica, just as the Germans live with the burden of Auschwitz."[39]

YOUNG PEOPLE TOGETHER

In some ways, there have been fewer obstacles to healthful interaction among young people who live in and around Srebrenica than among their elders, for a couple of reasons. First, they have fewer or no memories of the terror that took place as Srebrenica fell in 1995. Second, they live together and go to school together on a day-to-day basis, which gives them the opportunity to see how much they have in common.

During a visit to Srebrenica in 2010, I chatted with Marko and Zdravko, a couple of young musicians whose punk-rock band was based at the Youth Center. They were members of Zadnji Popis (the Last Census). It was one of these youths, speaking of the way young Bosniaks and Serbs get along in Srebrenica, who told me that "there's no hate here among us young people." I asked them how they, as young people, could influence the poor prospects in their town. One of them responded, "Voting doesn't seem to help anything. We have influence through music."

In 2006 a regular series of work camps was organized in various parts of Srebrenica municipality, starting in Sućeska, and later moving to Potočari. Recreational summer camps in the Srebrenica-Bratunac area became a regular event. In 2011 an annual "Kamp

Mira" (Peace Camp) was initiated by the NGO Za Srebrenicu (For Srebrenica). Located on Lake Perućac, thirty kilometers up the Drina River from Srebrenica, the camp was attended by more than one hundred youths from the entire region. One supporter, Federation of Bosnia vice president Svetozar Pudarić, commented, "Srebrenica is not only July 11th. People live in Srebrenica 365 days of the year, and it is important that projects to unite young people of different ethnicities and tear down barriers receive more attention."[40]

Speaking of efforts among young people to organize group events, activist Almir Salihović commented, "If you want to attend some cultural event, you have to make it happen yourself. We are simply trying to create an atmosphere where people will not judge each other by their ethnicity. We have returned here; we carry the burden of the past, and we simply must collaborate, to go to college together, and to spend time together, if we want to live a normal life."[41]

ODISEJ IN BRATUNAC

The grassroots organization Odisej, based in nearby Bratunac, provides a hopeful example of interethnic collaboration to make that "normal life" possible.

In the early part of the war, many members of the majority Bosniak population of Bratunac were killed, and the rest expelled. Local extreme Serb nationalist forces and paramilitaries carried out some particularly vicious atrocities against the non-Serb population.

Refugee return to Bratunac was underway by the early 2000s, in the face of great hostility and what has been called "low-intensity" terrorism, including occasional assassinations. Where the prewar Muslim population in the municipality was over twenty-one thousand (nearly two-thirds of the overall population), the return population has not amounted to much more than seven thousand. But for the Podrinje region where Bratunac and Srebrenica are located, in relative terms this is a significant return. Periodic elections have resulted in a minority of Bosniaks taking local office. At the same time, there is also a significant presence of Serbs who were displaced from the Federation.

The history of Bratunac has been closely intertwined with that of Srebrenica. Especially in the postwar period, the municipality has been favored by the Republika Srpska's nationalist political apparatus. The international community—especially via the UNDP—has crafted integrated development programs including Bratunac, Srebrenica, and Milići municipalities. Thus in various ways there has been ongoing economic, political, and social interaction between Bratunac and Srebrenica. Meanwhile, relations between Serbs and Bosniak returnees in Bratunac remained rather tense over the years. Young activists, on the other hand, have communicated relatively openly between Srebrenica and Bratunac.

It was in this context that young activists in Bratunac founded Odisej in 2001. Two of the leaders, Čedomir Glavaš and Miljan Vujević, had themselves been displaced from the Sarajevo suburb of Hadžići, when they were teenagers. They spoke with me at length about the history and activities of their organization, saying that at first, the atmosphere in Bratunac was too tense for the group to be able to reach across ethnic lines to Bosniak returnees. But after a couple of years, as the number of returnees increased, things began to change.

Miljan described a turning point for the organization in 2004:

> We had a small, intimate meeting, where we said, "What will we do? Will we work for integration? It will be very dangerous; they will put pressure on us, and we will be rejected socially." There were no Bosniaks in the group at that time, but we wanted to open up to them. It was a unanimous decision, to be better, to be different, not to be embarrassed to be able to say, "I have Bosniak friends," and for that to be an ordinary thing.
>
> When the first Muslims came back to Bratunac, we couldn't go in the kafanas with them. They would be kicked out. So we made a plan: we arranged for two of us to meet, a Serb and a Bosniak, and to have a big hug in a very public place. Then we went back into a kafana together. There, a Serb in the kafana criticized one of us for associating with Bosniaks. So then there was tension between Serbs; the Muslims weren't relevant. In a way, that was progress.
>
> We have gotten problems from other organizations, Serb NGOs that are only rhetorically "multiethnic." They criticized us when we called for the arrest of war criminals, and when we approved the arrest of Karadžić, they said that we were "politicizing the situation." Meanwhile, young Bosniaks who come to work with us have been criticized by their own people.

Outside Odisej's center stood a large mural of a policeman holding a flashlight and saying, "You from Odisej, again!" The caption read, "Let's help the police and beat ourselves."

The mural referred to a project that Odisej carried out in 2006, when activists put up posters in five municipalities. The poster's caption read, "Do you know who your war heroes are?" In one column, there were photographs of Radovan Karadžić, Naser Orić, and other war "heroes" (or war criminals, depending on one's outlook) from each of the three main ethnicities. In the other column, there were positive figures, such as the Nobel Prize–winning writer Ivo Andrić, popular athletes, musicians, and Bosnia's Oscar-winning filmmaker Danis Tanović.

At the end of the project, Miljan related:

> We held a party at our center that night. The police came and drove us out of the building. They brought some of us to the police station, and beat us. There was no legal process. They beat eight of us, brutally, all night.
>
> After that, we made a big noise about what happened, and since then, no police have come around here. Not when we need them, either.
>
> The local government gave us an office in an out-of-the-way place and blocked financial

resources. Then they harassed us by subjecting us to various inspections regarding clean-liness, bookkeeping, and similar things.

I asked if the government of Bratunac municipality gave any support to Odisej. Čedomir said, "We have good cooperation with the executive authorities, but bad cooperation with the municipal council. We presented a program that we called a 'peace initiative' to the local municipal assembly. But the council always rejects what we propose."

Miljan said, "Now we are working on youth policy, trying to get such projects financed, to promote reconciliation. They gave money for war; now they should give money for peace."

I asked the two to describe to me some of Odisej's more formal activities in con-fronting the past and clearing obstacles between young people of different ethnicities. Miljan explained, "What is essential is that we young people sit together, and share what we have experienced. People had the same experiences, hunger, and unemployment. Sharing these experiences has helped create respect for each other. We have visited each other's war memorials and cemeteries together, in the framework of a seminar. Around thirty people went to Potočari. People came from Vlasenica, Milići, Šekovići, Bratunac, and Srebrenica. We had prepared ourselves by reading reports from the ICTY."

I asked Čedomir and Miljan how they evaluated changes in the atmosphere in Bratunac in the past years since they opened up their organization. Miljan answered, "My opinion is that it has changed. A lot has changed. After the war, people were very homophobic."

I was surprised that Miljan would mention homophobia right off. This conversation took place in 2008 during days of great tension in Sarajevo, when extreme Islamists and street thugs violently attacked gay rights activists and shut down a queer festival. Miljan said,

It's horrible, what is going on. There has been a great degree of homophobia among na-tionalists. There was a gay parade in Belgrade in 2005, and they totally destroyed it. That event influenced the atmosphere here.

We have made progress here regarding nationalism; now there are not open conflicts or open expressions of hatred. People [both Bosniaks and Serbs] come here to our center to be together, to be in touch, to love each other. They go out together for coffee or to take a walk; they don't have any kind of problems. Once, this was unimaginable.

Regarding the ongoing work of Odisej and Čedomir and Miljan's hopes for the future, Miljan commented:

We need to broaden our work, to prepare young people. This is an ethnically mixed organization. Odisej was one of the first such groups in the country, along with a few non-governmental organizations. But we are the only local youth organization where every-thing has started from below.

We activists who are around twenty-five to thirty years old have no careers. We don't dare start raising a family. We are thinking about how to bring peace to the people, not how to buy our third car. We lost our childhood, our chance to go to the sea on holiday. But it is not in vain. It is not useless, because my child will be able to have a better life.

Some of the young people targeted by Odisej have publicly reflected on the impact of the group's work. A couple of Bosniak returnees to the Bratunac area, Almir and Ado, spoke with *Dani* in 2008. Almir, who was four years old at the beginning of the war, recalled that a Serb had saved him and his parents during the war, but that other Serbs had killed his two brothers, eleven and twelve years of age. Of Odisej, he recalled, "When I returned to Bratunac and when I learned of the organization Odisej, and that they had put up posters around Bratunac that spoke of the war crimes against Bosniaks, I could not believe that that existed."[42]

After Almir and Ado described improvements in the atmosphere in Bratunac, the *Dani* reporter asked them, "How do things stand with the girls?" Ado replied, "If only you knew how many secret connections there were in Bratunac."[43] Reading this, I recalled how Miljan had said to me, "Love, water, and money do not have borders."

Miljan said to the *Dani* reporter, "Do you know why we don't have problems with the youngsters? They simply do not see differences. Our biggest problem is with what happens when they go back home. There is pressure from the parents who then push nationalism on them, and they accept that, and then you've lost your work. But when you gather kids together in one place, they fall in love, they sing, and there is no kind of prejudice. . . . We have allowed people to say everything that they think, even the worst things—about how they hate Bosniaks, how they are guilty for everything. And then we ask them, "Why? What have they done to you? Little by little, we confront them with facts."[44]

Odisej has put "confrontation with the past" into practice on the most grassroots level. But Čedomir voiced an objection to what he called a "commercialization" of the process by nongovernmental organizations and political parties. In an environment where the majority of activists are ensconced in NGOs that receive funds from abroad or from their own government, there is a danger that those promoting "confrontation with the past" will be operating under someone else's agenda, without sensitivity to local conditions. Without sensitive grassroots action, no amount of governmental, nongovernmental, or international pressure or support can change society.

Odisej disbanded in the late 2000s because of shifting funding priorities and the personal needs of the group's leaders. But while Odisej is no more, it serves as an example, and it is clear that the work it performed in the first decade of the 2000s contributed to the cause of justice in Bratunac and beyond.

Organizations come and go, and grassroots campaigns in Bosnia are the most ephemeral. Some organizations disappear for lack of funds; others become co-opted by the very nature of funding. But the impulse for equal rights and justice among ordinary people never disappears; it reappears anew in another form, another organization.

AN EXAMPLE

In one manifestation of mutual understanding and empathy, a notably positive incident took place in Srebrenica in September 2014. It was a minor matter, but it was a hopeful thing. Ten members of Sana, an amateur multiethnic theater group based in Srebrenica, were invited by a Methodist Church group to come and visit four cities in England. Led by Imam Damir Peštalić and Serbian Orthodox priest Father Aleksandar Mlađenović, both of Srebrenica, members of the group submitted identical application forms with identical financial guarantees.

The Bosniaks of the group received visas, but the Serbs were rejected. In response, Imam Peštalić announced that the Bosniak members were not going to travel to England without their Serb colleagues. The Methodists apologized and promised to set things right. Mlađenović commented, "Many British diplomats and representatives of civil society come to Bosnia-Herzegovina to 'teach' us tolerance, reconciliation, and coexistence, but this example shows that they need to learn from us."[45]

The above examples of NGO and grassroots action point the way. They show that campaigns mounted from below can make a difference and are, indeed, an essential ingredient for change. However, there are severe limits to their effectiveness in the confines of the "Dayton straitjacket." This rigid, constitutionally enforced political structure continuously entrenches the position of the separatists who profit from the false divisions among the ordinary people of Bosnia.

International officials and "humanitarians" alike do not contribute to change when they restrict themselves to empty declarations about "tolerance" and "reconciliation." I also take exception to the discourse of "moving on." To the extent that this phrase calls for forgetting history, it is not realistic. The pain and loss created by the aggression against the multiethnic and multicultural state of Bosnia-Herzegovina, and by the genocide that took place during the war, is never truly left behind. The psychic damage from that loss "moves on" with the survivors forever. It is only to be hoped that the younger generation, which will also never forget the war crimes, can find within itself the strength to continue the struggle for truth and justice as the prerequisites to true reconciliation. Here, healing is an ongoing process, rather than a destination.

POSTWAR SREBRENICA

In contrast to gloomy evaluations of Srebrenica as a hopeless place, my own closer observations over the years find visible repair. Certainly this is true on the physical level, with the restoration of buildings in the city, and the repair of infrastructure throughout the municipality. It is true as well, to some extent, in the development of local institutions, a few amateur cultural organizations, and a number of effective NGOs.

There are two visions of Srebrenica: one that dwells in the past and one that looks to the future. They coexist and compete with each other, holding opposing visions of the fate of Srebrenica in their grip. The Srebrenica that dwells in the past necessarily recalls the atrocious wartime destruction of the community. The Memorial Center, whose population of reburied genocide victims roughly equals the live population of returnees to the municipality, embodies that Srebrenica. Unfortunately, few visitors to Srebrenica go beyond the cemetery.

That view of Srebrenica that is stuck in the tormented past dominates among the people who do not live there. On the other hand, the will to re-create a healthy and peaceful community in Srebrenica is indisputably present among the younger and more hopeful inhabitants of the municipality. Their actions vividly illustrate an innate awareness that all the residents of Srebrenica have the same needs and that the possibility of cooperation in the struggle for equality is something worth fighting for.

Speaking with Muhamed, an employee in the Srebrenica municipal government, I brought up my impression of these two visions. He responded, "No person is complete without carrying an involvement with the past, the present, and the future within him. Those of us who are still able to summon up any hope at all hold to the idea that the positive vision will prevail."

It is undeniable that division and bitterness still reside in Srebrenica. Part of the responsibility for divisiveness and obstruction of healing must be placed on the "stepmother" of Srebrenica, as former mayor Duraković has termed Banja Luka.[46] Provocations have continued, like the construction of crosses in inappropriate places such as Budak and Potočari, along with more ephemeral provocations such as the August 2013 celebration of an Orthodox holiday at the main church in the center of Srebrenica. On that occasion people at the church sang songs glorifying Ratko Mladić, Radovan Karadžić, and the World War II Chetnik leader Draža Mihailović.[47]

Denial of the genocide and war crimes continues among prominent figures in Srebrenica.[48] More pernicious is the ongoing job discrimination Serb officials practice against Bosniaks as employees or job applicants in local firms and institutions. Discrimination potentially affects all Bosniak returnees in Srebrenica, and unemployment and poor job prospects affect everyone. Young people, regardless of ethnicity, think about leaving; indeed, many of those who go to college in other places never return.

I was chatting with Džemila Spahić, who ran a long-lived café in Srebrenica with her husband Omer. Asked how she was, she answered, "Treba biti zadovoljna"—"One should be satisfied." But the Spahićs had employment, which so many others lack. Employment is available in politics and in the state-run institutions and industry, but corruption, discrimination, and obstruction have negative effects on the local economy. Unemployment has regularly been estimated to be at least 50 percent.

In spite of this, if one spends time in Srebrenica, it is not so hard to find people doing hopeful things, particularly among the young. Numerous local nongovernmental organizations continue their work. These activists and many in their broader circles manifest an opening between the ethnicities. In cooperation with the municipality, they continue to organize opportunities for the local population to interact in a positive and enjoyable way through musical events and an occasional festival.

The difficulties of life in a municipality burdened by its atrocious recent history continue. Side by side with the struggle for a decent life, activists continue the struggle for equal rights and justice. The key to recovery in Srebrenica is still, as before, economic recovery. In recent years there have been setbacks as well as small steps forward.

Obstruction of economic development continued in recent years, at times accompanied by a marked expression of anti-Bosniak prejudice. Cronyism in favor of Dodik's confederates, coupled with discrimination against Bosniaks, has significantly held back economic development in Srebrenica municipality. On the positive side, some new companies have established roots in Srebrenica with the sincere intention of contributing to the local economy.

In 2016 there was a glimmer of hope for development in Srebrenica. At a well-attended international donor conference held in the town in late 2015, funds were promised that rivaled those donated after the 2002 UNDP-sponsored donor conference. By spring of 2016, several million KM promised by the government of Serbia arrived in the municipality's coffers, and a couple of middle-sized reconstruction projects were underway.

However, toward the end of that year, then mayor of Srebrenica Ćamil Duraković complained bitterly that Banja Luka was still controlling economic development in Srebrenica municipality and, in large part, obstructing use of funds that had been donated. Duraković acknowledged funds that the RS government itself had donated but criticized the government for delaying approval of actual use of those funds.[49]

During a visit to Srebrenica in mid-2018, I sat at a sidewalk kafana with a friend and remarked on the clean look of the refurbished sidewalk nearby. My friend looked down and said, "Šminka"—makeup. As of 2018, significant economic growth had not blessed Srebrenica municipality.

PART IV

PRIJEDOR

Genocide, Return, and Apartheid

13

War and Postwar Events in Prijedor Municipality

THE MUNICIPALITY OF PRIJEDOR, IN THE KRAJINA, HAS BEEN the center of one of the most resolute struggles for rights and justice in all Bosnia-Herzegovina. In spite of having been the location of some of the greatest brutality during the war, Prijedor had one of the highest rates of "minority" return in the country. The twenty-year process of return, the fight against discrimination, and the movement for memorialization were all significant campaigns in the municipality. Because of both the struggle for rights in the postwar period and the atrocities that were committed in the area during the war, Prijedor deserves the attention of people who are interested in justice.

The 1991 prewar census reveals that Prijedor, a town of some 112,000, had a nearly evenly split Serb and Bosniak population, some 86 percent of the total. The remainder was composed of Croats and other ethnicities. A map of Bosnia shows that Prijedor was closer to Zagreb than to Sarajevo. And history reminds us that during World War II, under the leadership of the popular Partisan figure Dr. Mladen Stojanović, Serbs, Croats, and Muslims fought together against the Nazi occupiers and their collaborators.

In the first multiparty elections, in 1990, nationalist parties received well under one-third of the vote.[1] I have received descriptions of the relaxed atmosphere of coexistence in the municipality before the war similar to this one: "Before the war, people in this area behaved the same as in the most civilized places in Europe. There was no prejudice; we didn't even know who was of what ethnicity."[2]

With a background of multiculturalism and a strong legacy of antifascism, Prijedor and its surrounding towns and villages could have passed through a post-Yugoslav transitional phase to a peaceful and thriving future. But the war intervened, and, since the early 1990s, the municipality has been anything but a peaceful and thriving place.

Emsuda Mujagić, a Kozarac-based activist for return and recovery, spoke of the transformation in the atmosphere in Prijedor before the war, and of the murky preparations for war: "Beginning in 1990, you could notice polarization among the people. It was not too visible, but there was something in the air. Then in 1991 the wars in Slovenia and Croatia started, and there was preparation for war here. We didn't know it at the time, but looking back on it, the picture comes together."[3]

In developments that paralleled those in other parts of Bosnia-Herzegovina where Serb extremists planned to take power, Serb nationalists associated with SDS, the party of Radovan Karadžić, formed a "crisis staff" to organize the takeover of Prijedor municipality. Key figures in the takeover were, among others, Dr. Milomir Stakić, Dr. Milan Kovačević, the schoolteacher Slobodan Kuruzović, and the local police chief Simo Drljača.[4]

WARTIME EVENTS IN PRIJEDOR MUNICIPALITY

In April 1992, without prior notice, Muslim political officials were barred from performing their duties or even entering their offices. Croat and Muslim employees of state-run companies were dismissed from their jobs. At the end of the month the citizens of Prijedor woke up to the sound of gunfire and found their town sandbagged and occupied by extremist troops. The takeover had begun, and with it came the expulsion of non-Serbs and the violence that lasted throughout the war.

Not far from Prijedor, the town of Kozarac and its surrounding villages were home to some twenty-seven thousand inhabitants before the war. Around 95 percent were Muslim. In late May 1992 Serb forces surrounded Kozarac and began bombarding the town, with the intention of intimidating its citizens into submission so that they could be removed without resistance. After the shelling, the Serb army entered the town, killing some people and taking others away.

Emsuda Mujagić relates:

The war started in Kozarac with bombing from all sides. After forty-eight hours of bomb-ing, the army stopped to announce over a PA system that everyone should come out of their houses, that no one would touch them, and that we must leave and go to Prijedor. They said they would check everyone for weapons, and whoever did not have a weapon would have no problem. When people heard this announcement, they were less afraid, and then a river of people came out of their houses.

Then there was bombing again, and many people were killed. They separated the men from the women, and there were younger men who were not holding their heads down—these people had their throats cut or they were taken into houses and killed. This happened to four people I knew; two were cousins of mine, with two of their friends.

Everyone was driven toward Prijedor. They put people in buses and took them away. They called out people's names from the list, and naturally people didn't know what the list was about, so when they heard their names, they responded. They stole from people, tortured some of them, and then sent them to various prison camps: Omarska, Keraterm, Trnopolje, and other places. They split up families, sending a father to Omarska and a son to Trnopolje. There was a general panic, and in two days, Kozarac was empty.[5]

Muslims from the villages and towns fled Serb-controlled territory, but some tried to stay in Prijedor throughout the war. It was a miserable existence under pressure. Damir, who remained there with his family until he came of age for military conscrip-tion, told me of life in Prijedor during the war: "In Stari Grad [Old Town], 320 houses were burned in one night, then bulldozed. They made Muslims wear white armbands and put up white sheets on our windows. They ordered us to do this or else we would be taken away. There were checkpoints around the city, and if they caught a Muslim not wearing an armband, they would take him away to Keraterm.[6]

The Prijedor-based human rights activist Sudbin Musić explained to me the tra-jectory of the separatist assault on Prijedor:

There are three parts of Prijedor municipality; Kozarac was the first that was destroyed. Then the Old Town and other Muslim parts of the city. Then the villages of the Left Bank of the river Sana [the "Brdo" area including villages Bišćani, Hambarine, Čarakovo, and Zecovi] were destroyed between July 20 and 26, 1992.

There were seven hundred houses destroyed in Čarakovo; it looked like Hiroshima. In 1991, 2,417 people had lived there. The village was 99 percent Muslim, and 413 people from there were killed. The rest were taken to concentration camps, then deported to central Bosnia. Over 1,850 people were killed just in that part of the municipality; 95 percent of them were Muslim, including women, children, and old people.[7]

At least sixteen hundred of these victims were killed in just one day, on July 20, 1992.[8]

Mirsad Duratović, director of the Prijedor human rights organization Udruženje Logoraša Prijedor '92 (Association of Camp Survivors Prijedor '92), grew up in the village of Bišćani. "On May 22" Duratović told me, "the Serbs attacked my village. They killed my father and my fifteen-year-old brother, my grandfather as well, and three of my uncles. I am the only male survivor from that family."[9] All told, forty-seven members of his extended family were killed.

Compounding the terror of the attack, Duratović, then only seventeen, was used as human shield together with his younger brother and two cousins. They were taken through the village and forced to watch as soldiers killed their neighbors. In the course of this action Duratović's brother and one cousin were killed. Duratović was then taken to the prison camp that had been established at the mining complex in the village of Omarska. He was one of the youngest prisoners.[10] Later, he was transferred to a camp at Trnopolje.

In August 1992, the news media revealed the existence of Serb-run concentration camps. British journalists Penny Marshall, Ian Williams, and Ed Vulliamy released chilling stories of brutality at three camps near Prijedor. Marshall and Vulliamy managed to enter Omarska as well as the village of Trnopolje, where prisoners were being held in a former elementary school. American journalist Roy Gutman visited Manjača camp, south of Banja Luka and also recorded testimony from survivors he interviewed in refugee camps in Croatia. Ultimately it was revealed that some twenty concentration camps established for non-Serbs existed in the Prijedor area.[11]

Bosniaks and Croats from Prijedor and Kozarac were taken to Omarska, Keraterm, Trnopolje, and Manjača. At Omarska prisoners were divided into categories based on their status in the communities. Lists of non-Serb politicians, judges, lawyers, teachers, doctors, and company directors were drawn up and these people were eliminated, in a practice that has come to be called "elitocide." The vicious treatment practiced at the camps has been called "dirty and messy" in comparison with the organized Nazi extermination camps of World War II.[12]

Camp survivors' organizations estimate that over thirty thousand people were held in concentration camps in the Prijedor area.[13] It is reported that over thirty-three hundred people were held at Omarska,[14] and that well over twenty thousand passed through Trnopolje.[15] At Omarska it was not unusual for a few dozen people to be killed each day, with occasional larger massacres taking place.

It is hard to exaggerate the atrocities of the camps. Beatings were a daily occurrence, and prisoners were forced to beat each other when the guards tired. No one was fed well; often one bowl of thin soup was the daily meal, with an occasional loaf of bread divided among several people. Prisoners had to eat on the run. Starvation was part of the strategy of elimination. Gutman writes that in Omarska the prisoners, many of whom were living outdoors, had eaten all the grass.[16]

People were deported to the camps in sealed trains or covered trucks. Gutman writes of people dying from asphyxiation in cramped trucks on the way to Manjača.

There, inmates slept on ferns, eight persons in a space the size of a horse stall. A terrified prisoner, under observation by a nearby guard, told Gutman, "Everything is good; we have food and accommodations."[17]

In reality, the camps were places of rape and torture, where it seemed that sadism was practiced as recreation. Guards, policemen, and sometimes even neighboring Serb villagers tormented the prisoners; they burned some alive, castrated some, and decapitated some with chain saws. Policemen came to line-ups and asked each prisoner his occupation; those unlucky enough to say they had any political or professional employment were killed first.[18]

A massacre took place at Keraterm, a former ceramics factory on the main road between Kozarac and Banja Luka, one night in June 1992. Two hundred and fifty men were crammed into a room and beaten for hours. Then they were machine-gunned, and around 150 were killed. Other prisoners were forced to load the bodies onto trucks to be taken away.[19] Often, prisoners who did such work were then killed themselves.

The greatest amount of killing took place at Omarska. The Sarajevo-based Research and Documentation Center has established that more than thirty-two hundred Bosniaks and Croats were held captive there.[20] Murder and torture were practiced at Keraterm, Trnopolje, and Manjača as well. Trnopolje was a lower-security camp; at times some prisoners were allowed to leave, but there was nowhere to go. Vulliamy writes that although guards perpetrated violence against inmates there, some people arrived at Trnopolje voluntarily, because it was safer for them than remaining in their homes.[21]

After a period at Omarska, Mirsad Duratović was moved to the camp at Trnopolje. Of that camp, Duratović said, "Conditions at Trnopolje, where more than 6,000 people, including a great number of women and children, resided at one point, were horrific. People were not getting even one meal a day; water was lacking; and the sanitary situation was defeating. Along with all that, murders, beatings, and rapes were practically daily occurrences. The situation improved only in August, when members of the International Red Cross visited the camp."[22]

When international attention was focused on the three camps near Prijedor in the summer of 1992, Serb authorities took measures to close them down. Some prisoners were released in transfers coordinated by the Red Cross; most found themselves in refugee camps in nearby Croatia. Others were moved to Manjača, which was kept in operation until December of that year. Many were transported in the direction of central Bosnia, where they were compelled to walk long distances in order to reach safe territory.

Serb forces committed another atrocity as they removed prisoners from Trnopolje. On August 21, 1992, members of the Prijedor police force drove several busloads of male prisoners over Mount Vlašić, ostensibly taking them to Muslim-controlled territory in the direction of Travnik. However, the buses were stopped at the cliffside location of Korićanske Stijene. There, 224 men were shot and thrown over the cliff. In postwar court proceedings at the ICTY, one former policeman recalled how he and other police shot at civilians as they were kneeling. Another witness described a scene where, after the massacre, police were roasting meat on several spits, within sight of a pile of dead victims.[23]

The grim tally of war casualties notes more than three thousand people killed in Prijedor municipality.[24] At least half of these were killed in the initial assaults of Serb forces on the villages, and the most common estimate has approximately seven hundred more killed at Omarska camp alone.[25] Of the several thousand people killed, available figures say that 102 were children (of which the youngest was three months old) and 256 were women.[26] On top of the human loss, extremist forces demolished some thirty-two mosques and six Catholic churches in the municipality.[27]

CROATS TARGETED ALONG WITH MUSLIMS

The targets of ethnic cleansing in the Prijedor area included all non-Serbs, not only the Bosniaks. During the onslaught of Serb extremist forces, Croats were expelled as well, and their churches and property were destroyed or stolen. More Croats were killed in Prijedor municipality than in any other single municipality during the war.[28]

Croat villages in the Krajina were targeted along with those of the Bosniaks. One was Stara Rijeka, a primarily Croat settlement of some seventeen hundred, south of Prijedor. Father Iljo Arlović, Catholic priest of Stara Rijeka, recounted to me what happened to his village:

> We were bombarded, starting on May 20 of 1992. One day, on July 23, they started bombing with a howitzer when I was shaving. I was alone. Around thirty-five or forty soldiers came in and asked, "Who is the priest here?" They ransacked the church and the house. They held a gun to my back and followed me into the house. They took away beer, cigarettes, and money.
>
> They took me away. I wanted to dress, but they said not to worry about it, that I would be back soon. Altogether, they took away 107 people. We turned left before Sanski Most and went to Lušci Palanka, to the hall of a factory.
>
> There a Serb asked, "Are there any extremists here?" They took me and four others off, and beat us with clubs. They forced a son to hit the father. He hit him, and then the soldier hit him. There were also some Muslims, a total of around 220 Muslims and Croats together. There were Muslims who had already been mistreated and beaten. There was one man, around twenty-five, who was beaten and killed. I saw his brains.
>
> We were without food or water for about two days. Then they allowed the women to bring us some food, but no water. They beat everyone, but there was one commander who had worked with us in the mine, and when he was in charge, there was no beating. We got water, food, and cigarettes then. His name was Dragan. He allowed us to go outside. We were there for a total of twelve days. Two days before they were going to release us, there were no beatings.
>
> In ten days I was hit with the club three hundred times each day, from head to toe.

They singled me out because I was a "leader." I never fell while they were beating me; I didn't want to, and God gave me the strength. I didn't even cry out.

We slept on concrete. The Serbs danced on me, and sang Chetnik songs. They ordered me to repeat the songs, but I said that I didn't know them. When I got out, I had seven broken ribs. My pleura was broken, as well as a vertebra.

I returned to Stara Rijeka on September 13, 1992, and stayed another month. They had bombed the church. All the windows were broken. All the Croats left here in 1992. I went to Zagreb, and then to Germany for recovery.[29]

In the course of the war, approximately two hundred Croats were killed in Prijedor municipality.[30] Near Father Arlović's residence in Stara Rijeka stood the Croat village of Briševo. In July 1992, Serb forces carried out the largest massacre of Croats in the war. In that village of some four hundred inhabitants, sixty-eight Croats between the ages of fourteen and eighty-seven were killed. Surviving villagers were compelled to sign their property over "voluntarily" to Serb authorities as a condition for their departure.[31]

At the end of the war in late 1995, nearly all of Prijedor municipality's roughly fifty thousand Bosniaks had been killed or expelled, along with over sixty-three hundred Croats and ninety-two hundred others, including the Romani population. Only a few non-Serbs were left, while there had been an influx of Serbs displaced from central Bosnia and the Croatian Krajina to the west of Prijedor.[32]

POSTWAR RETURN TO PRIJEDOR MUNICIPALITY

What the caterpillar calls the end of the world, the butterfly calls the beginning.

—Russell, British visitor to a conference on rebuilding Kozarac, 1999

These words were spoken by a participant at an international conference in Kozarac organized by the local NGO Srcem do Mira (Through Heart to Peace) and held in that town, still mostly a place of rubble, in the spring of 1999. Then, most returnees to Bosnia who had been expelled from Kozarac were still living in nearby Sanski Most, on the other side of the interentity borderline between the Republika Srpska and the Federation. Preparations for return to their beloved Kozarac were well underway. While they may not have thought of the daunting task ahead of them in Russell's poetic terms, they were putting rebirth into concrete form.

At the end of the war, the soldiers and political leaders who worked to make Prijedor an ethnically homogenized territory had, in large part, succeeded. The Muslim population of the municipality was less than 1 percent.[33] The Muslim and Croat villages lay in ruins, as did Prijedor's formerly Muslim-inhabited Old Town. Most of the non-Serb citizens either were dead or had been expelled.

However, there was a will to return; many people insisted on going back to their ancestral homes. Ten years after the war's end, thousands of non-Serbs, mainly

Muslims, had returned to the municipality.[34] Return took place more quickly, and with somewhat less obstruction, than to eastern Bosnia. Prijedor was relatively close to a staging ground in the Federation where displaced people had started to gather after the war. There was well-organized leadership for the return movement.

Describing that well-organized leadership, Sebina Sivac-Bryant writes in *Re-Making Kozarac*, "Making the best of a bad situation, some veterans of the 17th Krajina Brigade stuck together as civilians and led the perilous and frustrating drive to return home. ... They had a clear shared vision and had been preparing for this moment since their expulsion in the summer of 1992. That they eventually achieved their goal is a remarkable story of patience, persistence and resilience."[35]

Sivac-Bryant notes that Sead Ćirkin, a commander in the Seventeenth Krajina Brigade and head of the wartime Prijedor presidency in exile, provided leadership for the return movement early in the postwar period. Ćirkin participated in negotiations with the Serb separatists who ruled Prijedor in that period; he endeavored to listen to the needs of those rulers, even though they were the ones who had expelled his community.[36]

One obstacle to participation by male veterans was that it was particularly dangerous, in the early postwar period, for men of military age to cross from Sanski Most into Prijedor municipality. This handicap left an opening for significant leadership of women, as embodied in the organization Srcem do Mira, in the return effort.

While the international community was at first reluctant to touch Prijedor, in response to pressure from would-be returnees it gradually became more involved, and more interested in putting pressure on the nationalist leaders, than was the case with much of the rest of the Republika Srpska.

By the peak of return, some ten thousand people had come back to Kozarac and its surrounding villages. Estimates for return to the entire municipality vary between twenty thousand and thirty thousand. It was overwhelmingly Muslims who returned, while Croats remained in their wartime places of refuge or moved abroad. Prijedor municipality registered one of the greatest numbers of return in the Republika Srpska. There, returnees have established a relatively visible community and have asserted themselves as a political and cultural presence.

Return was an uphill struggle for each family. Would-be returnees trying to reclaim their apartments in Prijedor found that they were occupied by displaced Serbs or, at times, officers from the Bosnian Serb army. Emsuda Mujagić spoke of a returnee who "camped in a hut in front of her house for two years. When she heard that the family was going to be evicted, she sat for three days watching the house. When the eviction took place, she received the key. She entered the house, and it was completely empty. Somehow, the family had taken everything."[37]

Such occurrences were common; in Kozarac the situation was challenging in a different way, as thousands of houses in that part of the municipality had been destroyed, and returnees had to find international agencies to sponsor their reconstruction. Against the odds, people returned, and by 2004, there were some twelve thousand returnees in the municipality.[38]

In the early days after the war, I had heard from displaced people from Kozarac of their desire to return to their home. They said, "To us, Kozarac is beautiful, even if it is in ruins," and "We will rebuild Kozarac; we built it ourselves before, so we can do it again." When I visited the destroyed town for the first time in early 1998, I was able to see what it was that was lovely about Kozarac, in spite of all the wrecked houses and buildings. Amid the expulsion and destruction, the extremists had not bothered to cut down the trees that still lined the long main street of the town. Would-be return-ees were beginning to remove the rubble from around their destroyed homes, and representatives of international relief agencies had set up an office from which they would begin to coordinate the repairs. A few hundred displaced Serbs temporarily formed the main population of the town. Most were housed in the former elementary school, converted into a collective center.

In the next couple of years return began in earnest. I visited one returnee, Sadija, in her semirestored brick house. Her husband and son had been taken away during the war, and she still did not know their fate. Some workmen were rebuilding Sadija's roof, expertly cutting thick rafter beams with a chain saw. Most of the house was still a construction zone; some of the rooms did not even have floors. Sadija had run a cable into her kitchen from outside. In the kitchen there was simple furniture, including a couple of cheap wooden beds made from kits. Returnees were living in their ancestral homes like pioneers.

Sadija sat on a stool and peeled onions as she spoke to me of her problems. She owned the house in front of hers as well as the house behind. Her son used to live in the front house, and her brother-in-law in the back one; both were missing. Some dis-placed Serbs from a town in the Federation now stayed in the back house.

In the front house, Sadija's son had built a kafana before the war. At the time of my visit it was occupied and run by a Serb from Banja Luka. The Prijedor municipal government had given him the right to run the venue for five years.

One day this man came to Sadija's door asking her to sign an agreement that would legitimize this arrangement. Sadija refused, saying, "You were in the army. How do I know you didn't kill my son? And now you expect to take his property? Is this yours? This is mine. Put yourself in my shoes."

A LOST URBAN SPIRIT

A few years after her return to Prijedor, I asked Mirjana (a retired economist of Bosnian Croat descent) whether she had found ways to revive her social life. She responded:

There is no one I can talk with among my old circle. Some have left, and most were killed in Omarska. I don't get together with my old friends; we aren't what we were. There is a lack of trust because of what happened. We don't have mutual subjects to talk about, because no one can understand about being in exile if they did not experience it. I would rather talk with the displaced Serbs.

Furthermore, here in my apartment building there are three Serbs, two Muslims, and me, and we are all afraid of crime. The criminals rule, and they have the support of the police department. You don't know who is a criminal and who is not. There is smuggling and corruption. Some people, the war profiteers, have five or six mansions. I am optimistic, however, that there will be change, but my generation won't see it. We have been set back fifty years.[39]

Unemployment in the Prijedor area, as throughout Bosnia-Herzegovina, discouraged return during the critical first years after the war. Discrimination against ethnic "minorities" and favoritism constituted implicit forms of obstruction. Gojko, a displaced Serb from nearby Sanski Most, provided relevant statistics, saying there were approximately twenty thousand displaced Serbs in the municipality, including nine thousand from Sanski Most. These people were experiencing obstruction in their attempts to return to that city, and this created a logjam that in turn prevented return to Prijedor.[40]

Anel Ališić returned a few years after the war, after having received an education abroad. In 2004 he recalled the atmosphere upon his return: "Many people had changed, and I didn't know how to communicate with them in a real way. There were people I had gone to school with, who had been acquaintances, but there was no longer a real kind of friendship. For many years, these people were in an isolated state. Their isolation created a weakness, and they really suffered economically. There were no computers, even in 2000. For them, to have a computer was a miracle, while I had already been using them for five years. In my time as a refugee I became more open, while here they were closed off from cultural currents in the world."[41]

Discussing the changes he had seen in the atmosphere since his return, Ališić said:

Now, many people have come back. Return to Kozarac definitely had an influence on return to Prijedor. In Kozarac, at times there would be twenty to thirty returnees in one house, which demonstrated people's determination.

In Prijedor, Serbs and Muslims have started to talk to each other, and Serbs have begun to travel, into the Federation, Croatia, and Serbia, and then Europe. They have started to talk differently, to stop generalizing about other ethnicities. People have opened up very rapidly, especially the younger people. Meanwhile, the media have changed; some of the media have become independent. You can buy newspapers from the Federation, and cigarettes from there as well. There is an aura around things from the Federation that there wasn't two years ago. Then, there had been problems at the kiosks; they would call them "Muslim cigarettes."

There is a bar owned by a Bosniak. This has happened in the last two or three years. Before that, a Muslim owner would have problems; people would break his windows, and it was risky. There has been some segregation, but that is changing, and Muslims and Serbs come to each others' kafanas—especially the younger people, if they learn to act this way from their parents.[42]

Vedran Grahovac, a young man of mixed ethnic background who remained in Prijedor throughout the war, analyzed the ideological manipulation that helped create the war, and how the residue of this madness weighed on people afterward:

Before the war we lived in a multiethnic society. That hate didn't exist before; it was artificially installed. It was all so unbelievable that at first, it seemed funny. The Nadrealisti [characters in a popular satirical television show] fought over the way to hold a shovel. In the most morbid way, through war, hunger, and poverty, hate became part of our everyday life. The emphasis on ethnicity and exclusion was so strong that ethnic hatred became normalized, and we lost the ability to have any communication among the different ethnicities.

There was an urban spirit here in the 1980s that was interregional and international in consciousness, but that is all gone now. There were bands from Zagreb, concerts, and theater. Now, our culture is a monster, a mutant, and Prijedor is crowded with roadside kafana-bordellos where turbo-folk music is popular, populated by people with tattoos and shaved heads, wearing gold chains. There are fights, even murder, in the kafanas. Elements of culture are mixed together in a monstrous way. The city is infected by an influx of villagers, people with an inferiority complex.

After the war, none of my friends who had been exiled returned. I am not in contact with them. Prijedor used to be nearly 50 percent Muslim, and most of them are gone, while many Serbs came. They are mostly villagers. We are lost between the city and the village.

What has happened here shows the absurdity of the whole nationalist program: we exist as ethnicities, not as people. This has only been possible through mass hysteria, through panic, political propaganda, and media campaigns. There has not been much change since the war; people have remained slaves to that struggle.

After 1992, time stopped. There are no more tanks and guns now, but there is no exit. People in government have no need for change, because they are getting rich. The three-member presidency is like a three-headed monster. The leaders are criminals, and there is nepotism in their families. Plunder is at the root of everything.

The main problem is the economy, and it can't get better as long as those who influenced the creation of this society are still in power. But we are stuck where we are because of fear and ideology. People follow blindly, without original thought. Things that aren't complicated become complicated. There is also the ideology of religion as nationality, which is entirely a virtual thing. Never has there been more religion and less faith, so to speak. As with the contrived "rural-urban" conflict, this is also not a matter of religious disputes or intricacies of interpretation of national histories. National and religious identities are openly used as weapons in the political arsenal. These things keep people in a condition of emptiness and spiritual poverty. Many Serbs here have made peace with the fact that they are part of a collectivity, instead of being individuals.

There is no end to the creation of propaganda constructs. The nationalist discourse is based on fine things like love and freedom, while the reality is crime and poverty. This paradox must be unmasked.

When I first met Vedran Grahovac in 2004, I asked him if the anger and violent incidents that had been taking place after the war had subsided. He answered that it had indeed, saying that there was "more compromise now than two years ago." I asked him, "Wouldn't you say that tolerance is a good first step?" "No," he answered. "It is not coexistence. People are still living as members of the SDS or some other nationalist formation, not as humans. Everyone is stuck on names and symbols. There has only been compromise, not a resolution. It is an agreement among the divided: tolerance is installed between ethnically separated people rather than a recognition of each other as human beings. These constructs promote a prison mentality: separation, the motionlessness of fixed identities. For me, every new thing is interesting. We must turn toward life. Why not, when we all live on the same planet, and breathe the same air?"[43]

RETURN TO STARI GRAD

In the city of Prijedor as in other urban centers, return was significantly more difficult than return to localities that had been nearly completely inhabited by Muslims before the war. Return was harder because so many formerly Croat- and Muslim-inhabited apartments were not devastated, but were usurped by Serb residents. In addition, in Prijedor the Stari Grad (Old Town) had been primarily Muslim inhabited, and that was torched and destroyed as its residents were being led off to captivity at the beginning of the war. A local businessman with political connections took advantage of the empty space to establish an open market in the area.

Very few Muslims were left in the city after the war. Only a handful had returned by the time of my first visit there in 1998, when I was given a tour by a return activist from Prijedor. Hasnija, living in Sanski Most at the time, walked me through the neighborhood.

Hasnija had grown up in Stari Grad when it was a pleasant neighborhood alongside the Sana River. At the time of my first visit it resembled a neglected urban green strip. Unlike in Kozarac, the rubble had been removed and hardly a trace of the old neighborhood remained. We crossed a rickety footbridge; a block ahead of us was a large vacant lot holding the outdoor market, and to our left was a forest of six-year-old trees. We took a path through the woods—a path that had once been a two-lane road through a residential district. Beside the path, one could barely make out the outline of a foundation concealed by nettles and thistles.

I was told that the houses in this neighborhood had been large and comfortable, and that many of them had belonged to the most prestigious members of Prijedor society: intellectuals, politicians, and company managers. These people were the first targets of the campaign to "ethnically cleanse" Prijedor. By chance we ran into Muharem Murselović, the city's deputy mayor. Murselović was a survivor of the concentration camps. Still living in Sanski Most, he was elected by the absentee vote of Muslims expelled from Prijedor.

Nearing the wide river, we walked along a pleasant footpath beside the overgrown banks, passing several park benches. Hasnija told me, "This riverside walkway was a favorite place for people of Prijedor to relax, especially on the weekends. We used to go swimming here when we were young; we didn't need the sea. We would come here with our sweethearts. The first kiss always happened here."

I said, "That is something that can never be forgotten." Hasnija replied, "And it can never be repeated."

In the years that followed, with a combination of international pressure, grassroots persistence, and assistance from relief agencies and the diaspora, displaced Prijedorans were able to start moving back into the city. A campaign to remove the illegal outdoor market ended in victory. By the end of the 1990s a visitor could see several dozen houses in Old Town in various stages of construction, and, by five years into the new century, scores of houses were restored. Upon one return, I sat by the dark, green, flowing river. Two fat ducks were lazing on the bank in the sun. Nearby stood some of the new houses, one built right up to the path along the riverbank and decorated with bright flower beds. The houses, not yet stuccoed, had been constructed with red cinderblocks and bricks.

A couple of men were fishing off a dock in the dusk. A cat kept them company. The Thursday night muezzin's call sounded. A little further down the river a couple of teenagers, around sixteen years old, were kissing on a bench.

DISPLACED SERBS IN PRIJEDOR MUNICIPALITY

The story of Prijedor involves more than Muslims and Croats who were displaced from the municipality: there are the Serbs who were displaced *to* Prijedor. While some Serbs had participated in the wartime atrocities, many others were simply victims. Thousands of Serbs were displaced from the Federation and from the Croatian part of the Krajina, a region that spans the Bosnia-Croatia border. Many of these unfortunate people ended up in Prijedor.

Soon after the war, I spoke with two men in Kozarac, Boro and Marko—one from Dabar, a predominantly Serb village near Sanski Most, and the other from Donji Lapac, a Serb village in Croatia. Both villages were emptied of Serbs in the same eastward military sweep of combined Croat/Croatian/Muslim forces that took place in the summer of 1995.

Many displaced Serbs were living in collective centers around Kozarac, but both Boro and Marko were living in the houses of Muslims who had fled in 1992. The future was uncertain for both of them, as they were aware that the owners of these houses would be returning. Boro was chopping wood in the back yard of a Muslim returnee when I spoke with him. He was a modest man with poor teeth and an unassuming smile. Marko was tall and slender, wore glasses, and had a more worldly air. Neither had had his fair share of good luck.

Boro told me, "I was a lumberman for twenty-five years, and now I have no way to earn a living. I get occasional odd jobs like this, chopping wood. I have a wife and two children. The owner of the house we live in is in the United States. He will probably return soon. The Republika Srpska government has promised people like me land to build a house. But I don't believe that the RS can build me a house. And work will still be a problem. What they really need to do is to build factories, so that we will be able to have economic security."

I asked Boro if he would have to leave his house, and he said, "Yes, but it is a problem. I don't know where I will go. I don't plan to go back to Dabar. There is no security there, and I could be attacked. If there were a mass return, that might be different." Asked whether he originally expected to be able to stay in this house, Boro said, "No, I never expected to stay. The owner's right to return is not in dispute. I don't want to live in someone else's house, anyway. When they come back, I'll leave."

Marko had a wife and a daughter. They left their home in Croatia in 1994, before the mass expulsion that took place during the "Oluja" (Storm) offensive of summer 1995. Marko hoped to emigrate to Australia, where he had relatives. He told me that he could return to Donji Lapac, but that the conditions for supporting a family there were poor.

"Have you read Jack London?" Marko asked me. "I am like one of his characters, who had no possibility to make a living. He went from washing laundry to smuggling, and so on. No one in my hometown is working, and they have no prospects."

Marko, unlike Boro, expected to be able to stay in his house in Kozarac. When he arrived, he invested around 3,000 DM (US$1,800) in its rehabilitation, repairing the roof and windows. Now he hopes that the international community will reimburse him if he leaves. He said, "The owner of the house is in Holland. I don't think he is going to return, but he will give his house to another Muslim. I had hoped to buy the house."

Speaking of tensions between Serbs and Muslims, Marko commented, "I read a book about World War II. The Americans and British fought the Germans and invaded at Normandy. Now, they all get along together very well. One day we will also solve our problems in a better way, but this is the hardest time."

About ten years after the war, I spoke with Gojko, a displaced Serb. A veteran, Gojko told a story that could represent thousands of displaced Serbs who found themselves in Prijedor.

Of his displacement from Sanski Most and his frustration at attempts to return, Gojko told me:

People in Sanski Most took away our houses, apartments, and land. They destroyed my house in 1996. There is obstruction everywhere, not just in Sanski Most. It is a mix of politics and legal problems. SDA doesn't want the Serbs to come back. There is much talk about return to Prijedor, but not about return to Sanski Most.

Before the war, there were around twenty-five thousand Serbs in Sanski Most. Some nine thousand of those were displaced to Prijedor. Between fifteen hundred and twenty-five hundred returned to their prewar homes. But many people are selling their property, because of the bad atmosphere there. A mosque doesn't bother me, as a mosque. But the new mosque in Sanski Most looks as if it were made in Tehran. It is like a message: "This is a Muslim city." Meanwhile, the younger people among us who were displaced have no connection with Sanski Most.

We Serbs who wish to return are talking with the OHR, the OSCE. There are four levels of court there: the municipal court, the cantonal, the federal, and the state. We have been in court for three years. It is very complicated, as if someone purposely arranged it this way to prevent it from functioning. It's not that I am in favor of conspiracy theories, as if we were controlled by buttons. We simply don't live in a legal state. If we were in a normal state, we would go to court and resolve our problems. In Sanski Most, the SDA controls the courts.

Also, there is no support for us Serb returnees from our own politicians. They treat our attempts to return as an act of treason. There are some financial donations from the RS government, but only as a result of international pressure.

Gojko relates:

My father died the very day that Croat and Muslim forces retook Sanski Most, on October 10, 1995. He had died that day at 2 p.m., and they entered at 5 p.m. My family, driven out of the city by the offensive, was forced to leave him there in his coffin. My mother left in her slippers. I spent time after the war seeking my father's body, which was found in November 1998.

The Muslims talk about how we made the aggression. All right, maybe there were units that came in from Yugoslavia; but there were mujahedeen also. But I lost my home, and then I'm the aggressor? Would you want your kids to go to school and learn that they were the aggressors?

This is not to compare with other people's problems. I am not trying to equate the victimhood on the different sides. The biggest victims were Muslims.

Gojko listed the main obstacle to return and reconciliation as unemployment: "The basic problem is the economy. With a better economy, the entities will lose their importance. I want to live like the Swedes, where they don't even know who is the president. Anyone who has the opportunity to start working and receiving a decent pay, they will forget things. As far as returning to Sanski Most is concerned, there is no work here *or* there, so people stay where they feel more comfortable. And there are long lines by the embassies, where people are seeking visas to emigrate."

Gojko took the international community and its agencies in Bosnia-Herzegovina to task as well, roundly condemning international officials, while simultaneously calling on them for more robust governance: "These have not been the years of return, but the years of talk about return. The local branch of the OSCE is not paying enough attention to the matter of return. They should be more responsible, but they have tolerated obstruction. They take what local officials say for granted, for example, when the Sanski Most SDA say that 'return is settled.'"[44]

GRADUAL RECOVERY IN KOZARAC

By a few years into the 2000s, Kozarac had largely been rebuilt. The homes and shops on the main street were mostly restored, with an occasional pile of rubble standing oddly between pristine houses. Many kafanas and other small businesses had been reestablished; the large mosque at the upper end of the town was refurbished. The old Austro-Hungarian-era elementary school in that section of town, which had stood in ruins since the war, was converted into a sparkling "House of Peace" and NGO center, thanks to the efforts of local activists. Thousands of Bosniaks returned to Kozarac and surrounding villages. Even a small shopping center was built.

Over a long period, returnees waged a successful struggle to reclaim their elementary school at the lower end of Kozarac from its use as a collective center for displaced Serbs. In 1999, the first year of return to Kozarac, I asked Emsuda Mujagić how returning parents would educate their young children, as the building was still occupied. She said, "They want us to send our children to the school in Trnopolje, six kilometers from here. That is not going to happen. Some of these children were four or five when that school was used as a prison camp, and they were held there. Some were even born there. I would be very guilty if I were to allow them to go back there. We will solve this in Kozarac."

Early on, Emsuda Mujagić and other return leaders in Kozarac spoke to me of the restoration of another former school, at the upper end of the town. At the time, their plans of restoration and conversion of the upper school into a "House of Peace" seemed a distant dream in the rubble of the town that had been bombarded and from which thousands of people had been expelled.

This building, like nearly every other structure in Kozarac, was torched and bombed during the war and left as a hulk. I was present on a dreary April day in 1998 when Emsuda, together with several dozen other members of Srcem do Mira and supporters, planted a "peace tree" next to the ruins of the building. At the time, the atmosphere in the ruined town was foreboding, but Emsuda declared that the building would be rebuilt as a community center. This was before any of the displaced Bosniaks had started to return to Kozarac. I thought Emsuda was fantasizing.

Not long afterward, someone ripped out the "tree of peace." However, after return to Kozarac got underway, the old school building was beautifully restored, and today it indeed serves as a center for nongovernmental activity. Seminars on coexistence and nonviolent communication are organized for students and activists there, and the House of Peace also occasionally serves as a haven for wandering visitors.

Today Kozarac has gone well beyond fulfilling those dreams. It has become a re-markably pleasant place—especially when compared with its dreadful appearance after the war—but it is like an enclave in a segregated entity controlled by profiteers and war criminals.

On a warm and pleasant summer day some ten years after the beginning of return to Kozarac, I sat at a sidewalk table in front of a kafana with Ervin Blažević, concentra-tion camp survivor and return activist. The long main street of the town was buzzing with activity as returnees and visitors walked from store to kafana and from school to mosque. All these buildings had been restored to their previous good condition or, in many cases, a considerably better one.

Ervin spoke to me of the situation behind what met the eye in Kozarac. He said:

We were all supposed to be killed. The camp at Omarska was near here. If it had remained open longer, we would have been killed. But Ed Vulliamy saved us [by making the ex-istence of the camps known around the world.] There was an entire logistical apparatus created to get rid of us. As a people, we have been decapitated. The elite of Kozarac were killed, and people like me were left to help with postwar recovery.

Today in Kozarac there is a *lažnji sjaj*, a false splendor; there are fine houses without water and electricity. A hundred years ago, we had a theater and a library; now we have kafanas. We have repaired things, but people have not come back. It is hard to return, after fifteen years. People are in Germany, in the United States.[45]

Along the way, Ervin spoke to me of his wartime experiences and his hopes for the future. He was eighteen when the war broke out. Of that moment in history, he told me, "They came here with tanks, and we had hunting rifles." Ervin was taken to the camp at Trnopolje, where he was held for two months. Upon his release, he was expelled to an area in central Bosnia controlled by the army of the government of Bosnia. He joined and fought in the Seventeenth Krajišnička Brigada—the Seventeenth Krajina Brigade. This was a brigade of displaced men from the Krajina who fought as a mobile forward operating force, wherever the Bosnian army needed them.

Of that period, Ervin told me, "I was always the second from the front in an offensive action, because I carried the RPG [rocket-propelled grenade launcher]. The person in the front was the commander." The commander was thus in the most dangerous position, and before it happened that Ervin might be promoted, he was transferred to the duty of cameraman—although that was also a very risky task.

Ervin told me that in the war, when they were in the trenches fighting, some soldiers would wear a scarf with perfume. At night in bed, they would cover their faces with that scarf to feel the sensation of something gentler than the brutality of war.

Reflecting on the war experience and present conditions, Ervin said, "I fought for Bosnia, not for the entities. The RS is a tumor. I don't like the Federation either. And Dodik is not fighting against the Federation, but against Bosnia."

The kafana where we sat chatting was at the lower end of Kozarac. Ervin pointed at a man across the street who was doing manual labor and said, "That man up the street, working on that house, he kicked me when I was a prisoner in the camp. Now he's just a *marginalac*—a person living on the margins of society. I look at him and I think, 'God, how the world has turned.' If I can ignore him, then I come out stronger."

Ervin Blažević is an example of the pozitivci I have mentioned earlier in this book—someone who thinks positively, does not dwell on his own victimization, and strives to improve the lot of his community. He says "If I don't hate people, it's for my own sake, so as not to carry the burden of that feeling."[46]

THE LEFT BANK IN POSTWAR YEARS

In the postwar period, the Left Bank of the Sana was the part of Prijedor municipality that took the longest to recover and experienced the greatest difficulties. This is no wonder if one considers that at least half the people killed during the ethnic cleansing—overwhelmingly civilians—lost their lives in a matter of a few days in July 1992. In the village of Čarakovo alone, over four hundred people were killed in a matter of hours.

Mentioning his family's fate here, at the beginning of the war, activist Sudbin Musić described his return to his home village:

> My father was killed in Čarakovo. I spent two years in Holland and four in Germany, and then I returned. I came to Sanski Most in 1998. Then I came back to Čarakovo with my family in 2000. There were two hundred families that wanted to return, but we were only able to get donations to repair forty houses.
>
> There were seven hundred houses destroyed in Čarakovo. It was like in Rwanda, you could find human bones everywhere. I found a skull in the garden. My first hobby was taking care of funeral arrangements—my God, what a hobby! I helped people identify the remains, coordinating with the ICMP.
>
> Three days after I returned, they called me into the army. A week after that, my father's body was discovered in a well. So there was no going-away party for me when I was drafted. Then I spent ten months in the army.[47]

Other villages on the Left Bank—Zecovi, Hambarine, Bišćani, Rizvanovići, and Rakovčani—fared the same as Čarakovo at the beginning of the war, and in the postwar period as well.[48] Today only an unpaved road leads to Zecovi, where some 150 people were killed in one day. In general, the villages are ghost towns with a few returnees each. Two decades after the war, there were more restored houses than inhabited ones, as some people have returned and then left, and other people living abroad have fixed their houses, only to visit them for a spell during the summer.

The overall population of six Left Bank villages was approximately sixteen thousand before the war; twenty-five years later it was reduced to a tenth of that number.[49] Rizvanovići, which was home to some eighteen hundred souls before the war, reported to house a mere ninety-seven people in 2015.[50] The nearby village of Tukovi, which suffered the same wartime fate as the rest of the area, is somewhat more lively; it has been repopulated by displaced Serbs from the Federation.[51]

It would be better to liken these partially restored villages to movie sets, in fact, rather than to call them "ghost towns," since their emptiness is masked somewhat by the appearance of repaired houses. During my visit in 2015, Sudbin Musić showed me around Čarakovo. There were no ruins of houses, only rebuilt ones—but most were unoccupied. Sudbin pointed out each house, saying that one owner now lives in Switzerland, another in the UK, and others in Australia, the United States, Germany, or Malaysia. A whole row of houses was owned by people now living in France. Most of the houses were completely restored, down to the vinyl windows and doors, the mortared walls, and the stainless steel fences. But the owners come back for a couple of weeks or, at most, a more extended part of the summer.

Activists say that they feel forgotten by those at the state level who should be concerned about their well-being. Often, the most significant assistance has come from the diaspora and from returnees themselves.

For example, funding for the construction of memorial cemeteries has largely come from the returnees. "Everything that has been done in this regard has been from personal donations financed by the families of the victims, local residents, and some voluntary contributions from abroad," Mirsad Duratović, director of the Association of Camp Survivors Prijedor '92, said. "The local communal administrations have not really had an ear for us. Not only the local communes, but also the state, federal government, and some ministries that are involved with return. We have addressed them and been rejected."

It further upsets the returnees that nationally prominent Bosniak representatives have largely ignored them. "I feel like the last Mohican," Sudbin Musić told me. He told a Banja Luka journalist, "They come here only for the anniversaries of the torment of the Bosniaks. One helicopter after another lands, Izetbegović, Lagumdžija, foreign ambassadors come to Keraterm and Omarska, have their pictures taken, and then they leave. We are left here, as if nothing had even happened."[52]

DISCRIMINATION IN PRIJEDOR MUNICIPALITY

In Prijedor municipality, as just about everywhere throughout Bosnia-Herzegovina, public services—financed as much by taxes paid by returnees as by anyone else—are allocated preferentially, with local Serbs and friends of those in power benefiting the most. Returnees who have managed to prosper have either earned sufficient money abroad, or are supported by connections in the diaspora, or are willing to do political favors for the local authorities. The only other option has been for people to mobilize and agitate for the services they merit simply as citizens.

Discrimination has been evident in preferential hiring of Serbs in both the government and private sectors. In 2006 Amnesty International published a report noting that non-Serb former employees of the mining complex in Ljubija were not rehired upon their return. Some two thousand Muslims and Croats had been fired from that state-owned company in May 1992; they were told that they were being sacked because they were not Serbs. As of the date of the report, none of those fired had been rehired nor given compensation.[53]

The Amnesty report noted that "workplaces have often remained largely mono-ethnic, and that "mechanisms to consider claims by former workers and to award compensation are not in place or are too limited."[54] As the government of the Republika Srpska moved toward privatizing Ljubija mine in 2019, there was no promise that the composition of the work force would be multiethnic.

In local government as well, only token numbers of non-Serbs have been hired. The exceptions have been a handful of returnees who were voted into public office by their own constituency.

After a decade of postwar domination by Karadžić's SDS party in Prijedor, power at the entity level was taken over by Dodik's SNSD, and at the municipal level in Prijedor by Marko Pavić's DNS. For the returnees, the change did not make much difference. The new leaders formed a power axis; as returnee to Kozarac Nedžad Bešić told me in 2008, "Dodik and Pavić are cooperating with regard to us. We are still in a phase of ethnic cleansing here. There was much hope before, but the RS was created for one people. Although it is not like it was here in 1996 and 1997, everything that is done here is to reduce the circumstances of our people."

Municipal resources overall have been allocated in a discriminatory manner. In 2009 the local politician Muharem Murselović cited the skewed budgetary priorities: "Of the 35 million KM municipal budget, returnees were first allocated 100,000 KM, and now 120,000 KM, which is ridiculously low if we take into account that in Prijedor alone more than 9,674 housing units owned by Bosniaks were destroyed." Murselović further noted that "in the municipality 169 kilometers of road were asphalted. However, of that, only two kilometers were asphalted in Bosniak return villages."[55]

Emsuda Mujagić elaborated on another aspect of discrimination, describing how Srcem do Mira was compelled to pay upward of 10,000 KM to a person who had previously done work to restore the old school building—but the work had been done in such a shoddy way that it all had to be done over again.

The organization was also required to pay extortionary sums just to submit plans and to secure permits to restore the House of Peace. Emsuda said:

There is the same obstruction when you go to register a car or a new business. Every other day the inspector comes to Bosniak companies, and taxes them 300 or 500 KM for something. Then with that money they fix the roads and clinics, the electricity, in the Serb villages, but nothing here. Bosniak returnees in villages near Kozarac have had difficulty in establishing telephone and electrical service unless Serbs live in the vicinity.

We are experiencing indirect kinds of pressure to leave Kozarac. There is some employment here, in construction, or small kafanas. It is OK to open a kafana here. But in order to start something that is productive, you have to pay the bureaucracy as it much as it would cost to start up the company itself. The alternative is to wait for ten or fifteen months, in which time you would be losing the business. We are opening some firms. But many people will not do so because of the inspections and unfair taxing: "I work, they take."[56]

It is apparent that the local powers perceive development projects as opportunities for graft and kickbacks. Often Muslims who have returned and wish to start a business are required to pay taxes that don't apply to Serbs. One way that returning Bosniaks who have started up businesses have avoided discriminatory taxation is to hire a local Serb.

I asked Mirsad Duratović whether he considered discriminatory conditions in Prijedor to amount to apartheid. He responded, "The government provides 500,000 KM for the victims of the war—but only for the Serbs, and this is written into the law. That money goes to five or six Serb veterans' organizations. We have six organizations here of Croats and Muslims. So this is legalized discrimination—and this is money that partially comes from the taxes that we pay. They also reserve funds for the monuments to the Serb soldiers, but nothing for our side."

Prijedor municipality does in fact apportion a relatively small sum to returnees, for example, for students' scholarships and for a few jobs in the municipality. This expenditure is an amount that appears to serve to keep some NGO activists in line as much as it helps them. Duratović explains, "There is fear. If the authorities see that your organization is mounting a protest, then the government says that you are 'rebels,' and you get no assistance from the municipality."

Under these conditions, Duratović says, "Some of the NGOs have become satellites of the government. You can criticize the government. But you have to choose between receiving money or being beaten. There is economic pressure, and when that doesn't work, there is physical pressure."

An additional problem that Duratović mentioned was the Republika Srpska government's failure to recognize victim status for concentration camp survivors. This status exists for civilian victims of war in both entities, but the RS does not include former camp prisoners in that category. Duratović explains the benefit of such status: "There is some material benefit, a pension. But we don't just need that material benefit; we also need the recognition of the pain in our souls. That's what hurts us. We need recognition from the government that crimes happened here. There is no amount of money that can assuage that pain."[57]

The most flagrant case of discrimination against victims of war crimes involves Hava Tatarević, mother of ten, of Zecovi village. Tatarević's husband and six of her sons were killed in one day at the beginning of the war, during the assault on the Left Bank region. For many years, all the way up until the fall of 2013, her sons and husband were simply "missing." Then their remains were finally discovered in a newly reopened mass grave at Tomašica.

Tatarević received civilian victim status in 2008 and was thus due to receive a stipend. For the next six years she was paid a monthly sum of 150 KM, equivalent to about one hundred dollars. When she sought a higher payment based on the number of immediate family members who had been killed, she was told, "With us it is 150 KM for one or for 10."[58]

In the summer of 2014, the relevant ministry conducted an audit of some of the civilian victim status cases, and it decided to cancel the status of Tatarević. Her small stipend was cut off. The ministry explained that it was necessary to prove that her sons and husband were killed by soldiers, and not in the course of a criminal act. The ministry's finding was quoted as saying that the evidence was "not sufficient to establish the circumstances of their disappearance or killing, or whether these persons died in relation to war operations or if the murders were a consequence of a criminal offence committed by unknown perpetrators."[59]

In his capacity as member of the Prijedor city council, Mirsad Duratović has reported periodically about the regular discrimination in funding of local services. Between 2012 and 2017 the city budget afforded more than 2 million KM for maintenance and reconstruction of local community centers, but only 5 percent of that sum went to return communities. And while no Orthodox churches in Prijedor were damaged during the war, well over two hundred mosques and related structures were destroyed—but between 2013 and 2016, the city allocated five times as much money to the restoration and construction of Orthodox churches as it did to Muslim or Catholic structures.

Parallel to the discrimination, numerous incidents of violence against the returnee population have taken place, especially in the first postwar years. They continued well into the 2000s, although decreasing in frequency. The incidents fall roughly under two categories: personal attacks against refugees and attacks against religious symbols. Most of those recorded were perpetrated against the Bosniak community.

MLADEN GRAHOVAC

The returnees to Prijedor municipality formed several robust human rights and survivors' organizations. Their struggle for justice includes the campaign for the restoration of an accurate memory of the war crimes. The number of local Serbs who were willing to participate in confronting the past has grown in recent years. In the early postwar period, one Prijedor Serb stood out for engaging in this struggle alongside the returnees, regardless of the risk. Mladen Grahovac held that the most important step toward recovery in Prijedor was to "look the truth in the eye." In his judgment, "only in this way could the Serb population begin to shed the great, unbearable burden of collective responsibility."[60]

Grahovac held that the imprisonment, murder, and expulsion of tens of thousands of non-Serbs from Prijedor fell within the definition of genocide, and that this brought up the question of the responsibility of ordinary citizens. He wondered "why such a large number of Prijedorans zealously entered into criminality, and it is this that speaks of the existence of collective guilt and responsibility. It is not just a question of the leadership of the SDS," he said, "nor just a matter of the military leadership—we are all witnesses that people took weapons and went to 'liberate' Kozarac to the ground; we are all witnesses to how many people participated in the cleansing and the plundering."[61]

In keeping with Prijedor's tradition, Mladen Grahovac was a lifelong antifascist. Before the war he had been an engineer at a local factory. He remained in Prijedor throughout the war with his Bosniak wife and his children. Because of his resolute antinationalist stance and his refusal to remain silent about the war crimes he had witnessed in Prijedor, Grahovac and his family were subjected to pressure and physical threats throughout the war and afterward.

After the war, Grahovac found it a moral necessity to make his positions known; on many occasions he publicly termed the postwar regime in Prijedor "nationalist-clero-fascist." In 1996, he was fired from his job as a result of his political heresy. In the early postwar period he was the only prominent Serb to acknowledge memorial observances at the former concentration camps. At Keraterm, Grahovac participated in one of the early attempts at memorialization on May 9, 2004, when he, together with activist Edin Ramulić, lay flowers and held a moment of silence.[62]

For a time, Grahovac believed that the Social Democratic Party of Bosnia-Herzegovina (SDP), led by Zlatko Lagumdžija, was an antifascist institution. A branch office was established in Prijedor in 2000, and he became a prominent activist in the party. Because of his intelligence and the respect of people in his community, he rose to leadership not only locally but nationally, soon becoming a member of the central administration of the party. In the next couple of years he distinguished himself as a fervent advocate for interethnic cooperation.

As evidence of Grahovac's eloquence on this matter, here is part of a campaign speech that he gave in 2002, drawing on his sense of the local and regional history that brought his fellow citizens together as Bosnians:

> Last night I dreamed of King Tvrtko [Bosnian king in the fifteenth century], who fought
> for the independence of Bosnia-Herzegovina and the Bosnian Church. From Rome,
> the pope threatened that if Tvrtko did not accept his crown and Catholicism, the Hun-
> garian king would attack him. Tvrtko accepted the crown. From the east, Orthodoxy
> made similar threats. He went to the monastery at Mileševo in Kosovo and was crowned

with the Orthodox crown. When he returned to Bosnia he melted the two crowns into one at Kreševo, and at Milač Polje [near today's city of Visoko], he was crowned king of Bosnia. . . .

Last night I dreamed of Dr. Mladen Stojanović, a Serb from Prijedor who in 1941 mounted an uprising [against the Nazis] at Mount Kozara. He called on Josip Mazar, a Croat from Banja Luka, and Osman Karabegović, a Muslim from Banja Luka, and in 1942 established the strongest Partisan detachment and the largest liberated territory in all of Europe. . . . They proved that these peoples can win only if they are all in the same army. If they divide on an ethnic basis and form separate armies, then the result is a fratricidal war and war crimes.

Because there are no "good" or "bad" peoples, only good or bad national elites who lead their people in a good or bad direction. In 1941, these peoples went in a good direction, fighting against fascism. But in 1990 the people of Bosnia-Herzegovina went in the wrong direction. . . . The result was war, murder, rape, camps, genocide, and the general destruction of the country.

Let us return to antifascism, because Bosnia-Herzegovina may survive only if we are together.[63]

At the time he delivered this speech, Grahovac was the only politician in Prijedor who was prepared to speak openly about the crimes of the Serb extremists in that city.

With his keen sense of justice, Grahovac pointed out corruption wherever he saw it. Neither was he averse to focusing his criticism on the multiethnic elite that joined to plunder Bosnia-Herzegovina's socially owned wealth after the war. In 2003 at the height of his activism with the SDP (he was, for a time, vice president of the party), Grahovac stated, "The current BiH [state] and entity authorities do not have the knowledge or the will to start resolving problems in the country. Together with the international community, they are preparing the final robbery of this country, with the ultimate aim of destroying Telekom, Elektroprivreda and water resources. We must and can stop them."[64]

By the mid-2000s Grahovac, like many other prominent and intelligent political activists, began to experience discomfort as a member of the Social Democratic Party. The SDP had represented hope for the antinationalists of the country, but it had failed to shed the authoritarian legacy of its predecessor, the Communist Party of Yugoslavia. It was also beginning to engage in profiteering and corrupt practices similar to the rest of the political parties. The autocratic Zlatko Lagumdžija was president of a party wherein activists either went along with his leadership or were shunned and removed. In that period an exodus of talented and qualified leaders from the party began.

Because Grahovac was, if anything, a man of principle, by 2007 he began to experience pressure from the party's leadership. In response, he said, "I will fight to my last breath for social democracy and the civic future of Bosnia . . . and will give my full contribution to the affirmation of the anti-fascist tradition of our country.[65] Grahovac was ultimately compelled to leave the party and to continue that struggle on other fronts.

Mladen Grahovac's principles cost him and his family dearly. He noted, almost with pride, that he was in debt. "Yes, this is true," he said, "and I am proud that I owe . . . and that I am not a 'well-heeled' politician. . . . I think that I was the only vice-president of a major party who did not have employment."[66]

Mladen Grahovac's last breath came too soon. He allowed his work and financial pressure to get in the way of taking care of his health. He was a fierce fighter for justice at a time when it cost the most. He was a patriot to his region, the Krajina, loyal to its history, and a proponent of a multicultural Bosnia-Herzegovina based on citizens' rights. It was left to younger activists to take up the fight for these principles.

After Grahovac's death the Sarajevo journalist Vildana Selimbegović wrote, "With his death this land has lost yet another true anti-fascist; the world a great humanist; and his family, their greatest friend."[67]

14

Corruption in the Republika Srpska and Prijedor

THROUGHOUT BOSNIA-HERZEGOVINA, ETHNONATIONALIST AND separatist leaders formed a new elite—a "tycoon class"—enriching themselves through plunder and other illicit means. This was one of the primary motivations, along with the urge for power, for the violence that destroyed the old order. Likewise, the regime of pervasive corruption continues to depress the living standard of ordinary citizens. The dynamics of plunder and postwar corruption influence the social environment in the Prijedor area no less than in the rest of the country.

We have examined, in the case of Srebrenica, the illicit enrichment of nationalist leaders and their cronies. Corrupt business practices and appropriation of socially owned wealth have been the drivers of political and economic policies in that municipality, as in all Bosnia-Herzegovina.

Throughout the country, at all political levels, the "partyocracy" (*strankokratija*) is the primary lever for governance in all its corruption. Under this model, there tends to be one "strong man" in each party to whom subordinate political operators pay obeisance and thereby receive favors. In a sense, this replicates the political dynamic of the Tito era. The ideology of socialism has been replaced by that of liberal democracy, but the ideology is a façade, and the governing mechanism sustains a hierarchy of power and accompanying privilege.

In the postwar system, ruling parties have the power to install governmental ministers, to appoint directors to companies that are still state owned, and to preside over the crooked privatization of those companies. Channeling economic power to relatives and political cronies of party leaders has led to the enrichment of the new managing elite, composed of former communists, former gangsters, former dissidents, and former military officers.

The new tycoons, each loyal to his respective political party, enrich themselves through corrupt practices while fostering ethnic divisions among those who should have the most in common: ordinary displaced and struggling citizens who have been conditioned to judge others according to their name or the religion of their grandparents.

Given the violence in the recent past and the ongoing fear-mongering by politicians and the media they control, sustaining this division is not difficult; to work for coexistence based on what should be an obvious commonality across ethnic lines is to go against the flow. In this vein, the Prijedor activist Damir said to me, "These days, nationalism is only for the little people. The big politicians are just criminals; corruption is their real work."

Touching on the wartime roots of the mafiocracy, Munir Alibabić described the actions of the ethnic-based military-gangster cliques that terrorized Bosnia-Herzegovina as the widespread plunder of everything "from industrial equipment to raw materials for energy production . . . [to] humanitarian relief contributions, and they controlled the trade of drugs and narco-routes, and took over housing and other state resources."[1]

This observation identifies the origins of the ongoing corruption that plagues Bosnia-Herzegovina today, providing a direct connection between wartime plunder and postwar practices. The ethnonationalist politics that reign in Bosnia today simply serve as a façade for profiteering.[2]

Bosnia-Herzegovina has the lowest living standard in Europe today.[3] In a country of less than four million, where over half a million are unemployed, and where it is nearly impossible to produce goods that can compete on the export market, there is practically no way for someone to attain affluence other than through corrupt practices.

Corruption exists at all levels, wherever the exchange of money for goods and services takes place. It is a notorious fact that hospital patients are compelled to pay bribes for preferential service and that university students pay bribes (or trade sex) for passing grades, even when they have earned those grades. Bent policemen rake off a small profit from arbitrary traffic tickets and other extortion. But to understand the scope of the perpetual national scandal, one must look at where the greatest amount of funds is involved. In a "transitional" society, recovering from the devastation of war and converting to a privatized economy, there are obvious venues for lucrative grand-scale transactions.

These opportunities include road construction, corporate privatization, and privatization of state-owned land. In each of these areas a tightly knit group of public officials makes decisions that make all the difference to the profiteers. A pyramidal infrastructure, with a party chief at the top, is composed of officials appointed by that leader to various positions, for example, in the Ministry of Transport and Communications; the Ministry for Physical Planning, Civil Engineering, and Ecology; the regional and entity prosecutorial offices and courts; the Ministry of Internal Affairs; the regional Center for Public Security and other police jurisdictions; the entity-based Telekom agency; and the management of energy plants.

The power of officials in such governmental agencies makes it possible for them to grant or deny concessions to road builders, shopping center developers, cell phone company operators, agricultural and industrial import-export businesses, timber companies, mine operators, and administrators of a host of other lucrative businesses. Furthermore, officials in law enforcement have the power to ignore or assist the transgressions of political cronies who break the law.

There is a limited set of circumstances where law enforcement agencies deem it appropriate to prosecute economic criminals. Prosecution may take place in instances where businessmen aligned with the political opposition make an easy target (such as in the case of Radojica Ratkovac, the Prnjavor businessman competing with Dodik's cronies in connection with development in Srebrenica). It may take place where a prominent politician has shown too much independence from party leadership, or where it becomes politically necessary to sacrifice an unusually corrupt operator.

There are also times when officials representing the international community have found it appropriate to pressure domestic officials to crack down on corruption—or at least appear to do so. However, it is generally the case that international officials are more comfortable ignoring high-end criminality—and conducting political negotiations with the kingpins—than confronting corruption. Periodic exhortations from international officials to combat corruption most often amount to mere rhetoric.

CORRUPTION IN THE REPUBLIKA SRPSKA

Moving to concrete illustrations, we will briefly examine corruption in the Republika Srpska, because corrupt dynamics in the Serb-controlled entity pertain directly to what goes on in Prijedor.

Two of the many notorious corruption scandals in the Republika Srpska have to do with construction deals the government arranged with close associates of RS prime minister, and then president, Milorad Dodik. One of those involved the construction of a portion of highway between the RS capital, Banja Luka, and Gradiška, on the border with Croatia. Sections of the roughly forty-kilometer stretch of road were opened between 2011 and early 2013, but not before millions of KM were misspent by building contractors.

The other case pertained to the construction of the new RS government building in Banja Luka. Both projects were characterized by dazzling cost overruns.

In mid-2009, after a couple of years of preliminary investigation, the state-level intelligence service SIPA (State Investigation and Protection Agency) called on the RS prosecutor to launch an investigation into the practices of Dodik, six RS ministers, and other high officials. Also named was Slobodan Stanković, owner of the construction firm Integral Inženjering.[4] Stanković hails from Dodik's hometown of Laktaši and has been the recipient of many construction contracts during the period of Dodik's tenure. It was Integral Inženjering that built much of the Banja Luka–Gradiška highway.

In the case of the highway, which took over seven years to build, each kilometer cost, on average, 20 million KM (ten million euros). Integral Inženjering began to implement the project without having to participate in any public tender procedure; this transparent favoritism is a common flaw in the allocation of public funds for big construction projects.[5] In construction of the Gradiška roadway, add-ons brought the cost overruns to some 115 million KM.[6]

Republika Srpska law on public procurement stipulates that such add-ons, called "annexes," may not be introduced without a public tender procedure if they increase the cost of the project by more than 50 percent of the original bid.[7] But this rule has commonly been ignored. Indeed, Integral Inženjering has won numerous contracts by placing the lowest bid—even below a credible level—and has then routinely reaped vast profits by piling on annexes and growing a project nearly beyond recognition.

In the case of the Gradiška roadway, costs were driven up by the arbitrary payment for private lands that were expropriated for the project. In cases where the owner of the land in question was someone who was close to the government, funds vastly higher than the legitimate price were paid. Some of the land owners purchased that land in advance, knowing that they would reap great benefits: they paid one or two KM per square meter, and received as much as 150 to 200 KM upon resale. In one case, the government paid 1.1 million KM for 124 square meters of land.[8]

Integral Inženjering also constructed Republika Srpska's scandal-ridden administrative "State Building" in Banja Luka. The building was originally intended for use by the entity's Telekom company, according to a contract drawn up in 2005. But when Milorad Dodik became prime minister the next year, the RS took over the contract and arranged for the building to house the entity's governmental offices. In the process, what began as a 34 million KM construction of one building quickly grew to two buildings with a projected cost of 220 million KM. This sum constituted one-sixth of the entity's annual budget.[9]

Add-ons to the project included furnishing of the interior and finishing the plaza in front of the building. The plaza added 14 million KM to the cost, and 11 million KM was added for "compensation for unforeseen expenses."[10] The project grew to include four fountains, underground passageways, and a hair salon.[11]

SIPA began examining the malversations of Dodik's cronies in connection with the government building as far back as 2007, after corrupt practices mushroomed in the RS. In 2009 the agency delivered a report that named Dodik; the minister for physical planning, civil engineering, and ecology; the finance minister; the minister for transportation and communication; some former ministers; and Slobodan Stanković, owner of Integral Inženjering. They were accused of "organized crime, tax evasion, money laundering, and several criminal acts under entity law, such as abuse of position."[12]

SIPA tried to acquire documentation about Dodik's financial dealings as head of the RS government. The agency was interested in the cases of the government building and the Gradiška highway, and in the suspicious privatization of formerly state-owned companies such as the oil refinery at Bosanski Brod, RS Telekom, and a power plant in Gacko. Dodik refused to cooperate with SIPA, warning that he would order RS police to physically resist agents if they dared to enter the government building. He also threatened to block participation of RS representatives in several state-level institutions—an ever-handy tactic in his obstructionist repertoire. True to custom, Dodik described SIPA's work not as an investigation into his crimes, but as "an attack on the Republika Srpska and on all Serbs."[13]

SIPA's report and inquiry into the corrupt practices of Dodik and his cronies ultimately did not result in criminal charges. Instead Dragan Lukač, the leader of SIPA's investigation and a second-rank official subordinate to the agency's director, was subjected to disciplinary procedures. It was alleged that he bypassed the director in conducting the investigation. Later in 2009, Lukač was removed from his position, a move that underscored Dodik's influence over the agency at that time.

Several years after the opening of the RS government's monumental administrative building, the independent journalist Nađa Diklić published leaked annexes that revealed the hidden sums that had mounted during the building's construction and furnishing, including a handcrafted president's chair at 36,000 euros, a television covering a full wall at US$105,000, and ashtrays at US$790 a piece—in a building where smoking is prohibited. The final reckoning added up to some 591 million KM, or roughly US$330 million.[14]

The investigation against Dodik and his business associates ended ingloriously. In mid-2009 SIPA, as a state-level agency, forwarded charges to the Bosnia-Herzegovina prosecutor alleging that the group had embezzled 145 million KM from the Republika Srpska budget. However, the prosecutor referred the case back to the RS special prosecutor. After quite some delay, in December 2011 the special prosecutor halted investigation into the case, stating that there was "insufficient evidence" that Dodik and his associates had committed a crime.

The notion of "insufficient evidence" is quite familiar to observers of criminal proceedings in Bosnia; it seems that it is more common for investigations to be aborted for this reason than for them to come to fruition, even in the most grave cases including murder. In any case, it was never realistic to expect that the RS prosecutor would prosecute his own master.

This sketch of two cases of corruption as perpetrated by the pyramid of operators under Milorad Dodik is but the tip of the iceberg. Other notorious cases include that of the "controversial businessman" Mile Radišić, former beneficiary of Dodik's favors, privatizer of companies in the Republika Srpska, and usurper and developer of erstwhile parkland in Banja Luka.[15]

Another illustrative case that has been swept under the rug was that of the murder of Milan Vukelić, a construction engineer in the employ of the Banja Luka Civil Engineering Institute. Vukelić went up against powerful forces in what he termed the "RS construction mafia" when he accused the head of this government agency of blackmail and abuse of office. He was killed when a bomb planted in his car exploded in November 2007. The case has never been solved.[16]

An understanding of the role of Milorad Dodik at the top of a criminal pyramid that rules in the Serb-controlled entity cannot be complete without mention of his holdings. A comprehensive description of Dodik's riches would include bad loans covered by assistance from the RS government. It would expose phantom companies formed to evade taxes and would reveal the fictitious ownership that is a common way of concealing wealth. However, it is beyond the scope of this writing to examine such holdings in detail.

Much of Dodik's wealth is legally registered under the names of his family members and close colleagues. But he is known, for example, to have significant ownership share in Integral Inženjering, and likewise to have a large share in numerous other companies. Just a few of these are the basketball team Igokea; Radio Čelinac; the Serbian fashion house Zekstra; a thermal spa in Laktaši; fruit orchards in Laktaši; and the Farmland company in Nova Topola.[17] To the above partial list of Dodik's holdings should be added numerous pieces of real estate.[18] One of the richest politicians in Bosnia-Herzegovina, Dodik is commonly said to be worth at least 200 million euro.[19]

In 2008 the returnee activist Anel Ališić said to me, "They will prosecute Dodik in five or seven years, but who cares? The damage will already have been done." Much time has passed since that statement. Dodik's political strength waxed and waned over the years, but his skill as a demagogue has kept him in power for well over a decade. In any case, he is also far richer than when he entered politics, and his fiefdom, correspondingly, is poorer.

CORRUPTION IN PRIJEDOR

One figure who closely collaborated with Dodik, and who benefited greatly from that relationship, was the three-term mayor Marko Pavić, the Dodik of Prijedor.

War starts with crimes and ends with crimes. These crimes are not limited to violence against people; just as rife is the practice of corruption, because law disappears during wartime. Better put, a new set of rules takes over; in the course of a war, the culture of corruption becomes institutionalized, and it is difficult to extirpate the practice afterward. Prijedor fits into this picture quite neatly.

In the early postwar period former police chief Simo Drljača personified that transition from wartime criminality to postwar corruption. He was nicknamed "Mr. Ten Percent" because of the obligatory rake-off that he received as extortion from many commercial establishments in Prijedor. Drljača's postwar power in the municipality, until his killing during an arrest attempt by British troops, was the logical continuation of the central role he had played in the wartime ethnic cleansing and the establishment of concentration camps.[20]

In the postwar environment of relative lawlessness, one particularly visible instance of corruption was the trafficking of women. On the outskirts of many towns in Bosnia one could spot motels, nightclubs, and small restaurants that bore colorful signs suggesting that prostitution was taking place. In the Prijedor area, such establishments had names such as "Maskarada," "Crazy Horse," or "Scharmant."[21] On the roads to the city one could see several such clubs with characteristic bright neon signs, often in pink and purple, with the eroticized form of a young woman. These nightclubs were "staffed" by young women from Moldova, Romania, and Ukraine—countries whose economies were in desperate straits and whose young women were susceptible to the deceptive lure of traffickers.

In the Prijedor area, the hotel Sherwood Castle was headquarters of one of the most notorious traffickers in the country, Milorad Milaković. Under his management, young women were bought and sold and treated as slaves. Traffickers would beat and rape newly arrived women, withhold their travel documents, and force them to work off the amount that was paid for their acquisition. Even then, rarely were the women paid, as they were also dunned the costs of their clothing and room and board.

The phenomenon of sex slavery in Bosnia-Herzegovina caused an international scandal in the early postwar period because it was clear that, to a significant extent, the industry of forced prostitution was supported by the thousands of foreign soldiers and international officials who were stationed in the country at that time. Kathryn Bolkovac, an employee of the United Nations–run International Police Task Force (IPTF), tried to blow the whistle on exploitation of trafficked women by her fellow officers in 2000 and was fired for her efforts. Bolkovac was vindicated in 2002, when she won a lawsuit against the company that recruited her, DynCorp. Her story was later portrayed in a movie, *The Whistleblower*.

It was not just foreigners who took advantage of the women trafficked into Bosnia; it was common to hear that among the "clients" were policemen and other local officials. Under Milaković, who ran at least three bordellos in Prijedor, an entire infrastructure supported his operations, right under the noses of the local authorities.

In response to scandals, the IPTF raided Milaković's nightclubs in November 2000, freeing over thirty entrapped young women. However, Milaković was not arrested then, and he even complained to the media about the expense incurred by the loss of his "employees." Finally, in May 2001 the Republika Srpska police raided Milaković's nightclubs again and arrested him.[22]

Milaković was charged with trafficking, holding women in slavery, and operating a prostitution business. The combined charges could have resulted in a twenty-year sentence for Milaković, but he pleaded guilty and cooperated with the court. In return, he was sentenced to nine years in prison, with the understanding that he would be paroled after three years.[23]

HIGH-END CORRUPTION

Corruption in the police department, a tradition enshrined by the deceased police chief Simo Drljača, continued to thrive, and official response to that corruption varied.

One example of corruption in the police department involved Draško Papak, head of the crime division until May 2013, when he was suspended from his position and arrested, together with several other officials. They were charged with "abuse of official position or authority"; receiving and giving bribes; revealing official secrets; illegal production and trafficking of weapons or explosive materials; and extortion.[24]

Another example of the on-and-off attention of the authorities where inappropriate police behavior is concerned is the case of Vojislav Pelkić, who was removed from a position of high authority not once, but twice. Pelkić had been under suspicion for involvement in the murder of prominent Bosniak citizens of Prijedor during the war, but he retained his position of authority after the war.[25]

In a staff shake-up, Pelkić was removed from his position as Prijedor's police chief in 2004 under accusation of "abuse of position and criminal activities." He was accused of using the services of a phantom organization to register hundreds of stolen automobiles for a lucrative fee. Higher legal authorities reduced charges from complicity in theft to corruption, and after numerous hearings over a five-year period, the charges were dropped altogether.[26]

Pelkić was an obedient functionary in the SNSD, the party of Dodik. Presumably this is the reason he was let off the hook—and some nine years later, in 2013, he was hired to a higher post as head of the newly formed regional Center for Public Security.

Corruption in Prijedor has, of course, not been limited to the police sector; it appears as well in the educational field, the health sector, and business in general. Of the university, Vedran Grahovac said, "The student population is passive. It's not important to them to stop corruption. They are thinking how to succeed in being more corrupt. This is the way things work." Grahovac elaborated by saying, "To pass a test in the medical faculty, it's a given that you have to slip 400 KM into the test booklet."[27] Such corruption as practiced by professors is indeed pretty much taken for granted throughout Bosnia-Herzegovina.

The practice of receiving kickbacks in return for employment surprises no one in Bosnia. The health care field offers another lucrative opportunity for graft and kickbacks; it is nearly proverbial that one pays a bribe in order to receive better service, whether at public or private institutions. For example, in Prijedor General Hospital, a doctor was charged with receiving bribes for charging a patient 200 KM for surgical thread.[28]

Dr. Mirko Sovilj was appointed director of the local hospital for two consecutive terms, and when his legal mandate expired, he remained in that position indefinitely as "acting director." He has been a member of Marko Pavić's party, the DNS, since the beginning of that party's existence and more recently headed its list in parliamentary elections. Dr. Sovilj was the subject of several charges of corruption for selling job placements, for which he was allegedly paid between 3,000 and 10,000 KM each.[29] However, each time that complaints were filed, the Banja Luka prosecutor's office decided against filing charges, because of "lack of evidence."

Sometimes it is easier to commit robbery without firearms than with them, especially if you have friends in high places. In Prijedor, Budimir Stanković "earned" 1.5 million KM simply by refusing to pay back a debt.

Budimir Stanković is a businessman who owns, among other holdings, the Prijedor-based trading company Trgoprodaja. He is often referred to as the "kum" of Milorad Dodik, referring to a very close relationship. The two were together in vocational high school. Stanković is a strongman of Dodik's SNSD by virtue of his position as president of the executive committee of that party in Laktaši, Dodik's hometown.

In 2010, Stanković engaged in dealings with the state agency Republika Srpska Administration for Geodetic and Property Affairs (Republička uprava za geodetske i imovinsko-pravne poslove, or RUGIP), which acts as administrator of real estate surveying, registration, archives, and property rights in the RS. When RUGIP needed to expand its administrative facilities, it made an arrangement with Stanković to buy a building of which he was part owner and gave him an advance of 1.5 million KM on the deal.

Meanwhile, it turned out that Stanković owed much more to the bank for his share of the building than he had revealed to RUGIP, so that RUGIP was not able to take possession of the building. However, Stanković never returned the 1.5 million KM that RUGIP had advanced him. When Tihomir Gligorić, the former director of RUGIP, attempted to redeem a voucher that had been given to an intermediary bank to guarantee Stanković's debt, it was revealed that the voucher had been falsely represented, and did not cover the sum of the debt.[30]

When this case was covered in the press three years later, Stanković had still not returned the debt he owed RUGIP. What is more, immediately after Tihomir Gligorić attempted to redeem Stanković's voucher, the Republika Srpska government removed Gligorić from his position as head of RUGIP and replaced him with someone who was not inclined to pursue Stanković's debt.[31]

There is evidence showing that in addition to his close connection with the president of the Republika Srpska, Budimir Stanković had other ways to throw his weight around. There are numerous media reports of his involvement in physical intimidation of his critics and threats against journalists who dare to discuss his corrupt practices; the affair with RUGIP is not even the most flagrant example. Tihomir Gligorić reported that he and his family were threatened when that scandal was exposed in the media.[32] And in July 2014 Stanković was accused of physically attacking an employee of RUGIP in Prijedor, warning that he would "break his spine" if he mentioned Stanković once more.[33]

Moving up to the top of the political food chain in Prijedor, it is noteworthy that during Milorad Dodik's first term as prime minister of Republika Srpska (1998–2000), Marko Pavić served as minister of transportation and communication. That ministry is a particularly lucrative one for corruption owing to its control over valuable contracts. The ministry not only controls entity agencies responsible for road construction and repair, but it also controls the railroad and postal services.[34]

In his capacity as minister, Pavić broke two laws while issuing permits for international transport. First, the income earned was required to be paid into the entity budget, but Pavić's ministry retained the funds instead. Second, the ministry used the funds to pay its own employees a bonus. In 2004 Pavić was charged with "abuse of official position or authority" for these offenses, which reduced income to the entity and state budgets by more than 900,000 KM.[35] Pavić admitted guilt; he was sentenced to three months in jail, but the sentence was converted to a period of probation, and Pavić was allowed to continue his career in politics unhindered.[36] By this time, he had been elected to his first term as mayor of Prijedor.

An examination of Pavić's behavior as mayor shows he lost no time in installing party favorites in positions of authority in his municipality. This refers not only to members of his party, the DNS, but also to Dodik's party, the SNSD. What is more, a good number of those installed by Pavić had a solid record of wartime operations similar to that of Pavić and, certainly in some cases, a more gruesome history.

For example, Pavić named Dragan Savanović, wartime vice mayor of Prijedor, as director of the municipal heating power plant. Similarly, during his tenure as minister Pavić had named Milan Kiković chief inspector for the Republika Srpska railroad system, and later executive director of that agency. During the war Kiković was the leader of military units involved in rampages both in Croatia and in the Prijedor area. Kiković was removed on suspicion of corruption after serving as executive director of the RS railways for a year.[37]

Regarding political appointments, a new regional Center for Public Security, with its administrative center in Prijedor, was created in 2013. It was created to coordinate police functions in the western part of northwest Bosnia, under an agreement crafted by Dodik and Pavić. In an illustration of the political nepotism that abounds in Bosnia-Herzegovina, it has been pointed out that fully 80 percent of the administrative staff of the Center for Public Security was filled by members of Dodik's SNSD party or persons very close to the party. This included the appointment of SNSD stalwart Vojislav Pelkić as director of the center, and other party figures in the positions of deputy director and director of the criminal police section, and in other positions as well. All this, in an institution that was supposed to be "depoliticized."[38]

Control over disposition of land owned by the municipality is one of the privileges exploited by the ruling elite in Prijedor. During Pavić's mandate, state-owned land was distributed illegally at a price far exceeding market value. Under entity law, the municipality has the power to act as administrator of land that is available for construction use, but it is not permitted to sell that land. This restriction covers publicly owned land.[39]

Sidestepping laws that cover public procurement, the Prijedor Bureau of City Development illegally sold portions of properties whose titles were illegally transferred from state agencies to that bureau after the war. The properties were sold at prices significantly higher than market scale; for example, a section of the building owned by war veterans was sold for 48,000 KM, rather than the market-based 20,000 KM. As one whistleblower said, "state-owned construction land in Prijedor is at the uncontrolled disposal of the Bureau of City Development, and it is selling that land through untendered contract, which is illegal."[40]

Thus Marko Pavić, in his Prijedor dominion, replicated the political/criminal paradigm as practiced throughout Bosnia-Herzegovina. He succeeded at this, on one hand, by employing like-minded colleagues, some of whom initiated their career of crime during the war. At the same time, the device of nationalism, so appropriately described as "only for the little people," served him well to keep divisions cemented among ordinary people. In these ways, Pavić enriched himself and his accomplices, while perpetuating the torment of displacement that began during the war.

It is interesting here to compare the "official story" of Prijedor with that of Srebrenica. As we have seen, until the election of a Serb mayor in 2016, Srebrenica was the location of a political conflict between its government, which was to some extent under the control of Bosniak returnees, and the central Republika Srpska government in Banja Luka. Banja Luka worked to keep Srebrenica impoverished and to withhold from local officials the power to exploit considerable available resources to improve the lot of all inhabitants of the municipality. Very rarely did the ruler of the entity even give lip service to the goal of helping Srebrenica.

On the other hand, Mayor Pavić habitually touted his economic accomplishments in his municipality, speaking of kilometers of road repaved, safe drinking water made available, street lighting in operation, and similar accomplishments. Indeed, the appearance of the city has improved—at least, the central pedestrian walkway has been refurbished and retiled, with fountains installed. A visitor who knew nothing of the recent history of the city—nor of the discrimination, the thousands of unemployed, and the repression of free speech—would find Prijedor a very pleasant place.

BOSNIAK COLLABORATION WITH PAVIĆ

There are some among the elected representatives of the Bosniak returnees who have used political position to their advantage. These officials have given in to the temptations of their own careerism, wherein a secure job and an income are more important than the rights of the returnees and the survivors of wartime atrocities. This is the case in spite of the fact that all those returnees who have collaborated with Pavić's political infrastructure are people who were expelled during the war. Some of them were even imprisoned in the concentration camps.

Of thirty-one representatives to the city council, for many years five have been Bosniaks, members of several of the "pro-Bosnia" parties. After the municipal elections in 2012, all five representatives agreed to enter into a political coalition with Pavić's government. The move was suggested by Mayor Pavić himself, with the explanation that a significant number of Bosniak returnees (and those in the diaspora) voted for him.[41] This number has been estimated variously between two thousand and five thousand voters.

The suggestion to form a local coalition between Pavić and the Bosniak representatives was accepted as a matter of expedience by the Bosniaks. One local Bosniak politician has explained that the only way that non-Serb representatives "can achieve something is if they are part of the system, and that means joining those in power."[42]

The Prijedor leader of the SDA stated that the Bosniak parties "do not have political power," and that it is necessary to make some compromises with the mayor. Similarly, the local leader of the Party for Bosnia noted that in exchange for membership in the mayor's coalition, Bosniaks were "thrown some crumbs"—but that for the time being, they were getting the maximum benefits that they could get. He added that Pavić "has never given us more than what he has now given," including government employment for five or six people, as well as resources for civilian war victims and NGOs.[43]

The financial assistance budgeted to local NGOs in 2013, after the formation of the new governing coalition, provides an example of what non-Serb returnees receive in comparison with the "politically favored" Serb organizations. Civilian war victims were allocated a total of 30,000 KM, while the Serb veterans' organizations were given 450,000 KM. Bosniak representatives voted for this budget along with their Serb coalition partners.[44] Such were the "crumbs" allocated to the constituency of the Bosniak representatives and, indeed, these came after quite some years wherein much less was granted.

Here perhaps is the best illustration of what Mirsad Duratović meant when he told me that, among activists, there is fear that the local government will refrain from providing assistance to local returnee organizations if it sees them as "rebels." The fact that the government can co-opt some of the leaders among the returnees and "throw some crumbs" creates a situation where activists have something to lose if they create a stir about discrimination. In this dynamic the mayor holds all the strings of power.

Discussing the collaboration by some non-Serb politicians, one commentator wrote, "This is good, perhaps, for some ten Bosniaks who are under the thumb of Pavić and Dodik; the rest of us are without a future. There is no force to create some kind of vision, there are just those who hustle and make deals for themselves."[45] Thus, one prominent Bosniak politician was able to own a restaurant and a couple of other properties in the center of Prijedor, and another owned a print shop that received contracts from the municipality.[46]

The collaboration with Pavić by Bosniak representatives put them on a collision course with local grassroots activists who were naturally in conflict with the mayor. Local activists have wondered publicly why central party organizations in Sarajevo have not spoken up against this collaboration. The apparent indifference of Sarajevo politicians, at least on the part of SDA leaders, was highlighted in mid-2013 when then SDA president Sulejman Tihić, during a visit to Prijedor on party business, praised Mayor Pavić. Tihić said, "If the local community is successful, then it is good for all of its citizens . . . and we hail the success realized in the resolution of life, existential, and human problems." He added that Prijedor should be seen as an example of good interethnic relations for other cities in Bosnia-Herzegovina.[47]

Tihić further commented that he was glad that criticisms of Pavić "had not adversely affected relations between our parties and our peoples." Tihić's statement was met with outrage among grassroots human rights activists concerned with Prijedor, who characterized his words as reaching "unheard of depths of hypocrisy." A public response to the statement recalled Pavić's sponsorship of discrimination against returnees and his government's acts of repression against activists.[48]

Keeping in mind that the Serbs have no monopoly on corruption and discrimination in Bosnia-Herzegovina, Tihić's position can be seen as a manifestation of the fact that the most powerful political parties in the country, regardless of their ethnic designation, have much in common. Orwell's *Animal Farm* continues to manifest in new forms. It is the grassroots activists who are the most aware of this.

15

War Crimes Prosecution and Justice in Prijedor

AFTER WELL OVER TWO DECADES SINCE THE END OF THE WAR, one can assess the achievements of Prijedor's separatist regime, whose roots were established at the beginning of the war. A majority of the top wartime leaders have been prosecuted or have died under a variety of circumstances. Some remain in prison, while many of those convicted have returned home after a nearly automatic one-third reduction of their prison sentence. They walk the streets freely, regularly confronting their wartime victims. Far more war criminals were never prosecuted. Meanwhile, the demographic makeup of the municipality progressively moves toward that envisioned by those very war criminals.

With displaced persons gradually coming back from exile to Prijedor municipality in the late 1990s, it was naturally a grave concern of the returnees to see their tormentors arrested and prosecuted for their crimes. Some were in hiding, but many were still walking the streets of Prijedor, regularly facing their former victims.

Activists in Prijedor mention that more war criminals from that region have been processed in the international and national courts than from any other part of Bosnia-Herzegovina. However, arrests and prosecutions were slow to start up in the period immediately following the war. The first trial regarding war crimes in Prijedor—and the first under the auspices of the ICTY—was the prosecution of Duško Tadić.

Born in Kozarac, Tadić was a leader of the SDS in that town at the outbreak of the war, and he was involved in the murder of two Bosniak policemen in Kozarac when it was initially under attack. He was also involved in the murder of five men in a village near Prijedor.[1] He was arrested in Germany before the end of the war and transported to The Hague to be tried there. In 1997 he was convicted of crimes against humanity and violations of the laws and customs of war, for forcibly transferring people to detention camps, and for murder.[2] He was sentenced to twenty years in prison and was released in 2008, whereupon he moved to Serbia.

In the early postwar years in Bosnia, there was very little attempt on the part of international forces, and none on the part of Republika Srpska authorities, to arrest any persons indicted for war crimes in Prijedor or anywhere else in the RS. So it created quite a ripple in the news when British SFOR troops attempted to arrest Simo Drljača in mid-1997.[3] Drljača was chief of police in Prijedor after the separatist takeover and, as such, had been accused of command responsibility for the cliffside massacre at Korićanske Stijene. He was involved in the establishment of Omarska, Keraterm, and Trnopolje concentration camps and was responsible for their administration throughout their duration in 1992.[4]

In 1996 the ICTY indicted Simo Drljača for genocide, crimes against humanity, and war crimes.[5] For the time being, he remained at large in Prijedor, retaining his status as one of the most powerful of the Serb extremists there. In that period, before minority return picked up significantly, and before the attempt to arrest him, it was reported that "Drljača personally obstructed freedom of movement and the return of refugees and displaced persons, going so far as to hand out weapons to the local population to threaten returnees."[6]

In the end, the arrest of Simo Drljača did not unfold as planned. British SAS troops confronted him at a lakeside fishing retreat. Drljača opened fire on the soldiers, who then shot and killed him. Drljača was buried with high honors in an Orthodox Christian cemetery in Banja Luka. Along with family members, the funeral was attended by some twenty thousand people including the president of the SDS, Serb member of the Bosnian state presidency Momčilo Krajišnik, and many other highly placed Serb separatists.

On the same day that Drljača was killed, Dr. Milan Kovačević was arrested without incident in the Prijedor hospital where he was employed as director. At the start of the war Kovačević was deputy head of the SDS-run Crisis Staff. He was closely involved, together with Drljača, in the round-up and expulsion of non-Serbs in Prijedor, and in the establishment of the concentration camps. Like Drljača, Kovačević remained at large and in a position of authority after the end of the war.

In February 1996, journalist Ed Vulliamy interviewed Kovačević. In a tortuous and unfocused conversation, Kovačević called Omarska "a terrible mistake," without quite admitting the dreadful nature of the camp. He continued by saying that Omarska "was planned as a camp, but was turned into something else because of this loss of control. I cannot explain the loss of control. You could call it collective madness."[7]

Kovačević called the mass murder at Omarska a mistake, but just the previous year, during a joint interview with Simo Drljača, he had taken quite the opposite position. In that interview, he bragged about how the takeover of Prijedor had been the result of meticulous planning that had started six months earlier.[8] This must be much closer to the truth, unless one can believe that concentration camps and mass expulsions are components of a strategy of "self-defense."

When Kovačević termed the horrors at Omarska "a mistake," this was one of the first instances of Serb war criminals finessing their crimes. In more recent years it has become customary for those suspected of command responsibility for wartime atrocities to attribute them to units that were "out of control," or "paramilitaries" not under army command, or, simply, to "criminals."

The ICTY indicted Kovačević for genocide and complicity in genocide, as well as for crimes against humanity including extermination, persecution, torture, and deportation, and for violations of the laws and customs of war.[9] A year after he was apprehended, Kovačević's trial began. However, less than a month later, he died of a heart attack.

For some years after Kovačević's death, he was memorialized by a photograph that was mounted at the hospital in Prijedor.[10]

Dr. Milomir Stakić, a physician from Omarska, was influential in the SDS-run Crisis Staff and was one of the key organizers of the separatist takeover of Prijedor. He held the post of president of Prijedor's municipal assembly during the war. In 2001 Stakić was arrested in Serbia and put on trial at The Hague. The prosecution in his case noted that "more than 1,500 non-Serbs were murdered in and around Prijedor; that rapes, sexual assaults, beating and torture took place regularly; and that a minimum of 20,000 people were deported between August and September 1992."[11]

Stakić was convicted of crimes against humanity and violations of the laws and customs of war for persecution, extermination, and murder. Found to be a member of a joint criminal enterprise (together with Dr. Kovačević), he was held responsible, as reported by the ICTY, not only for the murder of more than 1,500 people, but also for "the killing of around 120 men in Keraterm camp on 5 August 1992 and executions of approximately 200 people at Korićanske Stijene on Mount Vlašić on 21 August 1992."[12] Stakić was, however, acquitted of a charge of genocide, because, as one journalist reported "'specific intent to destroy, in whole or in part, a group as such' was not proven beyond a reasonable doubt."[13] He was sentenced to forty years in prison.

By 2012 about thirty persons were arrested on suspicion of war crimes committed in Prijedor municipality. Camp guards and commanders including Željko Mejakić were eventually apprehended. Several of those arrested died before completion of their trials; some others died without having been arrested.

The area on the Left Bank of the Sana River was attacked and its population expelled as a last "cleansing" operation by Serb troops in the Prijedor area in July 1992. Estimates of non-Serbs killed in just a few days range from 1,500 to 1,850. Survivors of the attacks on the Left Bank had to wait much longer than those from the rest of the municipality before they could see some of their killers taken to trial.

As late as 2012, the perpetrators of mass murder were walking free, their presence confronting the survivors. Zijad Bačić survived a crime that involved the murder of twenty-nine civilians in one house in Zecovi, including fifteen children between the ages of two and seventeen. Hidajet Horozović lost his mother, both grandmothers, and other relatives. Having returned to Zecovi after the war, he reports that "when we go to work, we see a man who participated in the killing. But what can you do? There is nothing you can do, just watch."[14]

Mirsad Duratović criticized the inaction of prosecutors regarding the crimes committed in his part of Prijedor: "No serious investigation of that question has been undertaken. Investigators keep changing; there were two prosecutors; they question witnesses; those don't wish to speak anymore, because they are constantly repeating the same story, and that, for ten times. And, for example, they never officially interviewed me, and everyone knows me and knows what I lived through, and I am a witness to murder. . . . There are, for example, people who that day in Bišćani recognized their work colleagues, neighbors from other villages, school friends. Those people have not been questioned."[15]

In late 2012, Bosnian national police from SIPA (State Investigation and Protection Agency) finally arrested three persons, Zoran Babić, Velemir Đurić, and Dragomir Soldat, in connection with the expulsion and murder of the inhabitants of Čarakovo. During the war, one of them was an intelligence officer, and the other two were military policemen. Among other crimes, they were accused of taking men, including an imam, from their homes and executing them in front of the village mosque. Those who survived shooting were placed inside the mosque, which was then set on fire. The three were charged with crimes against humanity and were put on trial in the spring of 2013.

The trial lasted exactly a year. During the procedure, one woman testified that she had come to the mosque after the murders with buckets of water to extinguish the flames of burning bodies.[16] Witnesses for the defense asserted that one of the defendants was a "decent man," and that he "caused no trouble."[17] Two of the defendants denied being in Čarakovo at the time of the assault.[18] But in March 2014, the three were convicted of their offenses and sentenced to twenty-one years each. In February 2015, the convictions were upheld upon appeal.

In September 2014 there was another arrest of persons implicated in the war crimes committed in the Left Bank villages. Bosnian police detained thirteen people and charged them, along with two more suspects who were already in prison for other crimes, with crimes against humanity including rape, torture, theft, destruction of property, and murder in the village of Zecovi. Three more suspects remained at large. In Zecovi over 150 people had been killed, including twenty-nine women and children, and many of the survivors were sent to concentration camps. The entire population of 701 people was expelled from the village.[19]

The trial promised to be Bosnia's most extensive to date. It continued throughout 2018 with chilling testimony from firsthand witnesses of the violence. Other trials continued as well, pertaining to crimes committed in Tukovi, Miska Glava, Ljubija, Prijedor, and Kozarac. A few new arrests were made.

All in all, the conviction of war criminals is absolutely necessary. But only the survivors of the crimes in Prijedor can say whether even a minimum of justice has been accomplished, for it is clear that no amount of prosecution of the murderers can balance the amount of misery and torment that they caused, for the rapes, the near-complete expulsion, the trauma and nightmares, and the pain that never really ceases.

Adding to the ongoing distress of the survivors is the fact that not only have some of their tormentors never been charged with any crimes, but others have served their prison sentences and returned to live among their victims. One of the more notorious examples of people who escaped punishment entirely was Major Slobodan Kuruzović, who had been the camp commander at Trnopolje.[20]

Before the war, Kuruzović was a math teacher. He became an influential member of the SDS-run Crisis Staff at the beginning of the war and was commander of the Trnopolje camp upon its formation. A common estimate holds that twenty-five thousand prisoners passed through that camp,[21] and it is estimated that approximately three hundred were killed there.[22] In addition, women and children as young as thirteen years old were raped in the camp.[23] Kuruzović, as camp commander, interrogated many of the incoming prisoners and was, in any case, responsible for their treatment.

Kuruzović testified on occasion in front of the ICTY at The Hague, but, curiously, he was never indicted for crimes that occurred at Trnopolje. Instead, he was made deputy director of an elementary school in Prijedor. While he may have been indicted eventually, he died of natural causes in 2005, escaping prosecution. His presence in Prijedor pained many a returnee who had survived the horrors at Trnopolje.

There are myriad cases of war crimes unpunished that fly in the face of justice and cause great anguish for the survivors who are forced, over and over, to see their former tormentors in positions of power. A document compiled by several Bosnian diaspora institutions presents the names of people involved just in the concentration camps around Prijedor. The lists presented in this document named 138 administrators, guards, interrogators, and other officials and employees who created camps or were employed at Omarska, Keraterm, and Trnopolje camps.[24] Most of these people were never questioned or charged with any crimes. The lists mentioned here did not include any of the people—numbering, at the very least, in the hundreds—involved in the mass murder and expulsion in Prijedor. And most of these people, especially those who were involved in the camps, have continued to reside in and around Prijedor.

Edin Ramulić spoke in 2015 about the number of war criminals from Prijedor, and the problem of their continued presence: "At this moment we have 34 binding convictions, and there are still proceedings at this time against 26. . . . For certain, we are one of the cities with the greatest number of war criminals in the world. That is a situation about which no one should remain indifferent, but in fact no one takes it seriously. . . . All of those people who committed crimes during the war are a danger to everyone, and there should be no indifference." Ramulić further noted that of the thirty-four people convicted of war crimes, twenty-eight of them had been policemen.[25]

I asked Ramulić how he felt living among war criminals who had returned from serving their sentences—and among those who had never been prosecuted. He answered, "Every day I pass the Butik, which is owned by a person who led the police and killed people. But I just pass by. People don't react anymore." I asked him, "Does that mean things are a little more normal than before?" He answered, "Maybe it is too normal for what happened. For example, Branko Topola was a guard in Trnopolje. He became the owner of a company that installed gutters on houses, and he was rebuilding returnees' houses."[26]

A short description of one figure closely involved in the separatist takeover of Prijedor, and never prosecuted, must not be left out: former mayor Marko Pavić himself. Pavić was elected mayor of Prijedor in 2004, and he served three consecutive terms before being replaced in 2016. Educated in law, in the prewar period Pavić served as head of the local branch of Državna Bezbjednost, the state security agency. That agency, which came under the control of the SDS before the war, played a crucial role in planning the ethnic cleansing that took place in the Prijedor area. It was also involved in setting up the Crisis Staff—including the recruitment of key separatist activists such as Milomir Stakić—and military formations that operated there.[27]

By the beginning of the war, Pavić had become director of the local branch of the PTT, the Post Office, Telephone, and Telegraph agency. There, he was able to work to the benefit of the forces that took over Prijedor by facilitating the laundering of funds through his office.[28] In addition, the PTT assisted the operation of ethnic cleansing in a sinister way; when the town of Kozarac came under attack, just at that time the telephone service was cut off. It has been widely reported that the same thing took place during attacks on several villages as well.[29]

During the war Pavić became a member of the Main Board of SDS, and for a period he also served as assistant commander for security for the Fifth Kozarac Brigade.[30]

Apparently, while Pavić's participation in the violent creation of the new, ethnically pure parastate was sufficient to come to the attention of Human Rights Watch, he did not rank high enough on the list of those involved in war crimes to merit the time and resources of the ICTY. Thus, he was able to move ahead in political life, capitalizing on his wartime record and his familiarity with the levers of power in Prijedor. Note, also, that in any officially sanctioned record of Pavić's career, there is no mention of his prewar work in the state security agency.

Another presence in Prijedor affects the atmosphere and torments the sensibilities of all survivors who have returned to that municipality: the convicted war criminals who have served part of their sentences and returned home, to walk the streets among their victims. One of those is Darko Mrđa, convicted in 2005 of murder and attempted murder for his participation in the massacre of over two hundred people at Korićanske Stijene. He was sentenced to seventeen years in prison, and released in late 2013, whereupon he resettled in the Left Bank village of Tukovi.

A measure of satisfaction was afforded to the returnee survivors in early 2016 when Mrđa was rearrested on suspicion of crimes against humanity for, among other things, murders he allegedly committed at Manjača concentration camp—but he was allowed to remain free in the course of his new trial. The trial began under the auspices of the Court of Bosnia-Herzegovina in the fall of that year and was concluded in late 2018.[31] Mrđa and his codefendant Zoran Babić were each given a fifteen-year sentence for the abuse of numerous people and for the murder of several non-Serb victims in the Prijedor area.[32]

Other war criminals returning home after serving reduced sentences included Mlađo Radić, Predrag Banović, Duško Sikirica, Miroslav Kvočka, Damir Došen, Dragoljub Prcač, and Dragan Kolundžija. Each of these convicts had been involved in the massive perpetration of abuses at Omarska and Keraterm.

Referring to the returned war criminals in an interview, Sudbin Musić commented, "Now they are enjoying their freedom, and the victims are condemned to build coexistence with them. It is terrible to come upon Darko Mrđa, the Banović brothers, or Tadić, every day."[33]

PUBLIC MONUMENTS AND HISTORICAL REVISIONISM

Throughout Prijedor municipality, public monuments to Serb fighters give concrete expression of the official narrative of the war, glorifying separatism and concealing local history. The most imposing of these stands in the center of Prijedor: a massive, seven-meter-high concrete monument in the shape of a cross, named Za Krst Časni— For the Holy Cross. The monument was unveiled on May 30, 2012, twenty years after the date that official Serb discourse holds to be the opening of wartime hostilities in the Prijedor region—this, even though by that date, hundreds of non-Serbs were already in the camps, and Kozarac already lay in ruins.

The monument is dedicated to the "fallen fighters and defenders of the city,"[34] who are understood to be Serbs. It describes them as having been killed "by Muslim extremists in the war of defense and liberation."[35] Another commemorative sculpture, the Kameni Cvijet (Stone Flower) bears the names of 575 fallen Serb soldiers.

One analyst estimates that there are at least sixty monuments to the "Serb defensive-liberation war" in Prijedor.[36] Damir, introduced in the previous chapter, researched monuments to the dead in the municipality under the auspices of the Sarajevo-based Research and Documentation Center. He stated that there were "perhaps around 100 Serbs killed, not more. But there is a monument to them in every local commune—even to people who were not killed in this municipality."[37]

Another reinforcement of official history is the renaming of the main square in the pedestrian zone of Prijedor, formerly Lenin Square, after the Serb fighter Zoran Karlica. Karlica had been a volunteer on the side of the Yugoslav National Army during its assault on Croatia in 1991. The next year, having achieved the rank of major in the Republika Srpska army, he participated in the ethnic cleansing of Prijedor municipality.[38] Karlica was a leader in the military assault on Kozarac in late May,[39] but soon afterward, he was wounded in fighting and died several days later.

Thus, in the city of Prijedor there are a number of prominent monuments that reinforce Serb nationalist historiography and efface the story of the suffering caused by the separatists who took over the city. A similar monument that perhaps causes the most pain to the survivors of wartime atrocities stands in the village of Trnopolje. The sculpture, a stylized eagle with a cross in the middle, stands about three meters tall. A plaque on the monument, located directly in front of the former concentration camp where some twenty thousand non-Serbs were held, dedicates the statue "to the fighters who built their lives into the foundation of the Republika Srpska."

Compounding the insult, in March 2016 the Organization of Veterans of the Army of the Republika Srpska opened a memorial center in the social hall at Trnopolje. This building formed part of the Trnopolje concentration camp where prisoners were held.[40]

In contrast, the few public monuments that have been permitted to commemorate the victimization of non-Serbs in Prijedor municipality are located in out-of-the-way places: cemeteries and returnee settlements where few Serbs frequent. Practically the only exception is the small plaque installed in front of the former Keraterm camp, now a business complex. In 2003, without official approval, activists from the survivor organization Izvor managed to place a memorial plaque in front of the building, commemorating the killed and disappeared camp inmates.

When I asked Izvor member Edin Ramulić how it was that the placement of the plaque was permitted—and never removed—he answered, "This is private property, and the owner is someone from Gradiška who does not feel guilty. It is still there, although there have been threats. This was the first time that any memorial has been placed anywhere other than at cemeteries. It is the first time that a memorial has been placed at the scene of a crime."[41]

Another monument to non-Serb victims stands at an intersection at the entrance to Kozarac. Completed in 2010, the monument is composed of a succession of vertical slabs of concrete arranged to stand in a circle. On the slabs are inscribed the names of 1,226 Bosniak and Croat civilians and soldiers from the Kozarac area who were killed during the war. A visitor can enter into the middle of the circle of slabs and ponder the long list of names.

Another manifestation of the revision of history in the Prijedor region—as throughout former Yugoslavia in the postwar period—is the destruction of Partisan monuments commemorating the antifascist struggle of World War II. To some extent, this has been a grassroots practice, an expression of the resentment of Titoist control of history in the service of promotion of the socialist regime. In the two decades since the dissolution of Yugoslavia, Partisan cemeteries and antifascist monuments alike have been desecrated or, at best, neglected and allowed to fall into ruin.

People in thrall to the nationalist leaders of the new era have taken the sledgehammer to the monuments to Bosnia-Herzegovina's antifascist past. Beyond the destruction of historical markers, there has been the organized co-optation of the antifascist history by leaders whose ideological sentiments are, in fact, much more in harmony with those of Goebbels than with those of the ordinary people of Bosnia who fought the Nazi occupation.

REWRITING HISTORY

The activist Ervin Blažević took me up to Mount Kozara, above Kozarac. There, at Mrakovica in Kozara National Park, stands a memorial to Partisan fighters and civilians killed by the Nazis after a siege during World War II. The memorial, a tall stack of concrete, is located in a very pleasant place at the top of a wooded hill. A memorial museum is located there as well. It has been rearranged to emphasize Serb victimization. A panel installed after the recent war focuses on damages that the Serbs of the region suffered during World War I and World War II and in the 1990s and describes Muslims and Croats as a danger to Serb survival. This part of the exhibition has been described as depicting the "genocide of the Serbs in the 20th century."[42]

Throughout Bosnia-Herzegovina there are local and entity-wide associations of participants in the Partisan antifascist struggle of World War II, staffed and led by survivors of that war and, increasingly, by their political heirs, as the generation that actively participated in that war disappears. Sadly, the Republika Srpska branch of the Partisan associations, and its Prijedor chapter, have adopted a revisionist version of World War II history along nationalist lines. In this "updated" interpretation of history, those who officially tasked themselves to commemorate the antifascist war have appropriated it in the cause of Serb nationalism.

Activist Goran Zorić noted, "Today in Prijedor Mladen Stojanović is exclusively a Serb hero, the liberation was exclusively a Serb thing, all public memory of heroes such as Esad Midžić, Franjo Kluzo, Muharem Suljanović, Atif Topić [World War II figures who were of Bosniak or Croat ethnicity] and others has been removed, the multi-ethnic character of the liberation war is completely denied, and the names of streets have been changed."[43]

In this way, nationalist propaganda distorts the significant contribution of the people of all ethnicities in the Prijedor region to the anti-Nazi struggle, that is, the antifascist heritage of all Prijedorans. It also extensively revises the history of the recent war. Meanwhile, postwar attempts by human rights activists to commemorate the heroism of non-Serbs in the framework of antifascist anniversaries have been thwarted by local authorities. Instead, for example, Mayor Pavić used the anniversary of the siege of Mount Kozara to refashion local history, declaring, "The [Serb] people are anti-fascists who have shown that they were freedom-loving then and now, and who always wish to extend the hand of reconciliation, a people who remember and wish to build their future in freedom."[44]

GENOCIDE IN PRIJEDOR

To the extent that people around the world think about the history of Bosnia-Herzegovina two decades after the war at all, they may particularly associate the concept of genocide with Srebrenica. Several high officers in the Bosnian Serb army have been convicted of the crime there. It is all but unknown that in 1997, the German Supreme State Court in Dusseldorf convicted a Bosnian Serb of genocide for murders he committed in the area around Doboj.[45] So for those not directly concerned with other parts of the country, the awareness of genocide in Bosnia starts and ends with Srebrenica. However, the Muslim and Croat survivors from Prijedor municipality do not accept the restriction of the concept of genocide to Srebrenica.

Even a very brief description of wartime events in Prijedor should prompt people to consider the question of genocide in that region. The systematic killing and expulsion of non-Serbs compels one to conclude that a concerted plan to commit genocide was implemented with intent, thus fulfilling not only the material requirement to establish the crime, but that of authorship as well.

We recall that, according to the UN Genocide Convention, "genocide means any of the following acts committed with intent to destroy, in whole or in part, a national, ethnical, racial or religious group, as such: killing members of the group; causing serious bodily or mental harm to members of the group; deliberately inflicting on the group conditions of life, calculated to bring about its physical destruction in whole or in part; imposing measures intended to prevent births within the group; [and] forcibly transferring children of the group to another group."[46]

There are two components to genocide identified in this seemingly simple language that must be present and proved in order for a court to arrive at a conclusion of genocide. One is evidence of commission of the physical acts such as killing members of a group or preventing births; the other is evidence that the intent to do so existed. In legal language referring to these two components, the physical act of the crime is termed "actus reus," and the "mental intent" to commit the crime is termed "mens rea." The latter is, of course, much more difficult to prove.

The sparse case law established to date that pertains to this crime has evolved as genocide cases are processed by the international courts. And the judgments to date have been so contradictory, counterintuitive, and even, apparently, whimsical, that it is difficult to avoid the conclusion that political considerations are at play. One explanation holds that, since the Genocide Convention requires states to intervene where genocide is perceived, the courts have avoided findings of genocide in order to avoid the obligation to intervene.

Case history nevertheless has supported the fact that actus reus, the physical commission of genocide, did take place in Prijedor as well as several other municipalities in addition to Srebrenica. In the pause between prosecution and defense testimony in the Milošević case, during the Rule 98 bis hearings that determined whether the prosecutor's case was strong enough to justify the continued pursuit of a given charge, presiding judges found that "sufficient evidence of a genocidal intent" had been demonstrated in the case of Prijedor and other municipalities.[47]

Although, in the middle of the trial, judges acknowledged that there was evidence of both genocide and genocidal intent, this did not necessarily signify that they would have found in favor of that argument, had Slobodan Milošević's trial been completed. Milošević died in detention before that was able to take place.

Momčilo Krajišnik, cofounder with Radovan Karadžić of the SDS and president of the Republika Srpska during part of the war, was later indicted for numerous war crimes including persecution, extermination, murder, deportation, inhumane acts, and genocide. The indictment covered crimes that were committed in thirty-five municipalities, including Prijedor.

In developments similar to those in the Milošević trial, deliberations on Rule 98 bis in Krajišnik's case found that evidence provided was "sufficient to infer genocidal intent in relation to both Bosnian Muslims and Bosnian Croats."[48] The finding also concluded that Krajišnik had been in collusion with other leaders who had acted with genocidal intent. At the end of the trial, judges found that acts of genocide had been committed in the areas mentioned in Krajišnik's charges, but that intent on his part could not be proved.[49]

Similar findings acknowledging genocidal actions in the Prijedor area were given in the case of Radoslav Brđanin, who had been president of the SDS-led Crisis Staff in the Krajina area. Brđanin's trial also concluded without a genocide conviction. This left the possibility for a finding of genocide in the Prijedor area dependent on the outcome of two trials: those of Radovan Karadžić and Ratko Mladić.

Karadžić was charged with genocide based on an acknowledgment of his numerous explicit statements to the effect that the Bosnian Muslims would be exterminated. One of these was uttered in Parliament on the eve of the war, when Karadžić said, "The path you have chosen is the same highway that led Croatia to hell, only that hell will be even worse in Bosnia, where the Muslims could cease to exist."[50] In May 2016 Karadžić was convicted on multiple charges and sentenced to forty years' imprisonment, but he was acquitted of genocide except in Srebrenica. Both Karadžić and the prosecutors appealed the conviction, and the appeal proceedings were concluded in the spring of 2019. At this time, the ICTY's successor institution, the Mechanism for International Criminal Tribunals (MICT), increased Karadžić's sentence to life but left all his convictions as they stood.[51]

The trial of Ratko Mladić lasted from 2012 to late 2017. It is noteworthy that near the beginning of the war, when Serb leaders were discussing the aim of ethnic cleansing, Mladić commented, "People are not little stones, or keys in someone's pocket, that can be moved from one place to another just like that. . . . Therefore, we cannot precisely arrange for only Serbs to stay in one part of the country while removing others painlessly. . . . That is genocide."[52] Notwithstanding this perception, Mladić proceeded to carry out the aims of his political leadership.

Mladić was tried for crimes against humanity, violations of the laws and customs of war, and, like Karadžić, two counts of genocide. These two counts pertained first of all to Srebrenica, and secondly to six other municipalities, including Prijedor. The first-instance verdict in Mladić's trial was delivered in November 2017. He was found guilty on ten charges, including genocide in Srebrenica, but, again like Karadžić, he was acquitted of genocide in the other municipalities.

It is a confounding situation that, so far, a number of legal proceedings have more or less found that genocide took place, without establishing that anyone intended it— therefore, genocide did not take place! To some extent this paradox is due to the fact that the wording of the UN Genocide Convention is unclear enough to leave space for varying interpretation by a succession of jurists. The period since the end of the Bosnian war has provided more opportunity for that varying interpretation than any other time since the adoption of the Convention. Case history has been interpreting the meaning of the original wording in a somewhat haphazard manner, with judges taking a series of decisions that have not always been in harmony with each other.

At issue is the possibility of determining genocidal intent without direct evidence of that intent, which is, naturally, rare because of the intellectual author's wish for concealment. One appeal of Karadžić's acquittal on one of the counts of genocide noted that clear indications of the intent of genocide (such as the threat quoted above) were known. It went on to quote an earlier ICTY finding that stated that "in the absence of direct explicit evidence, [proof of specific intent] may be inferred from a number of facts and circumstances, such as the general context, the perpetration of other culpable acts systematically directed against the same group, the scale of atrocities committed, the systematic targeting of victims on account of their membership of a particular group, or the repetition of destructive and discriminatory acts."[53]

In addition to explicit statements by convicted war criminals who threatened the disappearance of non-Serbs, the indirect evidence of intent as described is abundant in the case of Prijedor. However, the trend among judges has been to choose the minimum interpretation of the Genocide Convention. While law and human sensitivities are quite clearly two different realms, this trend damages the feelings of those who are informed about what happened in Prijedor, and especially those tens of thousands of survivors who were injured by the atrocities committed there.

As it happened, Ratko Mladić's acquittal of genocide in Prijedor and other municipalities constituted a rather perverse reversal of the ICTY's previous response to intent as discussed here. In fact, the court not only found that numerous non-Serbs were killed or physically harmed in the six municipalities in question; the majority of judges agreed that in five of the six municipalities, including Prijedor, perpetrators indeed "intended to destroy the Bosnian Muslims in those Municipalities as a part of the protected group." This should have been sufficient grounds for a conviction. But the court deemed that the victims "formed a relatively small part of the protected group," and thus decided against a conviction of genocide.[54]

This conclusion was strangely divorced from the reality of the Genocide Convention, whose wording clearly characterizes the crime of genocide as tied to intent and target, rather than the size of a given target. After the verdict's delivery, commentators called the verdict a "missed opportunity"; one writer stated, "By leaving Srebrenica as an isolated case, it diminishes the public understanding of what this war was about, and allows Srebrenica to be separated from the rest of the war, as a unique case of murderous and out of control military excess."[55]

Regardless of the legal outcome, the survivors know what they experienced and they know how to classify it. Ervin Blažević, native of Kozarac and a survivor of Trnopolje camp, returned to his hometown after the war. He has been working for its recovery and in promotion of human rights ever since. Addressing the question of genocide, Blažević told me, "If there was not genocide in Prijedor, then there is no such thing. I carry that genocide on my shoulders; I was in the camps, I saw the beatings and the killings. So I don't need there to be a decision in order to know there was genocide."[56]

16

Grassroots Activism for Justice in Prijedor

SINCE THE WAR, RETURNEES TO PRIJEDOR WHO SURVIVED THE worst atrocities and who lost many of their loved ones have formed the core of an activist community. Prijedor activist Mirsad Duratović summed up the needs of the community thus: "We need recognition from the government that crimes happened here. This is not about money, as there is no amount of money that can assuage our pain. If the government were to permit a memorial that commemorated the crimes to which we were subjected, that would be an admission. If this were to be done, then we would be able to move on. As it is now, I do not have the right in Prijedor to commemorate the day of the death of my parents."[1]

The compelling need for acknowledgment of wrongs done and for commemoration of that part of the war history are a requirement for justice in Prijedor. These requirements must be fulfilled on behalf of the victims, but also for the good of broader society, for there will be no chance for healing on all sides without recognition of the truth. Vedran Grahovac mentioned that in post–World War II Germany, "state-making was built on the notion of de-Nazification. Here in Prijedor," he continued, "it is exactly the opposite. The atmosphere here more closely resembles that of Spain, where there is no public memory. In Prijedor, there is no public discussion of the war crimes. We must publicly condemn what took place at the camp in Omarska, for example. However, there is no way that we can make progress on this problem while there are Serbs who were involved in war crimes who are still working in the public sphere."[2]

In the Prijedor area, two forces have been battling each other ever since the end of the war. On one side there is the corrupt ruling elite, and on the other side there are all those who have consciously struggled for some measure of justice over the years. That includes those who returned, knowing simply that they have a right to what is theirs. And it includes the grassroots activists, who articulate the rights and needs of the ordinary people— Serbs, Muslims, and Croats alike—and organize to fight for those rights and needs.

Everyone in Prijedor needs a secure life, with an honest government and, at the very least, with opportunities for education, employment, and good health care. Sadly, these things are so far from available under present conditions in the municipality as to sound like a far-fetched dream. But ordinary people innately know what their rights are, and so they continue to fight for these things.

Behind those elementary needs there is the need, just as in Srebrenica and in the rest of Bosnia-Herzegovina, for truth and justice. This phrase encompasses what Prijedor activists are fighting for: memory of the ills of the war needs to be preserved, and the right to memorialization of wartime events. That is, the survivors of war crimes and atrocities in the Prijedor region need to secure a public record of the wrong that was done to them, so the memory of that history does not go away. And they need public monuments, memorials that constitute an open acknowledgment of that time of torment. All these things are some of the prerequisites for the establishment of the healthy coexistence that is sometimes called reconciliation.

The demand for memorialization, which in Prijedor is obstructed at every turn, is an attempt to compel the political elite to admit that crimes were committed in order to establish and entrench the postwar order. The success of that violent endeavor requires the opposite of memory—amnesia—as the bulwark of the new social order.

Hariz Halilovich noted that memory is something actively performed in what he terms "interpretive reconstructions."[3] In a passage applicable both to Prijedor and to Srebrenica, he writes, "the memories of the survivors act as a form of defiance and resistance against the 'generic' nationalist histories that either exclude them or selectively include only fragments of memories that fit with the broader versions of nationalist narratives."[4]

When former Mayor Marko Pavić said that he was a "man of the present and the future, not of the past"[5]—and he found many ways to say this—it was a way of diverting attention from the legacy of thousands of murders committed in his dominion.

Thus not only is public memorialization important, but it also amounts to a call for a change of consciousness among the ordinary people. It is this consciousness that the grassroots activists of Prijedor are working to prompt, against great odds.

Starting a few years after the peak of return to Prijedor, activists, returnees, and survivors of the concentration camps began to mark a number of anniversaries: of the first assault on Kozarac; of the opening of the concentration camps and their discovery by international journalists; and of the closing of the camps. To the extent they have been permitted by the local authorities, activists have conducted memorial events at Omarska, at Trnopolje, and in front of the former Keraterm concentration camp.

In 2010 I met Satko Mujagić, originally from Kozarac. When he was twenty, he was held with his father in Omarska camp. He was kept in a series of camps over six months. After foreign journalists discovered the camps and informed the world during the summer of 1992, they were closed, and some of the surviving prisoners were released and expelled from the Republika Srpska. Others, including Satko, were transferred to Manjača camp. He was held there, together with thousands of other civilians. That camp was finally closed in December 1992, and Satko resettled in Western Europe and continued his education. Along the way, he became an energetic activist for the memorialization of the war crimes that he had experienced, often traveling back and forth between his new and old homes.

When I met him, Satko was taking a group of foreign students to Omarska, and I tagged along. We arrived at the spreading mine complex with its buildings of different sizes—buildings that meant one thing to the owners and workers there (since the war, exclusively Serbs), and another thing entirely to the survivors and activists.

Satko identified each building and told us what he remembered. Pointing to the "Red House," the biggest structure in the complex, he said

> We were in rooms in that building. From the windows, in the morning we could see the bodies of people who had been killed that night.
>
> There is a certain way that people scream when they know they are going to die. There was no way to know how to survive. There, in the space called the "garage," they crammed many people into a small room. No one could sit down. It became so hot that the paint melted. One night, a man died standing up. When people were allowed to move out of the room, they noticed that he had died. And in the "White House," people were tortured and killed nearly every night of that summer of 1992.
>
> We had to run along this building to the canteen there, for food. We only received one meal a day, but since there were thousands of us here, they were pretty much feeding people all the time. Sometimes they put out benches that we had to jump over or oil for us to slip on. The walkways were often covered in blood that we had to clean up.

At one point, Satko recalled, he was so weak that he could not move or talk. He noticed that his father was crying. His father had not even cried when his best friend was killed. Satko understood that his father thought Satko was dying. He whispered, "Dad, don't cry. This is your and my film. In a movie, the heroes always survive."

Returning to Kozarac from Omarska, we visited Kamičani, the local cemetery where Bosniak war victims whose remains had been found in mass graves were reburied. Hundreds of posts marked the graves; one bore the name of a woman with the dates 1892–1992. As we stood beside the rows of headstones, Satko said, "I am talking because I could be lying here under the ground, and these people cannot talk anymore."

Satko said, "I live to tell."[6]

Indeed, at that time Satko seemed to have a compulsion to recount the horrors that he had survived, to anyone who would listen. He told me that a friend of his, commenting on Satko's activism, once told him that he had "survivor's guilt." He responded, "I do not have survivor's guilt. I have survivor's responsibility."

In the evening after the tour, Satko and I sat together back in Kozarac. Satko was in a mood to sing. He made a remark that one hears more from older people—and those who have been very near death: "It is good to be alive."

WHITE ARMBANDS AND REPRESSION OF ACTIVISM

As survivors and their supporters were developing the tradition of commemorating important dates in wartime history by visiting the former concentration camps, groups of local activists were devising other modes of public remembrance in more central places. In early 2012 a coordinating body, the Twentieth Anniversary Committee for Commemoration of the Suffering of Prijedoran Civilians, was formed of eight local organizations from Prijedor and Kozarac.

In this period organizers cultivated a new tradition: wearing a white armband on May 31. That was the day, twenty years earlier, when the newly established Serb separatist regime in Prijedor issued a radio announcement, commanding the non-Serb population to hang white sheets in their windows and to wear white armbands whenever they went outside. The new requirement marked a heightening of the mistreatment of non-Serbs in the town.

Late May brings the anniversary of several assaults on the non-Serb population. On May 23, 1992, Serb forces carried out the first full-fledged attacked on a Muslim settlement in the Prijedor area. After an unsuccessful attempt on the part of local residents to resist harassment by Serb soldiers, Serb forces bombarded the village of Hambarine and then entered it with tanks, firing weapons and torching houses. Residents who did not succeed in fleeing were killed on the spot or taken away to concentration camps. Similar attacks on other non-Serb villages were repeated throughout the summer of that year.

Thus on the twentieth anniversary of those first attacks, the organizations Izvor and Association of Camp Survivors Prijedor '92 prepared not only the White Armband campaign slated for May 31, but also a gathering to be held on May 23, the Hambarine anniversary. The organizations planned to create a temporary sidewalk installation that displayed 266 white cloth sacks. The sacks symbolized the containers of exhumed remains of civilian war victims; in the Prijedor area 256 women were killed, ten girls as well.

In addition, the organizations planned to arrange more than a hundred school chairs on the street, representing the number of children who were killed during the war. However, local authorities banned the entire activity. After an unsuccessful appeal of the decision, activists continued with their plans for the armband commemoration.

The wearing of a white armband in Prijedor was a way of holding those days of mistreatment in the public memory. It was also a way of confronting ignorance and denial, letting other local people know that this history was not forgotten. Prijedor organizations posted an announcement of their plans with the slogan "Stop denial of genocide—support the victims' right to memory."

The public display of symbols marking the crimes of the early 1990s was an escalation by activists in response to repression they had experienced during the ongoing reign of Mayor Pavić. In previous years, the mayor had banned gatherings of survivors on anniversary days, saying that such activities would "hurt the town's reputation." He also objected to activists' use of the word "genocide" in reference to what had taken place in Prijedor. But as activist Refik Hodžić explained, "Marko Pavić cannot decide on behalf of the victims how they should name the commemoration of their suffering."[7]

Amid reports that local police were exerting surveillance over the city to learn whether activists would be distributing armbands in Prijedor, few people were seen wearing the symbol in town. It was a new, overt form of expression, and many people feared repercussions should they participate. But Mirsad Duratović, president of the Association of Camp Survivors Prijedor '92, described his feelings and the effect of international support: "All morning suffocating memories have been passing through my mind. I try to stop the tears, and what helps me is the fact that today, for the first time after all these years, I feel that I am not alone, and that we are not alone."[8]

On May 23 of the following year, the gathering that had been prohibited in 2012 was held. White cloth sacks bearing the names and ages of the women and girls who had been killed were arranged in five rows on the cobblestones of Prijedor's central square, and some dozens of activists stood solemnly among them in remembrance. Edin Ramulić spoke: "In this way we wish to show the citizens of Prijedor the extent of the crime that was committed, to call upon them to address this, and to cease the policy of denial of crimes that members of the army and police of the Republika Srpska committed."[9]

On May 31, 2013, the second annual White Armband Day was observed in Prijedor and, again, around the world. In Prijedor the commemoration took place in quite a different manner than the year before, with less fear and with significantly greater participation. This time, several hundred young people marched through the city. They carried 102 roses, for the number of children who were killed in the region during the war. The demonstration included not only Muslims, but also Serb activists from

Prijedor and nearby Banja Luka, as well as people who had arrived in solidarity from several cities in the Federation and from abroad.

A request for permission to make the march on May 31 was rejected by the city government. It was thus carried out without official permission, but police did not intervene. No representative from the city government participated. Shortly after the event, a journalist requested a comment from Mayor Pavić. He answered, "Prijedor municipality has nothing to do with that celebration." Surprised at Pavić's terminology, the journalist commented that it was not a celebration, but a remembrance of the more than three thousand people of Prijedor who had been killed during the war. Pavić then compounded the insult, saying, "Oh, that's just another gay parade!"[10]

The attitude of Prijedor officials did not change in the ensuing years, as the May 31 protests continued. Regarding the official stance, activist Emir Hodžić noted, "Prijedor authorities, the mayor, are simply people who are not prepared to change their politics, and [instead] see activists from Prijedor and elsewhere as provocateurs, Bosniak extremists, etc. The fact is that the majority of our activists are not even Bosniak."[11]

In December 2012 the Twentieth Anniversary Committee announced an event to be held on International Human Rights Day.

The committee designated December 10, the anniversary of the signing of the Universal Declaration of Human Rights, as a day to march in protest of discrimination against survivors and returnees in Prijedor. Recalling the robbery, rape, murder, and expulsion that took place during the war, an announcement of the event by the committee protested the fact that "employment taken away by force had never been returned, and municipal bodies invested the least in settlements where the infrastructure had been completely destroyed." The announcement stated that the goal of the gathering was to declare that it was "impermissible for people's rights to be curtailed simply because they belonged to different ethnic groups."[12]

The police quickly forbade the activity without explanation. When organizers discussed the prohibition with police authorities, they were told that the event could be held only as a stationary event on the main square. Edin Ramulić, noting that this was exactly what they had been prohibited from doing in May of the same year, commented, "They are literally playing with us."[13]

Police intensified their repression by calling some of the activists for "informational conversations," the euphemism for interrogation. Edin Ramulić simply refused to appear for this procedure. Ramulić said, "After all this it no longer makes sense to collaborate with the police, who have not had a single reason to prohibit our gathering."[14]

On December 10 some activists decided to violate the police order. Seven people marched on their predicted route. They wore tape covering their mouths, to symbolize the banning of freedom of expression. And they carried signs reading, "When civil rights are violated, civil disobedience becomes a duty."[15]

The December 10 protest in Prijedor passed without incident. On that day, Amnesty International issued a statement directed at Prijedor authorities, saying, "Rather than trying to clamp down on activist groups in Prijedor, the authorities should be heeding their calls for justice."[16] And the prominent German human rights organization Society for Threatened Peoples filed an appeal to the EU Parliament, stating, "It is scandalous that in the heart of Europe the Republika Srpska authorities are being allowed to create an apartheid system and intimidate the survivors of genocide in Bosnia."[17]

Meanwhile, in Banja Luka—not far from Prijedor, but as if in a separate universe— President Dodik greeted the citizens of the Republika Srpska the day before Human Rights Day and congratulated them. As a message covering his statement noted, "Dodik remarked that in recent years the Republika Srpska has created an environment in which all of her citizens will be able to realize their human and civil rights, as they are envisioned by the European Convention on Human Rights and other international documents."[18]

In a similar vein, as a late postscript to the December 10 repression, in early 2013 Mayor Pavić issued a related statement after meeting with Mary Ann Hennessey, head of the Council of Europe office in Bosnia-Herzegovina. The statement read, in part, "Today freedom of speech and freedom of assembly are implicit in this city"; also, "My goal is that no one forget anything, but that we all forgive and turn our sights toward the future."[19] Commentators found little need to filter Pavić's statements in order to present them satirically, calling him the "Wizard without an Oz," his statements "goodnight fairy tales," and Prijedor the "capital of human rights."[20]

BANNING USE OF THE WORD "GENOCIDE"

In 2005, Mayor Pavić stated, "I have to say that in Prijedor no one has been convicted of genocide. In all the misfortune that happened to our citizens, perhaps that is good. Perhaps in all that misfortune, we stopped, we did not go as far as some others went. Every crime, regardless of its intensity, is a crime. However, we have to know that genocide is the greatest crime."[21]

These words by Pavić, given at a conference organized by the ICTY in April 2005, implicitly admit that "we," that is, a group of people of whom Pavić was a part, committed crimes. It also admits that elsewhere, "some others" did commit genocide. That is not something that one will hear a member of the ruling infrastructure of the Republika Srpska say directly.

The survivors and activists had made up their own minds; they and their dear ones were the victims of genocide during the war. Activists have not held back from using the word "genocide" openly, and this disturbed the mayor. In 2012, in the midst of grassroots preparations for commemoration of the twentieth anniversary of the start of the war, Pavić banned the use of the word.

The Twentieth Anniversary Committee decided that the title of the series of events they were planning for spring of 2012 should be called "Genocide in Prijedor—20 Years." Mayor Pavić quickly called organizers to ask them not to use "genocide" in the name, saying that he would not allow events to take place under that title. He emphasized that organizations of Serb veterans had requested this of him.[22]

There followed a period of discussion among activists, returnees, leaders in the Muslim religious community, and the five elected returnee representatives in the municipal council. Disagreement was strong, with the Bosniak politicians forming the bloc that advocated changing the title of the events and finding "some adequate term that would not minimize the tragedy."[23]

Zinaida Hošić, Bosniak representative to the Prijedor municipal assembly and president of the local SDA, explained her colleagues' position on the prohibition, saying that they supported changing the title of the commemorations because they were "above all, legalists," and that it would be a step "in the interest of coexistence and trust that we are endeavoring to build" instead of "further complicating the situation."[24]

It appeared that the Bosniak municipal representatives were experiencing great difficulty, under pressure from both sides, and were finding it impossible to adhere consistently to a position of principle. Hošić and other representatives tried to convince the activists that they nevertheless supported the coordinating committee and that it was their right to determine the name of the commemorations. In the process, activists lost trust in their representatives.

The city authorities not only prohibited the May 23 commemoration, but survivors were also prevented from making a visit to the Omarska mining complex on May 9, the anniversary of the establishment of a concentration camp at that site.[25]

Mayor Pavić asked the activists to change their minds, saying, "I call on the Bosniaks in Prijedor, where we have made great progress, to give up this quasi-ideology and that we return to life in Prijedor and to the realization of our programs for the future."[26]

Shortly after the prohibition of the events in May 2012, the municipal assembly of Prijedor met and issued a harsh resolution. It requested that Mayor Pavić file criminal charges against organizers of programs bearing the word "genocide" in their title, for "fomenting hatred and causing great damage to the municipality." The resolution of the assembly also called for cancellation of any municipal funding to the local nongovernmental organizations involved in the events.[27]

The conflict carried on, with activists sometimes prohibited from organizing events, and other times allowed to organize events. The prohibition against the word "genocide" remained in place. A couple of months later it was implemented as events took an unpleasant turn. In the summer of 2012, the survivor association Izvor organized a commemoration under the title, "For Equality and the Right to Memory." The gathering was announced for August 5, the anniversary of the closing of concentration camp at Omarska. Organizers received permission to hold the event but were again forbidden from using the word "genocide."

For the gathering, activists inscribed the names of the more than one hundred children who had been killed in the Prijedor area during the war on a portable school blackboard. They also prepared schoolbags representing each of the children, to be arranged in a display on the central square of Prijedor. The word "genocide" was written on each bag.[28]

Several hundred activists and supporters participated in the commemorative gathering, accompanied by the British journalist Ed Vulliamy. The gathering took place peacefully; however, president of the Kozarac Association of Camp Survivors Sabahudin Garibović was arrested and charged for use of the word "genocide" on the schoolbags.

On the same day, when members of Izvor went to their office in the morning to pick up the props for the gathering, they found that every window of their office had been broken. The problem of the offending word was never resolved.

CONCENTRATION CAMPS AND THE CAMPAIGN FOR MEMORIALIZATION

Over the years after the war, the campaign for memorialization grew. This campaign, with its ebbs and flows, had as many forms and faces as there were activist organizations in the municipality.

There are annual visits, or attempted visits, to the former concentration camps on each of the anniversaries of their opening and closing. In 2000, Srcem do Mira began conducting annual visits to Omarska in May and August of each year.

There has been an ongoing, and so far largely unsuccessful, call for the erection of public monuments commemorating war crimes in the places where they were committed, and for the establishment of a museum that would illustrate this history. For a time, this campaign included the attempt to establish a memorial space at the former Omarska camp.

There have been successes and frustrations, but, over time, the campaign grew to include more young activists of different ethnicities. These include people who are native to Prijedor, those in the diaspora, and activists from Banja Luka and further afield. They share a common vision of truth revealed, justice established, and equality for all citizens of Prijedor.

In 2013 I revisited Omarska with some of these activists for the commemoration of the twenty-first anniversary of the closing of the camp. As we walked toward the Omarska mining complex I met an elderly woman who introduced herself to me as "Majka (mother) Mejra." She showed me two pendants around her neck, bearing the names of her son and daughter. She told me that both of them had been killed during the war, and that she had no grandchildren. She was living alone with her husband. The remains of her son and daughter, Edvin and Edna, were found in mass graves. It was the holy month of Ramadan, and Mother Mejra was fasting. As we walked, she was carrying some roses that she was going to lay in Omarska, in memory of her children.

We arrived at the center of the mining complex, the "Red House," a large and long building covered by red metal siding. In front of it stood the notorious "White House," a smaller structure where prisoners had been physically abused. Few survived to walk out of the White House alive. Off to the side was another mining facility that the survivors called the "restaurant," where people were fed. Activist Kemal Pervanić pointed out to me the balcony of the restaurant and explained that people were taken to that upper level to be interrogated.

I arrived to see a crowd of several hundred people huddled in the few feet of shade offered by the Red House. A speaker was intoning the names of those killed in Omarska. People said a silent prayer for the dead. There was a heaviness in the air.

Some fifteen hundred people gathered at the site that day. Sudbin Musić, then secretary of the Prijedor '92 organization of camp survivors, conducted the proceedings and introduced each speaker.

Looking at the crowd in the shade, I saw Fikret Alić, who had been made famous around the world by the iconic photograph of him, emaciated, taken at Trnopolje. We made eye contact, and he smiled a little smile.

That brief smile in this place of horror spoke volumes to me: that survival is possible, that people, though wounded, can find ways to function after trauma and to lead productive lives.

Mirsad Duratović, director of Prijedor '92, spoke about how the groups of concentration camp survivors may not and will not stop fighting for memory and memorialization. He emphasized that people have the right to truth, to commemoration, and to visit the place of their torment and their memories, as opposed to having those memories erased from history. Duratović called for the construction of a memorial center at Omarska.

Duratović quoted a line from the Croatian poet Vladimir Nazor: *Njih mrtvih ja sam živi spomenik*—"Of those who are dead, I am the living memorial."

The president of the national association of concentration camp survivors, Jasmin Mešković, spoke.

> It is a sad day as we remember those killed. The other night we visited the pit at Hrastova Glavica, twenty meters deep, where people were shot in the head and dumped. The truth comes out, and it comes out from the mass graves. The truth must be told not only about Prijedor but also about Batkovići, Lukavica, Vlasenica—and Čelebići. All of the former camps, regardless of whether they held Croats, Serbs, or Bosniaks, are places to be marked. In all these locations, the intent was the same: to kill. Only the numbers were different.
>
> In Bosnia there are laws. There are laws to protect dogs and horses. That is good. But it is sad that there is no law regarding the concentration camp survivors. There is no concern about us. For eighteen years we have been struggling for this, so that nothing like this can ever happen again in this country.

It is significant that Mešković mentioned not only the Serb-run camps at Lukavica and other places, but also Čelebići, a camp in central Bosnia run by progovernment forces, where Serbs were held and abused. Regarding this history, Ervin Blažević commented to me that it was appropriate that Čelebići should be mentioned and that those guilty should be prosecuted, because "they brought shame upon me and my people, and on the fight that I fought."[29]

In the same week, a different sort of commemoration took place at Trnopolje camp. The event took place on August 5, the anniversary of the day in 1992 that foreign journalists discovered the existence of this and other concentration camps in the Prijedor area.

I attended the gathering, held in the village of Trnopolje on the grounds of the devastated Dom Kulture (cultural center), adjacent to the school that had been used as a prisoner camp. The event, oriented toward young people from around Bosnia-Herzegovina and beyond, was designed to be something different from the yearly assemblies of survivors and families of the missing, although their presence was welcome. The evening's presentations, educational in nature, included an interactive lecture, a poetry reading, and a film screening. Emir Hodžić officiated.

Goran Šimić, a Sarajevo-based attorney and law professor, gave the first presentation. His specialties are criminal law and "transitional justice." In the Bosnian context the phrase refers to one very drawn-out process, the transition from a devastated postwar society to a peaceful and harmonious one, and to justice that is generally delayed and often denied.

Šimić focused on the court proceedings pertaining to war crimes, both at The Hague and in Bosnia. His main message, coming on the heels of the Hague court's acquittals of several people accused of war crimes, was that we expect too much from the courts. He said, "The courts are not involved in establishing the truth. They are involved in establishing whether there are sufficient facts to judge someone as guilty. We believe in the magic that the court will establish justice. But the court is involved in establishing guilt and responsibility. "Finally," Šimić explained, "in the whole legal process, there is no victim taken into consideration. The prosecutors think of these trials as cases with a number. But the victims do not think of it that way. No, these cases are part of our lives." He continued:

> It is not sufficient to judge the war criminals. We will get a maximum of 10 percent of what we want from the courts. From the court proceedings we acquire something like a mosaic that should have 6,000 pieces, but it only has 300. There is no picture that takes shape there.
>
> And what about the punishments that people are receiving? They are inadequate. Is this justice? There could be harsher punishments. They were raping twelve-year-olds, eight-year-olds, six-year-olds. The punishments given are like prescribing aspirin for a broken leg. There is no real punishment. The guilty should be required to pay into a fund that would help with reconstruction.

"Meanwhile," Šimić added, "there is denial. All sides are responsible for some crimes. There were crimes committed by Bosniaks in central Bosnia." He pointed out that people who actively participated in the war are now in political positions. Exhorting the audience to activism, he said, "There are around a hundred-thousand people in political positions, but there are three and a half million of us."

Šimić continued, "We don't want real confrontation with the past, but just the kind of confrontation where I was the victim and you were the war criminal. A real change would start with us, ourselves. It is easy just to criticize. We don't want to wait before getting to work on this change, because the potential for another conflict exists now."

The evening culminated with a moving moment as Izvor presented an award to Women in Black. Edin Ramulić presented the award to Staša Zajović, president of the organization, for the group's steadfast work against genocide denial. Receiving the award, Zajović spoke of personal responsibility, stating, "Justice comes from acting upon one's responsibility to one's fellow people, and from saying, 'These things shall not be done in our name.' I strongly rebel against the fact that I am a citizen of an aggressor state that changed the region into a concentration camp. . . . Participants in the crimes have now come to power in my country."[30]

In an interview on the same day, Zajović said, "Our obligation is to express empathy and solidarity with those who withstood horrible suffering and to express our deepest admiration for the fact that they have decided to struggle for justice. . . . We are on the same path, to create a culture of peace, justice, and trust."[31]

THE CAMPAIGN TO PRESERVE MEMORY IN OMARSKA

Over the years, a central focus of the campaign for memorialization was the attempt to preserve some part of the mining complex at Omarska as a facility that commemorates the use of the site as a prison camp. If it could be established, it would stand as a long-term recognition of the experience of the victims at that site, and as a physical refutation of the historical revisionism practiced by separatists and their sympathizers.

For nearly ten years after the war, the mining complex was the property of the Republika Srpska. In 2004, the RS sold a majority share to Mittal Steel, the world's biggest steel producer. (Upon its 2006 merger with the steel company Arcelor, the official name became ArcelorMittal.)

In 2005, Mittal promised not to touch the White House, and it appeared willing to foster negotiations leading to the establishment of a commemorative facility. That January, representatives of the survivors secured an agreement that Mittal would not restrict access to Omarska.[32] Negotiations resulted in a detailed plan for a memorial center, and Mittal announced that it would erect the center the following year. The announcement in late 2005 caused quite a media splash. However, as the facility's operational capacity was restored, renovation of the mining complex was undertaken.

The repairs left only the White House intact, making it impossible to use more of the complex for a memorial.[33]

Stalling of the memorial center has lasted to this day. Early on, ArcelorMittal announced that it was compelled to wait for approval from the local government in order to follow through with its plans. Approval was never forthcoming, and in February 2006 ArcelorMittal announced that it was "temporarily suspending" the memorial project, after it began to receive negative responses from local Serbs and authorities alike.

Responding to the proposal for a memorial center at Omarska, Mayor Pavić issued a dodgy statement that could have been addressed only to those who were unfamiliar with the state of relations in Prijedor: "I fear that the construction of a center for the victims of war in Omarska could destroy the now very good interethnic relations in Prijedor."[34] Pavić further commented that it was "too early" for a memorial in Omarska, saying, "I do not support that. Why [a monument] for dead Muslims and Croats here, and not for Serb victims in the Federation?"[35]

Activists continued to press for an opening of the center, lobbying before the OHR, writing petitions, and sending letters, but to no avail. In the course of the twentieth anniversary commemorations in 2012, ArcelorMittal reiterated that the company was "still ready to support the building of a memorial if the interested parties find agreement."[36] But ArcelorMittal meanwhile participated in the periodic obstruction of access to Omarska on dates when survivors and their supporters wished to visit the site. They allowed visitors in for the May anniversary in 2011, but in spring of 2012 they prevented visits from survivors and students, as well as a visit from solidarity activists from Belgrade.[37] Visits to Omarska on the August 6 anniversary of the closure of the concentration camp have continued each year.

Between ArcelorMittal, local authorities, and international officials, there seemed to be an abiding lack of concern about the needs of the survivors of Omarska. Mirsad Duratović commented, "Both the international community and ArcelorMittal seem to be neutral. In the Omarska case, being neutral . . . means taking a side. It means taking the side of a war crime."[38]

There is a question about the more widespread effect of memorialization, beyond the personal sphere of the survivors. Does public remembrance have any positive influence on the consciousness of those members of society who are steeped in denial, under the influence of the media controlled by the nationalists and separatists? We can see from the experience of Potočari that the answer is mixed. Local people in the Srebrenica area who deny the history of the crimes in the enclave are quite capable of passing the memorial center every day and still denying.

On the other hand, we have also seen that there are young people in the wider region around Srebrenica, including Bratunac, who are not under the burden of indoctrination, and Potočari has been an educational resource for them. There are similar people among the Serbs in Prijedor municipality.

In a more recent effort to establish a memorial, Prijedor activists proposed an idea that seemed difficult to oppose. In November 2014, parents of children killed during the war presented a petition, bearing nearly fifteen hundred signatures, to the city government requesting the construction of a monument dedicated to these children in the center of Prijedor. The parents' group was led by Fikret Bačić, from the village of Zecovi. His daughter, six, and son, twelve, were killed in July 1992, and overall, more than twenty of his relatives were killed.[39]

The petition proposed that the monument be inscribed with the name and birth year of each of the 102 children who were killed. Responding to the initiative, Mayor Pavić stated that he was "not opposed to the construction of such a monument, and that it needed to take place in the Federation" as well.[40]

He noted that it was up to the municipal assembly to make the decision.

Deliberations on the question were postponed for nearly two years. In mid-2016, the Prijedor municipal assembly finally discussed the proposal but declined to support a monument to the children. However, activists did not view this as a definitive defeat, first of all, because the discussion implicitly acknowledged that children were killed. Secondly, the assembly members did not object to the establishment of the monument per se, but to the proposed location.[41]

Negotiations for the memorial continued. Over time, activists had proposed a half dozen locations, but the municipal assembly rejected each one, saying that a monument at the proposed location "would not fit into the urban regulatory plan."[42] The activists thereupon proposed that the bridge from the main part of Prijedor crossing a stream into the Old Town be refurbished as a monument to the children victims.

Activists continued their campaign for a monument to the child victims, and there seemed to be progress in 2018. By this time, the notoriously obstructionist Mayor Pavić had retired, and the office was taken over by his fellow DNS party member Milenko Đaković. It appeared that Mayor Đaković wished to pursue a more cooperative approach to the commemoration project. In the course of a series of meetings with activists in 2018, Đaković proposed that there be erected a monument to commemorate all child victims of war throughout the twentieth century.

It was clear that Đaković's proposal was an attempt to co-opt the movement for a children's commemorative monument in such a way that the memory of the child victims of the 1990s war would be effaced. Nevertheless, activists for the project responded by accepting the idea—as long as the names and ages of their children were incorporated into the memorial. In early 2019 Mayor Đaković commented that "it is not a problem to erect a monument in Prijedor" but expressed the concern that such a monument would be "politicized" and become a venue for "pilgrimage."[43]

ADVOCATES FOR PUBLIC MEMORIALIZATION ARE AWARE that the monuments that have been erected can exert a divisive force, since they speak to only one side in a conflict that has not been resolved.[44] One activist told me, "That is not where the real message gets through—it is a message meant only for the victims, and the message from each side just bypasses the other side. So the function of the monument is lost."[45]

Furthermore, there is a danger that memorials can serve as instruments to nurture a "cult of victimhood." It should be possible to acknowledge this problem without denying the fact that survivors need public recognition of their suffering.

The creation of a law at the state level that would exert jurisdiction over all Bosnia-Herzegovina is probably the only action that can begin to resolve this problem. A campaign for such a law could be a useful focus for the attention of human rights advocates. However, ultimately much deeper legal changes are necessary: changes that would root out the criminal/political infrastructure that is the legacy of the war and that is safeguarded by the Dayton constitution.

While survivors have been prevented from constructing monuments in Prijedor, the opportunity has arisen to realize public memorialization in the form of group funerals of the remains of victims exhumed from mass graves. It became the custom to hold the mass burial on July 20 of each year. The largest to date occurred in 2006, when some 305 people were buried, including 302 Muslims (four of whom were Roma) and three Catholics. As of that year, fifty-three mass graves had been discovered in the area.[46] By the sixteenth annual funeral in 2015, the identified remains of over seven hundred victims had been reburied.

The reburial ceremonies, and the very visible funeral processions that led to them, afforded mourners a measure of public expression that had otherwise been denied them. The location of Kamičani on the main Banja Luka–Prijedor road, hard by the turnoff to Kozarac, also served as a convenient shrine for survivors whose loved ones were buried there.

17

The Missing, Kevljani, Survival, Emigration

WHEN SPEAKING TO PEOPLE WHO HAVE SURVIVED THE destruction of their village and their family, it is not unusual to hear shocking numbers. Nedžad Bešić told me, "Seventy-four of my relatives from here were killed,"[1] and Emsuda Mujagić said, "Forty-eight members of my family are gone."[2]

The matter of missing people is a painful issue of the greatest importance to survivors in Prijedor. As in Srebrenica, the discovery of hidden mass graves and the identification of the remaining missing victims have been a pressing concern and a main campaign point for human rights activists in the Prijedor area ever since the end of the war.

At the end of the war, some 31,500 people were counted as missing in Bosnia-Herzegovina. Through diligent and tortuous work in discovering and excavating mass graves over the years, by early 2015 the remains of some three-fourths of these people had been exhumed and identified.[3] Victims' remains were found in isolated burials, but most often in mass graves, which numbered upward of 750 throughout the country.[4]

By 2017, the number of those still missing was cited as approximately seven thousand.[5] At least one-tenth of those missing were from the Prijedor region. By this time the remains of some 2,325 of the missing had been identified, having been discovered in 450 different locations, including at least ninety-six mass graves. Nearly eight hundred were still missing.[6]

Discussing the problem of the missing, Edin Ramulić said, "Prijedor is still municipality number one per number of missing in Bosnia-Herzegovina, and thus in the region. Every tenth disappeared [person] is sought in Prijedor."[7]

On one occasion I was in Prijedor at the time of the major Muslim holiday Kurban Bajram. Many Muslims, whether observant or not, get together with their families on Bajram for a celebratory feast. But all too often, in the postwar period the holiday is a time that emphasizes how much of one's family is no more. During that visit, Mirsad Duratović said to me, "Now it is Bajram. I don't like this holiday. Ordinarily, it is a time when the whole family gets together, something like Christmas for the Catholics. But I am sitting with my mother alone, and it's sad."[8]

In a municipality where well over three thousand non-Serbs were killed, all the survivors and returnees would like to know the truth about their missing loved ones. Part of the organization Izvor's founding mission was to collect information about missing persons and to advocate for the rights of the relatives of the disappeared. In 1998 Izvor, in cooperation with Srcem do Mira, published a book containing information about the missing. *Ni Krivi ni Dužni* (Neither guilty nor obligated) contained personal data and, where possible, photographs of the missing persons.[9] The book includes data on 123 children and 228 women.[10]

In 2012 Edin Ramulić told me, "All of us have a relative who is missing. There were 3,176 people who were disappeared. We created a book of the disappeared; the first printing was the first evidence about the missing in Bosnia-Herzegovina. To that date, the government had done nothing."[11]

Mirsad Duratović criticized the lack of success in locating more of the missing:

> More than one thousand of those who were killed have not yet been found. There were drivers and other people who were involved, who were witnesses. There are people who know what was done. So why can't they find those missing people? There are at least five witnesses of what happened in my village who have already spoken. Some of them have testified in The Hague—but no prosecutor has taken any action.
>
> If you were in my place, what would you do? My grandmother, my other relatives, are gone. I must look for them and find them; then life can go on. Why is it like this? There are prosecutors in Sarajevo, at the state level, who could do something.[12]

Discovery of mass graves where the missing of Prijedor were concealed was slow. One of the first to be involved in this tormented and sometimes risky search was Jasmin Odobašić, himself a native of the Krajina and a former wartime prisoner of the Republika Srpska authorities in his hometown of Prnjavor. After the war Odobašić became deputy director of the Federal Commission on Missing Persons, and in that capacity he worked extensively in the field for many years.

By 2005 over fifty hidden graves, from single graves to some containing several hundred remains, were discovered and exhumed in the Prijedor area. Speaking of the very tense early postwar years, Odobašić recounted:

> We first went to Prijedor illegally, in 1998. There were state agencies that helped. There were traces of the remains; sometimes they were not even completely buried. You found a skull with gold teeth. There were more than three hundred graves, including pits. There was a five-month-old baby and a four-year-old boy. We found documents as well. There was the big grave in Stari Kevljani where hundreds of remains were recovered, and in Jakarina Kosa 373 remains were recovered. Of those, 296 were identified. In Stari Kevljani the graves were buried six meters under the surface. That mass grave was discovered in 2000, but not exhumed until 2004 because of lack of funding.[13]

I asked Odobašić how the mass graves were found: "I got information from survivors, witnesses, and returnees. There were some Serbs with a conscience. There were other Serbs who would give information in return for a favor. There were others who would get drunk and start bragging in a kafana, and someone would hear the information and convey it. And then there are people who will sell the information."

Odobašić spoke of political difficulties that he encountered during his work: "From 1996 to 1998 no one allowed me to exhume Serbs and Croats, nor were they allowed to exhume the others. But in one mass grave I found fifteen Muslims, eight Croats, and one Serb. We were not allowed to exhume at Briševo [where dozens of Croats had been killed]. But a victim is not an ethnicity; a victim is a victim. Every mother cries the same."

Over the years, workers continued to search and find new hidden graves. Numbers of graves, and of the remains found in them, are difficult to track because different organizations and activists recount varying figures, and those figures change with each new discovery. As with Srebrenica and other locations, secondary graves are part of the equation. Jakarina Kosa, near the town of Ljubija, was uncovered in 2001; some of the remains had been moved there from the larger site at Tomašica.

When Jakarina Kosa was discovered in 2001, altogether some seventeen hundred remains had been found in the region.[14] Jakarina Kosa was by far the largest gravesite discovered to that point. It should be noted that confusion is often generated around the number of bodies actually located in any given grave. In the next large mass grave to be uncovered, at Stari Kevljani in 2004, it is reported that 456 bodies were found, although these were not complete sets of remains.[15]

The search for the remains of those killed at Korićanske Stijene has been as perplexing as any other search. There, some two hundred men were taken out of buses, forced to kneel, and then shot and tossed over a steep cliff on August 21, 1992. These were people who had been evacuated from Trnopolje and were told that they were being driven to central Bosnia with other prisoners to be set free.

Some few remains were found in 2003, and an exploration of the dangerous terrain was undertaken in earnest, with ropes and ladders, in 2009 and 2010. With the search complicated by unexploded grenades, snakes, and unapproachable terrain, discovery of remains has been discouraging. By mid-2014 only about half of the victims' remains had been found and identified.[16] However, in September 2017 a well-hidden secondary mass grave—the sixth to be found in the area—was discovered under the cliffs.[17] Buried in a pit covered by tons of rocks, the grave revealed 137 clusters of bones including 86 skulls. It was expected that the find would provide the remains of more than one hundred additional missing victims.[18]

Dozens of smaller hidden graves have been discovered near the scenes of the crimes: at Hambarine, Hrastova Glavica, Čarakovo, Zecovi, Briševo, and many other locations including one near Omarska itself.[19] The remains exhumed at those locations were of people killed at Omarska, Trnopolje, and Keraterm, and in many of the towns and villages throughout Prijedor municipality, where people were often killed on the spot during initial assaults.

The number of those missing hovered around a thousand for nearly a decade. Then in the fall of 2013 another mass grave was discovered, or more accurately, rediscovered. This was the burial grounds at a mine that had been explored before, in the mainly Serb-populated village of Tomašica. Parts of Tomašica had been excavated in 2004, when the remains of twenty-four victims were exhumed, and in 2006, when another ten were found. Somehow, it was not understood that the extent of the burials was much greater than what had already been seen. It was thought that the majority of the remains from that location had been removed to Jakarina Kosa, where they had been uncovered ten years earlier. Thus for another seven years the place lay ignored, except by the occasional shepherd, grazing his flock on the surface above the bones of hundreds of victims.

More remains were discovered at Tomašica in 2013, when a couple of former soldiers in the Serb army tipped off authorities that the gravesite held far more victims than had been supposed. These soldiers had participated in the transporting of bodies to the site in 1992. One of them led investigators directly to the site of the mass grave. He was quoted as saying, "I can't comprehend what my people did to the Bosniak people." The soldier did not ask for money in return for revealing the grave, only that his name never be mentioned. He spoke of the neighbors who had protested about the grave in the postwar years, calling for it to be removed because of the odor that was reaching their houses even via the underground water. But they were not prepared to let the families of the missing know about this place.[20]

By early September 2013 some twenty remains were found that were thought to have been those of prisoners held at Keraterm and Trnopolje. A peculiar circumstance at Tomašica was that, because of the high composition of clay in the soil, the remains were relatively intact even after more than twenty years in the ground. Of the new discovery, Edin Ramulić said, "We hope that as many as 1,000 persons could be found in this grave, because in Prijedor we are still seeking 1,200 disappeared."[21]

The scope of this mass grave became clear only gradually. Excavation was taking place as deep as ten meters under the surface. More remains came to light every day, and some 271 victims were exhumed with identifying documents and personal effects such as watches and photographs. Early on, the grave was reported to cover an area of five thousand square meters, and in the course of the excavation new sections were uncovered.

When excavation was discontinued for the season because of rainy weather, the number of complete and partial remains had reached approximately 450. It is understood that Tomašica was a primary grave from which some remains were removed to Jakarina Kosa. Given this, its total original body count would have surpassed that of Crni Vrh, the mass grave holding 629 Srebrenica victims, exhumed in 2003. As some commentators have estimated, this makes Tomašica the largest single mass grave to be encountered in Europe since World War II.[22]

The revelations at Tomašica surpass the mere fact of numbers, staggering though they are. The uncovering is a painful experience for the survivors, and at the same time a bitter satisfaction. On one hand, it brings to the fore all the dreadful memories of the horror and atrocities that took place during the war, and it accentuates the feeling of injustice at the indifference and denial of citizens of Prijedor, from the neighbors of Tomašica on up to the highest local officials.

On the other hand, there is certainly satisfaction for many people who have been waiting for twenty years to bury their loved ones. Mirsad Duratović said, "This is a big relief for the families that have been searching for their missing loved ones for the last twenty years. After each funeral their fear increases, the fear that they will never find their disappeared relatives, and that is something that causes the greatest pain and fear among the families of the disappeared."[23]

Relatives of the missing, including activists, began visiting Tomašica as soon as the new excavations started. Unable to stay away even though they could not participate in the work, it was as if they felt that they must be involved, and that their relatives must be found. People from Left Bank villages came in the hope that their relatives who were killed in those villages, or taken away to be killed, would be discovered.

Periodic discoveries of buried victims have continued since Tomašica. In late 2015 it was announced that more than six hundred additional body parts were exhumed at Jakarina Kosa. This number was expected to represent a smaller total of complete remains, and investigators expected to find more.[24] All told, remains of victims had been discovered in ninety-six mass graves—even more graves than were found in the

Srebrenica area. But as recently as late 2018, some 760 victims from the Prijedor area were still missing.[25]

One of the most striking illustrations of suffering caused by the war and of longing for the truth about the missing was provided by the story of Hava Tatarević of Zecovi. When Serb forces attacked that village, they killed more than 150 residents (some estimates go as high as 250), including women, children, and elderly men.[26] Among them were Tatarević's husband and six of her sons, killed not far from their homes on July 23, 1992. Their remains were identified in the spring of 2014.[27]

When the remains of her sons and husband were discovered, Tatarević spoke of her long search for them: "They were together with their friends from our area. They took them away. . . . Since then I have had no trace of them. I tried to hear whatever I could about them, but it was of no use. I went to all the graves, went through clothing with my own hands, gave blood for identification, but there was no trace.

"I have no memento of my sons," Tatarević continued. "Just the two foundations of their wrecked houses remind me of them, and I have cleared them of weeds, hoping they would return. But as time goes by, my hope for their return fades more and more."[28]

Expressing her feelings upon the discovery of her missing loved ones, Tatarević commented, "I don't know which is worse: then, when there was the shock of them being taken away, or now, which is still greater." Her one surviving son, Suad, added, "I thought that I would feel better, but now it is worse; it is truly hard. I did not know that it would be this hard, especially when I see their bodies."[29]

On July 20, 2014, the identified remains of 284 people exhumed from Tomašica were reburied in several cemeteries in the Prijedor area. Among them were twenty-one members of the Hegić family from Bišćani village, as well as ten members of Mirsad Duratović's family.

In the heat of the autumn excavations at Tomašica, as hundreds of remains were being removed from under six meters of clay, a question was asked: "Why is this not widespread news in Bosnia-Herzegovina?" There are brave and honorable journalists in the Republika Srpska as well as in the Federation, but their message is confined to the Internet. They do not have mass outlets for their coverage, as those outlets are mostly controlled by the government.

Internet portals are the location of independent thought and critical commentary in Bosnia. Dragan Bursać, a professor of philosophy, is a columnist and journalist for one of those sites, the indispensable RS-based "Buka" (Noise).

Bursać castigated the mainstream RS press for ignoring Tomašica as much as it could, recalling how during World War II, Serbs themselves were killed in vast numbers in ways not much different from the more recent massacres. "Has this people perhaps forgotten?" Bursać asked and continued, "What is with all of us, 20 years after? Do we have the morality, the honor, and the humanity, to look at ourselves in the mirror and to seek forgiveness? . . . No, the media, raised on the fast food of nationalism, does not give this nation the chance even to look in that mirror of reality."

Addressing historical amnesia, Bursać wrote, "Remember, there is something worse than death. And that is death buried in oblivion and disinterest. In one way or another, at least this nearly one thousand people [referring to those exhumed at Tomašica] will be saved from that, and their families will give them a dignified burial. . . . But who will mourn for the chronically uninformed and uninterested, when they are no more, when they cross from physical obedience to eternity on the other side? Is that what they were born for, to keep silent and to be dead throughout their entire life?"[30]

As excavation activity at Tomašica wound down, there were still no convictions for genocide at Prijedor. But activists in the municipality considered Tomašica to be yet more evidence demonstrating that it was no less than genocide that had taken place. Edin Ramulić saw Tomašica as one of the clearest proofs that genocide was committed in Prijedor. "This is proof of the system," he stated, "because hundreds of people and machines had to have been involved in the creation of the mass grave. Military and civilian officials had to be there, from the civil defense and community services on down. This is one of the most obvious proofs that this was part of a joint criminal enterprise. . . . It will certainly be useful in the cases of Karadžić and Mladić, where [their indictments for genocide] include Prijedor."[31]

In late 2018 the government of the Republika Srpska initiated a move to privatize the long-idle mine complex at Ljubija, which encompasses Tomašica. A letter from concentration camp survivors cautioned the government not to let any such process endanger the commemoration of the victims at that mine, as had happened at Omarska.[32]

ONE MAN'S STORY: KEVLJANI

I was in Kozarac shortly before Tomašica was rediscovered, and I visited another mass grave, the one at Kevljani. Kemal Pervanić, survivor of Omarska, human rights activist, and native of the village, took me there.

The way Kemal Pervanić has come around to understanding his traumatic experience, using it to create something positive, is remarkable. He told me that in spite of the atrocities he has witnessed and lived through, he has forgiven. He quoted another man who had survived Omarska and also opposed revenge, saying, "A crime is a crime, no matter who commits it."

Kemal has said, "I didn't decide not to hate because I'm a good person. I decided not to hate because hating would have finished the job they'd started so successfully."[33]

Kevljani is located to the east of Kozarac, toward Banja Luka. Kemal called it "the village of mass graves," as that is where two of the larger mass graves of Prijedor municipality were found. But to Kemal it is, first of all, the place he came from, where he lived his formative years. He fondly remembered a rousing New Year's celebration on December 31, 1991, practically on the eve of a war that few expected. "It was a vibrant village with so many people," he said.

Kemal told me that Kevljani was a village of eight hundred people before the war, but now there are only around forty returnees living there permanently, including about eight children. There are more restored houses than people to live in them, and weddings and funerals take place there only rarely.

Kemal showed me around Kevljani. We sat in the house of Mevlida, one of Kemal's neighbors. There, we had a wide-ranging chat over coffee. Kemal's brother Kasim told me about an interaction that he had recently had with a person who had been a guard at Omarska and had mistreated people there. Now that person sells farming equipment at a store in the nearby village. Kasim went to purchase something there. The former guard said that he had had nothing to do with the mistreatment at Omarska. Kasim said, "You know that I was there, don't you? If everyone like you denies having participated, then who was it that did all that killing?" Kasim recounted that the man then looked down, ashamed.

As we walked around the village, Kemal said, "This village died before people came back, because only the older people returned." As we walked by houses that have been rebuilt but not re-inhabited, Kemal said, "This person is in Switzerland. That one's in Austria. That one's in Australia, and that one is in Germany."

After Kemal survived more than a half year in Omarska and Manjača concentration camps, he resettled in Great Britain, where he became the first in his village to finish a university degree. In 1999, already fluent in English, he published the book *The Killing Days: My Journey through the Bosnian War*.[34] The book remains a matter-of-fact but powerful witness to the torments that he and thousands of others experienced in Omarska, and a modest testimony to Kemal's strength of character as well.

Kemal remembered early scenes from the war. "Here is where they killed Šero, Mevlida's father, right outside this house. They shot him next to the tree in front of the house. He yelled to his son Hamed to run. Hamed ran down the street, but they caught him and killed him."

At the beginning of the war, Kevljani was shelled for two nights. No one was killed during that shelling, and only Šero and Hamed were killed in the village, Kemal told me. The rest were taken away and killed elsewhere, including about thirty-five of them in Omarska. More residents of Kevljani were taken to Trnopolje, and some of them ended up being killed in the massacre at Korićanske Stijene.

We walked past a shack, and Kemal told me that the first person who returned to Kevljani lived there alone for quite some time when he first came back to the village. That person told Kemal, "I had to sing to myself to keep from going crazy."

We walked to the two mass graves. The first one, Kevljani I, was a long, deep trench near the mosque. About 150 remains were exhumed from there. The site, discovered in the late 1990s, was both a primary and a secondary grave; some victims were buried there, and others had been moved there from elsewhere.

After the war the second grave, Kevljani II, just looked like a field to the returnees. Children played in that field, and people picked mushrooms and ate them. A cow grazed there. At some point Kemal's brother Kasim noticed a different kind of grass growing there, which made him suspect that the field covered a mass grave. It was investigated in 2004. Upon excavation, 456 bags of remains were uncovered. Until Tomašica was rediscovered, Kevljani II was the second largest mass grave in Bosnia-Herzegovina, and the largest in the Krajina region.

Along with the couple of out-of-the-way monuments and plaques that have been erected to memorialize the wartime trauma visited on non-Serbs in Prijedor, and the annual reburials, some of the mass gravesites also serve as memorials to the victims. The large site of Kevljani II is one.

On another day I was in Kevljani with Kemal and Satko Mujagić, who had also been a prisoner at Omarska. Standing by the former mass grave at Kevljani II Satko commented, "Of all these people who were found here, I must have known two hundred of them."

Thinking out loud about those traumatic days at Omarska, Satko winced and said, "I was supposed to end up here. Back in Omarska, I had had a vision of the future, that I was going to end up as bones, under the ground. Someone was pulling on my bones, pulling me apart. I said, 'Stop, I don't want to die. I don't want to end up as bones in a mass grave.'"

Kemal spoke of a man from Kevljani named Dževad Velić. He was taken to Omarska and severely mistreated, beaten there over a sustained period. At one point his brother, also a prisoner at the camp, passed him, and Dževad said to him, "mene više nema"—I am no more. Soon after that, he disappeared. Later his remains were found at Kevljani II. He had been buried about one hundred meters from the house he was born in.

Kemal told me, "Children born after the war have been named after Dževad and after others who were killed. So, they are living memorials to the victims."[35]

RETURNEES AND ECONOMIC SURVIVAL

In the preceding pages I have described a broad struggle on the part of the activists of Prijedor municipality: the campaigns against discrimination, for freedom of expression, and for justice, particularly in the realm of memorialization. One could say that these campaigns are a matter of moral survival, and that the returnees' and survivors' dignity depends on their success. At the same time, the Bosniak and Croat returnees to Prijedor must work in order to live, just as everyone must. So while activists have been fighting to locate their missing loved ones and to memorialize the atrocities of the 1990s war, ordinary people have also been struggling for material survival.

Author Sebina Sivac-Bryant notes that in the context of recovery in Kozarac, there is a dilemma; she asks, "What is the right balance between dwelling in the past, perhaps by campaigning for memorialisation, and simply getting on with normal life?" In a sense, efforts to foster economic development and thus provide employment for returnees is another stage in the fight for human rights because, among other things, it directly challenges the postwar discrimination described at the beginning of this section. Economic reconstruction contributes to what Sivac-Bryant calls "social reconstruction" (preferring this term to "reconciliation"), and it thwarts the goals of the separatists.[36]

The returnees to Prijedor are confronted with the same existential problems that face those who never left, and which face all ordinary citizens of Bosnia-Herzegovina. In early 2018 the official unemployment rate remained near 40 percent, nearly 480,000 people unemployed out of a population of less than four million. Industrial production was not increasing significantly, and export was decreasing. While the average monthly income was 850 to 950 KM (approximately US$600), that average was skewed by the number of people on the government payrolls; the income of people in the private sector was considerably less than this.[37]

In the same period, the average income was calculated as sufficient to cover less than half of the monthly basket of goods that a family needed.[38] In addition to the economic burden that all Bosnians share, returnees to Prijedor have been subject to widespread discrimination in hiring.

The benefit of remittances from the diaspora is quite significant, and nowhere is that more in evidence than in Kozarac. That town presents a mixed picture. On one hand, Sudbin Musić described it thus: "The return communities are like reservations. These are local microcosms with microeconomies. Kozarac is Dubai. It is the golden goose, based on good agricultural land, tourism, and agriculture, and some industry."[39]

Musić's comment reveals the economic advantages Kozarac enjoys. Sometimes called "an enclave of the Federation in the RS," Kozarac, with its relatively numerous and cohesive return population, enjoys some financial support from agencies in the Federation, and much more from the diaspora.

At the same time, a first impression of Kozarac presents a "false splendor" in a place where ordinary people—with or without special skills—are struggling to survive. Many returnees to the villages have resigned themselves to subsistence farming.

In spring of 2015, Maureen Cormack had been US ambassador to Bosnia-Herzegovina for three months. During an interview at that time, she commented that she was "already very frustrated" with the lack of progress in the country. She directed her criticism at the corrupt political infrastructure, saying that the great potential for tourism and development in the energy sector was being wasted "because of political corruption and obstacles that prevent it."[40]

There are, however, several instances of returnee-spurred development in the Kozarac area that have been able to develop with the help of the Kozarac diaspora and international development agencies. A Turkish credit fund for returnees helped farmer Mirnes Jakupović, twenty-five, to develop a farm that now sends tons of produce to Germany.[41] In the village of Džonlagići, a couple of kilometers away from Kozarac, a family returned from Switzerland to develop a touristic "ethno-village" in 2015. And a returnee from Austria, Enes Kahrimanović, founded the Kozarac-based company Austronet, producer and exporter of metal canopy frameworks, that employs over seventy workers.[42]

The largest and most successful returnee-based firm in Prijedor is certainly Arifagić Investment, which has gained acclaim for the establishment of a large dairy farm in the village of Trnopolje. The farm was founded in 2007 by Jusuf Arifagić, a returnee from Norway, with significant assistance from the governments of Norway and Turkey. Furnished with the most modern automated milking and sterilizing equipment, with over five hundred cows, this is the largest farm of Norwegian red cattle in the world. Arifagić, who in his fifteen years in Norwegian exile had become a successful businessman, characterized his farm as a "hotel for cows," where better conditions for the animals meant production of better milk.[43]

Sebina Sivac-Bryant outlines the postwar return and recovery process in the Prijedor region as taking place in three phases; the first is the establishment of a physical presence in one's prewar home, and the second is embodied in the campaign for memorialization. Sivac-Bryant characterizes the third phase as "securing the sustainability of the town in both the political and the economic realm,"[44] and she holds up Kahrimanović and Arifagić as exemplary individuals who have shown that it is possible to escape from a postwar paralysis and to create a better future for Bosnia's citizens.[45]

A NOTE ABOUT MAYORS

Earlier in this book I discussed not only the shady background of Prijedor's three-term mayor Marko Pavić, but also the extensive history of his obstruction of nearly all the aspirations of Prijedor's non-Serb returnees and human rights activists. After twelve years in office, Pavić relinquished his position, leaving it to his fellow DNS party member Milenko Đaković. As with any such change after a long, stagnant period of autocratic rule, there was hope that the new mayor would prove to be more open to the needs of the returnees, and willing to ameliorate the regime of discrimination that had pertained since the early 1990s.

Mayor Đaković gave an impression similar to that of Srebrenica's Mayor Grujičić, who came to office in the same electoral cycle. That is, Đaković presented himself as prepared to meet with local human rights activists and to listen to their needs. As mentioned previously, this indeed happened, and the mayor engaged in ongoing discussions with activists, for example, about the creation of a monument dedicated to the children killed during the war. In July 2017, unlike Grujičić, he even attended the commemorative reburial of non-Serb civilians who had been exhumed from mass graves and identified.

But, similar to Mayor Grujičić, Đaković had a nationalist background, and there were limits to the extent that he would accommodate the activists. He was, after all, a member of Pavić's party and subordinate to Pavić. In fact, well after his election he took the opportunity, more than once, to express his underlying, extreme nationalist position. For example, when Ratko Mladić was convicted of genocide in late 2017, Đaković declared, "We see General Mladić as a Serb hero and someone to whom our people are indebted. We know the General as an honorable person. . . . We consider that it would be appropriate to free him from his sentence and further imprisonment."[46] Đaković expressed great disdain for human rights activists in early 2019, characterizing their work as a "business" from which they make a comfortable living, while they do not actually care about the truth.[47]

During a visit to Prijedor in mid-2018, I asked local activist Goran Zorić for his opinion of the new mayor. Zorić replied, "Đaković is a bit more receptive than Pavić. But he still has to answer to his party boss, and to the members of the city council, most of whom are also members of Pavić's party."[48]

BETWEEN STAYING AND LEAVING

There are positive and negative aspects to the condition of Prijedor society. On the positive side, there are the returnees and the activists. Those who have returned have engaged in a hopeful act of trust in the future. It was a remarkable, positive thing to act out the belief that they could rebuild a life in their prewar homes after genocide. Added to that are the ongoing campaigns led by a small number of persistent people (returnees and their Serb colleagues alike) who have a strong sense of justice.

On the other side, we see the entrenched politicians who are carrying out the goals of their wartime predecessors through postwar means. They continue to skillfully impose a narrative of discord on uncritical citizens. Paradoxically, these people accept that narrative of hate even while they are aware their own representatives are robbing them.

In between these two poles of conscious activity, which signify life and death for Prijedor, there resides the mass of ordinary people who simply wish to live their lives realizing the same ambitions that everyone holds: to have a secure home and employment, and to make life better for themselves and their families.

At present, it is well-near impossible for ordinary people to fulfill those dreams, and many are leaving Prijedor. While the municipality is celebrated by virtue of the fact that some one-third of those expelled returned after the war, numbering between twenty thousand and twenty-five thousand, in fact many of those returnees have already left.

There are no hard statistics available regarding returnee figures, but according to a report issued in the spring of 2016, as many as thirty-three thousand people returned to Prijedor municipality—but that of that number, only between ten thousand and twelve thousand remained.[49] And in Prijedor proper, an estimated figure of twelve thousand to thirteen thousand returns was reduced, through emigration, to six thousand or seven thousand.[50]

On a cold November day, Mirsad Duratović graphically described to me the motivations for people's leaving, and the effects of that departure: "We have children. They want chocolate; they want a bicycle. If you have nothing to eat, you pack your trunks, and you leave. Whoever can leave is leaving. Regardless of how patriotic you are, you still have to have something to live on." Duratović looked out the window at the weather and concluded, "You can't live on snow."

Speaking about the Left Bank, Duratović painted a picture of decline:

In the last year there were thirty returnees who died, and no one was born. It's the third year that it's been like that. We have three schools in the six villages around my area. There were five schools, now there are three. When I was in first grade there, there were thirty-six students in the first grade. In those six villages there were 250 students in first grade.

Now there are thirteen. In the different schools, there is one student here, and maybe two there in first grade. Next year, altogether maybe there will be four students in the first grade. When we first returned, there were sixty students in the four-year elementary schools. Now there are thirty-six. Next year there will be fewer than thirty.

When those people reach the age of twenty, they go looking for work—not in Prijedor, but in Slovenia or Croatia, if not further abroad. They leave. In the last twelve years there have been hundreds of weddings here; all of those married couples left.[51]

Sudbin Musić provided an equally dark description of population decline in his village of Čarakovo:

The return process ended in 2003. And in that year, people started to leave. The older people are dying, and the younger ones are leaving if they can. They get married to someone abroad and then leave. In 2005 or 2006, France opened its borders to Bosniaks from the Republika Srpska, and then Finland did the same thing. This is the last phase of the ethnic cleansing.

In 1991, 2,417 people lived in Čarakovo. The village was 99 percent Muslim; 413 people from there were killed in the war. The rest were taken to concentration camps, then deported to central Bosnia, and they then left for Europe and elsewhere.

In 2003 there were 462 returnees. Now about 350 people live there. There are twenty-six children in the elementary school, first through fifth grade. That is a picture of the success of the ethnic cleansing.[52]

Among Croat returnees the picture is even darker. For example, before the war, the village of Šurkovac, not far from Ljubija, was home to some eleven hundred people, primarily Croats. The better part of their work force was employed in the Ljubija mines. Today approximately 150 people have returned, and they are faced with difficulties in water and electricity supply. Where there once were some two hundred pupils, today there are only a handful. The village also remains without a clinic or stores.[53]

Edin Ramulić stated, "No one has a real picture of how many people have left. . . . There are real indications that there are about 8,000 [remaining], but that number is still decreasing. There are many return communities in which no one is working. Everyone who is working is in farming or in some village store. No one goes to Prijedor, because for the returnees, there is no place [of employment] even for a doorman, a guard, or a cleaner."[54]

Since the war it has been common to hear that the goal of ethnic cleansing in Serb-controlled territory was that no more than a population of 5 percent non-Serbs should be permissible. There have even been reports that the Republika Srpska wartime parliament passed a resolution to this effect.[55] One can only ponder estimates that run between a 10 and 15 percent non-Serb population in the whole entity, without knowing whether they are accurate. However, with the present trend it is quite conceivable that the population of returnees in Prijedor will, before many more years pass, decrease to that level of 5 percent.

PART V

ATROCITY REVISIONISM

18

Denial of War Crimes at Srebrenica and Prijedor

THE STRUGGLE AGAINST HISTORICAL REVISIONISM IS A critical element of the ongoing campaign for truth and justice in Srebrenica, in Prijedor, and throughout Bosnia-Herzegovina. There is a widespread group of academics and other commentators who deny, in varying measure, that extreme nationalists committed aggression against the state of Bosnia-Herzegovina and that in the course of that aggression, they committed war crimes, expulsion, and genocide. This group includes self-identified Leftists who, for various reasons, openly or inadvertently ally themselves with criminal regimes in what they imagine is an expression of anti-imperialism.

To conceal or distort the truth about these war crimes is an offense to justice, and people concerned with human rights should be aware of such distortions.

Countless lies are the standard, necessary fare of the perpetrators of war crimes and their political heirs who are in power today. Among these are assertions to the effect that the Srebrenica genocide never happened; that the Markale bombings in Sarajevo were perpetrated by government forces against their own citizens to garner sympathy or prompt intervention; and that Trnopolje was, as typically worded, a "collection center set up for the safety of its inhabitants."

Historical distortions and enforced amnesia are promoted, first by the war criminals and their close collaborators, and then by the politicians and profiteers who have benefited vastly from the wartime actions of their predecessors. Political operators such as Milorad Dodik have everything to gain by pretending that the violent establishment of the Serb-controlled entity was somehow a just and necessary development.

Finally, the historical distortions are then repeated by misguided, dishonest, or fascist-leaning Western commentators and pundits whose positions range across a political spectrum from neo-Nazis to a fringe group that is sometimes called the "neo-Stalinist Left."

In the case of war crimes perpetrated in Bosnia, the comparison between Holocaust denial and revisionism is limited because Nazism was defeated, making it possible to prohibit Holocaust denial, and to punish pro-Nazi expressions (at least in Europe). No such thing took place in Bosnia, where the nationalists and separatists still reign.

In the West and elsewhere there is a circle of reactionary politicians and conservative ideologues—including Islamophobic commentators—who continue to deny the war crimes. For those of us concerned with human rights and the long-term struggle for justice, more disturbing are the members of the Left who participate in the denial. It is shocking to witness people who have been members of the worldwide movement for peace and justice grossly misreading the breakup of Yugoslavia and the Bosnian war.

While it is confounding to encounter atrocity revisionism on the part of progressive thinkers, it is possible to sort out several factors that contribute to their error. One is certainly the complicated history of Yugoslavia and its breakdown. A member of the Non-aligned Movement, Yugoslavia was part of neither the Warsaw Pact nor NATO. Its turbulent history tended to escape the attention of people focusing on Vietnam, then Central America, and other more prominent hot spots around the world.

Most Western progressives paid little attention to Yugoslavia as Tito died, economic crises struck, nationalism rose, and the country began to fall apart. Then, when the bloodshed began, it was all but too late to understand the situation without serious study. Quick primers that were produced at that time were insufficient and misleading.

In this vein, Western commentators prone to simplistic analysis repeated talk-show analyses along the lines of "It's an ancient ethnic problem, and there's nothing we can do about it," which absolved them of the responsibility to understand the situation further. Another popular and shallow explanation was that after the fall of the Berlin Wall in 1989, the West was eager to destabilize "the last socialist country in Europe." Purveyors of this analysis ignored the fact that the destabilization of Yugoslavia was at heart a domestic phenomenon, and that it began well before 1989.

As mainstream Western politicians, at least rhetorically, opposed Milošević's and then Tuđman's aggressive policies toward Bosnia-Herzegovina in the early 1990s, some Leftist commentators succumbed to another dangerous fallacy. They concluded, in effect, that they must necessarily defend Milošević since he was a target of the US administration. There are, of course, gradations on this theme, since it is not so easy to take the side of Milošević. But many Left pundits, in the habit of opposing all US policy regardless, found it impossible to hold two opposing thoughts simultaneously. It was, apparently, too complicated to understand that while the United States, as the lone superpower of the era, pursued a drive for increased influence around the world, there could at the same time be other actors who aspired to regional hegemony and whose policies were odious.

In the words of David Watson, a colleague in opposing revisionism:

> For the ostensibly radical antiwar Left, the wars in the former Yugoslavia have been a paradigm-wrecker. For example, the no-brainer that the US empire's motives are not humanitarian but cynical, hypocritical, and self-serving now passes in many quarters as proof of some coherent capitalist conspiracy to carve up the Balkans, and by extension, proof that Serbia was the innocent victim of the New World Order. While it is certainly true that capitalism is always and everywhere carving and re-carving, this one-dimensional anti-imperialism surrenders to what Slavoj Žižek has called the error of "double blackmail," the false choice between the empire and its enemies.[1]

Of course, there are reasons to oppose a broad range of US policies in the post–Cold War period. But on the question of the Bosnian war, members of the Left punditocracy tended to inform themselves inadequately, to participate in group-think, to quote and cite each other exclusively in their statements and writings, and to maintain an unfortunate distance from the reality of the atrocities.

This leads one to the conclusion that pundits are not to be trusted and should be taken off their pedestals; that facts must be checked; and that we must do our own work in understanding history.

Well-intentioned progressive people are sometimes confused when they hear that respected commentators such as Noam Chomsky or Michael Moore have expressed a mistaken position on the breakdown of Yugoslavia or the war in Bosnia. These are just a couple of examples from a longer list, and it is all the more unsettling because these two figures have done admirable work in the interest of justice over the years. It is disconcerting to observe that people with an antifascist background, who have consistently worked for justice, have fallen in with those whose policies have led to a devastated country dotted with mass graves.*

Confronting the Left deniers is all the more complicated because, in varying measure, there are points of political unity between them and progressives who advocate for truth and justice in Bosnia-Herzegovina. For example, among the two groups most people probably agree, at least in principle, that racism is wrong, that male supremacy is wrong, and that military aggression on any scale is wrong. Thus, while deniers on the Left seem incapable of simultaneously criticizing both US policy and some targets of that policy (such as Milošević), it is necessary for us to maintain clarity in the fight against atrocity revisionism.

Progressive thinkers who are familiar with regional dynamics in the western Balkans differ with the Left revisionists in our understanding of the causes of the dissolution of Yugoslavia. And some champions of human rights in that region have become so dismayed by the phenomenon of denial that they have been swayed to accept the characterization of "humanitarian intervention" to refer to the United States' and NATO's involvement in bringing the Bosnia war to an end. While the right and wrong of that intervention need not be sorted out here, it should be clear that morality is not a factor that influences the politics of a superpower. The deniers know this; we must not forget it.

Finally, coming back to Bosnia, the denial and distortion of the atrocities in Srebrenica and elsewhere is the utmost insult to the victims and the survivors of those crimes. Denial is of a piece with the vast crime of genocide, and it does no service to justice.

What follows is a brief overview introducing some of the deniers; only a sample of the most prominent figures will be introduced here.[2]

DENIAL OF THE SREBRENICA GENOCIDE

Where the war crimes that took place in Bosnia-Herzegovina are concerned, to a great extent the world's attention started and ended with the Srebrenica genocide, as if anything more than that was just too much for people to grasp. The crime at Srebrenica has served as a symbol for the entire range of war crimes throughout Bosnia, drawing much more attention than other crimes, such as those that were committed in the Prijedor area.

---

* Here I quote David Watson again: "One has to find this depressing in part because some of these people have had reasonable things to say about US support for dictatorships abroad, global capitalism, and other important related issues, and so they now function either to recruit the naturally skeptical into a counter-cult with its own authoritarian mystifications, or they simply discredit worthy opposition altogether through a kind of Gresham's law by which healthy ethical reasoning is driven out by paranoia and dogmatism."

Srebrenica is also an outsized focus of attention because it is the only case in which there have been criminal convictions for genocide. While there is a specifically worded legal definition of genocide, in common usage the word has a connotation of "the worst crime anyone can commit" and thus has more condemnatory impact than any other label. As such, it is more vehemently denied, and the interpretation of the concept of genocide is more enthusiastically distorted.

There is a close linkage between the history of the fall of Srebrenica and the conclusion of the war, which ended with the international recognition of the partition of Bosnia-Herzegovina. The two-entity system was legitimized by the Dayton agreement, and the Republika Srpska, where Srebrenica is located, also received political legitimacy through the consent of the majority of its inhabitants in the immediate postwar period. Given this, the political leaders of the RS have had a pronounced stake in cleaning up their history and denying the reality of Srebrenica.

This denial, at home and abroad, surfaces in many kinds of statements:

"There was no massacre at Srebrenica."

"The only people (or most of the people) who were killed were soldiers."

"Srebrenica was a base for Muslim military operations."

"A crime took place in Srebrenica, but it was the act of some individuals who did not answer to the RS army."

"A terrible crime took place in Srebrenica, but it was not genocide."

"The numbers of victims are inflated."

"People who were said to be killed in Srebrenica showed up later to vote in elections."

The variations on these themes of denial go on and on. The more subtle denial admits part of the history and calls the atrocity a "tragedy" rather than a "crime."

Likewise, there are numerous faces of Srebrenica genocide denial. The principal atrocity deniers are, understandably, the perpetrators themselves and their direct political heirs. A good example of their self-exoneration is the 2002 "unofficial" report on Srebrenica by Darko Trifunović, described in Chapter 8. Although the RS government distanced itself from this report and it was essentially refuted by the report of the Srebrenica Commission in 2004, its tenets have not lost currency among atrocity deniers.

Addressing the phenomenon of atrocity revisionism, Hariz Halilović has written, "What was ten years ago considered extremism is today accepted as a legitimate political attitude; hate speech is being presented as freedom of speech, and discrimination and racism are disguised as [an ethnicity's] vital national interest. In short, an all-encompassing domestication of evil and the rehabilitation of criminals . . . is in effect."[3]

One of the most prominent exponents of denial is Milorad Dodik, who has provided a textbook case of the manipulation of politics in the postwar period. What has been said of Slobodan Milošević could also be said of Dodik: that he did not start out as a nationalist, but he used extreme nationalism to attract votes and to consolidate power.

During Dodik's first term as RS prime minister, he acknowledged that a war crime had taken place at Srebrenica. Shortly after the first large commemoration of the massacre took place at Potočari in July 2000, he said, "We have to be aware that, according to available reports, a mass crime was perpetrated in Srebrenica, and people whose loved ones were killed there have an absolute right to mark this." Dodik's statement was calculated to endear him to the international community in a period when his popularity among RS voters was at a low point. Indeed, that year, he was defeated by an SDS candidate in an election for the RS presidency.[4]

In the five years that Dodik worked to return to power in the Republika Srpska, he modified his message to adhere to a line that proved successful with voters. In keeping with this strategy, Dodik's tone with regard to Srebrenica evolved.

In 2008, still implicitly acknowledging that an atrocious crime had taken place at Srebrenica, Dodik blamed it on Radovan Karadžić's SDS party. He stated that the killing had been organized "by local government officials and Bosnian Serb military leaders in the town of Bratunac," near Srebrenica.[5] In this vein, soon after the Srebrenica anniversary that year, he uttered the word "genocide," saying, "It is clear that what happened in Srebrenica was a local genocide committed by a small number of soldiers and army officers."[6]

From that point on, Dodik turned away from acknowledgment of genocide and worked to distort the definition of the term. There is one legal definition of genocide, as laid out in the 1948 UN Genocide Convention.[7] In early 2010 Dodik asserted that the characterization of the Srebrenica massacres as genocide was a political one. Ignoring the UN definition, he further stated that "when you look at textbook definitions of genocide, it is clear that it is difficult to find all their elements in the Srebrenica events. There was no intention to hurt children, women, and the elderly, and they were not hurt."[8]

Dodik's pronouncement was clearly directed at his domestic voting constituency in a general election year, and he hit on a successful strategy to maintain his popularity and power. In tandem with genocide denial, part of this strategy was to confuse and frighten his constituency by asserting that a determination of genocide was equivalent to tarring the entire Serbian people with collective guilt.[9] In fact, the ongoing judicial processes, ever since the end of the war, were engaged in establishing individual guilt. However, Dodik was not a scholar, but a politician. And in his use of the rhetoric of fear, he was proving to be the most skilled leader in Bosnia-Herzegovina.

By 2010, in addition to the finding of the International Court of Justice that acknowledged genocide in Srebrenica, several cases in the ICTY had resulted in convictions for genocide or aiding and abetting genocide as well. But by this time Dodik was regularly denying that genocide had taken place. Although he was willing to acknowledge that a "cruel crime" had taken place at Srebrenica, he periodically reiterated that it was not genocide. Dodik qualified the killings at Srebrenica as "revenge" for the earlier alleged attacks by Naser Orić against Serbs in the region.[10]

In the fall of 2010, writing for *Dani* magazine, Emir Imamović commented on the motivation for Dodik's evolution. In a speech in Srebrenica during his run for president of the Republika Srpska, Dodik declaimed, "It was not genocide here and we will not accept that it was genocide, because it was not genocide. More Bosniaks left Srebrenica during those months and went to Tuzla and Sarajevo than were killed here. So it was not genocide."

Imamović then described a conversation that had taken place between Dodik and SDA leader Sulejman Tihić after a particularly nationalistic outburst by Dodik. Tihić said to Dodik, "Why are you talking like this? I know you, Mile [nickname for Milorad], you're not like that." Dodik responded, "Fuck off, Suljo. I came to power by speaking this way, and that's how I'm going to stay in power."[11]

Another instance of Dodik's ideological evolution is demonstrated by his treatment of Radovan Karadžić. In earlier years Dodik had criticized him; after the war, Dodik had called Karadžić a "villain" and "an annoyance for the Serb people." While Karadžić was in hiding, Dodik had said that Karadžić and Mladić "had never been heroes" and called on them to turn themselves in.[12]

Dodik later softened his position, saying that Karadžić had "made mistakes, but should be credited with establishing Republika Srpska. RS was founded because of his courage."[13] He similarly called Karadžić a "historically important personality as he gathered a strong political force and mobilised people to defend the national interests" of Bosnia's Serbs.[14]

Taking his interpretation of history a step further, Dodik stated that if genocide had taken place in eastern Bosnia, "it was committed against Serb people of this region where women, children and the elderly were killed en masse."[15] In mid-2017, Dodik declared that textbooks in the Republika Srpska would never contain lessons about the siege of Sarajevo and Srebrenica, nor about the genocide of Bosniaks in Srebrenica.[16] And capping off his praise of war criminals, when Ratko Mladić was convicted of genocide and crimes against humanity in late 2017, Dodik called Mladić "a hero" and termed his conviction "a slap in the face to Serbs."[17]

In the summer of 2018, in the run-up to national elections in which Dodik was campaigning to become Serb member of the state-level presidency, he announced an initiative to annul the 2004 Srebrenica Commission report on the killings that took place on the fall of the Srebrenica enclave. In a clear ploy to gain popularity during the election campaign, Dodik asserted that the report had been "manipulated" and that it was "used to sentence many Serbs for war crimes at The Hague and in the Bosnian court."[18]

Dodik also stated that the figures in the report were "untrue," and that the Srebrenica Commission had "no evidence of guilt."[19] Both Bosniak and Serb opposition figures in the Republika Srpska decried the annulment, but it was carried out during a special session of the RS Parliament, in August 2018.[20] To enshrine Dodik's far-reaching revisionism, in early 2019 the RS government established two "investigative commissions," one to study the events surrounding the fall of Srebrenica, and another to examine the impact of the war on Serbs living in Sarajevo. The creation of these two commissions, complete with "international experts" selected by the RS government, flew in the face of more than two decades of investigation, producing tens of thousands of pages of evidence, by internationally respected courts.[21]

The US State Department, the OSCE, the UN High Commission for Human Rights, and other international bodies denounced the moves. Commentator Kemal Kurspahić wrote that the annulment of the 2004 report was an "escalation of the denial of the nature and extent of the crime [at Srebrenica]."[22]

Taking the "denial industry" into the "non-profit sector," the government of the Republika Srpska has provided funding to the "Srebrenica Historical Project," a "non-governmental organization" wholly devoted to revisionism. Between 2008 and 2012 the RS granted nearly US$1.1 million dollars to this outfit.[23] This Netherlands-based organization was headed by the Serbian American Stephen Karganović.

In March 2009, Karganović announced to news outlets that his organization was filing a lawsuit against the Dutch state and the United Nations for their "failure to protect Serbs" in the villages around Srebrenica. With this move, in an apparent imitation of the Srebrenica survivors' lawsuit, the Srebrenica Historical Project launched an attempt to equate Serb casualties with those of the Muslim population. Karganović's lawsuit argued that Dutchbat failed to protect Serbs from attacks launched by Muslim forces from Srebrenica.[24]

This argument turns history on its head by finessing the fact that Srebrenica was an enclave under siege. The lawsuit alleged that some thirty-five hundred Serbs were killed by raiding Muslims in the Srebrenica area.[25] While this figure has come into wide circulation among Serb revisionists, it is greatly distorted in the case of Srebrenica. It more accurately reflects the number of Serb casualties—both military and civilian—throughout the entire war in the broader Birač region encompassing Srebrenica, Vlasenica, Bratunac, and Zvornik.

In a sordid but unsurprising postscript to the story of Karganović's dishonesty in the service of war crimes revisionism, in spring 2016 the Republika Srpska filed tax evasion charges against its own protégé. The RS Ministry of the Interior reported that Karganović had failed to report his income from the years 2008 to 2014. Karganović had apparently evaded paying taxes in the amount of over 104,000 KM on the funds he had received from the RS government for his "NGO."[26]

The Serbian American Srdja Trifković is another person who has been very active in speaking up at The Hague for Serbs accused of war crimes, as well as making a career out of denying the fact of the atrocities committed by Serb extremists during the war. Trifković's work, in fact, goes beyond addressing those crimes to the construction of a rhetorical assault on Islam. In *The Sword of the Prophet*, Trifković presents Islam as a "violent religion" that is incompatible with the rest of civilization and that aims to impose itself on the entire world by any means necessary.[27] The book further asserts that Bosnia's Muslims constitute a threat to European civilization within its own borders.[28]

Trifković has a rich background in collaboration with war criminals and in the defense of persons accused of war crimes in Bosnia-Herzegovina. During the war he was a spokesman for Radovan Karadžić, and afterward he served as a consultant to Biljana Plavšić. He also worked at times as a spokesman for the Republika Srpska government.[29] Along the way, Trifković testified on behalf of several defendants at the ICTY, including people who were convicted of various crimes against humanity, genocide, murder, and extermination.

With such credentials, Trifković has apparently been sought after as a relevant analyst in the West, both in the media and in academic circles. He has worked consistently to deny the record of atrocities committed during the war by his confederates in Bosnia. He is quoted as saying, "Even if there was a massacre there, then there has been a grotesque distortion of the term 'genocide.'"[30]

Trifković has further described the Srebrenica enclave as an "armed camp used for attacks against Serb villages in the surrounding areas,"[31] ignoring the fact that Srebrenica was besieged for more than three years. Over the years, while admitting that a war crime took place at Srebrenica, he repeatedly asserts that the number of victims executed is inflated; that genocide did not take place; and that there is a "relentless Western campaign against the Serbs and in favor of their Muslim foes."[32]

Trifković implicitly revives the oft-repeated defense used by apologists for Serb extremists' war crimes: that Serbia serves as a Christian bulwark against Islam in Europe—a position that dates back to the time of the Crusades. Trifković goes so far as to say that Islam should be banned if it cannot be reformed: "We should not 'hate' [Islam], nor ban it, if it reforms itself to the standards of a civilized, that is, non-Muslim society. If it does not happen—and miracles are always possible—it should be banned, of course."[33]

In February 2011, Trifković was denied entry into Canada, where he was scheduled to give a lecture at the University of British Columbia in Vancouver. His lecture for the Serbian Students Association entitled "The Balkans: Uncertain Prospects for an Unstable Region" was blocked because he was deemed "inadmissible on grounds of violating human or international rights for being a proscribed senior official in the service of a government that, in the opinion of the minister, engages or has engaged in terrorism, systematic or gross human rights violations, or genocide, a war crime or a crime against humanity within the meaning of subsections 6 (3) to (5) of the Crimes Against Humanity and War Crimes Act."[34]

In a response to criticism of this decision Srdja Pavlović, a Serbian Canadian professor at the University of Alberta, commented that "denying genocide should not be called freedom of speech."[35] On appeal, the ban on Trifković's entry to Canada was lifted in mid-2015.

"PROGRESSIVE" ATROCITY DENIERS AND REVISIONISTS

The people described above who have been involved in denial and distortion of wartime atrocities escape public attention, for the most part, in the West. Their apologies for war crimes register as an insignificant phenomenon, if at all, on the radar of activists for human rights and justice around the world. However, there is also a network of Western commentators in the progressive community who defend or deny the war crimes that took place in Bosnia.

All but a handful of the Western atrocity revisionists are, again, unknown to the broad progressive community. Their stances vary from outright extreme nationalist, Islamophobic sympathy to disingenuous commentary. Such discourse surreptitiously distorts the reality of the war to the point that one can either assume that "all sides were equally guilty," or that the whole affair is too complicated to take time to sort out. However, there is an ideological space where this network of deniers overlaps with those who take the side of the war criminals. There, the rhetoric adopted by some is so similar to that of the war criminals and their local defenders that that such deniers appear to take their cues directly from those Bosnian and Serbian sources.

Given that human rights activists strive to support struggles for justice around the world, it is important that we be aware of those in our community who, through confusion, ideological bent, or ill will, are betraying decent values.

Diana Johnstone

Diana Johnstone was European correspondent for the progressive American magazine *In These Times* and periodically wrote for *counterpunch.org*. In 2002, Monthly Review Press published her book *Fools' Crusade: Yugoslavia, NATO and Western Delusions*. The book begins with a criticism of the American drive for increased worldwide military and economic influence in the period after the dissolution of the Soviet Union. This criticism has merit; however, the book goes on to defend targets of Western intervention as if it were necessary to exonerate every adversary of the United States, regardless of their behavior.

This reflexive binary thinking is a flaw among doctrinaire Leftists, leading them at times even to defend such figures as Saddam Hussein and others who are bona fide war criminals.

Johnstone's book is a low-grade polemic that takes the statements of people all the way up to Slobodan Milošević at face value when they support her positions, and that dismantles arguments with which she disagrees through sideswipes, prolific scare quotes, and insinuations along the lines of guilt by association. Along with denying or trivializing the use of rape as a war tactic,[36] and the establishment of Serb-run concentration camps,[37] Johnstone repeats many of the distortions about Srebrenica that have been introduced above.

Among other distortions, Johnstone states that the Srebrenica enclave was a "Muslim military base," ignoring the fact that the enclave was under a murderous starvation siege, and implying that the attempts by those penned up in the enclave to expand it from within—and to gather food—justified the subsequent massacres. She further mentions Naser Orić's early removal from the enclave and brings up rumors of a decision by Izetbegović to sacrifice Srebrenica, as if any of this could ameliorate the fact of the genocide. Johnstone calls the killings after the fall of Srebrenica "spontaneous revenge," ignoring the fact that such a large-scale operation of murder, burial, and covert reburial could not possibly have taken place without significant logistical planning—and that the planning is well-documented.[38] Finally, she puts the number of men who, to her mind, could be thought of as having been executed at 199, referring to the number of remains that had been, at the time of her writing, found bound and/or blindfolded.[39]

In more recent years Johnstone has exposed her distorted thinking by writing extensively in support of the extreme-right French politician Marine Le Pen.[40]

Edward Herman

Edward Herman was a retired professor of finance and a media analyst. Before his death in 2017, he distinguished himself in the progressive community by collaborating with Noam Chomsky. Over a period of a couple of decades from the late 1960s on, Chomsky and Herman coauthored several books, most prominently the 1988 volume *Manufacturing Consent: The Political Economy of the Mass Media*. Herman's association with Chomsky, though later terminated, afforded him familiarity in progressive circles.

Herman was for the most part an unknown figure in the mainstream, and, given this, it would seem that his voluminous work in atrocity denial and distortion of the history of the former Yugoslavia would not amount to much. However, there is a multiplier effect in which other deniers quoted Herman, he quoted other deniers, and together this network built a cache of falsified history that appeared, to the uninformed and to the willing followers, to have some respectable substance. For example, in 2002 Herman wrote the endorsement that is found on the opening page of Diana Johnstone's *Fools' Crusade*, which calls the book a "'must book' for progressives . . . an excitingly original and powerful book."

Edward Herman spent many years writing books and articles about the breakdown of Yugoslavia, in a rather casual style. His analysis resembled that found in the discredited 2002 Republika Srpska report on Srebrenica.

Just a few days before the tenth anniversary of the fall of Srebrenica, Herman came out with a twelve-page article titled "The Politics of the Srebrenica Massacre,"[41] a systematic compilation of distortions, unfounded theories, and misleading half-truths about the event. A few examples follow.

Herman regularly called into question the number of victims of the massacre and the nature of the remains found in mass graves. He asserted, as other deniers have done, that these graves contained both Muslim fighters and Serb soldiers. This has been firmly disproved by expert witnesses in numerous court proceedings in the ICTY. Conveniently, Herman also disputed the validity of all work of the ICTY, once even asserting that its staff "had been largely appointed" by Madeleine Albright.[42]

One of the more astonishing assertions by Herman in this article is his characterization of the Bosnian Muslims' "willingness to kill their own people" in order to prompt assistance from NATO.[43] Human rights advocates concerned with Bosnia-Herzegovina are familiar with this position, repeated by many figures from Radovan Karadžić on down; again, there is no basis in fact for this, and at least with regard to the Markale bomb massacres, it has been addressed and refuted numerous times in court.

Another gross distortion is the scenario of a large military force in the Srebrenica enclave. It is true that there were thousands of men in the besieged enclave; that some of them had arms; and that there was a military structure of a sort. But it is also true that the enclave was surrounded, that Serb forces outgunned and starved the population of Srebrenica, and that even Dutch UN forces undermined the local population's ability to defend itself. Herman suggested that the Srebrenica defense sacrificed itself, the enclave, and the civilian population in order to prompt a foreign intervention.[44] Such an assertion is not only an affront to decency, but it has also been refuted by the testimony of those who stayed in the Srebrenica enclave and defended themselves until the last possible minute.

A particularly amateurish distortion by Herman was the assertion that the numbers killed do not add up, since the population of Srebrenica municipality before the war is known to have been approximately thirty-seven thousand, and there were too many survivors for eight thousand to have been killed. Herman stated that these numbers "would require the prewar population of Srebrenica to have been 47,000 if 8,000 were executed," even though it is common knowledge that thousands of refugees from the entire Podrinje region had fled to Srebrenica as they were expelled from their homes. Many of those who were killed in the massacres were not originally from Srebrenica, but from Višegrad to Zvornik, and as far away as Vlasenica.

In 2007, the Old Left magazine *Monthly Review* shamed itself by devoting an entire issue to a forty-five-page (plus footnotes) article by Edward Herman and colleague David Peterson titled "The Dismantling of Yugoslavia."[45] In the section titled "The UN, ICTY, and the Srebrenica Massacre," the authors repeated their questioning of the numbers of the massacre and their anachronistic statement that in 2001 "Srebrenica-related gravesites had produced 2,028 sets of individual remains"—a figure that was significantly out of date by the time of the article.

In 2010, Herman and Peterson released their book *The Politics of Genocide*.[46] The volume was given a foreword by Noam Chomsky, and endorsed favorably by Diana Johnstone, as well as the journalists and analysts John Pilger, Norman Solomon, David Barsamian, and others. In the book, the authors present many of the disingenuous assertions about the Srebrenica massacre repeated by other revisionists. They particularly distort the definition of genocide beyond recognition, ignoring the UN Genocide Convention and insisting that the Nazi Holocaust is the only possible standard for such a definition.[47]

One can justifiably ask why so many progressive analysts, some of whom have made indisputably valuable contributions to knowledge and understanding of human rights issues, could venture to damage their reputations by falling in with Edward Herman. One possible reason is that some of the reviewers did not read the book or read it too quickly. Another is that some commentators—in any case not so well informed about the issue—are more concerned about their position in the network of pundits than they are concerned with the truth, and they are too comfortable in that club. And a third is that some analysts are so blinded by their anger at American policies that they have become incapable of recognizing that an opposing side in conflict with the West can also be wrong.

Noam Chomsky

In 2004, the writer M. Junaid Alam interviewed Noam Chomsky for the website Left Hook. The interview was published under the title "Civilization versus Barbarism?" During the interview, Chomsky provides a wide-ranging overview of war crimes, atrocities, and terrorist attacks, comparing various events that took place in Iraq, Chile, Nicaragua, Burundi, Germany, and Chechnya, among others. In his presentation Chomsky illustrates the scale of crimes perpetrated or supported by the United States as compared with those that come under the rubric of "Islamic terrorism," and shows the latter to be significantly smaller in scale. I do not argue with this overall presentation.

However, while mentioning the massacre at Fallujah, Iraq, which took place in the same year as this interview, Chomsky compares the event with the Srebrenica massacres. He comments that the military onslaught against Fallujah was "very much like Srebrenica—which is universally condemned as genocide—Srebrenica was an enclave, lightly protected by UN forces, which was being used as a base for attacking nearby Serb villages. It was known that there's going to be retaliation. When there was a retaliation, it was vicious. They trucked out all the women and children; they kept the men inside, and apparently slaughtered them. The estimates are thousands of people slaughtered."[48]

It is more than implicit in the wording of this statement that the Muslim population of the enclave was the aggressor in the conflict—practically inviting revenge. What is omitted is the entire background of the siege of Srebrenica and the development of the enclave. It would not have been necessary for Chomsky to stray far afield from the topic of the interview in order to make it clear that the inhabitants of the Srebrenica enclave were surrounded, besieged, starved, and shelled for several years. Instead, the impression an uninformed reader gets is that those inhabitants were aggressors and the provocateurs of their own massacre.

Toward the end of 2005 the journalist Emma Brockes published a controversial interview with Noam Chomsky in the British daily newspaper the *Guardian*. Owing to some unfortunate journalistic exaggeration on Brockes's part and a misleading pull quote, the interview was removed from circulation, but it is available on the Internet.[49] Parts of it are revealing of Chomsky's attitudes toward Bosnia and denial.

Chomsky has long presented himself as a defender of free speech, and there are other instances where he falls back on this stance in response to criticism of his apparent support for very offensive positions. In the interview with Brockes, Chomsky asserts, "And Diana Johnstone, whether you like it or not, has done serious, honest work." He also hedges, saying, "It may be wrong; but it is very careful and outstanding work." As Brockes expressed, it was difficult not to be confused about this statement.[50]

In the *Guardian* interview, one can observe that when pressed, Chomsky not only falls back on the freedom of speech defense but goes on the attack, calling critics "hysterical" and "irrational," saying, "if you depart a couple of millimetres from the party line, you're a traitor, you're destroyed. It's totally irrational."[51]

It is understandable that Chomsky wishes to make sure that ordinary observers of political events are aware of the scale of responsibility for atrocities that is borne by the United States, as the most powerful state in the world. But he has the unfortunate tendency to wander carelessly into discussion of history about which he is not an expert and, when confronted, to make matters worse by going on the offense and attacking the critic, making irrelevant and trivializing comparisons, or denying that he has taken positions he has undeniably taken.[52]

Noam Chomsky is not a flat-out atrocity denier, nor does he openly side with the war criminals and their supporters, as did Edward Herman. In an interview with Serbian television journalist Danilo Mandić, both Chomsky and Mandić openly refer to the Srebrenica massacres as such; Chomsky also slams Slobodan Milošević.[53] Given this, and given the fact that progressives and defenders of human rights tend to adore Chomsky, it is all the more confusing when he sides with those who deny the war crimes in the former Yugoslavia—which he does in the same interview, denying the vicious nature of the concentration camps around Prijedor.

In this vein, in an interview with Andrew Stephen of the *New Statesman* in June 2006, Chomsky acknowledges that Srebrenica was the "worst crime" (of the Bosnian war) but insists that Milošević had no responsibility for the atrocity, and that it was primarily the responsibility of the Dutch government. Chomsky gives undue weight to a Dutch report (without identifying the report), saying that it exonerates Milošević of responsibility for the massacres.[54] These statements reduce the atrocity to a Dutch mistake.

In mid-2011, the British activist and author George Monbiot took Noam Chomsky to task for having written the foreword to Edward Herman and David Peterson's book *The Politics of Genocide*. In a letter he asked, simply, whether Chomsky had read the book, and whether he considered his foreword an implicit endorsement of the book. He also asked whether Chomsky considered the book's description of the events at Srebrenica to be accurate.[55]

Writing a foreword to a book seems so obviously an endorsement of the same that, for my part, I would not have bothered to inquire of Chomsky about it. But the response from Chomsky, reproduced on Monbiot's website, is rather surprising. First, he denies that the word "genocide" applies to the case of Srebrenica. Then he characteristically goes on the counterattack by changing the subject and bringing up the denial of genocide in the United States, as if this denial cancels out that of Herman and Peterson. Subsequently, he openly rejects the idea that there is any implicit endorsement of a book involved in having written its foreword.[56]

On one hand, Chomsky praises the atrocity revisionists who have written a book of denial—which he refers to as a "powerful inquiry."[57] On the other hand, he denies having done so. In his final letter to Monbiot, Chomsky first trivializes the question of how many people the Serb forces killed at Srebrenica, and then states that it is not known, and can probably never be known. This, after numerous witnesses testified at war crimes trials, after dozens of mass graves were uncovered, and after thousands of victims were identified and reburied. The facts about the Srebrenica massacres are, to use one of Chomsky's stock phrases, a matter of public record.

The fact that over several decades Chomsky has become established as a venerable authority in progressive antiwar and human rights circles makes the impact of his revisionism powerful. A couple of generations of activists have grown up revering Chomsky for his clear and accurate description of, among many other things, what he has called an "intellectually totalitarian atmosphere" in the West. No other figure on the Left comes close to this man whom the *New York Times* described as "arguably the most important intellectual alive."[58]

Most readers do not have the time to check the facts behind what they are used to receiving as Chomsky's wisdom, and there is an entire coterie of writers and thinkers rhetorically situated around Chomsky, buttressing his positions. Some of these people do so intentionally, because they agree with his positions, and others do it unwittingly, because they are uninformed. Thus we are confronted with a serious absence of critical thinking in the presence of a revered analyst.

Referring to Noam Chomsky, David Watson wrote that "his role as a luminary itself is a central problem. Almost no one else can go around the world and speak to audiences looking for answers to their questions about everything from the economy to global warming to the situation in Nepal to Iraq to Latin America and on and on."[59]

Chomsky and the other revisionists described above are blinded by their anger at the United States as a perpetrator of large-scale military aggression. I share this revulsion. But the revisionists reflexively trivialize or deny the crimes of anyone who is an adversary of the United States.

There is in fact no contradiction between criticizing US war crimes and those of the smaller powers that the United States has targeted. Quite the contrary is true; what is at stake is moral consistency. It is a grave moral and intellectual failure on the part of Noam Chomsky and his admirers to miss this point.

In the case of Srebrenica, ultimately it is the survivors of the atrocity whose voices should be heard and with whom human rights advocates should stand in solidarity. In this vein, in 2006 Hasan Nuhanović, Srebrenica survivor and human rights activist, wrote an article titled "Who Is Noam Chomsky?"[60] Nuhanović outlines Chomsky's biography and then mentions some of the history of distortion that I have described above.

Nuhanović then poses several questions about Chomsky, wondering whether Chomsky was really convinced that the things that he said were true, or whether, alternatively, he had made mistakes and his ego would not let him admit it. Nuhanović notes that he wrote Chomsky via e-mail, offering to provide him with information about the case of Srebrenica. Chomsky "kindly responded," but did not wish to receive further information.

Nuhanović further wonders whether Chomsky was aware of how much damage he could create with his public statements. This point is critical to the discussion of revisionism. There are real people concerned, survivors who have lived through the atrocities and are seeking justice. For them, justice requires acknowledgment of the crimes that were committed, not denial and falsification of history. That falsification, first of all, works directly against the elucidation of the crimes and, for the victims, it adds insult to injury. And as Nuhanović noted in his article, it gives the perpetrators cause for celebration.[61]

ONE LAST POINT ABOUT DENIAL

It is more difficult to respond to the atrocity denial and revisionism as expressed by people who call themselves progressives, and are perceived as such by human rights activists, than it is to reject the distortions expressed by those, such as Karganović and Trifković, who openly sympathize with war criminals and support their actions. The most obvious obstacle to a clear understanding of what Western revisionists are doing is that, based on their past history as activists and analysts, we expect them to be working on the side of justice.

People who have fallen into the habit of admiring Left pundits without question may not notice when they have begun to stand on the wrong side of justice where the history is complicated. It is normal to trust people we consider to be intelligent and informed and look to them for analysis and answers, since no one has time to be well informed on all issues. But there is no substitute for questioning, and it is dangerous to be lulled into this kind of trusting mode.

We see that some prominent progressive analysts are essentially allying with the worst sort of human rights violators. When we discover this seemingly unlikely de facto alliance, we must expose it to an exacting public examination; this crucial work goes hand in hand with the entire struggle for truth and justice in the case of Srebrenica and Bosnia-Herzegovina in general.

Here, we see an added complication for progressive people who wish to understand and challenge the Left deniers, for those deniers are right about one thing. Many of the revisionists within the progressive community correctly perceive that after the breakup of Yugoslavia, the economies of its former republics have become ripe for plunder by international corporations, in collusion with domestic profiteers. This process of neo-liberal expansion into the weak states of the former Yugoslavia, and into their distressed economies, is quite clear.

We cannot deny that this process has taken place. The problem here is that in an exercise of the logical fallacy of *post hoc, ergo propter hoc*, the Left deniers assert that this was the plan all along. Here, they are retrofitting present reality to fit into their simplified anti-imperialist template, and that again puts them in alliance with the perpetrators of war crimes and nationalist expansionism who dishonestly declare that their fight is against Western imperialism.

But the breakup of Yugoslavia came from within, not as the result of an imperial plot. While some Western officials opposed the breakup at first, evidence shows that the international community exacerbated the process, unwittingly, through lack of organizational effort and lack of interest. It was only after the process was well underway that international corporations and governmental bodies began to find advantage in it.

Thus it is incumbent on those of us who are examining the work of the atrocity deniers and combating it to recognize that they are partly right: that the corporate and military components of the international community have taken advantage of the breakup of Yugoslavia. With a frank acknowledgment of this process, we can continue to expose the dishonesty of the deniers and the perpetuation of injustice that results from their analysis.

DENIAL OF WAR CRIMES IN PRIJEDOR

As with Srebrenica, denial of the crimes at Prijedor takes place on several levels. Perhaps the purest and most obvious denial, again, is heard in the courts. Then the lies radiate out from the perpetrators to their supporters and to gullible or murky personalities beyond, in Bosnia-Herzegovina and abroad.

The various lies belong to several categories, including the subject of who started the conflict in Prijedor and how it started; whether certain things (such as the existence of a concentration camp at Trnopolje) happened at all; what the nature of the camps was; and, of course, whether genocide was committed at Prijedor.

One of the more common tenets of denial, used in Prijedor as well as elsewhere, is that Serb forces organized to defend themselves against a "Muslim plan" to expel and destroy the Serbs. This position is used as a rationale for the legitimacy of the Republika Srpska as a separatist statelet. While it is a fact that even around Prijedor there were some small groupings of irregular fighters, including Muslims and Croats, who tried to defend themselves against the onslaught of Serb extremist forces in the spring of 1992, they were outnumbered and vastly outgunned and did not last very long.

The court record of the Serb organization and preparation for the takeover of Prijedor and the destruction of its non-Serb population, as led by the SDS and supported by Serbia's military infrastructure, is well documented and clear. There is no such record—especially in Prijedor—of significant support or advance preparation by the non-Serbs. Nevertheless, in an interview Dušan Berić, a key postwar leader of the Prijedor SDS, expressed the position aggressively. He asserted that Muslims in Kozarac had been "preparing the genocide of the Serbs. A list of Serbs to be liquidated was discovered in a mini-bunker."[62]

Similarly, during testimony for the defense at the trial of Radovan Karadžić, Boško Mandić, former vice president of Prijedor municipality and wartime member of the Crisis Staff, blamed the outbreak of the war on "Muslim extremists who killed soldiers at Hambarine and Kozarac in the spring of 1992." Mandić asserted that Muslims had "killed soldiers of the Yugoslav National Army, and police, and then refused to disarm; operations of the Serb forces followed this." Mandić went on to assert that "not a single governmental body organized nor supported the removal of non-Serbs from Prijedor."[63] And testifying for Ratko Mladić's defense, Zdravka Karlica, president of a Serb NGO in Prijedor, asserted that the conflict erupted when the "extreme part" of the SDA refused to disarm, and that "Muslim extremists were guilty of starting the conflict in Prijedor."[64]

Another revisionist version has it that non-Serbs were not expelled from the Prijedor region, but left of their own accord. Testifying during the defense phase of Radovan Karadžić's trial, Dragomir Keserović, introduced as a "military expert," asserted, "I believe that the population mostly moved out because war broke out in Bosnia, there was great insecurity, and everyone tried to leave and save themselves, their families and possessions. . . . The general conditions were the key cause for their moving out."[65] The explanation quoted here leaves the war in a wholly abstract context, as if it never happened that men with firearms came breaking down the doors of houses in villages around Prijedor and murdering civilians by the hundreds.

Another problematic construct that is often implicitly a tool in denial is the phrase "civil war." When the phrase is used by those who were involved in fomenting the war, and who manipulated ordinary people to serve as cannon fodder so that their superiors could entrench their power, then "civil war" is simply a cover-up. Again, the record of aggression, of the invasion of Bosnia-Herzegovina by Serbian troops at the beginning of the war and later, and of the generous sponsorship of Bosnian Serb separatists by the government of Serbia, has been clearly recorded in historical documentation that is available to everyone.[66]

There are those who use the phrase "civil war" from a distance, who perhaps are uninformed about the true nature of the war. They, the radio talk-show hosts and dilettante analysts, are unwittingly further propagating the lie. An overview of the war, its causes, and its planning supports the fact that it could not have happened without outside sponsorship, first from Serbia, and then from Croatia. So, to characterize the war as merely a "civil war" is a distortion, and often a conscious one.

A somewhat more subtle form of denial is the equation of guilt on all sides, accompanied by the phrase "war is war." I again quote Dušan Berić: "Alas! Crimes were committed on all sides."[67] It is not inaccurate to say that there were crimes committed on all sides, but this obscures the fact that planning, aggression, and intent were involved—disproportionately from one side—in the initiation of violence and the subsequent crimes. To say that "everyone was guilty" again places the scenario in an abstract realm, remote from the actual atrocities.

A somewhat more generous version of this distortion is the near-acknowledgment of some of the specific crimes in Prijedor, as we have seen in the case of Milan Kovačević. During Ratko Mladić's trial, Zdravka Karlica acknowledged that she had heard about the prison camps, and that non-Serb women and children had been killed during the war. This admission came on the heels of flagrantly inaccurate assertions that no non-Serbs were killed "where there were no attacks on Serb units."[68]

One of the more far-fetched distortions that cropped up in court testimony was that of a former security officer in the Serb army, Radomir Radinković, during Radovan Karadžić's trial. Speaking of the prison camp at Manjača, Radinković stated that the camp had the "highest standards of accommodation." He admitted that prisoners at Manjača were housed in cattle stalls but asserted that the hygienic conditions were suitable for human use.[69]

In fact, prisoners at Manjača, a camp where up to five thousand were interned from mid-1992 to the end of the year, often slept on concrete. They were fed poorly and beaten often.[70]

The distortions and untruths about Prijedor's war history expressed in court proceedings are repeated in the local and entity media, most of which are controlled by government and party infrastructures. From there the message filters into the consciousness of the ordinary people, many of whom, for various reasons, deny or distort what happened during the war.

There is much discussion about what ordinary Serbs knew or did not know about what was being done to non-Serbs. It is plausible that some Serbs did not know. Zdravka Karlica said that she was "shocked" when she learned of the Bosniak and Croat women and children who were killed during the war. Other Serbs were coping with their own trauma; there were, after all, thousands who had fled into the Prijedor area as refugees from other parts of Bosnia and from Croatia.

It is not credible, however, that no Serbs knew about what was taking place. The stories abound of neighbors and other people with a score to settle, and drunken people out of control, freely entering into the camps to abuse the prisoners. For example, Omarska is an isolated village in close proximity to the mining compound where atrocities were being committed continuously for several months running. In that area, denial at the ground level is complete. In a 2004 article, journalist Ed Vulliamy quotes mine security guards as saying, "There was no camp here. It was all lies, Muslim lies and forgery by the journalists."[71]

On the official level, citizens of Prijedor are often publicly encouraged to avoid confronting their recent past. Mayor Pavić, expressing an attitude familiar to other leaders who prefer to sweep crimes under the rug, said, "Prijedor and its youth need to move forward, to look to the future, and not turn toward the past."[72]

Addressing the pervasive denial promoted by local authorities, the Prijedor activist Sudbin Musić said, "Today we ask . . . how much more must the Sana flow before you comprehend that this dark stain on the reputation of the Serb people must be cleansed just like any other, and that the cry of horror from Omarska . . . burns our ears, seeking justice for all of the tears of the mothers, the fathers, the brothers, the sisters, and the little children whose dearest ended their days in this accursed place?"[73]

In the body of revisionism associated with the crimes against humanity that were committed in the Prijedor region, one instance of flagrant denial particularly stands out. That is the assertion that the camp at Trnopolje was a "collection center" where non-Serbs sought refuge voluntarily. This run-of-the-mill lie has distinguished itself by virtue of having spread out even beyond the local populace to the world at large. First uttered by the administrators of the camp, it was picked up and promoted by the international corps of deniers in Europe, people with murky motives who, intentionally or inadvertently, supported the rhetoric of the Serb separatists.

Former commander of Trnopolje Slobodan Kuruzović, in a reluctant 2003 interview with journalists from Sarajevo, first denied that he had ever been in charge of the camp. He added, "And that was no camp, it was an open center." He added, as if to provide conclusive proof, "It was written in English, 'Open Center.'"[74] Referring to Trnopolje during Ratko Mladić's trial, defense witness Slavko Puhalić stated that the camp was "intended for 'the removal of the non-Serb population from the combat zone . . . for their own protection.'"[75]

In the same trial, the former commander of the Serb territorial "defense force" in Prijedor, Rade Javorić, likewise asserted that non-Serbs were in the camps "of their own free will." Presiding Judge Alphons Orie challenged this statement, saying, "You have heard that people were raped and killed there, and you say that people went there voluntarily?"[76] Javorić elaborated, saying that "those who did not take up arms and did not participate in the fighting arrived there by themselves and were allowed to leave if they wanted, but those who were captured with arms or during fighting were not."[77]

The circumstances surrounding the camp at Trnopolje do not lend themselves freely to a black-and-white explanation; details can be picked out to support widely varying conclusions. It is true that a small number of terrified, displaced Bosniaks and Croats came to Trnopolje on their own steam. But this is not to say that they had any choice, when their homes were burning behind them and the region was crawling with deadly military forces. Given this, the term "voluntary" really has no application in connection with Trnopolje.

It is also true that, on occasion, guards gave permission to certain prisoners to leave the camp. There were evacuated houses nearby where people could bathe. And several survivors have told me that a guard accompanied them to their respective homes in Kozarac—before they were torched—in order to retrieve possessions. To some extent, this liberty was left up to the whim of a guard, and there were guards who allowed some leniency.

However, the fact that a few prisoners were allowed to go in and out of Trnopolje does not demonstrate that it was an "open camp"; survivor Kemal Pervanić explained to me that the entire village, in fact, was a "ghetto"—similar to the World War II ghetto where Jewish inhabitants had freedom of movement within specific confines. He said, "Everyone was herded there, not only to the camp, but also to the surrounding village. Some women could come and go with permission of the guards, but men could not go. They would be shot if they tried to leave."[78]

It has been documented, as mentioned in the section on war crimes in Prijedor, that several hundred people lost their lives in Trnopolje, in addition to widespread instances of beating, rape, and other abuse.

A team of journalists from the British Independent Television News (ITN) and Channel 4, led by Penny Marshall and Ian Williams and accompanied by Ed Vulliamy, visited Omarska and Trnopolje after having obtained permission to do so from Radovan Karadžić.[79] Ed Vulliamy reported in detail of the emaciated men he witnessed behind a barbed wire fence at Trnopolje. Photographs and video taken by the crew shocked the world with their grim resemblance to pictorial documentation from World War II. One of the photographs depicted prisoner Fikret Alić, from Kozarac, bare-chested and gaunt, with his ribs sticking out.

Fikret Alić had been transferred to Trnopolje from Keraterm shortly before the journalists arrived. Of life in Trnopolje, Alić later recounted, "We lay like cattle in the meadow. They had fenced us in with wires and told us that we would be a little better off there. But Trnopolje was a camp almost like Keraterm. Murders and rapes. They would take people into the woods and kill them, and then say that they had tried to escape."[80]

It was the reporting of the British journalists that forced international authorities into pressuring Serb leaders to close the camps, although that did not take place before hundreds more prisoners were quickly murdered.

While cover-up of the camps was perpetrated by Serb authorities from the beginning, it was not long before some foreign sympathizers took up the cause of denial.

The German writer Thomas Deichmann was one of those, attempting to testify for the defense in the trial of Duško Tadić. Just after the war, in 1996, Deichmann traveled to Bosnia to visit Trnopolje and to talk to wartime authorities who were still in control in the area. Soon afterward he wrote an article for a German magazine; that article was then translated and published in the British journal *Living Marxism* (*LM*) in early 1997. Titled "The Picture That Fooled the World," the article asserted that the photograph had been staged, and that it was the journalists who were, in fact, behind barbed wire and the prisoners had gathered to talk to them.[81]

There is a Serbian proverb, "A lie has short legs." The lie about the staging of the Trnopolje images has proven to be an exception to this adage. The Deichmann article was reprinted by Left apologists for Serbian atrocities in the West, including Diana Johnstone,[82] Edward Herman,[83] and the media watchdog Project Censored.[84]

In response to the attack on its journalistic integrity, lawyers representing ITN and the journalists involved filed a lawsuit for libel against *Living Marxism* in 1997. As the suit waited in the courts for the next three years, *LM* and other revisionists continued to promote their distortions and their condemnation of the journalists. When the lawsuit was finally resolved in favor of ITN in 2000, the penalty for damages on the finding of malicious libel was so high that *LM* was forced to go out of business.

In subsequent years Deichmann's story lived on, repeated by putative human rights advocates. Noam Chomsky supported it in more than one interview, stating that Ed Vulliamy's story was "probably not true," and lamenting that "a big corporation" put a "small newspaper out of business."[85] Using characteristically dodgy language, he stated that *LM* "was probably correct" about the fabrication of details about Trnopolje, and that "it was probably the reporters who were behind the barb-wire, and the place was ugly, but it was a refugee camp, I mean, people could leave if they wanted, and near the thin man was a fat man and so on."[86]

The by-now clichéd distortions about Trnopolje remained a favorite currency among people who testified in the defense of Ratko Mladić, whose charges included genocide in Prijedor. In March 2015, one Branko Berić testified and was quoted as saying that "no one as much as pulled the ear of an inmate in Trnopolje, let alone killed any civilians." He added that "conditions in Trnopolje were like in a Hyatt hotel," asserting that the prisoners had access, through Red Cross deliveries, to "better food than their Serb guards."[87]

It is notable that neither Deichmann, *LM*, Chomsky, nor any of the other commentators who supported Deichmann's denialism ever cited conversations with the original journalists involved or with survivors of Trnopolje.

The history of crimes against humanity in Prijedor is thus denied, and that denial is cemented by the fabrication of a cover story that talks about the "defense of the fatherland" (the newly formed Republika Srpska) from a Muslim threat. In that story, in the official discourse as articulated by the political leaders and the media, there is no room for the memory of the thousands of civilians killed and the tens of thousands expelled.

That culture of denial has been described well by the Bosnian artist and social commentator Nedim Seferović. He has written of denial of war crimes and the failure to confront the past, in the context of what he calls the "culture of collective moral indifference." Upon the discovery of a large mass grave at Tomašica in the Prijedor region, he criticized what he termed the "irrational denialist way of life of a great number of the inhabitants of Bosnia-Herzegovina [and] the apparent across-the-board disinterest in the repercussions of massive crimes committed not far from their doorstep."[88]

In his treatment of the phenomenon of mass denial, Seferović touches on the problem of collective responsibility, saying "that indifference is astonishing. . . . In its full capacity it is collective, pervasive, and loud in its silence." He elaborates further, saying, "In its totality the disconnect comprises the refusal to admit and accept the essential existence of Tomašica, not just as a heap of human bodies killed in the upwelling of an all-encompassing value system that justified and supported crime, but as the essence . . . of that system that was maintained for decades as normal, natural, regardless of how essentially inhuman, unnatural, and truly criminal it was."[89]

Seferović continues his commentary by describing the culture of denial as having a "Nazi-fascist character," and noting the "collective exaltation" upon the return of convicted war criminals after they had served their prison sentences. He locates denialism at the personal level, saying that "it can no longer be justified by an exceptional [wartime] social climate," and that "today it is a matter of choice."

There are, however, different kinds of choices, and people make many of those choices—very often unconsciously—based on a perception of risk and on the need to fit in with their peers. The matter of personal responsibility in moral questions brushes against all the evil that people do. Why does a foot soldier involved in aggressive military action not resist engaging in the organized perpetration of calamity, brutality, and mass murder—sometimes, at best, only to regret it afterward? What mother's son was raised to turn out this way? Where does guilt reside, and what is our portion as, very often, detached and indifferent citizens of a society that is committing crimes?

In this vein, it is appropriate to remember here the thinking of Karl Jaspers, who in his book *The Question of German Guilt* addressed the responsibility of Germany as a nation for the war crimes and atrocities that had been committed. Jaspers considered that all citizens of a state are in some way involved in the political conduct of that state, and given that, all citizens somehow experience the consequences of the state's policies.

To the extent that there has been collective involvement in crimes that a state has committed, then the citizens of that state have the moral obligation to own up to their participation in the crimes and to advocate for rectification of the damage done. Americans, for example, have this moral responsibility given the pervasive racism in the United States and the ongoing damage and violence caused by that racism.

Likewise, the citizens of Bosnia-Herzegovina—and not only the Bosnian Serbs—have the personal responsibility to examine the record of the crimes that were committed in their name, and to advocate for redressing the damage that was done. This would be part of the process of confronting the past (*suočavanje s prošlošću*), and it is, as expressed earlier, not only a prerequisite for justice, but also a precondition for the healing of society.

Commentator Eric Gordy has identified obstacles to this process, noting the boundary "between guilt and responsibility." He writes that examination of the past "confronts a whole set of ideas, orientations and conditions that are not crimes, but collectively contribute to constructing and maintaining an atmosphere in which crime is both possible and seen as necessary or normal. . . . These things comprise an unavoidable part of understanding how historical events occurred, as well as a potentially uncomfortable part of many people's personal memories." Rephrasing the thoughts of Karl Jaspers, Gordy concludes that "all members of a political community carry an obligation to understand the past, to recognize needs that derive from it, and to address those needs in the future."[90]

The denial of collective political and therefore moral responsibility is pervasive not only among Bosnian Serbs, but also among Bosnian Croats and Muslims as well. In this context, Nedim Seferović's characterization of denial as "Nazi-fascist" seems harsh. But it is necessary to confront the harsh reality manifested by the psychology of fascism, and to acknowledge that fear and lack of empathy, the seeds of fascism, are present in all of us.

There are rules governing the sometimes atrocious behavior of socialized humans that can be violated only at great risk. Dražen Erdemović chose to adhere to those rules, thus saving his skin and, with that understanding, earning leniency from the court. In pulling the trigger until his fingers were numb, he exemplified conformity to the norms of socially enforced brutality during war, and millions of Bosnians (like hundreds of millions of Americans) exemplify that same conformity in what passes for peacetime.

Here, the implication of collective responsibility, in the context of postwar Bosnia-Herzegovina, seems to find entire ethnic communities guilty. Pointing the finger at an entire ethnic group is likely simply to perpetuate anger among that group. The solution to this ongoing cycle of mistrust is, as has been noted periodically, the appearance of a Willy Brandt who will, in an act of catharsis that transfers to the mass, apologize in the name of his people. While it has been nearly exclusively members of one ethnicity calling for the appearance of Willy Brandt from another group, there have been instances, as mentioned above, of people advocating for confrontation with the truth from within their own community. This is the only way that the confrontation can take place—from within—but to date, there has been no indication of the catharsis taking place on a mass scale among any of the three main ethnic communities of Bosnia.

The contest that is playing out in Bosnia-Herzegovina between ordinary citizens with a well-developed conscience and the mainstream narrative of victimhood is thus heavily weighted toward the latter. That narrative serves the entrenched political class, which controls most of the press. But the number of people who are willing to take responsibility to confront their own history is growing.[91]

Epilogue

THE CONDITION OF BOSNIA-HERZEGOVINA AND
HOPES FOR ACTIVISM

AS WE ENTER THE 2020S, IT TAKES MORE AND MORE FAITH to believe in the ability of ordinary people to help Bosnia recover, because the preconditions for a decent life are as far away as ever.

The "Dayton straitjacket" described in this book continues to serve the elite well, with leading politicians on all sides profiting from the built-in divisions fostered by the constitutional order. Repetitious biennial elections continue to show that, without the possibility of a citizen-based movement coming to the fore, people carry on voting for their ethnonational "guardians." Those guardians are the same people, and their heirs, who fought for division during the war and, afterward, divided up the spoils.

With solutions seeming more remote, skepticism about the possibility of a turn-around is higher than ever. The attraction of the European Union as a panacea has dimmed, and instability in other parts of Eastern Europe and the Middle East have contributed to a feeling of insecurity at home.

My visits to Bosnia in the late 2010s revealed a depressing state, as expressed by my acquaintances. In Tuzla, Mirsada said to me, "Nothing has changed here in twenty-five years; it has only gotten worse. No one looks after the citizen. Prices are out of control, and they increase randomly. The leaders of all three ethnicities are na-tionalists. I'm Muslim, but Bakir [Izetbegović] doesn't represent me. Everyone under thirty, and many older people, are ready to leave. They have one foot on the road."

Nedžad said, "There's no hope for BiH at present. People just say, 'It's ok, as long as there's no shooting.' This is not a democracy, so you can't get anywhere. People can't organize. The only thing that can change things here is a revolution. And war is a revolution, but it would be led by the same profiteers that are running the country now."[1]

SOME KEY ECONOMIC AND DEMOGRAPHIC FACTORS

The 2013 census, delayed a decade by the war and instability, was not reported until three years later. Between 1991 and 2013, the population of Bosnia-Herzegovina fell by nearly 850,000.[2] The deaths of some during the war, at one hundred thousand, account for only a fraction of that number; emigration covers most of the remainder. What is more, in 2018 no one I spoke with believed the final tally of the census that cited a population of 3.53 million.[3]

As of that year there were no methodically collected data available to update the census. However, between the number of foreign residents from the Bosnian diaspora who padded the census, and citizens who left the country after 2013, the prevailing view was that the actual population numbered closer to three million. An investigation conducted by the Bosnia-Herzegovina Agency for Statistics in early 2019 came up with an even more drastic reduction, estimating the current population at 2.7 million. The agency further noted that while unemployment has decreased from 311,000 to 185,000, this is due to emigration rather than increased employment.[4]

Over the years since the end of the war, regular polls conducted by nongovernmental and intergovernmental agencies uniformly revealed a desire on the part of two-thirds or more of Bosnia's youth to leave the country, with many saying they did not wish to return. Recent years saw reports of varying numbers upward of forty thousand people leaving annually; a report in late 2018 stated that seventy thousand people left Bosnia in 2017.[5] In a development that makes emigration even easier, several West European countries are increasing their quotas for work visas in order to satisfy increasing demand for workers in many sectors.[6]

Emigration has been under way since the height of the return period, but it was starkly visible in 2018. A walk up the main street of Kozarac showed some 10 to 20 percent of shops and stores shuttered, with many "for sale" signs visible. The once-thriving Janj wood processing factory in Donji Vakuf, formerly employing more than six thousand workers, was broken up and no more than some three hundred people still worked there. Similar stories of depression and departure were repeated in a dozen towns and cities I visited.

In Sarajevo, I asked young Sanela if many of her friends were leaving. She answered, "The majority. Many of them are going up to Germany to work as nurses."[7] And Peđa, a Sarajevo journalist, told me that of the twenty-nine people in his high school graduating class in a central Bosnian town, only three remain in the country.[8]

Figures on emigration vary, but one report from 2014 had 150,000 young people leaving since the end of the war. And labor reports regularly announce that Bosnia, with approximately 50 percent youth unemployment, has the highest such rate in the world.[9] A recent study produced by a French demographer asserted that, with some 45 percent of its population living outside of the country, Bosnia-Herzegovina held the shocking position of first place in world emigration per capita.[10]

Youth unemployment and lack of hope are the main reasons for the emigration, but young people are also fed up with a government that is overladen with bureaucracy, in which only adherents of the "strankokratija," faithful members of a given political party, can get a job. Many students coming out of college have morals that prohibit them from joining a party just for personal interest. These people, and many more, seek better prospects in places as far-flung as New Zealand, Malaysia, and Western Europe.

Even those who have decent jobs are speaking of leaving, because they want better prospects, in a more stable country, for their children. Professionals and well-educated people are emigrating; it was reported, for example, that more than three hundred doctors left Bosnia in 2016.[11]

HOW THE TYCOON CLASS PRESERVES ITS POWER

I have discussed corruption extensively above; it is a pervasive dynamic that leads to a depression so overbearing that masses of people want to leave their homeland. It is thus worthwhile to review some of the mechanisms of political survival and domination employed by Bosnia's perennial rulers. Among those mechanisms are: historical denial; use of commemorations and monuments as propaganda; glorification of war criminals; low-intensity terror; extreme nationalist advocacy and separatism; militarism; and perhaps the most useful: elections.

Milorad Dodik, from 2019 enjoying his new position as Serb member of Bosnia's state-level three-part presidency, was arguably the country's most successful postwar politician. Perhaps because the Republika Srpska is more ethnically homogenous than the Croat-Muslim Federation, a version of McCarthyism is more effective in the Serb-controlled entity. There is no real political "opposition" in the RS; only a couple of parties on the outs, jealous that they are not in a position to engage in as much corruption and power-mongering as Dodik's party.

President Dodik thus has space to use his power flamboyantly and to manipulate the voting body in ways that, from any distance, can be seen as classic methods of divide and conquer. This is not by any means meant to imply that Croat and Bosniak leaders are not involved in similar maneuvers. And while Dodik's obvious manipulation provides a convenient bogeyman for his political adversaries, the same dynamic works for politicians in the other entity. Dodik and the Muslim leaders in the Federation, especially, are indispensable counterparts to each other.

The most flagrant of Dodik's divisive measures is the referendum, the use of which harks back to the ill-fated referendum of February–March 1992, which acted as a catalyst for war. Under a populist guise, referendums in Bosnia serve as a lever for escalated hostilities rather than as a means of conflict resolution. So President Dodik knew what he was doing when, in September 2016, he held a referendum to establish voters' support for the RS commemorative holiday of January 9.

On that date in 1992, Bosnian Serb separatists proclaimed the existence of the Republika Srpska. In more recent years January 9 was commemorated ostentatiously in the RS, whereupon non-Serbs filed a complaint with the Constitutional Court. Their objection was not only that the holiday, with all its connotations of discrimination and violence, did not appeal to non-Serb citizens of the RS, but also that January 9 was a Serbian Orthodox saint's day. This violated a constitutional prohibition of discriminatory holidays, and in November 2015, the Constitutional Court duly declared that January 9 must not be celebrated as a state holiday.

Not only did the Republika Srpska hold another gala anniversary celebration on January 9, 2016—attended by president of Serbia Aleksandar Vučić—but Dodik called a referendum on the matter, to be held that fall. When the time came, just short of 100 percent of RS voters approved the celebration, confirming its legitimacy, but only Serb voters participated in the referendum.

It is telling that this referendum was held just before the nationwide municipal elections of 2016. The campaign for the referendum was transparently a generator for hypernationalist support for Dodik and, by extension, his party officials running for office at the local level. It worked.

ELECTIONS AS NATIONALIST MANIPULATION

This brings up the matter of electoral campaigns generally, and the national parliamentary and presidential campaign of 2018. President Dodik, ever since 2006, has been skilled at raising and lowering the temperature of perceived crises with exquisite control. Elections, more than anything else, afford him the opportunity to make everyone in the country—and outside observers as well—worry about the survival of Bosnia-Herzegovina. Rumors of violence and dissolution become all the more dire in an election year, to the point where political prognoses seem to escape the orbit of rationality.

In 2018, the campaign seemed more repetitious, and the candidates more gray and less eminent, than ever. It is tempting to write off elections, as they seem perennially to present the same old soap opera, with the same results.

In the couple of years preceding the 2018 national elections, President Dodik and Dragan Čović had formed an open alliance that worked to destabilize Bosnia. This made sense, since their separatist agendas overlapped. Dodik has for at least a decade called for the secession of the RS, and Čović has, in one way or another, advocated for something approximating a "third entity," or a Croat version of the Republika Srpska. Such a political rearrangement would concentrate Croat nationalist power in a potential breakaway formation.

The 2018 elections provided another opportunity for nationalist leaders to stir up ethnic tension in the interest of preserving their positions of power. Dodik and Čović, both running for the presidency, swore to defend their ethnic constituencies. The Bosniaks running for that position promised to defend their followers from the Serbs and Croats.

In a constitutional order where it was the ethnic collectivities, rather than citizens per se, that had constitutional representation, the ethnonational conflict remained the predominant political dynamic. This works in favor of the nationalist leaders. In 2018 there was, as happened before, an apparent exception to this rule. That was the Croat social democrat Željko Komšić. Running for the Croat seat of the presidency as head of the Democratic Front, Komšić defeated Čović—with most of his two hundred thousand–odd votes coming from Bosniaks.

In the Republika Srpska, under the present constitution voters are allowed to select only the Serb member of the state-level presidency, and in the Federation, they are allowed to select only the Croat and Muslim members. Thus voters in the Federation, unlike in the RS, are able to vote across ethnic lines if they wish to. This is how thousands of Muslims voted for Komšić, outvoting the majority of Croats, who voted for Čović.

The scenario of a secular, socialist Croat defeating the nationalist Čović with non-Croat votes made it clear that many Bosnian Muslims were ready for a secular political system, where they would not have to vote for the likes of the SDA (Muslim nationalist) candidate. Komšić's election also played up the absurdity of the present system and, understandably, outraged the mass of Bosnian Croats loyal to Čović.

The outcome of the election gave Čović the opportunity to threaten to disrupt the functioning of both the Federation and the state-level parliament, and to exploit that most useful of political tools: the perceived victimization of his constituency.

There is an obvious solution to the "crisis" caused by the 2018 elections: to abolish the constitutionally imposed ethnic card, and to require that only secular parties representing concrete interests of the voters, for example, as workers, as women, as the poor, as farmers, be allowed to operate. This, clearly, will not happen soon. Rather, Čović and his successors will continue to exploit the victimology of his "flock," as will his counterparts among the Serbs and Muslims.

Each standstill in the functioning of Bosnia's government—and they are regular episodes—is termed a "crisis" by commentators and foreign journalists. The term came into regular use soon after Dodik became prime minister in 2006. However, it is more accurate to consider the Bosnian political system as in a state of permanent crisis, because that is a condition that is built into the constitution.

The recurrent sense of crisis is adeptly heightened or decreased through other means as well as referendums and elections. In the spring of 2018 the ongoing flow of migrants from the Middle East and North Africa changed routes and started passing through Bosnia-Herzegovina, instead of Serbia and Hungary, on the way to the European Union. When state authorities bused three hundred migrants (out of several thousand) to a camp near Mostar, Božo Ljubić, a prominent Bosnian Croat nationalist politician, declared that Sarajevo's goal was to destabilize Mostar and Herzegovina.[12] And President Dodik, refusing to allow the establishment of any refugee camps in the Republika Srpska, termed the influx of migrants an "intentional attempt by the Bosniak parties in Sarajevo to change the ethnic makeup of Bosnia-Herzegovina" by bringing in 150,000 migrants and providing them with citizenship so that they could vote in the upcoming elections.[13]

Alongside this kind of fear-mongering, Dodik has nicknamed Sarajevo "Tehran" and has warned of the danger of "terrorism in Bosnia" because of the perceived growth of a Wahhabi (Saudi-style Islamist) population.[14] And while engaging in such exaggeration, Dodik has also turned to praising the convicted war criminals among the Serbs. The Republika Srpska government has gone further than rhetorical statements to glorify the war criminals that founded the entity, by naming schools and institutions after them. In the spring of 2016, for example, President Dodik ceremonially opened a student dormitory at Pale, naming it after Radovan Karadžić.

This practice has been carried out among non-Serbs as well; in late 2016 school administrators changed the name of a Sarajevo elementary school to "Mustafa Busuladžić." Busuladžić was a prewar and World War II Muslim nationalist and anti-Semite who supported the wartime Ustasha regime in collaboration with the Nazis.[15] And in west Mostar, local Croat authorities changed the traditional names of several streets to commemorate World War II Ustasha collaborators.

Similar methods of reinforcing nationalist iconography have abounded on all sides through the erection of monuments, the placement of posters with likenesses of war criminals-cum-heroes, and the renaming of many public institutions.

Closely twinned with these practices is the continuation of war crimes denial and revisionism, which has seen no pause. On the part of the Serbs, a new instance of denial in extreme form was the 2018 revocation of the 2004 Srebrenica Commission Report. And former member of the presidency Dragan Čović, representing the Bosnian Croats, participated in a hero's welcome for convicted war criminal Dario Kordić, upon his prison release after serving a sentence for crimes against humanity.

It may seem an absurd leap from the glorification of war criminals to a discussion of sports as practiced in Bosnia-Herzegovina, but there is a strong element of nationalism attendant in the conduct of fans of professional sports. The behavior around prominent sports matches in Bosnia is similar to that of English or Russian "football hooligans," with a strong component of ethnic animosity. For example, when the Croatian soccer team won a World Cup match in 2014, Bosnian Croat fans burned the Bosnian flag in Mostar and Čapljina.[16] And during a celebration of the July 2018 second-place showing of the Croatian soccer team at the World Cup, fans in Mostar chanted the notorious "Nož, žica, Srebrenica" (Knife, wire, Srebrenica)[17]—as if this expression of hate toward Muslims had anything to do with the international soccer competition.

Sports matches have regularly been the occasion for such nationalist expression in every direction between the three ethnicities of Bosnia. Skirmishes seem to be particularly common between Croat and Muslim-dominated teams, perhaps because both are located in the Federation and have matches more often. Serb sports fans have expressed nationalist slogans at sports matches as well; for example, when a visiting team from Serbia played a Bosnian national team in the spring of 2014, local fans chanted the slogan pertaining to Srebrenica, as well as "Kill the Turk" and slogans lauding Ratko Mladić.[18] It appears that in Bosnia-Herzegovina sports are all too often the continuation of war by other means.

The nationalist eruptions at sports matches throughout Bosnia are an indication that ordinary people remain under the thrall of political manipulation. While the examples given here pertain to Croat and Serb expressions, their counterparts in Bosniak nationalism are just as present. The Bosniak elite, in power since the prewar elections, has as much stake in maintaining its position as do the Croat and Serb elites. Bosnian Muslims, while arriving a century late to nationalism, have created their own mythology and cult of victimhood that, in present times, promote exclusion just as effectively as do Serb and Croat nationalism. Altogether, the three nationalist tendencies cooperate to keep Bosnia-Herzegovina from transforming itself into a functional state.

One additional, starker aspect of the perpetuation of divisions is to be found in the practices of Milorad Dodik. That is the promotion of militarism, with an unspoken threat of violent resolution to the ongoing tensions present in Bosnian society. In his twelve years as prime minister and then president of the Republika Srpska, Dodik sponsored or promoted thinly veiled paramilitary formations. At first this practice was covert, with the formation of militarized "security" companies, and it gradually became more public as Dodik entrenched his power. In recent years he has invited Serbian and Russian paramilitary groups to Banja Luka.

Coupled with these threatening demonstrations of power has been the ostentatious arming of the police department in the Republika Srpska. In early 2018 the RS police force acquired twenty-five hundred automatic rifles from Serbia. In comparison, the entire Austrian police force has just four hundred such weapons. This unusual buildup of armaments prompted worry in Sarajevo and abroad.[19]

President Dodik has underscored his militarist leanings with public displays of armed groups marching through Banja Luka. One such group visiting from Serbia, the Russian-trained Srbska Čast (Serbian Honor), participated in the January 9, 2018, Republika Srpska anniversary parade. On this occasion officials as highly placed as Dragan Mektić, state-level minister of security, characterized Srbska Čast as a "criminal organization" guilty of violent crimes and drug trafficking. Mektić accused Dodik of promoting the founding of a branch of the organization in the RS with the goal of terrifying the opposition in that entity.[20]

In the run-up to the 2018 nationwide elections, saber-rattling in Banja Luka prompted widespread expressions of fear of an impending war. Sadly, history shows that it is never wise to rule out a war, but it is clear that the open displays of militarism by President Dodik served to boost his campaign for the state-level presidency.

BOSNIAN ELITES IN BED WITH REGIONAL POWERS: THE SERBS

In the minds of many Bosnians, for quite some years after the war, the idea of "going to Europe," that is, joining the European Union, was akin to going to heaven. People looked to EU membership as the guarantee of stability and a better living standard. More recently the EU's shine has become tarnished. Europe was not able to help Bosnia-Herzegovina recover swiftly from the worldwide recession of 2008. After "donor fatigue" came "expansion fatigue."

It became clear that EU accession was at best a distant dream, with all the other post-Yugoslav and Western Balkan states ahead of Bosnia in line. More recently, the planned departure of Great Britain from the EU has underscored Bosnia's sense of disappointment in the promise of the supranational organization.

Meanwhile, the rise of right-wing nationalism in the United States and much of Europe resonated among nationalists in Bosnia. Where domestic leaders had previously looked to the West for political sponsorship to enhance their legitimacy, more recently they turned to nearby authoritarian regimes for support. This applies to the ethnonationalist leaders of all three main ethnicities in Bosnia.

President Dodik and his supporters turned to Serbia and ascendant Russia to shore up their image. Dodik has been a frequent guest of Serbian president Vučić, with whom he regularly exchanges vows of loyalty and mutual support. President Vučić, in return, regularly attends high-visibility official functions, such as the January 9 commemoration, in the RS.

The relationship between Serbia and the RS goes beyond the rhetorical level. In recent years Serbia has donated or pledged millions to support infrastructure development projects including the development of the Banja Luka airport, five million euros for infrastructure development in ten RS towns,[21] and seven million euros for upgrading the RS defense industry.[22] Serbia's support of the RS is a practical matter, ensuring the RS's loyalty. It also perpetuates tension in Bosnia by virtue of Serbia's quite open support for President Dodik. And that support, both economic and rhetorical, helps Dodik stay in power.

Serbia and the Republika Srpska both look to Russia for support in their attempts to chart a path that is at least to some extent independent from Western influence. In Bosnia, at the street level, domestic interest in Russia is manifested in a proliferation of posters reading "Istočna Alternativa" (Eastern Alternative), often bearing the likeness of Russian president Putin, that show up on walls and signposts in many parts of the RS. The posters express support for an alliance between Bosnia and Russia.

At the top level of RS politics, President Dodik has ostentatiously fostered a friendship with Putin. Dodik visited Putin just before the Bosnian municipal elections in 2016, and shortly before the national elections in 2018.[23] In that same electoral period Russian foreign minister Sergei Lavrov visited Bosnia, paying special honors to the RS during a visit to Banja Luka. The honor was returned as Dodik accompanied Lavrov to the consecration of a Serbian-Russian cultural center and Orthodox church honoring Czar Nicholas II.

On one occasion Dodik announced, "True friends such as the Russian Federation and its President Vladimir Putin have helped us to clearly set our goals, get back self-confidence and fight for our original rights."[24]

On a much cruder level, Banja Luka hosted the Night Wolves, a band of Russian motorcyclists named known as "Putin's favorite bikers," that arrived in the RS ostensibly to tour sacred Orthodox sites. Members of the Night Wolves had participated in Russia's invasion of eastern Ukraine. Their leader, Aleksandr Zaldostanov, was blacklisted by the US Treasury,[25] but he was awarded the Medal of Honor by President Dodik.[26]

Dodik has acquired specially equipped helicopters and other military armaments from Russia for use by the RS police force.[27] In addition, the RS has sent special police forces to train in Russia.[28] The RS is also refurbishing a former army barracks at Zalužani, near Banja Luka; several analysts have asserted that Russian operatives will provide special police training there.[29]

Political commentator Srđan Šušnica, evaluating Dodik's cooperation with Russia, wrote, "Dodik has brought the game to a new, geopolitical level. He has forcefully dragged the Russians and Putin's regime into the still-frozen conflict. . . . He will prove to the Bosnian Serbs, that, see, we're not alone in this dangerous adventure."[30]

The displays of militarism and friendship with Russia and Serbia that Dodik flaunted throughout 2018 caused no end of dire pronouncements of impending war by foreign journalists and analysts, as well as by some combative Bosniak politicians in Bosnia-

Herzegovina. This scenario repeats itself every election year, when tensions are raised by politicians with Dodik at the fore. But after the October 2018 elections, tensions were quickly lowered, and there was no more talk of imminent violence. In this whole drama, the histrionics about potential war overshadowed the crucial dynamics underway: manufacturing and exploitation of fear in order to retain power. Those who were the most capable of that manipulation were reelected.

This is not to say that Serbia and Russia do not have designs on the Republika Srpska. Put briefly, both states wish to ensure an expanded sphere of influence and to prevent Bosnia-Herzegovina from joining the NATO alliance. But neither is in a position to bankroll a 1990s-style war in Bosnia, especially when local military strengths are much more proportionally even than they were in the 1990s.

BOSNIAN MUSLIM ELITE OUTREACH ABROAD

With much less explicit militarism, the Bosnian Muslim elite look to Turkey and beyond for economic and political support. Turkey has been an important investor in much of the former Yugoslavia in recent decades. In Bosnia, it has helped reconstruct mosques and infrastructure. And on the rhetorical level, the relationship between Bosniak nationalist leader Bakir Izetbegović and Turkish president Recep Tayyip Erdoğan is as cozy as that between Dodik and Putin.

When Erdoğan was banned from campaigning among Turkish diaspora communities in several European countries in 2018, he was welcomed by a crowd of fifteen thousand in Sarajevo. The crowd chanted Erdoğan's name, and Izetbegović declared that Erdoğan was a leader "sent by God."[31] In an indication that loyalty toward Turkey is not as monolithic as the Muslim elite would like, some leaders and many secular citizens among the Bosniak population were unhappy that Bosnia could be exploited by the Turkish autocrat.

Nevertheless, it is clear that as the strongest party among the Bosniaks, the SDA benefits from its association with the Turkish leader. There is also a warm relationship between the SDA and several Arab countries. Both Kuwait and Saudi Arabia have financed the restoration of numerous mosques around the Federation, along with the construction of several grandiose, Middle Eastern–style ones.

CROAT TIES ABROAD

Bosnia-Herzegovina's Croat elite has also found ways to enhance its image and longevity through association with foreign powers. In the case of HDZ chief Dragan Čović, the common goals he shares with President Dodik have led to cooperation between Russia and the Bosnian Croat elite as well. Russia and the HDZ have crafted mutually favorable economic arrangements, particularly with regard to the processing of aluminum.[32] Such deals between the Croat elite and Russia underscore Russia's partiality to Bosnian separatists of all stripes. That is, anything that furthers the goals of the separatists in weakening the Bosnian state also increases Russian influence in the country and, along the way, further discourages the possibility of Bosnian membership in NATO.

The strongest sponsor of Bosnian Croat nationalism is nearby Croatia. In a symbolic act in June 2018, in the run-up to Bosnia's national elections, Zagreb University awarded an honorary doctoral degree to Dragan Čović.[33] Čović's recurrent promotion of a "third entity," in earlier postwar years, took the form of attempts to revive the wartime Herceg-Bosna parastate. More recently, Čović proposed a constitutional change that would modify electoral law, concentrating Croat voting power in territories where non-Croats would effectively be disenfranchised. The Croatian government has often supported Čović's goals over the years.

Periodically, Croatia also stoked fears of "Islamic terrorism" to anyone who would listen. In late 2017, Croatian president Kolinda Grabar-Kitarović caused indignation among Bosnian Muslims by stating that, with "about 10,000 people in BiH with radical intentions even toward Croatia," Bosnia-Herzegovina constituted a "potential base for terrorists." The assertion was harshly criticized by commentators who noted that in Bosnia there have been no large-scale terrorist attacks similar to those that have taken place in Western Europe.[34]

Such propaganda moves by Croatian leaders have worked to shore up HDZ's image among its constituency. Although Dragan Čović lost his presidential seat in 2018 because of the Bosniak vote, among Bosnian Croats he actually garnered more votes than in the 2014 election.[35] Čović's 2018 tally of some 145,000 votes, however, was still a weak fraction of the Croat voting body of approximately five hundred thousand.[36]

Čović remains the most powerful leader among Croat nationalists, but he managed to dent his reputation by attending the 2019 celebration of the January 9 anniversary in Banja Luka. At the event, the RS president posthumously awarded the Karađorđe Star, one of the RS's highest honors, to a Yugoslav army officer and convicted war criminal, Slavko Lisica. Lisica had waged war against Croatia in the region around Šibenik in the early 1990s and was subsequently sentenced to fifteen years in prison upon conviction for shelling that city. The distastefulness of the Croat leader's presence at a ceremony honoring a war criminal who had attacked Croatian civilians was not lost on some Bosnian Croats.[37]

RISING AND FALLING INFLUENCE FROM THE EU AND THE UNITED STATES

After some fifteen years of relatively strong engagement, particularly during the term of High Representative Paddy Ashdown, Western involvement in Bosnia-Herzegovina tapered off. With the United States handing over its responsibilities to the EU, and that body's Bosnia policies in near chaos, Bosnia's elite received a particular message.

As expressed by Democratic Policy Council analyst Bodo Weber, "It was the EU's constant backing down in the face of domestic reform resistance out of political weakness—the lack of political will to seriously engage in Bosnia and Herzegovina—that lay at the core of its failure in the country. The EU had taught political elites in Bosnia and Herzegovina that if they postpone and ultimately resist reform conditions, the EU will ultimately back down."[38]

In late 2014, the EU adopted a package of economic reforms that it called the "Reform Agenda 2015–2018." Geared toward clearing the way for Bosnia-Herzegovina's accession to Europe, the reforms aimed to strike at the patronage system of governance wherein each party that holds any position in government has the privilege of rewarding its faithful. While there were desultory signs of cooperation in establishing the reforms, overall the Bosnian elite protected its interests through foot-dragging. The EU responded by softening its requirements.[39]

The EU displayed the same behavior in the realm of constitutional reform. In 2009 the European Court of Human Rights at Strasbourg heard the "Sejdić-Finci" case, in which a Bosnian Rom and a Bosnian Jew protested that the ethnic-based Dayton constitution prevented them from running for president, since only Serbs, Croats, and Muslims were counted as "constituent members" of the Bosnian polity. The court decided in their favor, finding that the constitution was discriminatory and in violation of the European Convention on Human Rights.[40]

In the ensuing years additional lawsuits at Strasbourg resulted in further findings of discrimination. However, in spite of economic sanctions, Bosnia's leaders never saw fit to undertake constitutional reform, and the EU simply downgraded its requirement for such reforms.

The general standstill in economic and constitutional reform in Bosnia-Herzegovina shows that talk of accession to the European Union is a charade, on both sides of the equation. On the domestic side, rhetoric in favor of EU accession is nearly unanimous on the part of the nationalist leaders. But the lack of interest in reform as evidenced in practice is also nearly universal.

On the European side, High Representative Valentin Inzko criticized Bosnian leadership, saying, "If the EU says to implement something in six months, even after nine years it won't be done." But in practice, Inzko maintained a strictly hands-off policy, leaving the Bosnians to chart their own course.[41]

Given that the course charted is one of stagnation, implicitly approved by the EU, it is clear that the international community is content with stability—with supporting "stabilocracy," one could say—regardless of the injustice and lack of democracy inherent in the Bosnian system.[42] We can predict that such stability is not a long-lasting thing.

The lack of effective engagement by the European Union was compounded by American disengagement during the term of President Obama, with the exception of sanctions placed on President Dodik after his referendum campaign in 2016. The aloof stance of the United States was then replaced by a chaotic one under the Trump presidency.

On one hand, the US Embassy announced that there were no plans to lift sanctions against Dodik.[43] On the other hand, in 2018 Trump's former staff members Steve Bannon and Corey Lewandowski met with Republika Srpska's then prime minister Željka Cvijanović (more recently RS president), a member of President Dodik's SNSD party, during a lobbying visit to Washington, DC. Other former Trump campaign assistants registered as lobbyists for the SNSD.[44] All this made sense, given the extreme right-wing nationalist point of view—and affinity for Vladimir Putin—held by both Trump and Dodik.

President Trump's staff supported Dodik's separatism in another way. In September 2018 John Bolton, Trump's national security adviser, stated that he "might support a plan to swap land between Kosovo and Serbia."[45] Such a plan portended disaster for Bosnia-Herzegovina, because it would constitute a precedent for secession by the Republika Srpska. For this reason, both Serbia and the RS leadership supported a land swap. Bolton's statement thus amounted to implicit support for the disintegration of Bosnia.

In contrast to the affinity for Dodik's policies that some followers of Trump expressed, Senator Roger Wicker, a Republican from Mississippi, wrote a reasoned statement encouraging American reengagement in Bosnia-Herzegovina and decrying the patronage and ethnic-based party system. Wicker called for a shift to citizen-based government and criticized the US stance, saying, "We, in my view, have been far too fatalistic about accepting in Bosnia what we are not willing to accept anywhere else."[46]

Wicker's approach, together with the US administration's resolve to maintain sanctions against President Dodik, directly conflicted with the US president's ethnic chauvinism and his affinity for autocrats. This conflict reinforced a perception of chaos in American policy.

If it happens that a more focused administration comes to power, one more in harmony with Senator Wicker's sentiments, then the United States should use its leverage to support constitutional reform in Bosnia. It should support the rule of law, and work to shore up grassroots engagement in democratic processes.

THE PURSUIT OF JUSTICE IN BOSNIA-HERZEGOVINA

A brief examination of court proceedings pertaining to Bosnia is useful to evaluate the possibilities for justice and rule of law in the 2020s.

The most notable recent event relevant to justice for Bosnia-Herzegovina was the closure of the ICTY. Residual court processes since this closure are undertaken by the UN's Mechanism for International Criminal Tribunals (MICT) and the state-level Court of Bosnia and Herzegovina. The MICT took over the Stanišić and Simatović retrial and the appeals of Radovan Karadžić and Ratko Mladić. The Bosnian court is processing many other cases domestically.

Evaluation of the ICTY upon its closure has been diverse. There can be little agreement as to its legacy; victims tend to feel that they have not been vindicated, and contrition among convicted war criminals is rare. It is customary among analysts to assert that the justice afforded by the findings of the ICTY is a prerequisite to reconciliation, but so many other developments are necessary for reconciliation that this assertion is unconvincing.

What is unquestionable is the value of millions of pages of case history garnered from testimony over the twenty-four-year run of the court. Calling on this indispensable source, historians will be able to mine volumes of primary documentation about war crimes committed in Bosnia and other parts of the former Yugoslavia.

Other elements of the ICTY's legacy are also valuable. The court indicted 161 suspects and convicted ninety of them, hearing from approximately five thousand witnesses.[47] For the first time, an international court acknowledged that systematic rape could be treated as a war crime. And the court validated the use of the concept of "joint criminal enterprise" to implicate politicians—both within Bosnia and in neighboring Croatia and Serbia—in war crimes that took place during the Bosnian war.

The ICTY was inevitably subject to accusations of the politicization of justice. This is most believable in its failure to find, despite overwhelming evidence, that Serbian officials were direct participants in the war. Sir Geoffrey Nice, prosecutor in the aborted case of Slobodan Milošević, was straightforward in his criticism, stating that there had been "no serious attempt in the cases of Karadžić and Mladić to show the ties [between Serbia and the war crimes committed in Bosnia and Croatia] and the judgments in both cases enabled Serbia to assert that it was not a party to the conflict."[48] As the ICTY closed, only in the retrial of Stanišić and Simatović in the MICT did the possibility remain for such a finding.

Another element of the ICTY's legacy was the manner in which it dealt with criminal responsibility in the instances where cases were successfully processed. All trials give a first and last name to the commission of a crime, rather than charging collective criminal responsibility, that is, tarring an entire ethnicity for an individual's crime. Unfortunately, commentators who wish to exploit people's feelings of victimization have often insisted that the ICTY's purpose was to condemn one entire national group. As analyst and former ICTY spokesperson Refik Hodžić noted, "Serbia has never accepted the Tribunal-offered individualization of responsibility for crimes its officials committed during the wars it led against its neighbors."[49]

The drive for individualization of criminal guilt as it pertained to Croat war criminals was thwarted as well, in the final case before the ICTY. In November 2017, in the "Prlić et al." case, the ICTY Appeals Chamber found six HVO members guilty of a joint criminal enterprise—critically, in collusion with Croatian officials—to "establish Croatian domination in the part of the Bosnia-Herzegovina's territory."[50] The Prlić group was found to have committed "crimes against humanity, violations of the laws or customs of war, and grave breaches of the Geneva Conventions, specifically murder, willful killing, persecutions on political, racial and religious grounds, deportation" and numerous additional crimes.[51]

One of the six HVO leaders, General Slobodan Praljak, committed an act that bizarrely punctuated the end of the ICTY's long run. Praljak, formerly a theater and film director by profession, had been implicated in the destruction of the Old Bridge at Mostar. In the courtroom, upon hearing the guilty verdict, Praljak drank a vial of poison that was smuggled into the room. The poison proved fatal. In the clamor following his dramatic suicide, hard-line Croatian nationalists portrayed Praljak as a martyr, commemorating him in Croatia and the Croat-controlled part of Bosnia-Herzegovina. Yet another episode proved that, at least among their own target audience, nationalist propagandists were able to control the narrative about collectivization of guilt.

In 2018, as the MICT covered residual appeals in the Ratko Mladić and Radovan Karadžić cases, a worrisome shuffling of personnel on the judge's panels foreshadowed a development that could do severe damage to the legacy of the ICTY. In September 2018, senior MICT judge Jean-Claude Antonetti removed three judges in response to a request by Mladić, who had been convicted of genocide, crimes against humanity, and war crimes, and sentenced to life in prison.

Judge Antonetti removed the three judges for possible bias, that is, not because of a certainty of bias, but because they had been involved in other court decisions related to the Srebrenica genocide; the outcomes of those cases implicated Mladić. Lawyers for Mladić, dissatisfied with that case history, accused Theodor Meron, Liu Daqun, and Carmel Agius of bias, and Antonetti acquiesced. The removal of the three, and their replacement by judges from Uganda, Madagascar, and Burkina Faso, meant that the appeal would not be concluded until at least the end of 2019. The addition of three judges entirely lacking in experience with major ICTY trials increased the concern, on the part of many observers, that the appeal could result in an acquittal.[52]

Soon afterward, Judge Meron decided also to withdraw from the appeals case of Radovan Karadžić, for the same reasons. This delayed the conclusion of Karadžić's appeal, which had been expected to wind up by the end of 2018.

The succession of removals developed into a sordid squabble at the highest level of the MICT, with two top judges competing for authority. At that point, the Office of the Prosecutor filed a motion to disqualify Judge Antonetti.[53] As of early 2019 this controversy placed the fate of the Mladić and Karadžić appeals in a disturbingly uncertain state. However, the qualms of some observers were assuaged in the case of the Karadžić appeal, when his conviction was upheld that spring. The Mladić case was still pending at the time of this writing.

Notwithstanding the disturbing shuffle of judges in the Mladić and Karadžić cases, overall the ICTY has been credited with helping to generate increased expectation in international justice. In this vein, professor of international law Diane Orentlicher commented, "All my students have grown up in a world where it's normal to think a mastermind of atrocities must be brought to book."[54] The legacy of the ICTY thus includes the formation of other international courts inspired by it. Not long after the ICTY was created, the UN also formed the ICTR to deal with war crimes cases in Rwanda. And several years later the International Criminal Court (ICC) was formed.

Professor Orentlicher also noted that the international courts can prompt domestic prosecutions.[55] The ICTY left an enormous caseload to the Bosnian court. According to Bruce Berton, head of the OSCE mission to Bosnia, in late 2018 over five thousand suspects, implicated in some twelve hundred war crimes cases, were still at large in the country. While nearly three thousand people have been convicted in domestic courts in Bosnia, Serbia, and Croatia, historian Iva Vukušić commented, "Sadly, the workload is such that there is no chance that all suspects will be prosecuted, not even most."[56]

One factor contributing to this defeat of justice is the fact that there are no extradition arrangements between the three countries. So dozens of persons suspected of war crimes in Bosnia can go on the lam in Croatia and Serbia, and live out their lives peacefully. Added to this is the discouraging fact that, as mentioned in the discussion of Prijedor's postwar history, numerous convicted war criminals have served their prison sentences and returned home—often to the places where they committed war crimes.

In the case of the Srebrenica genocide, among these are Vinko Pandurević, Ljubomir Borovčanin, Vidoje Blagojević, and Dragan Jokić, who resettled in the Republika Srpska. Others retired to Serbia.[57] In this vein, some fifty people campaigning in the municipal elections in 2016 had been convicted of war crimes or postwar corruption. It was legal for people with a criminal record to run for office, but people applying for state jobs must have a clean record.[58]

With regional cooperation on war crimes cases suffering, a poor rate of domestic prosecutions, and periodic chaos in the Bosnian court and prosecutorial infrastructure, citizens hoping for justice and the rule of law are discouraged.

There are lessons to be taken from the Bosnian postwar experience that could be useful to scholars, political analysts, international officials, and grassroots activists alike. Such lessons can apply to other "postconflict" venues around the world. (I put the term in quotation marks because, as is seen in Bosnia-Herzegovina, rarely is the conflict finished and resolved.)

Without pretending to be an expert on any other instance of postwar recovery, I'll venture to say that, with a great dose of local understanding, lessons learned in Bosnia are relevant to places as far-flung as Iraq and Syria (when the time comes), Rwanda, South Africa, Cambodia, and many others.

I am not breaking new ground by mentioning some of the grave mistakes that international officials made in Bosnia during and after the war, as described above: avoid a forced neutrality among international actors, which ends up aiding aggression; avoid validating war criminals by negotiating with them during and after war; do not partition a country based on war-drawn boundaries established through atrocities; *do* support grassroots peace initiatives, especially from multiethnic organizations; do not undermine such initiatives by ignoring or trivializing them; be careful in the use of the term "reconciliation" as a goal divorced from the achievement of justice and material recovery; support local economic initiatives by small business operators who are certifiably not corrupt; avoid and prevent regional and international profiteering on the corporate level, where such behavior serves not only to extract resources from a country, but also to render its population devoid of hope.

This is an incomplete list of things that have not been done well in pursuit of peace and recovery in Bosnia-Herzegovina. The result of these omissions and errors is the ongoing state failure that ordinary Bosnians often perceive as an "experiment" on their living conditions. The lessons taken from this quandary should be applicable in other parts of the world.

THE MANIFESTATION OF HOPE

This overview of the condition of Bosnia-Herzegovina portrays a land with a barely functional state apparatus, one that is oriented toward enriching three ethnonational elites and their crony networks. Ordinary people are left to manage with a low standard of living, with many affronts to their dignity, and with few prospects for improvement.

International officials and the states behind them have shown little other than rhetorical interest in helping ordinary people improve their lot. Rather—as was the case throughout most of the war—the internationals continue to collaborate with the domestic mafiocracy. The Bosnian profiteers benefit from this dynamic, and so do the regional and international corporations that have bought up significant portions of Bosnia's economic wealth.

All this leaves little for ordinary people to live on, and little reason for them to hope. In a region that has always been subject to the whim of empire, cynicism has been the default state of mind, and that attitude has intensified in recent years. During the war, one could hope that things would return to normal. But the new normal has been a long-term disappointment. In response, the only avenue for improvement that thousands of people have identified has been to leave the country for anywhere that there is promise of employment. Even some of the brightest and most capable activists are leaving. One activist asserted to me that "leaving is a form of rebellion." And for those who have not yet left, cynicism is compounded by depression.

During my mid-2018 visit to Bosnia, I spoke with my friend Miki in Sarajevo after returning from Kozarac. I described the closed shops and vacant homes I had seen in that town. Miki said, "Kozarac doesn't matter." I asked, "What matters?" He responded, "Nothing matters."[59]

I spent some time with an activist who is thinking about leaving Bosnia. She asked me, "What does Bosnia have to offer the world that is special, when high culture and sophisticated intellectual inquiry can be found in other centers, from Paris to Istanbul and beyond?"[60] In essence she was asking me why it matters that so many people are leaving. I responded that I looked at Bosnia a different way: that it is a beautiful country, with a rich history, and its people should have the possibility to contribute, to raise their families unmolested, and to cherish their culture.

For such a scenario of healing to happen—that is, for Bosnia-Herzegovina to survive the peace—it will be necessary for a new generation of grassroots activists to commit their lives to organizing for change. In the present atmosphere, even to suggest a glimmer of hope is to subject oneself to ridicule.

But one has to hope.

Recent history shows that grassroots organizing and protest in Bosnia are a strong current in the country's postwar history. Organizing and protest take place in cycles, with people mobilizing and then, sometimes, getting tired. Some activists become co-opted by NGO work or go into politics; others start a family or find a job that requires all their time and energy. Then other activists come up to replace them. Protest wells up in unexpected places for seemingly local, temporal reasons, but underlying discontent is universal within Bosnia. While local demagogues often manipulate people's fear and insecurity, in fact all the ordinary people of the country share that discontent, and at times they can unite around their resentment of their leaders and their common needs.

I have covered in detail the movements for refugee return in Bosnia-Herzegovina and the subsequent campaigns for memorialization and against the discrimination that, in some return communities, has amounted to apartheid. In the early years of the present century, there was a movement promoting conscientious objection, especially in Sarajevo. This drive became moot when Bosnia shifted to a volunteer army, but the campaign helped develop a core of experienced activists.

In early 2008, some of those activists mobilized a campaign against street violence after several incidents frightened the people of Sarajevo. One of the most upsetting of those was the casual murder of a teenager, Denis Mrnjavac, on a streetcar. While street violence appears not to be a political issue, it is a universal one that catalyzed discontent into action for several months.

In subsequent years, rare has been the season when there was no labor strike, pensioner's protest, or action by demobilized soldiers. Such actions, while periodically faced with reprisals by the authorities, have cut across ethnic lines.

As we have seen, 2012 saw concerted action by a group of bright young organizers to secure the election of a Muslim candidate for mayor in Srebrenica. This was essentially a movement for democracy and against war crimes denial. Repression, including the disenfranchisement of some returnees to Srebrenica, followed this victory. But the campaign also led to the creation of the March 1 campaign, active in the national elections two years later.

One might justifiably expect less activism in the Republika Srpska, where state control of the media is more widespread, and repression is more robust. But in 2012 there was an upwelling of dissent, complete with regular protest marches, against the corporate destruction of Picin Park, a cherished green space in the middle of Banja Luka. Again, a seemingly small issue was the catalyst for what was essentially a protest against corruption and autocracy. Protest leaders were singled out for harassment and abuse by the police, and the movement dwindled.

The next year, a politically engendered bureaucratic snafu turned newborn babies into noncitizens. This problem arose when Serb politicians demanded that the standardized citizens' number, known by the initials JMBG, reflect the entity in which an infant was born. For several months, no newborn was given an identification number, thus endangering the infant by preventing international travel if it became necessary for health reasons. At least one child died for this reason. In what came to be called the "Baby Revolution," some ten thousand protestors filled the streets of Sarajevo on several occasions, demanding the law be fixed. The demands escalated to include firing of prominent politicians, but again, with time the protests subsided.

The most widespread and turbulent series of demonstrations in recent history welled up in 2014, sparked by worker protests in Tuzla. In February of that year, workers at several large companies demonstrated against poor working conditions, late payment, and factory closures. Students and other citizens joined the workers and clashed with police; in the process, some protestors torched the Tuzla Canton government building. Many police and demonstrators were injured. The protests spread to nearly every city in the Federation, with arson and violence taking place in Sarajevo.

There were small demonstrations of solidarity across the interentity border in Banja Luka; resentment over the plight of workers was, after all, universal. In Bihać turbulence reached such a height that Hamdija Lipovača, prime minister of Una-Sana Canton, was forced to resign. In the face of several days of violence High Representative Inzko, showing where his sympathies ultimately lay, warned that it could become necessary to bring in international troops to preserve the peace.[61]

Meanwhile, Lipovača was briefly jailed for corruption. Other small concessions were given, including the end of an unseemly golden parachute for politicians upon retirement.

In the heat of the protests, leaders organized meetings they called plenums in several cities in the Federation. The plenums were an unusual practice of widely attended, open discussions where anyone present could voice grievances.

After giving Bosnia's leaders an attack of nerves for a few weeks, the protests dispersed. That moment of solidarity had an echo later in the spring of 2014, when widespread flooding caused landslides and massive damage in many parts of the country. Activists switched seamlessly from protest to grassroots aid work, crossing entity borders and ethnic lines to help whomever they could reach. On the other hand, in some areas local officials continued their discriminatory practices, providing aid to members of the preferred ethnicity and withholding it from returnees.[62]

In 2018, when the hope for activism seemed as far-fetched as could be, another sustained protest developed in the middle of Banja Luka. There, RS war veteran Davor Dragičević led a burgeoning protest against the murder of his son, allegedly carried out—and covered up—by local police. The protest resonated in the Federation, where more than one youth had been murdered in suspicious circumstances.

The unrest, in some ways echoing the Mrnjavac protests ten years earlier, brought together Bosniaks and Serbs across entity lines and generated by far the largest protests seen in Banja Luka since the war's end. As before, the obvious discontent was about endangered youth and mistrust of authorities, but about much more. The demonstrations, starting in the spring, straddled the October 2018 elections, but as soon as President Dodik's SNSD party confirmed its supremacy by winning the elections, repression set in, and, for example, employees of state-run companies found their jobs threatened.

This has been but a sketch of activism in postwar Bosnia-Herzegovina, with several omissions including student activism in Jajce, and sustained veterans' campaigns. But it points out the dissonance between overwhelming pessimism on the part of so many Bosnians, and what looks like an inevitable recurrence of action by people who know their rights and are determined to fight for dignity. Explicitly or not, the protests mentioned here constitute an expression of hope.

The activism described above can certainly be subject to criticism. The JMBG demonstrations tended to devolve into music festivals, with bands organized to play at the end of each event. Violence distorted the message of the 2014 protests, and the plenums of that year were characterized as "public therapy sessions." There was disappointment that the demands developed in the plenums were not pursued in an organized political campaign, and that no new, viable political party arose around some of the articulate leaders who rose to prominence.

An underlying problem hampering the campaigns was the lack of long-term strategy and ongoing, microlocal education and organizing of networks. So far, Bosnian activists have not succeeded in implementing the proven strategy of long-term neighborhood-level networking leading to sustained wider action. Instead, whenever a protest developed, it often happened that jealousy and competition for leadership undermined collaboration. These problems can be surmounted, but future activists will have to overcome widespread depression and cynicism. And, as everywhere, they will have to take risks.

There are great obstacles to activism, but among the people who remain in the country—because they cannot or will not leave—there is much love for Bosnia-Herzegovina. This is the force, together with intelligence and discipline, that will have to be harnessed for change. Until then, Bosnia will remain a kafana republic, governed by and for the elite. And when future rebellions arise, it will be necessary for international forces to support them by pressuring the domestic authorities in order to guarantee success.

Here too, the prospect is discouraging, because Western powers, so influential in Bosnia, have not shown that they sincerely wish to promote grassroots-based democracy.

THIS BOOK HAS BEEN A CHRONICLE OF ORDINARY Bosnians' reactions to the hand of cards they were dealt after the war, and their attempts to assert their rights. These attempts have not been the fruit of individual personalities alone.

During my years spent in Bosnia-Herzegovina I had hundreds of interviews and engaged in countless conversations. I periodically had occasion to try to explain to people that I was writing a book about postwar Bosnia. A couple of responses stand out.

One response was from those who justifiably distrust foreign writers, researchers, and commentators. All too often, such observers are naive or uninformed or, worst of all, write in order to confirm their own preconceptions or to argue in favor of their own worldview. In this vein I was admonished, "Do not write a book that prettifies Bosnia."

I was also told, "Please do not write a book that is fraught with gloom and pessimism."

Of course, there is still much in Bosnia-Herzegovina that is not only negative, but appalling. Nevertheless, the hopefulness characteristic of activists cannot entirely disappear. It is said that "the only concrete manifestation of hope is activism." And when that manifestation is found, it is an inspiring thing.

Thus there is both gloom and hope to be found in Bosnia. As an activist myself, I am distraught about the former and inspired by those who personify the latter.

Ultimately, it is they—Bosniaks, Serbs, Croats, and all the pozitivci of Bosnia—who are the true writers of this story. May their hopes prevail.

Notes

INTRODUCTION

1. Emsuda and Osman Mujagić, personal conversation, Sanski Most, May 22, 1998.
2. The Advocacy Project, *www.advocacynet.org*.
3. Robert Donia and John V. A. Fine Jr., *Bosnia and Hercegovina: A Tradition Betrayed* (New York: Columbia University Press, 1994), 245.
4. Mladen Lakic, "Bosnia 'Still Struggling' to Resolve Refugee Problem," Balkan Insight, December 27, 2017, *www.balkaninsight.com/en/article/bosnia-still-fails-to-resolve-question-of-refugees-12-27-2017*.
5. Maja Zuvela, "Displaced Bosnians Blame Politicians for Their Woes," Reuters, October 5, 2018, *widerimage.reuters.com/story/displaced-bosnians-blame-politicians-for-their-woes*.
6. "Ten Arrested for Banking Irregularities Worth 10 Percent of Bosnia's Budget," Reuters, March 31, 2016, *mobile.reuters.com/article/idUSKCN0WX1BA*.
7. Danijel Kovacevic, "Bosnia Police Arrest Bank Chief Linked to Dodik," Balkan Insight, February 11, 2016, *www.balkaninsight.com/en/article/bosnia-police-arrest-bank-chief-linked-to-dodik1-02-11-2016*.
8. Vildana Selimbegović, "Agencije za bankomatstvo" [Agency for ATMs], *Oslobodjenje*, May 29, 2017, *www.oslobodjenje.ba/dosjei/kolumne/agencije-za-bankomatstvo*.
9. Serbian Academy of Arts and Sciences, "Serbian Academy of Arts and Sciences (SANU) Memorandum, 1986," Making the History of 1989, item #674, *chnm.gmu.edu/1989/archive/files/sanu_memo_e3b3615076.pdf*.
10. Thomas S. Szayna, *Identifying Potential Ethnic Conflict: Application of a Process Model* (Santa Monica, CA: RAND, 2000), *www.rand.org/pubs/monograph_reports/MR1188.html*. See pages 8, 9, and 11 of chapter 3, "The Yugoslav Retrospective Case."
11. Thanks to Marko Atilla Hoare for clarifying this history.
12. Lenard J. Cohen, *Broken Bonds: The Disintegration of Yugoslavia* (Boulder, CO: Westview, 1993), 140.
13. Commission on Security and Cooperation in Europe, *The Referendum on Independence in Bosnia-Herzegovina: February 29-March 1, 1992* (Washington, DC: The Commission, 1992), 19. catalog. hathitrust.org/Record/008866183.
14. Laura Silber and Allan Little, *Yugoslavia: Death of a Nation* (New York: Penguin Books, 1997), 251.
15. Donia and Fine, *Bosnia and Hercegovina*, 245.
16. *Srebrenica: Remembrance for the Future* (Sarajevo: Heinrich Böll Foundation, 2005), 9.
17. UNSC Resolution 836, passed on June 4, 1992, *www.nato.int/ifor/un/u930604a.htm*. See paragraphs 5, 9, and 10.
18. "Dokazaću saučestništvo holandskog bataljona UN-a za genocid nad bošnjacima Srebrenice" [I will prove the participation of the UN Dutch battalion in the genocide of the Srebrenica Bosniaks], *Ljiljan*, no. 392 (July 17–24, 2000), 15.
19. Željko Ivanković personal interview, October 15, 2008.
20. Norman Cigar, *Genocide in Bosnia: The Policy of "Ethnic Cleansing"* (College Station: Texas A&M University Press, 1995), 137.
21. Silber and Little, *Yugoslavia*, 307–8.

22. Ed Vulliamy, *Seasons in Hell: Understanding Bosnia's War* (New York: St. Martin's, 1994), 332.

23. Adil Bašiç demobilized ARBiH veteran displaced from Gacko to Mostar. Conversation, Mostar, November 11, 1997.

24. "Slobodan Praljak: Defending Himself by Distorting History," Balkan Insight, December 4, 2017, *www.balkaninsight.com/en/article/slobodan-praljak-defending-himself-by-distorting-history-12–01–2017*.

25. Esad Hećimović, *Garibi: Mudžahedini u BiH 1992–1999* (Zenica: Fondacija Sina, 2006), 19.

26. Ian Traynor, "Search for the Missing Millions," *Guardian*, March 28, 2001, *www.theguardian.com/world/2001/mar/29/balkans.warcrimes*. See also R. Jeffery Smith, "The Hunt for Yugoslav Riches," *Washington Post*, March 11, 2001, *www.washingtonpost.com/archive/politics/2001/03/11/the-hunt-for-yugoslav-riches/62113b8f-79a0-4973-99f5-eda61b46d043*.

27. Gojko Berić, *Letters to the Celestial Serbs* (London: Saqi Books, 2002), 96.

28. Munir Alibabić, *U Kandžama KOS-a* (Sarajevo: Behar, 1996), 100–103.

29. Silber and Little, *Yugoslavia*, 352.

30. Richard Holbrooke, *To End a War* (1998; New York: Random House, 2006), 75.

31. Silber and Little, *Yugoslavia*, 350.

32. Hasan Nuhanović *Pod Zastavom UN-a* (Sarajevo: Preporod, 2005); also available in English as *Under the UN Flag: The International Community and the Srebrenica Genocide* (Sarajevo: DES, 2007), 70–71; and David Rohde, *Endgame* (Boulder, CO: Westview, 1997), 150.

33. Nuhanović *Pod Zastavom UN-a*, 56, 129, and 177.

34. Ibid., 321, 367.

35. Ibid., 323.

36. Ibid., 374–75.

37. Ibid., 327–28.

38. Silber and Little, *Yugoslavia*, 360.

39. Ibid., 358.

40. International Crisis Group's Balkans Report no. 80, "Is Dayton Failing?," October 28, 1998, *www.crisisgroup.org/europe-central-asia/balkans/bosnia-and-herzegovina/dayton-failing-bosnia-four-years-after-peace-agreement*.

41. Ibid. See footnote clxxiii: "Annex 6 of the Dayton constitution includes, among others, the 1951 Convention relating to the Status of Refugees; the 1965 International Convention on the Elimination of all Forms of Racial Discrimination; and the 1994 Framework Convention for the Protection of National Minorities."

42. Sumantra Bose, *Bosnia after Dayton: Nationalist Partition and International Intervention* (New York: Oxford University Press, 2002), 24–25, quoting Robert Hayden.

43. Alojz Čurić personal conversation, Banja Luka, May 27, 2004.

CHAPTER 1

1. Bosnia and Herzegovina Ministry for Human Rights and Refugees, Department for Housing Policy and Analytical Planning, *Housing and Urban Profile of Bosnia and Herzegovina: An Outline of Devastations, Recovery and Development Perspectives* (Sarajevo: Ministry for Human Rights and Refugees, May 2006), *www.mhrr.gov.ba/PDF/?id=243*.

2. ICJ judgment in the Bosnian genocide case, February 26, 2007, *www.icj-cij.org/files/case-related/91/091-20070226-JUD-01-00-EN.pdf*, paragraph 336.

3. "Bosnian Muslims Sue Serbs over Destroyed Heritage," Balkan Insight, April 10, 2008, *www.balkaninsight.com/en/article/bosnian-muslims-sue-serbs-over-destroyed-heritage*.

4. "I Srbi bježali iz RS" [Serbs fled from the RS too], *Oslobodjenje*, March 3, 1999.

5. "Raseljeni se teže vraćaju kućama" [Displaced returning home with difficulty], *Oslobodjenje*, March 4, 1999, lists figures for pre- and postwar populations.

6. "Grisly Clues in Bosnia's Largest Mass Grave," *Christian Science Monitor*, September 8, 2003, *www. csmonitor.com/2003/0908/p08s01-woeu.html*.

7. Ivica Bašić "Šta smo dobili a šta smo izgubili" [What we got and what we lost], printed in *Hrvatska Ljevica* [Croatian Left] 3 (2001).

8. Mirza, personal conversation, Tuzla, September 10, 1998.

9. Indira Čečo, personal interview, Sarajevo, May 4, 2004.

10. "Sex Slave: 'Every Day We Were Raped.'" CNN report, July 22, 2008, *edition.cnn.com/2008/WORLD/ europe/07/22/sarajevo.rape/index.html*.

11. "Bosnian Children Haunted by War Trauma," *Iran Daily*, May 15, 2005, via the Wayback Machine, *web.archive.org/web/20060322155215/www.iran-daily.com/1384/2274/html/politic.htm*.

12. Twenty percent: "Psychological Trauma among Former Yugoslavs," *Balkan Watch*, August 8, 2005. Fifty percent: "Šta nam je rat ostavio" [What the war left us], *Oslobodjenje*, February 2, 2007: "Dr. Senadin Ljubović, neuropsychologist at the Clinical Center of Sarajevo University, states that about fifty percent of Bosnian-Herzegovinan citizens have clinically expressed signs of post-traumatic stress disorder (PTSD)."

13. Vojislav Vujanović personal interview, Sarajevo, 1998.

14. Ivan Cvitković *Hrvatski Identitet u Bosni i Hercegovini* [Croat identity in Bosnia-Herzegovina] (Zagreb: Synopsis d.o.o., 2005), 165.

15. Ivan Lovrenović, *Bosna, Kraj Stoljeća* [Bosnia at the end of the century] (Zagreb: Durieux, 1996), 152.

16. Senka Kurtović "Pero s ovoga svijeta" [A feather from this world], *Oslobodjenje*, March 27, 2005, via Digitalni Arhiv Infobiro, *www.idoconline.info/article/31061*.

17. Lovrenović, *Bosna, Kraj Stoljeća*, 22.

18. Ibid., 25.

19. Ivan Lovrenović in conversation with Katarina Luketić, "The Monstrosity of 'Pure' National Culture," *Zarez*, November 6, 2003. Reprinted in *Bosnia Report*, no. 41, August–September 2004, *www. bosnia.org.uk/bosrep/report_format.cfm?articleid=1126&reportid=165*.

20. Hariz Halilovich, *Places of Pain* (New York: Berghahn Books, 2013), 79, 80. I note that Hariz Halilovich writes both in English and Bosnian and, depending on the language used, you will see his last name spelled as "Halilovich" or "Halilović," respectively.

21. Ibid., 56.

22. Berić, *Letters to the Celestial Serbs*, 255.

23. Ibid., 118.

24. Bose, *Bosnia after Dayton*, 3.

25. Ajka Baručić, "Neizvjesnost, stil života mladih u BiH" [Uncertainty, the lifestyle of youth in Bosnia-Herzegovina], *Oslobodjenje*, February 7, 2017, via BHRaja.ca, *bhraja.ca/ neizvjesnost-stil-zivota-mladih-u-bih*.

CHAPTER 2

1. Zehra, interview, Tuzla, February 24, 1999.

2. Chris Hedges, "On Bosnia's Ethnic Fault Lines, It's Still Tense, but World Is Silent," *New York Times*, February 28, 1997, *www.nytimes.com/1997/02/28/world/on-bosnia-s-ethnic-fault-lines-it-s-still-tense-but-world-is-silent.html*.

3. *Putokaz* (bulletin of the Coalition for Return), September 1997, 22.

4. "Impunity in Drvar," International Crisis Group Report no. 40, August 20, 1998, *www.crisisgroup.org/europe-central-asia/balkans/bosnia-and-herzegovina/impunity-drvar*.

5. Jacqueline Marino, "Croat Cardinal Seeks Help to Rebuild Church in Bosnia, *National Catholic Reporter*, October 30, 1998, *natcath.org/NCR_Online/archives2/1998d/103098/103098f.htm*. See also Sabrina Petra Ramet, *Balkan Babel: The Disintegration of Yugoslavia from the Death of Tito to the Fall of Milosevic*, 4th ed. (London: Routledge, 2018).

6. Marko Divković, "To Work Abroad, If Only in Belgrade," *Povratak*, March–June 2001, 61–62.

7. Sebina Sivac-Bryant, *Re-Making Kozarac* (London: Palgrave Macmillan, 2016). Chapter 2, titled "The Army of the Dispossessed," describes in detail the formation of the Seventeenth Krajina Brigade and its fortunes during the war. Sivac-Bryant writes, "Not having their own homes to defend created a sense that the only way for them to operate was as an offensive unit, in contrast to the largely defensive character of the Bosnian Army. Hence 'they had the courage of those with nothing to lose, with nowhere else to go' (McDonagh 1995). This gave them some of the characteristics and spirit of a liberation movement within the Bosnian Army" (44).

8. Vahid Kanlić, personal interview, Goražde, March 5, 1999.

9. Jelena Todorović, interview with Fadil Banjanović, *Povratak*, January–February 2001, 41–45.

10. Berić, *Letters to the Celestial Serbs*, 89.

11. Rada, personal interview, December 1999.

12. Berić, *Letters to the Celestial Serbs*, 35: "In this Alija Izetbegović assisted him to the best of his abilities. Happy that thanks to Dayton (in which he was a loser) 'Sarajevo has become ours,' meaning Bosniak, Izetbegović lost no time in announcing that every Serb from the suburbs of Sarajevo who had borne arms must be brought to justice. The message was clear: 'Get away as fast as you can, and don't wait for us to catch up with you.' Acts of violence against the few Serbs who remained in Vogošća, and the theft of what little remained to be looted, made this unspoken message a reality."

13. Holbrooke, *To End a War*, 336.

14. "Dialogue with Serbs in Brčko," *Oslobodjenje*, October 13, 2001.

15. "Pravo jednih da ostanu ne može poništiti pravo drugih da se vrate" [The right of some to remain may not annul the right of others to return], *Putokaz* 24 (October 2000), 24.

16. Interview with members of DISS, Sarajevo, February 2, 1999.

17. "Dialog with Serbs in Brčko," *Oslobodjenje*, October 13, 2001.

CHAPTER 3

1. Robert Gelbard, US special envoy to the former Yugoslavia, quoted in *Balkan Watch* 5, no. 5, February 3, 1998. Via the Wayback Machine at *web.archive.org/web/20050327081246/http://www.publicinternationallaw.org/programs/balkans/archives/1998/BW5-5.doc*.

2. Helena Holme-Pedersen, RRTF, personal interview, Sarajevo, May 1999.

3. For a comprehensive outline of international strategies for return, and obstruction to return, see Internal Displacement Monitoring Centre, *Bosnia and Herzegovina: Sectarian Divide Continues to Hamper Residual Return and Reintegration of the Displaced: A Profile of the Internal Displacement Situation*, (Geneva: Internal Displacement Monitoring Centre, 2006), *www.refworld.org/pdfid/45505b864.pdf*.

4. *Putokaz*, September 1997, 20.

5. The International Criminal Tribunal for the former Yugoslavia, or ICTY, was created by the United Nations in the spring of 1993 (UNSC Resolution 827) to prosecute those accused of committing war crimes during the wars of Yugoslav dissolution throughout the 1990s See *www.icty.org*. The court operated until 2017, when it was replaced by the United Nations International Residual Mechanism

for Criminal Tribunals, or MICT. See *www.irmct.org/en*. The statute for the ICTY gives the court the power to prosecute "serious violations of international law committed on the territory of the former Yugoslavia since 1991," including grave breaches of the Geneva Conventions of 1949; violations of the laws or customs of war; genocide; and crimes against humanity. See "Updated Statute of the International Criminal Tribunal for the Former Yugoslavia," July 7, 2009, *www.icty.org/x/file/Legal%20 Library/Statute/statute_sept09_en.pdf*.

6. *Oslobodjenje*, May 26, 1998.

7. "Human Rights Watch Applauds NATO Efforts to Apprehend War Criminals," Human Rights Watch, July 10, 1997, *www.hrw.org/news/1997/07/10/human-rights-watch-applauds-nato-efforts-apprehend-war-criminals*.

8. Nigel Moore, RRTF, interview, Mostar, December 1999.

9. "Summary of Registered and Estimated Returns of Displaced Persons within Bosnia and Herzegovina," UNHCR, released early 2001. Document on file with author.

10. "Preventing Minority Return in Bosnia and Herzegovina: The Anatomy of Hate and Fear," ICG Report no. 73, August 2, 1999, *www.ecoi.net/en/file/local/1270057/2107_1305882624_bosnia-39.pdf*. See also "Minority Return or Mass Relocation?" ICG, May 14, 1998, *www.crisisgroup.org /europe-central-asia/balkans/bosnia-and-herzegovina/minority-return-or-mass-relocation*.

11. Jelena Todorović, interview with Fadil Banjanović, *Povratak*, January–February 2001, 41–45.

12. Interview with Olivier Mouquet, Mostar, December 1999.

13. The "reported thousand refugees" figure is taken from speech to the Permanent Council of the OSCE by OSCE head of mission Robert Barry, June 10, 1999. Transcript of the speech is available on the Internet by searching in the JUSTWATCH archive at *listserv.buffalo.edu/cgi-bin/wa? REPORT&z=4&1=JUSTWATCH-L&L=JUSTWATCH-L* for "OSCE HoM Speech."

14. "Republika Srpska in the Post-Kosovo Era," International Crisis Group, July 5, 1999, *www.crisisgroup .org/europe-central-asia/balkans/kosovo/republika-srpska-post-kosovo-era*.

15. *Oslobodjenje*, April 7, 1999.

16. *Oslobodjenje*, March 31, 1999.

17. "Grenade Launchers against Bosniaks," *Večernje Novine*, Sarajevo, April 15, 1999.

18. *Putokaz*, April 10, 1999, 5.

19. Charles Philpott, *Journal of Refugee Studies*, February 2005, quoted in report by the Internal Displacement Monitoring Centre, *Bosnia and Herzegovina*, 164.

20. David Howitt, OHR, personal interview, Sarajevo, November 1999.

21. Alexandra Stieglmayer, spokesperson for OHR, NATO press conference, Sarajevo, October 28, 1999.

22. "Unacceptably slow implementation of property laws," *Oslobodjenje*, March 15, 2000.

23. Interview with Stieglmayer: "Scandalous Disrespect for Basic Human Rights," *Putokaz* 23 (July 2000), 8.

24. Catherine Phuong, *Forced Migration Review*, April 2000, quoted in report by the Internal Displacement Monitoring Centre, *Bosnia and Herzegovina*, 166.

25. Mentioned by Simon Haselock, OHR, during NATO Joint Press Conference on September 10, 1999, referring to a statement by then President Alija Izetbegović that "no one was going to be thrown out into the street in order to let 'some grandmother' return." Via SFOR Press Releases & Transcripts of the International Community Press Conferences, *www.nato.int/sfor/trans/1999/t990910a.htm*.

26. Mentioned by Stefo Lehmann, UN Mission in Bosnia spokesman, during a NATO Joint Press Conference on March 21, 2002. Via SFOR Press Releases & Transcripts of the International Community Press Conferences, *www.nato.int/sfor/trans/2002/t020321a.htm*.

27. *Nezavisne Novine*, May 17, 2005.

28. "Assault on Housing Official Condemned," March 26, 2003, UNHCR online news report. Via Wayback Machine, *web.archive.org/web/20030501035642/http://www.unhcr.ba /press/2003pr/260303.htm*.

29. *Putokaz* 12 (June 5, 1998), 8.

30. Carlotta Gall, "Bosnians, Ending Exile, Cope with Old Hatreds," *New York Times*, July 30, 2000, *www.nytimes.com/2000/07/30/world/bosnians-ending-exile-cope-with-old-hatreds.html*.

31. *Putokaz* 25 (December 2000), 9.

32. OHR spokesperson Alexandra Stieglmayer, interviewed in *Putokaz* 23 (July 2000), 8–11.

33. Internal Displacement Monitoring Centre, *Bosnia and Herzegovina*, 169.

34. Interview with Fadil Banjanović, *Povratak*, January–February 2001, 43.

35. *Oslobodjenje*, January 25, 2001.

36. *Putokaz* 23 (July 2000), 13.

37. Gall, "Bosnians, Ending Exile, Cope with Old Hatreds."

38. Supplement to *Povratak* 16 (March–June 2001), 12.

39. Father Radman, personal conversation, Sarajevo, September 18, 2001.

40. Ibid.

41. "The Western Gate of Central Bosnia: The Politics of Return in Bugojno and Prozor-Rama," ICG report, July 31, 1998, *www.refworld.org/docid/3ae6a6d14.html*.

42. "4222 Croats Returned to Bugojno," *Slobodna Dalmacija* (Croatian daily, split), March 5, 2000.

43. ICG report, December 13, 2002, quoted in report by Internal Displacement Monitoring Centre, *Bosnia and Herzegovina*, 150.

44. Vlado Azinović, *Al-Qaeda U Bosni: Mit ili stvarna opasnost?* [Al-Qaeda in Bosnia: Myth or present danger?] (Prague: Radio Free Europe, 2007), Chapter 8, p. 1. Entire book accessible at *www .slobodnaevropa.org/specials/al_kaida/index.htm*.

45. Ibid., 2.

46. Hećimović, *Garibi*, 183–84.

47. United States Committee for Refugees and Immigrants, "U.S. Committee for Refugees World Refugee Survey 1999—Bosnia and Herzegovina," January 1, 1999, *www.refworld.org/docid/3ae6a8d230. html*.

48. Office of the High Representative, "Statistics: Implementation of the Property Laws," December 31, 2000, *www.ohr.int/plip/pdf/PLIP12.00.PDF*.

49. UNHCR, "Registered Minority Returns from 01/01/2001 to 31/12/2001 in Bosnia and Herzegovina," *Statistics Package*, Table 3. Via the Wayback Machine, *web.archive.org/web/20041026185542/http:// www.unhcr.ba/return/pdf%202001/SP_12_01.pdf*.

CHAPTER 4

1. Milan Jovičić, personal interview, Mostar, autumn 1999.

2. Repatriation Information Centre, 1998: of a remaining population of approximately 106,000, some 47,000 Croats now lived on the west side of Mostar, and 49,000 Bosniaks on the east side. Of a prewar population of nearly 24,000 Serbs, only slightly over 2,000 remained. The Repatriation Information Center website is discontinued, but the document is on file with author.

3. Zinka Cerić, interview, March 26, 1999.

4. For example, BosNet news digest reported the torching of a Bosniak-owned house in west Mostar on June 8, 1998.

5. International Crisis Group, "Reunifying Mostar: Opportunities for Progress," ICG Balkans Report no. 90, April 19, 2000, *www.crisisgroup.org/europe-central-asia/balkans/bosnia-and-herzegovina /reunifying-mostar-opportunities-progress.*

6. Ibid.

7. Olivier Mouquet, interview, Mostar, December 1999.

8. "Hrvatska: Otmica koja je digla prašinu u Hrvatskoj i Bosni i Hercegovini" [Croatia: A kidnapping that raised a fuss in Croatia and Bosnia-Herzegovina"), *Dani* 618 (April 17, 2009), *www.bhdani.ba /portal/izdanje/618.*

9. Verdict in corruption case against Ante Jelavić from November 4, 2005, Case KPV-10/04, "Verdict," 58–63, *www.sudbih.gov.ba/files/docs/presude/2005/Jelavic_ENG_KPV_10_04.pdf.*

10. International Crisis Group, "Turning Strife to Advantage: A Blueprint to Integrate the Croats in Bosnia and Herzegovina," ICG Report no. 106, March 15, 2001, *www.refworld.org/docid/3de20e394 .html,* 10.

11. "Verdict in Corruption Case against Ante Jelavić," *Oslobodjenje*, November 4, 2005. Among the companies that founded the new bank were Aluminij, the huge Mostar-based aluminum-manufacturing plant; the Mostar-based aircraft plant Soko, directed by HDZ functionary Dragan Čović; and INA-BiH, an oil company. Hercegovačka Gradnja, a private Bosnian construction subsidiary of Monitor M, was at 1.5 million DM (approximately US$900,000) the single largest contributor for the capitalization of the bank.

12. "Former Bosnian President Sentenced to 10 Years," ISN Security Watch, October 7, 2005, *129.132.112.238/news/sw/details_print.cfm?id=13072.* This article is no longer accessible online, as of January 2018, but is on file with the author.

13. Ibid.

14. Sead Numanović, "Bosnia: Bank Fraud Revelations; Probe into Hercegovacka Bank Scandal Implicates Top Bosnian Croat leaders," IWPR report, December 21, 2002, *iwpr.net/global-voices /bosnia-bank-fraud-revelations.*

15. International Crisis Group, "Reunifying Mostar: Opportunities for Progress," ICG Balkans Report no. 90, April 19, 2000, 34. *www.crisisgroup.org/europe-central-asia/balkans/bosnia-and-herzegovina /reunifying-mostar-opportunities-progress.*

16. Mile Stojić, "Jelavić," *Dani* 618 (April 17, 2009), *www.bhdani.ba/portal/izdanje/618.*

17. Alibabić, *U Kandžama KOS-a*, 233.

18. International Crisis Group, "Turning Strife to Advantage: A Blueprint to Integrate the Croats in Bosnia and Herzegovina," ICG Report no. 106, March 15, 2001, *www.refworld.org/docid/3de20e394 .html,* 2.

19. Beth Kampschror, "SFOR Raids Croat Bank—Take Two," Central Europe Review, April 20, 2001, *www.ce-review.org/01/14/bosnianews14.html.* See also "SFOR Raids Bosnian Bank," News 24 Archives, April 18, 2001, *www.news24.com/xArchive/Archive/SFOR-raids-Bosnian-bank-20010418*; and "21 Hurt in NATO Raid on a Bosnian Bank," *Deseret News*, April 6, 2001, *www.deseretnews.com /article/835576/21-hurt-in-NATO-raid-on-a-Bosnian-bank.html.*

20. Verdict in corruption case against Ante Jelavić from November 4, 2005, Case KPV-10/04, "Verdict," 58–63, *www.sudbih.gov.ba/files/docs/presude/2005/Jelavic_ENG_KPV_10_04.pdf.*

21. Letter from Association of Residents of Šantićeva Street to Mostar Mayor, October 10, 2000, on file with the author.

22. "Ostajte u Santicevoj" [Stay at Šantićeva], *Žena 21*, September 2001.

23. Ignacio Matteini, UNHCR, interview, Mostar, September 24, 2001.

24. Report from UN Mission in Bosnia in transcript from SFOR Press Conference, December 19, 2000.

Via SFOR Press Releases & Transcripts of the International Community Press Conferences, *www .nato.int/sfor/trans/2000/t001219a.htm.*

25. Milenko Milanović, director, Gacko Department for Refugees and Displaced Persons, *Glas Srpske,* Banja Luka, December 12, 2003.

26. Richard Black, Marita Eastmond, and Saskia Gent, "Introduction: Sustainable Return in the Balkans: Beyond Property Restitution and Policy," *International Migration* 44 (2006): 8 (table 1), doi: 10.1111/j.1468-2435.2006.00369.x.

27. Edin Beća, Coalition for Return, interview, September 4, 2001.

28. Ibid.

29. Internal Displacement Monitoring Centre, *Bosnia and Herzegovina,* 183.

30. Ibid., 205-6.

31. Ibid., chart on 41.

32. "Analysis of the State of Human Rights in Bosnia and Herzegovina (Monitoring Covered the Period 1 January – 1 December 2001)" Helsinki Committee for Human Rights in Bosnia and Herzegovina, Decemeber 2001. Via the Wayback Machine, *web.archive.org/web/20060214224330/http://www .bh-hchr.org/Reports/reportHR2001.htm.*

33. *Putokaz* 26 (March 2001), 20.

34. Ibid.

35. Ibid.

CHAPTER 5

1. *Oslobodjenje,* May 13, 2004.

2. Albina Sorguc, "Females Were 'Youngest and Oldest Victims' of Srebrenica," Balkan Insight, July 5, 2018, *www.balkaninsight.com/en/article/females-were-youngest-and-oldest-victims-of-srebrenica-07-04-2018.*

3. Nagorka Idrizović, "Srebrenica: Deset godina poslije" [Srebrenica: Ten years after], *Oslobodjenje,* July 11, 2005.

4. Sadeta Dizdarević, interview, Tuzla, May 2003.

5. Nura Suljić, interview, Tuzla, May 2003.

6. Ibran Mustafić, interviewed in "Presidency and Army Command Sacrificed Srebrenica," *Slobodna Bosna,* July 14, 1996, *www.ex-yupress.com/slobos/slobos4.html.* Mustafić here repeats many conspiracy theories that were popular shortly after the war and which have never entirely gone out of circulation.

7. Muša, interview, May 31, 1998.

8. Report from Physicians for Human Rights delivered at ICVA (International Council of Voluntary Agencies, an NGO network) interagency meeting in Tuzla, May 1998.

9. Report by Srebrenica Regional Recovery Programme outlining a Strategic Action Plan for return to and from Srebrenica, May 14, 2001, 2. Report is on file with the author.

10. This incident was described in a letter from Fadila Memišević sent to the author on November 21, 2003.

11. Fatima Huseinović, interview, Sarajevo, March 1999.

12. Vesna Mustafić, interviewed in *Povratak,* August–September 1999, 28.

13. Vesna Mustafić, interview, December 1999.

14. "Trust, and Then Renewal." *Oslobodjenje,* June 9, 1999.

15. Ibrahim Hadžić, interview, Tuzla, December 1999.

16. Dragan Jevtić, interview, Srebrenica, December 14, 1999. Jevtić's name is also often spelled "Jeftić."

He is said to have commanded Serb special forces in Sarajevo during the war; see "The Lost City Of Srebrenica," by Zoran Tmušić for IWPR, July 16, 1999, *iwpr.net/global-voices/lost-city-srebrenica*.

17. See "Bosnian Serbs Stone Buses," *New York Times*, May 12, 2000, *www.nytimes.com/2000/05/12 /world/bosnian-serbs-stone-buses.html*.

18. Šaćir and Mevlida Halilović, interview, Srebrenica, April 23, 2003.

19. Vesna Mustafić, interview, July 2000.

20. KM stands for konvertabilna marka—convertible marks. The value of one KM has varied over the years between US$0.60 and US$0.75.

21. Report by Srebrenica Regional Recovery Programme outlining a Strategic Action Plan for return to and from Srebrenica, May 14, 2001, 4. The same report counts Bosniak returnees in early 2002 at between 180 and 500, while Serbs in the municipality numbered between 6,000 and 7,000, of whom 4,000 to 6,000 were displaced persons. Report is on file with the author.

22. "A Total of 240 Houses Are Waiting to Be Donated" (reported in *Tuzla Night Owl* [TNO], SFOR news digest), *Oslobodjenje*, August 3, 2000.

23. Ibid.

24. "Bosniaks Submitted 300 Requests for the Return of Their Property in Srebrenica," *TNO*, SFOR news digest, January 30, 2000.

25. Quote of US Army captain Ossy Penny, *TNO*, January 28, 2000.

26. "Safety Situation in Srebrenica Worsened," *TNO*, February 28, 2000.

27. *Oslobodjenje*, August 3, 2000.

28. *TNO* quoting *Oslobodjenje*, July 24, 2000.

29. "Appointment of the Wartime Presidency of Srebrenica Municipality—Confidential Directive No. 01–1371/95," Institute for Research on Suffering of the Serbs in XX c., June 12, 2009, *www.serb -victims.org/en/index.php?option=com_content&task=view&id=175&Itemid=47*. Directive issued by Radovan Karadzic on July 14, 1995.

30. "Animosities Prevail as Bosnian Elections Begin," *Los Angeles Times*, September 14, 1997, *articles. latimes.com/1997/sep/14/news/mn-32234*. "'Either you remove the [Muslim] names from the voter lists and we win, or you remove the stigma that says we killed these people,' said Momčilo Cvijeti-nović, the local SDS chief and the party's leading candidate in the city council elections." See also Ger Duijzings, "Commemorating Srebrenica: Histories of Violence and the Politics of Memory in Eastern Bosnia," in Xavier Bougarel, Elissa Helms, and Ger Duijzings, eds., *The New Bosnian Mosaic: Identities, Memories and Moral Claims in a Post-war Society* (Aldershot: Ashgate, 2007), 161. Duijzings here refers to denial expressed by Cvijetinović in the year 2000.

31. International Crisis Group, "War Criminals in Bosnia's Republika Srpska: Who Are the People in Your Neighbourhood?" ICG Balkans Report no. 103, November 2, 2000, *xyzcontagion.files .wordpress.com/2016/03/international-crisis-group-war-criminals-in-bosnias-republika-srpska-who- are-the-people-in-your-neighbourhood-europe-balkans-report-no103-november-2000-bosnia-39.pdf*.

32. Ibid.,67.

33. Momir Nikolić, testimony quoted in *Dani* 309 (December 2002–July 2003), translated and pub-lished in Bosnia Report (Bosnia Institute), May 16, 2003, *www.bosnia.org.uk/bosrep/report_format .cfm?articleid=944&reportid=157*.

34. "Optuženi za genocid u PSBiH?" [Genocide suspect in the Bosnia-Herzegovina Parliament?], *Oslo-bodjenje*, July 3, 2018, *www.oslobodjenje.ba/dosjei/teme/optuzeni-za-genocid-u-psbih-375752*.

35. "Koalicija 'Pod lupom' traži poništavanje izbora u Zvorniku" [Coalition Pod Lupom (Under the Magnifying Glass) seeks annulment of elections in Zvornik], *Oslobodjenje*, October 25, 2018, *www .oslobodjenje.ba/vijesti/bih/koalicija-pod-lupom-trazi-ponistavanje-izbora-u-zvorniku-404081*. See

also Vildana Selimbegović, "CIK: Centralna izborna krađa" [CIK (Central Election Commission) central election theft], *Oslobodjenje*, October 29, 2018, *www.oslobodjenje.ba/dosjei/kolumne/cik -centralna-izborna-krada-404575*. Discussing the election fraud, Selimbegović writes, "Of 88 polling places, in 64 of them candidates from Zvornik have 100% of the votes."

36. *Povratak* (returnee magazine), August–September 1999, 29.

37. Hasan Hadžić, *Dani* 78 (June 22, 1998), *www.bhdani.ba/portal/arhiva_67_281/78*. "They were here, but didn't return." "Those who were expelled from Bijeljina, Zvornik, Vlasenica . . . have their activists in the Offices for Return. The activists are mainly SDA, . . . and most of them have become well-ensconced in the Federation or they have already traded homes and property with Serbs."

38. Hasan Hadžić, "Dani Dossier: How the SDA Undermined Return of Bosniaks to the Republika Srpska; Purveyors of Confusion and Sellouts of Their Own People," *Dani* 641 (September 25, 2009), *www.bhdani.ba/portal/izdanje/641*.

39. Hasan Hadžić, "Zašto izbori u Srebrenici nisu i ne mogu biti ovjera genocida?!" [Why elections in Srebrenica are not and cannot be a certification of genocide?!], Depo, May 22, 2012, *depo.ba/ clanak/71529/zasto-izbori-u-srebrenici-nisu-i-ne-mogu-biti-ovjera-genocida*.

40. Ibid.

41. Hakija Meholjić, interview, July 2000.

42. Eleanor Gordon, interview, Srebrenica, July 2000.

43. *Dnevni Avaz* (Sarajevo newspaper), July 19, 2000.

44. *Dani* 107 (June 18, 1999), *www.bhdani.ba/portal/arhiva_67_281/107*.

45. *Oslobodjenje*, June 12, 1998.

46. Wolfgang Petritsch, "Decision removing Mr. Miodrag Josipović from his position of Mayor of Bratunac and further banning him from holding any official, elective or appointive public office," OHR report, January 6, 2001, *www.ohr.int/?p=67224*.

47. Report by Srebrenica Regional Recovery Programme outlining a Strategic Action Plan for return to and from Srebrenica, May 14, 2001, 12.

48. Ibid., 4.

49. Ibid.

50. "Field Progress Report as at 28 February 2002," report by the OHR's Srebrenica field representative Charlie Powell.

CHAPTER 6

First epigraph: Sakib Smajlović, "Mirni protesti majki Srebrenice i Podrinja" [Peaceful protest of mothers of Srebrenica and Podrinje], *Oslobodjenje*, October 12, 2004. Reposted in *Tuzlarije.net, bhstring.net /tuzlauslikama/tuzlarije/viewnewnewsb.php?id=2538*. Second epigraph: Bogdan Bogdanović, "On This and That Side of the River Drina," in *Srebrenica: Remembrance for the Future*, ed. Heinrich Boll Foundation (Sarajevo: Heinrich Böll Foundation, 2005), 119.

1. Meeting with representatives of Women of Srebrenica, July 3, 2000.

2. Kada Hotić, interview, Sarajevo, September 4, 2006.

3. Sakib Smajlović, "Sedam godina obilježavanja srebrenicke tragedije" [Seven years of commemoration of the Srebrenica tragedy], *Oslobodjenje*, July 7, 2004.

4. Movement of the Mothers of Srebrenica and Žepa Enclaves, interview, Sarajevo, November 28, 2003.

5. Interview, November 28, 2003.

6. Duijzings, "Commemorating Srebrenica," 162.

7. Srebrenica municipal assembly document no. 01–022–44/2002, "Rezolucija o posebnom tremanu

područja opštine Srebrenica" [Resolution on special treatment of the region of the Srebrenica municipality], issued March 11, 2002, and signed by president of the municipal assembly Desnica Radivojević.

8. Personal letter from Munira Beba Hadžić, early March 2003.

9. Information about the March 31 event received in a personal letter from Angelina Hodžić, April 1, 2003.

10. Personal letter from Vesna Mustafić, April 1, 2003.

11. Amnesty International, "Bosnia-Herzegovina: Human Rights Chamber Decision on Srebrenica—a First Step to Justice" (press release), March 7, 2003, *reliefweb.int/report/bosnia-and-herzegovina /bosnia-herzegovina-human-rights-chamber-decision-srebrenica-first-step*.

12. Interview with Movement of the Mothers of Srebrenica and Žepa Enclaves, Sarajevo, November 28, 2003.

13. *Oslobodjenje*, December 18, 2002.

14. Information provided by Sarah Wagner.

15. Nura Begović, interview, Tuzla, July 3, 2000.

16. International Comission of Missing Persons, "Missing Persons Institute" (press release), *www .icmp.int/press-releases/missing-persons-institute*.

17. Ivana Avramović, "DNA Technique Allows Identification of Bosnian Victims in Mass Graves," *Stars and Stripes*, May 11, 2003.

18. "Finding the Bodies to Fill the Bosnia Graves," *The Scotsman*, March 14, 2007, *www.scotsman.com /news/international/finding-the-bodies-to-fill-the-bosnia-graves-1–690822*.

19. Avramović, "DNA Technique"; quoting Šehida Abdurahmanović, aunt of one victim reburied in March 2003.

20. "Finding the Bodies."

21. Daniel Simpson, "DNA Tests Help Some Families of Bosnia Victims, but Not Most, *New York Times*, December 23, 2002, *www.nytimes.com/2002/12/23/international/europe/23BOSN.html*.

22. Zenicablog, "Iako je u BiH pronađeno 750 masovnih grobnica: Dio nestalih nikada neće biti pronađen" [Although 750 mass graves have been discovered in BiH, some of the missing never will be found], Zenicablog, August 2, 2018, *www.zenicablog.com/ iako-je-u-bih-pronadjeno-750-masovnih-grobnica-dio-nestalih-nikada-nece-biti-pronadjen*.

23. Anes Alić and Dragan Stanimirović, "Imaginary Massacres?," *Time Magazine*, September 11, 2002, *www.time.com/time/world/article/0,8599,349957,00.html*.

24. Agence France Presse, "More Than 400 Missing from Bosnia War Exhumed in 2011," February 1, 2012.

25. "The Events in and around Srebrenica between 10th and 19th July 1995," June 11, 2004, *balkanwitness.glypx.com/srebrenica_report2004.pdf*. Report drafted by the Commission for Investigation of the Events in and around Srebrenica between 10th and 19th July 1995, or simply the Srebrenica Commission, sponsored by the Republika Srpska government.

26. Agence France Presse, "Hundreds of Skeletons Found in Bosnian Mass Grave," July 27, 2006, reposted by the Bosnian Institute, *www.bosnia.org.uk/news/news_body.cfm?nesid=2214*. It should be noted that while Crni Vrh was originally thought to contain the remains of victims from the 1995 killings, it was later determined that the overwhelming number were victims of the violence in 1992 at the outset of the war.

27. "881 Remains Exhumed from Srebrenica Grave," Balkan Insight, December 11, 2008, *balkaninsight .com/2008/12/11/881-remains-exhumed-from-srebrenica-grave*.

28. Sakib Smajlović, "U Srebrenici postoje jos 22 masovne grobnice" [Still 22 mass graves in Srebrenica], *Oslobodjenje*, April 27, 2005.

29. Amnesty International, "Bosnia-Herzegovina: Redress for Srebrenica," ReliefWeb, EUR 63/011/2002, July 11, 2002, *reliefweb.int/report/bosnia-and-herzegovina/bosnia-herzegovina-redress-srebrenica*.

30. Avramović, "DNA Technique."

31. Ibid.

32. Ed Vulliamy, "Most Victims Still Nameless—Local Forensic Investigation Teams Attempt to Return Victims' Bodies to Grieving Relatives," July 6, 2005, *iwpr.net/report-news/most-victims-still-nameless-0*.

33. Aida Čerkez-Robinson, "In Bosnia, Each Funeral Never Ends," *Independent*, July 12, 2009, *www.independent.co.uk/news/world/europe/in-bosnia-each-funeral-never-ends-1742767.html*. This article refers to one victim whose remains were discovered in five locations and arrived for analysis in eleven different body bags.

34. Vulliamy, "Most Victims Still Nameless."

35. "Finding the Bodies." Also, the ICMP created an infographic about missing and identified victims pertaining to Srebrenica, "Srebrenica Figures as of 26 June 2018," ICMP, July 2018, *www.icmp.int/wp-content/uploads/2017/06/srebrenica-english-2018.pdf*.

36. Aida Alić and Merima Husejnović, "Uncertainty Ends for Families of Some Bosnian Missing," Balkan Insight, September 3, 2009, *www.balkaninsight.com/en/article/uncertainty-ends-for-families-of-some-bosnian-missing*.

37. Thanks to Sarah Wagner for pointing this out (and for other comments related to this section) in personal correspondence.

38. "Burying a Child One Bone at a Time," *Dawn*, July 11, 2009, *www.dawn.com/news/824384*.

39. Alić and Husejnović, "Uncertainty Ends."

40. Zdravko Ljubas, "Bosnia Unveils Complete List of Missing Persons," Balkan Insight, February 4, 2011, *www.balkaninsight.com/en/article/bosnia-s-central-records-on-missing-persons-introduced*.

41. Vesna Besic and Lejla Biogradlija, "Over 7,000 Victims of Bosnian War Still Missing," Anadolu Agency, July 21, 2018, *www.aa.com.tr/en/europe/over-7-000-victims-of-bosnian-war-still-missing/1210377*.

42. Almir Šečkanović, "Mirni protest Podrinjki u Tuzli: Trebaju li majke same traziti grobnice?" [Peaceful protest of Podrinje women in Tuzla: Do the mothers themselves have to search for graves?"], *Oslobodjenje*, December 12, 2011.

43. Zana Kovačević, "Bosnian Burial Sites Uncovered for Cash," Institute for War and Peace Reporting, June 16, 2008, *iwpr.net/report-news/bosnian-burial-sites-uncovered-cash*.

44. "Dvadeset Godina Nakon Početka Rata: U BiH mrtvačnicama 2.500 neidentificiranih ostataka" [Twenty years after the beginning of the war: In Bosnia-Herzegovina mortuaries hold 2,500 unidentified remains], *Oslobodjenje*, June 28, 2012.

45. "Karadžić Contests Number of Srebrenica Victims," ICTY report, Sense Agency, April 10, 2012, *www.sense-agency.com/icty/karadzic-contests-number-of-srebrenica-victims.29.html?news_id=13811&cat_id=1*.

46. "Srebrenica Figures as of 26 June 2018," ICMP, July 2018, *www.icmp.int/wp-content/uploads/2017/06/srebrenica-english-2018.pdf*. See also "Srebrenica Memorial Day: Identifying Bosnia's missing thousands," ICMP blog, July 11, 2014, *hmd.org.uk/news/srebrenica-memorial-day-identifying-bosnias-missing-thousands*.

47. "Čengić: Još se traga za najmanje 1.100 žrtava genocida" [Čengić: Still searching for at least 1,100 genocide victims], *Oslobodjenje*, March 31, 2016, reposted at *vijesti.ba/clanak/303775/cengic-jos-se-traga-za-najmanje-1-100-zrtava-genocida*. See also Zenicablog, "Iako je u BiH." For figures on the reburial ceremony in 2017, see, for example, "Thousands Remember 22nd Anniversary of Srebrenica Massacre," Reuters, July 11, 2017, *www.rtklive.com/en/news-single.php?ID=8935*.

48. "Čengić: Još se traga."

49. Christopher Bobyn, "If Bones Could Talk: Reassembling the Remains of Srebrenica," *Balkanist Magazine*, July 11, 2016, *balkanist.net/if-bones-could-talk-srebrenica.*

50. Nicholas Wood, "Bosnian Police Find 2 Bombs Near Memorial," *New York Times*, July 6, 2005, *www .nytimes.com/2005/07/06/international/europe/06bosnia.html.*

51. Snježana Karić, "Istraga tapka u mjestu" [Investigation at a standstill], *Nezavisne Novine*, May 6, 2007, *www.nezavisne.com/novosti/hronika/Istraga-tapka-u-mjestu/9260.*

52. Samir Karić and Almir Šečkanović, "Povratak u 1995. godinu: Četnici pjevali Srebrenicom" [Return to 1995: Chetniks sing in Srebrenica], *Oslobodjenje*, July 13, 2009.

53. "Proslava genocida u Srebrenici" [Commemoration of genocide in Srebrenica], Elektronske Novine, July 7, 2007, *www.e-novine.com/srbija/vesti/48955-Proslava-genocida-Srebrenici.html.*

54. D. Brkić, "U Srebrenici puštali četnicke pjesme" [In Srebrenica, Chetnik songs played], Klix.ba, July 4, 2011, *www.klix.ba/vijesti/bih/u-srebrenici-pustali-cetnicke-pjesme/110704153.*

55. "Bosnian Serb Club Banned from Ground," ESPN Soccernet, November 13, 2002, *www.espnfc.com /europe/news/2002/1113/20021113boracbanjaluka.html.* See also "Violence Forces Borac Ground Closure," UEFA, November 13, 2002, *www.uefa.com/memberassociations/news/newsid=42246.html;* and "Borac Banja Luka Punished after Nationalist Violence," ESPN Soccernet, November 14, 2002, *www .espnfc.com/europe/news/2002/1114/20021114boracbanja.html.*

CHAPTER 7

1. Daniel Williams, "Experts Doubt Top Suspects Will Be Tried before U.N. Court Is Scheduled to Expire," *Washington Post*, June 30, 2005.

2. Hariz Halilović, "Dječije kosti uzidane u temelje Šumske; Tako se kalio Dodikov Reich" [Children's bones built into the foundations of the Forest Republic; That's how Dodik's Reich was reinforced], Elektronske Novine, January 12, 2012, *www.e-novine.com/stav/56862-Djeije-kosti-uzidane-temelje-umske.html.*

3. Michael Farquhar, "Srebrenica: Anatomy of a Massacre," IWPR, August 3, 2006, *iwpr.net/global-voices/srebrenica-anatomy-massacre.*

4. Marlise Simons, "Tribunal in Hague Finds Bosnia Serb Guilty of Genocide, *New York Times*, August 3, 2001, *www.nytimes.com/2001/08/03/world/tribunal-in-hague-finds-bosnia-serb-guilty-of-genocide. html?ref=radislavkrstic.*

5. Munira Subašić, quoted in *Oslobodjenje*, April 20, 2004.

6. Emir Suljagić, "Fresh Assault on Srebrenica," *Dani* 407 (April 1, 2005), *www.bhdani.ba/portal/ izdanje/407.*

7. John Tagliabue, "Former Bosnian Serb Officer Admits Guilt in '95 Massacre," *New York Times*, May 7, 2003, *www.nytimes.com/2003/05/07/world/former-bosnian-serb-officer-admits-guilt-in-95-massacre.html.*

8. Munira Subašić, interview, Sarajevo, May 2003.

9. Emir Suljagić, "Truth at The Hague," *New York Times*, June 1, 2003, *www.nytimes.com/2003/06/01 /opinion/truth-at-the-hague.html.*

10. Emir Suljagić, "Operation Exterminate," *Dani* 308 (May 9, 2003), *www.bhdani.ba/portal/izdanje/308.* For English translation, see "'Operation Exterminate' at Srebrenica," Bosnia Report, no. 32–34 (December–July 2003), *www.bosnia.org.uk/bosrep/report_format.cfm?articleid=942&reportid=157.* For the complete guilt admission of Momir Nikolić, included in his written plea agreement, see "Joint Motion for Consideration of Plea Agreement between Momir Nikolić and the Office of the Prosecutor" (Legal Tools Database record no. 149796, Case number: IT-02-60, *www.legal-tools.org /doc/369725*), especially the "Statement of Facts and Acceptance of Responsibility." The relevant passage starts at page 19.

11. Farquhar, "Srebrenica: Anatomy of a Massacre."

12. "Penitent Witness," Sense Agency, April 4, 2011, *www.sense-agency.com/icty/penitent-witness.29.
html?news_id=12674&cat_id=1.*

13. "Case Information Sheet: Slobodan Milošević," ICTY, 2006, *www.icty.org/x/cases/slobodan_
milosevic/cis/en/cis_milosevic_slobodan_en.pdf.*

14. "ICTY: Milošević Trial Exposed Belgrade's Role in Wars," Human Rights Watch, December 14, 2006,
www.hrw.org/news/2006/12/13/icty-milosevic-trial-exposed-belgrade-s-role-wars.

15. "Weighing the Evidence: Lessons from the Slobodan Milošević Trial," Human Rights Watch, December 14, 2006, pg. 2, *www.hrw.org/en/reports/2006/12/13/weighing-evidence-0.*

16. Emir Suljagić, "Milošević Linked to Srebrenica Massacre; Document Reveals Milošević Account-
ability for Worst Atrocity of the Balkan Wars," Institute for War and Peace Reporting, April 30, 2005,
iwpr.net/report-news/milosevic-linked-srebrenica-massacre.

17. For information on the Scorpion film, see "Former 'Scorpion' Soldier Testifies about Links with
Serbian Secret Police," Sense Agency, December 14, 2010, *www.sense-agency.com/icty/former
-'scorpion'-soldier-testifies-about-links-with-serbian-secret-police.29.html?cat_id=1&news_id=12365.*
See also Tim Judah and Daniel Sunter, "How Video That Put Serbia in Dock Was Brought to Light,"
Observer, June 4, 2005, *www.guardian.co.uk/world/2005/jun/05/balkans.warcrimes.*

18. "Miloševiću 'sumnjivi' videosnimci likvidacije mladića iz Srebrenice" [Videotapes of the liquidation
of the youths from Srebrenica are "suspicious" to Milošević], *Avaz,* June 9, 2005.

19. Anes Alić, "Serbia Sentences Its Scorpions," Spero NewsApril 17, 2007, *www.speroforum.com/a/9071
/Serbia-sentences-its-Scorpions.*

20. Rachel S. Taylor, "Genocide Charges against Ex-Serb Leader to Stay," IWPR, November 9, 2005.
Reposted in JUSTWATCH-L Archives, *listserv.buffalo.edu/cgi-bin/wa?A2=JUSTWATCH
-L;bd5ff8f.0406.*

21. "Serbia and Montenegro on Trial for Genocide," IWPR, March 1, 2006, *iwpr.net/report-news
/serbia-and-montenegro-trial-genocide.*

22. "Application of the Convention on the Prevention and Punishment of the Crime of Genocide," press
release from the ICJ, December 8, 2004, *www.icj-cij.org/files/case-related/91/091–20041208
-PRE-01-00-EN.pdf.*

23. "Verbatim record 2006/3," from public sitting of International Court of Justice, February 28, 2006,
in the case concerning the Application of the Convention on the Prevention and Punishment of the
Crime of Genocide (Bosnia and Herzegovina v. Serbia and Montenegro), *www.icj-cij.org/files
/case-related/91/091–20060228-ORA-01-01-BI.pdf.*

24. "Witnesses in Bosnia ICJ Case Offer Few Surprises," IWPR, April 7, 2006, *iwpr.net/report-news
/witnesses-bosnia-icj-case-offer-few-surprises.*

25. International Court of Justice press release 2007/8, February 26, 2007, *www.icj-cij.org/files/case-
related/91/091–20070226-PRE-01-00-EN.pdf.* For the full ICJ decision, see "Judgement of 26 February
2007," in the case concerning the Application of the Convention on the Prevention and Punishment
of the Crime of Genocide (Bosnia and Herzegovina v. Serbia and Montenegro), International Court
of Justice, February 26, 2007, *www.icj-cij.org/files/case-related/91/091–20070226-JUD-01-00-EN.pdf.*

26. Nidžara Ahmetašević, "Serbia Faces Trial for Bosnia Genocide," Balkan Insight, February 22, 2006,
www.balkaninsight.com/en/article/serbia-faces-trial-for-bosnia-genocide.

27. "Perišić, Momčilo," The Hague Justice Portal, March 3, 2017. Via Wayback Machine, *web.archive.org
/web/20170303095932/www.haguejusticeportal.net/index.php?id=6060.*

28. "Army That Is 'Sort of Here, and in Fact It Is There': Documents from the Supreme Defense Council
about the Personnel Support Provided by the VJ to the Serb Armies in Bosnia and Krajina," Sense

Agency, May 16, 2011, *www.sense-agency.com/icty/army-that-is-'sort-of-here-and-in-fact-it-is-there'.29.html?news_id=12793&cat_id=1*. Minutes of the Supreme Defense Council meetings are accessible at *www.sense-agency.com/home/icty.59.html*.

29. Dženana Karup-Druško, "Ekskluzivno: Zapisnici Vrhovnog saveta odbrane SR Jugoslavije: Srbija i Haški tribunal protiv BiH" [Exclusive: Notes of the Supreme Defence Council of the SR Yugoslavia: Serbia and the Hague Tribunal against Bosnia-Herzegovina], *Dani* 667 (March 26, 2010), *www.bhdani.ba/portal/izdanje/667*.

30. Munira Subašić, interview, Sarajevo, 2003.

31. Zulfo Salihović, interview, Srebrenica, summer 2004.

32. "Naser Orić–Heroj i simbol otpora i opstanka Bosnjaka u Podrinju" [Naser Orić, hero and symbol of resistance and survival of the Bosniaks in Podrinje], *Bilten Srebrenica* 16 (June 2001), 7, published by Žene Srebrenice.

33. Merdijana Sadović, "Orić Lawyers Call for Acquittal; Case against Bosnian Muslim Commander Criticised as 'Weak' and 'Sloppy'," *TRI* 409 (November 17, 2005), *iwpr.net/report-news/oric-laywers-call-acquittal*.

34. See, for example, Dženana Karup, "Bošnjačka Cosa nostra: Družba Cele Kvržice," *Dani* 76 (May 25, 1998), *www.bhdani.ba/portal/arhiva_67_281/76*.

35. "UN Court Refuses to Prevent Naser Oric Trial," Balkan Insight, December 10, 2015, *www.balkaninsight.com/en/article/hague-judge-denies-naser-oric-s-request-12–10–2015*.

36. ICTY judgment in the case of Vidoje Blagović and Dragan Jokić (IT-02–60), International Court of Justice, January 17, 2005, *www.icty.org/x/cases/blagojevic_jokic/tjug/en/bla-050117e.pdf*, 110.

37. ICTY, "Judgement Summary for Popović et al.," June 10, 2010, *www.icty.org/x/cases/popovic/tjug/en/100610summary.pdf*.

38. Zoran Živanovič, attorney for Vujadin Popović, quoted by Velma Šarić, "Prosecution Demands Life for Srebrenica Accused," *ICTY Tribunal Watch* 615 (September 11, 2009), *iwpr.net/report-news/prosecution-demands-life-srebrenica-accused*.

39. Adam LeBor, "Senior Yugoslav Army Officer Momčilo Perišić Goes on Trial," *Times* (UK), October 3, 2008, *www.thetimes.co.uk/tto/news/world/europe/article2597953.ece*.

40. Ibid.

41. David Rohde, "Serbia Held Responsible for Massacre of Bosnians," *Christian Science Monitor*, October 24, 1995, *www.csmonitor.com/1995/1024/24013.html*.

42. "Tribunal Convicts Momčilo Perišić for Crimes in Bosnia and Herzegovina and Croatia," ICTY press release, September 6, 2011, *www.icty.org/sid/10793*.

43. "Perišić's Defence Says Waging War Declared a Crime," Hrvatska izvještajna novinska agencija (Croatian informational news agency, HINA), November 8, 2011.

44. Caroline Tosh, "Tolimir Trial May Shed New Light on Srebrenica," IWPR, June 4, 2007, *iwpr.net/report-news/tolimir-trial-may-shed-new-light-srebrenica*.

45. Ibid.

46. Arthur Max, "UN Prosecutor Opens Genocide Case, Says Bosnian Serb General Supervised Execution of Thousands," *StarTribune*, February 26, 2010, *www.startribune.com/templates/Print_This_Story?sid=85477792*.

47. "Salvation or a Military Operation?," Sense Agency, March 7, 2011, *www.sense-agency.com/icty/salvation-or-a-military-operation.29.html?news_id=12586*.

48. "Insider from the VRS Main Staff Gives Evidence," Sense Agency, June 9, 2011, *www.sense-agency.com/icty/insider-from-the-vrs-main-staff-gives-evidence.29.html?news_id=12895&cat_id=1*.

49. See UN General Assembly Resolution 260, Convention on the Prevention and Punishment of the

Crime of Genocide, Human Rights Web, last edited January 27, 1997, *www.hrweb.org/legal/genocide
.html*. See also "How Do You Define Genocide?," BBC, March 17, 2016, *www.bbc.co.uk/news/world
-11108059*.

50. Eric Gordy, "Hague Verdicts Allow Commanders to Evade Justice," Balkan Insight, March 1, 2013,
www.balkaninsight.com/en/article/hague-verdicts-allow-commanders-to-evade-justice.

51. "Serbian Relief at Perišić Ruling," IWPR, March 4, 2013, *iwpr.net/report-news/
serbian-relief-perisic-ruling*.

52. "Jovica Stanišić and Franko Simatović Acquitted of All Charges," ICTY press release, May 30, 2013,
www.icty.org/sid/11329.

53. Velma Šarić, "Serb Special Forces Created 'Disorder' in Krajina," IWPR, February 15, 2010, *iwpr.net
/report-news/serb-special-forces-created-disorder-krajina*.

54. "Jovica Stanišić and Franko Simatović Acquitted," Sense Agency, May 30, 2013, *www.sense-agency
.com/icty/jovica-stanisic-and-franko-simatovic-acquitted.29.html?news_id=14999*.

55. "Serbian Security Chiefs Acquitted of War Crimes," Balkan Insight, May 30, 2013, *www
.balkaninsight.com/en/article/stanisic-and-simatovic-sentenced-for-war-crimes*.

56. Dženana Karabegović and Ognjen Zorić, "Bosnian Consternation at Serbian Security Officers' Acquittal," IWPR, June 3, 2013, *iwpr.net/global-voices/consternation-serbian-security-officers-acquittal*.

57. James Stewart, "'Specific Direction' Is Unprecedented: Results from Two Empirical Studies,"
September 4, 2013, *www.ejiltalk.org/specific-direction-is-unprecedented-results-from-two-
empirical-studies*.

58. "Appeals Chamber Orders Retrial of Jovica Stanišić and Franko Simatović," ICTY press release,
December 15, 2015, *www.icty.org/en/press/appeals-chamber-orders-retrial-jovica-stanišić-and
-franko-simatović*.

59. "Reakcije Na Presudu Suda U Haagu—Porodice ubijenih u šoku nakon oslobađanja Perišića"
[Reactions to the judgment of the court at The Hague—families of those killed in shock after the
release of Perišić], *Oslobodjenje*, February 28, 2013.

60. Ajla Gezo and Emina Dizdarevic, "Srebrenica Court Verdicts: Do They Make
Sense?," Balkan Insight, July 9, 2018, *www.balkaninsight.com/en/article/
srebrenica-court-verdicts-do-they-make-sense—07-05-2018*.

61. "Mladic Verdict Highlights Bosnia's Ethnic Divisions," Balkan Insight, November 22, 2017, *www
.balkaninsight.com/en/article/mladic-verdict-highlights-bosnia-s-ethnic-divisions-11-22-2017*.

62. Dražen Remiković, "BiH Releases More War Crime Convicts Based on EU Ruling," *Southeast European Times*, December 2, 2013, *web.archive.org/web/20140209124708/http://www.setimes.com/cocoon
/setimes/xhtml/en_GB/features/setimes/features/2013/12/02/feature-01*. "In the past eight years, BiH
courts have closed 206 war crimes cases and sentenced 229 people to a total of 2,224 years in prison,
but 1,300 cases are still pending."

63. Denis Džidić and Marija Tausan, "Most Hague Tribunal Convicts Already Free," Balkan Insight,
February 14, 2014, *www.balkaninsight.com/en/article/early-release-means-most-convicts-are-free*.

64. Filip Rudić and Erna Mačkić, "Srebrenica Suspects Find Safe Haven in Serbia," Balkan Insight, July
6, 2018, *www.balkaninsight.com/en/article/srebrenica-suspects-find-safe-haven-in-serbia-07-04-2018*.

65. Srđa Pavlović and Christophe Solioz, "Requiem for a Court," March 5, 2013, *www.opendemocracy.
net/sr%C4%91-pavlovi%C4%87-christophe-solioz/requiem-for-court*.

66. "Prvi mart: Beara u zatvoru, a 400 saučesnika u javnim službama" [March 1st Coalition: Beara in
prison, but 400 collaborators in public service], *Oslobodjenje*, January 30, 2015, reposted at Patria
Novinska Agencija, *nap.ba/news/7762*.

67. Eric Gordy, "Chronicle of an Arrest Foretold and a Process Foreshortened," *Croatian Political*

Science Review, March 18, 2015, *politickamisao.com/chronicle-of-an-arrest-foretold-and-a-process-foreshortened.*

CHAPTER 8

1. The Contact Group, including the United States, Russia, Germany, France, and Great Britain, was established in the spring of 1994 to arrange a peace agreement between the Federation and the Bosnian Serbs. See "Bosnia: The Road to Dayton," US Department of State Fact Sheet, November 1, 1995, via the Wayback Machine, *web.archive.org/web/20100620173052/http://dosfan.lib.uic.edu/ERC/bureaus/eur/releases/951101BosniaRoad.html.*

2. "Report of the Secretary-General Pursuant to General Assembly Resolution 53/35: The Fall of Srebrenica." UN document no. A/54/549. November 15, 1999, *www.refworld.org/docid/3ae6afb34.html*, paragraph 502, p. 111.

3. Ibid., paragraph 488.

4. Ibid., paragraph 479.

5. Judy Aita, "Report on Srebrenica: UN Failed to Confront Evil," UN correspondent, November 16, 1999, *danieltoljaga.wordpress.com/2011/09/18/analysis-of-the-1999-un-report-on-srebrenica*. Via Wayback Machine, *web.archive.org/web/20130304211526/http://danieltoljaga.wordpress.com/2011/09/18/analysis-of-the-1999-un-report-on-srebrenica.*

6. Ibid.

7. "Report of the Secretary-General Pursuant to General Assembly Resolution 53/35," paragraph 480.

8. Letter from American lawyer, professor Francis Boyle, to Del Ponte on behalf of the Bosnian NGO, the Citizens Association of Mothers of Srebrenica and Podrinje, *republic-bosnia-herzegovina.com/arhiva/?p=611.*

9. "NIOD Srebrenica Report: Summary for the Press," NIOD, April 10, 2002, *www.niod.nl/en/srebrenica-report/summary-press*. For the full NIOD report, see NIOD, April 10, 2002, *www.niod.nl/en/srebrenica-report.*

10. "NIOD Srebrenica Report: Summary."

11. Ibid. See also Don Hill, "Bosnia: Report on Massacre at Srebrenica Condemns Dutch Military 'Errors,'" Radio Free Europe, April 10, 2002, *www.rferl.org/content/article/1099363.html.*

12. Karen Meirik, "Controversial Srebrenica Report Back on Table," IWPR, February 6, 2004, *iwpr.net/report-news/controversial-srebrenica-report-back-table.*

13. Alain van der Horst, "Secret—The True Story behind the Srebrenica Report," *De Tijd*, December 12, 2003.

14. "Srebrenica Report Spreads Blame, but Angry Victims Say It's Too Mild," Associated Press, April 11, 2002. Via Wayback Machine, *web.archive.org/web/20151016175048/http://staugustine.com/stories/041102/wor_635177.shtml.*

15. "Dutch Government Quits over Srebrenica," BBC, April 16, 2002, *news.bbc.co.uk/2/hi/europe/1933144.stm.*

16. "Srebrenica Report Spreads Blame."

17. "Dutch Government Quits over Srebrenica."

18. Nedim Dervišbegović, "Dutch PM to Bosnia: Don't Blame Us for Srebrenica," Reuters, June 11, 2002.

19. Sheri Fink, *War Hospital: A True Story of Surgery and Survival* (New York: Public Affairs, 2003), 347.

20. "Dutch Report Blasts U.N. Actions in Srebrenica," UN news posting, January 27, 2003. Via Wayback Machine, *web.archive.org/web/20091125101519/http://www.unwire.org/unwire/20030127/31682_story.asp*. Also available at *balkanwitness.glypx.com/un-wire2003-01-27.htm.*

21. Othon Zimmermann, "Srebrenica Comes Back to Haunt Netherlands; Dutch Parliament Again

Probes Government Responsibility for Srebrenica Massacre," *TRI* 316 (May 1, 2005), *iwpr.net /global-voices/srebrenica-comes-back-haunt-netherlands.*

22. Михайлов Андрей, "Another Version of Srebrenica," *Pravda*, November 23, 2004, *www .pravdareport.com/opinion/7266-srebrenica.* This article, posted in response to the release of a subsequent, more-revealing report by the RS, provided a link to a poorly translated version of the 2002 report.

23. "Pulling Rotten Teeth," *Transitions Online*, October 20, 2003, *www.tol.org/client/article/10827-pulling -rotten-teeth.html.*

24. "Report about Case Srebrenica" [*sic*], p. 47, RS Bureau for Cooperation with the ICTY, September 2002, *www.slobodan-milosevic.org/documents/srebrenica.pdf* (linked at *www.pravdareport.com /opinion/7266-srebrenica*).

25. Ibid., 44–45.

26. Ibid., 34.

27. Ibid., 31–32.

28. Minutes of Joint OHR, NATO, and SFOR conference, Sarajevo, September 3, 2002, *www.nato.int /sfor/trans/2002/t020903a.htm.*

29. "High Representative Condemns Srebrenica Report," OHR, Sarajevo, September 3, 2002. Via Way-back Machine, *web.archive.org/web/20021129091139/http://www.ohr.int/ohr-dept/presso/pressr/default. asp?content_id=27845.*

30. Ibid.

31. Isabelle Wesselingh and Arnaud Vaulerin, *Raw Memory: Prijedor, Laboratory of Ethnic Cleansing* (London: Saqi Books, 2005), 78.

32. "Bosnia-Herzegovina: Human Rights Chamber Decision on Srebrenica—A First Step to Justice," Amnesty International, March 7, 2003, *reliefweb.int/report/bosnia-and-herzegovina/bosnia-herzegovina-human-rights-chamber-decision-srebrenica-first-step.* See also Daniel Simpson, "Bosnian Serbs Ordered to Pay $2 Million for Srebrenica Massacre," *New York Times*, March 8, 2003, *www.nytimes .com/2003/03/08/world/bosnian-serbs-told-to-pay-2-million-for-srebrenica-massacre.html.*

33. *Oslobodjenje*, April 29, 2004.

34. Internal Displacement Monitoring Centre, "Overview," *Bosnia and Herzegovina: Sectarian Divide Continues to Hamper Residual Return and Reintegration of the Displaced: A Profile of the Internal Displacement Situation* (Geneva: Internal Displacement Monitoring Centre, 2006), 9–15. *www .refworld.org/pdfid/45505b864.pdf.*

35. Nicholas Wood, "Bosnian Serbs Admit Responsibility for the Massacre of 7,000," *New York Times*, June 12, 2004, *www.nytimes.com/2004/06/12/world/bosnian-serbs-admit-responsibility-for-the-massacre-of-7000.html.*

36. Ibid.

37. Irena Gajić, "Bosnian Serb President Expresses Regrets for a Wartime Massacre of Muslims," Associated Press, June 22, 2004. See also "Serb Leader's Srebrenica Regret," BBC News, June 23, 2004, *news.bbc.co.uk/2/hi/europe/3831599.stm.*

38. "Prvi mart: Beara u zatvoru, a 400 saučesnika u javnim službama" [March 1st Coalition: Beara in prison, but 400 participants in public service], *Oslobodjenje*, January 30, 2015, reposted at Patria Novinska Agencija, *nap.ba/news/7762.*

39. S. Rožajac, "Zavrsni izvjestaj Komisije Vlade Republike Srpske o Srebrenici" [Final report of the Republika Srpska Government Commission on Srebrenica], *Oslobodjenje*, October 15, 2004.

40. Munira Subašić, interview, Sarajevo, May 7, 2004.

41. Lisa Clifford, "Srebrenica Survivors Sue Dutch and UN," IWPR, June 9, 2007, *iwpr.net/report-news /srebrenica-survivors-sue-dutch-and-un.*

42. Radio Netherlands interview with attorney Liesbeth Zegveld, published October 30, 2003, *fr.groups .yahoo.com/group/eur-engl/message/401?var=1.*

43. Ibid.

44. Harro ten Wolde, "Srebrenica Families Sue Dutch State, U.N.," Reuters, June 4, 2007, *www.reuters .com/article/2007/06/04/us-dutch-srebrenica-idUSL0437048320070604.*

45. Convention on the Privileges and Immunities of the United Nations, adopted February 13, 1946, *www.un.org/en/ethics/pdf/convention.pdf.*

46. "Dutch Court Rules Srebrenica Families Can Sue U.N.," Reuters, November 27, 2007, *www.reuters .com/article/2007/11/27/us-bosnia-srebrenica-court-idUSL2712448720071127.*

47. Ibid.

48. "UN Ruled Immune from Srebrenica Prosecution," IWPR, April 3, 2010, *iwpr.net/report-news/un -ruled-immune-srebrenica-prosecution.*

49. *Oslobodjenje,* December 20, 2012.

50. "Complaint about UN's Immunity from National Jurisdiction in Civil Case Concerning Srebrenica Massacre Declared Inadmissible," European Court of Human Rights press release, June 27, 2013, *hudoc.echr.coe.int/webservices/content/pdf/003–4416460–5307356.*

51. "Court Rules Dutch State Liable for 300 Srebrenica Deaths," Reuters, July 16, 2004, *www.reuters. com/article/2014/07/16/us-dutch-srebrenica-ruling-idUSKBN0FL0ZJ20140716.*

52. "Dutch State Liable for 300 Srebrenica Massacre Deaths," *Guardian,* July 16, 2014, *www.theguardian .com/world/2014/jul/16/dutch-liable-srebrenica-massacre-deaths.*

53. Ibid.

54. "Srebrenica Massacre: Dutch Government 'Partially Liable' for Murder of 300 Muslim Men, Court Finds," *Independent,* June 27, 2017, *www.independent.co.uk/news/world/europe/srebrenica-massacre-dutch-peacekeepers-murder-300-muslim-men-serbia-bosnia-war-1995-appeals-court-a7809806.html.*

55. "Dutch State Not Liable for 300 Srebrenica Deaths, Says Supreme Court Advisor," *DutchNews.nl,* February 1, 2019, *www.dutchnews.nl/news/2019/02/dutch-state-not-liable-for-300-srebrenica-deaths-says-supreme-court-advisor.*

56. Marlise Simons, "2 Bosnian Muslim Families Sue Dutch over Srebrenica Massacre," *New York Times,* May 13, 2005, *www.nytimes.com/2005/05/13/international/europe/13balkans.html.*

57. Ian Traynor, "Netherlands in the Dock over Bosnia Massacre," *Guardian,* May 13, 2005, *www .theguardian.com/world/2005/may/13/warcrimes.iantraynor.*

58. "Dutch in Dock for Srebrenica Crimes," Al Jazeera, June 16, 2008, *www.aljazeera.com/news/europe /2008/06/2008619122811348441.html.*

59. For a detailed discussion of this decision, see "Dual Attribution: Liability of the Netherlands for Removal of Individuals from the Compound of Dutchbat," by Shares—Research Project on Shared Responsibility in International Law, July 8, 2011, *www.sharesproject.nl/dual-attribution-liability-of-the-netherlands-for-removal-of-individuals-from-the-compound-of-dutchbat.*

60. Hasan Nuhanović, interview, Sarajevo, July 25, 2013.

61. "'Dutch Sent Family to Their Deaths' at Srebrenica, Court Told," ICTJ, January 18, 2013, *www.ictj.org /es/node/16460.*

62. Ibid.

63. A Resolution Expressing the Sense of the Senate Regarding the Massacre at Srebrenica in July 1995, S. Res. 134, 109th Cong. (2005), *www.congress.gov/bill/109th-congress/senate-resolution/134.*

64. European Parliament Resolution of 15 January 2009 on Srebrenica, P6_TA(2009)0028, *www
.europarl.europa.eu/sides/getDoc.do?type=TA&reference=P6-TA-2009-0028&language=EN.*

65. "Bosnian Serbs Reject EU Srebrenica Resolution," Balkan Insight, January 16, 2009, *www
.balkaninsight.com/en/article/bosnian-serbs-reject-eu-srebrenica-resolution/1422/4.*

66. Bojana Barlovac, "Serbia Parliament to Vote on Srebrenica Resolution," Balkan Insight, March 30,
2010, *www.balkaninsight.com/en/article/serbia-parliament-to-vote-on-srebrenica-resolution.*

67. Ibid.

68. Stephanie van den Berg, "Serbia Holds Landmark Srebrenica Debate," Agence France-Presse, March
30, 2010. See also Daniel McLaughlin, "Politicians in Serbia Divided over Srebrenica," *Irish Times*,
March 31, 2010, *www.irishtimes.com/news/politicians-in-serbia-divided-over-srebrenica-1.646010.*

69. Neil MacDonald, "Srebrenica Apology Angers Bosnian Muslims," *Financial Times*, March 31, 2010,
www.ft.com/content/2fa7745c-3c4f-11df-b316-00144feabdco?o=%2Fworld.

70. Ibid.

71. Dan Bilefsky, "E.U. Finds Serbia's Apology Lacking," *New York Times*, April 1, 2010, *www.nytimes
.com/2010/04/01/world/europe/01iht-serbia.html.*

72. Bojana Barlovac and Sabina Arslanagić, "Mixed Reactions in Serbia, Bosnia to Srebrenica Resolution," Balkan Insight, April 1, 2010, *www.balkaninsight.com/en/article/mixed-reactions-in-serbia
-bosnia-to-srebrenica-resolution.*

CHAPTER 9

1. "Implementation of the Property Laws in Bosnia and Herzegovina," Office of the High Representative/
Commission for Real Property Claims, December 31, 2003. Via Wayback Machine, *web.archive.org
/web/20041028095139/http://www.ohr.int/plip/pdf/plip_12.03.PDF.*

2. Internal Displacement Monitoring, *Bosnia And Herzegovina*, 10.

3. "Povratak u Opštinu Srebrenica" [Return to Srebrenica municipality], by Unija za održivi povratak
i integracije u Bosni i Hercegovini (Union for Sustainable Return and Integration in Bosnia-
Herzegovina), *uzopibih.com.ba/povratak/srebrenica.html.* Accessed January 16, 2018.

4. Sakib Salimović and Miro Pejić, *Srebrenica, Povratak Života* [Srebrenica, the return of life] (Srebrenica: Srebrenica Municipality, 2006); quote is of Muška Krdžić, from the article "Selo povratnika i
vikendaša" [A village of returnees and weekenders], 65.

5. For more information on the SRRP program and its funding, see "Summative Evaluation Report of
Srebrenica Regional Recovery Programme and Birač Region Development and Cooperation Project,"
Hamid R. Chaudhry, International Evaluation Consultant, July 2018, *erc.undp.org/evaluation
/documents/download/12106.*

6. *Oslobodjenje*, November 22, 2002.

7. *Oslobodjenje*, December 18, 2002.

8. Arundhati Roy, "The NGO-ization of Resistance," *beautifulrising.org/tool/the-ngo-ization-of-
resistance.* Accessed March 15, 2018. Excerpted from Arundhati Roy, *The End of Imagination*
(Chicago: Haymarket Books, 2016).

9. Marija Arnautović, "Bosnia's War Victims Let Down by NGOs; Funding for Victim Support Does
Not Always Translate into Visible Change for Vulnerable Groups," IWPR, December 28, 2011, *iwpr
.net/report-news/bosnias-war-victims-let-down-ngos.*

10. *Oslobodjenje*, June 11, 2003.

11. For Prijatelji's website, see *www.prijateljisrebrenice.org.* The site features day-to-day information
from Srebrenica municipality.

12. Amil Dučić, "Privredni uspon jedne siromašne regije" [Economic rise in one poor region], *Oslobodjenje*, October 19, 2006.

CHAPTER 10

1. The Repatriation Information Centre (RIC), based in Sarajevo, described itself as "serv[ing] as a comprehensive clearing-house for information related to all aspects of repatriation and return movements of refugees and displaced persons within and to Bosnia and Herzegovina, with the aim of facilitating the decision-making process of relevant and interested institutions, organisations and individuals, both inside and outside Bosnia and Herzegovina." For about five years after the war, the RIC regularly posted statistical reports about many municipalities throughout Bosnia-Herzegovina. Ultimately its web page was removed, and its documentation is no longer accessible, to my knowledge. The 1999 report, and any others in my possession, are available to the reader upon request.

2. UNDP statement published in May 2002 describing projects to be launched under the auspices of the Srebrenica Regional Recovery Programme. Document on file with the author.

3. Ibid.

4. Ibrahim Hadžić, interview, Tuzla, December 1999.

5. Svetlana Buca Jukić, interview, Srebrenica, April 2, 2002.

6. Senad Subašić, interview, Srebrenica, May 29, 2004.

7. Munira Subašić, interview, Sarajevo, July 31, 2014.

8. Hakija Meholjić, interview, Srebrenica, July 2006.

9. Aleksa Milanović, interview, Srebrenica, April 9, 2002.

10. Statements by Ibrahim Hadžić, Svetlana Jukić, Senad Subašić, Hakija Meholjić, Aleksa Milanović, and Enes Đozić all come from interviews in Srebrenica between 1999 and 2006.

11. US$3,000 to US$10,000.

12. Albina Beganović, interview, Srebrenica, September 23, 2008.

13. Hakija Meholjić, interview, Srebrenica, July 9, 2006.

14. Approximately US$25 million. One DM (deutschmark) and one KM (Bosnian konvertabilna marka, or convertible mark) hold roughly the same value, which fluctuates between US$0.60 and US$0.70.

15. Ibrahim Hadžić, interview, Srebrenica, April 9, 2002.

16. Approximately US$600 billion.

17. Eldin Karić, "Korupcija pojede 47 KM u sekundi" [Corruption eats up 47 KM each second], *Nezavisne Novine*, September 2, 2013, *www.nezavisne.com/novosti/intervju/ Eldin-Karic-Korupcija-pojede-47-KM-u-sekundi/207410*.

18. Hadžić, "Zašto izbori u Srebrenici."

19. J. Šarac, "Ko i kako je trosio donacije za obnovu Srebrenice" [Who spent donations for the renewal of Srebrenica, and how], *Nezavisne Novine*, October 1, 2005.

20. Selma Lemo, "Sarajevo: Do 2010. godine u Srebrenicu će biti uloženo 70 miliona KM" [Sarajevo: By 2010 70 million KM to be invested in Srebrenica], Kliker, July 4, 2007, *kliker.info/sarajevo-do-2010 -godine-u-srebrenicu-ce-biti-ulozeno-70-miliona-km*.

21. "Predistrazne radnje Kantonalnog tužilaštva Tuzla o pronevjeri donatorske pomoci za Srebrenicu— Ne zna se ko je potrosio saudijsku donaciju od 130 miliona dolara" [Preliminary investigation by Tuzla Canton Prosecution about embezzlement of donor assistance for Srebrenica—it is not known who spent the Saudi donation of $130 million], *Nezavisne Novine*, January 4, 2005.

22. "Dutch Aid to Srebrenica Questioned," OCCRP, July 18, 2013, *reportingproject.net/occrp/index.php /en/ccwatch/cc-watch-briefs/2063-dutch-aid-to-srebrenica-questioned*.

23. "Bosnia and Herzegovina: More Than 36.5 Million Euros for Srebrenica," UNDP Report,

July 5, 2007, *reliefweb.int/report/bosnia-and-herzegovina/bosnia-and-herzegovina-more-365-million-euros-srebrenica.*

24. "Ko je odgovoran za propast srebreničkog rudnika Sase? Uništi, pa rasprodaj" [Who is responsible for the downfall of the Srebrenica mines at Sase? Destroy, and sell off], *Dani* 609 (February 13, 2009), *www.bhdani.ba/portal/izdanje/609.*

25. "Sve teža situacija u privredi Srebrenice; Rudnik olova i cinka zatrpan kreditima" [Ever harder situation in the Srebrenica economy; Lead and zinc mines burdened with debt], *Nezavisne Novine,* February 17, 2003.

26. A. Šišic, "Nakon što su 'Nezavisne' objavile odredbe nepovoljnog ugovora Vlade RS i ruske firme o upravljanju Rudnikom Sase" [After "Nezavisne" published the contents of the unfavorable agreement between the RS government and the Russian company about administration of the Sase mine], *Nezavisne Novine,* January 7, 2005.

27. Ibid.

28. Ibid.

29. D. Risojević, "Osnovni sud u Banjoj Luci donio privremenu odluku o slucaju 'Sase'; Rusima zabranjeno upravljanje Rudnikom" [Basic court in Banja Luka takes temporary decision in the case of "Sase"; Russians forbidden to run mine], *Nezavisne Novine,* October 19, 2005.

30. D. Risojević, "Rusi za porez duguju 630.000 KM" [Russians owe 630,000 KM in taxes], *Nezavisne Novine,* October 19, 2005.

31. J. Šarac, "Predsjednik Sindikata Rudnika olova i cinka u Srebrenici: 'Vladu nije briga za nezakonitosti'" [President of the union of lead and zinc miners in Srebrenica: "The government does not care about the illegalities"], *Nezavisne Novine,* February 12, 2006.

32. Ibid.

33. "Uprkos sudskoj zabrani iz Rudnika Sase u Srbiju izvezena vrijedna ruda; Odvezeno 450 tona olova iz Rudnika Sase" [In spite of a court prohibition valuable ore exported to Serbia; 450 tons of lead transported from Sase mine], *Nezavisne Novine,* March 23, 2006.

34. A. Šišic, "Osumnjiceni za mito i bankrot Rudnika Sase" [Suspected of bribery and bankrupt of the Sase mines], *Nezavisne Novine,* December 10, 2006.

35. Ibid.

36. Ibid.

37. Ibid.

38. Milan Malenović, "Stečajna mafija: Organizovani kriminal uz blagoslov ili prećutnu saglasnost vlasti" [The bankruptcy mafia: Organized crime with the blessing or silent agreement of the authorities], *Tabloid* 217 (August 14, 2010), *www.magazin-tabloid.com/casopis/?id=06&br=217&c1=12.*

39. "Radnici Rudnika olova i cinka 'Sase' u stečaju traže isplatu dugovanja od oko 500 000 KM" [Workers from the "Sase" lead and zinc mine in bankruptcy seek payment of debts of about 500,000 KM], Prijatelji Srebrenice, February 17, 2014.

40. "Srebrenički rudnik Sase: Poslovanje pozitivno, planovi kao prošle godine" [Srebrenica mine at Sase: Business in the black, plans like last year], SRNA (Novinska Agencija Republike Srpske, Republika Srpska News Agency), February 26, 2016, *www.klix.ba/biznis/privreda/srebrenicki-rudnik-sase-poslovanje-pozitivno-planovi-kao-prosle-godine/160226009.*

41. D. Risojević, "Rudniku boksita 'Srebrenica' zabranjen rad" [Work at Srebrenica bauxite mine prohibited], *Nezavisne Novine,* October 4, 2006, *www.nezavisne.com/novosti/bih/Rudniku-boksita-Srebrenica-zabranjen-rad/731.*

42. Z. Kusmuk and P. Klincov, "Milionska prevara" [Millions in embezzlement], *Nezavisne Novine,* May 31, 2007, *www.nezavisne.com/ekonomija/privreda/Milionska-prevara/10216.*

43. "Mineco Had Troubled History," Organized Crime and Corruption Reporting Project, July 23, 2013, *www.reportingproject.net/minecoproject/*.

44. Marinko Sekulić, "Ljekovite vode Banje Guber nada su brojnim bolesnicima" [The healing waters of Guber spa are the hope of many patients], *klix.ba*, November 24, 2010, *www.klix.ba/vijesti/bih /ljekovite-vode-banje-guber-nada-su-brojnim-bolesnicima/101124006*.

45. Ibid. See also "'Argentum 09' dobio koncesiju za ljekovitu vodu Guber" ["Argentum 09" received concession for the healing waters of Guber], Srna news agency, August 23, 2012, *www.capital.ba /argentum-09-dobio-koncesiju-za-ljekovitu-vodu-guber*.

46. Sekulić, "Ljekovite vode Banje Guber nada su brojnim bolesnicima."

47. Ibid.

48. "Ko se danas bori protiv Srebrenice?" [Who today is fighting against Srebrenica?], tacnonet-deutsche-welle, May 18, 2011, *tacno.net/novosti/ko-se-danas-bori-protiv-srebrenice*.

49. "Pokrenut prekršajni postupak protiv nadležnih u Srebrenici u slučaju Banja 'Guber'" [Infractionary proceedings initiated against Srebrenica authorities in Guber spa case], May 11, 2011, *informer.ba /tekstovi/vijesti/pokrenut-prekrsajni-postupak-protiv-nadleznih-u-srebrenici-u-slucaju-banja -guber*.

50. Maja Bjelajac "Ministarstvo i dalje sprečava obnovu banje Guber" [Ministry still preventing renewal of Guber spa], August 6, 2014, *www.slobodnaevropa.org/content/ministarstvo_i_dalje_sprecava_ obnovu_banje_guber/24183685.html*.

51. Selma Milovanović, "Borba za vlast u podijeljenom gradu" [Struggle for power in divided city], Al Jazeera Balkans, July 11, 2012, *balkans.aljazeera.net/vijesti/borba-za-vlast-u-podijeljenom-gradu*.

52. "Ambition and Vision Are the Only Realistic Hope for Change in BiH," from the blog of the grassroots organization Koalicija 143, summer 2014. Via Wayback Machine, *web.archive.org /web/20160409063305/http://k143.org/en/blog.html*.

53. Krstina Ćirković, "Ratkovac bez dozvole gradi na tuđoj zemlji" [Ratkovac builds on someone else's land without permission], December 12, 2012, *www.glassrpske.com/drustvo/panorama/Ratkovac -bez-dozvole-gradi-na-tudjoj-zemlji/lat/102944.html*.

54. Ibid.

55. Marinko Sekulić, "Banja Guber—Nada bolesnicima i Srebreničanima" [Guber spa—The hope of patients and Srebrenicans], by November 24, 2013, *www.dw.de/banja-guber-nada-bolesnicima -i-srebreni%C4%8Danima/a-17248768*.

56. Jelena Bjelica, "Otkrivamo: Lekovita voda Banje Guber u rukama Milorada Motike" [Uncovered: Healing waters of Guber spa in the hands of Milorad Motika], *Blic.rs*, July 22, 2016, *www.blic.rs /vesti/republika-srpska/otkrivamo-lekovita-voda-banje-guber-u-rukama-milorada-motike/5v10d4k*.

57. Amer Kapetanović, "Lijepe fabrike lijepo gore" [Pretty factories, pretty flames], *Dani* 165 (July 28, 2000), *www.bhdani.ba/portal/arhiva_67_281/165*.

58. Robert Donia, *Sarajevo: A Biography* (Ann Arbor: University of Michigan Press, 2006), 290, quoting April 1998 testimony in the ICJ during Bosnia's genocide lawsuit against Yugoslavia.

59. Transcript of testimony by Berko Zečević, Humanitarian Law Center, January 16, 2004, *www .hlc-rdc.org/Transkripti/Milosevic/_Milosevic.html*.

60. "Karadzic and Krajisnik for EU in Balkans," Sense Agency, November 21, 2013, *www.sense-agency .com/icty/karadzic-and-krajisnik-for-eu-in-balkans.29.html?news_id=15518&cat_id=1*.

61. Kapetanović, "Lijepe fabrike lijepo gore."

62. Ibid.

63. Ibid.

64. Ibid.

65. "Srpskoj preti višemilionski gubitak" [Multimillion KM loss threatens Srpska], Press RS, December 21, 2013. Via Wayback Machine, *web.archive.org/web/20131223114103/http://www.pressrs.ba/sr/vesti /vesti_dana/story/51606/Ratkovac++napla%C4%87uje++6.000.000+KM!.html*.

66. "Krivična prijava protiv vlasnika 'Gubera'" [Criminal charges against the owner of Guber], Press RS, September 20, 2012. Via Wayback Machine, *web.archive.org/web/20120921005312/http://www.pressrs .ba/sr/vesti/vesti_dana/story/23856/Ratkovac+oteo+dr%C5%BEavnu+zemlju.html*.

See Žana Gauk, "Dok gura 'Aluminu' u stečaj, Motika kupuje luksuzni mercedes od 200.000 KM!" [While pushing Alumina into bankruptcy, Motika buys a luxurious Mercedes for 200,000 KM!], *Capital*, June 3, 2017, *www.capital.ba/dok-gura-aluminu-u-stecaj-motika-kupuje-luksuzni -mercedes-od-200-000-km*. I note that with Motika at the helm, and in spite of financial pressures, Alumina continued to register profits into 2019. (See "Motika: Plan proizvodnje ostvaren sa 97 odsto" [Motika: Production plan 97 percent realized], *Capital.ba*, January 2, 2019, *www.capital.ba /motika-plan-proizvodnje-ostvaren-sa-97-odsto.*)

67. Early that year, it was announced that Motika was planning to retire. (See "Motika ide u penziju" [Motika to retire], *zvono.media*, February 27, 2019, *zvono.media/sr/motika-ide-u-penziju.*)

68. Sekulić, "Banja Guber—Nada bolesnicima i Srebreničanima."

69. Sadmir Nukić, quoted in ibid.

70. Petra Živić and Stefan Veselinović, "Banja Guber, još jedan propali srebrenički san" [Guber spa, yet another failed Srebrenica dream], July 10, 2015, *www.vice.com/rs/read/banja-guber.* See also the enthusiastic but inaccurate prediction of resumption of construction in 2018: E. Trako, "Čuveno lječilište Guber na proljeće počinje s radom!" [Famed Guber spa to continue work in the spring!], in the Sarajevo daily *Avaz*, February 1, 2018, *avaz.ba/vijesti/bih/346426/ cuveno-ljeciliste-guber-na-proljece-pocinje-s-radom.*

71. Anadolija, "Srebrenica: Banja Guber mogla bi početi sa radom tokom 2019. godine" [Srebrenica: Banja Guber could start functioning during the year 2019], N1 BiH (Bosnian, Serbian, and Croatian news service), January 27, 2019, *ba.n1info.com/Vijesti/a312059/Srebrenica-Banja-Guber-mogla-bi -poceti-sa-radom-tokom-2019.-godine.html.*

72. Conversation with Subašić, July 31, 2013.

73. Sekulić, "Banja Guber—Nada bolesnicima i Srebreničanima."

74. "Zatvorena jedina mesara i poljoprivredna prodavnica u Srebrenici" [The only butcher shop and farm outlet in Srebrenica closed], Srna press agency, *Oslobodjenje*, August 4, 2016, reposted at *www .klix.ba/biznis/privreda/zatvorene-jedina-mesara-i-poljoprivredna-prodavnica-u-srebrenici/160804014.*

CHAPTER 11

1. Roberta Biagiarelli, "Le mucche della Val Rendena, a Srebrenica" [The cows of Val Rendena, to Srebrenica], December 22, 2010, *www.balcanicaucaso.org/aree/Bosnia-Erzegovina/Le-mucche-della -Val-Rendena-a-Srebrenica-85899.*

2. "Bosniaks Do Not Want to Go Home," *Večernje Novosti* (Belgrade), July 25, 2001.

3. Samir Karić, "U Potočarima do sada ukopane 4.524 žrtve: Srebrenica mora ostati urezana u pamćenje" [In Potočari to date 4,524 victims buried; Srebrenica must remain engraved in memory], *Oslobodjenje*, July 12, 2010.

4. For details about the murder of Hasan Nuhanović's family and the discovery of their remains, see Lauren Comiteau, "Survivor of the Genocide," March 5, 2010, *www.thedailybeast.com/survivor -of-the-genocide*, and Michael Dobbs, "Who Killed Muhamed Nuhanović?," March 26, 2012, *foreignpolicy.com/2012/03/26/who-killed-muhamed-nuhanovic.*

5. Halilovich, *Places of Pain*, 93–94.

6. Hariz Halilović, *Kako Opisati Srebrenicu* [Writing after Srebrenica] (Sarajevo: Buybook, 2017), 67.

7. Iva Martinovic, "Serbs Honor Srebrenica Victims with Shoe Memorial," Radio Free Europe / Radio Liberty, July 12, 2010, *www.rferl.org/content/Serbs_Honor_Srebrenica_Victims_With_Shoe_Memorial/2096026.html.*

8. Faruk Borić, "Sila Dodika ne moli" [Power does not pray to Dodik], *Oslobodjenje*, July 13, 2010, reposted at *www.idoconline.info/article/721941.*

9. Nerma Jelacic, "Serbs Subvert Srebrenica Commemoration," IWPR, August 2, 2005, *iwpr.net/report-news/serbs-subvert-srebrenica-commemoration.*

10. The Cyrillic "C" is equivalent to the Latin "S," and in this slogan it stands for "Samo sloga Srbina spašava," i.e., "Only unity saves the Serb."

11. "Bosnian Serb Leader Denies Srebrenica Genocide," Agence France-Presse, July 12, 2010, reposted in JUSTWATCH Archives, *listserv.buffalo.edu/cgi-bin/wa?A2=ind1007&L=JUSTWATCH-L&F=&S=&P=108908.*

12. Srđan Puhalo, "Zašto se manipuliše srpskim žrtvama u regionu Srebrenice?" [Why are the Serb victims in the Srebrenica region manipulated?], Portal Frontal, August 22, 2014, *www.frontal.ba/blogovi/blog/60306/zasto-se-manipulise-srpskim-zrtvama-u-regionu-srebrenice.* Quoting Glas Srpske (Voice of Srpska).

13. Puhalo, "Zašto se manipuliše."

14. Nidžara Ahmetašević, "Bosnia's Book of the Dead," Justice Report, June 21, 2007, *www.academia.edu/1083734/Justice_Report_Bosnias_Book_of_the_Dead.* Information on the parallel count by the ICTY is available at Jan Zwierzchowski and Ewa Tabeau, "The 1992–95 War in Bosnia and Herzegovina: Census-Based Multiple System Estimation of Casualties Undercount," February 1, 2010. *www.icty.org/x/file/About/OTP/War_Demographics/en/bih_casualty_undercount_conf_paper_100201.pdf.*

15. Lara J. Nettelfield and Sarah E. Wagner, *Srebrenica in the Aftermath of* Genocide (New York: Cambridge University Press, 2014), 273. The relevant passage on this page refers to a website entry from the RDC that is no longer available on the Internet, but it is summarized in the Srebrenica Genocide Blog website in the article, "The Myth of Bratunac: A Blatant Numbers Game," May 15, 2006, *srebrenica-genocide.blogspot.com/2006/05/myth-about-serb-casualties-around.html.*

16. Puhalo, "Zašto se manipuliše."

17. Conversation with Vanja, April 12, 2002.

18. Vanja's description of the transformation of her identity, and her self-examination in the course of that transformation, illustrate well Hariz Halilovich's characterization of identity changes among displaced people: "In some instances, identities of the displaced have been partially or completely replaced, adapted, hybridised and entangled with new identities, roles and places, while in other instances there is a prevalent feeling of permanent 'misplacement', with an inability to reconstruct a sense of belonging in a new social environment." Halilovich, *Places of Pain*, 54.

19. Conversation with Vanja, September 22, 2008.

CHAPTER 12

1. Emin Mahmutović and Nedim Jahić, interview, Bratunac, October 2, 2012.

2. "Pritisak na aktiviste inicijative 'Glasajmo za Srebrenicu,'" [Pressure on activists from the initiative "Let's [sic] Vote for Srebrenica"], *Oslobodjenje*, June 20, 2012, reposted at *vijesti.ba/clanak/92807/suljagic-pritisak-na-aktiviste-quot-glasajmo-za-srebrenicu-quot.* For the record, the name of the organization this title means to refer to is actually "*Glasaću* za Srebrenicu," meaning "*I Will Vote* for Srebrenica."

3. "Inicijativa 'Glasaću za Srebrenicu'" ["I will vote for Srebrenica" Initiative], *Oslobodjenje*, August 24, 2012.

4. Nedim Jahić, "Kafka u Srebrenici" [Kafka in Srebrenica], *Oslobodjenje*, August 6, 2012, reposted at *www.mediaonline.ba/ba/pdf.asp?ID=482&n=%8ATAMPA%200%20LJUDSKIM%20PRAVIMA*.

5. "Čađo da odgovori ko će odgovarati za dijeljenje nelegalnih državljanstava, pa i Legiji" [Čađo must respond who will answer for the distribution of illegal citizenship, even to Legija], *Oslobodjenje*, August 27, 2012, reposted at *24sata.info/vijesti/bosna-i-hercegovina/109952-suljagic-cadjo-da-odgovori-ko-ce-odgovarati-za-dijeljenje-nelegalnih-drzavljanstava-pa-i-legiji.html*.

6. "Bliži smo tome da se ne izađe na izbore u Srebrenici" [We are closer to not participating in the elections in Srebrenica], Federation of Bosnia News Agency (FENA), May 8, 2012, *vijesti.ba/clanak/85955/izetbegovic-blizi-smo-tome-da-se-ne-izade-na-izbore-u-srebrenici*.

7. "Danas neće biti saopšteni rezultati za Srebrenicu" [Results for Srebrenica will not be announced today], Srna news agency, *Nezavisne Novine*, November 11, 2012, *www.nezavisne.com/novosti/bih/Danas-nece-biti-saopsteni-rezultati-za-Srebrenicu/166100*.

8. "Srebrenička udruženja: Zaustavite kršenja ljudskih prava povratnika" [Srebrenica associations: Stop violations of human rights of returnees], *Oslobodjenje*, January 14, 2013.

9. "Ljudi koji ostaju bez identiteta" [People who are left without identity], *Oslobodjenje*, February 18, 2013, reposted at *www.trt.net.tr/bosanski/bosna-i-hercegovina/2013/02/18/ljudi-koji-ostaju-bez-identiteta-16223*.

10. Ibid.

11. "Dodik: Bit će procesuirani oni koji su lažno glasali u Srebrenici" [Dodik: Those who voted illegally in Srebrenica will be processed], *Oslobodjenje*, January 8, 2013, reposted at *vijesti.ba/clanak/124455/quot-bit-ce-procesuirani-oni-koji-su-lazno-glasali-u-srebrenici-quot*.

12. "Pravo na slobodu kretanja i prebivališta ne može ograničavati niko, pa ni Dodik" [No one can curtail the right to freedom of movement, not even Dodik], *klix.ba*, April 6, 2013, *www.klix.ba/vijesti/bih/suljagic-pravo-na-slobodu-kretanja-i-prebivalista-ne-moze-ogranicavati-niko-pa-ni-dodik/130406055*.

13. Elvira Jukić, "Inzko Raises Bosnian Serb Residence Checks," Balkan Insight, May 14, 2014, *www.balkaninsight.com/en/article/bosnia-residence-issue-related-to-elections*.

14. Mirsada Lingo-Demirović, "Ukinuti Odluka o prebivalištu i Zakon o povratnicama" [Annul decision on residency and law about returnees], *Nezavisne Novine*, July 4, 2014.

15. Such visits are described in Nettelfield and Wagner, *Srebrenica in the Aftermath of Genocide*, 62.

16. "Majke Srebrenice poručile da će po svaku cijenu ući u Kravicu" [Mothers of Srebrenica announced that they will enter Kravica at all costs], *Oslobodjenje*, June 26, 2013.

17. The description of the incident at Kravica is taken from several sources including the following: "Bosnia: Women Break through Police Cordon to Lay Flowers at Srebrenica Massacre Site," Associated Press, July 13, 2013, *www.startribune.com/lifestyle/215372261.html*; Sadik Salimović, "Nekoliko Srebreničanki povrijeđeno u sukobu sa policijom u Kravici" [Several Srebrenican women injured in conflict with police at Kravica], Radio Free Europe, July 13, 2013, *www.slobodnaevropa.org/content/nekoliko-srebrenicanki-povrijedjeno-u-sukobu-sa-policijom-u-kravici/25045026.html*; "Muniri Subašić povrijeđeni ruka i stomak u komešanju prilikom ulaska u hangar u Kravici" [Munira Subašić injured in the arm and stomach in tussle upon entrance to the hangar at Kravica], *Oslobodjenje*, July 13, 2013, reposted at *www.haber.ba/vijesti/bih/49015-muniri-subasic-povrijedjena-ruka-i-stomak-u-naguravanju-priliko-ulaska-u-hanagar-u-kravici*.

18. Samir Karić, "Srebreničankama stižu pozivi na sud: Tu je moja zjenica ubijena" [Summons to court

arrive to Srebrenican women: The apple of my eye was killed there], *Oslobodjenje*, March 21, 2014, reposted at *www.nkp.ba/srebrenicankama-stizu-pozivi-na-sud-tu-je-moja-zjenica-ubijena.*

19. Igor Spaić, "Srebrenica's Serb Mayor Repeats Denial of Genocide," Balkan Insight, April 13, 2017, *www.balkaninsight.com/en/article/srebrenica-s-serb-mayor-repeats-denial-of-genocide-04–13–2017.*

20. Ervin Mušinović, "Kako je FBiH prevarila Srebrenicu: Ćamil Duraković bi mogao izgubiti izbore za načelnika" [How FbiH deceived Srebrenica: Ćamil Duraković could lose the mayoral election], *klix.ba*, April 19, 2016, *www.klix.ba/vijesti/bih/kako-je-fbih-prevarila-srebrenicu-camil-durakovic-bi-mogao-izgubiti-izbore-za-nacelnika/160418071.*

21. "Srebrenica: Do 15.00 sati izlaznost 49 posto; Glasa 3.000 ljudi iz Srbije?" [Srebrenica: By 15:00 49 percent turnout; 3,000 votes from Serbia?], *Vijesti.ba*, October 2, 2016, *hamdocamo.wordpress. com/2016/10/02/srebrenica-do-15–00-sati-izlaznost-49-posto.*

22. "Duraković: Birači iz Srbije su dobivali po 20 eura da glasaju u Srebrenici" [Duraković: Voters from Serbia were paid 20 euros each to vote in Srebrenica], *Oslobodjenje*, October 10, 2016, reposted at *glasbosne.com/durakovic-biraci-iz-srbije-su-dobivali-po-20-eura-da-glasaju-u-srebrenici.*

23. Zulfo Salihović, interview, Srebrenica, June 19, 2018.

24. "Ne mogu prihvatiti da se u Srebrenici desio genocid" [I cannot accept that genocide took place in Srebrenica], N1 BiH, April 12, 2017, *ba.n1info.com/a148458/Vijesti/Vijesti/Ne-mogu-prihvatiti-da-se-u-Srebrenici-desio-genocid.html.*

25. "Načelnik Srebrenice Grujičić: Nije bio genocid i to je moj stav dok sam živ" [Srebrenica Mayor Grujičić: There was no genocide and that is my position as long as I live], *Faktor.ba*, July 10, 2018, *faktor.ba/vijest/naelnik-srebrenice-grujii-nije-bio-genocid-i-to-je-moj-stav-dok-sam-iv-302969.*

26. "Mladic Verdict Highlights Bosnia's Ethnic Divisions," Balkan Insight, November 22, 2017, *www .balkaninsight.com/en/article/mladic-verdict-highlights-bosnia-s-ethnic-divisions-11–22–2017.*

27. "Srebrenica to Honour Bosnian Serb Leader Dodik," Balkan Insight, March 6, 2018, *www .balkaninsight.com/en/article/bosnian-serb-leader-dodik-to-be-awarded-in-srebrenica-03–06–2018.*

28. Zulfo Salihović, interview, Srebrenica, June 19, 2018.

29. Senad Subašić, interview, Srebrenica, June 19, 2018.

30. "Srebrenica zaslužuje poseban status u BiH" [Srebrenica deserves special status in BiH], Vildana Selimbegović, *Oslobodjenje*, November 6, 2016.

31. Munira Hadžić, interview, Sarajevo, November 23, 2002.

32. "Bosniak Students Protest Pro-genocide Serb Education Curriculum," *Today's Zaman*, March 19, 2012.

33. Ibid.

34. "Srebrenica: Od ponedjeljka bošnjačka djeca ponovo u klupama" [Srebrenica: From Monday, Bosniak children back on their benches], Srna press agency, March 16, 2012, *www.24sata.info/vijesti /bosna-i-hercegovina/91676-postignut-dogovor-od-ponedjeljka-bosnjacki-ucenici-u-srebrenici -ponovo-u-klupama.html.*

35. "'Petar Petrović Njegoš' više nije naziv osnovne škole u Srebrenici" ["Petar Petrović Njegoš" is no longer the name of the elementary school in Srebrenica], *Prijatelji of Srebrenica*, October 29, 2012.

36. "Srebrenica: Roditelji odbijaju da se u knjižice upiše jezik bošnjačkog naroda" [Srebrenica: Parents reject entrance of Bosniak language in school curriculum], *Oslobodjenje*, June 13, 2016, reposted at *www.radiosarajevo.ba/vijesti/bosna-i-hercegovina/roditelji-odbijaju -da-se-u-knjizice-upise-jezik-bosnjackog-naroda/228798.*

37. Stevan Weine, *When History Is a Nightmare: Lives and Memories of Ethnic Cleansing in Bosnia-Herzegovina* (New Brunswick, NJ: Rutgers University Press, 1999), 166.

38. "Rasprave i poruke uz desetogodišnjicu genocida u Srebrenici" [Discussions and messages on the tenth anniversary of the genocide in Srebrenica], A. Bečirović, *Oslobodjenje*, June 20, 2005, reposted at *bhstring.net/tuzlauslikama/tuzlarije/viewnewnewsb.php?id=6035*.

39. "Bijes umjesto stida" [Fury instead of shame], by Gojko Berić, *Oslobodjenje*, July 7, 2005, reposted at *www.pcnen.com/portal/2005/07/07/bijes-umjesto-stida*.

40. "Kamp mira u Srebrenici zaslužuje više pažnje" [Peace Camp in Srebrenica merits more attention], Office of the Vice President of FBiH, March 3, 2012.

41. "Nije nas strah priznati da želimo mir" [We are not afraid to admit that we wish for peace], *Dani* 663 (February 26, 2010), *www.bhdani.ba/portal/izdanje/663*.

42. "Reportaža: Dani u Bratuncu i Srebrenici—Slamanje aparthejda" [Reportage: Dani in Bratunac and Srebrenica—smashing apartheid], *Dani* 600 (December 12, 2008), *www.bhdani.ba/portal/clanak/600/arhiva/slamanje-aparthejda-*.

43. Ibid.

44. Ibid.

45. "Čudo U Srebrenici: Hodža odbio da ide u Englesku bez pravoslavnog popa" [Wonder in Srebrenica: Imam refuses to go to England without Orthodox priest], *Telegraf*, September 19, 2014, *www.telegraf.rs/vesti/1233422-cudo-u-srebrenici-hodza-odbio-da-ide-u-englesku-bez-pravoslavnog-popa*.

46. Samir Karić, "Valentin Inzko poručio: Srebrenicu okrenuti budućnosti" [Valentin Inzko message: Srebrenica face the future], *Oslobodjenje*, February 1, 2013, reposted at *ba.n1info.com/Vijesti/a113884/Inzko-BiH-se-mora-okrenuti-buducnosti.html*.

47. "Na slavi u Srebrenici veličani Mladić i Karadžić" [Mladić and Karadžić glorified during celebration in Srebrenica], *Oslobodjenje*, August 19, 2013, reposted at *minber.ba/na-slavi-u-srebrenici-velicani-mladic-i-karadzic*.

48. Ed Vulliamy, "After the Massacre, a Homecoming," *Guardian*, April 30, 2005, *www.theguardian.com/lifeandstyle/2005/apr/30/weekend.edvulliamy*. In 2005 Miloš Milovanović, president of the Serb veterans organization and representative for Dodik's SNSD to the Srebrenica municipal council, called the fall of Srebrenica a "liberation," and the genocide "a lie." During an interview in 2013, Milovanović similarly stated that the "Hague tribunal works against the Serbs and that is why I do not agree with its judgments," adding, "genocide did not take place here." Also see Paulina Janusz, "Beleške sa sednice Skupštine opštine u Srebrenici" [Notes from municipal assembly meeting in Srebrenica], *e-novine*, February 7, 2013, *www.e-novine.com/index.php?news=78674*.

49. See "Duraković: Vlada RS blokira razvoj Srebrenice" [Duraković: RS government blocking development of Srebrenica], *Oslobodjenje*, September 7, 2016, reposted at *ba.n1info.com/Vijesti/a111971/Camil-Durakovic-Vlada-RS-blokira-razvoj-Srebrenice.html*.

CHAPTER 13

1. Wesselingh and Vaulerin, *Raw Memory*, 38.

2. E.g., Emsuda and Osman Mujagić, personal conversation, Sanski Most, May 22, 1998.

3. Emsuda Mujagić, interview, Kozarac, April 1999.

4. Wesselingh and Vaulerin, *Raw Memory*, 41.

5. Emsuda Mujagić, interview, Kozarac, April 1999.

6. Damir, interview, Prijedor, September 22, 2006.

7. Sudbin Music, interview, Prijedor, October 28, 2012.

8. "Kozarac: Klanjana dženaza i obavljen ukop za osam žrtava zločina u Prijedoru" [Kozarac: Funeral held and burials for eight victims of the crimes in Prijedor], Anadolija press agency, *Oslobodjenje*,

July 20, 2016, reposted at *miruhbosne.wordpress.com/2016/07/20/kozarac-klanjana-dzenaza-i -obavljen-ukop-za-osam-zrtava-zlocina-u-prijedoru.*

9. Mirsad Duratović, interview, Prijedor, October 29, 2012.

10. "Kosti bez grobova, zločin bez kazne" [Bones without graves, crime without punishment], by Paulina Janusz, *e-novine.com*, December 19, 2012, *www.e-novine.com/region/region-bosna/76358 -Kosti-bez-grobova-zloin-bez-kazne.html.*

11. "Povratnički život u Prijedoru uz političke i etničke podjele" [Returnee life in Prijedor, with political and ethnic divisions], *Deutsche Welle*, March 21, 2016, *www.dw.com/bs/povratnicki-zivot-u -prijedoru-uz-politicke-i-etnicke-podjele/a-19130261.*

12. Omer Bartov and Phyllis Mack, eds., *In God's Name: Genocide and Religion in the Twentieth Century* (New York: Berghahn Books, 2001), 189.

13. "Prijedor: Roditelji ubijene djece traže izgradnju spomenika" [Prijedor: Parents of killed children seek construction of monument], *Mostarski.ba*, May 31, 2018, *mostarski.ba/ prijedor-roditelji-ubijene-djece-traze-izgradnju-spomenika.*

14. Eldin Hadžović, "Fabrika smrti" [Death factory], *Dani* 687 (August 13, 2010), *www.bhdani.ba/portal /izdanje/687.*

15. Sudbin Musić, "30.maj—Dan oslobađanja Prijedora" [May 30—Liberation Day of Prijedor], *MojPrijedor.com*, May 31, 2010. Via Wayback Machine, *web.archive.org/web/20140617133329 /http://www.rakovcani.ba/index.php/vijesti/iz-rakovcana/110–30maj-dan-oslobaanja-prijedora.*

16. Roy Gutman, *Witness to Genocide* (New York: Macmillan, 1993), ix.

17. Ibid., 29.

18. Ibid., 55–58 and 95–98.

19. Vulliamy, *Seasons in Hell*, 111–12.

20. Eldin Hadžović, "Godišnjice: Dani u Prijedoru; Ponovo na ukletom mjestu" [Anniversaries: Dani in Prijedor; at the accursed place again], *Dani* 635 (August 14, 2009), *www.bhdani.ba/portal/izdanje /635.*

21. Vulliamy, *Seasons in Hell*, 105.

22. "Logoraši pozdravljaju pronalaženje bivšeg čuvara u Trnopolju" [Camp survivors hail discovery of former camp guard], *klix.ba*, September 26, 2012, *www.klix.ba/vijesti/bih/logorasi-pozdravljaju -pronalazenje-bivseg-cuvara-u-trnopolju/120925127.*

23. Mirsad Duratović, "Korićanske stijene—simbol zločina Interventnog voda prijedorske policije" [Korićanske stijene—symbol of the crimes of the Response Team of the Prijedor Police], Sanainfo, August 22, 2018, *sanainfo.ba/index.php/vijesti/item/1454-koricanske-stijene-simbol-zlocina-i -zlocinaca-interventnog-voda-prijedorske-policije.*

24. N.S., "Istina o zločinima u Tomašici se pokušava ubiti i nakon 22 godine" [In Tomašica, even 22 years later they are trying to kill the truth about crimes], July 20, 2014, *vijesti.ba/clanak/228613 /istina-o-zlocinima-u-tomasici-se-pokusava-ubiti-i-nakon-22-godine.* A similar number is quoted as the estimate of the Prijedor-based human rights organization Izvor in Haris Subašić, "The Culture of Denial in Prijedor," *Transconflict*, January 29, 2013, *www.transconflict.com/2013/01/the-culture -of-denial-in-prijedor-291.*

25. The number of those killed at Omarska is commonly stated to be impossible to estimate. At the same time, the estimate given by more dispassionate analysts falls roughly around seven hundred or, at times, between five hundred and nine hundred. Higher estimates are also seen. See, for example, the website of Forensic Architecture, "Living Death Camps," *www.forensic-architecture.org/case /living-death-camps.*

26. "Dan bijelih traka u Prijedoru: 102 ruže za ubijenu djecu" [White armband day in Prijedor: 102

roses for children killed], *Oslobodjenje*, May 31, 2017, *www.oslobodjenje.ba/vijesti/bih/dan-bijelih-traka-u-prijedoru-102-ruze-za-ubijenu-djecu*. See also "Duratović: U Prijedoru je ubijeno 3.176 civila nesrpske nacionalosti od kojih je 102 djece i 256 žena" [Duratović: 3,176 non-Serb civilians killed in Prijedor, of which 102 were children and 256 women], *BNN.ba*, November 27, 2017, *bnn.ba/vijesti /duratovic-u-prijedoru-je-ubijeno-3176-civila-nesrpske-nacionalosti-od-kojih-je-102-djece-i*.

27. Halilović, *Kako Opisati Srebrenicu*, 110.

28. Ibid., 10. Author Halilović attributes the fact that this is so little known to the separatist leanings of Bosnian Croat nationalist leaders, who focus on concentrating their power and their domain in western Herzegovina, to the detriment of the memory of Croat victims in Republika Srpska.

29. Father Iljo Arlović, interview, Stara Rijeka, September 23, 2006.

30. "Nekažnjen zločin u nestalom selu" [Unpunished crime in a vanished village], by Esad Hećimovič, *Dani* 633 (July 31, 2009), *www.bhdani.ba/portal/izdanje/633*. See also "Briševo Commemorates 67 War Victims," HINA (Croatian news agency), July 25, 2012, *listserv.buffalo.edu/cgi-bin/wa?A2= JUSTWATCH-L;10e4d6ff.1207*.

31. "Karadžić: Murder of Civilians in Villages near Prijedor," Justice Report, October 21, 2011. Reposted in JUSTWATCH-L archives, *listserv.buffalo.edu/cgi-bin/wa?A2=JUSTWATCH-L;179ad8e0.1110*.

32. Figures from the 1991 Bosnian census. See, for example, the Prijedor section of the 1997 Human Rights Report on Bosnia at *www.hrw.org/reports/1997/bosnia/Bosnia-02.htm*, giving much detail on the prewar and postwar ethnic breakdown of the municipality.

33. Wesselingh and Vaulerin, *Raw Memory*, 35.

34. Ibid., 92.

35. Sivac-Bryant, *Re-Making Kozarac*, 64. Chapter 3, titled "Return," discusses the role of demobilized soldiers of the Seventeenth Krajina Brigade.

36. Ibid., 77.

37. Emsuda Mujagić, interview, Kozarac, September 12, 2001.

38. Wesselingh and Vaulerin, *Raw Memory*, 92.

39. Mirjana, interview, Prijedor, May 23, 2004.

40. Gojko, interview, Prijedor, May 26, 2004.

41. AnelAlišić, interview, Prijedor, May 27, 2004.

42. Ibid.

43. Vedran Grahovac, interviews in Prijedor on May 24, 2004, and September 21, 2006.

44. Gojko, interview, Prijedor, May 26, 2004.

45. Ervin Blažević, interview, Kozarac, October 10, 2008.

46. All quotes from conversations with Blažević in Kozarac between 2008 and 2013.

47. Sudbin Musić, interview, Prijedor, October 28, 2012.

48. Denis Džidić, "Bosnia Charges 15 Serbs for Zecovi Massacre," Balkan Insight, December 12, 2014, *www.balkaninsight.com/en/article/zecovi-massacre-indictment-raised*.

49. Sudbin Musić, personal correspondence, October 26, 2018.

50. Dražen Huterer and Nejra Suljović, "Survival, Not Revival for War-Torn Bosnian Village," Institute for War and Peace Reporting, May 29, 2013, *iwpr.net/report-news/survival-not-revival-war-torn-bosnian-village*. Information updated by Sudbin Musić, interview, Prijedor, October 1, 2015.

51. Paulina Janusz, "Kosti bez grobova, zločin bez kazne" [Bones without graves, crime without punishment], *e-novine.com*, December 19, 2012, *www.e-novine.com/region/region-bosna/76358-Kosti-bez -grobova-zloin-bez-kazne.html*.

52. Nađa Diklić, "Prijedor: Grad u kojem se zabranjuju i sjećanja" [Prijedor: City in which even remembering is prohibited], *Slobodna Bosna*, August 20, 2013. *kasaba.blogger.ba/arhiva/2013/08/20/3578007*.

53. N. Krsman, "Otpuštani zbog nacionalnosti" [Fired because of ethnicity], *Nezavisne Novine*, January 26, 2006.

54. "Bosnia and Herzegovina: Behind Closed Gates—Ethnic Discrimination in Employment," Amnesty International, January 26, 2006, *www.amnesty.org/fr/documents/EUR63/001/2006/en.*

55. "Prijedor: Diskriminacija povratnika" [Prijedor: Discrimination against returnees], *Dani* 621 (May 5, 2009), *www.bhdani.ba/portal/izdanje/621.*

56. Emsuda Mujagić, interviews, Kozarac, September 12, 2001, and October 9, 2008.

57. Mirsad Duratović, interview, Prijedor, October 29, 2012.

58. "Odbijena žalba Have Tatarević" [Hava Tatarević appeal rejected], Al Jazeera Balkans, August 14, 2014, *balkans.aljazeera.net/vijesti/odbijena-zalba-have-tatarevic.*

59. "The Case of Hava Tatarević," Prijedor Genocide Research, August 17, 2014, *www.facebook.com /coe.sarajevo/posts/750521024994900.* See also Dragan Bursać, "Koliko košta smrt šest sinova Have Tatarević?" [How much does the death of Hava Tatarević's six sons cost?], August 16, 2014, *www.e-novine.com/stav/107904-Koliko-kota-smrt-est-sinova-Have-Tatarevi.html.*

60. Oći u oći sa upravnikom koncentracionog logora" [Face to face with the administrator of a concentration camp], by Vildana Selimbegović, *Dani* 247 (March 8, 2002), *www.bhdani.ba/portal/arhiva_67_281/247.*

61. Ibid.

62. *Oslobodjenje*, May 10, 2004. This event was similarly described to me by Ramulić.

63. Mladen document, in possession of the author.

64. "Robbery of Big Companies Is Being Prepared," *Oslobodjenje*, June 30, 2003. Quote is provided in translation by SFOR news digest, *www.nato.int/sfor/media/2003/ms030630t.htm.*

65. Vildana Selimbegović, "Odlazi nam raja" [Our crowd is leaving], *Dani* 503 (February 2, 2007), *www.bhdani.ba/portal/izdanje/503.*

66. Ibid.

67. Vildana Selimbegović, "Mladen Grahovac, priča o životu" [Mladen Grahovac, a life story], *Oslobodjenje*, December 7, 2009, reposted at *www.idoconline.info/article/653387.*

CHAPTER 14

1. Alibabić, *U Kandžama KOS-a*, 233.

2. For a compelling early postwar report on the plunder of private and socially owned property in the Prijedor area during and after the war, see "The Unindicted: Reaping the Rewards of 'Ethnic Cleansing,'" Human Rights Watch, January 1997, *www.hrw.org/reports/1997/bosnia2.*

3. Eldar Dizdarević, "Kako smo se uklopili u divlji kapitalizam" [How we have fit ourselves into wild capitalism], *Oslobodjenje*, March 17, 2015, 11–12, reposted at *docs.rferl.org/sh-SH/2015/12/16/158d866a-1459–415f-9e72-d901741cd5e5.pdf.*

4. A.M., "Sve više prijava korupcije-sve manje suđenja" [More and more corruption complaints and fewer and fewer sentences], *bljesak.info*, June 14, 2011, *www.capital.ba/sve-vise-prijava-korupcije -%E2%80%93-sve-manje-sudenja.*

5. Dragan Maksimović, "Milijarde maraka se kradu kroz javne (ne)nabavke" [Billions of marks are stolen through public procurements], *Deutsche Welle*, December 9, 2013, *www.dw.de/milijarde -maraka-se-kradu-kroz-javne-nenabavke/a-17280001.*

6. A.M., "Sve više prijava korupcije-sve manje suđenja."

7. "Istragom državnog tužilaštva obuhvaćeni ugovori sa građevinskom kompanijom" [Contracts with construction company included in investigation by state prosecutor], Center for Investigative Journalism, September 15, 2008, *www.cin.ba/istragom-drzavnog-tuzilastva-obuhvaceni-ugovori-sa -gradevinskom-kompanijom.*

8. Slobodan Vasković, "Eksproprijacija zemljišta za autoput Banjaluka-Gradiška: Za 124 m2 RS platila milion i sto hiljada KM" [Expropriation of land for autoput Banjaluka-Gradiška: For 124 square meters RS paid 1,100,000 KM], Slobodan Vasković—Sa druge strane . . . (blog), February 17, 2013, *slobodanvaskovic.blogspot.com/2013/02/eksproprijacija-zemljista-za-autoput.html*.

9. "Banja Luka: Nova zgrada Vlade RS šest puta skuplja" [Banja Luka: New RS government building six times more expensive], *kliker.info*, September 14, 2007, *kliker.info/banja-luka-nova-zgrada-vlade-rs-sest-puta-skuplja*.

10. "Istragom državnog tužilaštva."

11. "Banja Luka: Nova zgrada Vlade RS šest puta skuplja."

12. Senad Pećanin, "Povratak u predvečerje rata" [Return to the eve of the war], *Dani* 611 (February 27, 2009), *www.bhdani.ba/portal/izdanje/611*.

13. Ibid.

14. Nađa Diklić, "Ekskluzivno: Izgradnja zgrade vlade RS koštala 591 milion maraka" [Exclusive: Construction of RS government building cost 591 million KM], *Politički Meridijan*, February 11, 2015.

15. For background on Milorad Dodik's best man and sometime collaborator in economic corruption, see the following articles: "Dodikov kum pobjegao u Srbiju da ne ide u zatvor: Policiji poručio da se ne vraća u BiH" [Dodik's best man fled to Serbia to avoid prison: Notified police that he is not returning to Bosnia], *faktor.ba*, March 13, 2015, *faktor.ba/vijest/dodikov-kum-pobjegao-u-srbiju-da-ne-ide-u-zatvor-policiji-porucio-da-se-ne-vraca-u-bih-158560*; Milorad Milojević, "Uhapšen Dodikov kum Mile Radišić" [Dodik's best man Mile Radišić arrested], Radio Free Europe, November 18, 2015, *www.slobodnaevropa.org/a/uhappsen-dodikov-kum-mile-radisic/27373474.html*; "Mile Radišić 'otvorio dušu': Dodik u zgradu 'Grand trejda' uložio 15 miliona" [Mile Radišić "opened his heart": Dodik invested 15 million [KM] in construction of "Grand Trade."] BN Radio-Television, March 28, 2019, *www.rtvbn.com/360736/Mile-Radisic-otvorio-dusu-Dodik-u-zgradu-Grand-trejda-ulozio-15-miliona*; "Mile Radišić izašao iz zatvora" [Mile Radišić left prison], *Nezavisne novine*, October 6, 2017, *www.nezavisne.com/novosti/hronika/Mile-Radisic-izasao-iz-zatvora/446094*.

16. For background on the case of Milan Vukelić, see "Bosnian City Demands Answers for Whistle-Blower's Killing," Balkan Insight, November 6, 2017, *balkaninsight.com/2017/11/06/bosnian-city-demands-answers-for-whistle-blower-s-killing-11–06–2017*; Dragan Risojevic, "Na tragu ubicama Milana Vukelica" [On the trail of the killers of Milan Vukelić], *Nezavisne Novine*, August 6, 2008, *www.nezavisne.com/novosti/bih/Na-tragu-ubicama-Milana-Vukelica/26883*.

17. Dženana Karup-Druško, "Dodikova imperija" [Dodik's empire], *Dani* 629, *www.bhdani.ba/portal/izdanje/629* (July 3, 2009). See also Hana Mujić, "Bahati milijarder iz Laktaša" [Arrogant billionaire from Laktaši], *e-novine.com*, September 19, 2012, *www.e-novine.com/region/region-bosna/71638-Bahati-milijarder-Laktaa.html*.

18. Slobodan Vasković, "Imperija Dodik 4" [Dodik Empire 4], January 19, 2013, *slobodanvaskovic.blogspot.com/2013/01/imperija-dodik-4.html*.

19. Dženana Karup-Druško, "Dodikova imperija" [Dodik's empire], *Dani* 629 (July 3, 2009), *www.bhdani.ba/portal/izdanje/629*. See also Mujić, "Bahati milijarder iz Laktaša."

20. Lawrence Weschler, "High Noon at Twin Peaks," *New Yorker*, August 18, 1997, *www.newyorker.com/magazine/1997/08/18/high-noon-at-twin-peaks*.

21. "Hopes Betrayed: Trafficking of Women and Girls to Bosnia and Herzegovina for Forced Prostitution." *Human Rights Watch* 14, no. 9 (December 2002), *www.hrw.org/report/2002/11/26/hopes-betrayed/trafficking-women-and-girls-post-conflict-bosnia-and-herzegovina*.

22. Andrew Cockburn, "21st-Century Slaves," *National Geographic*, September 2003, 2–25.

23. "Crna Bosna: Kriminal, korupcija, zločini, ubistva, droga, terorizam i crne liste 2002–2004" [Black Bosnia: Criminality, corruption, crimes, murders, drugs, terrorism, and blacklists 2002–2004], *Nezavisne Novine* special edition, September 14, 2004.

24. "Uhapšen Draško Papak, načelnik Kriminalističke policije u Prijedoru" [Draško Papak, crime police chief in Prijedor, arrested], Center for Investigative Journalism, May 23, 2013, *www.cin.ba/uhapsen-drasko-papak-nacelnik-kriminalisticke-policije-u-prijedoru*.

25. Vildana Selimbegović, "Oči u oči sa upravnikom koncentracionog logora [Face to face with concentration camp administrator], *Dani* 247 (March 8, 2002), *www.bhdani.ba/portal/arhiva_67_281/247*.

26. Open letter to Republika Srpska Minister of Internal Affairs R. Jovičić, written by the NGO Demokratska javnost grada Prijedora (Democratic public of Prijedor city), April 28, 2014. Document in possession of the author.

27. Vedran Grahovac, interview, Prijedor, September 21, 2006.

28. "Ljekarima mito i do 2.500 maraka" [Bribes to doctors up to 2,500 KM], *Nezavisne Novine*, October 12, 2004.

29. Personal correspondence and interviews with Mladen Žabić, an independent investigator of corruption in Prijedor, July and October 2015.

30. Ljiljana Kovačević, "Scenarij Prevare: Kako je Dodikov kum Budimir Stanković ukrao 1,5 milion maraka" [Scenario of deception: How Dodik's 'kum' Budimir Stanković stole 1.5 million KM], *zurnal.ba*, August 27, 2013, *zurnal.ba/novost/17345/scenarij-prevare-kako-je-dodikov-kum-budimir-stankovic-ukrao-15-milion-maraka*. Accessed January 18, 2018.

31. Ibid.

32. Ljiljana Kovačević, "Život mi je ugrožen zato što sam rekao da je car go!" [My life is in danger because I said that the emperor is naked!], *zurnal.ba*, October 25, 2013, *zurnal.ba/novost/17530/zivot-mi-je-ugrozen-zato-sto-sam-rekao-da-je-car-go*.

33. "Fizički obračun Budimira Stankovića" [Physical showdown of Budimir Stanković], BN Televizija, July 19, 2014, *www.rtvbn.com/312368/Dodikov-kum-Budimir-Stankovic-fizicki-napao-sluzbenika-Geodetske-uprave*.

34. Ljiljana Kovačević, "Kakva vlast takva i opozicija: Kako je 'neutralni' Pavić godinama pljačkao državu" [As the government is, so is the opposition: How 'neutral' Pavić robbed the state for years], *zurnal.ba*, September 9, 2014, *zurnal.ba/novost/18268/kakva-vlast-takva-i-opozicija-kako-je-neutralni-pavic-godinama-pljackao-drzavu*.

35. Sn.K., "Dokić i Pavić osumnjičeni da su prisvojili 900.000 KM" [Dokić and Pavić accused of appropriating 900,000 KM], *Nezavisne Novine*, February 12, 2004, *www.idoconline.info/article/13069*.

36. Kovačević, "Kakva vlast takva i opozicija."

37. Hasan Hadžić, "Vlasnik Prijedora i kontrolor RS-a" [The owner of Prijedor and the controller of RS], *Dani* 646 (October 30, 2009), *www.bhdani.ba/portal/izdanje/646*.

38. Slobodan Vasković, "Neđu Ilića štiti 'srbački klan'; Jovičić radi Sizifov posao" ["Srbac clan" protecting Neđo Ilić; Jovičić is doing a Sisyphean task], January 17, 2014, *slobodanvaskovic.blogspot.com/2014/01/neu-ilica-stiti-srbacki-klan-jovicic.html*.

39. Hadžić, "Vlasnik Prijedora i kontrolor RS-a."

40. Ibid.

41. Paulina Janusz, "Gradonačelnik Prijedora i njegovi bošnjački partneri" [Mayor of Prijedor and his Bosniak partners], *e-novine.com*, February 15, 2013, *www.e-novine.com/region/region-bosna/79080-Podguzne-muhe-borbi-ljudska-prava.html*.

42. Nihad Forić, quoted in unpublished overview of a doctoral dissertation by Sebina Sivac-Bryant,

doctoral student at University College London, Anthropology Department, in chapter 6, "Survival and Future." Sivac-Bryant's dissertation was later developed into the book *Re-Making Kozarac*.

43. Janusz, "Gradonačelnik Prijedora i njegovi bošnjački partneri."
44. "Saopštenje za javnost udruženja logoraša Prijedor92" [Public announcement by Association of Concentration Camp survivors Prijedor92], posted by Sudbin Musić, *mojprijedor.com*, September 1, 2013, *www.mojprijedor.com/saopstenje-za-javnost-udruzenja-logorasa-prijedor92*.
45. Hadžić, "Vlasnik Prijedora i kontrolor RS-a."
46. Paulina Janusz, "Daleko je Prijedor" [Faraway is Prijedor], *e-novine.com*, August 7, 2013, *www .e-novine.com/region/region-bosna/88955-Daleko-Prijedor.html*.
47. Ibid.
48. Comment on Tihić's statement posted by Refik Hodžić in Facebook group "Genocide in Prijedor: 20 Years," July 8, 2013. Document on file with author.

CHAPTER 15

1. ICTY case information sheet on Tadić, *www.icty.org/x/cases/tadic/cis/en/cis_tadic_en.pdf*. Accessed January 18, 2018.
2. "Conference in Prijedor," ICTY (press release), June 24, 2005, *www.icty.org/sid/8575*.
3. "Korićanske stijene: Smjena po depeši" [Korićanske stijene: Sacking by dépêche], *e-novine.com*, April 12, 2012, *www.e-novine.com/region/region-bosna/36534-Korianske-stijene-Smjena-depei.html*.
4. "Human Rights Watch Applauds NATO Efforts to Apprehend War Criminals," July 11, 1997, *www.hrw.org/news/1997/07/09/human-rights-watch-applauds-nato-efforts-to-apprehend-war-criminals*. See also "Mejakić: We were Ordered to Give 'Official Version,'" Sense Agency, November 29, 2013, *www.sense-agency.com/icty/mejakic-we-were-ordered-to-give-'official-version'.29.html? news_id=15544&cat_id=1*.
5. "The Prijedor Genocide," Institute for Research of Genocide, Canada, January 2012, *instituteforgenocide.org/en/wp-content/uploads/2012/01/THE-PRIJEDOR-GENOCIDE-1.pdf*.
6. "Human Rights Watch Applauds NATO Efforts to Apprehend War Criminals."
7. Ed Vulliamy, "Middle Managers of Genocide," *Nation*, June 10, 1996, *www.barnsdle.demon .co.uk/bosnia/Vulliamy.html*.
8. Wesselingh and Vaulerin, *Raw Memory*, 37.
9. ICTY case sheet for Milan Kovačević, 2005, *www.icty.org/x/cases/milan_kovacevic/cis/en/cis_kovacevic_milan_en.pdf*.
10. Wesselingh and Vaulerin, *Raw Memory*, 79.
11. Nerma Jelačić and Mirna Mekić, "Stakić Sentence Appeal Plays on Victims Nerves," IWPR Tribunal no. 440, February 17, 2006. Archived by JUSTWATCH-L, *listserv.buffalo.edu/cgi-bin/wa?A2= JUSTWATCH-L;d1277cee.0602*.
12. ICTY case information sheet on Stakić, *www.icty.org/x/cases/stakic/cis/en/cis_stakic.pdf*.
13. Adrienne N. Kitchen, "Stakić: Defence Appeal against Length of Sentence, but Prosecution Suggests It Wasn't Long Enough," IWPR, November 20, 2005, *iwpr.net/global-voices/stakic*.
14. Aida Alić, "Perpetrators Walk Freely," Justice Report, October 26, 2010, *www.justice-report.com/en /articles/perpetrators-walk-freely*.
15. Paulina Janusz, "Kosti bez grobova, zločin bez kazne" [Bones without graves, crime without punishment, *e-novine.com*, December 19, 2012, *www.e-novine.com/region/region-bosna/76358-Kosti-bez-grobova-zloin-bez-kazne.html*.
16. "Witness 'Extinguished Burning Bodies outside Bosnia Mosque,'" Balkan Insight, September 30, 2013, *www.balkaninsight.com/en/article/prosecution-rests-its-case-on-carakovo-murders*.

17. "Bosnia Mosque Murders Defendant 'a Decent Man,'" Balkan Insight, October 8, 2013, *www*
    .balkaninsight.com/en/article/defendant-soldat-responsible-and-professional.

18. Mirna Buljugić, "Indictees Testify That They Were Not in Čarakovo," Justice Report, February 3,
    2014, *www.justice-report.com/en/articles/indictees-testify-that-they-were-not-in-carakovo.*

19. Denis Džidić, "Bosnia Charges 15 Serbs for Zecovi Massacre," Balkan Insight, December 12, 2014,
    www.balkaninsight.com/en/article/zecovi-massacre-indictment-raised.

20. Kuruzović had been an officer in the Serb-controlled Yugoslav National Army during the war in
    Croatia, and he had returned from there, by more than one account, with stolen cars and furniture
    to sell in Prijedor. See Vildana Selimbegović, "Oći u oći sa upravnikom koncentracionog logora"
    [Face to face with the administrator of a concentration camp], *Dani* 247 (March 8, 2002), *www.*
    bhdani.ba/portal/arhiva_67_281/247. See also "The Unindicted: Reaping the Rewards of 'Ethnic
    Cleansing' in Prijedor," Human Rights Watch, January 1, 1997, D901, *www.refworld.org/docid*
    /3ae6a8368.html.

21. Katarina Panić, "Bosnia's Notorious Trnopolje Jail Camp Remembered," Balkan Insight, May 26,
    2015, *www.balkaninsight.com/en/article/bosnia-s-infamous-pow-camp-remembered.*

22. Milorad Milojević, "Sjećanje na žrtve logora Omarska i Trnopolje" [Commemoration of victims
    at Omarska and Trnopolje camps], August 11, 2013, *www.slobodnaevropa.org/content/sjecanje-na*
    -ubijene-u-logorima-omarska-i-trnopolje/25071701.html.

23. Edin Ramulić, "Trnopolje na godišnjicu uspostave logora" [Trnopolje upon anniversary of establish-
    ment of camp], *mojprijedor.com*, May 26, 2014, *www.mojprijedor.com/trnopolje-na-godisnjicu*
    -uspostave-logora-2.

24. "Pokretanje odgovornosti protiv Marka Pavića, za planiranje i izvršenje zločina genocida" [Initiation
    of culpability against Marko Pavić for planning and commission of the crime of genocide], *B.net*,
    April 7, 2010, *bosnjaci.net/prilog.php?pid=37323.* Organizations involved in compiling and posting this
    list included the Bosnian Academic Circle, Bosniak Academic Forum, Bosnian-American Institute,
    and Institute for Genocide Research, Canada. The lists named eight "main organizers," fourteen
    "implementers," five "perpetrators of crimes," three "organizers and sponsors" of Omarska camp;
    four administrators of Omarska; six employees of the Ljubija mine corporation who abused people at
    Omarska; sixty-three guards, interrogators, and other officials involved with Omarska; twenty guards,
    administrators, and interrogators at Keraterm; and fifteen figures similarly involved with Trnopolje.

25. Edin Barimac, "U posjeti: Svaki deseti nestali traži se u Prijedoru" [In a visit: Every tenth missing
    person is sought for in Prijedor], *Oslobodjenje*, March 23, 2015, reposted at *www.mojprijedor*
    .com/u-posjeti-svaki-deseti-nestali-trazi-se-u-prijedoru. A year after this report, Ramulić upped
    the figure of binding convictions to thirty-eight, adding that approximately another one hundred
    people were still under suspicion, named in a variety of cases. See Erduan Katana, "Politike u BiH
    i danas provode Karadžićev strateški cilj" [Policies in Bosnia-Herzegovina today are implementing
    Karadžić's war goals], interview of Edin Ramulić, Radio Free Europe, March 25, 2016, *www*
    .slobodnaevropa.org/content/politike-u-bih-i-danas-provode-karadzicev-strateski-cilj/27635756.html.

26. Edin Ramulić, interview, Prijedor, May 27, 2010. For information on Branko Topola, see brief profile
    by TRIAL (Track Impunity Always—Swiss agency that fights impunity), *trialinternational.org*
    /latest-post/branko-topola.

27. Hasan Hadžić, "Vlasnik Prijedora i kontrolor RS-a" [Owner of Prijedor and controller of the RS],
    Dani 646 (October 30, 2009). See also Paulina Janusz, "Neautorizivana ratna biografija gradonačel-
    nika Prijedora; Marko Pavić—karijerista, ne zločinac" [Unauthorized war biography of mayor of
    Prijedor; Marko Pavić—careerist, not criminal], *e-novine.com*, August 4, 2013, *www.e-novine.com*
    /region/region-licnosti/88857-Marko-Pavi—karijerista-zloinac.html.

28. "The Unindicted: Reaping the Rewards of Ethnic Cleansing," *Human Rights Watch Report for Bosnia-Herzegovina* 9, no. 1 (January 1997), *www.hrw.org/reports/pdfs/b/bosnia/bosnia971.pdf*. Also quoted in Janusz, "Neautorizivana ratna biografija."

29. For example, see Janusz: "Neautorizivana ratna biografija."

30. Hadžić, "Vlasnik Prijedora i kontrolor RS-a."

31. "Cases at Court of Bosnia and Herzegovina: S1 1 K 020819 16 KrI—Darko Mrđa et al.," *www.sudbih .gov.ba/predmet/3590/show*.

32. Marija Tausan, "Two Bosnian Serb Ex-Policemen Convicted of War Crimes," Balkan Insight, November 30, 2018, *www.balkaninsight.com/en/article/ two-bosnian-serb-ex-policemen-convicted-of-war-crimes-11–30–2018*.

33. "Sudbin Musić: Strašno je svakodnevno se susretati s Mrđom, braćom Banović, Tadićem" [Sudbin Musić: It is terrible to come upon Darko Mrđa, the Banović brothers, or Tadić, every day], *kozarac. ba*, August 5, 2014, *www.radiosarajevo.ba/vijesti/bosna-i-hercegovina/sudbin-music-strasno-je -svakodnevno-se-susretati-s-mrdom-bracom-banovic-tadicem/160967*. For more information on the Crisis Staff, the organization of the separatist takeover of Prijedor, and the war criminals involved, see International Crisis Group, "War Criminals in Bosnia's Republika Srpska." In early 2016, Darko Mrđa was arrested on fresh charges of crimes committed early in the war, including torturing and killing at least ten non-Serb prisoners in 1992.

34. "Приједор обиљежава 20 година одбране" [Prijedor marks 20 years of defense], Radio Television Republika Srpska, May 30, 2012, *www.rtrs.tv/vijesti/vijest.php?id=62522*.

35. Haris Subašić, "The Culture of Denial in Prijedor," *TransConflict*, January 29, 2013, *www.transconflict .com/2013/01/the-culture-of-denial-in-prijedor-291*.

36. Ibid.

37. Damir, interview, Prijedor, May 27, 2010.

38. Saša Ilić, "Prijedorski hologrami" [Prijedor holograms], *pescanik.net*, July 3, 2014, *pescanik. net/2014/07/prijedorski-hologrami*.

39. Jasmin Medić, "Kozarac: Prve optužnice tek nakon 22 godine" [Kozarac: First indictments only after 22 years], June 6, 2014, *www.mojprijedor.com/kozarac-prve-optuznice-tek-nakon-22-godine*.

40. "Još jedna uvreda za logoraše i žrtve zločina: U Trnopolju postavljen spomenik vojnicima RS-a" [Yet another insult to camp survivors and war crimes victims], *Faktor.ba*, March 19, 2016, *faktor.ba/vijest /jos-jedna-uvreda-za-logorase-i-zrtve-zlocina-u-trnopolju-postavljen-spomenik-vojnicima-rs-a-183973*.

41. Edin Ramulić, interview, Prijedor, October 29, 2012.

42. Sarah Correia, "Remembering War in Bosnia: Monuments and Commemorations in the Area of Prijedor," presented at Annual Conference of the American Association for the Advancement of Slavic Studies, Los Angeles, November 19, 2009.

43. "Goran Zorić: Borimo se protiv revizije istorije" [Goran Zorić: We are fighting against the revision of history], interview by Oštra Nula, June 16, 2015, *ostranula.org/goran-zoric-borimo-se-protiv- revizije-istorije*.

44. Srđan Puhalo, "Falsifikovanje Kozare" [Falsification of Kozara], July 9, 2014, *www.frontal.ba/blogovi /blog/60273/falsifikovanje-kozare*.

45. Allen Cowell, "German Court Sentences Serb to Life for Genocide in Bosnia," New York Times, September 27, 1997, *www.nytimes.com/1997/09/27/world/german-court-sentences-serb-to-life-for- genocide-in-bosnia.html*. See also "Federal High Court Makes Basic Ruling on Genocide," press release, Federal High Court of Germany, April 30, 1999, *www.preventgenocide.org/punish /GermanFederalCourt.htm*.

46. See UN General Assembly Resolution 260, Convention on the Prevention and Punishment of the

Crime of Genocide, *www.hrweb.org/legal/genocide.html*. See also "How Do You Define Genocide?," BBC, March 17, 2016, *www.bbc.co.uk/news/world-11108059*.

47. Prosecutor v. Slobodan Milošević Decision on Motion for Judgement of Acquittal, ICTY, June 16, 2004, *www.icty.org/x/cases/slobodan_milosevic/tdec/en/040616.htm* (section 289). See also Rachel S. Taylor, "Genocide Charges against Ex-Serb Leader to Stay," IWPR Tribunal update, June 18, 2004, archived by JUSTWATCH-L, *listserv.buffalo.edu/cgi-bin/wa?A2=JUSTWATCH-L;bd5ff8f.0406*.

48. Transcript of proceedings in the Krajišnik case, page 17130, line 20, through page 17131, line 11, August 19, 2005, *www.icty.org/x/cases/krajisnik/trans/en/050819IT.htm*.

49. ICTY trial judgment in the case of Momčilo Krajišnik, September 27, 2006, *www.icty.org/x/cases /krajisnik/tjug/en/kra-jud060927e.pdf*, page 305.

50. Berić, *Letters to the Celestial Serbs*, 41. See also a report on preparations for Karadžić trial: Ana Uzelac, "A Mountain of Evidence Pointing to Genocide," Balkan Insight, August 23, 2008, "'They [Muslims] will disappear, that people will disappear from the face of the Earth . . . ,' he confided in a telephone conversation with poet Gojko Djogo already in October 1991, months before the outbreak of war in Bosnia, in an intercept recently admitted into evidence in the Milosevic case." *www. balkaninsight.com/en/article/a-mountain-of-evidence-pointing-to-genocide*. See also Silber and Little, *Yugoslavia*, 215; Cigar, *Genocide in Bosnia*, 37.

51. Marlise Simons, "Radovan Karadzic Sentenced to Life for Bosnian War Crimes," *New York Times*, March 20, 2019, *www.nytimes.com/2019/03/20/world/europe/radovan-karadzic-bosnia-un-tribunal. html*.

52. Quoted by Edina Bećirević in "Bosnia's Accidental Genocide," Bosnian Institute, September 30, 2006, *www.bosnia.org.uk/news/news_body.cfm?newsid=2229*.

53. Quoted in "Application for Leave to Submit an Amicus Brief on Behalf of Satko Mujagić, Fikret Alić, and the Association of Witnesses and Survivors of Genocide concerning Judgement of Acquittal under Rule 98 *bis*," Institute for Research of Genocide, Canada, August 31, 2012, *instituteforgenocide.org/en /wp-content/uploads/2012/09/Request-for-leave-to-file-amicus-in-Karadzic.zip*, paragraph 35, page 10.

54. Trial Judgement Summary for Ratko Mladić, ICTY, November 22, 2017, *www.icty.org/x/cases/mladic /tjug/en/171122-summary-en.pdf*.

55. Jelena Subotic, "After Mladic's Conviction, Can Serbia Face Its Past?," Balkan Insight, November 23, *www.balkaninsight.com/2017/11/23/after-mladic-s-conviction-can-serbia-face-its-past-11-22-2017*.

56. Ervin Blažević, interview, Kozarac, October 30, 2012.

CHAPTER 16

1. Mirsad Duratović, interview, Prijedor, October 29, 2012.

2. Vedran Grahovac, interview, Prijedor, June 18, 2010.

3. Halilovich, *Places of Pain*, 56.

4. Ibid., 97.

5. Dražen Huterer, "Film remeti šutnju o zločinima u Prijedoru" [Film disturbs silence about crimes in Prijedor], Radio Free Europe, March 23, 2015, *www.slobodnaevropa.org/content/film-remeti -sutnju-o-zlocincima-u-prijedoru/26907391.html*.

6. This visit to Omarska took place on May 24, 2010.

7. Denis Džidić and Marija Ristić, "White Ribbons against Genocide Denial," Balkan Insight, May 31, 2012, *www.balkaninsight.com/en/article/the-white-ribbons-against-genocide-denial*.

8. "Policija RS-a tragala ko nosi bijele trake" [RS police tracking who wears white armbands], Al Jazeera Balkans, May 31, 2012, *balkans.aljazeera.net/vijesti/policija-rs-tragala-ko-nosi-bijele-trake*.

9. "Sjećanje na prijedorske žrtve" [Remembrance of Prijedor victims], Anadolija press agency, May 23, 2013. Via Wayback Machine, *web.archive.org/web/20130615025207/http://www.e-novine.com/region /region-bosna/84745-Sjeanje-prijedorske-rtve.html*.

10. Refik Hodžić, "Srami se, Marko Paviću: Gradonačelnik Prijedora: Bijele trake su 'gej parada'" [Shame on you, Marko Pavić: Mayor of Prijedor: White Armbands Are "Gay Parade"), Facebook post, June 1, 2013, reproduced by tacno.net, *tacno.net/novosti/srami-se-marko-pavicu-gradonacelnik-prijedora-bijele-trake-su-gej-parada*.

11. Selma Milovanovic, "Bosnians Mark a Painful Chapter with White Armband Day," Al Jazeera America, May 30, 2014, *america.aljazeera.com/articles/2014/5/30/for-bosnians-whitearmbandday markspainfulchapter.html*.

12. "Mirni protest u povodu kršenja ljudskih prava u Prijedoru" [Peaceful protest of violation of human rights in Prijedor], Twentieth Anniversary Committee (committee for observance of the twentieth anniversary of the killing of Prijedorans), December 5, 2012. Via Wayback Machine, *web.archive.org /web/20121220063118/http://stopgenocidedenial.org/2012/12/05/mirni-protest-u-povodu-krsenja -ljudskih-prava-u-prijedoru*.

13. Edita Gorinjac, "Demokratija u RS-u: Četnički pokret maršira kroz Prijedor, udruženja žrtava ne mogu" [Democracy in RS: Četnik movement marches through Prijedor, victims associations cannot], *klix.ba*, December 9, 2012, *www.klix.ba/vijesti/bih/demokratija-u-rs-u-cetnicki-pokret-marsira -kroz-prijedor-udruzenja-zrtava-ne-mogu/121209076*.

14. Ibid.

15. "Prijedor: Protest Walk Despite Police Ban," *Oslobodjenje*, December 10, 2012 Via Wayback Machine, *web.archive.org/web/20121213024849/http://www.oslobodjenje.ba/daily-news/prijedor-protest -walk-despite-police-ban*.

16. "Bosnia: Banning of Human Rights March Is 'Unacceptable,'" Amnesty International, December 10, 2012, *www.amnesty.ca/news/news-releases/republika-srpska-banning-of-human-rights-march- unacceptable*.

17. "Appeal to Members of the EU Parliament, the Council of Europe and the European Union Agency for Fundamental Rights in Vienna," Society for Threatened Peoples, Göttingen, December 10, 2012, *www.gfbv.de/en/news/appeal-to-members-of-the-eu-parliament-the-council-of-europe-and-the- european-union-agency-for-fundamental-rights-in-vienna-5756*.

18. "Dodik: Pokazati spremnost za provođenje presude Sejdić-Finci" [Dodik: Showing preparedness to implement Sejdić-Finci finding], SRNA agency, *Nezavisne Novine*, December 9, 2012, *www.nezavisne .com/novosti/bih/Dodik-Pokazati-spremnost-za-provodjenje-presude-Sejdic-Finci-170737.html*.

19. "U Prijedoru se sloboda govora i okupljanja podrazumijevaju" [In Prijedor freedom of speech and freedom of assembly are implicit], Prijedor official city portal, August 2, 2013, *kozarac .ba/2013/02/09/6195-794-u-prijedoru-se-sloboda-govora-i-okupljanja-podrazumijevaju*.

20. "Prijedor, prestonica ljudskih prava" [Prijedor, capital of human rights], *e-Novine.com*, February 10, 2013, *www.e-novine.com/region/region-bosna/78794-Prijedor-prestonica-ljudskih-prava.html*.

21. Quoted by Edin Ramulić, in "Povijest Prijedora u kandžama Pavića Marka" [History of Prijedor in the grip of Marko Pavić], December 1, 2011, *kozarac. ba/2011/12/01/5362-474-povijest-prijedora-u-kandzama-pavica-marka*.

22. Edin Ramulić, "20 godina genocida—Saopštenje za javnost" [20 years of genocide—public announcement], April 26, 2012, *www.bosnjaci.net/prilog.php?pid=4558&prijedor_je_bio_najstras- nije_mjesto_na_planeti,_sa_najgorim_logorima_smrti_-_i_tu_je_pocinjen_genocid!!!*

23. Ibid.

24. Elvir Padalović, "Prijedor, zabranjena riječ" [Prijedor, forbidden word], Buka portal, May 29, 2012, Edin Ramulić, *www.6yka.com/novost/24204/Prijedor-zabranjena-rijec*.

25. Discussing official resistance to commemoration of the atrocities at Omarska, Hariz Halilovich writes, "RS authorities, as both a legacy and a direct product of 'Omarska policies,' have political reasons to oppose such an idea [memorialization of Omarska as a concentration camp]—it may undermine the legitimacy of RS if Omarska were to become known as a 'genocidal entity'—while many ordinary Serbs from Prijedor who were in the Serb army and police during the war prefer to close that chapter of their lives." Halilovich, *Places of Pain*, 87.

26. Ibid.

27. "Dodik: Ljudska prava cvjetaju u RS" [Dodik: Human rights are blossoming in RS], *istinomjer.ba*, December 10, 2012, *istinomjer.ba/dodik-ljudska-prava-cvjetaju-u-rs*.

28. "Priveden zbog riječi genocid" [Detained because of the word "genocide"], *klix.ba*, August 5, 2012, *www.e-novine.com/region/region-bosna/69143-Priveden-zbog-rijei-genocid.html*.

29. Ervin Blažević, interview, Kozarac, August 6, 2013.

30. I have reproduced this excerpt of Zajović's words here based on the notes I took at the time of her presentation at Trnopolje, August 5, 2013.

31. "Noć sjećanja na logor Trnopolje" [Night of commemoration of Trnopolje camp], Anadolija press agency, *Oslobodjenje*, August 5, 2013, reposted at *vijesti.ba/clanak/160086/ljudi-iz-cijele-regije-se-sjecaju-zrtava-trnopolja*.

32. For a full account of the negotiation process between advocates for a memorial at Omarska and ArcelorMittal, see Sebina Sivac-Bryant, "The Omarska Memorial Project as an Example of How Transitional Justice Interventions Can Produce Hidden Harms," *International Journal of Transitional Justice*, December 3, 2014, 1–11, *academic.oup.com/ijtj/article/9/1/170/678030*.

33. "Burying the Memory of Omarska," by David Mutton, Index on Censorship, November 29, 2005, *listserv.buffalo.edu/cgi-bin/wa?A2=JUSTWATCH-L;ba77323b.0511*. See also "Mittal to Erect War Memorial in Bosnia Mines," Reuters, December 1, 2005, archived at *listserv.buffalo.edu/cgi-bin/wa?A2=JUSTWATCH-L;be5b37ef.0512*.

34. D. Kovačević, "Čeka se odobrenje lokalnih vlasti" [Awaiting approval of local government], *Nezavisne Novine*, December 27, 2005, *kozarac.ba/2005/12/28/410-58-ceka-se-odobrenje-lokalnih-vlasti*.

35. "Omarska, 15 godina kasnije" [Omarska, 15 years later], by Chris Keulemans, *Dani* 522 (June 15, 2007), *www.bhdani.ba/portal/izdanje/522*.

36. Daria Sito-Sucic, "Bosnia Camp Survivors Protest for Memorial at ArcelorMittal Mine," Reuters, August 6, 2012, *in.reuters.com/article/2012/08/06/bosnia-camp-idINL6E8J6ARC20120806*.

37. Letter from the Advisory Council for Bosnia and Herzegovina to ArcelorMittal regarding the "Omarska" concentration camp, May 12, 2012, *bosniak.org/2012/05/12/letter-to-arcelormittal-regarding-the-omarska-concentration-camp*. See also Hariz Halilovich's discussion of Mittal's role: "Mittal Steel has not been indifferent to the construction of a memorial at Omarska but, on the contrary, has been collaborating with the RS authorities in keeping Omarska survivors away from the site." Halilovich, *Places of Pain*, 89.

38. Katarina Panic, "Selective Memory," Balkan Insight, November 22, 2013, *www.balkaninsight.com/en/article/selective-memory*.

39. "Fikret Bacic—Bosnia and Herzegovina," ICTJ Gallery (International Center for Transitional Justice), *www.ictj.org/gallery-items/fikret-bacic-bosnia-and-herzegovina*.

40. "Da li će Prijedor podići spomenik ubijenoj djeci?" [Will Prijedor erect a monument to the murdered children?], *Portal kozarac.ba*, January 27, 2016, *kozarac.ba/vijesti/prijedor/item/7660-da-li-ce-prijedor-podici-spomenik-ubijenoj-djeci*.

41. Katarina Panic, "Prijedor's Serbs Reject Memorial to Killed Children," Balkan Insight, June 29, 2016, *www.balkaninsight.com/en/article/prijedor-assembly-rejects-memorial-to-killed-children-06-29-2016*.

See also Edin Ramulić, "Prijedorski Parlament Prihvatio Zločin Nad Djecom" [Prijedor Parliament acknowledged crime against children], Kozarac.eu, June 29, 2016, *kozarac.eu/index.php/kolumne /1736-prijedorski-parlament-prihvatio-zlocin-nad-djecom.html*.

42. For example, see "Povratnički život u Prijedoru."

43. "Bačić: Nudi nam se neki spomenik bez imena djece ubijene u Prijedoru" [Bačić: They are offering us some monument without the names of the children killed in Prijedor], Faktor, June 4, 2018, *faktor.ba/vijest/bai-nudi-nam-se-neki-spomenik-bez-imena-djece-ubijene-u-prijedoru-298456*. See also "Đaković: Nije problem gradnja spomenika u Prijedoru, želja mi je da ljudi razgovaraju i jedni druge razumiju" [Đaković: Building a monument in Prijedor is not a problem; my wish is that people talk and understand each other], *Oslobodjenje*, January 17, 2019, *www.oslobodjenje.ba/vijesti /bih/dakovic-nije-problem-gradnja-spomenika-u-prijedoru-zelja-mi-je-da-ljudi-razgovaraju-i-jedni -druge-razumiju-426051*.

44. Rachel Irwin and Velma Saric, "Calls for War Memorials Divide Bosnia," IWPR, December 6, 2010, *iwpr.net/global-voices/calls-war-memorials-divide-bosnia*.

45. Edin Ramulić, interview, Prijedor, May 27, 2010.

46. "Bosnian Ethnic Cleansing Casualties Finally Laid to Rest," AP, *Sydney Morning Herald*, July 21, 2006, *www.smh.com.au/news/world/bosnian-ethnic-cleansing-casualties-finally-laid-to-rest /2006/07/20/1153166525875.html*.

CHAPTER 17

1. Nedžad Bešić, interview, Kozarac, October 9, 2008.

2. Emsuda Mujagić, interview, Kozarac, September 24, 2006.

3. Marek Kohn, "Šejla Kamerić: An Artist's Search for Bosnia's Missing," *FT Magazine*, January 30, 2015, *www.ft.com/content/3c851938-a741-11e4-8a71-00144feab7de*. See also "Bosnian Missing Persons Hunt Praised as Success," Balkan Insight, December 5, 2013, *www.balkaninsight.com/en/article /bosnian-lessons-in-search-for-the-missing*.

4. Vesna Besic and Lejla Biogradlija, "Over 7,000 Victims of Bosnian War Still Missing," Anadolu Agency, July 21, 2018, *www.aa.com.tr/en/europe/ over-7-000-victims-of-bosnian-war-still-missing/1210377*.

5. "Čengić: Do sada pronađeno i identificirano više od 22.500 nestalih osoba" [Čengić: To date more than 22,500 missing persons discovered and identified], *Oslobodjenje*, March 5, 2017, reposted at *jajce-online.com/2017/03/06/cengic-do-sada-pronadeno-i-identificirano-vise-od-22-500-nestalih- osoba*.

6. "Zajednička Dženaza U Prijedoru Najmlađa žrtva petogodišnja Emira Mulalić" [Joint funeral in Prijedor; youngest victim five-year-old Emira Mulalić], *Dnevni Avaz*, July 19, 2016, *www.avaz.ba/clanak/246849 /zajednicka-dzenaza-u-prijedoru-najmlada-zrtva-petogodisnja-emira-mulalic?url=clanak/246849 /zajednicka-dzenaza-u-prijedoru-najmlada-zrtva-petogodisnja-emira-mulalic*.

7. Edin Barimac, "U posjeti: Svaki deseti nestali traži se u Prijedoru" [In a visit: Every tenth missing person is sought for in Prijedor], *Oslobodjenje*, March 23, 2015, reposted at *www.mojprijedor .com/u-posjeti-svaki-deseti-nestali-trazi-se-u-prijedoru*.

8. Mirsad Duratović, interview, Prijedor, October 29, 2012.

9. *Ni Krivi Ni Dužni—Knjiga Nestalih Općine Prijedor* [Neither guilty nor obligated]. For a facsimile of the second (2000) edition, which lists 3,227 missing, see *www.scribd.com/doc/51727802/Ni- Krivi-Ni-Duzni-Knjiga-Nestalih-Opcine-Prijedor#scribd*. For an announcement of the third edition, which lists 3,173 missing, see "Prijedor-Promocija knjige nestalih Ni krivi ni dužni" [Prijedor— promotion of book of disappeared neither guilty nor responsible], June 15, 2012, *www.gradprijedor .com/drustvo/prijedor-promocija-knjige-nestalih-ni-krivi-ni-duzni*.

10. Katherine Boyle, "Bosnia: A House Divided," January 18, 2007, *www.bosnia.org.uk/news/news_body* *.cfm?newsid=2244.*

11. Edin Ramulić, interview, Prijedor, October 29, 2012.

12. Mirsad Duratović, interview, Prijedor, October 29, 2012.

13. Jasmin Odobašić, interview, Sarajevo, November 1, 2012.

14. Besima Kahrimanović, "U nasoj zemlji do sada ekshumirano 14.500 zrtava" [In our country 14,500 victims have been exhumed to date]. Interview with Jasmin Odobašić, deputy president of State Commission for the Disappeared, *Oslobodjenje*, August 19, 2002.

15. Kemal Pervanić, interview, Kevljani, August 4, 2013.

16. K.K., "Korićanske stijene: Dževad Smajić pozvao prijedorske policajce da olakšaju dušu i progovore" [Korićanske stijene: Dževad Smajić called on Prijedor police to relieve their souls and speak out], *Dnevni Avaz*, August 21, 2014, *avaz.ba/vijesti/bih/131657/koricanske-stijene-dzevad-smajic* *-pozvao-prijedorske-policajce-da-olaksaju-dusu-i-progovore.*

17. "Danas ukop tri žrtve zločina na području Prijedora: Kavazović predvodi dženazu" [Today burial of three victims of the crimes in the area of Prijedor: Kavazović to conduct the funeral], *Oslobodjenje*, July 20, 2018, *www.oslobodjenje.ba/vijesti/bih/danas-ukop-tri-zrtve-zlocina-na-podrucju-prijedora* *-kavazovic-predvodi-dzenazu-380337.*

18. "Mass Grave with Nearly 100 Victims Found in Bosnia," Agence France-Presse, September 21, 2017, *nation.com.pk/international/22-Sep-2017/mass-grave-with-nearly-100-victims-found-in-bosnia.*

19. See map showing distribution of mass graves in Prijedor, see Fontbonne University, "The Search for the Missing," *photos.fontbonne.edu/Academics/Honors-Program/The-Search-for-the-Missing/* *i-wQPkkzm.* Accessed January 18, 2018.

20. "Brammertz: Otkrića u Tomašici dokazi u optužnicama" [Brammertz: Discovery at Tomašica [to be used as] evidence in indictments], Al Jazeera Balkans, November 8, 2013, *balkans.aljazeera.net* */vijesti/brammertz-otkrica-u-tomasici-dokazi-u-optuznicama.*

21. "Amor Mašović: Vjerujem da smo pronašli žrtve logora Keraterm i Trnopolje" [Amor Mašović: I believe that we have discovered victims of Keraterm and Trnopolje camps], *Oslobodjenje*, September 6, 2013, reposted at *www.klix.ba/vijesti/bih/amor-masovic-vjerujem-da-smo-pronasli* *-zrtve-logora-keraterm-i-trnopolje/130906099.*

22. "Huge Bosnia Mass Grave Excavated at Tomasica," BBC, November 1, 2013, *www.bbc.com/news* */world-europe-24778713.*

23. Nedim Botić, "Mirsad Duratović—'Nakon Tomašice niko nema pravo da kaže da se u Prijedoru nije desio genocid!'" [Mirsad Duratović—"after Tomašica no one has the right to say that in Prijedor genocide did not happen!"], *Haber.ba*, November 14, 2013, *www.haber.ba/vijesti/bih/63734* *-nakon-tomasice-niko-nema-pravo-da-kaze-da-se-u-prijedoru-nije-desio-genocid.html.*

24. Denis Džidić, "Bosnia Finds 600 Body Parts in Mass Grave" Balkan Insight, October 29, 2015, *www* *.balkaninsight.com/en/article/six-hundred-mortal-remains-found-in-bosnia-grave-10-29-2015.*

25. E. Duvnjak-Šalaka, "Još oko sedam hiljada ljudi u masovnim grobnicama: Zločinci šute, umjesto pijeteta ubijeni dobijaju smeće" [Still about seven thousand people in mass graves: The criminals remain silent; instead of respect, those killed are receiving garbage], *Faktor.ba*, April 2, 2016, *www.* *faktor.ba/vijest/jos-oko-sedam-hiljada-ljudi-u-masovnim-grobnicama-zlocinci-sute-umjesto-pijeteta-* *ubijeni-dobijaju-smece-191752.* See also Vesna Besic and Lejla Biogradlija, "Over 7,000 victims of Bosnian war still missing," Anadolu Agency, July 21, 2018, *www.aa.com.tr/en/europe/over-7-000-* *victims-of-bosnian-war-still-missing/1210377.*

26. Denis Džidić, "Bosnia Charges 15 Serbs for Zecovi Massacre," Balkan Insight, December 12, 2014, *www.balkaninsight.com/en/article/zecovi-massacre-indictment-raised.*

27. Faruk Vele, "Nakon 22 godine: Šest sinova i muž majke Have Tatarević pronađeni u Tomašici!"

[After 22 years: Six sons and husband of mother Hava Tatarević discovered at Tomašica!], April 2, 2014, *www.klix.ba/vijesti/bih/nakon-22-godine-sest-sinova-i-muz-majke-have-tatarevic-pronadjeni-u-tomasici/140402062*.

28. Ibid.

29. "Posmrtni ostaci pripadaju Tatarevićima" [Mortal remains belong to the Tatarevićes], Al Jazeera Balkans, April 22, 2014, *balkans.aljazeera.net/vijesti/posmrtni-ostaci-pripadaju-tatarevicima*.

30. Dragan Bursać, "Tomašica, mrtvi ljudi i živi mrtvaci!" [Tomašica, dead people and the living dead], Buka, July 20, 2014, *www.6yka.com/novost/46557/dragan-bursac-tomasica-mrtvi-ljudi-i-zivi-mrtvaci*.

31. A.A., "Ramulić: Zašto još niko nije uhapšen za Tomašicu?" [Ramulić: Why is there still no one arrested for Tomašica?], November 8, 2013, *vijesti.ba/clanak/177140/ramulic-zasto-jos-niko-nije-uhapsen-za-tomasicu*.

32. Mirsad Duratović, "Udruženje Logoraša Banja Luka uputilo otvoreno pismo Vladi Rs-A o privatizaciji Rudnika Ljubija" [Association of Concentration Camp Survivors of the Banja Luka region addressed open letter to the RS government about the privatization of Ljubija mine], *hayat.ba*, October 19, 2018, *www.hayat.ba/vijest.php?id=136322*.

33. Kemal Pervanic, Forgiveness Project, *www.theforgivenessproject.com/kemal-pervanic*. Accessed March 27, 2019.

34. Kemal Pervanić, *The Killing Days: My Journey through the Bosnian War* (London: Blake, 1999). For an excerpt from the book, see "Case Study: Kemal Pervanić," *av.hmd.org.uk/1256561497–101.pdf*.

35. This visit to Kevljani and the conversations recounted here took place on August 4, 2013.

36. Sivac-Bryant, *Re-Making Kozarac*, 155. In chapter 6, titled "Kozarac.ba: Online Community as a Network Bridge," Sivac-Bryant describes the valuable project of Kozarac.ba, a virtual online community led by Ervin "Švabo" Blažević. During a crucial period in the return process, Kozarac.ba provided a communication link between returnees and their friends and relatives in the widespread diaspora. This network played an important part in facilitating economic development in Kozarac through remittances and investment (149–66).

37. See "Bosnia and Herzegovina Unemployment Rate 2007–2018," *www.tradingeconomics.com/bosnia-and-herzegovina/unemployment-rate*. See also "Najniže plate i penzije u Evropi" [Lowest wages and pensions in Europe], by Eldar Dizdarević, *Oslobodjenje*, October 4, 2017, *www.oslobodjenje.ba/dosjei/kolumne/najnize-plate-i-penzije-u-evropi*.

38. "U RS-u prosječna plaća za samo 45 posto potrošačke korpe" [In RS average pay only enough for 45 percent of consumer basket], FENA news agency, June 26, 2014, *www.klix.ba/biznis/u-rs-u-prosjecna-placa-za-samo-45-posto-potrosacke-korpe/140626045*.

39. Sudbin Musić, interview, Prijedor, October 28, 2012.

40. "Cormack: Potential Untapped Due to Political Corruption," *Oslobodjenje*, English digest, April 16, 2015. Via Wayback Machine, *web.archive.org/web/20150422032702/http://www.Oslobodjenje.ba/daily-news/cormack-potential-untapped-due-to-political-corruption*.

41. "Povratnici kozaračku regiju podigli iz pepela: Budućnost su poljoprivreda i male farme" [Returnees to Kozarac region up from the ashes: Agriculture and small farms are the future], *Oslobodjenje*, April 18, 2015, reposted at *www.trt.net.tr/bosanski/bosna-i-hercegovina/2015/04/18/povratnici-kozaracku-regiju-podigli-iz-pepela-buducnost-su-poljoprivreda-i-male-farme-42502*.

42. Nijaz Huremović, "Kozarački 'Austronet' planira proširenje proizvodnje" [Kozarac "Austronet" plans expanded production], Kozarac.eu, January 20, 2015, *www.kozarac.eu/index.php/novosti/tekuce-vijesti/723-kozaraki-austronet-planira-proirenje-proizvodnje.html*.

43. Elvir Padalović, "Čudo iz Kozarca: Otvorena najveća farma za uzgoj norveškog govečeta na svijetu!" [Wonder from Kozarac: Biggest farm in the world opened for breeding of

Norwegian red cattle!], Buka, November 27, 2014, *www.6yka.com/novost/69064/cudo-iz-kozarca*
-otvorena-najveca-farma-za-uzgoj-norveskog-goveceta-na-svijetu.

44. Sivac-Bryant, *Re-Making Kozarac*, 197.

45. Ibid. In chapter 7, titled "Economic Sustainability in a Land of Corruption," the author notes that there is a younger generation of returnees in Kozarac who are more interested in economic opportunities than in memorialization and other campaigns. The chapter describes Kahrimanović's and Arifagić's endeavors in more detail than possible in this book, and it notes these entrepreneurs' wisdom in striving to work for the good of all local residents, rather than only for the Bosniak returnees. Sivac-Bryant quotes Kahrimanović: "It is not a question of whether one hates Serbs, or whether one can forget the past; according to him, forgetting is impossible and hating those who committed the worst crimes is to be expected; but it should not influence our relationship with other Serbs who were not involved" (180).

This approach to living and working together points to a manner of reconciliation that is much more realistic and concrete than the one that resides in the dreams of many international officials and NGOs. Sivac-Bryant notes attempts by internationals to bring former adversaries together in a "sterile environment" where they can "perform" reconciliation. Sivac-Bryant contrasts this kind of performance with the hard work of actual return and living together. Only in that endeavor, she writes, can people experience a postwar reality that is healthy enough and mutually supportive enough to engender a more sustainable reconciliation "according to local social norms, rather than an external frame of reference" (15).

46. "Đaković: Generala Mladića doživljavamo kao srpskog heroja" [Đaković: We consider General Mladić to be a Serb hero], N1 BiH, November 22, 2017, *ba.n1info.com/a228288/Vijesti/Vijesti*
/Djakovic-Generala-Mladica-dozivljavamo-kao-srpskog-heroja.html.

47. "Gradonačelnik Prijedora Milenko Đaković: Mi smo grad međaš Republike Srpske" [Mayor of Prijedor Milenko Đaković: We are a landmark city of the Republika Srpska], interview with *Srbija Danas*, March 2, 2019, *prijedor24h.net/2019/03/02/gradonacelnik-prijedora-milenko-dakovic-mi*
-smo-grad-medas-republike-srpske.

48. Goran Zorić, interview, Prijedor, June 26, 2018.

49. "Povratnički život u Prijedoru."

50. Erduan Katana, interview with Edin Ramulić, "Politike u BiH i danas provode Karadžićev strateški cilj" [Policies in BiH today carry out Karadžić's strategic goal], Radio Free Europe, March 25, 2016, *www.slobodnaevropa.org/content/politike-u-bih-i-danas-provode-karadzicev-strateski-cilj/27635756*
.html.

51. Mirsad Duratović, interview, Prijedor, October 29, 2012.

52. Sudbin Musić, interview, Prijedor, October 28, 2012.

53. "Povratnici kozaračku regiju podigli iz pepela: Budućnost su poljoprivreda i male farme" [Returnees to Kozarac region up from the ashes: Agriculture and small farms are the future], *Oslobodjenje*, April 18, 2015, reposted at *www.trt.net.tr/bosanski/bosna-i-hercegovina/2015/04/18/*
povratnici-kozaracku-regiju-podigli-iz-pepela-buducnost-su-poljoprivreda-i-male-farme-42502.

54. "U posjeti: Svaki deseti nestali traži se u Prijedoru."

55. Jusuf Trbić, "Genocid" [Genocide], Preporod Bijeljina, July 15, 2013, *preporodbn.com/genocid.*

CHAPTER 18

1. David Watson, "The Balkan Wars and the New World Dis/Order," *Fifth Estate*, Spring 2002. *balkanwitness.glypx.com/watson.htm.*

2. For an extensive source of information on atrocity revisionism concerning Bosnia-Herzegovina and Kosovo, see the Balkan Witness website for "News, Background, and Progressive Perspectives on

the Yugoslav Wars," *balkanwitness.glypx.com/articles-deniers.htm*. This website has been carefully compiled and maintained by my brother, Roger Lippman, since 1999.

3. Halilović, *Kako Opisati Srebrenicu*, 24.

4. Željko Cvijanović, "Dodik Owns Up to Srebrenica," IWPR, July 17, 2000, *iwpr.net/report-news/ dodik-owns-srebrenica*.

5. "Bosnian Serb PM Blames Rivals for Srebrenica," Balkan Insight, May 8, 2008, *www.balkaninsight. com/en/article/bosnian-serb-pm-blames-rivals-for-srebrenica*.

6. Edina Bećirević, "More Than a 'Local Genocide,'" IWPR, July 25, 2008, *iwpr.net/report-news/ more-"local-genocide"*.

7. "Convention on the Prevention and Punishment of the Crime of Genocide," Human Rights Web, last edited January 27, 1997, *www.hrweb.org/legal/genocide.html*. See particularly the definition in Article 2.

8. "Bosnian Serb Leader Disputes Srebrenica Genocide 'Definition,'" BBC Monitoring Newsfile, April 8, 2010. Excerpt from a report by Bosnian Serb news agency SRNA. Article on file with author.

9. Ibid.

10. From Bosnia Press Review, Balkan Insight, July 6, 2010, quoting the Sarajevo daily *Oslobodjenje*, *www.balkaninsight.com/en/article/bosnia-press-review-july-6-2010*.

11. Emir Imamović, "Srebrenica: Milorad Dodik nastavio negirati genocid" [Srebrenica: Milorad Dodik continued to deny genocide], *Dani* 693 (September 24, 2010), *www.bhdani.ba/portal /izdanje/693*.

12. Maja Bjelajac, "Bosnian Serb Leader Opportunistic or Committed Nationalist?," IWPR, March 2, 2012, *iwpr.net/report-news/bosnian-serb-leader-opportunistic-or-committed-nationalist*.

13. Ibid.

14. "Bosnian Serb Leader to Testify for Karadzic's Defence," Agence France-Presse, February 28, 2013. Article on file with author.

15. "Srebrenica Massacre 'Not Genocide,'" *Sydney Morning Herald*, July 13, 2010, *news.smh.com.au /breaking-news-world/srebrenica-massacre-not-genocide-20100713–1083q.html*.

16. "Bosnian Serbs to Ban Lessons on Srebrenica Genocide," Balkan Insight, June 6, 2017, *www .balkaninsight.com/en/article/bosnian-serbs-to-ban-lectures-on-srebrenica-sarajevo-siege-06–06–2017*.

17. Srdjan Garcevic, "Confronting the Shame of Nationalism after Mladic Verdict," Balkan Insight, December 7, 2017, *www.balkaninsight.com/en/blog/ confronting-the-shame-of-nationalism-after-mladic-verdict-12–04–2017*.

18. Mladen Dragojlovic, "Dodik Determined to Annul the Srebrenica Report," IBNA Independent Balkan News Agency, July 20, 2018, *www.balkaneu.com/dodik-determined-to-annul-the- srebrenica-report*.

19. Mladen Lakic, "Bosnian Serb Assembly to Annul Report on Srebrenica," Balkan Insight, July 23, 2018, *www.balkaninsight.com/en/article/bosnian-serbs-to-annul-report-on-srebrenica-07–23–2018*.

20. David Brunnstrom, "U.S. Criticizes Serb Vote to Overturn Srebrenica Massacre Report," Reuters, *uk.reuters.com/article/uk-bosnia-serbs-usa/u-s-criticizes-serb-vote-to-overturn-srebrenica -massacre-report-idUKKBN1L02CA*.

21. "Bosnian Serbs Form New Panels to Re-examine Srebrenica, Sarajevo Victims," Reuters, February 7, 2019, *www.reuters.com/article/us-bosnia-serbs-srebrenica/bosnian-serbs-form-new-panels-to-re- examine-srebrenica-sarajevo-victims-idUSKCN1PW1TD*. See also S. H., "Dugoročna opasnost revizionističke politike vlasti RS-a o agresiji na BiH i genocidu u Srebrenici" [Long-term danger of revisionist policies of the RS government about aggression against BiH and genocide in Srebrenica], *klix.ba*, February 8, 2019, *www.klix.ba/vijesti/bih/dugorocna-opasnost-revizionisticke-politike-vlasti-*

rs-a-o-agresiji-na-bih-i-genocidu-u-srebrenici/190208049; and Daniel McLaughlin, "US Denounces Bosnian Serb Bid to Reassess 1990s War Crimes," *Irish Times*, February 8, 2019, *www.irishtimes.com/ news/world/europe/us-denounces-bosnian-serb-bid-to-reassess-1990s-war-crimes-1.3787180*.

22. Kemal Kurspahić, "Kurspahić: Istorija po narudžbi" [Kurspahić: History made to order], Radio Free Europe, August 17, 2018, *www.slobodnaevropa.org/a/kurspahic-istorija-narudzba/29438666.html*.

23. Michael Dobbs, "The Wages of Genocide Denial," July 5, 2012, *dobbs.foreignpolicy.com/posts/2012 /06/29/the_wages_of_genocide_denial*.

24. "Bosnian Serbs Sue UN, Netherlands over 1992–95 War," Unified Communications, March 2, 2009, *unified-communications.tmcnet.com/news/2009/03/02/4023912.htm*.

25. Ibid.

26. "MUP podnio krivičnu prijavu protiv Karganovića zbog utaje poreza" [Ministry of Interior filed criminal charges against Karganović for tax evasion], Buka portal, April 5, 2016, *www.6yka.com/ novost/102711/mup-podnio-krivicnu-prijavu-protiv-karganovica-zbog-utaje-poreza*.

27. Trifković provides sections of his book on his website, *www.trifkovic.mysite.com*, on the page titled "The Sword of the Prophet: Islam; History, Theology, Impact on the World" (*www.trifkovic.mysite. com/article.html*). One passage on this page reads, "There is a huge problem for all Muslims—the violent message of the Kuran."

28. Lee Jay Walker, "Bosnia: The Myths of Peaceful Islam and the Hidden Islamic Ji-had," *Modern Tokyo Times*, January 14, 2011, *islamicinquisition.wordpress.com/tag/ serge-trifkovic-and-the-sword-of-the-prophet*.

29. See Trifković's testimony at the ICTY in the case of Milomir Stakić, March 18, 2003, *www.icty. org/x/cases/stakic/trans/en/030318IT.htm*, page 13714 and *www.icty.org/x/cases/stakic/trans/ en/030313ED.htm*, page 13580. See also Richard Miron, "Mixed Views on Balkans Pair," BBC, July 5, 2001, *news.bbc.co.uk/1/hi/world/europe/1423835.stm*; Božo Nikolić, "Serbia Is Sick with Indifference," Bosnian Institute, January–May 2002, *www.bosnia.org.uk/bosrep/report_format. cfm?articleid=846&reportid=153*.

30. Senad Pečanin, "Nepodnošljiva lakoća negacionizma" [The unbearable lightness of denialism], *Dani* 630 (July 10, 2009), *www.bhdani.ba/portal/izdanje/630*.

31. Srdja Trifković, "'Srebrenica' as Holocaust: Trifković, the 'Genocide Denier,'" April 27, 2012, *www. chroniclesmagazine.org/srebrenica-as-holocaust-trifkovic-the-genocide-denier*.

32. Ibid.

33. "The Meaning of the Myth," by Srdja Trifković, July 14, 2010. Via Wayback Machine, *web.archive.org /web/20100721063422/http://www.balkanstudies.org/articles/meaning-myth*. As stated previously, there is apparently no end to the ongoing denial by Trifković. For an earlier example from soon after the war, see "The Hague Tribunal: Bad Justice, Worse Politics," a reproduction of an article originally published in *Chronicles* in August 1996 (archived at *web.archive.org/web/20040820152416/http://www .srpska-mreza.com/WarCrime/ST-Hague.html*). There, Trifković brazenly asserts that the breadline and Markale bomb massacres, in which dozens of Sarajevans were killed during the war, were per-petrated by Bosnian government forces against their own population. Trifković also strives in this article to discredit the ICTY, calling it a "farce" and describing it as stacked with anti-Serb judges.

34. Robyn Urback, "Guest UBC Lecturer Denied Entry to Canada," February 27, 2011, *oncampus .macleans.ca/education/2011/02/27/guest-ubc-lecturer-denied-entry-to-canada*.

35. Srđa Pavlović, "Does Denying Genocide Counts [*sic*] as Free Speech?," March 5, 2011, *pescanik .net/does-denying-genocide-counts-as-free-speech*.

36. Diana Johnstone, *Fools' Crusade: Yugoslavia, NATO and Western Delusions* (New York: Monthly Review Press, 2002), 78. Here Johnstone asserts that the use of the accusation of mass rape

was calculated to engage women's rights groups in the West. Her third paragraph begins, "Women are raped every day in peacetime in the most 'advanced' societies," going on to say that evidence for rape is hard to come by. Indeed, while admitting that rape happened, she subsequently takes apart several stories of wartime rape. She further attempts to undermine the significance of the rape of Jadranka Cigelj (79–81) through character assassination of that activist.

37. Ibid., 71. Here and in subsequent pages Johnstone repeats the discredited lie by independent German journalist Thomas Deichmann that the famous photograph of the war prisoner at Trnopolje, Fikret Alić, was a forgery and that that concentration camp was, actually, merely a "collection center" for the safety of its inhabitants.

38. Ibid., 109–18. Note that Johnstone repeatedly uses quotation marks around the phrases "mass grave," "Srebrenica massacre," and "genocide," among others.

39. Ibid., 115.

40. Diana Johnstone, "The Main Issue in the French Presidential Election: National Sovereignty," Counterpunch, April 21, 2017, *www.counterpunch.org/2017/04/21/the-main-issue-in-the-french-presidential-election-national-sovereignty*.

41. Edward S. Herman, "The Politics of the Srebrenica Massacre," Global Research, July 2005, *www.globalresearch.ca/the-politics-of-the-srebrenica-massacre/660*.

42. From press conference announcement: "Researchers and Former UN Officials Challenge Portrayal of Events at Srebrenica," balkan.info (blog), July 12, 2005, *balkaninfo-emre.blogspot.com/2006/07/researchers-and-former-un-officials.html*.

43. Herman, "Politics of the Srebrenica Massacre."

44. Ibid.

45. "The Dismantling of Yugoslavia," *Monthly Review* 59, no. 5 (October 29, 2007), *monthlyreview.org/2007/10/01/the-dismantling-of-yugoslavia*.

46. Edward S. Herman and David Peterson, *The Politics of Genocide* (New York: Monthly Review Press, 2010, new ed., December 2011). The 2010 edition of this book is available in its entirety as a pdf at *libcom.org/files/Edward_Herman_and_David_Peterson_The_Politics_of_Genocide__2010.pdf*.

47. Ibid., 47.

48. Noam Chomsky interviewed by M. Junaid Alam, "Civilization versus Barbarism?" Left Hook, December 17, 2004. Via chomsky.info, *chomsky.info/20041217-2*.

49. "The Greatest Intellectual? Noam Chomsky Interviewed by Emma Brockes," *Guardian*, October 31, 2005, *chomsky.info/20051031*.

50. Ibid.

51. Ibid.

52. For more on the Brockes episode, see "Focus: Chomsky Interview Controversy," Balkan Insight, December 23, 2005. Via Wayback Machine, *web.archive.org/web/20060213175353/http://cm.greekhelsinki.gr/index.php?sec=194&cid=1557*. Also available at *courses.wcupa.edu/rbove/eco343/050Compecon/Centeur/BalkanInsight/Balkan%20Insight%20No.15.txt*. See also Noam Chomsky, "Open Letter to *The Guardian*," ZNet, November 13, 2005 (viachomsky.info, *www.chomsky.info/letters/20051113.htm*); Oliver Kamm, "Chomsky's Complaints," November 15, 2005, *oliverkamm.typepad.com/blog/2005/11/chomskys_compla.html*; "Corrections and Clarifications—*The Guardian* and Noam Chomsky," *Guardian*, November 17, 2005, *ww.theguardian.com/media/2005/nov/17/pressandpublishing.corrections*; Dr. Marko Attila Hoare, "Chomsky's Genocidal Denial," Srebrenica Genocide Blog, December 17, 2005, *srebrenica-genocide.blogspot.com/2005/12/chomskys-genocidal-denial.html*.

53. Noam Chomsky interviewed by Danilo Mandić, "On the NATO Bombing of Yugoslavia," RTS Online, April 25, 2006. For the transcript, see *www.chomsky.info/interviews/20060425.htm*. For the video, see *www.youtube.com/watch?v=Iq-3ZJFH35w*.

54. Andrew Stephen, "NS Interview—Chomsky," *New Statesman*, June 19, 2006, *www.newstatesman .com/node/164578*.

55. George Monbiot, "Correspondence with Noam Chomsky," supporting material for the article "See No Evil," May 21, 2012, *www.monbiot.com/2012/05/21/2181*.

56. Ibid.

57. Herman and Peterson, *Politics of Genocide*, 7.

58. Paul Robinson, "The Chomsky Problem," *New York Times*, February 25, 1979, *www.nytimes. com/1979/02/25/archives/the-chomsky-problem-chomsky.html*.

59. From personal correspondence with David Watson. Reprinted with permission.

60. Hasan Nuhanović, "Ko je Noam Chomsky?" [Who is Noam Chomsky?], *Bilten Srebrenica* (Bulletin of the Tuzla-based Srebrenica survivors organization Žene Srebrenice [Women of Srebrenica]) 36 (February 2006), 2–3.

61. Ibid. All paraphrases and quotations from this article are my own translations.

62. Wesselingh and Vaulerin, *Raw Memory*, 74.

63. Radoša Milutinović, "Svjedok: Bolje u Trnopolju nego na ulici" [Witness: Better in Trnopolje than on the street], MojPrijedor, January 29, 2014, *www.mojprijedor.com/svjedok-bolje-u-trnopolju -nego-na-ulici*.

64. "Mladić Witness: Extremists Guilty of Prijedor Conflict," Balkan Insight, January 19, 2015, *www .balkaninsight.com/en/article/extremists-guilty-of-prijedor-conflict*.

65. "Radovan Karadžić 'Always Wanted Peaceful Solutions,'" Balkan Insight, July 12, 2013, *www .balkaninsight.com/en/article/karadzic-always-wanted-peaceful-solutions*. It is worth noting that, in June 2004, then High Representative Paddy Ashdown added Dragomir Keserović to the European Union's Visa Ban List and removed him from his position as head of the Department for Intelligence and Security, Republika Srpska Ministry of Defense, for "helping ICTY indictees evade justice or otherwise acting in a matter which could obstruct the ICTY in its work." See *CEPS Europa South-East Monitor* 56 (June 30, 2004), *unpan1.un.org/intradoc/groups/public/documents/untc/unpan018282 .pdf*.

66. Hariz Halilović calls the use of the phrase "civil war" an "old mantra," writing, "The intent of these lies is, in retroactively changing the character of the war, to also change the character of the crimes." Halilović, *Kako Opisati Srebrenicu*, 79.

67. Wesselingh and Vaulerin, *Raw Memory*, 75.

68. "Why and When Did Muslims Leave Prijedor?," Sense Agency, January 19, 2015, *www.sense-agency .com/icty/why-and-when-did-muslims-leave-prijedor.29.html?news_id=16359&cat_id=1*.

69. "Mladić in Focus," Sense Agency, February 15, 2015, *www.sense-agency.com/icty/mladic-in-focus.29 .html?news_id=16425&cat_id=1*.

70. Denis Džidić, "Haunted by Hearing Brother Being Killed in Manjaca" Justice Report, May 28, 2010, *www.justice-report.com/en/articles/for-the-record-haunted-by-hearing-brother-being-killed-in- manjaca*. See also Peter Maass, "Away from Guards, Inmates Whisper of Abuse," *Washington Post*, August 11, 1992, *www.washingtonpost.com/archive/politics/1992/08/11/away-from-guards-inmates- whisper-of-abuse/ac3f1ac5-c230–48f8–95c4-a805f4dcda89*.

71. Ed Vulliamy, "We Can't Forget," *Guardian*, September 1, 2004, *www.theguardian.com/world/2004 /sep/01/warcrimes.balkans*.

72. Gordana Katana, "Odbrana konc-logorima" [In defense of concentration camps], *Oslobodjenje*, May 31, 2012, reposted at *www.ww.w.idoconline.info/article/891952*.

73. Eldin Hadžović, "Godišnjice: Dani u Prijedoru; Ponovo na ukletom mjestu" [Anniversaries: *Dani* in Prijedor; at the accursed place again], *Dani* 635 (August 14, 2009), *www.bhdani.ba/portal/ izdanje/635*.

74. Vildana Selimbegović, "Oći u oći sa upravnikom koncentracionog logora" [Face to face with the administrator of a concentration camp], *Dani* 247 (March 8, 2003), *www.bhdani.ba/portal/arhiva _67_281/247*. See also "The Unindicted: Reaping the Rewards of 'Ethnic Cleansing' in Prijedor," Human Rights Watch, January 1, 1997, D901, *www.refworld.org/docid/3ae6a8368.html*.

75. "Serbs Detained Bosniaks 'for Their Own Protection,'" Balkan Insight, February 12, 2015, *www .balkaninsight.com/en/article/ratko-mladic-trnopolje-camp-prijedor*.

76. Goran Jungvirth, "Svjedok obrane o 'dobrovoljnom' odlasku u prijedorske logore" [Defense witness on "voluntary" departure to Prijedor camps], Radio Free Europe, February 10, 2015, *www.slobodnaevropa .org/content/svjedok-obrane-o-dobrovoljnom-odlasku-u-prijedorske-logore/26840134.html*.

77. "Mladić Witness: Bosniaks Entered Detention Centres 'Voluntarily,'" Balkan Insight, February 10, 2015, *www.balkaninsight.com/en/article/voluntary-departure-to-community-centers*.

78. Kemal Pervanić, interview, Kevljani, August 4, 2013.

79. David Campbell, "Atrocity, Memory, Photography: Imaging the Concentration Camps of Bosnia— the Case of ITN versus Living Marxism, Part 1," *Journal of Human Rights* 1, no. 1 (March 2002), *www.david-campbell.org/wp-content/documents/Atrocity_memory_photography_1.pdf*.

80. Vuk Bačanović, "Priča o dva logora" [A story of two camps], *Dani* 682 (July 9, 2010), *www.bhdani .ba/portal/izdanje/682*.

81. An English translation of Deichmann's article is available online at *www.whatreallyhappened.com /RANCHO/LIE/BOSNIA_PHOTO/bosnia.html*.

82. Johnstone, *Fools' Crusade*, 72–73.

83. Edward S. Herman and David Peterson, "Vulliamy's Smears," CounterPunch, November 23, 2009, *www.counterpunch.org/2009/11/23/vulliamy-s-smears*.

84. David Walls, "Dubious Sources: How Project Censored Joined the Whitewash of Serb Atrocities," *New Politics* 33 (Summer 2002), *nova.wpunj.edu/newpolitics/issue33/walls33.htm*.

85. "Greatest Intellectual?"

86. David Campbell, "Chomsky's Bosnian Shame," David-Campbell.org, November 14, 2009, *www .david-campbell.org/2009/11/14/chomskys-bosnian-shame*.

87. "The Hyatt Hotel in Trnopolje," Sense Agency, March 10, 2015, *www.sense-agency.com/icty/the-hyatt-hotel-in-trnopolje.29.html?news_id=16480&cat_id=1*.

88. Nedim Seferović, "Kultura kolektivne moralne ravnodušnosti" [Culture of collective moral indiffer-ence], Elektronske Novine, December 2, 2013, *www.e-novine.com/stav/94761-Tomaica-jedina -objektivna-realnost.html*.

89. Ibid.

90. Eric Gordy, "Chronicle of an Arrest Foretold and a Process Foreshortened," *Croatian Political Sci-ence Review*, March 18, 2015, *politickamisao.com/chronicle-of-an-arrest-foretold-and-a-process -foreshortened*.

91. Not all Prijedor Serbs, thus, have buried their heads in the sand of denial. Especially in more recent years, a number of local young men and woman of Serb descent have come to engage themselves actively, in solidarity with returnee activists, in all the ongoing campaigns for justice in the Prijedor region and beyond. In addition to working in solidarity with returnees and non-Serb war victims, some local Serbs have called for a public admission of the war crimes that were committed in Prijedor.

One of these people, the pathologist Dr. Nikolina Balaban, posted a compelling comment on genocide, denial, and personal responsibility. Balaban published her statement in response to the viewing in Prijedor of a new film, *Zemlja Tvrda, a Nebo Visoko* (The land is hard and the sky is high), in February 2015. The film examines the lives of people who have returned to the municipality since the war and addresses questions of coexistence and "confrontation with the past."

In a forceful article titled "Genocide in Prijedor: I Admit It; You Admit It Too!" Dr. Balaban wrote, "I would rather say that we need to talk about a *public admission* that in Prijedor there happened a truly monstrous crime, genocide. About a collective admission, of those who were directly a part of the ethnic cleansing, murder, torture, and expulsion . . . of civilians, citizens of Prijedor, Bosniaks, but also about a public admission of all of us who were indirectly part of all that . . . and I was." See "Genocid u Prijedoru: Ja priznajem, priznajte i vi!," by Dr. Nikolina Balaban, Novi Horizonti, February 28, 2015, *www.novihorizonti.ba/ja-priznajem-priznajte-i-vi*. A couple of years later, Dr. Balaban came under legal scrutiny for inappropriate and dangerous medical practices in another city. However, her legal troubles do not negate the value of her earlier statements.

EPILOGUE

1. Mirsada and Nedžad, personal conversations, Tuzla, June 10 and 11, 2018.
2. Rodolfo Toè, "Census Results Highlight Impact of Bosnian War," Balkan Insight, July 1, 2016, *www.balkaninsight.com/en/article/census-highlights-impact-of-bosnian-conflict-on-population-07–01–2016*.
3. Rodolfo Toè, "Census Reveals Bosnia's Changed Demography," Balkan Insight, June 30, 2016, *www.balkaninsight.com/en/article/new-demographic-picture-of-bosnia-finally-revealed-06–30–2016*.
4. "Zapanjujući podaci: Novi pokazatelji otkrivaju koliko u BiH zaista ima stanovnika" [Astonishing data: New indicators uncover how many residents BiH really has], *Oslobodjenje*, January 28, 2019, *www.oslobodjenje.ba/vijesti/bih/zapanjujuci-podaci-novi-pokazatelji-otkrivaju-koliko-u-bih-zaista-ima-stanovnika-429025*.
5. Minela Pamuk, "BiH lani napustilo 70.000 ljudi, sve manje prijava za posao u našoj zemlji" [Last year 70,000 people left BiH; fewer and fewer applications for work in our country], *Oslobodjenje*, October 17, 2018, reposted at *mojusk.ba/bih-lani-napustilo-70–000-ljudi-sve-manje-prijava-za-posao-u-nasoj-zemlji*.
6. Vedrana Maglajlija, "Novi val iseljavanja iz BiH: Potraga za 'normalnim' životom" [New wave of emigration from BiH: Search for 'normal' life], Al Jazeera Balkans, October 14, 2018, *balkans.aljazeera.net/vijesti/novi-val-iseljavanja-iz-bih-potraga-za-normalnim-zivotom*.
7. Sanela, personal conversation, Sarajevo, June 14, 2018.
8. Peđa, interview, Sarajevo, June 17, 2018.
9. Velma Saric and Elizabeth D. Herman, "Why Bosnia Has the World's Highest Youth Unemployment Rate," Balkan Insight, October 9, 2014, *www.pri.org/stories/2014–10–09/why-bosnia-has-worlds-highest-youth-unemployment-rate*. Some analysts cite a much higher youth unemployment rate, reaching as much as 65 percent.
10. "Istraživanje: Bosna i Hercegovina prva po izvozu, ali stanovnika" [Research: Bosnia-Herzegovina first in exports—of its residents], *Oslobodjenje*, March 24, 2019, *www.oslobodjenje.ba/vijesti/bih/istrazivanje-bosna-i-hecegovina-prva-po-izvozu-ali-stanovnika-443847*.
11. "Oko 300 ljekara napustilo FBiH prošle godine" [About 300 doctors left FBIH last year], *Oslobodjenje*, January 16, 2017, reposted at *www.fokus.ba/vijesti/bih/oko-300-ljekara-prosle-godine-napustilo-fbih/594262*.
12. "Božo Ljubić: Migranti su tu zbog destabilizacije Mostara i Hercegovine" [Božo Ljubić: Migrants are there to destabilize Mostar and Herzegovina], pogled.ba, May 22, 2018, *m.pogled.ba/clanak/bozo-ljubic-migranti-su-tu-zbog-destabilizacije-mostara-i-hercegovine/142350*.

13. "Dodik: Sarajevo migrantima menja etničku sliku BiH" [Dodik: Sarajevo is changing the ethnic structure of BiH with migrants], Sputnik Srbija, June 23, 2018, *sptnkne.ws/hRNp*.

14. "Dodik: Postoji veoma realna opasnost od terorizma u BiH" [Dodik: There is a very real danger of terrorism in BiH], Blic, January 12, 2016, *www.blic.rs/vesti/politika/sirenje-vehabizma-dodik -postoji-veoma-realna-opasnost-od-terorizma-u-bih/1eh56hy*.

15. "Preimenovanja škola i ulica: OŠ Dobroševići postala OŠ Mustafa Busuladžić" [School and street renamed: Elementary school Dobroševići becomes elementary school Mustafa Busuladžić], Radio Sarajevo, October 26, 2016, *www.radiosarajevo.ba/vijesti/lokalne-teme/preimenovanja-skola-i -ulica-os-dobrosevici-postala-os-mustafa-busuladzic/242385*.

16. Denis Džidić, "Bosnia Probes Flag-Burning during World Cup," Balkan Insight, June 20, 2014, *www .balkaninsight.com/en/article/bosnia-investigates-ethnic-and-religious-incidents*.

17. "Bruka: Dječak u Mostaru na proslavi pobjede Hrvatske skandirao 'Nož, žica, Srebrenica'" [Scandal: Youth in Mostar at celebration of Croatian victory chanted "Knife, wire, Srebrenica"], *faktor.ba*, July 12, 2018, *faktor.ba/vijest/bruka-i-sramota-djecak-u-mostaru-tokom-proslave-pobjede-hrvatske -skandirao-noz-zica-srebrenica-303265*.

18. "Serb Hate Speech Brings Bosnia Match to Halt," Balkan Insight, March 12, 2014, *www.balkaninsight .com/en/article/bosnia-serbia-match-stopped-over-nationalistic-slogans*.

19. Gordana Katanac, "Talk of Paramilitaries, Real or Imagined, Could Fuel Division," Radio Free Europe, February 21, 2018, *www.rferl.org/a/balkans-talk-of-paramilitaries-fuel-division/29055292.html*.

20. Gojko Veselinović, "Da li Dodik pravi paravojne formacije?" [Is Dodik creating paramilitary formations?], Radio Slobodna Europa, January 15, 2018, *www.slobodnaevropa.org/a/dodik-pravi-paravojne -formacije/28976938.html*.

21. "Vučić: Srbija će donirati Republici Srpskoj 5 miliona evra" [Vučić: Serbia will donate 5 million euros to the Republika Srpska], *Kurir.rs*, March 3, 2018, *www.kurir.rs/vesti/politika/3023919 /vucic-srbija-ce-donirati-republici-srpskoj-5-miliona-evra*.

22. "Serbia to Fund RS Military Industry with EUR 7.2 Million," N1 Sarajevo, June 18, 2018, *ba.n1info. com/a267228/English/NEWS/Serbia-to-fund-RS-military-industry-with-EUR-7.2-million.html*.

23. David Salvo and Stephanie De Leon, "Russia's Efforts to Destabilize Bosnia and Herzegovina," Alliance for Securing Democracy, April 25, 2018, *securingdemocracy.gmfus.org/russias-efforts -to-destabilize-bosnia-and-herzegovina*.

24. Daria Sito-Sucic, "Bosnian Serbs Roll Out Red Carpet for Russian Delegation," Reuters, April 24, 2018, *www.reuters.com/article/us-bosnia-russia/bosnian-serbs-roll-out-red-carpet-for-russian- delegation-idUSKBN1HV27Z*.

25. The resulting sanctions blocked Zaldostanov's access to any assets held in the United States and prohibited business transactions with US persons. "Treasury Designates Individuals and Entities Involved in the Ongoing Conflict in Ukraine," US Department of the Treasury, press release, June 20, 2017, *www.treasury.gov/press-center/press-releases/pages/sm0114.aspx*.

26. A. Avdić, "Putinovi Noćni Vukovi: Za Obamu teroristi, za Dodika humanisti!" [Putin's Night Wolves: For Obama terrorists, for Dodik humanists], Žurnal, January 17, 2018, *www.zurnal.info /novost/20922/za-obamu-teroristi-za-dodika-humanisti*.

27. "Republika Srpska kupuje tri helikoptera od Rusa" [Republika Srpska buys three helicopters from Russians], Oslobodjenje, August 25, 2018, *www.oslobodjenje.ba/vijesti/bih/republika-srpska-kupuje -tri-helikoptera-od-rusa-388329*.

28. Rodolfo Toè, "Russia to Train Bosnian Serb Special Police," Balkan Insight, February 19, 2016, *www .balkaninsight.com/en/article/republika-srpska-police-to-get-trained-in-russia-02-19-2016*.

29. Vera Mironova and Bogdan Zawadewicz, "Putin Is Building a Bosnian Paramilitary Force," *Foreign Policy*, August 8, 2018, *foreignpolicy.com/2018/08/08/putin-is-building-a-bosnian-paramilitary-force*.

See also Mladen Lakic, "New Weapons for RS Police Make Bosnia Jittery," Balkan Insight, February 9, 2018, *www.balkaninsight.com/en/article/bosnian-serb-police-gets-new-weapons-02–09–2018.*

30. Srđan Šušnica, "Kako se otresti velikosrpske mitomanije?" [How to shake off Greater Serbian mythomania?], *kliker.info*, October 18, 2018, *kliker.info/srdjan-susnica-publicista-iz-banja-luke-kako -se-otresti-velikosrpske-mitomanije.*

31. Mark MacKinnon, "In Bosnia-Herzegovina, Fears Are Growing That the Carefully Constructed Peace Is Starting to Unravel," *Globe and Mail*, May 24, 2018, *www.theglobeandmail.com/world /article-in-bosnia-serb-nationalists-see-putin-and-trump-as-their-tickets-to.*

32. David Salvo and Stephanie De Leon, "Russia's Efforts to Destabilize Bosnia and Herzegovina," Alliance for Securing Democracy, April 25, 2018, *securingdemocracy.gmfus.org/russias-efforts-to- destabilize-bosnia-and-herzegovina.* See also Drago Pilsel, "Pogled iz Hrvatske: Uloga Kolinde GK, Brkića, Čovića i Dodika u ruskom porobljavanju BiH" [The view from Croatia: The role of Kolinda GK, Brkić, Čović, and Dodik in the Russian plunder of BiH], *Oslobodjenje*, October 29, 2018, *www .oslobodjenje.ba/vijesti/bih/pogled-iz-hrvatske-uloga-kolinde-gk-brkica-covica-i-dodika-u-ruskom -porobljavanju-bih-404827.*

33. "Draganu Čoviću dodijeljen počasni doktorat" [Dragan Čović awarded honorary doctorate], Večernji List, June 19, 2018, *www.vecernji.hr/vijesti/draganu-covicu-dodijeljen-pocasni-doktorat -1253122.*

34. Katarina Anđelković, "Is Bosnia and Herzegovina Really a 'Terrorist Haven'?," European Western Balkans, November 13, 2017, *europeanwesternbalkans.com/2017/11/13/bosnia-herzegovina-really -terrorist-haven.*

35. Čović received 145,319 votes in 2018, as compared to 128,053 votes in 2014. See "Confirmed Results of General Election, 2014," Central Election Commission, November 11, 2014, *www.izbori.ba /Potvrdjeni2014/Finalni/PredsjednistvoBiH/Default.aspx*, and "Preliminary Results for 2018 General Elections" as of October 18, 2018, at *www.izbori.ba/rezultati_izbora?resId=25&langId=4#/1/1/0/0/702.*

36. A.V., "Mobilizacija glasačkog tijela: Čović iz Zagreba poručio da građanska BiH znači islamska država" [Mobilization of the voting body: From Zagreb, Čović announces that a civic BiH means an Islamic state], Patria Novinska Agencija, February 2, 2018, *www.nap.ba/new/vijest.php?id=42714.* The 2013 census shows a Croat population of 544,000; accounting for persons not of voting age, and for subsequent emigration, the voting body should have still been roughly 500,000 in late 2018.

37. Ky Krauthamer, "Croatian Rain Falls on Bosnian Parade," Transitions Online, January 11, 2019, *www .tol.org/client/article/28160-croatia-bosnia-war-veterans-yugoslavia-ivan-del-vechio.html.* See also "HRS: 'Čoviću nije bilo mjesto u Banjoj Luci, gazi se dostojanstvo Hrvata'" ["Čović's place was not in Banja Luka, he tramples the dignity of Croats"], Jabuka TV, January 10, 2019, *www.jabuka.tv /hrs-covicu-nije-bilo-mjesto-u-banjoj-luci-gazi-se-dostojanstvo-hrvata.*

38. Aleksandra Radu, "[EWB Interview] Weber: Western Balkans Has Never Been Priority for the EU," European Western Balkans, April 24, 2017, *europeanwesternbalkans.com/2017/04/24/ ewb-intreview-bodo-weber-western-balkans-has-never-been-priority-for-the-eu.*

39. Bodo Weber, "Brussels Is Letting Bosnia's Reform Agenda Slip Away," Balkan Insight, April 6, 2017, *www.balkaninsight.com/en/article/brussels-is-letting-bosnia-s-reform-agenda-slip-away-04–05–2017.*

40. "Bosnia and Herzegovina: Ensuring the Political Participation of Minorities," Minority Rights Group, November 20, 2016, *minorityrights.org/law-and-legal-cases/finci-v-bosnia-and-herzegovina.*

41. Krithika Varagur, "Why Bannon Is Meddling with Bosnia," *New York Review of Books*, September 5, 2018, *www.nybooks.com/daily/2018/09/05/why-bannon-is-meddling-with-bosnia.*

42. In Jasmin Mujanović, *Hunger and Fury: The Crisis of Democracy in the Balkans* (New York: Oxford University Press, 2018), author Mujanović discusses the "postwar stability consensus that Western governments reached with nationalist leaders." See pages 13 and 132.

43. "Dodik's Ambitious 'Reforms' Threaten to Shake Bosnia," Balkan Insight, December 3, 2018, *www .balkaninsight.com/en/article/dodik-s-ambitious-reforms-threaten-to-shake-bosnia-11–30–2018*.

44. Varagur, "Why Bannon Is Meddling with Bosnia."

45. Emily Tamkin, "Kosovo's Prime Minister Warned the US Not to Back a Land Swap with Serbia," Buzzfeed, September 28, 2018, *www.buzzfeednews.com/article/emilytamkin/kosovo-land -swap-serbia-warns-against-prime-minister*.

46. Senator Roger Wicker, press statement, *Congressional Record* 164, no. 152 (September 12, 2018), *www .csce.gov/international-impact/press-and-media/statements/bosnia-herzegovina*.

47. Marlise Simons, "Yugoslavia Tribunal Leaves Rich Legacy, but 'Immense' Challenges Remain," *New York Times*, December 23, 2017, *www.nytimes.com/2017/12/23/world/europe/yugoslavia-tribunal-hague.html*.

48. Sir Geoffrey Nice: "Zapadne sile su se pobrinule da se Srbiji ne sudi za genocid" [Western powers took care not to condemn Serbia for genocide], Jutarnji List, December 30, 2017, *www.jutarnji.hr /vijesti/hrvatska/sir-geoffrey-nice-zapadne-sile-su-se-pobrinule-da-se-srbiji-ne-sudi-za-genocid /6888225*.

49. Refik Hodžić, "Serbia, the ICTY and Reconciliation: The Terrifying New Era of 'Quiet Pride,'" Peščanik, November 28, 2017, *pescanik.net/serbia-the-icty-and-reconciliation-the-terrifying-new-era-of-quiet-pride*.

50. "Drama as Tribunal Delivers Its Last Verdict," Sense Agency, November 29, 2017, *www.sense-agency .com/icty/drama-as-tribunal-delivers-its-last-verdict.29.html?news_id=17235*.

51. "The ICTY Renders Its Final Judgement in the Prlić et al. Appeal Case," press release, ICTY, November 29, 2017, *www.icty.org/en/press/the-icty-renders-its-final-judgement-in-the-prlic-et-al-appeal-case*.

52. Denis Džidić, "Hague Tribunal Replaces 'Biased' Judges in Mladic Case," Balkan Insight, September 18, 2018, *www.balkaninsight.com/en/article/hague-tribunal-changes-judge-panel-in-mladic-case-09–05–2018*. See also "Bivši haški sudija: Antonetti priprema teren za oslobađanje Mladića i Karadžića" [Former Hague judge: Antonetti is preparing the ground for the liberation of Mladić and Karadžić], Faktor, January 30, 2019, *faktor.ba/vijest/bivsi-haski-sudija-antonetti-priprema-teren -za-oslobadanje-mladica-i-karadzica/21352*. This article points out that it was also Judge Antonetti who prematurely freed Vojislav Šešelj.

53. Stephanie Van Den Berg, "Damaging Power Struggle Engulfs the Former ICTY," JusticeInfo.net, October 29, 2018, *www.justiceinfo.net/en/tribunals/icty/39367-damaging-power-struggle-engulfs-the -former-icty.html*.

54. Simons, "Yugoslavia Tribunal Leaves."

55. Diane Orentlicher, "25 Years of Contemporary War Crimes Tribunals," Oxford University Press blog, May 25, 2018, *blog.oup.com/2018/05/25-years-contemporary-war-crimes-tribunals*.

56. Cain Burdeau, "Experts Say Many Balkan War Crimes Will Never Be Prosecuted," Courthouse News Service, September 18, 2018, *www.courthousenews.com/experts-say-many-balkan-war-crimes -will-never-be-prosecuted*.

57. Admir Muslimovic and Filip Rudic, "Srebrenica Genocide Convicts Return to Freedom," Balkan Insight, July 7, 2017, *www.balkaninsight.com/en/article/srebrenica-genocide-convicts-return-to -freedom-07–06–2017*.

58. Srdjan Kureljusic, "Bosnian Mayoral Hopefuls Tainted by Crime Claims," Balkan Insight, September 20, 2016, *www.balkaninsight.com/en/article/bosnian-mayoral-hopefuls-tainted-by-crime-claims- 09–19–2016*.

59. Miki, personal conversation, Sarajevo, July 7, 2018.

60. Informal conversation with a respondent who wished to remain anonymous, Tuzla, June 12, 2018.

61. "International Envoy Warns against Bosnian Escalation," Radio Free Europe, February 9, 2014, *www.rferl.org/a/bosnia-inzko-warning-troops/25258191.html.*

62. "Duraković: Dosad nije bilo konkretne pomoći od strane Vlade RS-a" [Duraković: So far there has not been concrete help from the RS government], Vijesti.ba, May 20, 2014, *vijesti.ba/clanak/216357 /durakovic-dosad-nije-bilo-konkretne-pomoci-od-strane-vlade-rs-a.*

Selected Bibliography

Ali, Rabia, and Lawrence Lifschultz, eds. *Why Bosnia? Writings on the Balkan War.* Stony Creek, CT: Pamphleteer's, 1993.

Alibabić, Munir. *U Kandžama KOS-a.* Sarajevo: Behar, 1996.

Andreas, Peter. *Blue Helmets and Black Markets: The Business of Survival in the Siege of Sarajevo.* Ithaca, NY: Cornell University Press, 2008.

Azinović, Vlado. *Al-Qaeda U Bosni: Mit ili stvarna opasnost?* [Al-Qaeda in Bosnia: Myth or Present Danger?]. Prague: Radio Free Europe, 2007. Entire book accessible at *www.slobodnaevropa.org /specials/al_kaida/index.htm.*

Bakšić, Hamza. *Sarajeva Više Nema.* Sarajevo: *Oslobodjenje* (Radio Free Europe), 1997.

Bartov, Omer, and Phyllis Mack, eds. *In God's Name: Genocide and Religion in the Twentieth Century.* New York: Berghahn Books, 2001.

Bećirević, Edina. *Na Drini Genocid: Istraživanje Organiziranog Zločina u Istočnoj Bosni.* Sarajevo: Buybook, 2009.

Berić, Gojko. *Letters to the Celestial Serbs.* London: Saqi Books, 2002.

Bieber, Florian. *Post-war Bosnia: Ethnicity, Inequality and Public Sector Governance.* Basingstoke: Palgrave Macmillan, 2005.

Bose, Sumantra. *Bosnia after Dayton: Nationalist Partition and International Intervention.* New York: Oxford University Press, 2002.

Bougarel, Xavier, Elissa Helms, and Ger Duijzings, eds. *The New Bosnian Mosaic: Identities, Memories and Moral Claims in a Post-War Society.* Aldershot, England: Ashgate, 2007.

Bringa, Tone. *Being Muslim the Bosnian Way: Identity and Community in a Central Bosnian Village.* Princeton, NJ: Princeton University Press, 2005.

Broz, Svetlana. *Good People in an Evil Time: Portraits of Complicity and Resistance in the Bosnian War.* New York: Other, 2004.

Cigar, Norman. *Genocide in Bosnia: The Policy of "Ethnic Cleansing."* College Station: Texas A&M University Press, 1995.

Cohen, Lenard J. *Broken Bonds: The Disintegration of Yugoslavia.* Boulder, CO: Westview, 1993.

Cohen, Roger. *Hearts Grown Brutal: Sagas of Sarajevo.* New York: Random House, 1998.

Cvitković, Ivan. *Hrvatski Identitet u Bosni i Hercegovini* [Croat identity in Bosnia-Herzegovina]. Zagreb: Synopsis d.o.o., 2005.

―――. *Hrvatski Identitet u Bosni I Hercegovini: Hrvati između nacionalnog i Građanskog.* Zagreb-Sarajevo: Synopsis, 2006.

Demick, Barbara. *Logavina Street: Life and Death in a Sarajevo Neighborhood.* Kansas City, MO: Andrews and McMeel, 1996.

Denitch, Bogdan. *Ethnic Nationalism: The Tragic Death of Yugoslavia.* Minneapolis: University of Minnesota Press, 1994.

Dervisevic-Cesic, Jasmina. *The River Runs Salt, Runs Sweet: A Memoir of Visegrad, Bosnia.* Eugene: Panisphere Books, 1994.

Đilas, Milovan, and Nadežda Gaće. *Bošnjak: Adil Zulfikarpašić.* Zurich: Bošnjački Institut, 1994.

Dizdar, Mehmed. *Stolac, Virtualni Zavičaj.* Mostar: Smart d.o.o., 2006.

———. *Suđeni Stolac.* Sarajevo: Kuća Bosanska, 1996.

Donia, Robert. *Radovan Karadžić: Architect of the Bosnian Genocide.* New York: Cambridge University Press, 2015.

———. *Sarajevo: A Biography.* Ann Arbor: University of Michigan Press, 2006.

Donia, Robert, and John V. A. Fine Jr. *Bosnia and Hercegovina: A Tradition Betrayed.* New York: Columbia University Press, 1994.

Drakulić, Slavenka. *They Would Never Hurt a Fly: War Criminals on Trial in The Hague.* New York: Penguin Books, 2004.

Fine, John V. A. *The Bosnian Church: A New Interpretation.* New York: Columbia University Press, 1975.

Fink, Sheri. *War Hospital: A True Story of Surgery and Survival.* New York: Public Affairs, 2003.

Glenny, Misha. *The Fall of Yugoslavia: The Third Balkan War.* New York: Penguin Books, 1992.

Gunić, Vehid. *Doktor Eso.* Sarajevo: Bemust, 2009.

Gutman, Roy. *Witness to Genocide.* New York: Macmillan, 1993.

Halilović, Hariz. *Kako Opisati Srebrenicu* [Writing after Srebrenica]. Sarajevo: Buybook, 2017.

Halilovich, Hariz. *Places of Pain.* New York: Berghahn Books, 2013.

Hećimović, Esad. *Garibi: Mudžahedini u BiH 1992–1999.* Zenica: Fondacija Sina, 2006.

Hensman, Rohini. *Indefensible: Democracy, Counterrevolution, and the Rhetoric of Anti-imperialism,* Chicago: Haymarket, 2018.

Holbrooke, Richard. *To End a War.* 1998. New York: Random House, 2006.

Honig, Jan Willem, and Norbert Both. *Srebrenica: Record of a War Crime.* New York: Penguin Books, 1996.

Hukanović, Rezak. *The Tenth Circle of Hell: A Memoir of Life in the Death Camps of Bosnia.* New York: Basic Books, 1996.

Jergović, Miljenko. *Sarajevski Marlboro.* Zagreb: Durieux, 1994.

Johnstone, Diana. *Fools' Crusade: Yugoslavia, NATO and Western Delusions.* New York: Monthly Review Press, 2002.

Karahasan, Dževad. *Sarajevo: Exodus of a City.* New York: Kodansha America, 1994.

Kordić, Ivan. *Sarajevo Post Bellum 1991–2004.* Sarajevo: Šahinpašić, 2004.

Lieblich, Julia, and Esad Boškailo. *Wounded I Am More Awake: Finding Meaning after Terror.* Nashville, TN: Vanderbilt University Press, 2012.

Lovrenović, Ivan. *Bosna, Kraj Stoljeća* [Bosnia at the end of the century]. Zagreb: Durieux, 1996.

———. *Bosnia: A Cultural History.* New York: New York University Press, 2001.

Loyd, Anthony. *My War Gone By, I Miss It So.* New York: Penguin Books, 1999.

Maass, Peter. *Love Thy Neighbor: A Story of War.* New York: Vintage Books, 1997.

Magaš, Branka. *The Destruction of Yugoslavia: Tracking the Break-Up 1980–92.* London: Verso, 1993.

Mahmutćehajić, Rusmir. *Bosnia the Good: Tolerance and Tradition.* Budapest: Central European University Press, 2000.

Malcolm, Noel. *Bosnia: A Short History.* New York: New York University Press, 1996.

Mappes-Niediek, Norbert. *Balkanska Mafija—Države u Rukama Zločina: Opasnost za Europu.* Zagreb: Durieux, 2003.

Marić, Mišo. *Mostarenje.* Sarajevo: Rabic, 2006.

Maric, Vesna. *Bluebird: A Memoir*. New York: Soft Skull, 2009.

Medić, Jasmin. *Genocid u Prijedoru*. Cazin: Grafis d.o.o., 2003.

Mujanovic, Jasmin. *Hunger and Fury: The Crisis of Democracy in the Balkans*. London: Hurst, 2018.

Nettelfield, Lara J. *Courting Democracy in Bosnia and Herzegovina*. New York: Cambridge University Press, 2010.

Nettelfield, Lara J., and Sarah E. Wagner. *Srebrenica in the Aftermath of Genocide*. New York: Cambridge University Press, 2014.

Neuffer, Elizabeth. *The Key to My Neighbor's House: Seeking Justice in Bosnia and Rwanda*. New York: Picador, 2002.

Nuhanović, Hasan. *Pod Zastavom UN-a*. Sarajevo: Preporod, 2005. Also available in English as *Under the UN Flag: The International Community and the Srebrenica Genocide*. Sarajevo: DES, 2007.

———. *Zbijeg: Put u Srebrenicu*. Sarajevo: Mediacentar, 2012.

Odobašić, Jasmin. *Sjaj i Bijeda Ekshumacija*. Sarajevo: Sak Trade, 2012.

Pervanić, Kemal. *The Killing Days: My Journey through the Bosnian War*. London: Blake, 1999.

Pinson, Mark, ed. *The Muslims of Bosnia-Herzegovina: Their Historic Development from the Middle Ages to the Dissolution of Yugoslavia*. Cambridge, MA: Harvard University Press, 1993.

Rieff, David. *Slaughterhouse: Bosnia and the Failure of the West*. New York: Touchstone/Simon and Schuster, 1995.

Rohde, David. *Endgame*. Boulder, CO: Westview, 1997.

Rusinow, Dennison. *The Yugoslav Experiment 1948–1974*. Berkeley: University of California Press, 1977.

Salimović, Sakib, and Miro Pejić. *Srebrenica, Povratak Života* [*Srebrenica*, the return of life]. Srebrenica: Srebrenica Municipality, 2006.

Sells, Michael. *The Bridge Betrayed: Religion and Genocide in Bosnia*. Berkeley: University of California Press, 1998.

Silber, Laura, and Allan Little. *Yugoslavia: Death of a Nation*. New York: Penguin Books, 1997.

Sivac-Bryant, Sebina. *Re-Making Kozarac*. London: Palgrave Macmillan, 2016.

Srebrenica: Remembrance for the Future. Sarajevo: Heinrich Böll Foundation, 2005.

Srpsko Građansko Vijeće–Tuzla. *Bosno, i Mi Smo Tvoj Narod*. Tuzla: SGV, 2004.

Stiglmayer, Alexandra, ed. *Mass Rape: The War against Women in Bosnia-Herzegovina*. Lincoln: University of Nebraska Press, 1994.

Sudetic, Chuck. *Blood and Vengeance: One Family's Story of the War in Bosnia*. New York: Penguin Books, 1998.

Suljagić, Emir. *Postcards from the Grave*. London: Saqi, 2005.

Terry, Sara. *Aftermath: Bosnia's Long Road to Peace*. New York: Channel Photographics, 2005.

Toal, Gerard, and Carl Dahlman. *Bosnia Remade: Ethnic Cleansing and Its Reversal*. New York: Oxford University Press, 2011.

Trbić, Jusuf. *Gluho Doba*. Lukavac: Kujundžić, 2006.

———. *Majstori Mraka I*. Lukavac: Kujundžić, 2007.

———. *Majstori Mraka II*. Lukavac: Kujundžić, 2007.

Vuksanović, Mladen. *From Enemy Territory: Pale Diary*. London: Saqi, 2004.

Vulliamy, Ed. *Seasons in Hell: Understanding Bosnia's War*. New York: St. Martin's, 1994.

———. *The War Is Dead, Long Live the War—Bosnia: The Reckoning*. London: Bodley Head, 2012.

Wagner, Sarah. *To Know Where He Lies: DNA Technology and the Search for Srebrenica's Missing*. Berkeley: University of California Press, 2008.

Weine, Stevan. *When History Is a Nightmare: Lives and Memories of Ethnic Cleansing in Bosnia-Herzegovina*. New Brunswick, NJ: Rutgers University Press, 1999.

Wesselingh, Isabelle, and Arnaud Vaulerin. *Raw Memory: Prijedor, Laboratory of Ethnic Cleansing.*
    London: Saqi Books, 2005.

Zaimović, Karim. *Tajna Džema od Malina.* Sarajevo: Zid, 1997.

Zimmerman, Warren. *Origins of a Catastrophe: Yugoslavia and Its Destroyers.* New York:
    Times Books, 1999.

Index

In Appreciation

LIST OF INTERVIEWEES AND HELPERS

Thanks go to my brothers, Roger, David, and George, with me always in human rights activism.

Special thanks to Vesna Ljubić for guidance from the beginning to the end in my attempt to understand Bosnia-Herzegovina.

Thanks to Valerie Schloredt, my editor, and to Jen Marlowe, for critical advice along the way.

And particular thanks to my dear Leslie Nelson for all her support.

The following is a partial list acknowledging people who have been important in one way or another in the couple of decades leading up to this publication. Some of them are people whom I interviewed either formally or for background information over the past twenty-two years. Others are friends in Bosnia-Herzegovina and in the United States who gave me support and encouragement. I regret the inevitable omissions.

Ronelle Alexander, Anel Ališić, Father Iljo Arlović, Rosemary Armao, Judith Armatta, Damir Arsenijević, Zoran Badrić, Himzo Bajrović, Fadil Banjanović, Ševko Bajić, Denis Bašić, Kurt Bassuener, Mirna Bauk, Edin Beća, Meho Bećirević, Albina Beganović, Nura Begović, Owen Beith, Jovan Belenzada, Nedžad Bešić, Darjan Bilić, Werner Blatter, Ervin Blažević, Lynda Boose, Lamia Borić, Mišo Božić, Darko Brkan, Alojz Čakarić, Aline Cateux, Zinka Cerić, Indira Čečo, Nina Čizmić, Salem Čorbo, Mustafa Ćorić, Sarah Correia, Ismet Ćosović, Dražen Crnomat, Alojz Ćurić, Damir, Bembo Davies, Momir Dejanović, Massimo Diana, Mehmed Dizdar, Nerin Dizdar, Sadeta Dizdarević, Tanya Domi, Enes Đozić, Nada Đukanović, Mirsad Duratović, Srpko Đurić, Zehra Ferhatbegović, Amanda Franklin, Vanja Gagić-Lazić, Sajma Gajetić, Jure Galić, Fata Ganić, Riza Ganić, Čedo Glavaš, Michel Gliha, Eleanor Gordon, Mladen Grahovac, Vedran Grahovac, Zachary Gresham, Adila Grebović, Avdo Grebović, Ekrem Grebović, Kasim Grebović, Iain Guest, Hasan Hadžić, Ibrahim Hadžić, Mirsada Hadžić, Munira Hadžić, Milenko Hadživuković, Hariz Halilović, Mevlida Halilović, Nurija Halilović, Šaćir Halilović, Zejna Halilović, Suleyman Hangun, Beth Harris, Azra Hasanbegović, Elissa Helms, Marko Hoare, Emir Hodžić, Helena Holme-Pedersen, Kada Hotić, David Howitt, Meagan Hrle, Suleiman Hrle, Rozalija Hrustić, Carla Hurt, Fatima Huseinović, Nedžad Ibrahimović, Slobodanka Ilić, Milenko Iliktarević, Izet Imamović, Zekira

Imamović, Gordan Isabegović, Željko Ivanković, Nedim Jahić, Robert Jandrić, Jovo Janjić, Emina Jašarević, Irena Javor, Nermina Jelačić, Mirjana Jokanović, Dragana Jovanović, Milan Jovičić, Svetlana Jukić, Hamdija Kandžić, Vahid Kanlić, Hikmet Karčić, Slavko Klisura, Krešimir Krtalić, Nedžmija Kukričar, Elmina Kulašić, Dražana Lepir, Dženita Lončarević, Emin Mahmutović, Father Mirko Majdandžić, Cvijetin Maksimović, Melika Malešević, Željko Marić, Fra Ivo Marković, Father Petar Matanovic, Ignacio Matteini, Naftali McGill, Amer Medar, Jasmin Vedran Mehičević, Hakija Meholjić, Dževad Memić, Silva Memić, Fadila Memišić, Gojko Mijatović, Milutin Mikerić, Aleksa Milanović, Jadranka Miličević, Jonathan Moore, Nigel Moore, Olivier Mouquet, Emsuda Mujagić, Satko Mujagić, Milorad Muratović, Sudbin Music, Vesna Mustafić, Lara Nettelson, Milena Nikolić, Dan Nord, Hasan Nuhanović, Jasmin Odobašić, Husein Oručević, Arifana Pašalić, Ibro Pašalić, Magbula Pašalić, Suljo Pašalić, Daniel Perez, Vjekoslava Perković, Valery Perry, Kemal Pervanić, Aleksandar Pevendić, David Pettigrew, Selma Porobić, Charlie Powell, Father Franjo Radman, Miro Raguž, Edin Ramulić, Wendy Rappeport, Midhat Riđanović, András Riedlmayer, Aleksandar Šakota, Zulfo Salihović, Robert Sandrić, Sandro Sarić, Aleksandra Savić, Marta Schaaf, Priscilla Sears, Esma Šehović, Marinko Sekulic, Danijel Senkić, Burhan Shehu, Andrea Siegl, Novak Simić, Sebina Sivac, Željka Slišković, Alison Sluiter, Ted Soden-Bird, Božidar Stanojević, Blažo Stevović, Krsto Stjepanović, Milena Stjepanović, Mahmud Strik, Munira Subašić, Senad Subašić, Amir Sućeska, Nura Suljić, Drew Sullivan, Susan Sunflower, Mira Tahirović, Nesim Tahirović, Eli Tauber, Pero Todorović, Marko Tomaš, Jusuf Trbić, Vesna Tustonja, Sedat Uysal, Behija Vajzović, Kemal Vajzović, Mirjana Vehabić, Vladislav Vlajić, Ivan Vrhunc, Vojislav Vujanović, Miljan Vujičić, Sarah Wagner, David Watson, Mark Wheeler, Mladen Žabić, Dunja Zaklan, Meng Zhang, Belma Žiga, Ahmo Žigojević, Goran Zorić, Mirhunisa Zukić-Komarica, Predrag Zvijerac.

About the Author

Peter Lippman, born in Seattle, is a journalist and human rights activist. A fascination with the ethnography of southeast Europe led him to Yugoslavia in the early 1980s. He lived and worked in Bosnia-Herzegovina for two years after the war and has returned many times since then. Over more than two decades, he has closely followed the efforts of grassroots activists to return to their prewar homes, to fight corruption and discrimination, and to regain their rights.